I0890675

Entrepreneurial Resilience in Turbulent Globalized Economies

Georgios A. Deirmentzoglou
https://orcid.org/0000-0003-1687-0708
Neapolis University Pafos, Cyprus

Eleni E. Anastasopoulou
Neapolis University Pafos, Cyprus

Valeska V. Geldres-Weiss
Universidad de La Frontera, Chile

Bojan Jovanovski
FH JOANNEUM University of Applied Sciences, Austria

Andreas Masouras
https://orcid.org/0000-0001-8989-3930
Neapolis University Pafos, Cyprus

IGI Global
Scientific Publishing
Publishing Tomorrow's Research Today

Vice President of Editorial Melissa Wagner
Director of Acquisitions Mikaela Felty
Director of Book Development Jocelynn Hessler
Production Manager Mike Brehm
Cover Design Jose Rosado

Published in the United States of America by
IGI Global Scientific Publishing
701 East Chocolate Avenue
Hershey, PA, 17033, USA
Tel: 717-533-8845 | Fax: 717-533-7115
Website: https://www.igi-global.com E-mail: cust@igi-global.com

Library of Congress Cataloging-in-Publication Data

LCCN: 2025053780 (CIP Data Pending)
ISBN13: 979-8-3373-6991-4
Isbn13Softcover: 979-8-3373-6992-1
EISBN13: 979-8-3373-6993-8

British Cataloguing in Publication Data
A Cataloguing in Publication record for this book is available from the British Library.

For Maria-Magdalena,
for the futures yet to be shaped

Table of Contents

Detailed Table of Contents

This chapter offers an integrative overview of entrepreneurial resilience in turbulent globalized economies. It situates entrepreneurship within a context of overlapping crises, such as financial shocks, pandemics, geopolitical tensions, climate risks and rapid technological change; and conceptualises entrepreneurial resilience as a dynamic, multilevel process through which entrepreneurs and ventures absorb shocks, adapt and sometimes transform. The chapter synthesises key drivers at three levels: individual psychological resources and learning-oriented mindsets; firm-level capabilities related to strategic flexibility, innovation, digitalisation and financial management; and ecosystem-level conditions. It also highlights major conceptual and methodological gaps, including fragmented definitions, reliance on cross-sectional designs and limited attention to marginalised contexts. The chapter concludes by outlining research directions linking resilience to digital and green entrepreneurship, crisis-prone and emerging economies and AI-enabled ecosystems.

Global crises such as pandemics, geopolitical conflicts, and digital disruptions have fundamentally redefined the structure of entrepreneurial ecosystems. An integrative conceptual framework is developed to explain how policy coherence and institutional capacity enhance entrepreneurial resilience. Resilience is understood not merely as the ability of individuals to adapt, but as a systemic process arising from coordinated policy design, institutional learning, and cross-sectoral collaboration. The framework emphasizes the interdependence between public policy, institutional strength, and entrepreneurial behavior as key mechanisms sustaining innovation and long-term recovery. It also illustrates that adaptive governance and institutional flexibility are critical in transforming crises into opportunities for renewal and inclusive growth. Conceptually, this study advances institutional theory by linking it to dynamic governance and policy learning, providing strategic insights for building sustainable, resilient, and innovation-driven entrepreneurial systems amid global uncertainty.

This chapter explores how education strengthens entrepreneurs' resilience and competitiveness in today's global economy. Entrepreneurs face rapid market shifts and rising uncertainties, and education formal, informal, and experiential merges as a key driver of adaptability and success. Using an exploratory approach based on secondary data (literature, policy reports, and global indices), the chapter highlights the transformative role of education in building skills, strategic thinking, and sustainable growth.

In a world increasingly defined by systemic turbulence, the traditional governance and development models are no longer suitable. Conventionally existing methods are becoming less responsive to these new and multifaceted challenges. The current chapter focuses on social entrepreneurship as a systemic solution to development of resilience and inclusion in such uncertain environments based on knowledge. The analysis will focus on three dynamics that are interconnected, namely inclusive participation as a source of distributed intelligence, reflective learning as a crisis-to-innovation transformation and digital transformation as a social impact amplifier. The chapter also questions under what circumstances social entrepreneurship is likely to succeed. Finally, the chapter claims that a more adaptive and inclusive system should be formed through social entrepreneurship. Through this, it gives a vision of generating value that puts an emphasis over learning, equity, and long-term well-being rather than narrow economic indicators.

Social, inclusive, and community-based entrepreneurship (SICE) is an entrepreneurship practice to tackle poverty; inequalities; systemic discrimination; and socio-economic exclusion. SICE approaches focus on inclusive participation, collaborative decision making to address socio-economic inequalities and to promote sustainability. The chapter explains that SICE actions are especially beneficial in areas with socio-economic fragility or economically or infrastructurally poor areas due to their aggregated governance, embedded social networks, and variegated resource systems, which allow communities to endure shocks and recover from crises including pandemics, climate emergencies, and economic breakdowns. Additionally, the chapter discusses the essential contribution of governmental and bureaucratic actors, the private sector, educational institutes and the multi-polar systems of SICE. To summarize, this book chapter explains how SICE provides a transformative blueprint which is capable of linking grassroots innovation with societal, national and global sustainability agendas.

Purpose Entrepreneurship in the informal economy is highly vulnerable to systemic shocks, as evident during the COVID-19 pandemic. Urban street vendors, who constitute one of the most visible segments of India's informal workforce, faced severe livelihood disruptions due to mobility restrictions and market closures. In response, the Government of India introduced the Pradhan Mantri Street Vendor's AtmaNirbhar Nidhi (PM SVANidhi) scheme in June 2020, designed to provide collateral-free microcredit, promote digital financial inclusion, and stabilize vendor incomes. This chapter examines the implementation and impact of PM SVANidhi in the state of Haryana through secondary data analysis, positioning it within the broader discourse on entrepreneurial resilience. The purpose is twofold: (a) to assess the scale and effectiveness of the scheme in Haryana compared to national trends, and (b) to link these findings with theoretical discussions on informal entrepreneurship, resilience, and financial inclusion.

traditional commercial function to become a socio-political practice that builds trust, signals legitimacy, and connects local firms to global markets. Case studies from Syria, Palestine, and sub-saharan Africa illustrate how entrepreneurs deploy marketing to navigate conflict, sanctions, and institutional weakness. Integrating insights from scholars and contemporary entrepreneurship research, the chapter highlights how branding can function as informal governance, a trust architecture, and a bridge to international solidarity and investment.

Agrifood value chains operate in an increasingly turbulent global environment where exchange rate volatility interacts with climate shocks, input price surges, and geopolitical disruptions. Although agricultural trade is highly sensitive to currency movements, the implications of exchange rate shocks for entrepreneurs embedded in agrifood chains remain insufficiently examined. This chapter analyses how currency fluctuations affect costs, revenues, competitiveness, and strategic decision-making across farming, processing, and distribution activities. It highlights the uneven exposure of firms, especially small and medium-sized enterprises that rely on imported inputs and possess limited financial and organisational buffers. By integrating insights from exchange-rate economics, value-chain resilience, and entrepreneurship research, the chapter develops a conceptual understanding of how agrifood entrepreneurs sense, absorb, and adapt to exchange-rate-induced disruptions. The analysis identifies key gaps in current scholarship and outlines future research opportunities.

Tourism is faced with ongoing shocks—pandemics to weather risks—that undermine its capacity to innovate and sustain development. Here, this chapter argues that two levers—foreign direct investment (FDI) and artificial intelligence (AI)—combined can render the sector resilient and expand in the long term if combined with sound policy and sustainability goals. Integrating new evidence from advanced economies, small island, and transition economies, is presented how FDI increases productive capacity, improves infrastructure, and disseminates know-how as AI re-engineers demand creation, operations, and management into smarter, greener tourism. Generative AI travel companions shape trust, interaction, and the capacity

The results underscore resilience as a dynamic, entrepreneurial process fueled by learning, innovation, and networked collaboration. By reconceptualizing destination competitiveness via adaptive capacity, this work advances theoretical dialogues on resilience while equipping destination management organizations, policymakers, and entrepreneurs with pragmatic strategies for regenerative recovery and enduring viability in hyper-connected global markets.

Preface

Entrepreneurship today unfolds in an era defined by turbulence. Globalized economies are increasingly shaped by overlapping shocks, financial crises, geopolitical tensions, pandemics, climate change, technological disruption, and institutional fragility. In this environment, resilience has emerged not merely as a desirable trait, but as a defining capability for entrepreneurs, firms, and ecosystems striving to survive, adapt, and grow. This volume, Entrepreneurial Resilience in Turbulent Globalized Economies, responds to this pressing reality by offering a multidimensional exploration of how resilience is built, enacted, and sustained across diverse contexts, sectors, and levels of analysis.

The book brings together conceptual, empirical, and policy-oriented perspectives to advance understanding of entrepreneurial resilience as a dynamic and systemic process. Rather than treating resilience as simple recovery from crisis, the chapters collectively emphasize learning, innovation, strategic adaptation, and transformation. They examine how entrepreneurs respond to volatility in markets, institutions, and resources, while also highlighting the critical roles of governance, education, finance, technology, and social inclusion.

Spanning developed, emerging, and fragile economies, the contributions address resilience in startups, agrifood systems, tourism, informal economies, social enterprises, and community-based initiatives. By integrating insights from entrepreneurship, economics, management, policy studies, and sustainability research, the volume seeks to bridge fragmented literatures and stimulate future research agendas. At the same time, it offers practical frameworks and evidence-based insights for entrepreneurs, policymakers, educators, and development practitioners navigating uncertainty in an interconnected world.

CHAPTER OVERVIEW

The volume opens by introducing entrepreneurial resilience in turbulent globalized economies and establishing a unifying theoretical foundation for the book. Resilience is conceptualized as a multilevel process spanning individuals, firms, and entrepreneurial ecosystems, while entrepreneurship is situated within an environment shaped by overlapping global crises. By synthesizing prior scholarship and highlighting conceptual and methodological gaps, the first chapter advances a forward-looking research agenda that connects resilience to digital transformation, green entrepreneurship, emerging economies, and AI-enabled ecosystems.

Building on this foundation, the second chapter addresses the policy and institutional conditions that shape entrepreneurial resilience in periods of global disruption. It develops an integrative framework that foregrounds coordinated policy design, institutional learning, and adaptive governance as drivers of recovery, innovation, and inclusive growth, positioning resilience as a systemic outcome rather than an individual attribute.

The third chapter turns to human capital and learning, demonstrating how education strengthens entrepreneurial adaptability and competitiveness in a rapidly evolving global economy. Emphasis is placed on formal, informal, and experiential learning as pathways through which entrepreneurs build capabilities for opportunity recognition, strategic renewal, and sustainable performance under uncertainty.

Extending the discussion toward inclusion and social value creation, the fourth chapter reconsiders social entrepreneurship through the lenses of knowledge, social inclusion, and digital transformation. It positions social entrepreneurship as a systemic response to turbulence, highlighting its potential to address complex social needs while contributing to long-term well-being and resilient development trajectories.

The fifth chapter broadens the inclusive perspective by focusing on social, inclusive, and community-based entrepreneurship in global contexts. It emphasizes collective governance, embedded social networks, and multi-actor collaboration as foundations of community resilience, particularly in socio-economically fragile settings where entrepreneurship can mitigate exclusion and strengthen local capacity.

Complementing these insights with a policy-embedded case, the sixth chapter focuses on entrepreneurial resilience among urban street vendors through the lens of financial inclusion. Drawing on evidence from a large-scale microcredit initiative, it illustrates how institutional support and access to finance can stabilize livelihoods, reduce vulnerability, and enhance adaptive capacity within the informal economy during systemic shocks.

Shifting to firm-level strategy, the seventh chapter explores how consulting firms help startups navigate the tension between internationalization and innovation. The analysis highlights the contribution of external advisors in providing strategic knowledge, experiential learning, and risk mitigation capabilities that enable young firms to pursue cross-border growth while sustaining innovation under conditions of uncertainty.

The eighth chapter brings the discussion to organizational resilience and managerial practice, focusing on strategic shifts in management control systems during times of crisis. Based on evidence from companies operating in adverse conditions, it shows how adjustments in control practices can strengthen responsiveness, improve processes, and support organizational adaptability, reinforcing resilience as an integrated managerial capability.

Turning to contexts of acute instability, the ninth chapter foregrounds marketing and branding as entrepreneurial coping mechanisms in fragile and conflict-affected states. Marketing is reframed as a socio-political practice that builds trust, legitimacy, and global connectivity, demonstrating how entrepreneurs navigate institutional voids, sanctions, and geopolitical uncertainty while sustaining resilience and, in some cases, fostering international solidarity.

From there, the tenth chapter addresses macroeconomic turbulence through the lens of exchange rate shocks in agrifood value chains. Integrating exchange-rate economics with value-chain resilience perspectives, it outlines how currency volatility reshapes costs, competitiveness, and strategic decision-making, particularly for small and medium-sized enterprises with limited buffers, and proposes a conceptual framework to explain adaptive responses to macroeconomic disruption.

The eleventh chapter then turns to tourism-sector resilience, highlighting the combined role of foreign direct investment and artificial intelligence in strengthening development pathways. It shows how investment and technology jointly enhance productivity, support innovation, improve risk management, and advance sustainability objectives within tourism ecosystems facing accelerating change.

Focusing on the built environment of tourism, the twelfth chapter introduces a KPI- and ESG-based framework for resilience in tourism real estate and mixed-use developments. It offers a practical, data-light approach that links performance indicators with sustainability goals and managerial decision-making, supporting more robust strategic planning and disruption management.

The volume concludes with destination-level perspectives on resilience, drawing on insights from the Greek experience to illuminate processes of strategic adaptation. The final chapter emphasizes learning, innovation, and networked collaboration as key drivers of adaptive capacity and long-term competitiveness, demonstrating how destination resilience emerges through coordinated stakeholder action and continuous renewal in response to evolving external pressures.

Chapter 1
Introducing Entrepreneurial Resilience in Turbulent Globalized Economies:
Theory, Context, and a Research Agenda

Eleni E. Anastasopoulou
https://orcid.org/0000-0002-0918-8527
Neapolis University Pafos, Cyprus

Georgios A. Deirmentzoglou
https://orcid.org/0000-0003-1687-0708
Neapolis University Pafos, Cyprus

Ioannis Anastasopoulos
https://orcid.org/0009-0003-6430-5831
University of Piraeus, Greece

Valeska V. Geldres-Weiss
Universidad de La Frontera, Chile

ABSTRACT

This chapter offers an integrative overview of entrepreneurial resilience in turbulent globalized economies. It situates entrepreneurship within a context of overlapping crises, such as financial shocks, pandemics, geopolitical tensions, climate risks and rapid technological change; and conceptualises entrepreneurial resilience as

DOI: 10.4018/979-8-3373-6991-4.ch001

a dynamic, multilevel process through which entrepreneurs and ventures absorb shocks, adapt and sometimes transform. The chapter synthesises key drivers at three levels: individual psychological resources and learning-oriented mindsets; firm-level capabilities related to strategic flexibility, innovation, digitalisation and financial management; and ecosystem-level conditions. It also highlights major conceptual and methodological gaps, including fragmented definitions, reliance on cross-sectional designs and limited attention to marginalised contexts. The chapter concludes by outlining research directions linking resilience to digital and green entrepreneurship, crisis-prone and emerging economies and AI-enabled ecosystems.

1. INTRODUCTION

Entrepreneurship has long been recognised as a critical engine of job creation, innovation and structural transformation. Small and medium-sized enterprises (SMEs) alone account for around 90% of firms and more than half of global employment, meaning that the fortunes of entrepreneurs are tightly intertwined with broader societal prosperity. Yet the conditions under which entrepreneurs operate have become more volatile and difficult to diagnose. The contemporary environment is often described as 'VUCA' (volatile, uncertain, complex and ambiguous) capturing forms of unpredictability that roil markets and complicate strategic planning, shaped in part by globalization and rapid technological change (Bennett & Lemoine, 2014). In this context, the capacity of entrepreneurs and their ventures to withstand, adapt to and even leverage adversity has moved from a desirable attribute to an essential prerequisite for survival and long-term value creation.

Recent crises have made this imperative visible. The global financial crisis, the COVID-19 pandemic, geopolitical conflicts, energy price spikes and climate-related disasters have exposed the fragility of interconnected value chains and the vulnerability of firms to abrupt demand collapses, supply disruptions and credit constraints (Deirmentzoglou et al., 2025; Deirmentzoglou et al., 2024). For instance, reviews of the pandemic's economic effects conclude that COVID-19 constituted an unprecedented shock for entrepreneurship, simultaneously threatening existing ventures and opening new market opportunities (Belitski et al., 2022). Firm-level micro-data show that SMEs experienced sharper sales declines than large firms during COVID-19 across multiple developing countries, and US evidence indicates high closure risk and severe financial fragility among small businesses. These patterns are consistent with thinner liquidity buffers and greater financing/support frictions for smaller firms (Amin et al., 2023; Bartik et al., 2020). These patterns underline that shocks in turbulent globalized economies are not "great equalisers":

they disproportionately test the resilience of entrepreneurs and SMEs that already operate at the margins of financial and institutional systems.

Against this backdrop, resilience has emerged as a central construct in management and entrepreneurship research. In management research, resilience has often been defined as the ability to recover or 'bounce back' after shocks, while more recent conceptualizations emphasize resilience as a dynamic attribute involving absorption, adaptation, and in some accounts transformative responses over time (Conz & Magnani, 2020). Entrepreneurship scholars have imported and extended these ideas, arguing that the entrepreneurial process is inherently fraught with uncertainty, setbacks and resource scarcity, so that understanding why some entrepreneurs persist, learn and grow through adversity while others exit is fundamental to explaining entrepreneurial success. Systematic reviews show that SME/business resilience remains conceptually fragmented: it is variously framed as bounce-back/survival and recovery, as adaptability and responsiveness, as maintaining positive performance/growth, and, in more dynamic conceptualizations, as the capability to develop new capabilities and seize opportunities under turbulence (e.g. Saad et al., 2021).

A rapidly growing literature has begun to unpack these layers. At the individual level, research on entrepreneurs' psychological resilience examines how affective, cognitive and behavioural resources, such as optimism, self-efficacy, emotion regulation and coping strategies, enable founders to maintain functioning and continue opportunity pursuit under stress (Ahmed et al., 2022; Hartmann et al., 2022). This work shows that resilient entrepreneurs are better able to reframe adversity, sustain motivation and mobilise social support, which in turn is associated with higher venture persistence and well-being. At the firm level, SME resilience is increasingly conceptualized as a dynamic, time-dependent process that unfolds before, during, and after disruptions (Conz & Magnani, 2020). Emerging research on entrepreneurial ecosystems indicates that place-based networks and institutional conditions shape entrepreneurs' access to resources and knowledge, and that stronger local ecosystems are associated with greater regional economic resilience to shocks (e.g. Iacobucci & Perugini, 2021; Roundy, 2022).

The salience of resilience is heightened by the changing nature of globalization. Deep integration into global value chains has increased efficiency and opened new markets for entrepreneurs, but it has also created complex exposure to geographically distant shocks, whether in the form of logistics bottlenecks, trade disputes, sanctions or sudden regulatory shifts. In such a "polycrisis" environment, entrepreneurial resilience is not only about surviving discrete shocks but about navigating overlapping and interacting disruptions over time. At the same time, turbulence can act as a powerful selection and learning mechanism in entrepreneurial ecosystems. Crises often trigger the exit of less productive firms while creating niches for innovative business models, new technologies and novel forms of organising. However, the ability to "pivot" under such pressure depends strongly on prior investments in capabilities, access to finance and supportive policy frameworks. This makes resilience a relational and distributed phenomenon rather than a purely individual attribute: it is produced through interactions among entrepreneurs, teams, organisations and institutions.

It is therefore unsurprising that resilience has become a focal point for policy debates around inclusive and sustainable recovery (World Economic Forum, 2023). This emphasis is strongly echoed by the World Economic Forum, which positions resilience as a central pillar of sustainable and inclusive economic recovery. The Forum argues that governments and international organisations must strengthen SME support, innovation-oriented policy instruments and coordinated public–private strategies in order to build entrepreneurial ecosystems that can absorb shocks, sustain employment and function under conditions of ongoing disruption. In the same spirit, the World Economic Forum's Resilience Consortium frames resilience as an "imperative condition" for securing a sustainable and inclusive future, stressing that coordinated action is needed to ensure SMEs can adapt to intersecting pressures arising from climate risks, technological disruption, geopolitical instability and recurrent supply-chain disturbances. This policy framing reinforces the chapter's argument that entrepreneurial resilience is not solely an individual or firm-level attribute, but a systemic capability shaped by ecosystem design, institutional capacity and multi-actor coordination.

Governments and international organisations increasingly frame SME support, innovation policy and place-based industrial strategies in terms of building resilient entrepreneurial ecosystems that can better absorb shocks and sustain employment. Research synthesizing COVID-19 policy responses indicates that governments deployed a broad toolkit, including job-retention/wage-subsidy schemes, loan guarantees and other emergency finance, and tax-related relief—to protect SME liquidity and employment. Evidence also suggests that such interventions could improve short-run survival prospects for some SMEs, but their effectiveness was uneven and often depended on targeting and implementation, with some groups (e.g., self-employed or otherwise vulnerable entrepreneurs) not fully reached by initial policy designs (Belitski et al., 2022; Amin et al., 2023). Understanding entrepreneurial resilience in turbulent globalised economies thus has direct implications for how support schemes are designed, targeted and evaluated.

This chapter responds to these developments by offering an integrative, multi-level introduction to entrepreneurial resilience in turbulent globalized economies. Drawing on recent systematic reviews and empirical studies in entrepreneurship, SME research and strategic management, it first situates entrepreneurial resilience within the broader landscape of globalization-induced turbulence, highlighting key sources of volatility and uncertainty for entrepreneurs. It then disentangles the concept of entrepreneurial resilience, clarifying how it relates to, but differs from, organisational resilience and other adjacent constructs such as agility or adaptability. Subsequent sections synthesise evidence on the drivers and determinants of entrepreneurial resilience at individual, firm and ecosystem levels, before outlining emerging research directions that connect resilience to digitalisation, sustainability, crisis-prone contexts and AI-enabled entrepreneurial ecosystems. By foregrounding resilience as both an outcome and a process embedded in multi-scalar systems, the chapter aims to advance scholarly understanding and provide a conceptual foundation for researchers, educators and policymakers seeking to foster more robust and opportunity-oriented forms of entrepreneurship in an increasingly turbulent world.

2. UNDERSTANDING TURBULENCE IN THE GLOBALIZED ECONOMY

2.1 Defining Turbulence: Volatility, Uncertainty, Complexity and Ambiguity (VUCA)

The contemporary global economy is frequently described through the VUCA lens to capture the intensity and multidimensional nature of turbulence that confronts firms and entrepreneurs. Originally coined in military strategy and later adopted in management research, the VUCA framework highlights how rapid, nonlinear change, incomplete information, dense interdependencies and equivocal signals combine to make environments increasingly difficult to interpret and predict (Dziak, 2024; Bennett & Lemoine, 2014). Volatility refers to the speed and magnitude of change in key variables such as prices, exchange rates or demand conditions. Uncertainty reflects the limited ability to forecast future events or their impacts, even when probabilities are hard to assign. Complexity stems from the dense networks of actors, institutions and technologies that shape outcomes, while ambiguity points to situations in which causal relationships are unclear or contested.

Recent systematic work has clarified that VUCA is not just a loose metaphor but a set of related yet analytically distinct dimensions that characterise contemporary business environments. Taskan et al. (2022), for example, show that volatility is typically operationalised as rapid and unstable change, uncertainty as information gaps and unpredictable outcomes, complexity as numerous interconnected factors and relationships, and ambiguity as situations where events admit multiple, competing interpretations (Taskan et al., 2022). Although these insights emerge from broader organizational and leadership studies, they are highly relevant for entrepreneurship: founders must commit resources, design business models and mobilize stakeholders precisely in contexts where signals are noisy and conditions change faster than learning cycles. The VUCA framing thus offers a conceptual bridge between macro-level turbulence and micro-level entrepreneurial decision-making.

2.2 Global Shocks Affecting Entrepreneurial Ecosystems

In the last two decades, entrepreneurial ecosystems have been repeatedly exposed to large-scale economic crises. The 2008 global financial crisis, the eurozone sovereign debt crisis and, more recently, the COVID-19 pandemic all produced sudden collapses in demand, liquidity constraints and credit tightening that directly affected venture formation and growth. Synthesizing 26 systematic reviews on COVID-19 and small and medium-sized enterprises (SMEs), Kádár and Jáki (2024) document widespread revenue declines, liquidity and cash-flow constraints, and heightened risks to firm survival, while also highlighting heterogeneous resilience strategies, including digitalization, supply chain adaptation and business model innovation. At the level of entrepreneurial finance, Brown and Rocha (2020) show that the early stages of the COVID-19 pandemic coincided with a sharp contraction in venture capital and other equity deals in China, with especially severe declines in seed and early-stage investments as heightened uncertainty disrupted the market for entrepreneurial finance. These dynamics illustrate how macroeconomic shocks filter through financial markets into entrepreneurial ecosystems, reshaping opportunity sets and survival probabilities.

Geopolitical instability has emerged as an equally salient source of turbulence. Geopolitical tensions and conflicts, including the Russia–Ukraine war and escalating U.S.–China rivalry, have heightened uncertainty, altered risk perceptions and reconfigured global value chains. Recent analyses show that rising geopolitical tensions propagate through global value chains, magnifying uncertainty, creating contagion across sectors and countries, and contributing to trade slowdowns, bottlenecks and reduced investment. (Bo, & Ankai, 2021). Recent research on SMEs and geopolitical risk shows that such tensions affect the performance and volatility of SME equity indexes and that their impact can differ across major crises such as COVID-19 and the Russia–Ukraine war, reinforcing the view that geopolitical risk is now a central element of the SME and entrepreneurial environment (Choudhury et al., 2025). Entrepreneurs operating in export-oriented or internationally networked sectors must therefore navigate not only market volatility but also sanctions regimes, trade restrictions and fluctuating security conditions.

Pandemics and public health crises constitute another category of global shocks with profound entrepreneurial implications. COVID-19 produced simultaneous supply and demand shocks: mandatory lockdowns and mobility restrictions constrained production and service delivery, while consumer uncertainty depressed discretionary spending. A growing body of research shows that SMEs were particularly exposed to revenue collapse, supply chain interruptions and workforce disruptions, but also that many developed adaptive responses such as digitalization, product–service reconfiguration and new forms of collaboration (Kádár & Jáki 2024; Mishra & Singh, 2023; Santos et al. 2023). Studies of entrepreneurial uncertainty argue that crisis events like COVID-19 generate chronic uncertainty in the business environment and in entrepreneurial finance, heightening unpredictability around economic and policy developments and making it harder for entrepreneurs to secure funding and pursue growth-oriented investments (Brown & Rocha, 2020).

Climate change and environmental disruptions add a slower-burning but increasingly acute dimension of turbulence. Empirical work by Han and Zhou (2025) shows that climate-related disasters reduce firm entry and increase firm exits in the short term, and that cumulative disaster losses are associated with higher exit rates and shorter firm survival in the long term, while cities with denser local financial institutions display greater entrepreneurial resilience. Broader analyses of climate risk for business highlight both physical risks, such as damage to assets and infrastructure, supply interruptions and productivity losses, and transition risks related to carbon pricing, regulation and shifting consumer preferences. For entrepreneurs, these dynamics simultaneously threaten existing models and generate new opportunities in renewable energy, climate services, circular economy solutions and nature-based tourism.

Technological disruptions associated with digitalization and artificial intelligence are increasingly reshaping entrepreneurial ecosystems by changing business models, transaction costs and competitive conditions. Using panel data for 34 countries between 2015 and 2018, Dabbous et al. (2023) find that digitalization has a positive effect on both entrepreneurial activity and sustainable competitiveness, with connectivity, internet use and the integration of digital technologies emerging as particularly important drivers. At the same time, scholarship on digital entrepreneurship stresses that rapid technological change generates risks, including heightened competition, cybersecurity threats, data privacy concerns and the constant need for organizational learning to avoid business model obsolescence. In crisis situations such as COVID-19, digital technologies have been shown to "reinvent" entrepreneurial resilience by enabling new channels for value creation and stakeholder engagement, from platform-based business models to remote service delivery (Santos et al., 2023).

2.3 How Turbulence Affects Markets, Supply Chains and Entrepreneurial Opportunities

Turbulence of the kind described above affects markets by increasing demand volatility and shortening firms' planning horizons. During the pandemic, severe drops in demand in sectors such as hospitality, tourism and other face-to-face services put intense pressure on SMEs. Recent studies document how these demand shocks translated into revenue losses, cash-flow instability, liquidity shortages and heightened bankruptcy risk, particularly for SMEs with limited financial reserves or restricted access to external finance (e.g. Kádár & Jáki, 2024). At the same time, policy interventions such as credit and cash support and wage subsidies helped firms address liquidity constraints and retain workers in some contexts, but cross-country evidence shows that government support had heterogeneous effects across firm sizes and regions, generating complex policy–market interactions that firms had to navigate during the crisis (Amin et al., 2023). Economic crises and geopolitical shocks also interact with exchange rate movements and commodity price swings, influencing cost structures and profit margins in ways that are particularly salient for internationally oriented ventures.

Trade policy volatility has also re-emerged as a distinct source of turbulence in the world economic order. Recent U.S. actions introduced a broad-based tariff structure, featuring a baseline tariff applied across trading partners alongside differentiated "reciprocal" rates, thereby increasing uncertainty for firms engaged in international sourcing and exporting (White House, 2025; KPMG, 2025). This matters for entrepreneurship because trade policy uncertainty tends to dampen new firm formation and to weaken firms' performance through operational channels such as reduced innovation and lower supply-chain efficiency, effects that are especially consequential for resource-constrained SMEs. In practical terms, tariff shocks propagate quickly into pricing, contracting and working-capital needs, and they interact with other disruption channels (logistics bottlenecks, geopolitical risk, and regulatory shifts), amplifying planning difficulties for internationally exposed ventures.

Supply chains are a critical transmission mechanism linking global shocks to entrepreneurial outcomes. Early COVID-19 disruptions, followed by logistics bottlenecks and geopolitical conflicts, exposed the vulnerability of highly specialized, geographically dispersed value chains. Reviews of global supply chain shocks indicate that pandemics and conflicts led to shortages of key inputs, shipping delays and rising transportation costs, forcing firms to reconsider sourcing strategies, inventory policies and geographic concentration (Mishra et al., 2025). The OECD's (2025) recent analysis of economic security similarly highlights that deep international supply-chain integration, while a source of efficiency and innovation, creates systemic vulnerabilities when shocks occur in locations that are critical nodes for semiconductors, critical raw materials or strategic goods. For entrepreneurs, particularly in manufacturing, agrifood and technology sectors, these disruptions can delay product launches, increase working capital requirements and erode competitiveness.

Yet turbulence also reshapes entrepreneurial opportunities. Research on supply chain resilience in SMEs shows that crises have accelerated experimentation with supplier and customer diversification, more flexible sourcing and logistics arrangements, and the adoption of Industry 4.0 technologies that enhance supply-chain visibility, transparency and real-time monitoring (Mishra & Singh, 2023). Entrepreneurs who can orchestrate flexible networks and leverage digital tools, such as e-commerce platforms, data analytics and cloud-based coordination, are often better positioned to convert supply chain redesign into competitive advantage. Santos et al. (2023) illustrate how entrepreneurs during COVID-19 exploited digital infrastructures to pivot into new markets, redesign revenue models and sustain stakeholder relationships under conditions of extreme uncertainty. In this sense, turbulence not only constrains but also reconfigures the opportunity landscape, privileging capabilities in scanning, recombination and rapid implementation.

3. CONCEPTUALIZING ENTREPRENEURIAL RESILIENCE

Entrepreneurial resilience has emerged as a central construct in explaining why some entrepreneurs and their ventures withstand adversity, recover from shocks and even grow through crises, while others exit or stagnate. Yet, despite its popularity, the concept is far from settled. Resilience has travelled from ecology and developmental psychology into management and entrepreneurship, accumulating multiple and sometimes inconsistent meanings along the way. In this section, entrepreneurial resilience is disentangled conceptually by tracing its definitional evolution, distinguishing it from organizational resilience, and clarifying its psychological, strategic and ecosystem dimensions, before differentiating it from related constructs such as adaptability, agility, absorptive capacity and entrepreneurial orientation.

3.1 Definitions and Conceptual Evolution of Resilience

Early work in psychology defined resilience as "positive adaptation despite adversity", emphasizing individuals' ability to maintain or regain functioning in the face of risk and stress. In management and organization studies, resilience was initially understood as a capability to withstand disruption and bounce back to prior performance levels, but has gradually shifted towards more dynamic conceptualizations that highlight learning, transformation and even growth through adversity (Todt et al., 2024; Martinelli et al., 2018).

Entrepreneurship scholars began to adopt the concept as they recognized that launching and growing ventures exposes founders to unusually high levels of uncertainty, setbacks and failure. Systematic reviews show that entrepreneurial resilience has been conceptualized variously as a personal trait, a set of psychological resources, and an adaptive process unfolding over time (Korber & McNaughton,

2017; Hartmann et al., 2022; Nautiyal & Pathak, 2023). Building on this work, some authors further treat entrepreneurial resilience as a dynamic capability of the entrepreneur–venture system, enabling the reconfiguration of resources in the face of adversity. Across these perspectives, three common elements can be identified: the presence of significant adversity or turbulence; a pattern of constructive coping, adaptation or resource mobilization; and relatively positive outcomes such as venture survival, opportunity pursuit, well-being or learning.

The two constructs are linked but not interchangeable. Founders' resilience can "spill over" into the venture by shaping culture, decision-making and the development of adaptive capabilities, yet resilient individuals may not always build resilient organizations if structures remain fragile or overly dependent on heroic leadership. Conversely, organizations may institutionalize resilience through robust processes and slack resources even when individual entrepreneurs experience strain. Conceptually distinguishing entrepreneurial from organizational resilience allows scholars to examine cross-level mechanisms, how micro-level psychological resilience aggregates into meso- and macro-level resilience, and where misalignments between resilient individuals and vulnerable organizations arise.

3.2 The Psychological Dimension: Persistence, Grit and Cognitive Adaptability

At its core, entrepreneurial resilience has a psychological foundation. Entrepreneurship requires sustained effort under uncertainty, so resilient entrepreneurs must regulate emotions, maintain motivation and adapt their cognitions when confronted with setbacks. Hartmann et al.'s (2022) review shows that empirical studies typically conceptualize entrepreneurs' psychological resilience as a process grounded in affective, cognitive and behavioral resources, such as optimism, self-efficacy, emotional regulation and persistence, which support continued entrepreneurial action despite adversity.

Grit, the tendency to sustain passion and perseverance for long-term goals, has been increasingly examined as a key ingredient of entrepreneurial resilience. Studies in the broader literature on grit and entrepreneurship suggest that gritty founders are more likely to persist with their ventures, recover from failure and invest in learning after negative outcomes, though excessive persistence can sometimes lock entrepreneurs into unviable paths (Todt et al., 2018; Hartmann et al., 2022). Cognitive adaptability is another critical element: existing work suggests that resilient entrepreneurs show flexibility in how they frame problems, drawing on both causal and effectual logics, using cognitive coping strategies to revise their interpretations of adversity and to identify new opportunities through creative recombination of resources and information (Ahmed et al., 2022; Hartmann et al., 2022).

Psychological resilience is not purely dispositional but can be developed over time through experience, reflection and social support. Entrepreneurs' engagement with challenging events can build resilience by expanding their repertoire of coping strategies and strengthening self-efficacy, provided that adversity does not become overwhelming. At the same time, there is growing awareness of the "dark side" of resilience: overly resilient entrepreneurs may tolerate harmful conditions, neglect well-being or persist with failing ideas, with negative implications for themselves and their teams.

3.3 The Strategic Dimension: Pivoting, Opportunity Recognition and Resource Recombination

Entrepreneurial resilience is also expressed in strategic behaviour. Resilient entrepreneurs do not only endure shocks; they adapt their business models, reorient markets and creatively reconfigure resources. Studies of small firms in turbulent and crisis conditions highlight how resilient ventures leverage digital channels, data-driven marketing and resourcefulness to pivot towards emerging customer needs. (Branicki et al., 2018; Hokmabadi et al., 2024).

Opportunity recognition is central in this strategic dimension. From a resilience lens, adverse events can reveal new opportunities, such as unmet needs created by disrupted supply chains or damaged infrastructures. Research on entrepreneurship in disaster and other adverse contexts shows that entrepreneurs who interpret such situations as openings for value creation engage in opportunity search, improvisation and various forms of bricolage, which can support both their own recovery and the resilience of affected communities. (Monllor & Murphy, 2017; Shepherd & Williams, 2020).

Bricolage and resource recombination are key mechanisms through which strategic resilience is enacted. Linna's (2013) study of innovator-entrepreneurs at the base of the pyramid shows how they "make do with resources at hand," improvising and recombining locally available materials and knowledge to create low-cost innovations, with resource scarcity functioning as a driver of creative experimentation rather than simply a barrier. A recent systematic review of entrepreneurial bricolage shows that such improvisational combining of resources can underpin resilience by enabling ventures to adapt in turbulent conditions without relying on large new financial investments, especially under the resource constraints typical of start-ups and small firms (Aaouid et al., 2024).

In digital contexts, strategic resilience is increasingly linked to the ability to leverage digital transformation and marketing capabilities. Hokmabadi et al. (2024) show, based on a systematic review, that small firms can strengthen business resilience by deploying digital technologies to transform their operations and business models, reach new markets and increase agility, but only when these technologies are supported by organizational capabilities, such as ambidexterity, agility and digital skills, that enable firms to sense and respond to rapidly changing environments.

3.4 The Ecosystem Dimension: Networks, Institutions and Policy Environments

Entrepreneurial resilience does not develop in isolation; it is shaped by contextual resources in entrepreneurs' environments, particularly their business networks. These network ties provide access to information, socioemotional support and advice that help buffer stress and adversity. Newman et al. (2018) show that entrepreneurs' effective use of business networks enhances both their psychological resilience and subjective well-being, indicating that relational resources are a crucial underpinning of resilience.

At the organizational level, studies of small and medium-sized enterprises (SMEs) show that resilience is facilitated by external institutional support and collaborative networks. Government programs, SME support schemes and supply-chain partners can provide financial assistance, training and improved market connections that help firms cope with shocks such as COVID-19 (e.g. Damiano & Valenza, 2025). Policy environments also matter: subsidies, emergency loans, regulatory flexibility and targeted entrepreneurship support programs can help ventures absorb shocks and invest in adaptation. Conversely, institutional voids, political instability or weak rule of law can undermine resilience by increasing unpredictability and limiting access to formal support mechanisms, pushing entrepreneurs to rely more heavily on informal networks and strategies such as bricolage.

This ecosystem perspective underscores that entrepreneurial resilience is co-produced through interactions between actors and contexts. Networks and institutions can either amplify entrepreneurs' psychological and strategic resilience or constrain their ability to mobilize resources and exploit opportunities.

4. DRIVERS AND DETERMINANTS OF ENTREPRENEURIAL RESILIENCE

Entrepreneurial resilience is increasingly understood as a multilevel phenomenon shaped by the interaction of individual, organizational and ecosystem-level factors rather than as a fixed personal trait. Recent reviews of resilience in entrepreneurship and SMEs highlight that resilient outcomes emerge from the alignment of psychological resources, firm capabilities and external support structures that enable ventures to anticipate, absorb and adapt to shocks over time (e.g. Koporcic et al., 2025). In this sense, resilience is not merely a capacity to "bounce back," but a dynamic process through which entrepreneurs recombine resources, revise strategies and reconfigure relationships in response to turbulence. The following subsections synthesize evidence on key individual, firm and ecosystem drivers that underpin this process.

4.1 Individual-Level Drivers

At the individual level, psychological capital (PsyCap), a developable positive psychological state, has been proposed as an important personal resource for performance and coping in challenging contexts. PsyCap comprises hope, self-efficacy, resiliency, and optimism, which together can support goal pursuit and bouncing back from adversity under uncertainty. (Luthans & Youssef, 2007). Conceptual and empirical work shows that these components are highly relevant in entrepreneurial settings characterized by ambiguity, setbacks and prolonged effort. Hope supports goal-directed energy and flexible pathways thinking; self-efficacy underpins confidence in mobilizing resources; resilience facilitates recovery from failure; and optimism sustains positive expectations about future outcomes. Synthesizing this literature, PsyCap helps entrepreneurs manage stressors more effectively, engage in adaptive coping and maintain functioning during crises, thereby acting as a psychological backbone of resilience.

Longitudinal evidence links resilience-related psychological resources to entrepreneurial success. Ayala and Manzano (2014), studying established entrepreneurs in the Spanish tourism sector, show that hardiness, resourcefulness, and optimism measured earlier significantly predict both objective and subjective business growth over time, with resourcefulness emerging as the strongest predictor. Moreover, Bullough and Renko (2013) find that among participants in Afghanistan and the U.S., entrepreneurial self-efficacy and resilience are positively associated with entrepreneurial intentions; moreover, in the Afghan (higher-adversity) context, the interaction of self-efficacy and resilience is significant, suggesting these psychological resources are especially important for sustaining entrepreneurial intentions under severe conditions. Together, these studies suggest that PsyCap and related resilience dimensions increase the likelihood that entrepreneurs will persist through shocks and convert adversity into learning and growth rather than exit.

Closely related is the entrepreneurial mindset, particularly growth-oriented and learning-oriented cognitions. Research on entrepreneurial learning shows that the ability to extract lessons from failures and crises is crucial for building resilient trajectories. Cope (2011) shows that learning from venture failure can trigger higher-order learning (e.g., transformative, double-loop, and generative learning), fostering deeper self-awareness and more sophisticated entrepreneurial mental models, alongside future-oriented preparedness and heightened sensitivity to 'warning signals' in subsequent entrepreneurial activity. During the COVID-19 crisis, Orth and Schuldis (2021) find that organizational learning capability is positively associated with organizational resilience, with particularly strong effects on the adaptive capacity component. Although these studies focus partly at the organizational level, they underline the importance of individual-level learning orientation and cognitive flexibility for resilience, as entrepreneurs must be willing to revise assumptions, experiment with alternative solutions and incorporate feedback from turbulent environments. In this sense, a resilient entrepreneurial mindset combines persistence with openness to change rather than rigid tenacity.

Leadership and crisis-time decision-making are pivotal in shaping SME responses to turbulence. Koporcic et al. (2025) synthesize evidence linking individual characteristics such as strong leadership, rapid decision-making, and motivated individuals to SME resilience, and highlight that ineffective leadership can impede crisis response, supporting the view that leaders' actions under pressure materially influence organizational outcomes. Entrepreneurship resilience research highlights the importance of emotion-focused coping, including emotion regulation, for managing the negative emotions associated with adversity and failure, and for enabling sensemaking and (re)engagement over time. Ahmed et al. (2022) further emphasize appraisal and re/appraisal processes and meaning-making narratives as mechanisms shaping how entrepreneurs cope and build psychological resilience. Empirical work in organizational psychology suggests that leaders' self-efficacy and emotional stability are associated with higher follower well-being and adaptability, which are themselves foundational to collective resilience. While more domain-specific studies are needed in entrepreneurship, existing evidence indicates that resilient leadership, characterized by calm under pressure, constructive framing of adversity and supportive interaction with stakeholders, amplifies the effects of individual PsyCap and learning orientation, and transmits resilience throughout the venture.

4.2 Firm-Level Drivers

Individual capacities translate into sustainable resilience only when supported by firm-level routines and capabilities. Strategic flexibility and innovation capability are especially salient in this regard. Building on a dynamic capabilities view, Ibora et al. (2020) argue that SME resilience under turbulence depends on firm-level capabilities that combine experimentation and reliability. In Spanish manufacturing SMEs during the Global Financial Crisis, organizational ambidexterity (exploration and exploitation) is positively associated with resilience, measured as survival and sales recovery, while strategic consistency in the exploration–exploitation trajectory mainly supports recovery (with a modest effect) and strengthens the ambidexterity–

recovery relationship. Bhamra et al. (2011) review organizational resilience as involving preparedness, response/adaptation, and recovery, emphasizing adaptive capacity and system characteristics such as diversity and adaptability (flexibility). They suggest resilience is strengthened when organizations can absorb disturbances while reconfiguring in changing environments, rather than relying solely on stability-oriented approaches. Recent systematic reviews of SME resilience confirm recurring coping strategies including business continuity planning, technology adoption/technological innovation, and proactive production strategies (Koporcic et al., 2025).

Digital transformation and technological integration have become increasingly central firm-level drivers of resilience. Khurana et al. (2022), studying Indian SMEs during COVID-19, show that adopting digital technologies enabled firms to enact sensing, seizing and transforming activities; through this crisis-driven digital transformation, resilience emerged as a second-order, multilevel dynamic capability spanning entrepreneur, organization and ecosystem levels. Complementary evidence from Browder et al. (2024) indicates that digital transformation promotes organizational resilience by enhancing firms' ability to adapt, reconfigure and innovate in response to shocks, effectively "upgrading" their adaptive capacity. Collectively, the literature suggests that digital technologies function not only as operational tools but as enablers of dynamic capabilities, widening the strategic menu of responses available to entrepreneurial ventures in crisis.

Financial resource management constitutes another critical firm-level determinant of resilience. Financial constraints repeatedly emerge as a key barrier to SME resilience, limiting preparedness and recovery options (Koporcic et al., 2025). Shojaee and Mirzaei (2024) provide direct empirical evidence by showing that financial flexibility, measured through indicators such as liquidity and financial stability, has a strong positive effect on the financial resilience of Iranian SMEs facing economic shocks, and that higher financial resilience is associated with a reduction in the adverse impact of economic shocks. While other studies identify proactive financial management, such as building emergency reserves, diversifying funding sources and cultivating strong relationships with financial institutions, as a central coping strategy for SMEs (e.g. Koporcic et al., 2025). For entrepreneurial ventures, disciplined financial planning, scenario analysis and the maintenance of flexible financing arrangements can therefore be understood as integral parts of resilience-building, rather than purely administrative tasks.

4.3 Ecosystem and Environmental Drivers

Beyond the individual firm, the broader entrepreneurial ecosystem exerts a powerful influence on resilience. Entrepreneurial ecosystems consist of interconnected actors, institutions and cultural norms that jointly shape entrepreneurial opportunities and constraints. Roundy et al. (2017) conceptualize the 'resilience of entrepreneurial ecosystems' and argue that ecosystems with diverse participants, ventures, business models, and support organizations, together with coherence around shared values and connectivity among actors, are better able to recover from and adapt to shocks while sustaining entrepreneurial activity. Their framework suggests that ecosystem resilience is rooted in system-level properties, particularly diversity and coherence/connectivity (shared values, common logics, and coordination among ecosystem actors), which can provide ventures with access to resources and support during and after shocks. Iacobucci and Perugini (2021) link the strength of local entrepreneurial ecosystems to territorial economic resilience in Italian provinces, showing that a multidimensional EE index, capturing institutional quality and ecosystem resource conditions (including finance and new knowledge proxies), is positively associated with provinces' resistance to and recovery from downturns.

Government policy and crisis-response frameworks form a second key pillar of ecosystem-level drivers. Evidence during COVID-19 suggests that crisis-response policy design can shape firms' expected survival and employment decisions (Bartik et al., 2020). Koporcic et al. (2025) underscore that external ecosystem conditions, especially strategic collaborations with stakeholders (including government bodies and NGOs), can support SME resilience by facilitating resource exchange and knowledge co-creation, while also calling for more research on how government policies and programs influence SME resilience during crises. The same review highlights SMEs' resource constraints and argues that resilience strategies should be tailored to sectoral and operational realities, while emphasizing the importance of strengthening access to finance. It also calls for further research on how the timing and nature of government interventions shape SME recovery and resilience after crises.

Finally, social networks and community support underpin entrepreneurial resilience by providing access to information, resources and emotional support. Newman et al. (2018) find that entrepreneurs' business network utilization is positively related to self-efficacy and resilience, which in turn enhance subjective well-being, highlighting networks as contextual resources that provide socioemotional support, advice and industry-relevant information that help build entrepreneurs' psychological resources. At the organizational level, Ozanne et al. (2022) show that internal social capital directly strengthens SME organizational resilience during COVID-19, while customer-focused external social capital contributes to resilience indirectly through dynamic capabilities (sensing, seizing, and reconfiguring) that enable firms to mobilize relational resources. Their analysis highlights how strong internal ties facilitate rapid information sharing and coordinated response, and how external customer ties become resilience-enhancing when translated into action via dynamic capabilities.

In summary, entrepreneurial resilience arises from the interaction of individual psychological resources, firm-level capabilities and ecosystem supports. Psychological capital, resilient mindsets and effective leadership shape how entrepreneurs perceive and respond to adversity; strategic flexibility, digital transformation and prudent financial management determine the range and quality of organizational responses; and supportive ecosystems, policies and networks provide the external scaffolding that allows ventures to withstand and adapt to shocks. Understanding these multilevel drivers is essential for designing interventions—whether training programs, organizational practices or policy frameworks—that seek not only to help entrepreneurs survive turbulence, but to build more adaptive, innovative and socially embedded forms of entrepreneurship in an increasingly volatile global economy.

5. RESEARCH AGENDA FOR ADVANCING THE FIELD

5.1 Conceptual Gaps in the Literature

Although work on entrepreneurial resilience has expanded rapidly, the construct remains conceptually fragmented. Reviews by Korber and McNaughton (2017) and Conduah and Essiaw (2022) indicate that entrepreneurial resilience research remains conceptually fragmented: resilience is variously treated as an ex ante trait-like capacity, as a set of resources/capabilities, as an outcome reflected in survival or performance, and as a dynamic process of recovery and transformation. This plurality has enabled the concept to travel across subfields, but it also creates ambiguity in definitions and measurement; both reviews call for clearer conceptualization and more multi-level, longitudinal theorizing across individual, firm, and broader system contexts. Future research needs more explicit theorisation of "what" is resilient, entrepreneur, team, venture, or ecosystem, and of how these levels interrelate. Pennetta et al.'s (2025) systematic review of entrepreneurial resilience under recent global disruptions similarly calls for multi-level models that connect psychological, organisational and contextual dimensions, instead of analysing them in isolation.

A second key gap is that resilience research is often not sufficiently process-anchored and theoretically precise. Hartmann et al. (2022) therefore call for stronger integration of entrepreneurs' psychological resilience with the new venture development process, including clearer theorizing of how resilience operates across initiation, engagement, and performance stages, and more designs that capture its dynamic nature over time. Likewise, Saad et al.'s (2021) systematic review highlights that SME resilience remains conceptually fragmented, with studies using divergent definitions and operationalizations and offering inconclusive evidence on key influencing factors. They also note that most contributions are conceptual or case-based and that longitudinal and interaction-focused empirical studies are relatively rare, limitations that constrain cumulative theory-building and a clearer understanding of how resilience develops over time. Conceptual work is needed that embeds entrepreneurial resilience in process theories of venturing, dynamic capabilities and strategic renewal, specifying when resilience facilitates persistence and when it may instead delay necessary exit or transformation.

Third, the literature remains biased toward entrepreneurs in advanced economies and formal sectors. Conduah and Essiaw's (2022) systematic review shows that resilience–entrepreneurship research remains fragmented across multiple tributaries, including a distinct stream on entrepreneurship and culture. They also note that the evidence base is skewed toward Western contexts, which may limit generalizability given potential cultural differences in how entrepreneurial resilience is constructed, and they call for more inclusive, multi-dimensional and longitudinal research. Evidence from informal artisan entrepreneurs in Kenya's tourism sector shows that resilience extends beyond individual traits and is strongly shaped by cultural and social norms, tacit knowledge, and collective arrangements (e.g., family/friend networks and social capital) that enable resourcing and coping through adversity (Kiptoo et al., 2024). Future theorising should therefore adopt a more critical lens, viewing entrepreneurial resilience not only as an admirable capability but also as an adaptation to structural precarity, and examining how institutions, power relations and policy choices make resilience more or less necessary for different groups.

Finally, the relationship between resilience and other key constructs, such as well-being, identity work, sustainability, digitalisation and innovation, remains under-specified. Reviews show that resilience is often positioned as a mediator between resources and performance, yet empirical studies rarely unpack potential trade-offs, for example when sustained effort under adversity erodes health or family life, or when short-term coping strategies undermine long-term environmental or social goals. Conceptual models that simultaneously incorporate resilience, well-being, purpose and sustainability could clarify when resilience is developmentally "healthy" and when it becomes a form of endurance in unsustainable conditions.

5.2 Methodological Opportunities

Methodologically, resilience research in SMEs is still heavily skewed toward cross-sectional designs. Reviews by Saad et al. (2021) and Conz and Magnani (2020) argue that this limits insight into causal processes and temporal dynamics of resilience, and that definitional and measurement overlap with survival and performance can blur resilience with simple success outcomes. Longitudinal and process-oriented studies, using panel data, event history analysis, diary methods or narrative approaches, are needed to follow entrepreneurs across the full arc of crises, recovery and potential transformation.

A second methodological gap lies in the limited use of multi-level and cross-country designs. Most existing studies analyse individual-level data or single firms, while treating the institutional and ecosystem context as background. Future research could leverage hierarchical modelling, network analysis and configurational methods to examine how combinations of personal resources (e.g., psychological capital), organisational capabilities (e.g., dynamic capabilities, digital readiness) and contextual factors (e.g., policy support, social safety nets) jointly produce resilient outcomes. Comparative work across advanced, emerging and conflict-affected economies would further clarify which drivers of resilience are universal and which are context-specific.

There is also considerable scope for methodological pluralism. Mixed-methods designs can triangulate survey measures of resilience with in-depth qualitative data on coping strategies, identity work and relational dynamics. Experimental and quasi-experimental studies, such as randomised trials of resilience-building training, mentoring schemes or digital support platforms, would allow scholars to test the effectiveness of specific interventions and move beyond merely documenting correlations. Malik and Terzidis (2025), using a TCCM-based review, argue that progress in resilience and strategic adaptation research requires greater theoretical integration, broader contextual coverage beyond Western- and MNC-centric settings, and stronger methodological pluralism (e.g., longitudinal, multi-level, configurational and mixed-method designs) to improve generalizability and capture resilience dynamics. Finally, advances in digital trace data and computational methods open opportunities to study entrepreneurial responses to shocks in real time, for example by analysing online platform activity, crowdfunding campaigns or social-media narratives during crises.

5.3 The Future of Entrepreneurial Resilience in Key Domains

Promising new research frontiers are emerging at the intersection of entrepreneurial resilience with digital entrepreneurship, sustainable and green entrepreneurship, crisis-prone and emerging economies, and AI-enabled ecosystems. In digital entrepreneurship, the COVID-19 pandemic has highlighted how digital artefacts, platforms and infrastructures can "reinvent" entrepreneurial resilience by enabling rapid business model pivots, access to new markets and reconfiguration of value creation under mobility restrictions. Santos et al. (2023), analysing reflective interviews with entrepreneurs from the "How I Built This – Resilience Series" podcast, show how entrepreneurs used digital tools to experiment with new offerings, maintain customer relationships and orchestrate partnerships, thereby transforming constraints into opportunities. Audretsch et al. (2024) similar argue that digitally advanced entrepreneurship can enhance resilience because digital tools strengthen firms' proactive, adaptive/absorptive, robustness and revitalization capacities. They also note that digitalization introduces new vulnerabilities, particularly around cybersecurity (and related technology-induced strains), which require greater attention in research and practice. Future research should therefore examine how different forms of digitalisation, platform participation, data analytics, automation, remote work, shape resilience, and how digital entrepreneurs build dynamic capabilities to cope with "polycrisis" environments.

In sustainable and green entrepreneurship, resilience is increasingly linked to the capacity of ventures to pursue economic viability while addressing environmental and social challenges. Studies of green entrepreneurial orientation and sustainable entrepreneurial orientation show that entrepreneurs who integrate environmental and social values into their strategies often rely on resilience to withstand regulatory uncertainty, technology risk and scepticism from investors or customers. Alshebami (2025) frames purpose-driven resilience in micro- and small enterprises in terms of defining a clear core purpose—articulating mission, vision, and values, which helps guide decision-making and sustain commitment during adversity. Empirically, defining core purpose (along with coping with unexpected challenges) is positively associated with business resilience and business economic sustainability. Korry & Wijayanti (2024) find that entrepreneurial resilience significantly contributes to SMEs' sustainable competitive advantage. They further show that financial, human, and social capital shape entrepreneurial resilience, while local cultural values strengthen the resilience–competitive advantage relationship by reinforcing entrepreneurs' confidence and support through alignment with local norms. Future work could explore how resilience enables experimentation with circular business models, low-carbon technologies and inclusive value chains, and whether there are tensions between resilience and deep sustainability transformations, for instance when resilience strategies prioritise incremental adaptation over more radical system change.

Crisis-prone and emerging economies constitute another critical domain. Research on entrepreneurial resilience in conflict zones, fragile states and informal economies illustrates how entrepreneurs operate under persistent threats, ranging from violence and political instability to weak institutions and infrastructural deficits. Future research should deepen understanding of how macro-level shocks (armed conflict, currency crises, climate extremes) interact with micro-level coping strategies, and how policy interventions can move beyond generic SME support to address the specific constraints of entrepreneurs operating in informal, rural or marginalised urban settings.

Finally, the rise of artificial intelligence (AI) creates a new frontier for entrepreneurial resilience and ecosystem research. At the individual level, Liu et al. (2025) show that entrepreneurs' AI literacy is positively associated with entrepreneurial resilience, partly because greater understanding of AI reduces AI-related anxiety and preserves psychological resources. Qualitative work and conceptual papers argue that AI tools, from predictive analytics to generative AI, can enhance resilience by improving opportunity recognition, scenario planning, resource optimisation and post-adversity learning, while also posing new challenges related to ethical risks, data privacy and algorithmic bias (Quahi et al., 2026; Hanif et al. 2024). At the ecosystem level, Roundy (2022) and Ştefan et al. (2025) push entrepreneurship research to theorize AI in relation to entrepreneurial ecosystems. Roundy (2022) explains how entrepreneurs' use of AI can substitute for local ecosystem interactions, reshaping ecosystem social, knowledge, and cultural coordination, with implications for entrepreneurs' access to ecosystem resources. Ştefan et al. (2025) introduce an 'AI-based entrepreneurial ecosystem' framework and show that ecosystem conditions, together with social influence and entrepreneurs' openness/performance expectations, shape AI entrepreneurial intentions. Future work should investigate how AI-driven policy mapping, accelerator programmes and platform governance influence the resilience of entire entrepreneurial communities, and how to design AI systems that amplify, rather than erode, inclusive and sustainable forms of entrepreneurial resilience.

6. CONCLUSION

6.1 Summary of Key Insights

This chapter has argued that entrepreneurial resilience is best understood as a dynamic, multilevel phenomenon that emerges from the interaction of individuals, organisations and their broader ecosystems. At the individual level, psychological resources such as hope, self-efficacy, optimism and the capacity to regulate emotions underpin entrepreneurs' ability to sustain effort in the face of uncertainty and failure. These resources are reinforced by a growth-oriented mindset and a willingness to learn from setbacks, which enable entrepreneurs to convert adverse experiences into new capabilities rather than treating them as terminal events.

At the firm level, resilience is rooted in strategic flexibility, innovation capability, digital transformation and prudent financial management. Ventures that invest in adaptive routines, maintain diverse revenue and supply bases, and use digital technologies to sense and respond to change are better able to withstand shocks and seize emergent opportunities. Financial resilience, through liquidity buffers, flexible financing arrangements and careful risk management, provides the slack needed to experiment and adjust without jeopardising survival.

Ecosystem and environmental drivers further shape how resilience is developed and deployed. Supportive entrepreneurial ecosystems provide access to knowledge, finance, networks and institutional support that amplify firm-level capabilities. Government policy and crisis-response frameworks can either buffer or exacerbate shocks, depending on their design and accessibility. Social networks and community support act as critical channels for information, resources and emotional sustenance, particularly for smaller and more vulnerable ventures. Finally, the chapter highlighted future research directions that link entrepreneurial resilience to digital entrepreneurship, sustainable and green ventures, crisis-prone and emerging economies, and AI-enabled ecosystems, while also calling for richer conceptual and methodological approaches.

6.2 Reaffirming the Importance of Resilience for Entrepreneurship in Global Turbulence

The need for entrepreneurial resilience has never been greater. Entrepreneurs today operate in a world characterised by overlapping crises, rapid technological disruption and dense cross-border interdependencies. Shocks travel quickly through global value chains and financial systems, often reaching even small, locally oriented ventures. In such an environment, traditional notions of stability and linear growth are increasingly unrealistic. The capacity to absorb disruption, adapt business models and, where necessary, transform or recombine ventures has become central to entrepreneurial success.

Resilience, however, is not only about surviving turbulent episodes. It is intimately connected with the opportunity-seeking nature of entrepreneurship. By enabling entrepreneurs to remain engaged, to tolerate ambiguity and to experiment under pressure, resilience supports the discovery of new solutions to emergent societal and market challenges. This is particularly evident in domains such as digital and sustainable entrepreneurship, where founders must continuously navigate regulatory uncertainty, technological change and shifting stakeholder expectations. Resilient entrepreneurs are better positioned to contribute to inclusive and sustainable growth, precisely because they can persist and innovate in contexts that might otherwise drive withdrawal or passivity.

Crucially, the chapter has emphasized that resilience should not be romanticised as individual heroism. It is shaped by structural conditions, institutions and power relations that distribute risks and buffers unevenly across different groups of entrepreneurs. Recognising this complexity does not diminish the value of resilience; rather, it highlights the importance of designing systems in which resilience is cultivated and shared, rather than demanded as a private obligation from those with the fewest resources.

6.3 Implications for Policymakers, Educators, and Ecosystem Designers

For policymakers, the analysis underscores that building resilient entrepreneurship requires more than ad hoc crisis interventions. It calls for coherent policy portfolios that strengthen financial resilience, incentivise innovation and digitalisation, and provide timely, accessible support mechanisms during shocks. Policies should be designed with attention to the heterogeneity of entrepreneurial populations, ensuring that micro-firms, informal entrepreneurs and underrepresented groups can access assistance and not only well-connected or larger SMEs. Long-term investments in infrastructure, social protection and institutional quality are likewise essential, as they reduce the background volatility that entrepreneurs must absorb and create more predictable conditions for experimentation and growth.

For educators and those designing entrepreneurship training, the chapter suggests the importance of integrating resilience explicitly into curricula and pedagogical practices. This involves going beyond technical skills and business planning to cultivate psychological resources, reflective practice and coping strategies. Experiential learning methods, such as simulations, serious games, project-based courses and failure-based cases, can help students rehearse decision-making under uncertainty and learn how to extract lessons from setbacks. Embedding themes of well-being, purpose and sustainability into entrepreneurship education can also foster a more balanced understanding of resilience, one that values endurance but also recognises the legitimacy of strategic exit and reorientation.

For ecosystem designers, leaders of incubators, accelerators, investor networks and support organisations—, he chapter highlights the role of relational and structural conditions in enabling resilience. Effective ecosystems are characterised by dense yet open networks, diverse support actors and mechanisms that encourage collaboration rather than zero-sum competition. Designing programmes that facilitate peer learning, mentoring relationships and cross-sector partnerships can create reservoirs of social capital that entrepreneurs draw upon during crises. At the same time, ecosystem actors need to reflect on how their own practices, such as funding cycles, performance metrics or platform rules, may inadvertently amplify vulnerability or short-termism.

Taken together, these implications point toward a collective agenda: cultivating entrepreneurial resilience as a shared capacity embedded in people, organisations and places. In turbulent globalized economies, such an agenda is not merely defensive. It is a proactive strategy to harness uncertainty as a catalyst for innovation, inclusion and sustainable transformation, ensuring that entrepreneurship continues to contribute meaningfully to economic and societal resilience in the years ahead.

ACKNOWLEDGMENT

During the preparation of this manuscript, the authors employed ChatGPT (OpenAI) solely to assist with language refinement and improvement of readability. The authors have reviewed and edited the output and take full responsibility for the content of this publication.

REFERENCES

Aaouid, B., Elboussadi, A., Boubker, O., & Nejjari, Z. (2024). Entrepreneurial bricolage: A systematic literature network analysis and TCCM approach. *Scientific African*, *26*, e02474. DOI: 10.1016/j.sciaf.2024.e02474

Ahmed, A. E., Ucbasaran, D., Cacciotti, G., & Williams, T. A. (2022). Integrating psychological resilience, stress, and coping in entrepreneurship: A critical review and research agenda. *Entrepreneurship Theory and Practice*, *46*(3), 497–538. DOI: 10.1177/10422587211046542

Alshebami, A. S. (2025). Purpose-Driven Resilience: A Blueprint for Sustainable Growth in Micro-and Small Enterprises in Turbulent Contexts. *Sustainability*, *17*(5), 2308. DOI: 10.3390/su17052308

Amin, M., Jolevski, F., & Islam, A. M. (2023). *The Resilience of SMEs and Large Firms in the COVID-19 Pandemic*. World Bank.

Ayala, J. C., & Manzano, G. (2014). The resilience of the entrepreneur. Influence on the success of the business. A longitudinal analysis. *Journal of Economic Psychology*, *42*, 126–135. DOI: 10.1016/j.joep.2014.02.004

Bartik, A. W., Bertrand, M., Cullen, Z., Glaeser, E. L., Luca, M., & Stanton, C. (2020). The impact of COVID-19 on small business outcomes and expectations. *Proceedings of the National Academy of Sciences of the United States of America*, *117*(30), 17656–17666. DOI: 10.1073/pnas.2006991117 PMID: 32651281

Belitski, M., Guenther, C., Kritikos, A. S., & Thurik, R. (2022). Economic effects of the COVID-19 pandemic on entrepreneurship and small businesses. *Small Business Economics*, *58*(2), 593–609. DOI: 10.1007/s11187-021-00544-y PMID: 38624899

Bennett, N., & Lemoine, G. J. (2014). What a difference a word makes: Understanding threats to performance in a VUCA world. *Business Horizons*, *57*(3), 311–317. DOI: 10.1016/j.bushor.2014.01.001

Bhamra, R., Dani, S., & Burnard, K. (2011). Resilience: The concept, a literature review and future directions. *International Journal of Production Research, 49*(18), 5375–5393. DOI: 10.1080/00207543.2011.563826

Branicki, L. J., Sullivan-Taylor, B., & Livschitz, S. R. (2018). How entrepreneurial resilience generates resilient SMEs. *International Journal of Entrepreneurial Behaviour & Research, 24*(7), 1244–1263. DOI: 10.1108/IJEBR-11-2016-0396

Browder, R. E., Dwyer, S. M., & Koch, H. (2024). Upgrading adaptation: How digital transformation promotes organizational resilience. *Strategic Entrepreneurship Journal, 18*(1), 128–164. DOI: 10.1002/sej.1483

Brown, R., & Rocha, A. (2020). Entrepreneurial uncertainty during the Covid-19 crisis: Mapping the temporal dynamics of entrepreneurial finance. *Journal of Business Venturing Insights, 14*, e00174. DOI: 10.1016/j.jbvi.2020.e00174

Bullough, A., & Renko, M. (2013). Entrepreneurial resilience during challenging times. *Business Horizons, 56*(3), 343–350. DOI: 10.1016/j.bushor.2013.01.001

Choudhury, T., Al Fadli, A., Butros, N., & Fadul, A. (2025). SME, Crisis and Geopolitical Risk: Lessons from COVID-19 and War. *Journal of Risk and Financial Management, 18*(11), 645. DOI: 10.3390/jrfm18110645

Conduah, A. K., & Essiaw, M. N. (2022). Resilience and entrepreneurship: A systematic review. *F1000 Research, 11*, 348. DOI: 10.12688/f1000research.75473.1

Conz, E., & Magnani, G. (2020). A dynamic perspective on the resilience of firms: A systematic literature review and a framework for future research. *European Management Journal, 38*(3), 400–412. DOI: 10.1016/j.emj.2019.12.004

Cope, J. (2011). Entrepreneurial learning from failure: An interpretative phenomenological analysis. *Journal of Business Venturing, 26*(6), 604–623. DOI: 10.1016/j.jbusvent.2010.06.002

Dabbous, A., Barakat, K. A., & Kraus, S. (2023). The impact of digitalization on entrepreneurial activity and sustainable competitiveness: A panel data analysis. *Technology in Society, 73*, 102224. DOI: 10.1016/j.techsoc.2023.102224

Damiano, R., & Valenza, G. (2025). Enacting resilience in small and medium enterprises following the sustainability path: A systematic literature review. *Strategic Change, 34*(2), 237–252. DOI: 10.1002/jsc.2608

Deirmentzoglou, G. A., Anastasopoulou, E. E., & Sklias, P. (2024). International economic relations and energy security in the European Union: A systematic literature review. *International Journal of Sustainable Energy, 43*(1), 2385682. DOI: 10.1080/14786451.2024.2385682

Deirmentzoglou, G. A., Anastasopoulou, E. E., & Theodorakopoulos, N. (2025, September). Geopolitical Risks: Threats or Opportunities in Shaping Entrepreneurial Intentions? In *European Conference on Innovation and Entrepreneurship* (pp. 184-190). Academic Conferences International Limited. https://doi.org/DOI: 10.34190/ecie.20.1.3660

Dziak, M. (2024). Volatility, uncertainty, complexity and ambiguity (VUCA). Retrieved from https://www.ebsco.com/research-starters/politics-and-government/volatility-uncertainty-complexity-and-ambiguity-vuca (Accessed on 20/12/2025).

Han, S., & Zhou, M. (2025). Assessing the impact of climate change on entrepreneurship: Short-term and long-term effects. *Humanities & Social Sciences Communications, 12*(1), 1–8. DOI: 10.1057/s41599-025-04763-6

Hanif, R., Khalique, M., Pierotti, M., Goyipnazarov, S., Ngah, R., & Ermatov, T. (2024, December). Impact of Artificial Intelligence on Organizational Resilience and Sustainable Performance. In *Proceedings of the 8th International Conference on Future Networks & Distributed Systems* (pp. 465-471). https://doi.org/DOI: 10.1145/3726122.3726189

Hartmann, S., Backmann, J., Newman, A., Brykman, K. M., & Pidduck, R. J. (2022). Psychological resilience of entrepreneurs: A review and agenda for future research. *Journal of Small Business Management, 60*(5), 1041–1079. DOI: 10.1080/00472778.2021.2024216

Hokmabadi, H., Rezvani, S. M., & de Matos, C. A. (2024). Business resilience for small and medium enterprises and startups by digital transformation and the role of marketing capabilities—A systematic review. *Systems, 12*(6), 220. DOI: 10.3390/systems12060220

Iacobucci, D., & Perugini, F. (2021). Entrepreneurial ecosystems and economic resilience at local level. *Entrepreneurship and Regional Development, 33*(9-10), 689–716. DOI: 10.1080/08985626.2021.1888318

Iborra, M., Safón, V., & Dolz, C. (2020). What explains the resilience of SMEs? Ambidexterity capability and strategic consistency. *Long Range Planning, 53*(6), 101947. DOI: 10.1016/j.lrp.2019.101947

Kádár, B., & Jáki, E. (2024). COVID-19 and SMEs: An umbrella review of systematic literature (2020–2024) and future directions for entrepreneurship: Introduction to the "The Entrepreneurial Landscape in the Post-COVID Era: Insights, Challenges, and Future Perspectives" special issue. *Society and Economy*, *46*(4), 323–341. DOI: 10.1556/204.2024.00017

Khurana, I., Dutta, D. K., & Ghura, A. S. (2022). SMEs and digital transformation during a crisis: The emergence of resilience as a second-order dynamic capability in an entrepreneurial ecosystem. *Journal of Business Research*, *150*, 623–641. DOI: 10.1016/j.jbusres.2022.06.048

Kiptoo, M., Sambajee, P., & Baum, T. (2024). Resilience through adversity: A case of informal artisan entrepreneurs in Kenya. *International Journal of Entrepreneurial Behaviour & Research*, *30*(11), 446–465. DOI: 10.1108/IJEBR-07-2023-0762

Koporcic, N., Kukkamalla, P. K., Markovic, S., & Maran, T. (2025). Resilience of small and medium-sized enterprises in times of crisis: An umbrella review. *Review of Managerial Science*, •••, 1–29. DOI: 10.1007/s11846-025-00883-0

Korber, S., & McNaughton, R. B. (2017). Resilience and entrepreneurship: A systematic literature review. *International Journal of Entrepreneurial Behaviour & Research*, *24*(7), 1129–1154. DOI: 10.1108/IJEBR-10-2016-0356

Korry, P. D. P., & Wijayanti, R. (2024). Investigating entrepreneurial resilience toward sustainable competitive advantage: Does local culture matter? *Uncertain Supply Chain Management*, *12*(2), 801–814. DOI: 10.5267/j.uscm.2024.1.006

KPMG. (2025). US Tariffs – Understanding the Implications for Ireland and the EU. Retrieved from https://kpmg.com/ie/en/insights/tax/us-tariffs.html (Accessed on 22/12/2025).

Linna, P. (2013). Bricolage as a means of innovating in a resource-scarce environment: A study of innovator-entrepreneurs at the BOP. *Journal of Developmental Entrepreneurship*, *18*(03), 1350015. DOI: 10.1142/S1084946713500155

Liu, Y., Hu, H., & Kong, W. (2025). The Impact of Entrepreneurs' AI Literacy on Entrepreneurial Resilience: The Role of AI Anxiety and Social Support. *Behavioral Sciences (Basel, Switzerland)*. PMID: 41464084

Luthans, F., & Youssef, C. M. (2007). Emerging positive organizational behavior. *Journal of Management*, *33*(3), 321–349. DOI: 10.1177/0149206307300814

Malik, F. S., & Terzidis, O. (2025). Thriving in turbulence: Resilience and strategic adaptation in global business. *Review of Managerial Science*, •••, 1–46. DOI: 10.1007/s11846-025-00940-8

Martinelli, E., Tagliazucchi, G., & Marchi, G. (2018). The resilient retail entrepreneur: Dynamic capabilities for facing natural disasters. *International Journal of Entrepreneurial Behaviour & Research*, *24*(7), 1222–1243. DOI: 10.1108/IJEBR-11-2016-0386

Mishra, R., & Singh, R. K. (2023). A systematic literature review on supply chain resilience in SMEs: Learnings from COVID-19 pandemic. *International Journal of Quality & Reliability Management*, *40*(5), 1172–1202. DOI: 10.1108/IJQRM-03-2022-0108

Mishra, V., Sharma, P., Khound, K., Mishra, V., Sharma, P., & Khound, K. (2025). Global Supply Chain Shocks and Trade Resilience: A Review Post-Covid and Ukraine Crisis. *Journal of Marketing & Social Research*, *2*, 336–348. DOI: 10.61336/jmsr/25-05-38

Monllor, J., & Murphy, P. J. (2017). Natural disasters, entrepreneurship, and creation after destruction: A conceptual approach. *International Journal of Entrepreneurial Behaviour & Research*, *23*(4), 618–637. DOI: 10.1108/IJEBR-02-2016-0050

Nautiyal, S., & Pathak, P. (2023). Resilience through the lens of entrepreneurship: A bibliometric analysis and network mapping of the emerging research field. *The International Journal of Organizational Analysis*. Advance online publication. DOI: 10.1108/IJOA-12-2022-3540

Newman, A., Mole, K. F., Ucbasaran, D., Subramanian, N., & Lockett, A. (2018). Can your network make you happy? Entrepreneurs' business network utilization and subjective well-being. *British Journal of Management*, *29*(4), 613–633. DOI: 10.1111/1467-8551.12270

OECD. (2025), Economic Security in a Changing World, New Approaches to Economic Challenges, OECD Publishing, Paris. https://doi.org/DOI: 10.1787/4eac89c7-en

Orth, D., & Schuldis, P. M. (2021). Organizational learning and unlearning capabilities for resilience during COVID-19. *The Learning Organization*, *28*(6), 509–522. DOI: 10.1108/TLO-07-2020-0130

Ozanne, L. K., Chowdhury, M., Prayag, G., & Mollenkopf, D. A. (2022). SMEs navigating COVID-19: The influence of social capital and dynamic capabilities on organizational resilience. *Industrial Marketing Management*, *104*, 116–135. DOI: 10.1016/j.indmarman.2022.04.009

Pennetta, S., Anglani, F., Reaiche, C., & Boyle, S. (2025). Entrepreneurial agility in a disrupted world: Redefining entrepreneurial resilience for global business success. *The Journal of Entrepreneurship*, *34*(2), 221–267. DOI: 10.1177/09713557251352283

Roundy, P. T. (2022). Artificial intelligence and entrepreneurial ecosystems: Understanding the implications of algorithmic decision-making for startup communities. *Journal of Ethics in Entrepreneurship and Technology*, *2*(1), 23–38. DOI: 10.1108/JEET-07-2022-0011

Roundy, P. T., Brockman, B. K., & Bradshaw, M. (2017). The resilience of entrepreneurial ecosystems. *Journal of Business Venturing Insights*, *8*, 99–104. DOI: 10.1016/j.jbvi.2017.08.002

Saad, M. H., Hagelaar, G., Van Der Velde, G., & Omta, S. W. F. (2021). Conceptualization of SMEs' business resilience: A systematic literature review. *Cogent Business & Management*, *8*(1), 1938347. DOI: 10.1080/23311975.2021.1938347

Santos, S. C., Liguori, E. W., & Garvey, E. (2023). How digitalization reinvented entrepreneurial resilience during COVID-19. *Technological Forecasting and Social Change*, *189*, 122398. DOI: 10.1016/j.techfore.2023.122398 PMID: 36778643

Shepherd, D. A., & Williams, T. (2020). Entrepreneurship responding to adversity: Equilibrating adverse events and disequilibrating persistent adversity. *Organization Theory*, *1*(4), 2631787720967678. DOI: 10.1177/2631787720967678

Shojaee, S., & Mirzaei, I. (2024). The Impact of Financial Flexibility on the Resilience of Small and Medium Enterprises in the Face of Economic Shocks. *Business, Marketing, and Finance Open*, *1*(2), 150–159. DOI: 10.61838/bmfopen.1.2.13

tefan, S. C., Popa, I., & Breazu, A. (2025). A new framework for the artificial intelligence entrepreneurship ecosystem. *Journal of Innovation & Knowledge*, *10*(6), 100850. DOI: 10.1016/j.jik.2025.100850

Taskan, B., Junça-Silva, A., & Caetano, A. (2022). Clarifying the conceptual map of VUCA: A systematic review. *The International Journal of Organizational Analysis*, *30*(7), 196–217. DOI: 10.1108/IJOA-02-2022-3136

Todt, G., Wolf, B., & Maisch, B. (2024). Navigating Peaks and Valleys-Fostering Resilience via Entrepreneurial Life Design. *CERN ideaSquare Journal of Experimental Innovation*, *8*(3), 28–35. DOI: 10.23726/cij.2024.1578

White House. (2025). Further Modifying the Reciprocal Tariff Rates. Retrieved from https://www.whitehouse.gov/presidential-actions/2025/07/further-modifying-the-reciprocal-tariff-rates/ (Accessed on 22/12/2025).

World Economic Forum. (2023). Seizing the Momentum to Build Resilience for a Future of Sustainable Inclusive Growth (White paper). World Economic Forum & McKinsey & Company. Retrieved from https://www3.weforum.org/docs/WEF_Resilience_Consortium_2023.pdf (Accessed on 23/12/2025).

Chapter 2
Policy and Institutional Frameworks for Strengthening Entrepreneurial Resilience in Global Crises

Wahyu Wibowo
https://orcid.org/0009-0000-5176-7103
Sunan Kalijaga State Islamic University, Yogyakarta, Indonesia

ABSTRACT

Global crises such as pandemics, geopolitical conflicts, and digital disruptions have fundamentally redefined the structure of entrepreneurial ecosystems. An integrative conceptual framework is developed to explain how policy coherence and institutional capacity enhance entrepreneurial resilience. Resilience is understood not merely as the ability of individuals to adapt, but as a systemic process arising from coordinated policy design, institutional learning, and cross-sectoral collaboration. The framework emphasizes the interdependence between public policy, institutional strength, and entrepreneurial behavior as key mechanisms sustaining innovation and long-term recovery. It also illustrates that adaptive governance and institutional flexibility are critical in transforming crises into opportunities for renewal and inclusive growth. Conceptually, this study advances institutional theory by linking it to dynamic governance and policy learning, providing strategic insights for building sustainable, resilient, and innovation-driven entrepreneurial systems amid global uncertainty.

DOI: 10.4018/979-8-3373-6991-4.ch002

INTRODUCTION

The current global environment is characterized by a series of multi-layered crises, ranging from the COVID-19 pandemic, geopolitical tensions, global supply chain disruptions, accelerating digital disruption, to climate change. The complexity of the crisis not only tests the resilience of macroeconomic structures, but also pressures the sustainability of micro, small, and medium enterprises (MSMEs) and startups that often lack financial reserves and adaptive capacity (Koporcic et al., 2025; Sakib & Rahman, 2024). In such a situation, the MSME sector is the most vulnerable group to supply chain shocks, declining liquidity, and uncertainty over mobility restriction policies. Therefore, digitalization-based adaptation strategies, business model innovation, and emergency financing mechanisms are important elements to maintain business sustainability (Kádár & Jáki, 2024; Vasi et al., 2024; Koporcic et al., 2025; Scheidgen et al., 2025).

However, a number of recent studies show that behind these vulnerabilities, MSMEs also have significant adaptive potential and can act as a motor of post-crisis economic recovery if supported by responsive public policies and a strong institutional ecosystem (Hokmabadi et al., 2024; Petropoulou et al., 2024). Recent literature confirms that formal and informal policy support has a central role in strengthening entrepreneurial resilience. Governments that provide financial incentives, digital training, and social protection for business actors are able to improve entrepreneurial orientation and business performance both directly and indirectly (Prasannath et al., 2024).

On the other hand, normative and cognitive dimensions such as sustainability culture, collaborative values, and collective perceptions of innovation are believed to play an equally important role with regulations in shaping entrepreneurial adaptive behavior (Maaßen et al., 2025). In certain contexts, formal regulation can lose effectiveness when it is not supported by social norms and collective consciousness conducive to innovation. In this context, Vargas-Zeledon & Lee (2024) emphasizing that entrepreneurial resilience is the result of collective interaction between public policies, financing systems, and educational institutions that work within a specific institutional framework.

Although research on entrepreneurial resilience is growing rapidly, most studies still focus on the micro level, namely business adaptation strategies, business model innovation, and digital technology adoption (Vasi et al., 2024; Koporcic et al., 2025). This approach does provide important insights into the internal dynamics of small firms, but it still lacks the relevance to the structural factors that shape the macro environment such as national policies, institutional capacity, and regulatory dynamics. Study by Balzano et al. (2025) shows that institutional theory has been widely used to explain innovation and sustainability, but has not yet fully integrated policy dimensions, crisis dynamics, and long-term resilience outcomes systematically.

This understanding gap shows that entrepreneurial resilience cannot be explained through micro approaches alone, but requires a more comprehensive analysis of how national policies, financing institutions, and educational institutions interact to form a resilient entrepreneurial ecosystem (Chavira et al., 2023; Deirmentzoglou et al., 2024). When public policy is not aligned with institutional capacity, the resulting resilience efforts tend to be temporary and fragile when faced with the next crisis.

Entrepreneurial resilience is shaped not only by domestic policies, but also by the global economic governance structures governed by various international organizations. The Association of Southeast Asian Nations (ASEAN) is a regional organization that has a mandate to encourage regional economic integration, harmonization of SME policies, and accelerate digital transformation through the ASEAN Strategic Action Plan for SME Development 2016-2025 document (Asean, 2025). World Trade Organization (WTO) regulating multilateral trading systems that affect market stability, tariffs, and MSMEs' trade access to global value chains (WTO, 2025). Meanwhile, the International Monetary Fund (IMF) is responsible for maintaining global macroeconomic stability and providing financing facilities such as the Resilience and Sustainability Trust that help developing countries increase their economic adaptation capacity (IMF, 2022). Understanding the mandates of these institutions is important because entrepreneurial resilience in the era of polycrises is influenced by the interaction of national policies and the global economic architecture.

Indonesia is a very relevant research context to understand entrepreneurial resilience because of its economic structure that relies heavily on MSMEs. There are more than 64.2 million MSMEs that contribute about 61% of the national GDP, absorb 97% of the workforce, and play an important role in domestic economic stability (KEMENKO, 2021; Junaidi, 2024). The impact of global crises such as COVID-19, food and energy crises, and climate change risks is strongly felt by business actors in this sector. In addition, Indonesia faces various forms of polycrises, including international supply chain volatility, natural disaster risk, and geopolitical uncertainty.

In terms of digital transformation, Indonesia recorded the highest acceleration of digital technology adoption in Southeast Asia in the 2020–2023 period, reflected in the increase in the adoption of digital platforms by MSMEs by 26% (Arief, 2024). The Government of Indonesia has also implemented policy innovations such as the People's Business Credit (KUR), the National Economic Recovery Program (PEN), and the OSS-RBA licensing system that accelerates digital integration for business actors. This combination of structural and policy factors makes Indonesia an ideal policy laboratory to understand how public policies, institutional capacity, and institutional dynamics shape the resilience of MSMEs.

Considering these complexities, there is a need to understand more comprehensively why the integration between public policy and institutional frameworks is the main foundation in strengthening entrepreneurial resilience. Global crises are systemic, multidimensional, and long-term, so policy responses are not sufficiently partial or sectoral. Without institutional coordination and policy learning mechanisms, public policies tend to be reactive and unsustainable.

Conceptually, contemporary entrepreneurial literature emphasizes the importance of public policies and institutional frameworks in shaping business resilience (Bachtiar et al., 2023). However, much of the literature is still dominated by micro-studies that highlight individual capabilities, product innovation, and technology adoption without regard to how national policies, financial institutions, and educational institutions work in a coordinated manner (Deirmentzoglou et al., 2024; Chavira et al., 2023). This condition creates a conceptual gap between the adaptive strategies of business actors and the policy structures that support them.

This theoretical gap raises several important research gaps. First, there is limited longitudinal research that explores the long-term impact of policy and institutional integration on entrepreneurial resilience (Koporcic et al., 2025; Sakib & Rahman, 2024). Second, the lack of cross-country and cross-regional comparative studies limits understanding of the variation in policy and institutional models between developed and developing countries (Vargas-Zeledon & Lee, 2024; Balzano et al., 2025; Maaßen et al., 2025). Third, although the literature emphasizes the importance of adaptive regulation and public-private partnerships, there is still little research that understands how interactions between institutional elements work in the context of multiple global crises (Prasannath et al., 2024; Vasi et al., 2024).

In response to these gaps, this paper offers a conceptual framework that integrates entrepreneurial theory, institutional theory, and public policy in one comprehensive analytical system. This approach places entrepreneurial resilience as the result of a dynamic interaction between policies, social norms, and institutional capacity (Prasannath et al., 2024; Balzano et al., 2025; Lestari & Choirunissa, 2025). Thus, strengthening entrepreneurial resilience is not enough through individual strategies, but must be built through inclusive policy design, effective institutional coordination, and adaptive learning mechanisms.

This paper contributes through three main tracks. First, broaden the understanding of entrepreneurial resilience from a systemic perspective that includes the reciprocal relationship between public policy, institutional capacity, and entrepreneurial adaptive strategies. Second, it offers a cross-level approach that connects the micro (individual), meso (institutional), and macro (regulatory) dimensions. Third, it opens up research opportunities to test this model empirically in various contexts of countries and economic sectors.

In addition to academic contributions, this paper has significant practical value for policymakers, financial institutions, and business actors. This analysis is expected to be a reference in designing inclusive, innovative, and sustainable economic resilience strategies. The emphasis is directed on the importance of adaptive institutional design, cross-actor collaboration, and policy learning systems that allow policy responses to continue to be adapted to the dynamics of global crises.

THEORETICAL FRAMEWORK AND CONCEPTUAL FOUNDATIONS

Institutional theory provides an important foundation for understanding how social structures, norms, and public policies shape entrepreneurial behavior in the context of a global crisis. North (1990) defines an institution as a set of formal and informal rules that govern human interaction, while Scott (1987) emphasizing that institutions consist of three main pillars, namely regulative, normative, and cognitive, which work simultaneously to provide stability and meaning to social actions. In the realm of entrepreneurship, this theory explains how policies, social values, and collective perceptions interact with each other to form innovative behavior and adaptive capacity of business actors. This framework is particularly relevant for MSMEs operating in high-risk environments and often experiencing resource constraints, so it relies more on institutional stability to navigate uncertainty.

The regulatory pillar represents the formal policies, laws, and rules that direct economic activity, including fiscal and monetary policies that are adaptive to the crisis. The normative pillar deals with the social values, justice, and business ethics that form the social legitimacy of entrepreneurial behavior, while the cognitive pillar reflects the shared perception and frame of mind that determines how business actors view risks and opportunities (Scott, 1987). The three pillars work as a system that strengthens each other when facing a global crisis. In a pandemic and economic disruption situation, responsive public policies, collaborative values in society, and positive perceptions of innovation are synergistic factors that strengthen the resilience of entrepreneurship (Basri et al., 2022; Maaßen et al., 2025). The interaction of these three pillars also affects how MSMEs build new capabilities, modify internal procedures, or access external resources when faced with prolonged stress.

Institutions not only limit economic behavior, but also provide legitimacy and incentives for innovative actions. In the entrepreneurial ecosystem, institutions such as universities, financial institutions, business incubators, and industry associations act as a liaison between business actors and government policies (Li & Bosma, 2023). Research by Basri et al. (2022) about social entrepreneurship organizations in Indonesia shows that normative and regulatory pressures significantly affect the socio-economic orientation of business actors, showing that social norms and public expectations can be the drivers of social innovation during times of crisis. At the macro level, Topcu & Gulsen (2025) found that the success of fiscal stimulus depends not only on the size of the budget, but on institutional capacity, transparency, and accountable governance. In the context of MSMEs, the existence of credible institutions increases the sense of security of business actors to take risks, invest, and expand.

Institutional theory also highlights the importance of the interrelationship between formal regulation and social norms in shaping public trust in economic systems. When governments implement adaptive fiscal policies accompanied by social legitimacy and transparency, the entrepreneurial ecosystem tends to be more resilient. On the other hand, if the policy is reactive and not integrated with institutional capacity, then the impact is temporary (IMF, 2024; EIB, 2025). This is where institutional theory helps explain that entrepreneurial resilience cannot be separated from the stability of the institutional system that underpins trust, coordination, and adaptive learning. In this context, MSMEs operating in a stable institutional environment are much better able to control risk and innovate compared to business actors who are in a fragile system.

The concept of entrepreneurial resilience itself is rooted in the theory of organizational adaptation and positive psychology, which focuses on the ability of individuals and systems to recover from disruption and create new value. Shore et al. (2024) Define entrepreneurial resilience as the capacity of business actors to anticipate, absorb, and adapt to external shocks without losing their strategic orientation. The indicators include risk management capabilities, business model flexibility, social network strength, financial readiness, and adoption of digital technologies (Aaouid et al., 2025; Ma'amor et al., 2025; Shore et al., 2024). This perspective is increasingly important in a regional environment such as Southeast Asia, where economic volatility and external pressures often occur simultaneously.

From the context of Southeast Asia, research by Poolsawat & Rinthaisong (2025) shows that resilience functions as a mediator between entrepreneurial orientation, self-efficacy, as well as external support such as public policy on the performance of MSMEs. The research confirms that the psychological strength of individuals needs to be supported by a stable policy system and institutions in order for business resilience to be realized. Hokmabadi et al. (2024) adding that organizational learning and cross-network collaboration are the main sources of post-critical adaptive capacity. Findings by Aaouid et al. (2025) Through bibliometric analysis, a surge in publications on post-pandemic resilience is shown, with the main topics involving the relationship between digitalization, sustainability, and institutional factors. This indicates a growing academic attention to the integration between individual capacities and institutional structures.

The convergence of institutional theory and the concept of resilience opens up opportunities to formulate an integrative conceptual framework. In this framework, public policy acts as a policy trigger that forms institutional capacity, and this institutional capacity becomes the foundation for strengthening entrepreneurial resilience. IMF (2025) and Syahribulan et al. (2024) It shows that instruments such as fiscal stimulus, adaptive liquidity, and regulatory reform serve not only as a short-term response, but also as a tool to shape a more shock-resistant economic structure. This conceptual model describes sequential relationships in which each component reinforces each other through institutional learning mechanisms, as follows:

Policy Frameworks → Institutional Capacity → Entrepreneurial Resilience → Economic Recovery

Adaptive public policies increase institutional capacity to manage risks, strengthen inter-agency coordination, and provide supporting infrastructure. Strong institutional capacity creates an entrepreneurial ecosystem that is more legitimate, innovative, and responsive to market changes. When business actors operate in a stable institutional environment, they are better able to innovate, expand networks, and accelerate the economic recovery process. This cycle is reciprocal because increasing entrepreneurial resilience also strengthens institutional legitimacy and encourages policy sustainability.

This integrative approach expands the understanding of institutional theory from the framework of stability to the dynamics of adaptation. If classical institutional theory emphasizes the consistency of rules and norms, then the context of *a polycrisis economy* demands institutional flexibility that is able to adapt quickly to global disruptions. Through cross-level interactions ranging from micro (individual capabilities), meso (institutional networks), and macro (public policy), this model places entrepreneurial resilience as a systemic outcome, not just an individual reaction to a crisis (Bachtiar et al., 2023).

The theoretical contribution of this framework lies in the integration between institutional theory and entrepreneurial resilience through policy learning mechanisms and *institutional complementarity* (Elert et al., 2017). This integration expands the boundaries of entrepreneurship theory that has been focusing on individual strategies into a systemic perspective that highlights how policies and institutions together shape economic adaptivity. In the context of developing countries such as Indonesia, where global crises, climate change, and digital disruption occur simultaneously, this model emphasizes the need for learning, inclusion, and sustainability-oriented governance.

In practical terms, this conceptual model provides guidance for policy makers and business support agencies to view economic interventions not as a momentary response, but as a long-term investment in building ecosystem resilience. Cross-actor collaboration between governments, financial institutions, academics, and business actors, is at the heart of an adaptive system that enables sustainable innovation (Syahribulan et al., 2024; IMF, 2025). Thus, entrepreneurial resilience emerges as a result of multi-level interactions that link micro-strategies with macro governance, strengthening the link between public policy and economic sustainability in the face of global uncertainty.

Crises are thus not only a threat, but also an arena of institutional learning. Policy systems and institutions that are able to adapt, experiment, and build new legitimacy will result in a more resilient economic structure. In the era of polycrisis, the integration of adaptive policies, institutional capacity, and entrepreneurial innovation is the foundation for resilient, inclusive, and future-oriented economic development.

THE ROLE OF PUBLIC POLICY IN ENTREPRENEURIAL RESILIENCE

The role of public policy in strengthening entrepreneurial resilience is a key element in ensuring economic sustainability, especially when MSMEs face major shocks such as pandemics, geopolitical tensions, energy crises, and global supply chain disruptions. Conceptually, public policy can serve as a shock absorber through three main mechanisms: fiscal and monetary interventions, adaptive regulatory reforms, and international trade policies that encourage market diversification and cross-border collaboration. These three dimensions interact with each other in determining national capacity to maintain entrepreneurial resilience and reduce the destructive impact of the global crisis on the small-scale business sector.

Fiscal and monetary instruments are fundamental components that determine the state's ability to maintain the sustainability of economic activities, especially for MSMEs that have limited capital, digital capacity, and access to financing. According to Supari & Anton (2022), The combination of new credit, credit restructuring, and interest subsidies in the National Economic Recovery Program (PEN) in Indonesia significantly reduced the risk of bankruptcy and improved the cash flow of MSMEs during the pandemic. This success is not only due to the large amount of stimulus, but also due to the digitization of the aid distribution process and coordination between financial institutions, the central government, and local governments. The effectiveness of the PEN program is in line with the findings by Sakib & Rahman (2024), which shows through a systematic review of more than 831 international publications that sectoral fiscal policies, emergency financing programs, and credit easing are the most significant factors in increasing the resilience of MSMEs to external pressures.

However, the effectiveness of fiscal stimulus is highly dependent on the fiscal capacity and quality of governance of the implementing country. Countries with limited fiscal capacity often face distribution gaps, delays in distribution, and lack of oversight, reducing policy effectiveness. On the other hand, countries with strong fiscal governance are able to distribute stimulus in a targeted manner and maintain the sustainability of support until the recovery phase. The IMF report shows that while liquidity stimulus and restructuring in the EU have been successful in reducing the insolvency rate of small businesses, their impact on new business creation tends to be limited due to regulatory asynchrony between member states (IMF, 2024). This underscores the need for structural reforms that strengthen the investment climate, fiscal governance, and local innovation so that fiscal stimulus plays a role not only as a short-term response, but also as a catalyst for economic transformation.

Indonesia's context shows that fiscal policy design involving microfinance institutions, state-owned enterprises, and digital platforms has succeeded in extending policy impact to the informal sector, which is the backbone of the national economy. Such an integrative model is an example of policy adaptation that is relevant for developing countries with fiscal and infrastructure limitations (Supari & Anton, 2022). A similar pattern exists in a number of Southeast Asian countries, where the involvement of local community institutions and regional banks accelerates post-crisis recovery and encourages new entrepreneurial participation at the local level (Poolsawat & Rinthaisong, 2025).

In addition to fiscal intervention, adaptive regulation is a crucial dimension in strengthening entrepreneurial resilience. Rigid regulations can be an obstacle for business actors to pivot when the crisis demands a change in strategy and business model. Conversely, legal flexibility and ease of administration accelerate operational transformation and innovation. Mishrif & Khan (2023) emphasized that the adaptation of regulations related to digitalization, taxation, and business licensing accelerated the transition to a more resilient business model during the pandemic. Findings by Syahribulan et al. (2024) It shows that adaptive institutional pressures, such as regulations that support policy experimentation and public–private partnerships, have a significant influence on improving entrepreneurial resilience at the local level.

The effectiveness of adaptive regulation is reflected in the Kurzarbeit policy in Germany, which provides wage subsidies for workers with a reduction in working hours. Study by Zimmermann & Köhler-Geib (2023) It shows that these policies not only protect the workforce, but also maintain the liquidity of small businesses and prevent waves of bankruptcy. Although it focuses on social protection, the policy has a direct effect on the stability of entrepreneurship and the sustainability of MSMEs' supply networks. The KfW SME Panel 2024 report reinforces these findings by showing that while wage subsidies and soft credit maintain the stability of small businesses, energy cost pressures and inflation remain key challenges for the sustainability of small businesses in Germany. This indicates that regulatory policies must take into account the character of the sector and the long-term economic dynamics (KfW, 2024).

The third dimension is international trade policy and regional economic cooperation. In a highly connected global economy, cross-border supply chains are a vital factor for the resilience of small industries. Countries with open trade policies, strong logistics infrastructure, and stable regional agreements tend to recover faster from global crises. Sakib & Rahman (2024) demonstrate that countries with access to efficient regional trade agreements are able to support MSMEs in accessing new markets, diversifying risks, and adapting to fluctuating global demand.

Overall, the effectiveness of public policies in strengthening entrepreneurial resilience relies heavily on three interconnected pillars: (1) responsive fiscal and monetary capacity, (2) adaptive regulations that support innovation and business flexibility, and (3) international trade integration that expands the space for adaptation and growth. The experiences of various countries, ranging from Kurzarbeit in Germany, the PEN Program in Indonesia, to responsive fiscal policies in the ASEAN region, show that the success of entrepreneurial resilience is not only determined by the amount of stimulus, but also by the quality of policy design, the level of adaptivity, and its suitability to local and global dynamics.

THE ROLE OF INSTITUTIONS IN BUILDING RESILIENCE

Institutions play an important role in building entrepreneurial resilience through the provision of access to inclusive finance, a supportive innovation ecosystem, business networks that strengthen markets, and policy support from regional and global institutions. This role includes financial institutions (banks, venture capital, microfinance, and fintech), innovation ecosystems (incubators, accelerators, universities, research institutes), business communities and industry associations, as well as regional/global institutions such as ASEAN, WTO, IMF, and the World Bank. Each institution has complementary functions that form the foundation for structural and adaptive resilience for MSMEs.

Traditional financial institutions and fintechs play a role in expanding liquidity and providing financing instruments that enable MSMEs to absorb economic shocks more effectively. Microfinance has a strategic function as a safety net for micro businesses that are often beyond the reach of conventional banking (Gatto & Sadik-Zada, 2022; Zhou & Sun, 2024). Study by Sarfo et al. (2024) demonstrating that positive perceptions of microfinance encourage exploratory innovation and improve business performance in Ghana, showing that microfinance is not only a liquidity tool but also a stimulus for innovation.

In Indonesia, Islamic financial institutions contribute to business resilience through community-based financial inclusion. Research by Salma et al. (2023) shows that strengthening the role of Baitul Maal and Baitul Tamwil increases access to financing for micro enterprises that are depressed by the crisis. Venture capital and private investors also play an important role, although their distribution tends to be concentrated in developed countries and certain regions of Asia. Syahribulan et al. (2024) emphasizing that venture capital is an important element in the innovation system, especially when the ecosystem is supported by conducive regulations and market integration.

The innovation ecosystem is the main driver that provides intellectual capital, technology access, mentorship, and prototyping facilities that accelerate the ability to pivot businesses. Incubators supported by strong human capital such as managerial capacity, technical expertise, and professional networks that are able to increase the effectiveness of incubation schemes in Indonesia (Imelda & Susiang, 2024; Máté et al., 2024). In addition, the research Persada et al. (2025) shows that incubators and accelerators provide digitalization facilities such as online market analysis, digital marketing platforms, and technology education that are very crucial during times of mobility restrictions and operational disruptions. Universities and research institutions play a role in providing space for collaboration, knowledge transfer, and the development of new technologies that can support business diversification and business model adaptation for MSMEs affected by the crisis.

Business communities, industry associations, and diaspora networks strengthen resilience through increased social capital, dissemination of market information, and the expansion of cross-border networks. Business associations often serve as policy advocacy providers, industry data centers, and best practice sharing spaces, which become essential when businesses face rapidly changing market conditions. Diaspora networks contribute in the form of international market access, export opportunities, funding networks, and knowledge about global trends. These aspects become social capital that cannot be provided by financial institutions or formal regulations alone.

Regional and global institutions play a strategic role in expanding the scale of support, policy harmonization, and cross-border learning. ASEAN's digital initiatives to support MSMEs, for example, strengthen regional connectivity and facilitate access to cross-border markets (World Bank, 2022; ERIA, 2023). Business networks, industry associations, diaspora, and professional communities are often important drivers of social capital and access to information during crises. Communities such as diasporas bring access to foreign markets, non-financial capital such as knowledge, and networking development opportunities.

Regional and global institutions are able to expand the scale of cross-border policy support and coordination, especially for SMEs related to international supply chains and market digitalization. A chapter in the book Open Innovation Ecosystem in Asia, Endress (2023) shows how collaboration between governments, universities, incubators, and research institutions is shaping an innovation ecosystem in Southeast Asia that enables MSMEs to access global technology and markets. In addition, institutions such as the World Bank, IMF, and ERIA provide development financing, digital training programs, and institutional capacity that drive the modernization of economic structures in developing countries.

From these various findings, several conceptual points can be summarized. First, access to financing is not enough without regulatory support and social capital that ensures the productive use of capital. The role of financial institutions must be combined with social legitimacy, public trust, and regulatory certainty so that investment and business expansion can run sustainably. Second, innovation ecosystems work most effectively when there are connections between universities, incubators, the private sector, and governments which ensures the relevance of innovation and ease of technology adoption at the small business level. Third, the cooperation of the business community accelerates the flow of information and facilitates the exchange of knowledge so as to increase the adaptive capacity of MSMEs in conditions of high uncertainty. Fourth, regional and global institutions provide economies of scale, international learning, and sometimes regulatory harmonization that allows MSMEs actors to expand the market despite policy differences between countries.

Overall, the literature shows that institutions are not only providers of resources, but also structural architects of entrepreneurial resilience. This resilience is built through a combination of financial capacity, social capital, regulatory support, and regional/global connectivity that collectively shape an adaptive and innovative business environment. To strengthen systemic resilience, inclusive and responsive institutions are needed that are able to bridge local resources with global opportunities. Further research needs to examine how these institutions work in diverse local cultural contexts, regulations, and capacities, particularly in developing countries facing polycrisis dynamics.

CHALLENGES AND GAPS IN STRENGTHENING ENTREPRENEURIAL RESILIENCE

While policies and institutions are geared towards strengthening entrepreneurial resilience, a number of structural and operational challenges remain and have the potential to undermine the effectiveness of these efforts. These challenges include gaps in policy implementation, barriers faced by informal businesses, reliance on global supply chains, and weak coordination of institutional governance. If not taken seriously, these barriers can hinder the ability of MSMEs to recover from the crisis, adapt, and grow sustainably.

One of the biggest issues is the gap between formal policy and field implementation. Many government programs designed to support MSMEs, whether in the form of financing, fiscal incentives, or digital training, do not fully reach micro and informal enterprises, especially those in rural or suburban areas. Cruz et al. (2023) noted that pro-MSMEs interventions often stop at regulatory documents and do not undergo meaningful operational transformation. This happens due to bureaucratic practices that are still hierarchical, limited regional resources, lack of local administrative capacity, and administrative obstacles such as business legality requirements that are difficult for micro actors to meet.

Prasannath et al. (2024) menambahkan bahwa kebijakan publik, baik yang bersifat finansial maupun non-finansial, menghasilkan dampak berbeda tergantung pada tingkat adaptasi lokal. Ketika kebijakan tidak diterjemahkan ke dalam mekanisme pelaksanaan yang responsif terhadap konteks daerah, maka manfaat kebijakan sering kali tidak dirasakan oleh pelaku usaha yang paling rentan. Di sejumlah daerah, program pembiayaan misalnya, lebih mudah diakses oleh usaha kecil menengah formal dibandingkan usaha mikro karena prasyarat seperti laporan keuangan, akun digital, atau bukti legalitas tidak dapat dipenuhi secara cepat. Hal ini menandakan perlunya kebijakan yang lebih adaptif terhadap karakteristik sosial-ekonomi lokal.

Selain itu, penelitian oleh Hess et al. (2025) shows that there is a significant gap between policy research at the theoretical level and policy implementation in local contexts. Policy theory often reflects an ideal framework, but implementation requires adjustments to the capacity of local institutions, digital infrastructure, and the competence of public administrators. Differences in capacity between regions make some regions unable to utilize assistance or program schemes optimally, thus creating inequality in resilience between regions. MSMEs in rural areas, for example, often operate far from government administrative service centers, face digital literacy constraints, and lack of supporting facilities such as internet access or companion agencies.

Another major challenge arises from the informal business sector, which is significant in developing countries including Indonesia. Informal businesses face major barriers in accessing formal financing because they do not have the collateral, legal documentation, or credit track record required by financial institutions. According to the SME Finance Gap report by World Bank (2025) estimates that the global financing gap for MSMEs stands at US$ 5.7 trillion, with most of the shortfall coming from the informal sector. This gap severely affects the ability of informal businesses to build resilience to shocks such as pandemics, supply chain disruptions, or rising production costs.

Research by Zhao & Zhang (2025) Clarifying this barrier by showing that hard information such as formal financial data and soft information such as business reputation or social relations are equally difficult to collect from informal actors. These data collection challenges are a major barrier to access formal credit. As a result, many informal MSMEs rely on informal loans, which often have high interest rates, short tenors, and the risk of default that can worsen their business conditions in times of economic crisis.

The next challenge is the dependence of MSMEs on global supply chains. Connectivity with international suppliers does open up opportunities for cost efficiency and access to cheap raw materials, but at the same time makes MSMEs vulnerable to global fluctuations. Research by Kanyepe et al. (2025) indicates that supply chain risks such as supply delays, input price volatility, and supplier failures can disrupt operations and affect the performance of manufacturing MSMEs. Technology capabilities are an important moderation factor that helps MSMEs respond to disruptions through better demand planning, inventory digitization, and the use of supplier management applications.

In this context, the concept of supply chain finance (SCF) began to be introduced as a solution to strengthen the financial resilience of small suppliers. Analysis by Asifulla & Basha (2023) emphasized that SCF allows financing to be channeled to small suppliers based on the credibility of the anchor company, rather than solely on collateral. Although SCF is still a conceptual framework in many developing countries, this approach has the potential to improve MSMEs' cash flows and reduce reliance on informal credit. However, the implementation of SCF requires digital system readiness, banking coordination, and supply chain data integration—factors that are still weak in many developing countries.

In addition to these challenges, coordination across domestic and regional institutions is also a serious obstacle. Fragmentation of tasks between public agencies, duplication of programs, and weak synergy mechanisms between the central government, regions, financial institutions, and the private sector often cause policy responses to be out of sync or late. Hess et al. (2025) emphasizing that the entrepreneurial ecosystem requires close collaboration between stakeholders—governments, universities, industry, and local communities—with clear coordination mechanisms to avoid policy overlap. Misalignments in fiscal policies, digitalization assistance, and financing support can create confusion for MSMEs and undermine the effectiveness of resilience-building strategies.

This governance gap also arises in a regional context, where policy harmonization and market integration between countries are still not optimal. In the context of ASEAN, for example, digital integration efforts and trade facilitation for MSMEs still face differences in domestic regulations, uneven digital infrastructure, and varying institutional capacities. In fact, regional collaboration can open up new market opportunities, encourage cross-border learning, and increase MSMEs' access to technology and international supply networks.

Overall, these challenges and gaps suggest that entrepreneurial resilience depends not only on the policy design or internal capacity of MSMEs, but also on the effectiveness of institutional governance, financing inclusivity, and systemic readiness in managing global dynamics. Overcoming implementation gaps, strengthening access to formal financing, building resilient supply chains, and creating effective inter-agency coordination will be an important foundation to ensure that resilience policies can be truly operationalized down to the small and micro enterprise level.

POLICY AND MANAGERIAL IMPLICATIONS

Policy and managerial implications emerge in response to the various challenges and gaps identified in efforts to strengthen entrepreneurial resilience. The main focus is on how to design interventions that are not only reactive to the crisis, but also build long-term foundations through adaptive institutional reform, cross-sector collaboration, and the integration of Environmental, Social, and Governance (ESG) principles into entrepreneurial policies and practices. A systemic and evidence-based approach is needed for public policy to function as an instrument of sustained institutional learning, not just as a temporary response to economic shocks.

First, a synergistic *policy mix* between fiscal, monetary, and regulatory policies is needed to strengthen institutional structures and entrepreneurial capabilities at the local level. Fiscal incentives such as tax relief, interest subsidies, and microfinance need to be integrated with non-fiscal policies such as business assistance, digitalization, and improving human resource competence. Study by Tunçalp (2025) affirming that resilient entrepreneurship combines improvised actions to survive and strategic planning to grow. Therefore, public policy must function not only as a crisis mitigation tool, but also as part of an innovation- and sustainability-oriented entrepreneurial development roadmap.

Policy interventions need to be designed with a long-term evaluation framework so that their effectiveness can be measured periodically. Entrepreneurship education, digital literacy, and business infrastructure development should be positioned as strategic investments. The government also needs to develop an integrated data system to monitor policy implementation in a sustainable manner. This system is the foundation for the implementation *of evidence-based policies*, which connect policy, research, and field practice in an adaptive manner. Policy sustainability is ultimately determined not only by the duration of the program, but by the ability of the system to learn from the experience of the crisis and adapt to global economic dynamics.

Second, public and regulatory institutional reform is a prerequisite for the effectiveness of entrepreneurial policies, especially in diverse local contexts. Public institutions need to increase adaptive capacity to global dynamics, such as supply chain disruptions, digital transformation, and rapidly changing economic climate pressures. This reform includes accelerating the licensing process, increasing transparency in decision-making, and flexibility in responding to the needs of business actors. Research by Wahrudin & Sutrisno (2025) shows that institutions that are able to speed up the regulatory process and reduce the bureaucratic burden on the innovation sector and MSMEs experience increased competitiveness and accelerated technology adoption. Therefore, local governments need to be strengthened through apparatus training, cross-agency coordination mechanisms, and the preparation of adaptive regulations that adjust to the capacity and needs of the local entrepreneurial ecosystem.

Strengthening *institutional governance* also requires a performance-based incentive system and participatory supervision mechanisms. Business actors, academics, and civil society organizations need to be involved in policy evaluations so that public accountability increases. This approach not only increases the legitimacy of public institutions, but also fosters social trust that is an important foundation for entrepreneurial sustainability at the local level.

Third, *public-private partnerships* (PPPs) play a strategic role in expanding access to resources, technology, and financing for MSMEs. In the midst of the government's limited fiscal capacity, PPP is an important mechanism to provide innovative solutions that are efficient and sustainable. Systematic study by Bramantyo et al. (2025) highlighted a number of PPP challenges in Asia, ranging from unbalanced risk sharing to limited political support. However, when implemented effectively, PPPs can result in improved efficiency of public services, strengthen local production capacity, and expand MSMEs' access to technology and global markets.

In this context, MSMEs managers should be proactive in building networks with financial institutions, universities, investors, and the business community to gain capital support, social legitimacy, and collaborative opportunities. The government acts as *an enabler* that provides conducive regulations and facilitates inter-stakeholder relations. PPPs also serve as a medium of knowledge transfer, where MSMEs can access innovations and best practices from the corporate sector, while large companies gain social legitimacy from their contribution to strengthening the local economy. Thus, PPP is not only a technocratic instrument, but a strategic mechanism to increase the systemic competitiveness of national entrepreneurship.

Fourth, the integration of ESG principles is becoming increasingly important in the policy design and managerial practices of MSMEs. Global pressure on sustainability, social responsibility, and *good governance* issues makes ESG a distinguishing element in modern business competition. Research by Shalhoob & Hussainey (2022) shows that ESG disclosure improves the sustainability performance of MSMEs, both in terms of reputation, customer satisfaction, and export competitiveness. Next Mathuros et al. (2025) added that ESG strategies open up new market access, expand opportunities for international collaboration, and increase the likelihood of obtaining environmental policy support in the ASEAN region.

For policymakers, ESG integration implies the need for a regulatory framework that facilitates the application of sustainability principles through instruments such as green tax incentives, carbon credit schemes, or subsidies for green investments. Meanwhile, for MSME managers, ESG implementation can include transformation of production processes, inclusive social practices, and accountable internal governance. ESG is not just a disclosure obligation, but a long-term business strategy that drives innovation, efficiency, and sustainability competitiveness.

Overall, the effectiveness of entrepreneurial resilience policies is determined not only by the quality of program design, but also by the extent to which it can be operationalized through cross-level coordination and active participation of the non-state sector. Evidence-based approaches and cross-crisis institutional learning are essential for any intervention to transform from a temporary response to a sustainable adaptive system.

The combination of *an integrated policy mix*, adaptive institutional reforms, public-private partnerships, and ESG implementation forms a new foundation for the sustainable entrepreneurship resilience paradigm. By adopting a resilient, innovative, and collaborative mindset, policymakers and business actors can create an entrepreneurial ecosystem that is not only able to survive crises, but also grow through sustainable transformation amid global uncertainty.

FUTURE RESEARCH DIRECTION

Future research directions need to be focused on empirical testing and longitudinal evaluation of the effectiveness of entrepreneurial policies in diverse contexts, both in developed and developing countries. So far, most of the research is still descriptive and short-term, so it has not fully mapped how adaptive policies affect entrepreneurial resilience in long-term dynamics. Longitudinal studies that track policy changes, MSMEs' performance, and institutional adaptation from the crisis phase to the recovery phase will be critical to understanding complex cause-and-effect mechanisms. This approach can enrich theoretical models of *entrepreneurial resilience* by integrating macro variables such as regulatory stability, fiscal support, and institutional capacity with micro variables such as innovation, organizational learning, and adaptive strategies of business actors.

In addition to the temporal dimension, future research also needs to adopt a cross-contextual comparative perspective to identify similarities, differences, and patterns of policy adaptation in various regions. Comparative studies between ASEAN, Africa, and Latin American countries will provide deeper insights into how culture, economic structure, and capacity of public institutions affect policy effectiveness. In the ASEAN region, for example, the government emphasizes more on the digitalization of MSMEs as a post-pandemic recovery strategy, while in Africa the informal sector is the main pillar of local economic resilience. In Latin America, political dynamics and policy volatility are often limiting factors for the stability of MSMEs. By understanding these differences, further research can formulate the concept of "contextual entrepreneurial resilience," which is a framework that emphasizes that resilience is strongly influenced by the unique social and institutional structures in each region.

Along with technological changes, the exploration of the role of *digital governance* is a very promising research agenda. Digital transformation is not only changing business operational behavior, but also the way governments design and implement policies. Effective digital governance enables cross-sector data integration, strengthens transparency, and improves accountability in aid distribution. However, the digital divide, especially in developing countries, can create new inequalities between business actors who have access to technology and those who do not. Therefore, future research needs to examine how inclusive digital governance designs can address these inequalities through data-driven mechanisms, *real-time feedback*, and digital monitoring systems to assess the effectiveness of policies for MSMEs.

Interdisciplinary research agendas are also increasingly relevant. The integration between public policy, the digital economy, organizational behavior, and technological innovation can enrich analytical approaches in understanding entrepreneurial behavior in the midst of global uncertainty. For example, research can incorporate *system dynamics modeling* to simulate the impact of fiscal policy on the resilience of business ecosystems, or use *machine learning* to map the adaptation patterns of MSMEs during crises. In addition, a *mixed methods* approach that combines long-term quantitative analysis with in-depth qualitative interviews will provide a more comprehensive picture of how MSMEs are adapting and how they perceive the impact of public policies at the operational level.

At the micro level, future research needs to strengthen the focus on the psychological and behavioral aspects of entrepreneurship as the foundation of long-term resilience. Aspects such as *entrepreneurial mindset*, psychological resilience, digital literacy, and collaborative ability greatly determine the adaptive capacity of MSMEs in the face of repeated shocks. In-depth research on this aspect will help explain why two businesses facing similar conditions can produce very different levels of resilience. This kind of research can also enrich the design of mentoring and entrepreneurship training programs that are more targeted.

At the meso level, research can be directed at the role of digital communities, business incubators, research centers, and local ecosystems as mediators between public policy and business resilience. Local entrepreneurial ecosystems often form social capital, trust, and networks that encourage collaboration in the face of crises. Research on the relationship between the power of local networks and the effectiveness of public policies can provide valuable insights into how to strengthen collective capacity in building resilience.

The sustainability dimension also needs to continue to be a priority in future research. With the increasing impacts of climate change, geopolitical volatility, and environmental risks, the integration of ESG principles has become relevant not only as a compliance obligation, but also as a crucial business strategy and policy. Further research can explore the extent to which ESG implementation, both at the policy level and at the corporate level, can improve the long-term resilience of MSMEs. This approach can be done through cross-sector studies or region-based case studies to see how environmental, social, and governance variables affect business performance and sustainability.

Overall, the direction of entrepreneurship research in the future is expected to produce more adaptive, collaborative, and transformative theories and policy models. Research that considers the multi-level dynamics of business actors, local communities, and global policy systems will open up opportunities to build a more inclusive, equitable, and sustainability-oriented entrepreneurial resilience framework. Through the development of comprehensive and contextual research, the entrepreneurial ecosystem can be strengthened not only to deal with the current crisis, but also to prepare for future challenges.

CONCLUSION

Entrepreneurial resilience is the result of a dynamic interaction between individual capacity, institutional support, and mutually reinforcing public policy frameworks. This study emphasizes that the resilience of business actors, especially MSMEs, cannot be separated from the quality of regulatory governance and the effectiveness of policy implementation at the national and local levels. The experience of Indonesia, ASEAN countries, and Germany shows that flexible, inclusive, and collaborative public policies can be a driver of economic recovery and a catalyst for entrepreneurial transformation in the midst of global uncertainty.

Building the resilience of MSMEs requires solid synergy between three strategic components. First, adaptive policies that are prepared based on empirical evidence so that they are able to respond appropriately to crisis dynamics and structural changes. Second, an entrepreneurial ecosystem that encourages innovation, digitalization, and technological integration is the foundation for business actors to increase efficiency and expand market opportunities. Third, cross-border collaboration involving government, the private sector, financial institutions, academia, and civil society is an important mechanism to strengthen support networks and expand access to resources.

Strengthening institutional capacity, expanding digital literacy and inclusion, and authentically applying ESG principles contribute to the formation of entrepreneurial resilience that is not only reactive, but develops into a long-term strategy that supports sustainable economic growth. With a resilient, collaborative, and future-oriented approach, the MSMEs ecosystem can transform into a key pillar of economic development that is resilient, inclusive, and adaptive to global change.

REFERENCES

Aaouid, B., Elboussadi, A., & Boubker, O. (2025). Entrepreneurial Resilience in Times of Crisis: A Bibliometric Analysis. *Entrepreneurial Business and Economics Review, 13*(3), 55–75. DOI: 10.15678/EBER.2025.130303

Arief, A. M. (2024). *Tantangan UMKM Bukan Digitalisasi, Tapi Daya Saing.* Katadata.Co.Id. https://katadata.co.id/berita/industri/66a0b52c6b5b5/menkop-teten-tantangan-umkm-bukan-digitalisasi-tapi-daya-saing

Asean, A. (2025). *ASEAN Strategic Action Plan for SME Development 2016-2025.* 1–10. https://asean.org/book/asean-strategic-action-plan-for-sme-development-2016-2025/

Asifulla, A., & Basha, H. M. (2023). Supply Chain Finance in SMEs A Conceptual Analysis. *Journal of Informatics Education and Research, 3*(2), 2181–2187. DOI: 10.52783/JIER.V3I2.365

Bachtiar, N. K., Setiawan, A., Prastyan, G. A., & Kijkasiwat, P. (2023). Business Resilience and Growth Strategy Transformation Post Crisis. *Journal of Innovation and Entrepreneurship, 12*(1), 1–25. DOI: 10.1186/S13731-023-00345-5/FIGURES/3

Balzano, M., Marzi, G., & Turzo, T. (2025). SMEs and Institutional Theory: Major Inroads and Opportunities Ahead. *Management Decision, 63*(13), 1–27. DOI: 10.1108/MD-05-2023-0734

Basri, Y. M., Taufik, T., Yasni, H., & Putri, R. I. (2022). Institutional Pressure and Social Entrepreneurship Orientation: Their Impact on The Performance of Social Enterprises. *Jurnal Reviu Akuntansi Dan Keuangan, 12*(3), 545–559. DOI: 10.22219/JRAK.V12I3.23425

Bramantyo, H. B., Sumartono, Muluk, M. R. K., & Mindarti, L. I. (2025). Public-Private Partnerships for Infrastructure in Developing Asia: A Systematic Review of Challenges and Future Research Agendas. *Lex Localis - Journal of Local Self-Government, 23*(11), 20–46. https://doi.org/DOI: 10.52152/801711

Chavira, P. C., Shamsuzzoha, A., Kuusniemi, H., & Jovanovski, B. (2023). Defining Green Innovation, Its Impact, and Cycle – A Literature Analysis. *Cleaner Engineering and Technology, 17*, 100693. DOI: 10.1016/J.CLET.2023.100693

Deirmentzoglou, G. A., Anastasopoulou, E. E., & Sklias, P. (2024). International Economic Relations and Energy Security in the European Union: A Systematic Literature Review. *International Journal of Sustainable Energy, 43*(1). Advance online publication. DOI: 10.1080/14786451.2024.2385682

EIB. (2025). *EIB Investment Report 2024/2025: Innovation, Integration and Simplification in Europe.* https://www.eib.org/en/publications/20240354-investment-report-2024

Elert, N., Henrekson, M., & Stenkula, M. (2017). *Innovation, Entrepreneurship and the Complementary Skill Structure.* 9–23. https://doi.org/DOI: 10.1007/978-3-319-55092-3_2

Endress, T. (2023). Open Innovation Ecosystem in Asia. *Business and Management in Asia: Digital Innovation and Sustainability*, 35–48. https://doi.org/DOI: 10.1007/978-981-19-6418-3_3

ERIA. (2023). ASEAN's Digital Integration: Evolution of Framework Documents. *Books.* https://ideas.repec.org//b/era/eriabk/2023-10-oct-asean-digital-integration-evolution-of-framework-documents.html

Gatto, A., & Sadik-Zada, E. R. (2022). Access to Microfinance as a Resilience Policy to Address Sustainable Development Goals: A Content Analysis. *Heliyon*, *8*(10), e10860. DOI: 10.1016/J.HELIYON.2022.E10860 PMID: 36267370

Hess, S., Wurth, B., Stam, E., Giones, F., Fini, R., Cavallo, A., Wahl, A., Bosma, N., Theodoraki, C., Chabaud, D., Brem, A., & Kuckertz, A. (2025). The Future of Entrepreneurial Ecosystems Research: Toward a Policy-Oriented Research Agenda. *Journal of Business Venturing Insights*, *23*, e00538. DOI: 10.1016/J.JBVI.2025.E00538

Hokmabadi, H., Rezvani, S. M. H. S., & de Matos, C. A. (2024). Business Resilience for Small and Medium Enterprises and Startups by Digital Transformation and the Role of Marketing Capabilities—A Systematic Review. *Systems 2024, Vol. 12, Page 220, 12*(6), 220. https://doi.org/DOI: 10.3390/SYSTEMS12060220

Imelda, M., & Susiang, N. (2024). Business Incubators In The Entrepreneurship Ecosystem In Indonesia Mediated By Government Support And Intellectual Capital. *Commercium : Journal of Business and Management*, *2*(2), 67–81. DOI: 10.61978/COMMERCIUM.V2I2.215

IMF. (2022). *IMF Executive Board Approves Establishment of the Resilience and Sustainability Trust.* https://www.imf.org/en/news/articles/2022/04/18/pr22119-imf-executive-board-approves-establishment-of-the-rst

IMF. (2024). *Regional Economic Outlook for Europe, October 2024: A Recovery Short of Europe's Full Potential.* https://www.imf.org/en/Publications/REO/EU/Issues/2024/10/24/regional-economic-outlook-Europe-october-2024

IMF. (2025). *IMF Resilience and Sustainability Trust*. https://www.imf.org/en/Topics/Resilience-and-Sustainability-Trust

Junaidi, M. (2024). *UMKM Hebat, Perekonomian Nasional Meningkat*. https://djpb.kemenkeu.go.id/kppn/curup/id/data-publikasi/artikel/2885-umkm-hebat%2C-perekonomian-nasional-meningkat.html

Kádár, B., & Jáki, E. (2024). COVID-19 and SMEs: An Umbrella Review of Systematic Literature (2020–2024) and Future Directions for Entrepreneurship. *Society and Economy*, *46*(4), 323–341. DOI: 10.1556/204.2024.00017

Kanyepe, J., Musasa, T., & Wilbert, M. (2025). Supply Chain Risk Factors, Technological Capabilities, and Firm Performance of Small to Medium Enterprises (SMEs). *Journal of Small Business Strategy*, *35*(1), 115–128. DOI: 10.53703/001C.125910

KEMENKO. (2021). *UMKM Menjadi Pilar Penting dalam Perekonomian Indonesia*. https://ekon.go.id/publikasi/detail/2969/umkm-menjadi-pilar-penting-%20dalam-perekonomian-indonesia

KfW. (2024). *KfW SME Panel 2024: The business environment puts pressure on companies*. https://www.kfw.de/About-KfW/Newsroom/Latest-News/Pressemitteilungen-Details_825024.html

Koporcic, N., Kukkamalla, P. K., Markovic, S., & Maran, T. (2025). Resilience of Small and Medium-Sized Enterprises in Times of Crisis: An Umbrella Review. *Review of Managerial Science*, •••, 1–29. DOI: 10.1007/S11846-025-00883-0/TABLES/2

Lestari, N. P., & Choirunissa, Z. (2025). Transformasi Digital dan Ketahanan UMKM: Systematic Literature Review (SLR). *Jambura Economic Education Journal*, *7*(1), 355–372. DOI: 10.37479/JEEJ.V7I1.26333

Li, X., & Bosma, N. (2023). Institutional Theory in Social Entrepreneurship: A Review and Consideration of Ethics. SSRN *Electronic Journal*. https://doi.org/DOI: 10.2139/SSRN.5043847

Ma'amor, H., Badrolhisam, N. I., & Munir, R. (2025). Entrepreneurial Resilience in SMEs: A Bibliometric Perspective. *Information Management and Business Review*, *17*(3(I)), 252–265. DOI: 10.22610/imbr.v17i3(I).4701

Maaßen, C., Lopez, T., & Urbano, D. (2025). Institutional Enablers for Sustainable Entrepreneurship: A Configurational Analysis. *Small Business Economics*, •••, 1–22. DOI: 10.1007/S11187-025-01076-5/TABLES/5

Máté, D., Estiyanti, N. M., & Novotny, A. (2024). How to Support Innovative Small Firms? Bibliometric Analysis and Visualization of Start-Up Incubation. *Journal of Innovation and Entrepreneurship, 13*(1), 1–26. DOI: 10.1186/S13731-024-00361-Z/TABLES/3

Mathuros, S., Kuljittree, S., & Wongkamhaengharn, K. (2025). *Sustainability Strategies for SME Business Development Applying ESG Concepts to Create Competitive Advantage*. Arts of Management Journal. https://so02.tci-thaijo.org/index.php/jam/article/view/278541

Mishrif, A., & Khan, A. (2023). Technology Adoption as Survival Strategy for Small and Medium Enterprises during COVID-19. *Journal of Innovation and Entrepreneurship, 12*(1), 1–23. DOI: 10.1186/S13731-023-00317-9/TABLES/4

North, D. C. (1990). *Institutions, Institutional Change, and Economic Performance*. Cambridge University Press., https://doi.org/https://doi.org/10.1017/CBO9780511808678

Persada, A. R., Mulyadi, H., Jajang, A., Mahri, W., & Furqon, C. (2025). Digital Transformation and Business Incubation on SME Performance in Indonesia. *Jurnal Ilmiah Manajemen Kesatuan, 13*(4), 2183–2194. DOI: 10.37641/JIMKES.V13I4.3441

Petropoulou, A., Angelaki, E., Rompogiannakis, I., Passas, I., Garefalakis, A., & Thanasas, G. (2024). Digital Transformation in SMEs: Pre- and Post-COVID-19 Era: A Comparative Bibliometric Analysis. *Sustainability 2024, Vol. 16, Page 10536, 16*(23), 10536. https://doi.org/DOI: 10.3390/SU162310536

Poolsawat, P., & Rinthaisong, I. (2025). The Mediating Role of Entrepreneurial Resilience and Self-Efficacy in Enhancing SMEs Performance in Thailand. *Journal of Business* [JBIS]. *Innovation and Sustainability*, *20*(2). Advance online publication. DOI: 10.71185/JBIS.2025.276235

Prasannath, V., Adhikari, R. P., Gronum, S., & Miles, M. P. (2024). Impact of Government Support Policies on Entrepreneurial Orientation and SME Performance. *The International Entrepreneurship and Management Journal*, *20*(3), 1533–1595. DOI: 10.1007/S11365-024-00993-3

Sakib, Md. N., & Rahman, Md. M. (2024a). Mitigating the Impact of COVID-19 on SMEs Through Government Policy Intervention: A Systematic Literature Review and Bibliometric Analysis. *Future Business Journal 2024 10:1, 10*(1), 1–11. https://doi.org/DOI: 10.1186/S43093-024-00346-0

Sakib, Md. N., & Rahman, Md. M. (2024b). Mitigating the Impact of COVID-19 on SMEs Through Government Policy Intervention: A Systematic Literature Review and Bibliometric Analysis. *Future Business Journal 2024 10:1, 10*(1), 1–11. https://doi.org/DOI: 10.1186/S43093-024-00346-0

Salma, D. F., Nuryartono, N., & Purwanto, B. (2023). Sharia Financial Inclusion to Build Economic Resilience of Micro Small Enterprises During COVID-19. *Jurnal Manajemen Dan Organisasi, 14*(4), 430–439. DOI: 10.29244/JMO.V14I4.47631

Sarfo, C., Zhang, J. A., O'Kane, C., & O'Kane, P. (2024). Perceived Value of Microfinance and SME Performance: The Role of Exploratory Innovation. *International Journal of Innovation Studies, 8*(2), 172–185. DOI: 10.1016/J.IJIS.2024.02.003

Scheidgen, K., Günzel-Jensen, F., & Schmidt, S. L. (2025). Entrepreneurial Resourcefulness Throughout Crisis. *Entrepreneurship Theory and Practice, 49*(2), 502–538. DOI: 10.1177/10422587241269067

Scott, W. R. (1987). The Adolescence of Institutional Theory. *Administrative Science Quarterly, 32*(4), 493. DOI: 10.2307/2392880

Shalhoob, H., & Hussainey, K. (2022). Environmental, Social and Governance (ESG) Disclosure and the Small and Medium Enterprises (SMEs) Sustainability Performance. *Sustainability 2023, Vol. 15, Page 200, 15*(1), 200. https://doi.org/DOI: 10.3390/SU15010200

Shore, A., Tiwari, M., Tandon, P., & Foropon, C. (2024). Building Entrepreneurial Resilience during Crisis Using Generative AI: An Empirical Study on SMEs. *Technovation, 135*, 103063. DOI: 10.1016/J.TECHNOVATION.2024.103063

Supari, S., & Anton, H. (2022). The Impact of the National Economic Recovery Program and Digitalization on MSME Resilience during the COVID-19 Pandemic: A Case Study of Bank Rakyat Indonesia. *Economies 2022, Vol. 10, Page 160, 10*(7), 160. https://doi.org/DOI: 10.3390/ECONOMIES10070160

Syahribulan, S., Lasaksi, P., Samuddin, S. F., Souisa, W., & Hafid, A. (2024). Entrepreneurial Resilience and Adaptation in Times of Crisis: A Bibliometric Study on Business Continuity in SMEs. *West Science Social and Humanities Studies, 2*(05), 728–738. DOI: 10.58812/WSSHS.V2I05.875

Topcu, M., & Gulsen, M. A. (2025). Governance Quality Vs. Stimulus Size: Fiscal Policy Effectiveness During the COVID-19 Pandemic. *Public Sector Economics - Submission Site, 49*(2), 251–272. https://doi.org/DOI: 10.3326/PSE.49.2.4

Tunçalp, D. (2025). Entrepreneurial Resilience in Polycrisis: Adaptation Via Improvizational Action, Institutional Workarounds, and Strategic Reconfiguration. *Journal of Management & Organization*, •••, 1–23. DOI: 10.1017/JMO.2025.10040

Vargas-Zeledon, A. A., & Lee, S. Y. (2024). Configurations of Institutional Enablers that Foster Inclusive Entrepreneurship: A Fuzzy-Set Qualitative Comparative Analysis. *Journal of Innovation and Knowledge*, *9*(4). Advance online publication. DOI: 10.1016/J.JIK.2024.100549

Vasi, M., Sansone, G., & English, V. (2024). Exogenous Crises and SMEs Resilience: The Dynamic Open Innovation Funnel. *Technovation*, *129*, 102886. DOI: 10.1016/J.TECHNOVATION.2023.102886

Wahrudin, B., & Sutrisno. (2025). Public Policy Strategies for Enhancing Innovation and SME Competitiveness in Emerging Economies. *International Journal of Economics and Development, 1*(1), 63–78. https://journal.as-salafiyah.id/index.php/ijed/article/view/348

World Bank. (2022). *World Development Report 2022: Finance for an Equitable Recovery*. https://www.worldbank.org/en/publication/wdr2022

World Bank. (2025). *World Bank SME Finance*. https://www.worldbank.org/en/topic/smefinance

WTO. (2025). *The WTO in brief*. https://www.wto.org/english/thewto_e/whatis_e/inbrief_e/inbr_e.htm

Zhao, X., & Zhang, L. (2025). How to Improve the Financing Availability of Transport Smes? A Survey Based on Supply Chain Relationship-Logistics Capability-Information Traceability. *Research in Transportation Business & Management*, *62*, 101421. DOI: 10.1016/J.RTBM.2025.101421

Zhou, N., & Sun, R. (2024). Coping with the Storm: The Role of Fintech in SME Survival. *International Review of Financial Analysis*, *93*, 103157. DOI: 10.1016/J.IRFA.2024.103157

Zimmermann, V., & Köhler-Geib, F. (2023). Impact of the COVID-19 Pandemic on Different Groups of SMEs in Germany and Their Recovery. *Inter Economics*, *58*(6), 333–341. DOI: 10.2478/IE-2023-0068

Chapter 3
Empowering Entrepreneurs Through Education Resilience and Competitiveness in a Global Economy

Laveena Pareek
https://orcid.org/0009-0009-2096-8653
Institute of Management Studies, Noida, India

Aradhana Kumari
https://orcid.org/0009-0008-1455-2267
Institute of Management Studies, Noida, India

Vaishali Mogha
https://orcid.org/0009-0003-6803-4231
Institute of Management Studies, Noida, India

Muskan Wadhwa
https://orcid.org/0009-0000-8012-4924
Institute of Management Studies, Noida, India

ABSTRACT

This chapter explores how education strengthens entrepreneurs' resilience and competitiveness in today's global economy. Entrepreneurs face rapid market shifts and rising uncertainties, and education formal, informal, and experiential merges as a key driver of adaptability and success. Using an exploratory approach based

DOI: 10.4018/979-8-3373-6991-4.ch003

on secondary data (literature, policy reports, and global indices), the chapter highlights the transformative role of education in building skills, strategic thinking, and sustainable growth.

1. INTRODUCTION: ENTREPRENEURSHIP IN THE GLOBAL ECONOMY

The role of entrepreneurship in today's world goes far beyond starting a business; it is central to driving innovation, generating employment, and fostering sustainable development. In the 21st century, as economies become more interconnected and technology continues to evolve rapidly, entrepreneurs face environments marked by volatility, uncertainty, complexity, and ambiguity (the VUCA world). This reality means that success now depends not only on having a viable business idea or technical expertise but also on the ability to be resilient, flexible, and creative in the face of change. Education formal, informal, and experiential serves as a key enabler in this process. Formal education, such as business schools and university programs, provides foundational knowledge in areas like finance, marketing, and strategic management. Meanwhile, informal learning, which occurs through mentorship, peer networks, and professional communities, allows entrepreneurs to gain practical insights and develop real-world problem-solving skills. Experiential learning, including internships, startup incubators, and hands-on projects, helps entrepreneurs test their ideas, learn from failure, and adapt their strategies in dynamic contexts. By integrating these different forms of learning, entrepreneurship education cultivates an entrepreneurial mindset encouraging innovation, risk-taking, and continuous improvement. It also equips individuals to identify and exploit emerging opportunities despite uncertainty, fostering both personal and economic resilience. Ultimately, education not only shapes competent business founders but also adaptive leaders who can contribute to sustainable development and inclusive economic growth on a global scale.

Education serves as a powerful driver of entrepreneurial success by developing the knowledge, skills, and mindsets necessary for identifying and exploiting opportunities. It does more than teach business fundamentals; it shapes how individuals think, act, and respond to challenges. Through structured learning and experiential engagement, education helps entrepreneurs cultivate cognitive abilities such as critical thinking, creativity, and strategic decision-making competencies vital for navigating the unpredictable business environment of the modern world.

Moreover, entrepreneurial education plays a key role in nurturing behavioral and emotional traits that are equally critical to success. It encourages learners to adopt a growth mindset, view failure as a learning experience, and remain adaptable when confronted with uncertainty or disruption. By focusing on resilience and problem-solving, educational programs prepare entrepreneurs to respond constructively to technological changes, market fluctuations, and crises that might otherwise threaten their ventures.

In an era where knowledge drives economic progress, the connection between education and entrepreneurship becomes indispensable for sustainable development. Knowledge-based economies rely heavily on innovation and the continuous generation of new ideas, both of which stem from an educated and entrepreneurial workforce. Thus, well-designed entrepreneurial education not only empowers individuals to create and sustain businesses but also strengthens national competitiveness, fosters inclusive development, and contributes to long-term global prosperity. The relationship between education and entrepreneurship is multidimensional. Formal education systems such as universities and vocational institutes provide structured learning environments that develop managerial and technical capabilities. Informal education, including mentoring, peer learning, and community networks, fosters experiential understanding and social capital (Baporikar, 2020). Experiential learning, on the other hand, enables entrepreneurs to learn by doing business simulations, internships, and real-world problem-solving which strengthens resilience and adaptability in uncertain markets (Kolb, 2015; Rae, 2010).

In an increasingly globalized economy, competitiveness is not solely determined by access to capital or technology but by the capacity for continuous learning and innovation (Audretsch & Belitski, 2021). Education cultivates this capacity by promoting strategic thinking, digital literacy, and global awareness among entrepreneurs, enabling them to leverage cross-border networks, adopt sustainable practices, and adapt to emerging trends such as digital transformation and green entrepreneurship (European Commission, 2022). Furthermore, resilient entrepreneurs contribute to inclusive economic growth by generating employment and fostering community-based innovation, underscoring the social dimension of education-driven entrepreneurship (OECD, 2021).

Despite the evident benefits, significant gaps persist in existing educational frameworks. Many educational institutions continue to emphasize theoretical business knowledge over practical, experience-based learning. Moreover, entrepreneurship education often fails to address the challenges faced by marginalized groups, including women, rural populations, and youth in developing economies (Brush et al., 2019). Bridging these gaps requires reimagining educational systems to integrate experiential learning, mentorship, and global exposure that collectively build entrepreneurial resilience and competitiveness.

Thus, this chapter seeks to examine the intricate relationship between education and entrepreneurial resilience, explore the role of education in enhancing global competitiveness, identify shortcomings in current educational approaches, and propose strategies for strengthening education-driven entrepreneurship. By drawing on secondary data including scholarly literature, policy reports, and global competitiveness indices this chapter aims to contribute to the growing discourse on how education serves as both a foundation and a transformative force for entrepreneurial success in the global economy.

2. EDUCATION, RESILIENCE, AND COMPETITIVENESS CONCEPTUAL LINKAGES

2.1 Conceptual Foundations

2.1.1 Education

Education is not merely a structured system of learning confined to classrooms and textbooks; it is a lifelong, dynamic, and transformative journey that molds individuals and civilizations alike. It encompasses the vast spectrum of formalized schooling, non-formal community-based instruction, and experiential, real-world learning all synergistically contributing to the expansion of human potential, intellectual agility, and economic vitality (Business Case Studies, 2025; OECD, 2024).

Drawing upon the foundational insights of Becker's Human Capital Theory (1993), education stands as perhaps the single most powerful investment a society can make in its future. Every lesson learned, skill mastered, and curiosity pursued acts as a catalyst for individual empowerment and collective advancement. Through deliberate investments in education, nations sculpt a resilient, innovative, and adaptive workforce capable of pioneering technological revolutions, confronting global challenges, and redefining the boundaries of possibility (Business Case Studies, 2025; Investopedia, n.d.; Frontiers in Psychology, n.d.).

In the modern world, where information evolves at lightning speed and industries transform almost overnight, education emerges as the cornerstone of progress. Societies that channel resources into cultivating knowledge and skills are not only securing their economic competitiveness but are also advancing the broader cause of human civilization. They nurture critical thinkers who question convention, innovators who disrupt stagnation, and leaders who envision alternative futures (Frontiers in Psychology, n.d.; ADB Blog, n.d.).

Ultimately, education is the great equalizer and the eternal engine of progress. It transcends borders, dismantles barriers, and fuels the collective ambition of humankind to reach higher, see farther, and achieve what once seemed impossible. In investing in education, humanity invests in itself a boundless reservoir of creativity, resilience, and progress without which societies would drift aimlessly in the tide of mediocrity and decline.

Crucially, education extends its impact beyond technical know-how by nurturing socio-emotional strengths such as self-efficacy and adaptability, which are increasingly essential in managing uncertainty and disruption (OECD, 2024). In a knowledge-driven global economy, these capacities enable individuals and societies to overcome unpredictable challenges and seize emerging opportunities (OECD, 2024).

2.1.2 Resilience

Resilience is far more than mere endurance it is the dynamic essence of recovery, reinvention, and growth in the face of adversity. It embodies the extraordinary human and organizational capacity to not only withstand turbulence but to emerge from it stronger, wiser, and more adaptable than before. Within the domains of business and entrepreneurship, resilience represents the beating heart of sustained success, capturing the indomitable persistence, flexibility, and ingenuity that empower individuals and enterprises to navigate crises, reorganize amid uncertainty, and turn chaos into opportunity (Korber & McNaughton, 2018).

Bhamra et al. (2011) conceptualize resilience as both a continuous process and a tangible outcome, a dual-force mechanism through which learning from disruption becomes a source of strategic renewal. In this light, resilience is not a passive defense mechanism but a proactive philosophy- a deliberate, cultivated capacity to anticipate, absorb, and adapt to shocks of any scale. Whether confronting economic downturns, technological upheavals, or global crises, resilient organizations transform adversity into a catalyst for reinvention, leveraging disruption as a proving ground for innovation and leadership.

At its core, resilience is the intellectual and emotional infrastructure of progress. It demands creativity under pressure, unity amid fragmentation, and an unrelenting pursuit of purpose when conditions seem insurmountable. Businesses that embody resilience don't merely survive turbulent markets they redefine them. They evolve, recalibrate, and sow the seeds of their future success in the very soil of their setbacks.

In essence, resilience is both shield and spark the shield that protects against breakdown and the spark that ignites transformation. It is the hallmark of visionary entrepreneurs and forward-thinking organizations, a testament to the human spirit's ability to persist, adapt, and flourish even when the world seems to conspire against it.

2.1.3 Competitiveness

Competitiveness refers to the enduring ability of a nation, region, or enterprise to generate higher levels of productivity, innovation, and prosperity compared with its peers (Porter, 1990). It is a dynamic and multidimensional construct that transcends mere short-term profitability, encompassing structural efficiency, innovation capacity, technological advancement, and the effective mobilization of human and institutional capital. A truly competitive economy or firm consistently adapts to evolving market forces, leverages its unique strengths, and sustains growth even amid global uncertainty.

While traditional economic perspectives often highlight physical capital, infrastructure, and technology as key determinants of competitiveness, modern frameworks recognize the pivotal role of human resources and institutional quality. A skilled and creative workforce fuels innovation and productivity, while transparent and efficient institutions establish the foundation for trust, fair competition, and sustained investment. These elements act in concert to promote agility, entrepreneurial vitality, and continuous improvement—core attributes of competitiveness in an increasingly interconnected world.

The World Economic Forum's Global Competitiveness Index underscores this holistic view by identifying education, skills development, and training as indispensable pillars of productivity and innovation (Schwab, 2023). Through education, individuals acquire not only technical expertise but also the critical thinking and adaptability required to drive technological change and economic transformation. When coupled with effective governance, robust infrastructure, and an enabling business environment, such human capital investments create an ecosystem where innovation flourishes and competitiveness compounds.

Ultimately, competitiveness is both the product and the process of perpetual refinement. It demands foresight, collaboration, and resilience—qualities that empower nations and organizations to sustain excellence, expand opportunity, and forge a lasting position of leadership in the global economy.

3. THEORETICAL LINKAGES

Education, resilience, and competitiveness are interlinked through a powerful tapestry of foundational theories, each revealing how learning acts as the catalyst for sustainable success and enduring advantage in today's unpredictable world. To fully appreciate their connection and its implications, it is essential to explore, expand, and dramatize the central themes these theories present.

3.1 Human Capital Theory: Education as the Engine of Excellence

Human capital theory positions education not just as a means of personal advancement, but as the very engine that propels societies and organizations toward unrivaled productivity and breakthrough innovation. Through the systematic acquisition of knowledge and skills, individuals are transformed into dynamic sources of growth who multiply value wherever they go. Every skill learned, every insight gained, and every innovative mindset fostered through education acts as a force multiplier, generating competitive advantage from local contexts to the global stage.

3.2 Resource-Based View: People as Strategic Powerhouses

Barney's resource-based view redefines educated human resources as invaluable treasures—the rare jewels of modern organizations. These talented individuals are not easily replicable, making them a driving force behind sustained competitiveness. With education, firms become repositories of unique know-how, creativity, and expertise that rivals simply cannot imitate. In this way, education becomes the foundation of a strategic arsenal, unlocking a competitive edge that is as enduring as it is unassailable.

3.3 Dynamic Capabilities: Education Fuels Resilience and Agility

The dynamic capabilities framework (Teece, 2018) brings education to the forefront as the enabler of senses, responses, and transformation. In turbulent markets and disruptive environments, educated leaders and teams can anticipate change, adapt strategies, and reinvent their organizations with remarkable agility. Education strengthens not just the core but the connective tissue of resilience—allowing businesses (and entire economies) to flex, reset, and seize new opportunities even when faced with the fiercest headwinds.

3.4 Learning Perspective: Education as a Springboard for Innovation

From a learning perspective, education is the perpetual renewable resource that keeps the fires of innovation burning bright. As knowledge creation accelerates and capability building becomes ingrained, entrepreneurs and organizations cultivate cultures of boundary-pushing curiosity and iterative experimentation. Education acts as the springboard from which new ideas leap into existence and continuous improvement becomes a way of life.

3.4 Converging Forces: The Virtuous Cycle

When these theories are woven together, a virtuous cycle emerges. Education amplifies human capabilities, which fuel resilience, which in turn sustains competitiveness across ever-changing landscapes. The result is an unstoppable force—a nation, firm, or individual equipped not only to survive, but to thrive, redefine possibility, and lead the charge into an unknown future.

(i) Empirical Evidence: Education and Competitiveness

Empirical findings consistently link educational attainment and quality with economic competitiveness. Cross-country analyses by the OECD (2024) show that nations investing in equitable, skills-oriented education systems report higher productivity growth and innovation capacity. Similarly, the World Bank (2020) underscores education as a core determinant of human capital accumulation, which directly contributes to global competitiveness.

At the firm level, education and training improve organizational performance by enhancing employees' technical proficiency and adaptability. Studies indicate that ongoing workforce upskilling correlates with higher innovation output and export competitiveness (Piva & Vivarelli, 2018). Universities also play a regional role by supplying skilled labor and promoting research-industry collaboration that strengthens local innovation ecosystems (Audretsch et al., 2020). Porter's (1990) framework highlights such clusters where education and business interacts engines of national advantage.

(ii) Empirical Evidence: Education and Resilience

Research linking education and resilience has expanded in recent years. Entrepreneurial education has been shown to foster persistence, creativity, and coping capacity in uncertain contexts. Korber and McNaughton (2018) demonstrated that entrepreneurship education enhances opportunity recognition and adaptive problem-solving, enabling entrepreneurs to recover from failure. Anwar et al. (2023) found that educational interventions nurturing self-efficacy and passion significantly predict entrepreneurial resilience among students and early-stage founders.

At the regional level, education supports socioeconomic recovery after crises. Rose (2017) argued that human capital accumulation facilitates faster post-disaster recovery by increasing adaptability and innovation potential. Education also contributes to psychological resilience through socio-emotional learning, improving individuals' capacity to manage stress and uncertainty (Montoro-Fernández et al., 2022). These findings position education as both a preventive and adaptive mechanism for dealing with turbulence.

4. MECHANISMS CONNECTING EDUCATION, RESILIENCE, AND COMPETITIVENESS

Four primary mechanisms explain the interdependence among these constructs:

1. Skill acquisition – Education develops cognitive, technical, and problem-solving skills that drive productivity and innovation (competitiveness) while enhancing adaptive responses to shocks (resilience) (OECD, 2024).
2. Socio-emotional competencies – Emotional intelligence, self-efficacy, and teamwork fostered by education strengthen persistence and adaptive thinking (Montoro-Fernández et al., 2022).
3. Social capital and networks – Educational environments provide networks of peers, mentors, and institutional partners that serve as informational and emotional resources during crises and as collaboration channels in competitive markets (Audretsch et al., 2020).
4. Institutional signaling – Educational credentials act as signals of competence and reliability, facilitating access to markets, funding, and partnerships that sustain competitiveness and resilience (Barney, 1991).

5. EVIDENCE FROM SECONDARY DATA

Evidence drawn from global datasets, institutional reports, and peer-reviewed studies provides strong support for the role of education in shaping resilience and competitiveness across individual, organizational, and national spheres. Secondary sources such as the OECD, World Bank, and World Economic Forum, along with empirical studies spanning entrepreneurship, human capital, and innovation systems, collectively demonstrate that education enhances productivity, adaptability, and long-term economic performance (OECD, 2024; Schwab, 2023; World Bank, 2020). This body of evidence substantiates the theoretical linkages outlined earlier and offers a robust empirical foundation for understanding how education operates as a strategic driver of resilience and sustained competitive advantage.

5.1 Evidence Linking Education and Competitiveness

Education emerges as a central driver of competitiveness at multiple levels, with cross-country evidence showing that the quality of education systems, fair access to skills development, and robust human capital formation are key determinants of national competitive strength (OECD, 2024; World Bank, 2020; Schwab, 2023). At the organizational level, firms that prioritize employee education and ongoing training tend to achieve higher productivity, stronger innovation performance, and greater export success, particularly when they foster learning-oriented cultures that support continuous skill-building and knowledge sharing (Piva & Vivarelli, 2018). In addition, education underpins regional innovation and cluster development, as universities not only supply skilled graduates but also engage in research partnerships with industry, positioning higher education institutions as core nodes in regional knowledge networks in line with Porter's (1990) conceptualization of national competitive advantage (Audretsch et al., 2020; Porter, 1990)

5.2 Evidence Linking Education and Resilience

Entrepreneurship scholarship increasingly demonstrates that education is a crucial lever for strengthening resilience at the individual, organizational, and societal levels, particularly under conditions of uncertainty and volatility (Korber & McNaughton, 2018; Anwar et al., 2023). At the entrepreneurial level, targeted learning experiences help cultivate opportunity recognition, creative problem-solving, adaptive thinking, self-efficacy, and passion, all of which underpin persistence and recovery in the face of setbacks (Korber & McNaughton, 2018; Anwar et al., 2023). Beyond individuals, higher stocks of human capital enable regions to rebound more quickly after crises because better educated populations possess stronger learning capacities, innovation potential, and labour-market flexibility, making education both a preventive buffer and an adaptive resource for socio-economic reorganization (Rose, 2017). Complementing these structural effects, socio-emotional learning initiatives that build emotional intelligence, self-belief, and stress-management skills have been shown to enhance people's ability to cope with adversity, with such competencies now recognized as essential for functioning effectively in a fast-changing, knowledge-intensive global economy (Montoro-Fernández et al., 2022; OECD, 2024).

6. CROSS-VARIABLE SYNTHESIS: MECHANISMS CONNECTING EDUCATION, RESILIENCE, AND COMPETITIVENESS

Secondary evidence converges on four primary mechanisms through which education fosters both resilience and competitiveness.

1. Skill Acquisition: Cognitive, technical, and problem-solving skills developed through education directly increase productivity and innovation while enabling individuals and firms to adapt effectively to disruptions (OECD, 2024).
2. Socio-Emotional Competencies: Education nurtures emotional intelligence, teamwork, and self-efficacy—capabilities essential for resilience and valuable for organizational competitiveness (Montoro-Fernández et al., 2022).
3. Social Capital and Networks: Educational settings provide access to peer networks, mentors, and institutional partnerships that support both crisis coping and competitive collaboration (Audretsch et al., 2020).
4. Institutional Signaling: Academic credentials signal competence, reliability, and skill quality, facilitating access to opportunities, funding, and markets that reinforce competitive and resilient outcomes (Barney, 1991).

These mechanisms collectively illustrate how education functions as a foundational resource that strengthens adaptive capacity while simultaneously enabling innovation, productivity, and competitive performance.

6.1 Integrative Analytical Summary

The secondary evidence demonstrates a consistent and reinforcing connection among education, resilience, and competitiveness. Global data, institutional analyses, and empirical studies converge to show that investments in education yield stronger human capabilities, greater adaptability, and enhanced innovative capacity. Through skill development, socio-emotional growth, network formation, and signaling effects, education initiates a virtuous cycle wherein individuals, firms, and nations become more resilient to turbulence while securing long-term competitive advantage. This synthesis provides robust empirical validation for the theoretical propositions linking education, resilience, and competitiveness.

Table 1. Summary of Secondary Evidence Linking Education, Resilience, and Competitiveness

Theme	Key Findings from Secondary Data	Supporting Sources (APA)
1. Education → Competitiveness	**Macro-Level Evidence**: Strong education systems correlate with higher national productivity, innovation capacity, and competitiveness.	OECD (2024); World Bank (2020); Schwab (2023)
	Organizational-Level Evidence: Firms investing in employee education and upskilling show higher innovation output, improved productivity, and superior export performance.	Piva & Vivarelli (2018)
	Regional Innovation Systems: Universities strengthen regional clusters through talent supply and research-industry collaboration, reinforcing national competitive advantage.	Audretsch et al. (2020); Porter (1990)
2. Education → Resilience	**Entrepreneurial Resilience**: Entrepreneurship education enhances opportunity recognition, adaptive thinking, creative problem-solving, and persistence in uncertain contexts.	Korber & McNaughton (2018); Anwar et al. (2023)
	Socio-economic Resilience: Human capital accelerates regional recovery after crises by enabling adaptability and innovation.	Rose (2017)
	Psychological & Socio-emotional Resilience: SEL (socio-emotional learning) programs improve self-efficacy, emotional regulation, and stress management, strengthening resilience.	Montoro-Fernández et al. (2022); OECD (2024)
3. Mechanisms Linking Education, Resilience & Competitiveness	**Skill Acquisition**: Education builds cognitive, technical, and problem-solving skills that drive productivity, innovation, and crisis adaptability.	OECD (2024)
	Socio-emotional Competencies: Emotional intelligence, self-efficacy, and teamwork enhance resilience and contribute to organizational performance.	Montoro-Fernández et al. (2022)
	Social Capital & Networks: Educational environments create networks that support crisis coping and competitive collaboration.	Audretsch et al. (2020)
	Institutional Signaling: Educational credentials signal competence and reliability, improving access to opportunities that enhance resilience and competitiveness.	Barney (1991)
4. Integrative Summary	Education triggers a "virtuous cycle" where human capability development leads to greater adaptability (resilience) and superior innovation and productivity (competitiveness).	Synthesis of above evidence

7. GAPS, CHALLENGES, AND RESEARCH DIRECTIONS

Although a substantial body of literature confirms a positive association between education, entrepreneurial resilience, and competitiveness, several conceptual, methodological, and contextual challenges persist. One major limitation lies in establishing causality. Much of the existing evidence relies on cross-sectional correlations rather than robust longitudinal designs, making it difficult to determine whether education directly enhances resilience and competitiveness over time or merely coincides with them (Korber & McNaughton, 2018). This short-term focus is particularly evident in studies emphasizing entrepreneurial intention or immediate skill acquisition, while long-term outcomes such as business sustainability, adaptive capacity, and survival in volatile global markets remain underexplored.

Measurement inconsistencies further complicate the literature. Entrepreneurial resilience is variably conceptualized as psychological endurance, firm-level survival, or regional economic recovery, while competitiveness is measured using diverse indicators such as productivity, innovation output, export performance, or market growth. The absence of standardized frameworks or validated metrics has resulted in reliance on subjective or self-reported measures, limiting comparability and the reliability of findings across studies. Consequently, assessing the true impact of education on entrepreneurs' adaptability and crisis response capabilities remains challenging.

Contextual variation represents another significant gap. The influence of education is not uniform, as curriculum relevance, institutional quality, and alignment with labor-market needs strongly mediate outcomes (World Bank, 2020). Moreover, most empirical studies originate from developed economies, with comparatively limited evidence from developing and emerging contexts. Given differences in socio-economic structures, cultural norms, and institutional ecosystems, there is a pressing need to understand how education-driven entrepreneurship functions across diverse economic and cultural environments. Comparative analyses are essential to clarify how institutional settings and policy frameworks condition the relationship between education, resilience, and competitiveness (OECD, 2024; Audretsch & Belitski, 2021).

Another notable limitation is the predominant focus on formal education models. Research largely centers on university-based or institutional entrepreneurship programs, often neglecting the growing role of informal and non-traditional learning pathways such as mentorship, experiential learning, online platforms, incubators, and peer networks. These alternative modes of learning increasingly shape entrepreneurial capabilities, yet their contribution to resilience and competitiveness remains insufficiently examined.

The integration of digital and global perspectives within entrepreneurship education is also underdeveloped. In an era characterized by digital globalization, remote business models, and rapid technological change, relatively few studies investigate how digital literacy, cross-border collaboration, and exposure to global markets are embedded within educational curricula. This gap limits understanding of how education prepares entrepreneurs to compete and adapt in digitally networked and internationally competitive environments.

Issues of gender and inclusivity further underscore existing research gaps. The intersection of entrepreneurship education with gender, social inclusion, and marginalization has received limited scholarly attention. Women and underrepresented groups often face distinct barriers in accessing education, finance, and entrepreneurial networks, yet these challenges are not adequately reflected in mainstream research. Greater emphasis on inclusive educational strategies is required to support more equitable entrepreneurial participation and outcomes (Brush et al., 2019).

Finally, current scholarship often adopts narrowly defined educational or economic perspectives, overlooking the psychological, sociological, and technological dimensions of entrepreneurial development. There is a clear need for multidisciplinary approaches that integrate insights from education, innovation studies, behavioral sciences, and digital technologies. In addition, while governments worldwide promote entrepreneurship education through policy initiatives, incubators, and academia–industry partnerships, empirical evaluations of their effectiveness remain limited. More rigorous research is needed to assess how policy interventions and institutional ecosystems translate into sustained entrepreneurial resilience and competitiveness.

Addressing these gaps requires future research to employ longitudinal and mixed-method designs that track entrepreneurs over time and combine quantitative evidence with qualitative insights. Such approaches can illuminate how specific educational experiences such as experiential entrepreneurship training, digital literacy programs, leadership development, and emotional-intelligence-oriented pedagogy shape resilience and competitiveness trajectories (Korber & McNaughton, 2018; Anwar et al., 2023). Comparative studies across emerging and developed economies can further clarify contextual and institutional influences, while greater attention to curriculum relevance, inclusivity, and interdisciplinary integration will strengthen both theory and practice in education-driven entrepreneurship research.

8. POLICY AND PRACTICE RECOMMENDATIONS

8.1 Financial Literacy

Every organization requires finance as it makes it easier to handle accounts, including cash flow, banking, and budgeting. Effective financial management reduces risks and improves the company's overall stability. The foundation of effective money management techniques that promote the expansion as well as sustainability of businesses is financial literacy. Educating young entrepreneurs financial education is essential because it gives them the tools they need to restart and refocus their enterprises for greater future growth. Additionally, pupils who receive early financial education are better equipped to manage financial emergencies.

There are numerous both traditional and digital financial awareness initiatives. Through the growth of financial skills, free programs and courses on websites like Coursera and Udemy, as well as government programs like Startup India, promote entrepreneurship. By boosting long-term sustainability and enhancing liquidity management, these approaches have a favorable impact on firms. On the other side, people who lack financial literacy frequently find themselves in debt traps or suffering significant losses. Many small business owners in India operate without an effective understanding of financial management, which impedes the expansion and durability of their companies. Maravilla and Flores (2025) claim that when entrepreneurs integrate financial literacy with skills like strategic planning and decision-making, their resilience is much increased, which eventually improves sustainable performance.

The development of entrepreneurship is further aided by the inclusion of financial literacy in educational institutions. In Finland, entrepreneurial education is integrated into a number of topics to foster critical thinking, creativity, and problem-solving abilities from a young age. Students build mini-businesses, participate in project-based learning, and acquire financial literacy. Comparably, the Network for Teaching Entrepreneurship (NFTE) in the US provides elective entrepreneurship courses that cover financial literacy, idea generating, and company skill development. As stated by Bozward (2024), these courses expose students to real-world experiences through mentorship programs and business plan competitions.

Financial literacy, which is an essential part of economic education, gives people the power to make wise choices about borrowing, spending, investing, and saving. Such information lowers poverty, encourages entrepreneurship, and boosts economic resilience in emerging countries, where financial inclusion is still developing (Vega, 2025).

8.2 A creative and successful workforce

By encouraging productivity and creativity, an inventive and productive staff accelerates corporate growth. Economic education gives people the critical thinking, problem-solving, and resource management abilities that are necessary for both developed and emerging economies to experience long-term economic growth as stated by Goduni, 2024. Building leadership skills and an entrepreneurial perspective—which are crucial for handling uncertainty and fostering innovation—is facilitated by creating a welcoming, learning-focused culture that promotes entrepreneurship through practical problem-solving initiatives and ideation workshops. These programs enable young people to see their potential beyond traditional business skills, as noted by O'Mahony (2025).

Resilient and entrepreneurial workforces may lead successfully in difficult times, innovate in response to changing circumstances, retain flexibility for long-term growth, and lower risk while promoting recovery from failures. While continuous training combined with mentorship improves engagement, adaptability, and resilience, experiential learning through entrepreneurial projects fosters creativity and practical problem-solving abilities. Open communication, idea sharing, and a "fail-fast" strategy are all facilitated by fostering psychological safety, which encourages creativity without fear of failure. Workforce resilience and productivity are increased when employee well-being is prioritized through work-life balance and mental health care. This integrated approach creates a workforce that is robust enough to maintain organizational growth, innovation, and leadership that is suited to the demands of the future economy.

8.3 Higher education in entrepreneurship

Numerous organizations provide a variety of entrepreneurship programs to help them grow their companies. Through project-based learning, case studies, and practical exercises, it fosters critical thinking, creativity, innovation, risk management, and problem-solving abilities. Higher education programs that integrate entrepreneurship enhance students' understanding of market circumstances, financial literacy, and business operations, preparing them to contribute significantly to economic development. Additionally, entrepreneurial education promotes resilience and adaptability, two traits that are essential for navigating volatility in the modern business world.

Educational institutions should incorporate entrepreneurship electives that allow students to explore their interests through specialized courses in entrepreneurship and core business principles, while also offering flexible pathways such as business-oriented streams or dedicated entrepreneurship programs to align with diverse career aspirations. Complementing this, universities ought to establish on-campus incubation centers to nurture student-led ventures and entrepreneurial initiatives, alongside arranging internships and apprenticeships through partnerships with local firms to deliver hands-on mentorship and real-world exposure. Furthermore, curricula should integrate business plan development exercises, enabling students to create comprehensive and actionable plans, and encourage participation in regional or national business plan competitions to hone their skills and gain visibility.

8.4 Personality traits: Leadership, Self-worth, and Creativity

Leadership is essential for entrepreneurial resilience because it enables business owners to make courageous strategic choices in the face of uncertainty and successfully mentor others to identify and assess opportunities. Self-esteem fosters the confidence required for taking risks and solving problems successfully, both of which are essential for avoiding bad choices that could endanger the company. Innovation is fostered by creativity, which enables business owners to provide distinctive goods or services and take advantage of new opportunities by seeing signs of shifts in the international market. By improving cognitive maturity and decision-making skills, age-appropriate capabilities reinforce these abilities. This reflects a mature thought process that is necessary for managing a business with flexibility and resilience against disturbances.

However, entrepreneurial resilience is less common in India, where institutions have just recently started emphasizing the development of personality attributes in addition to entrepreneurship abilities. There are issues including a lack of entrepreneurial culture and inadequate incubation facilities. Therefore, substantial attempts to create an entrepreneurial ecosystem, including advantageous tax and regulatory frameworks and competitive conditions that foster growth, are necessary to encourage entrepreneurial resilience (OECD, n.d.).

This integrated perspective is consistent with research demonstrating that resilient entrepreneurs are capable of anticipating and effectively managing challenges in a volatile global economy because they possess dynamic adaptability, cross-cultural communication skills, emotional intelligence, and digital proficiency as stated by Pennetta, 2025.These qualities show up as a collection of skills that enable business owners to continuously innovate, learn from mistakes, and create networks of support—all of which are critical for long-term success and expansion in today's interconnected marketplaces.

8.5 The Role of Mentoring in Promoting Entrepreneurial Success

Direct assistance and mentoring are extremely beneficial to entrepreneurs, as seasoned mentors offer insightful advice when business plans fail to produce the desired outcomes. Having access to experienced founders' perspectives speeds up the development of entrepreneurial skills and helps avoid costly missteps. Many people fail to see how important timely, high-quality advice can be to their success in both their personal and professional lives.

Programs that are specifically targeted are essential for developing entrepreneurial talent, particularly for students. These programs can concentrate on useful business skills that are now crucial to contemporary business management, like hiring tactics and the efficient use of AI tools. In today's digital marketplace, being able to use digital technology improves visibility and competitiveness in addition to enhancing operational efficiency.

8.6 Leveraging Digital Literacy for business efficiency

Digital literacy, which includes website management and online business abilities, should be included in entrepreneurship education. Since global expertise is essential for industries like logistics that operate internationally, entrepreneurs must also keep up with changes in national and international legal frameworks and regulations.

All things considered, focused mentoring, meaningful educational programs, and exposure to technological and legal developments enable entrepreneurs to run their companies more successfully and sustainably in the quickly evolving global market.

8.7 Improving Students' Entrepreneurial Attitudes / Motivation Creative Methods to Boost the Effectiveness of Entrepreneurship Education

Drawing on qualitative and quantitative research findings on entrepreneurship education (EEd) in Nigerian higher education, and considering persistent challenges such as the gap between educators and practicing entrepreneurs as well as students' ineffective entrepreneurial attitude development, several practice-oriented recommendations emerge.

First, stronger cooperation with businesses and entrepreneurs is essential. Academic institutions should establish robust partnerships with regional businesses and entrepreneurial networks to create opportunities for mentorship, guest lectures, internships, and real-world problem-solving experiences. Such collaborations help bridge the gap between theoretical instruction and the practical realities of entrepreneurship, thereby enhancing students' applied learning and industry relevance (Oyinlola, 2024).

Second, targeted training and capacity building for faculty must be prioritized. Continuous professional development initiatives should be implemented to equip entrepreneurship educators with contemporary pedagogical approaches, digital teaching tools, and practical entrepreneurial competencies. Enhancing faculty capability is critical for delivering relevant and engaging entrepreneurship education that reflects current market dynamics (Adenike, 2016; Oluwafunmilola, 2024).

Third, the development of comprehensive entrepreneurial ecosystems within higher education institutions is recommended. Universities should establish innovation hubs, business incubators, and accelerator programs to support student-led ventures and entrepreneurial experimentation. Improving access to markets, professional networks, and funding opportunities can significantly strengthen students' ability to transform ideas into viable enterprises (Oyinlola, 2024).

In addition, entrepreneurship education should place greater emphasis on motivation and entrepreneurial attitude formation. Educational initiatives should integrate workshops, coaching sessions, and experiential activities that foster key psychological attributes such as resilience, risk tolerance, and achievement motivation. These elements are crucial for nurturing adaptive and opportunity-driven entrepreneurial mindsets (Liu et al., 2019).

Furthermore, the inclusion of financial and digital literacy is increasingly important. Entrepreneurship curricula should incorporate structured training on financial management, online marketing, artificial intelligence applications, and digital business tools to prepare students for participation in digitally enabled and competitive markets (Balogun, 2023).

Finally, continuous evaluation and feedback mechanisms should be institutionalized. Regular monitoring, assessment, and feedback loops involving students, educators, and entrepreneurs are necessary to ensure curriculum relevance, pedagogical effectiveness, and alignment with evolving entrepreneurial ecosystems. Such iterative evaluation supports continuous improvement in both curriculum design and delivery (San-Martín et al., 2019).

9. POLICY RECOMMENDATIONS:

Strengthening entrepreneurship education requires supportive policy frameworks and sustained institutional commitment. Governments should ensure sufficient infrastructure and funding by investing in the establishment of entrepreneurial centers, the provision of relevant instructional materials, and the renovation of physical and digital infrastructure that enables hands-on and experiential learning (Adenike,

2016). In addition, there is a need to design and implement a comprehensive national strategy for entrepreneurship education. Such a strategy should provide a cohesive framework with clearly defined competency objectives, standardized pedagogical approaches, and robust quality assurance mechanisms to guide educational institutions and ensure consistency in delivery (Oyinlola, 2024).

Furthermore, public–private collaborations should be actively encouraged to strengthen entrepreneurship ecosystems. Partnerships among academic institutions, businesses, government agencies, and financial institutions can help mobilize resources, expand access to entrepreneurial opportunities, and enhance students' exposure to real-world business environments (Oyinlola, 2024). Equally important is the inclusion of gender-responsive programs. Policy interventions should deliberately support women-focused initiatives that address gender disparities in access to entrepreneurship education and create enabling conditions for the development of women entrepreneurs (Adenike, 2016).

10. IDEAS FOR IMPROVING THE EFFECTIVENESS OF EED

Improving the effectiveness of entrepreneurship education (EEd) in today's dynamic and competitive environment requires innovative and learner-centered strategies that equip students with practical skills, real-world exposure, and psychological resilience. One effective approach is the organization of entrepreneurship challenge competitions. Annual startup competitions provide students with opportunities to pitch their business ideas to real investors and business leaders, fostering experiential learning by requiring the application of classroom knowledge to authentic entrepreneurial contexts. Such competitions enhance public speaking, persuasion, and creative problem-solving skills while allowing participants to adapt constructively to feedback. Direct exposure to investment evaluation processes and entrepreneurial networking further motivates students, stimulates innovative thinking, and can lead to actual venture creation. Research indicates that participation in these competitions increases enthusiasm, confidence, and long-term entrepreneurial career prospects.

Another critical strategy involves practical focus and curriculum reform. Entrepreneurship education should shift from predominantly theoretical instruction toward hands-on, experiential learning models. Integrating business simulations, internships, live startup projects, and venture-based assignments helps cultivate entrepreneurial mindsets and strengthens the connection between theory and practice. This experiential orientation encourages active learning, opportunity recognition, and skill application in real-world settings, thereby enhancing the overall effectiveness of entrepreneurship education (Okolie et al., 2023; Oluwafunmilola, 2024).

The use of platforms for virtual mentoring also represents a valuable innovation. Virtual mentoring systems connect students with experienced entrepreneurs and industry professionals across different geographical locations, expanding access to guidance and expertise. Features such as structured mentor–mentee matching, flexible scheduling, goal-oriented interactions, and community discussion forums support personalized skill development and sustained engagement. These platforms democratize mentorship opportunities and provide timely, context-specific advice on entrepreneurial challenges. Evidence suggests that well-designed virtual mentoring programs result in high levels of participation, enhanced knowledge acquisition, and measurable progress toward individual development goals.

Incorporating local context into entrepreneurship education is equally important. Adapting case studies, examples, and learning materials to reflect local economic, cultural, and social realities enhances relevance and practical applicability. Context-sensitive content enables students to identify region-specific opportunities and constraints, connect theoretical concepts to lived experiences, and design solutions that address community needs. This approach fosters deeper engagement, critical thinking, and the capacity to navigate diverse entrepreneurial environments.

Additionally, utilizing artificial intelligence and advanced technologies can significantly strengthen entrepreneurship education delivery. AI-driven personalized learning tools and simulation technologies offer adaptive exercises, individualized feedback, and interactive representations of entrepreneurial scenarios. These innovations accommodate diverse learning styles, encourage experimentation without real-world risk, and accelerate the mastery of complex entrepreneurial concepts. Research highlights that technology-enhanced entrepreneurship education improves motivation, learning retention, and scalable customization for large student cohorts.

Finally, workshops on mental resilience play a crucial role in preparing students for entrepreneurial uncertainty and failure. Structured resilience-building programs teach coping strategies, stress management techniques, and adaptive thinking skills essential for navigating adversity. Through practical exercises, mindfulness practices, and reflective activities, students develop self-efficacy, emotional intelligence, and persistence. Empirical evidence indicates that resilience training within educational settings enhances opportunity recognition, sustained entrepreneurial effort, and overall well-being among aspiring entrepreneurs.

11. CONCLUSION

Entrepreneurship education is increasingly recognized as a strategic investment in human capital that generates not only technical and managerial skills but also the socio-emotional capacities required to withstand, adapt to, and grow from adversity in volatile and uncertain environments (Becker, 1993; Korber & McNaughton, 2018; OECD, 2024). Anchored in human capital theory, the resource-based view, dynamic capabilities, and learning perspectives, this study synthesizes secondary evidence to demonstrate that well-designed educational experiences formal, informal, and experiential play a pivotal role in strengthening entrepreneurial resilience and sustaining competitiveness across firm, regional, and national contexts (Barney, 1991; Audretsch et al., 2020; Teece, 2018; World Bank, 2020).

The integrative findings of this paper confirm that education operates through a set of mutually reinforcing mechanisms, including skill acquisition, socio-emotional capability development, social capital formation, and institutional signaling. Cognitive, technical, and problem-solving competencies enhance productivity and innovation while enabling adaptive responses to disruption. Simultaneously, socio-emotional attributes such as self-efficacy, emotional intelligence, and collaborative capacity reinforce psychological resilience and organizational performance. Educational institutions also function as platforms for network building and legitimacy signaling, facilitating access to markets, finance, and knowledge ecosystems that strengthen both resilience and competitive advantage. Collectively, these mechanisms create a virtuous cycle in which learning-driven capability development enhances adaptability and long-term performance.

Empirical evidence drawn from global competitiveness indices, post-crisis recovery analyses, and entrepreneurship education interventions further reinforces this cycle. Skills-oriented, inclusive, and context-sensitive educational programmes are consistently associated with higher innovation output, faster recovery from economic shocks, and superior long-term outcomes, particularly when curricula integrate financial literacy, digital capabilities, experiential learning, and socio-emotional development (Anwar et al., 2023; Piva & Vivarelli, 2018; Rose, 2017; Schwab, 2023). These findings highlight the importance of aligning entrepreneurship education with evolving technological, institutional, and labor-market conditions to maximize its resilience- and competitiveness-enhancing effects.

At the same time, the synthesis reveals persistent challenges related to causality, measurement inconsistency, contextual variation, and limited attention to informal learning pathways and inclusivity. Addressing these gaps requires longitudinal and mixed-method research designs, comparative analysis across developed and emerging economies, and multidisciplinary frameworks that integrate educational, psychological, technological, and policy dimensions. From a policy and practice perspective, the evidence underscores the need for coordinated investments in financial and digital literacy, mentoring systems, experiential learning infrastructures, and supportive entrepreneurial ecosystems, alongside inclusive and gender-responsive strategies.

In conclusion, this paper affirms that entrepreneurship education extends beyond skill formation to function as a core mechanism for building adaptive capacity and competitive strength in an increasingly turbulent global economy. When education systems intentionally integrate experiential pedagogy, socio-emotional learning, digital competence, and ecosystem support, they enable entrepreneurs and organizations not only to survive disruption but to innovate, grow, and sustain competitive advantage over time.

REFERENCES

Blog, A. D. B. (n.d.). What role does human capital play in innovation? https://blogs.adb.org/blog/what-role-does-human-capital-play-innovation

Adenike, O. (2016). Challenges of entrepreneurship education in Nigeria. *Journal of Business and Management, 8*(3), 12–25. DOI-DOI: 10.5901/jesr.2016.v6nip208

Anwar, I., Khan, S. Z., & Gomathi,S. (2023). Role of entrepreneurial passion and self-efficacy in fostering resilience. *Business Case Studies*, 2025.

Audretsch, D. B., & Belitski, M. (2021). Entrepreneurial ecosystems in cities: The role of institutions. *World Bank Working Paper*.DOI:DOI: 10.1007/s10961-016-9473-8

Audretsch, D. B., Belitski, M., & Desai, S. (2020). National business regulations and city entrepreneurship in Europe: A multilevel spatial analysis. *Entrepreneurship Theory and Practice*, *44*(6), 1121–1145.

Audretsch, D. B., Belitski, M., & Desai, S. (2020). National business regulations and city-level entrepreneurship. *Small Business Economics*, *54*(4), 1107–1128. DOI: 10.1007/s11187-018-01136-6

Audretsch, D. B., Lehmann, E. E., & Seitz, N. (2020). Universities as anchors of high-tech regional development: The case of university–industry knowledge transfer. *Regional Studies*, *54*(7), 999–1008.

Balogun, M. (2023). Strategies to promote entrepreneurship education in Nigerian higher institutions. *Education Journal*, *15*(2), 35–48.

Baporikar, N. (2020). *Entrepreneurship Education and Training: The Issue of Effectiveness*. IGI Global.

Barney, J. (1991). Firm resources and sustained competitive advantage. *Journal of Management*, *17*(1), 99–120. DOI: 10.1177/014920639101700108

Becker, G. S. (1993). *Human capital: A theoretical and empirical analysis with special reference to education* (3rd ed.). University of Chicago Press.

Bhamra, R., Dani, S., & Burnard, K. (2011). Resilience: The concept, a literature review, and future directions. *International Journal of Production Research*, *49*(18), 5375–5393. DOI: 10.1080/00207543.2011.563826

Bozward, D. (2024, January). Election 2024: Entrepreneurship and enterprise education policy for the English Education Ministry. Retrieved from https://david.bozward.com/2024/01/election-2024-entrepreneurship-and-enterprise-education-policy-for-the-english-education-ministry/

Brush, C. G., Edelman, L. F., Manolova, T. S., & Welter, F. (2019). A gendered look at entrepreneurship ecosystems. *Small Business Economics*, *53*, 393–408.

Business Case Studies. (2025, March 16). Human Capital Theory: Education & Training. https://businesscasestudies.co.uk/human-capital-theory-education-training

European Commission. (2022). Entrepreneurship and digital transformation: Policy brief. Brussels.

Frontiers in Psychology. (n.d.). Innovation capabilities and human development. https://www.frontiersin.org/articles/10.3389/fpsyg.2021.736618/full

Goduni, A. (2024). Empowering growth: How economic education can drive global economic development. Academy of Economics Journal. Retrieved from https://www.abacademies.org/articles/empowering-growth-how-economic-education-can-drive-global-economic-development-17651.html#r4

Investopedia. (n.d.). Understanding human capital theory: Importance and impact. https://www.investopedia.com/terms/h/human-capital-theory.asp

Kolb, D. A. (2015). *Experiential learning: Experience as the source of learning and development* (2nd ed.). Pearson Education.

Korber, S., & McNaughton, R. B. (2018). Resilience and entrepreneurship: A systematic literature review. *International Journal of Entrepreneurial Behaviour & Research*, *24*(7), 1129–1154. DOI: 10.1108/IJEBR-10-2016-0356

Liu, Z., & San-Martín, S., & Others. (2019). Contextual uniqueness in entrepreneurship education: A review. *International Journal of Entrepreneurial Education*, *22*(1), 41–60.

Maravilla, V. S.Jr, & Flores, G. (2025). Entrepreneurial competency, resilience, and financial literacy: Drivers of sustainable performance in SMEs for societal welfare. *Journal of Sustainability, Society, and Eco-Welfare*, *2*(2), 159–176. DOI: 10.61511/jssew.v2i2.2025.1374

Montoro-Fernández, E., Palomares-Montero, D., & Rubio-Navarro, A. (2022). Entrepreneurial resilience: A case study of university entrepreneurship education. *Sustainability*, *14*(18), 11523. DOI: 10.3390/su141811523

Montoro-Fernández, E., Palomares-Montero, D., & Rubio-Navarro, A. (2022). Entrepreneurial resilience: A case study of university entrepreneurship education. *Sustainability*, *14*(18), 11523.

Montoro-Fernández, M., Fernández-Muñoz, J. J., & Ruiz-Montero, M. (2022). Socio-emotional competence, self-efficacy, and resilience in higher education students. *Frontiers in Psychology*, *13*, 834521.

OECD. (2021; 2024). Education and Skills: OECD Education at a Glance. Paris.

OECD. (2024). *Education at a glance 2024: OECD indicators*. OECD Publishing., DOI: 10.1787/eag-2024-en

OECD. (2024, December 18). Human capital and educational policies. https://www.oecd.org/education/human-capital-and-educational-policies.htm

OECD. (n.d.). International compendium of entrepreneurship policies. Retrieved from https://www.oecd.org/en/publications/international-compendium-of-entrepreneurship-policies_338f1873-en.html

Okolie, J.. (2023). Impact of entrepreneurship education on competencies of Nigerian university students. *American Journal of Entrepreneurship*, *5*(4), 77–90.

Oluwafunmilola, R. O. (2024). The contemporary issues and technological gaps in entrepreneurship education in Nigerian higher institutions. *European Journal of Business and Innovation Research*, *12*(5), 80–89.

Organisation for Economic Co-operation and Development (OECD). (2021). *Entrepreneurship Education: A Road to Success*. OECD Publishing.

Oyinlola, M. (2024). Entrepreneurship and innovation in Nigerian universities. *Journal of African Educational Research*, *9*(1), 105–125.

Pennetta, S. (2025). Redefining Entrepreneurial Resilience for Global Business. *The Journal of Entrepreneurship*, *34*(2), 221–267. DOI: 10.1177/0971355720957889

Piva, M., & Vivarelli, M. (2018). Technological change and employment: Is Europe ready for the challenge? *Economics of Innovation and New Technology*, *27*(1), 1–19. DOI: 10.1080/10438599.2017.1250189

Piva, M., &Vivarelli, M. (2018). Technological change and employment: Is Europe ready for the challenge? *Economics of Innovation and New Technology, 27*(2), 95–113. Doi: https://DOI: 10.1007/s40821-017-0100-x

Porter, M. E. (1990). *The competitive advantage of nations*. Free Press.

Rae, D. (2010). Entrepreneurial learning: Educating for ambition and aspiration. *Education + Training, 52*(8/9), 722–740.

Rose, A. (2017). Defining and measuring economic resilience to disasters. *Disaster Prevention and Management, 26*(1), 2–13. DOI: 10.1108/DPM-02-2016-0043

Rose, A. (2017). *Economic resilience: Definition and measurement. Community and Regional Resilience Institute (CARRI) Research Report*. Oak Ridge National Laboratory.

Rose, A. (2017). *Human capital and recovery after disaster: Evidence and policy implications*. ADB Blog.

San-Martín, S.. (2019). The effectiveness of entrepreneurship education programs. *Education + Training, 61*(7/8), 872–887.

Schwab, K. (2023). The Global Competitiveness Report 2023. World Economic Forum. https://www.weforum.org

Teece, D. J. (2018). Business models and dynamic capabilities. *Long Range Planning, 51*(1), 40–49. DOI: 10.1016/j.lrp.2017.06.007

Vega, B. (2025). Empowering growth: How economic education can drive global economic development. *Journal of Economics and Economic Education Research, 26*(S3), 1–3. https://www.abacademies.org/articles/empowering-growth-how-economic-education-can-drive-global-economic-development-17651.html#r3

World Bank. (2020). *The Human Capital Index 2020: Human capital in the time of COVID-19*. World Bank Publications.

World Bank. (2020). *The Human Capital Project 2.0: Investing in people to build resilience and productivity*. World Bank Publications., DOI: 10.1596/978-1-4648-1520-3

World Bank. (2020). *The human capital project 2.0: Investing in people to build resilience and productivity*.

World Bank. (2020). *World Development Report 2020: Trading for Development in the Age of Global Value Chains*. World Bank Group.

World Economic Forum. (2023). The global competitiveness report. https://www.weforum.org/reports/global-competitiveness-report-2023/

World Economic Forum. (2025, June 21). Youth innovation builds workforce resilience through entrepreneurship. Retrieved from https://www.weforum.org/stories/2025/06/youth-innovation-builds-workforce-resilience-through-entrepreneurship/

KEY TERMS AND DEFINITIONS

Entrepreneurship Education: Learning programs and experiences that help people understand how to start, manage, and grow a business by teaching practical skills, problem-solving, and creativity needed for entrepreneurship.

Global Competitiveness: How well a person, business, or country can compete with others worldwide, usually by being innovative, productive, and able to meet international standards in products or services.

Inclusivity Gaps: Differences or inequalities in access, opportunities, and participation among various groups in society, meaning some people are left out or do not benefit equally from resources, services, or education.

Resilience Building: The process of strengthening a person's ability to recover, adapt, and keep going when faced with difficulties, setbacks, or changes, especially in challenging environments.

Chapter 4
Knowledge, Social Inclusion, and the Dynamics of Resilience:
Rethinking the Role of Social Entrepreneurship in Turbulent Economies

Konstantina Agoraki
https://orcid.org/0009-0007-5135-3091
University of Piraeus, Greece

Apostolos Skotis
https://orcid.org/0000-0002-7393-5793
University of Piraeus, Greece

Panos Chountalas
University of Piraeus, Greece

Ioannis Katsanakis
https://orcid.org/0000-0002-3603-5470
University of Piraeus, Greece

ABSTRACT

In a world increasingly defined by systemic turbulence, the traditional governance and development models are no longer suitable. Conventionally existing methods are becoming less responsive to these new and multifaceted challenges. The current chapter focuses on social entrepreneurship as a systemic solution to development of resilience and inclusion in such uncertain environments based on knowledge.

DOI: 10.4018/979-8-3373-6991-4.ch004

The analysis will focus on three dynamics that are interconnected, namely inclusive participation as a source of distributed intelligence, reflective learning as a crisis-to-innovation transformation and digital transformation as a social impact amplifier. The chapter also questions under what circumstances social entrepreneurship is likely to succeed. Finally, the chapter claims that a more adaptive and inclusive system should be formed through social entrepreneurship. Through this, it gives a vision of generating value that puts an emphasis over learning, equity, and long-term well-being rather than narrow economic indicators.

1. INTRODUCTION

In a world that is becoming increasingly uncertain due to economic volatility, climate change, social tensions and the pace of technological disruption, conventional modes of governance and development proved inadequate (Gul et al., 2024). The twenty-first century has been marked by profound social and economic disruptions that have reshaped the foundations of global economies and local communities alike. From financial crises to pandemics and environmental disasters, societies have been compelled to develop new mechanisms of adaptation and recovery. Entrepreneurship has long been known as innovation, economic and social change catalyst (Audretsch et al., 2020). However, entrepreneurship is often called to overcome systemic weakness, create inclusion and build resilience in society. Social entrepreneurship provides both the moral and practical agenda for creating sustainable value (Diaz-Sarachaga & Ariza-Montes, 2022; García-Jurado et al., 2021; Haugh, 2005). In this environment, knowledge is the foundation in shaping the way social enterprises create, adapt and maintain resilience (Satar et al., 2023; Solomon et al., 2019). Moreover, resilience and social inclusion have emerged as critical dimensions of sustainable development, demanding innovative approaches that transcend traditional policy or market solutions (Folke, 2016; Hall, Daneke, & Lenox, 2010). Drawing from the knowledge-based perspective of the firm, resilience thinking, and institutional entrepreneurship, the chapter considers social enterprises as spaces of creating and practicing knowledge. Such resilience knowledge systems connect regional experiences with global systems, which allow a community and a group to adapt and evolve through disruption (Argote et al., 2000; Audretsch et al., 2020).

This chapter examines the crucial role that social entrepreneurship provides in the formation of more resilient, inclusive and knowledge-based communities, especially in environments of uncertainty and volatility. It places social entrepreneurship not simply as an economic endeavor, but as a social and cultural process that generates new organizational processes. In place of profit maximization, social entrepreneurs seek to create favorable social impact while keeping their operations efficient (Leadbeater, 1997). Social entrepreneurs tend to operate in areas that regular businesses have left behind, like education, health, or climate adaptability. In doing so, they form the hub of local and regional change.

Central to understanding how social enterprises navigate turbulent environments is the role of knowledge (Ndou, 2021). Knowledge is not merely a resource for operational efficiency but it functions as a strategic asset that shapes problem-solving capacity, adaptive behaviors, and collective learning. The ability to generate, share, and apply knowledge effectively determines how individuals and organizations adapt to turbulence and uncertainty (Nonaka, Toyama, & Konno, 2000; Gul, 2025). Therefore, situating knowledge management within the broader context of social entrepreneurship allows us to understand how resilience is produced and sustained (Halberstadt et al., 2019; Uygur & Marcoux, 2013). Social enterprises that cultivate learning-oriented cultures and inclusive knowledge systems are better positioned to anticipate challenges and develop context-specific responses (Vázquez-Parra et al., 2020; Worsham, 2012). In this regard, knowledge management serves not merely as an operational tool but as a strategic enabler of resilience and inclusion.

In the broader context, knowledge is a constitutive element, not just a resource to be delivered, but as a process of collective creation (Darroch, 2005). Comprehending how social enterprises build, transform and maintain resilience in turbulent settings entails a broader exploration of how they create, share and use knowledge at various levels. In the current chapter, the essential role that social entrepreneurship holds in the formation of resilient, inclusive and knowledge-based communities, especially under circumstances of uncertainty and volatility, is examined. Social entrepreneurship is framed not simply as an economic mechanism but as a social and cultural process. The current chapter analyses the relationship knowledge, social inclusion and resilience (Elkhidir, et al., 2022; Kabir, 2019; Vizcaíno et al., 2020) This framework is not prescriptive, but an interpretative guide for the multi-layered role of social enterprises in turbulent environments.

Knowledge, in the case of entrepreneurship, is no longer an asset but is considered as a dynamic ability that facilitates learning process, adaptation and innovation. Social entrepreneurs engage in settings where informal structures are common and uncertainty exists, so knowledge becomes the platform through which resilience is practiced (Maalaoui et al., 2020; Scuotto et al., 2022). The knowledge in place is not technical or market-based, yet it can also be relational, contextual and experiential. It entails the awareness of the needs and the tacit knowledge inherent in social networks. In that case, the production and diffusion of knowledge create the foundation on which resilience-oriented entrepreneurship is built.

In turbulent economies, social entrepreneurs are confronted with multidimensional challenges. However, the challenging conditions also breed creativity and adaptive intelligence. The ability of social enterprises to withstand comes not from the avoidance of shocks, but from the ability to learn from them. Here, knowledge acts as a feedback mechanism, connecting the past experience to future action. By incorporating reflective practice, sharing of knowledge and group learning, social enterprises convert uncertainty to opportunity and adversity to innovation.

Inclusion is central to this process. Inclusion broadens the set of voices, views and experiences at an ecosystem or an organization. A diverse society creates a more extensive set of problem-solving tactics and a more extensive range of resilience mechanisms. Inclusive entrepreneurship, then, is considered as an organizational structure that enhances adaptability. By bringing marginalized populations into the entrepreneurial process, diversity is converted into an engine of group intelligence and systemic resilience.

Knowledge and inclusion come together in the formation and maintenance of networks by social entrepreneurs. These networks tend to be hybrid networks, both formal and informal (Elkhidir et al., 2022). In these networks, knowledge is coming from various sources, from local communities to institutional actors, from practice to policy and from micro-projects to broad-based frameworks at the macro-level. In the multilevel framework, social enterprises can integrate local environment with broad-based challenges and make resilience based on practical experience yet spreadable because of learning and networking.

Resilience creates new knowledge, as communities and organizations respond to and learn from crises. Successive rounds of disruption and recovery add to a dynamic set of experience, lessons and best practices. By sharing and embedding knowledge, social enterprises contribute to the creation of what can be termed as resilience knowledge systems. These systems reach beyond the individual organizations to the overall ecosystem of entrepreneurship and impact policy, education and inter-organizational cooperation (Ali et al., 2021).

Theoretically, the dynamic can be translated in the frames of knowledge-based and systems-based perspective entrepreneurship. The knowledge-based perspective claims that organizational competitive and adaptive advantage focuses on the capability to create, integrate and use knowledge efficiently. In social entrepreneurship, the perspective assumes a broader social dimension where the knowledge is not limited to the business but is shared, co-generated and democratized. On the other hand, the system-based perspective, underlines the interconnectivity how the actors, institutions and networks engage in sustaining resilience at various scales. Together, both perspectives show that resilience is not an inherent quality of the individual but an aggregate quality arising out of distributed learning processes (Argote et al., 2000).

The function of social entrepreneurship in volatile economies, thus, is double (Wallace, 1999). It is both a source and a disseminator of resilience. As a source, it creates adaptive practices, innovative models and inclusive opportunities. As a disseminator, it spreads diffusion and resilience capacities across the system, having an impact both on the policy setups and the market actions, as well as the social norms in communities. The merger of the application of knowledge to social entrepreneurship also redesigns the concept of value creation. Conventional entrepreneurship measures success mostly in economic terms, while social entrepreneurship integrates value in the social, cultural, as well as ecologic sphere (Wang et al., 2022). The role of knowledge in this case is the bridging element that connects the sectors so that both economic viability and social mission are performed at the same time. The ability to learn, to transform knowledge into practice and to disseminate it widely becomes the most sustainable resource of competitive advantage (Halberstadt, 2019).

Furthermore, digital transformation enhances the knowledge-resilience nexus. New technologies like artificial intelligence, big data analytics and online collaboration tools, accelerate, expand and make inclusive faster and broader-based sharing of knowledge. Digitalized ecosystem supports the co-creation of the solution beyond geographies and sectors, making the resilience a local as well as a globalized phenomenon. However, digitalization also creates new inequalities as well as risks. Therefore, inclusive knowledge management is needed in order to ensure that the technological advancement strengthens, instead of weakening, social cohesion as well as equity (Đalic & Erceg, 2024; Gigauri et al., 2023).

Social entrepreneurship captures that concept by creating contexts in which knowledge is leveraged not only to recover but to redesign the circumstances that create vulnerability in the first place. By education, mentoring and learning by experience, social entrepreneurs cultivate a culture of resilience, considering uncertainty as a source of cooperation. Equally essential is the dimension of social inclusion. Social enterprises often operate in contexts marked by marginalization, unequal access to resources, and limited participation in decision-making processes (Short, 2009). By prioritizing inclusive practices, these organizations help democratize the flow of knowledge and empower under-represented groups to become active contributors rather than passive beneficiaries. Social inclusion is thus not simply an ethical imperative but a mechanism through which communities build capacity and resilience. When marginalized groups are engaged as co-creators of solutions, they contribute unique forms of tacit knowledge that can strengthen adaptive responses and foster cohesion in times of crisis (Maalaoui et al., 2019).

The connection among knowledge, social inclusion and resilience implicates a change in the way we conceptualize entrepreneurship. Entrepreneurs are considered not only as innovators or market disrupters but also as players in complex adaptive systems, influencing and being influenced by knowledge, values and relationships. Social entrepreneurship, based in knowledge management and inclusion, is a model of regenerative development, that prepares societies to handle uncertainty. Social entrepreneurship has increasingly been recognized as a key driver in this transformation, combining entrepreneurial innovation with a mission of social value creation (Maalaoui et al., 2019). Rather than viewing profit and purpose as incompatible, social entrepreneurs leverage knowledge, networks, and creativity to tackle systemic inequalities and promote inclusive growth (Defourny & Nyssens, 2017; Santos, 2012). By integrating social innovation into dynamic market structures, these actors enhance community resilience and foster the co-creation of sustainable livelihoods, particularly in economically and institutionally fragile environments (Seelos & Mair, 2005).

In conclusion, turbulent economies require innovative business models as well as resilient mindsets and knowledge ecosystems. Social entrepreneurship leads the transformation process, by bringing together knowledge creation and social inclusion to create resilience that is both adaptive and generative. As the global challenges escalate, the ability to learn together and transfer knowledge into shared resilience will shape the future of entrepreneurship and sustainable development. This chapter seeks to explore how knowledge dynamics intersect with social inclusion to reinforce resilience in turbulent economies. It considers the role of social entrepreneurship as a bridge between innovation and social transformation, emphasizing how knowledge-sharing practices can empower marginalized communities, strengthen adaptive capacity, and contribute to more equitable and sustainable societies. The chapter concludes by reflecting the wider conditions needed to enable and maintain social entrepreneurship as a driver of inclusion, resilience and knowledge. These challenges require investment in inclusive education, adaptable regulations, sources and the adaptation of diverse knowledge systems.

2. SOCIAL ENTREPRENEURSHIP IN AN ERA OF TURBULENCE

Contemporary economies are increasingly defined by turbulence, uncertainty, and multidimensional crises. Economic instability, social fragmentation, climate-related disruptions, and rapid technological transformations have collectively reshaped the conditions under which organizations and communities operate. In this shifting landscape, traditional market mechanisms and state-led interventions often prove insufficient to address persistent inequalities, vulnerabilities, and systemic risks (Santos, 2012). Social entrepreneurship has emerged as a critical force that bridges economic activity with social purpose, mobilizing innovation, community engagement, and hybrid value creation (Certo & Miller, 2008). Yet, despite its growing visibility, the role of social entrepreneurship in fostering resilience remains inconsistently defined and conceptually fragmented (Saebi et al., 2019).

The lack of a unified understanding creates challenges not only for researchers, but also for educators seeking to teach the subject effectively (Lawrence et al., 2012; Choi & Majumdar, 2014). At its core, social entrepreneurship blends elements of business innovation with social impact, yet the scope and boundaries of this blend remain contested. According to Johnson (2000), social entrepreneurship represents a vital means of tackling multifaceted social issues in a creative and efficient way.

A review of the literature reveals a wide spectrum of definitions, varying in complexity and breadth. Some definitions are minimal, describing social entrepreneurship as any initiative with a social aim (Baron, 2007; Solomon et al., 2019). Others argue that economic sustainability must be an inherent component, placing value creation for society alongside financial viability (Dacin et al., 2010). Broader perspectives, such as those proposed by Pomerantz (2003) and Zahra et al. (2009), include any business, model—profit or non-profit, that seeks to address social problems through entrepreneurial approaches.

This conceptual ambiguity has prompted scholars to categorize the existing definitions. Dacin et al. (2010), in their extensive review of 37 definitions, noted that most emphasize the mobilization of resources to address social needs, yet few agree on how this is to be achieved. Tracey and Phillips (2007) identified two overarching interpretations, one centered on social change regardless of the organizational form, and another emphasizing the generation of economic value in pursuit of social outcomes.

Historically defined as a source of innovation and economic growth, entrepreneurship is currently reconceived to be a source of systemic change and social stability. Social entrepreneurship in its turn is challenging but may be used as an alternative to leading models that are market-oriented (Portales, 2019; Steiner et al., 2018). It actively incorporates social purpose into its fundamental practices, both to achieve financial sustainability and to attain quantifiable social benefit, community empowerment and ecological restoration. This orientation is particularly crucial in areas where the traditional institutions failed in their duties or missed in needs such as the informal education, healthcare, climate adaptation, and rural development, where social entrepreneurs fail to improve institutional gaps, but rather design inclusive and regenerative systems (Pérez-Barea, 2025). The main feature of this new paradigm is a change of the concept of knowledge itself. Rather than being just a static asset or technical input to competitive advantage, however, knowledge is now being viewed as a dynamic process, socially embedded. It is developed by participatory participation, lived experience and shared meaning-making. This reconceptualization challenges dominant assumptions in traditional entrepreneurship theory, which tend to privilege formal, market-based knowledge. In contrast, social entrepreneurs very much rely on the contextual, tacit, and relational levels of knowing and operating at hybrid networks (Kraus et al., 2017). They will bring the wisdom gained through experience into resiliency-building and long-term influence strategies.

At the same time, the issue of inclusion cannot be considered only as a question of morality, but as an adequate requirement of flexibility and creativity. Incorporation of diversity of opinion, knowledge systems as well as lived experiences increases the ability of creative problem-solving and strengthening of organisations and communities. Inclusion creates distributed intelligence, where learning and innovations are not centralised but brought about through the interaction of various actors situated in the unique socio-cultural contexts (de Bruin et al., 2024; Smith & Woodworth, 2012). It is especially in this interdependence of participation and knowledge co-creation that social entrepreneurship can play a system-building role to a wider and more adaptable future.

Social entrepreneurship cannot solely be regarded as an instrument of economic development or intervention into society but as a cultural and systemic process that helps communities to develop resilience by creating and mobilising knowledge- particularly in unpredictable or volatile circumstances (Rey-Martí, 2016). Analyzing the way social entrepreneurs work under complicated circumstances, the research focuses on considering three interconnected areas: knowledge, inclusion, and resilience.

3. THEORETICAL BACKGROUND: SOCIAL ENTREPRENEURSHIP AS A KNOWLEDGE-BASED RESILIENCE MECHANISM

In this chapter, we combine three mutually reinforcing perspectives to understand the contribution of social enterprises in providing resilience to turbulent environments: the knowledge-based view (KBV) of entrepreneurship, systems and resilience theory and the recent emergent discipline of institutional and social entrepreneurship. These three perspectives allow a better understanding of the relationship linkages between knowledge, inclusion and adaptability in activities of social entrepreneurship. The pillar of the framework is the KBV of the firm. According to KBV, the first idea of competitive advantage of a firm lies in its ability to create, combine, and apply knowledge (Grant, 1996). Although initial conceptions of KBV focused on formal systems of learning, technical resources as well as codified information, recent developments have expanded the coverage to include tacit, experiential, and relational knowledge. Furthermore, the knowledge is not limited in the company or its entrepreneur (Solomon et al., 2019). In this case knowledge is distributed socially and collectively and negotiated by interaction with diverse stakeholders.

Social enterprises operate in environments like informal and rural settlements, and post-war or climate-prone areas where institutions are relatively weak, infrastructure is untrustworthy, and there is limited access to formal education. Despite the important challenges that these settings have, they operate as good environments of adaptive experience, cultural awareness, and local knowledge (Wang et al., 2022). These social entrepreneurs that can manage to fit such knowledge forms in their organizational strategies are the ones who succeed in such environments. Knowledge, in this framing, becomes a means for inclusion and resilience. KBV emphasizes the importance of knowledge to entrepreneurial success whereas resilience theory helps to explain the capacity to increase adaptability of an organization and community through knowledge (Elkhidir et al., 2022). Resilience theory focuses on cyclical and networked models of transformation instead of on linear models of growth. According to Folke et al. (2010), resilience refers to the ability to absorb the disturbances, reorganize, and maintain the core functions and structure thus allowing to survive through continuous learning and adaptation This systems-based approach urges a re-evaluation of the function of the entrepreneur when applied to business. This reframing is especially relevant to social entrepreneur who have their projects often framed in the more institutional and natural environment (Vázquez-Parra et al., 2020).

The third element emphasizes the ability of the actors to act within, across, and outside the existing institutional structures. According to Battilana et al. (2009), an institutional entrepreneur innovates in the institutional settings, in some instances through legitimacy, and cultural frames. Social entrepreneurs mediate institutional gaps and contradictions in particular cases, when the provision of vital services by public institutions is malfunctioning or when the mechanisms of the market lead to an increase in inequalities. Social entrepreneurs in those settings are also seen to stand out, not only due to their ingenuity, but also due to the fact that they can operate under hybrid institutional structures (Zahra et al., 2019). These propositions combine social value and economic efficiency, combine the formal policy frameworks with informal conventions.

The convergence of resilience theory, institutional entrepreneurship and the KBV contributes to creating a new intellectual approach that defines the resilience knowledge system. This system merges a group of connected people, events, and tools that create, share, and use knowledge to help the system be more resilient. In such systems, learning is an ongoing process where everyone participates (Wang et al., 2022). Learning in these systems is a continual process and it includes all the participants. In such systems, social entrepreneurs act as both catalysts and channels. Such intellectual systems help companies thrive over the long-run and at the same time enhance the stability of whole ecosystems and societies.

The propensity to separate the cognitive and structural aspects of the entrepreneurship is challenged by this framing. Knowledge creation in social entrepreneurship is embodied and often generated as a need. Resilience is developed in the process of relationship, and shared values and spontaneous action, instead of being a deterministic result or natural talent (Folke, 2016). Conceptualizing social entrepreneurship in reference to knowledge-based system of building resilience, in a practical context, emphasizes the role of inclusive education, participatory governance, and digital platforms of knowledge generation (Ali et al., 2021). Overall, the main concept in this theoretical approach is the complexity of social entrepreneurship, which combines a systemic knowledge building process with social impacts.

4. KNOWLEDGE, INCLUSION, AND THE ARCHITECTURE OF RESILIENCE

Resilience in social entrepreneurship is built by the active interplay of knowledge production, inclusive involvement, and flexible system building. Rather than running by themselves, these factors comprise a co-constitutive triad that helps social businesses to flourish in volatile and unstable settings (Elkhidir et al., 2022). From this perspective, resiliency is a developing ability developed by means of strategic adaptation, community involvement, and relational learning. Each aspect is thoroughly examined in this section along with examples showing how they combine to form the basis of resilience knowledge systems.

Knowledge used in social entrepreneurship differs from the typical idea of market intelligence or technical competence (Gul et al., 2024). It covers a wider range including community-based, contextual, experiential, and tacit types of knowledge. Social entrepreneurs typically operate in fields where institutions are weak, formal statistics is limited, and life experience serves as the main resource. In such settings, learning from direct contact with the community becomes more important than theoretical concepts or written instructions (Johnson, 2000). This form of learning is inherently situated, tied to place, culture, and specific historical trajectories, and is often transmitted through narrative, mentoring, and embodied practice.

What distinguishes knowledge within social entrepreneurship is its relational and recursive nature. It is not produced by isolated experts but co-created through interaction (Halberstadt et al., 2019). Through active listening, participatory design, and iterative experimentation, social entrepreneurs integrate diverse perspectives into problem-solving frameworks. Knowledge, then, functions not as a fixed input but as a continuous feedback loop, connecting past experiences with present needs and future possibilities. It enables the conversion of disruption into learning, and of adversity into innovation (Maalaoui et al., 2020).

Inclusion plays a pivotal role in the construction of this knowledge. Far from being an add-on or an ethical afterthought, inclusion is the very condition that makes knowledge meaningful and actionable in diverse settings (Cornelius-Hernandez & Clarke, 2024). When knowledge is generated in exclusionary or top-down ways, it often fails to resonate with those it intends to serve. By contrast, when knowledge is co-created through inclusive processes, it becomes both more relevant and more resilient. Social entrepreneurship provides a platform through which marginalized voices can actively shape the solutions that affect their lives.

Inclusive participation enhances the quality and diversity of ideas, fostering what can be described as distributed intelligence. This distribution is not only horizontal, involving peer networks and communities, but also vertical, linking grassroots actors with institutional stakeholders and policy frameworks. In this multi-level configuration, social entrepreneurs become mediators of knowledge flow, connecting informal knowers with formal institutions and translating between different epistemic communities. The capacity to navigate these knowledge ecologies, where information is held in stories, rituals, data, or policy, is central to building collective resilience (Greer & Egan, 2019).

The convergence of knowledge and inclusion gives rise to systemic resilience. Resilience here is not a matter of organizational endurance alone but a property that emerges from ongoing, inclusive, and adaptive interactions among actors embedded in complex systems. Social entrepreneurs do not merely withstand disruption; they actively participate in reshaping the conditions that produce vulnerability. This is evident in their efforts to transform educational systems in underserved areas, to co-design climate adaptation strategies with vulnerable communities, or to redesign economic models in regions abandoned by traditional industry (Greer & Egan, 2019).

In each case, resilience is generated not by avoiding failure but by learning through it. The entrepreneurial process becomes a space of experimentation, where failure is not a verdict but a source of insight. Reflective practice, peer learning, and collective sense-making turn these failures into feedback, a resource that feeds the recursive nature of resilience. Over time, this leads to the formation of resilience knowledge systems: institutional and social ecosystems where knowledge is not only accumulated but diffused, where inclusion is not only practiced but structured, and where adaptation becomes part of the culture.

In the context of digital transformation, these dynamics are further amplified. Digital platforms enable social entrepreneurs to scale their learning processes, to include dispersed communities in real time, and to share resilience practices across borders (Đalic & Erceg, 2024). However, they also introduce new forms of exclusion and epistemic inequality, as access to technology remains uneven and algorithmic systems often reflect dominant knowledge hierarchies. Thus, the digital must be embedded within inclusive and context-aware strategies, ensuring that technological scaling does not undermine the social foundations of resilience (Đalic & Erceg, 2024; Gigauri et al., 2023).

Ultimately, the interplay between knowledge, inclusion, and resilience redefines the practice of entrepreneurship itself. It shifts the focus from value extraction to value co-creation, from product innovation to systemic transformation, and from isolated success to collective adaptation. It also challenges us to rethink the criteria by which entrepreneurial success is measured. Instead of return on investment alone, new indicators are needed, that capture learning outcomes, community empowerment, knowledge circulation, and structural change.

Social entrepreneurship, viewed through this lens, emerges as a regenerative force. It cultivates not only new solutions, but new ways of knowing, relating, and evolving together in a world that demands both imagination and endurance (Borzaga & Santuari, 2003). By positioning knowledge as a dynamic process, inclusion as a strategic asset, and resilience as a systemic outcome, this framework offers a pathway for navigating uncertainty (Greer & Egan, 2019).

5. SOCIAL ENTREPRENEURSHIP AS SYSTEMIC INFRASTRUCTURE

In the analysis above, it is evident that social entrepreneurship is not merely a local innovation mechanism (Portales, 2019). However, it is an emerging force in the creation of adaptive, knowledge-based and inclusive systems. As opposed to being suppliers or providers of solutions to problems, social enterprises can be viewed as part of the wider social structures, which in turn determine the conditions within which resilience can be created, maintained, as well as reproduced. The wider implications of the systemic contribution of social entrepreneurship revolves around three interconnected areas: the re-frame of entrepreneurship, the re-definitions of resilience, and value creation reshaping (Zhao, 2021).

Social entrepreneurship forces a re-examination of the concept of entrepreneurship. In these frames, an entrepreneur is represented as a disrupter, an innovator, or a rational risk-taker who is acting in the framework of well-defined institutional settings (Steiner et al., 2018; Vázquez-Parra et al., 2020). Social entrepreneurship predicts a relational, embedded, and systemic agency. This re-framing entails a significant shift. Instead of considering entrepreneurship as the result of decisions made in isolation, it should be regarded as the emergence of novel socio-technical configurations that occur through learning in groups and interaction with the community. Second, social entrepreneurship contributes to a redefinition of resilience, which can be regarded as a generative capacity that is based on diversity, learning, and collaboration.

By engaging directly with affected communities, social entrepreneurs develop the culture of reflective practice, where failure is a source of learning, and uncertainty is embracing innovation. They also emphasize relational resilience, the idea that flexibility and change are not only shaped by personal strength (Godwin & Amah, 2013).

Third, and, perhaps most importantly, social entrepreneurship triggers a value-creation transformation. Under the dominant economic logic, value has become narrows and quantified in terms of efficiency, profitability and market growth. In its turn, social entrepreneurship demands a multidimensional understanding of value that integrates the combination of social equity, cultural meaning, sustainability and emotional well-being (De Ruysscher et al., 2017). Knowledge creation, trust building, and resilience empowering community are the core of the social and environmental prosperity in the long run (Elkhidir et al., 2022). It is in this paradox that social entrepreneurs exist, by struggling to strike a balance between financial viability and the greater public benefit.

Moreover, there are opportunities and threats posed by the transition toward digitally mediated ecosystems. Digital technologies allow social entrepreneurs to expand on a larger scope, engage more participants and learn faster. Distributed co-creation occurs in open-source platforms, through online communities of practice and in participatory data infrastructures. Digital transformation should be considered as a tool that requires a careful design to enhance inclusivity, equity, and resilience (Đalic & Erceg, 2024; Gigauri et al., 2023).

6. DIGITAL TRANSFORMATION AND THE EVOLUTION OF SOCIAL ENTREPRENEURSHIP

The digital transformation has started to rapidly rearrange the operational environment of social entrepreneurship permanently. Originally viewed as a process of improving the efficiency of operations and making communication more straightforward, digital transformation has turned into a structural necessity that transforms the channels of value creation and resilience in social enterprises (Canestrino et al., 2024). Data analytics, artificial intelligence, blockchain, mobile applications, platforms of online collaboration, and data technologies have moved into central place in the social entrepreneurial ecosystem. The new technologies support new forms of connection, education, and inclusion, contributing to the possible expansion of the mission-driven organizations in unstable and uncertain environments (Gigauri et al., 2023).

Digitization magnifies the knowledge-based and systemic aspects of social entrepreneurship. Digital infrastructures function as distributed repositories of knowledge, where information is constantly generated, processed, and shared across networks (Cheng et al., 2023). Social enterprises that make good use of these infrastructures can transform their visions into collective knowledge and understanding. These dynamic interactions enable social entrepreneurs to make more adaptive and evidence-based decisions and at the same time democratize access to knowledge among communities traditionally locked out of the traditional knowledge systems (Shrivastav et al., 2025). At the same time, digitalization introduces profound challenges and contradictions.

Uneven distribution of technology, digital literacy, and connectivity continue to sustain pre-existing social inequalities. In addition, the high rate of technological shift creates new forms of dependencies and vulnerabilities, which may destroy local knowledge systems, and cultural practices (Cheng et al., 2025).

To navigate these complexities, social entrepreneurs are increasingly acting as digital intermediaries, bridging the gap between technological potential and social purpose.

In addition, the digital transformation restructures both time and space of social entrepreneurship (Chebo & Dhliwayo, 2024; Khanzada, et al., 2023). It allows the horizontality of initiatives across communities and territories by means of imitation and open access. Finally, digital platforms act as amplifiers of collective learning, enabling the rapid adaptation of solutions to new contexts, within a short period.

7. CONCLUSION

Social entrepreneurship emerges as a practice that not only produces solutions but orchestrates systems of learning and adaptation, especially within environments characterized by uncertainty and institutional fragility. In that sense, there is no proprietary and pure technical knowledge but relational, contextual, and created by the lived experience of the different actors. Moreover, resilience is not just the ability to survive but the ability to reinvent, based on reflective practice.

In this analysis, resilience knowledge systems have been discussed as the way to view the special role that social entrepreneurship plays in turbulent situations. This is a network of actors and infrastructures, which are adaptive, inclusive and generative. The mediators linking these systems are social entrepreneurs who channel the wisdom, provide feedback, and combine the small-scale experiences with the large-scale change.

However, the transformative nature of social entrepreneurship depends upon a policy and institutional environment that offers substantive resources. Even though social entrepreneurs play a crucial role in developing adaptive solutions, the sustainability and systemic impact of their activities is subject to the context of systems that promote knowledge and coordinating resources through various levels. Governance in this respect is no longer just a case of regulatory adherence but the creation of facilitating infrastructures which are necessary to align innovation with inclusiveness and resilience. The current policy frameworks usually adopt linear and sectoral approaches that separate the economic, social, and environmental goals, constraining the integrative nature of social entrepreneurship.

At the national level, governments can play a catalytic role by institutionalising ecosystem-based support systems such as innovation hub, social enterprise incubation, and cross-sectoral co-operations which line up entrepreneurs to the universities, municipalities and community organisations. Funding mechanisms need to be designed in such a way as to reward teamwork, experimentation and social value-generation rather than immediate economic performance. Blended finance, and social impact bonds are funding instruments that align social innovation and financial sustainability. Finally, inter-organisational, transnational, and multi stakeholder alliances are becoming increasingly essential in the process of sharing knowledge and harmonising policies. Initiatives such as the UN Sustainable Development Goals (SDGs) provide normative and functional benchmarks on which the expansion of social entrepreneurship can be performed.

The findings of this theoretical inquiry suggest several implications for future research. First, there is a need to develop new metrics and evaluative frameworks that capture the non-linear, systemic, and relational nature of social entrepreneurial impact. Conventionally used performance measures do not indicate the value added by the diffusion of knowledge, social inclusion and the empowerment of communities. In addition, longitudinal and transdisciplinary studies could illuminate how social enterprises not only survive disruption but enable broader institutional renewal.

In conclusion, this chapter has argued that social entrepreneurship, when conceptualized through the interconnection of knowledge and inclusion represents an emergent infrastructure for regenerative development.

REFERENCES

Ali, I., Golgeci, I., & Arslan, A. (2021). Achieving resilience through knowledge management practices and risk management culture in agri-food supply chains. *Supply Chain Management, 28*(2), 284–299.

Argote, L., Ingram, P., Levine, J. M., & Moreland, R. L. (2000). Knowledge transfer in organizations: Learning from the experience of others. *Organizational Behavior and Human Decision Processes, 82*(1), 1–8.

Audretsch, D. B., Belitski, M., Caiazza, R., & Lehmann, E. E. (2020). Knowledge management and entrepreneurship. *The International Entrepreneurship and Management Journal, 16*(2), 373–385.

Baron, D. P. (2007). Corporate social responsibility and social entrepreneurship. *Journal of Economics & Management Strategy, 16*(3), 683–717.

Battilana, J., Leca, B., & Boxenbaum, E. (2009). 2 how actors change institutions: Towards a theory of institutional entrepreneurship. *The Academy of Management Annals, 3*(1), 65–107.

Borzaga, C., & Santuari, A. (2003). New trends in the non-profit sector in Europe: The emergence of social entrepreneurship. *The non-profit sector in a changing economy*, 31-59.

Canestrino, R., Magliocca, P., & Ćwiklicki, M. (2024). Digital Transformation for a Better Society: The Role of Digital Social Entrepreneurship. In *Humane Entrepreneurship and Innovation*(pp. 153-173). Emerald Publishing Limited.

Certo, S. T., & Miller, T. (2008). Social entrepreneurship: Key issues and concepts. *Business Horizons, 51*(4), 267–271.

Chebo, A. K., & Dhliwayo, S. (2024). Scientific mapping and thematic progression of digitalization of social entrepreneurship in developing countries. *Sustainable Futures : An Applied Journal of Technology, Environment and Society*, *7*, 100153.

Cheng, Q., Liu, Y., Peng, C., He, X., Qu, Z., & Dong, Q. (2023). Knowledge digitization: Characteristics, knowledge advantage and innovation performance. *Journal of Business Research, 163*, 113915.

Cheng, Q., Wan, H., & Ju, H. (2025). Analysis of factors contributing to the efficiency of tackling critical technologies: From a knowledge digitisation perspective. *Technology Analysis and Strategic Management*, •••, 1–15.

Choi, N., & Majumdar, S. (2014). Social entrepreneurship as an essentially contested concept: Opening a new avenue for systematic future research. *Journal of Business Venturing*, *29*(3), 363–376.

Cornelius-Hernandez, T., & Clarke, A. (2024). The current state of integrating equity, diversity and inclusion into knowledge mobilization: A systematic literature review. *Equality, Diversity and Inclusion*.

Dacin, P. A., Dacin, M. T., & Matear, M. (2010). Social entrepreneurship: Why we don't need a new theory and how we move forward from here. *The Academy of Management Perspectives*, *24*(3), 37–57.

Đalic, I., & Erceg, Ž. (2024). The impact of motivation to decision on digital transformation of social entrepreneurship. *Strategic Management-International Journal of Strategic Management and Decision Support Systems in Strategic Management*, *29*(3).

Darroch, J. (2005). Knowledge management, innovation and firm performance. *Journal of Knowledge Management*, *9*(3), 101–115.

De Bruin, A., Eversole, R., & Woods, C. (2024). Guest editorial: Gender and social entrepreneurship: building cumulative knowledge. *International Journal of Gender and Entrepreneurship*, *16*(1), 1–6.

De Ruysscher, C., Claes, C., Lee, T., Cui, F., Van Loon, J., De Maeyer, J., & Schalock, R. (2017). A systems approach to social entrepreneurship. *Voluntas*, *28*(6), 2530–2545.

Defourny, J., & Nyssens, M. (2017). Fundamentals for an international typology of social enterprise models. *Voluntas*, *28*(6), 2469–2497.

Diaz-Sarachaga, J. M., & Ariza-Montes, A. (2022). The role of social entrepreneurship in the attainment of the sustainable development goals. *Journal of Business Research*, *152*, 242–250.

Elkhidir, E., Mannakkara, S., Henning, T. F., & Wilkinson, S. (2022). Knowledge types and knowledge transfer mechanisms for effective resilience knowledge-sharing between cities–A case study of New Zealand. *International Journal of Disaster Risk Reduction*, *70*, 102790.

Folke, C. (2016). Resilience (Republished). *Ecology and Society*, *21*(4), 44.

García-Jurado, A., Pérez-Barea, J. J., & Nova, R. J. (2021). A new approach to social entrepreneurship: A systematic review and meta-analysis. *Sustainability*, *13*(5), 2754.

Gigauri, I., Apostu, S. A., & Popescu, C. (2023). Digital transformation: Threats and opportunities for social entrepreneurship. In *Two faces of digital transformation: Technological opportunities versus social threats* (pp. 1–17). Emerald Publishing Limited.

Godwin, I., & Amah, E. (2013). Knowledge management and organizational resilience in Nigerian manufacturing organizations. *Developing Country Studies*, *3*(9), 104–120.

Grant, R. M. (1996). Toward a knowledge-based theory of the firm. *Strategic Management Journal*, *17*(S2), 109–122.

Greer, T. W., & Egan, T. M. (2019). Knowledge management for organizational success: Valuing diversity and inclusion across stakeholders, structures, and sectors. In *Connecting adult learning and knowledge management: Strategies for learning and change in higher education and organizations* (pp. 119–136). Springer International Publishing.

Gul, S., Limongi, R., & Syed, H. W. U. (2024). Unraveling the nexus: Social entrepreneur intention and socioeconomic development with mediating role of entrepreneurial knowledge. *Kybernetes*.

Halberstadt, J., Timm, J. M., Kraus, S., & Gundolf, K. (2019). Skills and knowledge management in higher education: How service learning can contribute to social entrepreneurial competence development. *Journal of Knowledge Management*, *23*(10), 1925–1948.

Halberstadt, J., Timm, J. M., Kraus, S., & Gundolf, K. (2019). Skills and knowledge management in higher education: How service learning can contribute to social entrepreneurial competence development. *Journal of Knowledge Management*, *23*(10), 1925–1948.

Hall, J. K., Daneke, G. A., & Lenox, M. J. (2010). Sustainable development and entrepreneurship: Past contributions and future directions. *Journal of Business Venturing*, *25*(5), 439–448.

Haugh, H. (2005). A research agenda for social entrepreneurship. *Social Enterprise Journal*, *1*(1), 1–12.

Johnson, S. (2000). *Literature Review on Social Entrepreneurship*. Canadian Centre for Social Entrepreneurship.

Kabir, M. N. (2019). *Knowledge-based social entrepreneurship*. Palgrave Macmillan.

Khanzada, A. A., Hasnain, A., Narejo, S., Chowdhry, B. S., & Laxmi, L. (2023). Impact of digitalization on social entrepreneurship. In *Two Faces of Digital Transformation* (pp. 19–29). Emerald Publishing Limited.

Kraus, S., Niemand, T., Halberstadt, J., Shaw, E., & Syrjä, P. (2017). Social entrepreneurship orientation: Development of a measurement scale. *International Journal of Entrepreneurial Behaviour & Research, 23*(6), 977–997.

Lawrence, T., Phillips, N., & Tracey, P. (2012). From the guest editors: Educating social entrepreneurs and social innovators. *Academy of Management Learning & Education, 11*(3), 319–323.

Leadbeater, C. (1997). *The Rise of the Social Entrepreneur*. Demos.

Maalaoui, A., Le Loarne-Lemaire, S., & Razgallah, M. (2020). Does knowledge management explain the poor growth of social enterprises? Key insights from a systematic literature review on knowledge management and social entrepreneurship. *Journal of Knowledge Management, 24*(7), 1513–1532.

Ndou, V. (2021). Social entrepreneurship education: A combination of knowledge exploitation and exploration processes. *Administrative Sciences, 11*(4), 112.

Nonaka, I., Toyama, R., & Konno, N. (2000). SECI, Ba and leadership: A unified model of dynamic knowledge creation. *Long Range Planning, 33*(1), 5–34.

Pérez-Barea, J. J. (2025). The Evolution of Social Entrepreneurship: Broadening the Framework for the Digital and Sustainable Era. *Administrative Sciences, 15*(2), 55.

Pomerantz, M. (2003). The business of social entrepreneurship in a down economy. *In Business, 25*(3), 25–30.

Portales, L. (2019). Social innovation: Origins, definitions, and main elements. In *Social innovation and social entrepreneurship: fundamentals, concepts, and tools* (pp. 1–14). Springer International Publishing.

Rey-Martí, A., Ribeiro-Soriano, D., & Palacios-Marqués, D. (2016). A bibliometric analysis of social entrepreneurship. *Journal of Business Research, 69*(5), 1651–1655.

Saebi, T., Foss, N. J., & Linder, S. (2019). Social entrepreneurship research: Past achievements and future promises. *Journal of Management, 45*(1), 70–95.

Santos, F. M. (2012). A positive theory of social entrepreneurship. *Journal of Business Ethics, 111*(3), 335–351.

Satar, M. S., Aggarwal, D., Bansal, R., & Alarifi, G. (2023). Mapping the knowledge structure and unveiling the research trends in social entrepreneurship and inclusive development: A bibliometric analysis. *Sustainability, 15*(7), 5626.

Scuotto, V., Lemaire, S. L. L., Magni, D., & Maalaoui, A. (2022). Extending knowledge-based view: Future trends of corporate social entrepreneurship to fight the gig economy challenges. *Journal of Business Research, 139*, 1111–1122.

Seelos, C., & Mair, J. (2005). Social entrepreneurship: Creating new business models to serve the poor. *Business Horizons, 48*(3), 241–246.

Short, J. C., Moss, T. W., & Lumpkin, G. T. (2009). Research in social entrepreneurship: Past contributions and future opportunities. *Strategic Entrepreneurship Journal, 3*(2), 161–194.

Shrivastav, S. K., Bag, S., & Bhattacharya, R. (2025). Sustainable knowledge management in the digital era: Leveraging natural language processing to identify trends, challenges and future directions. *Journal of Knowledge Management, 29*(9), 2843–2872.

Smith, I. H., & Woodworth, W. P. (2012). Developing social entrepreneurs and social innovators: A social identity and self-efficacy approach. *Academy of Management Learning & Education, 11*(3), 390–407. DOI: 10.5465/amle.2011.0016

Solomon, G. T., Alabduljader, N., & Ramani, R. S. (2019). Knowledge management and social entrepreneurship education: Lessons learned from an exploratory two-country study. *Journal of Knowledge Management, 23*(10), 1853–1873. DOI: 10.1108/JKM-12-2018-0743

Steiner, S., Brock, D., Pittz, T., & Liguori, E. (2018). Multi-disciplinary involvement in social entrepreneurship education: A uniquely threaded ecosystem. *Journal of Ethics and Entrepreneurship, 8*, 73–91.

Tracey, P., & Phillips, N. (2007). The distinctive challenge of educating social entrepreneurs: A postscript and rejoinder to the special issue on entrepreneurship education. *Academy of Management Learning & Education, 6*(2), 264–271.

Uygur, U., & Marcoux, A. M. (2013). The added complexity of social entrepreneurship: A knowledge-based approach. *Journal of Social Entrepreneurship, 4*(2), 132–152.

Vázquez-Parra, J. C., García-González, A., & Ramírez-Montoya, M. S. (2020). Social entrepreneurship competency: An approach by discipline and gender. *Journal of Applied Research in Higher Education.*

Vizcaíno, F. V., Cardenas, J. J., & Cardenas, M. (2020). A look at the social entrepreneur: The effects of resilience and power distance personality traits on consumers' perceptions of corporate social sustainability. *The International Entrepreneurship and Management Journal*, *17*, 83–103.

Wallace, S. L. (1999). Social Entrepreneurship: The role of social purpose enterprises in facilitating community economic development. *Journal of Developmental Entrepreneurship*, *4*(2), 153–174.

Wang, M., Rasoolimanesh, S. M., & Kunasekaran, P. (2022). A review of social entrepreneurship research in tourism: Knowledge map, operational experiences, and roadmaps. *Journal of Sustainable Tourism*, *30*(8), 1777–1798.

Worsham, E. L. (2012). Reflections and insights on teaching social entrepreneurship: An interview with Greg Dees. *Academy of Management Learning & Education*, *11*(3), 442–452.

Zahra, S. A., Gedajlovic, E., Neubaum, D. O., & Shulman, J. M. (2009). A typology of social entrepreneurs: Motives, search processes, and ethical challenges. *Journal of Business Venturing*, *24*(5), 519–532.

Zhao, M. (2021). Social entrepreneurship for systemic change: The case of Southeast and South Asian countries. *Journal of Asian Public Policy*, *14*(2), 225–250.

Chapter 5
Social, Inclusive, and Community-Based Entrepreneurship in Global Contexts

Akhil Anand
https://orcid.org/0009-0007-4656-4601
Indian Institute of Technology, Jodhpur, India

Prajna Jha
https://orcid.org/0000-0002-2937-2487
Amity University, Mumbai, India

ABSTRACT

Social, inclusive, and community-based entrepreneurship (SICE) is an entrepreneurship practice to tackle poverty; inequalities; systemic discrimination; and socio-economic exclusion. SICE approaches focus on inclusive participation, collaborative decision making to address socio-economic inequalities and to promote sustainability. The chapter explains that SICE actions are especially beneficial in areas with socio-economic fragility or economically or infrastructurally poor areas due to their aggregated governance, embedded social networks, and variegated resource systems, which allow communities to endure shocks and recover from crises including pandemics, climate emergencies, and economic breakdowns. Additionally, the chapter discusses the essential contribution of governmental and bureaucratic actors, the private sector, educational institutes and the multi-polar systems of SICE. To summarize, this book chapter explains how SICE provides a transformative blueprint which is capable of linking grassroots innovation with societal, national and global sustainability agendas.

DOI: 10.4018/979-8-3373-6991-4.ch005

1. INTRODUCTION

The early twenty-first century provides critical contrast in the development of economic strategies. On one hand the strategies opened a wide range of opportunities for economic advancement with technical inclusion (Apatan *et al.*, 2025). However, on the other hand, these strategies increased the social, economic gap in the low-income, daily wagers (Cash, 2025). This gap is further accentuated by the geographical and environmental issues that were not adequately addressed in any previous economic models. With the increasing rise in the number of people living around the poverty-line, ever-broadening income gaps among middle class families and capitalists, persistent discrimination, eroding cultural diversity, and escalating climate disruption compel fresh analytical and practical frameworks. Early entrepreneurial methods were developed solely for the purpose of increasing private profit of large organizations, by enhancing their operational efficiency and expanding their capital market (Knight, 1942). Even though these methods led to marginal growth in the economy, yet often that growth has imposed hidden tolls on equity, environment, and social cohesion. In this diagnostic aperture, social, inclusive, and community-based entrepreneurship (SICE) has crystallized into a coherent alternative, reformulating entrepreneurship as a disciplined vehicle for reconstituted public opportunity, social justice, and sustainable coexistence.

Social, inclusive, and community-based entrepreneurship (SICE) is an emergent paradigm with potential to tackle entrenched poverty; rising inequalities; systemic discrimination; and socio-economic exclusion and crises in sustainability within the 21st century. Social, inclusive and community-based entrepreneurship is unlike other forms of traditional entrepreneurship strategies which focuses on individual profit maximization and commercialization, economic rapid growth and individual ownership. Social, inclusive and community-based approaches focus on inclusive participation, democratic value and decision making, socio-economic inequalities in communities, and sustainable ecology. By incorporating the foundations of SICE as a base, entrepreneurship becomes both economically and socially just while promoting environmental stewardship.

1.1 Salient features of the SICE

The chapter focuses theoretically and analytically on the linkages of social entrepreneurship with inclusive and community entrepreneurship in the global context, and the synergy of all three to construct local resilience and global pathways. Based on an extensive review of literature related to SICE social entrepreneurship as inclusive growth (Hall, 2012), it is observed that the SICE addresses the multiple dimensions of inclusive growth, such as the creation of social work, economic and social support of the marginalized. SICE assembles the socio-economic cohesive democratic governance and addresses the requirement of participatory social entrepreneurship and collaborative governance. The results explain that the SICE framework is beneficial, especially in areas with socio-economic fragility. It serves as a better alternative for economically or infrastructurally disadvantaged regions due to its aggregated governance, embedded social networks, and variegated resource systems, which enable communities to endure shocks and recover from crisis, including pandemics, climate emergencies, and economic downturns.

The chapter discusses the essential role that the governmental and bureaucratic organizations (such as the central and state governments, civil society, the private sector, educational institutes, and the multi-polar systems) will contribute towards the development of SICE, such as the ecosystem construction, policy design and implementation. The chapter also discusses how the SICE framework assists in considering strategic entrepreneurship decisions, which includes systematic capacity augmentation, inclusive financial mechanisms, infrastructure integration, technology enablement, and sustained ecosystem for cooperative arrangements that enable community entrepreneurship.

With the SICE thinking pillars contextualized around the cross-disciplinary Sustainable Development Goals (SDGs), entrepreneurship theories, systems theory, governance, and resilience, this chapter proposes a conceptual theory for SICE as an aggregated enterprise strategy system to a structural development paradigm that can redistribute development capacity at the grassroot level, democratize resource allocation, restore livelihoods, and address the research and policy gaps on global sustainable development.

This chapter introduces Systematic Inclusive Capacity of SICE Entrepreneurship strategy as a rigorously grounded theoretical construct that departs from the dominant finance-led interpretation of entrepreneurship. The prevailing entrepreneurship schema encourages credit access and firm expansion as primary mechanisms for growth (Schulman *et al.*,2011), often overlooking deeper structural conditions. SICE provides an alternative logic, asserting that sustainable and just development emerges from collective entrepreneurial systems characterized by shared-ownership of productive assets, community-embedded governance structures, and more equitable distributions of authority within decision-making processes. Through this orientation, enterprise activity is positioned as a means of simultaneously generating economic value, strengthening local capacity, and reducing social and environmental harm.

Drawing on an integrated review of theory, comparative international experiences, and policy reflection [Alka *et al.*, 2025], the chapter demonstrates that SICE functions across diverse socio-economic and cultural contexts. Rather than being confined to specific regions or institutional settings, the framework is shown to operate effectively in rural and urban environments and within both formalized and informal economic systems. This adaptability reinforces SICE's relevance as a broadly applicable model for entrepreneurship. The chapter further conceptualizes SICE as a foundational mechanism for inclusive development and systemic resilience, particularly under conditions of external stress such as economic volatility, ecological disruption, or technological change. In this way, growth is reinterpreted as a collaborative and regenerative process rather than a narrowly defined metric of scale or profitability.

In addition, the chapter offers a practical and policy-oriented framework for stakeholders—including governments, educators, development agencies, and practitioners—seeking to operationalize SICE. It emphasizes the role of enabling regulatory environments, inclusive fiscal policies, and coordinated ecosystem partnerships in supporting the expansion of SICE-based initiatives without compromising their equity-driven foundations. The chapter situates SICE within broader aspects of entrepreneurship on sustainable development, highlighting its capacity to integrate economic performance with social inclusion and environmental stewardship, while actively addressing the historical exclusion of marginalized groups from entrepreneurial opportunity.

The chapter concludes by positioning SICE as a strategic vehicle for transformative change, capable of supporting digital innovation, strengthening collective governance, and enhancing cultural resilience. It also calls for further scholarly inquiry into adaptive entrepreneurial paradigms aligned with inclusive sustainability. Overall, the chapter articulates how SICE provides a comprehensive framework that connects localized entrepreneurial practices with national and global sustainability agendas, offering a compelling alternative to extractive and exclusionary models of development.

1.2 Concept behind Social, Inclusive Community-based Entrepreneurship

SICE refers to organized entrepreneurial activity that is (a) collective within a community, a group, or a federation, (b) intentionally inclusive (intentionally designed to broaden participation, access, and decision-making to historically marginalized groups), and (c) entrepreneurial, applying market-driven and sustained value capture of economically productive and socially responsible ventures. In short, SICE includes collective ownership, deliberate inclusion, and sustainable market engagement (respectfully termed as collective social entrepreneurship). This framework is developed on the "collective social entrepreneurship" literature that shifts focus from heroic individuals to actors in collaboration, alongside policy streams on inclusive entrepreneurship. The value creation mechanism of SICE can be understood from Figure 1.

Figure 1. Value creation through social, inclusive, and community-based entrepreneurship (SICE)

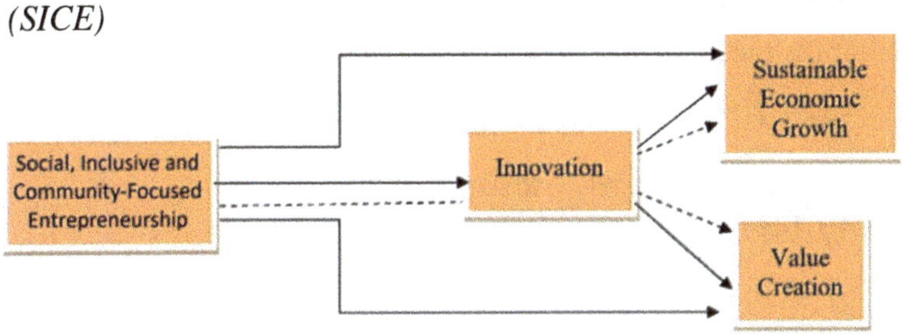

[Source: Authors' own creation]

The 21st century began with the paradox of having the greatest technological advancements in history while also having unprecedented economic inequality, social inequity, ecological degradation, and persistent worldwide inequities. The first few decades of the 21st Century was characterized by the optimism of globalization, technological advancements, and the free market (Loku & Loku, 2025). Unfortunately, most of the world's population suffers from economic and social structural barriers that limit economic engagement.

For decades, entrepreneurship and business were assumed to be the most important drivers of economic and social progress. These, historically, were based on self-interested, profit-maximizing motives. Unfortunately, while self-interested entrepreneurial activity has historically been important for industrial progress and wealth generation for some, they also failed miserably to significantly impact the reduction of wealth and social inequality, the democratization of wealth and social opportunity, solve inequities in social problems, and the socio-ecological imbalances in communities. The emergence of social, inclusive, and community-based entrepreneurship is, thus, the first ever counter to the dominant theory on development, innovation, and economic progress in the world.

SICE is not just an idea or a statement of policy, but an ideology based on the realities of suffering people, grassroots movements, and organizations in various parts of the world. SICE conceptualizes and redefines entrepreneurial activity as and for complex, collaborative, justice-seeking, system-changing sustainable acts, in the practice of remapping economic power and broadening the ownership of economic instruments. Unlike mainstream entrepreneurship, SICE eludes the individualistic obsession of the 'success' and monetary wealth, to focus on the collective 'successful' production of diverse goods and services, the just and sustained benefit of resilient people of the community, and on the socio-ecological systemic balance of the community. SICE's alternative economic logic is anchored on the inescapable reality of the interconnectedness of the socio-ecological system, and the fact that it is a system that deteriorates or gets exhausted on the economic system continues to exclude a significant part of the people. SICE, therefore, instead and firstly points to human dignity, participation, stewardship, pluralism, and sustainable ecological balance.

1.3 Importance of Social, Inclusive Community-based Entrepreneurship

The present state of the world heightens the need for such an option even more. Existing paradigms of development fall short because of climate change driven displacement, youth unemployment, gender -based inequality in job opportunities, the fragility of the global supply chain, and widening wealth gaps. In the face of climate vulnerability, socio-political instability, and economic precarity, the integrated crisis response of traditional business ecosystems remains lacking. On the other hand, the global development policies including the Sustainable Development Goals (SDG) (Mahajan *et al.*, 2024) have, on multiple occasions, highlighted the need for creative and place-based solutions that synergistically integrate economic growth with social equity and ecological balance. SICE provides that very solution, being situated at the crossroads of local input, participatory governance, and models of sustainable enterprise.

One of the most important functions of SICE is its challenging of the assumption that innovative potential is limited to privileged elite, urbanized, and formally educated groupings of society. SICE recognizes and uplifts the innovative, latent, and problem-solving abilities of communities that have been excluded and marginalized from society, such as women's self-help groups, youth networks, indigenous peoples, workers in the informal economy, rural producers, minorities, migrants, people with psychosocial disabilities, etc. These communities have been historically sidelined from offered entrepreneurial activities. By categorizing these communities as actors, rather than passive participants in the development processes, SICE confronts the deeply rooted development hierarchy of profit-based entrepreneurship and broadens entrepreneurship reachability to potential entrepreneurs without biasness (Kalkanci *et al.*, 2019). SICE entrepreneurship is innovative, participative, and flexible to the realities of multiple communities, focusing on entrepreneurship for the collective longevity of these communities.

SICE's ability to integrate and mobilize different resources using flexible governance mechanisms and multi-actor partnerships. Traditional market enterprises are less flexible in times of crises due to their hierarchical organizational structures, dependence on outside capital, and low levels of community embeddedness. In contrast, SICE entities (i.e., cooperatives, social enterprises, community-owned businesses, and federated networks) exhibit decentralized governance, trust-based partnerships, and mutual ownership arrangements. These characteristics make them flexible in times of crises. Recent global crises, including the COVID-19 pandemic, demonstrated the capacity of community-rooted enterprises to stay flexible and maintain essential services, protect livelihoods, and facilitate the distribution of resources. Their ability to access locally complex social ecosystems allows these enterprises to mobilize resources quickly. Their ability to create socially inclusive solutions from locally embedded ecosystems is particularly valuable.

Moreover, SICE confronts the misunderstanding of entrepreneurship being exclusively economic or business-related. SICE recontextualizes entrepreneurial action as integration of social, cultural and ecological processes. Communities exercise agency in determining their social and economic development, protecting their cultural heritage, and managing local ecological assets. For example, within indigenous communities, entrepreneurship can be a means to self-affirm identity, resist systems of exploitation, and safeguard traditional knowledge. Moreover, for women and marginalized workers, the acts of entrepreneurship offer means for social and political empowerment and greater participation (Thomas, 2024). Given this, SICE is redefining entrepreneurship to include the processes of building community and inclusive, sustainable transformation, rather than the sole creation of a business venture.

The potential SICE has to transform societies and economies will be further enhanced by how it contributes to globally defined targets in sustainability and SDGs, particularly under such targets as poverty, gender, social, democratic and environmental governance. Within the confines of ecological sustainability, SICE demonstrates how the reduction of social inequalities and the provision of social equity is possible. SICE resolves the profit-purpose dualism by integrating social equity and ecological sustainability with economic growth. SICE entities do this through socio-economic hybrid structures that invest their surplus in social community economic development, promote circular economies, and create local economic systems that decrease the predation of global economic systems.

Although the institutional environment presents challenges, SICE is tempered by uneven funding in SICE, limited access to financial markets, weak integration in global markets, and inadequate policy support and neglect to promote community-oriented enterprises. Furthermore, in the academic and business community dominated by the discourse of entrepreneurial individualism, PMC (full form?) is celebrated, and collective frameworks are sidelined while local knowledge systems are disparaged. To alleviate these constraints, the interplay of the systems of support surrounding the entrepreneurial ideas and teaching must also change along with the support structures built around the systems of SICE. For SICE to be a part of the new economic development, social equity paradigm, SICE must be recognized by governments, NGOs, academia, and the business community as a core activity and not an ancillary one.

Also, the fast growth of digital technologies presents both positives and negatives to SICE. For example, SICE can now facilitate more accessible and inclusive digital channels of market access, financial services, and information for disadvantaged entrepreneurs. Nonetheless, the digital divides related to differential access, lower levels of connectedness and affordability, and lower levels of digital literacy might exacerbate existing gaps. Thus, the application of digital tools within SICE systems needs to be looked into for the inclusive innovation perspective, ensuring that technological responses fit the purpose of and are co-developed with the communities aligned to the context. When fairly implemented, digital shifts can enhance community governance, promote visibility and inclusiveness of communities in the policy spectrum, strengthen interinstitutional partnerships for climate resilience, and facilitate seamless transparent value chain flows.

Evolving socio-cultural changes in the world's approach toward development and collective wellbeing explain the increasing relevance of SICE. All over the world, new generations advocate for climate justice and broaden and deepen social changes, while demanding ethical and just consumption practices and challenging the extractive character of economies. Such changes amplify the momentum of SICE and new generations create social movements, new market opportunities, and advocate for community-based enterprises. When social innovation, entrepreneurship, sustainability and SICE are incorporated into the curricula of educational institutions, future, and present, leaders are provided with the knowledge and skills required to implement SICE in various contexts.

SICE's role in increasing locality's resilience in the face of global risk is another critical dimension of the global relevance of SICE. While globalization has integrated economies, it has also created systemic risks: rising commodity prices, supply chain disruptions, geo-political tensions, and climate-induced disasters. Communities with external dependencies for employment and resources are particularly vulnerable to shocks. On the other hand, SICE fosters community-based economic activities that circulate value, promote interdependence, and diversify livelihood opportunities in the community. Such embedded economic systems improve the community's ability to withstand and recover from disruptions, and to sustain social cohesion.

SICE is obligated to be a constructive reaction to the intricate issues posed by the present day. It has the capacity to add unique ways to the community self-determination, the entrepreneurial ecosystem equity has broadened, the resistance to negative development processes, and the entrepreneurial self-determination has been increased. When the collective action and inclusive governance of communities is made visible, SICE has the capacity to reframe the concept of entrepreneurship and its achievements when based on compassion toward communities, fairness among economically different social groups, and a longer time horizon for sustainability. The longer introduction is deserving of this particular explanation to open the following part of the chapter, examining how SICE can empower communities and contribute to a sustainable future, during a time of crisis and social interdependence.

1.4 Key Features of Social, Inclusive Community-based Entrepreneurship

Following are some key features of SICE as explained in Figure 2:

1. Collective governance and federative structures — SICE enterprises often leverage collective ownership (e.g., cooperatives, federations, SHGs) that are accompanied with democratic governance principles of local legitimization and rapid, decentralized decision-making. Empirically documented collective social entrepreneurship and cooperative resilience highlight these governance structures as durable.
2. Deliberate inclusion of social outsiders — SICE participation targets women, youth, ethnic minorities, migrants, and people with disabilities through membership, quota systems, capacity-building, and financial access. The OECD Missing Entrepreneurs program and the literature on inclusive entrepreneurship map policies and more systematic frameworks designed for such inclusion.
3. Hybrid economic models (market and mission)—SICE organizations are known to integrate social initiatives with (surplus) generating ventures (sales, service provision, and social enterprise models), reinvesting profits into the mission and not the other way around.
4. Economic linkages — SICE relies on place-based value chains (local procurement, local labour, circular economy activities) that keep value circulating within the community and strengthen local multiplier effects. This economic embeddedness is supported by many community entrepreneurship case studies such as Dharavi's recycling ecology.
5. Support cradle-to-scale ecosystem—SICE requires multi-actor support (government facilitation, catalytic capital from NGOs/impact investors, higher-education partnerships, federative cooperative networks). Governance and policy analyses assert that these ecosystem functions enhance replicability and depth which increases governance and policy gaps and constraints.
6. Resilience & shock absorption — Collectively governed and inclusive enterprises in the literature on cooperatives, mutual aid and community networks absorb shocks (2008 financial crisis, pandemics, climate events) better through resource pooling, employment redistribution and local demand substitution.

Figure 2. Key features of SICE

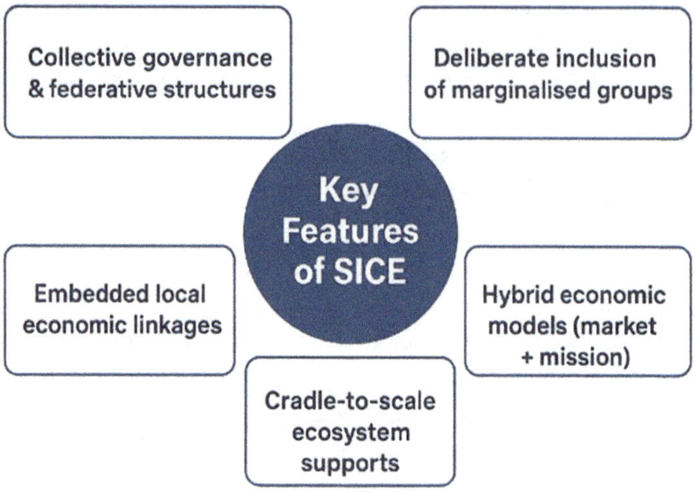

Figure 2
Key features of SICE

[Source: Author's own creation]

SICE encompasses value production beyond financial metrics, explicitly pursuing social, cultural, and environmental dividends. By centering collective participation, shared stewardship, and mutual accountability, SICE articulates a multidimensional and context-rooted alternative to mainstream entrepreneurial logic. Its core purpose is to knit tighter social networks, safeguard cultural heritage, secure fair and universal access to assets and pathways, and steward ecosystems for successive generations. Consequently, SICE is designed not merely to fill market voids, but to confront the structural impediments for which dominant market paradigms have remained inadequate. Given the world's deep commitment towards the United Nations Sustainable Development Goals, SICE emerges as a decisive vehicle for advancing both localized equity and planetary sustainability in the twenty-first century (Nagdev *et al.*, 2025).

The Global Relevance of SICE

SICE is, in real terms, well beyond traditional entrepreneurship cases. Although globalization has integrated many economies and societies, it has simultaneously exacerbated disparities between economies by categorizing them as 'developed' and 'developing' economies. Continuing experiences of economic marginalization, involuntary migration, gender asymmetries, and climate-induced vulnerability, persuaded the policymakers to understand that market mechanisms alone prove insufficient.

Variants of entrepreneurship that are explicitly community-centered and inclusive provide practical countermeasures by translating marginalized communities into active economic and social participants. The phenomena are observable in women-managed rural cooperatives (example, Self-Employed Women's Association (SEWA), which financially supports self-employed women through cooperative societies), indigenous-led entrepreneurial networks, and community-centered social ventures, whose effects include the generation of income, the transmission of cultural heritage, and the reinforcement of social bonds and agency.

Contemporary and recurrent crises, such as geopolitical uncertainties, exemplified by the COVID-19 pandemic and by disasters attributable to climate change, have exposed the brittleness of dominant economic arrangements. Evidence collected during these crises shows that locally managed enterprises frequently performed the role of initial responders, supplying wage opportunities, essential goods and services, and expressions of social solidarity amid widespread insecurity. Such instances underscore that entrepreneurship designed upon inclusive modalities and rooted in participatory governance possesses the potential to operate as a resilient vector, capable of sustaining both local and extended economic networks in periods of perturbation.

2. CONCEPTUAL UNDERPINNINGS OF SOCIAL, INCLUSIVE, AND COMMUNITY-BASED ENTREPRENEURSHIP

SICE synthesizes three interdependent, yet conceptually distinct, traditions: social entrepreneurship, inclusive entrepreneurship, and community-centered entrepreneurship, the interactions of which clarify the normative and operational contours of a more equitable economic order. SICE integrates three areas of entrepreneurship which has been explain in this chapter: collective social entrepreneurship (shifting the unit of analysis from heroic individuals to federated, multi-actor structures), inclusive entrepreneurship (policy and program efforts to open opportunity to underserved populations), and community-based/place-based enterprise (economic activities situated within specific locations). Empirical evidence from Kudumbashree in Kerala (multi-million membership network), SEWA (multi-million women-member federation with parametric insurance pilots), the Mondragon cooperatives (federative resilience during systemic shocks), and place-based clusters such as Dharavi (USD ~0.6–1.0 billion informal turnover and significant employment in the recycling industry) illustrate the impact of the integration of these elements: collective governance, purposeful integration, and market access. The impact is clear: enhanced employment continuity, improved household resilience during shocks, retention of local economic value, and demonstrable improvements in gender and poverty metrics. Such evidence supports SICE as a policy goal and a descriptive category.

2.1. Social Entrepreneurship

Definition & Core Imperative

Social entrepreneurship consists of dual objectives of generating social value and achieving sustainable economic feasibility. It involves creating and utilizing opportunities to bring social change and then organising resources and business strategies to deliver that change in an economically sustainable way (instead of entirely philanthropic). For example, as Zahra et al. (2009) have written, "activities and processes undertaken to discover, define, and exploit opportunities to enhance social wealth by creating new ventures or managing existing organizations in an innovative manner". Similarly, Peredo & McLean (2006) as cited in Dumay (2009) have written it as "a unique blend of vision, innovation, and risk-taking to set up social change". As a result, social entrepreneurs focus on social issues that public or private entities have neglected and/or underinvested in, such as poverty, inequity, education and health access, environmental issues, and others, all while keeping a financially sustainable and responsible model.

At this point, certain unique properties of SICE have been identified, which makes the strategy unique and different in its own way. SICE is primarily focused on a social mission, within which the profit generated is often needed to sustain the enterprise and/or is reinvested for mission activities.It employs market-based, innovative approaches, such as strategically applying business logic and market mechanisms to social issues (B-Corps, hybrid model). It pursues systemic change and scalability, as opposed to the mere incremental provision of social services. It functions in all three sectors: non-profit, for-profit, and blended cross-sectors.

Types/Formats

The literature identifies a number of typologies/formats of social entrepreneurship, such as

1. **Integrated social entrepreneurship:** It is for-profit corporate activity that also produces social benefit (profit + mission).
2. **Reinterpretation model:** It is mostly applied in non-profit organizations to re-interpret and/or adopt revenue diversification/business logic in order to support the mission.

3. **Complementary social entrepreneurship:** Here nonprofit entities engage in profit-seeking activities to cross-subsidize the social mission.

More broadly, venture-creation, intra-enterprise innovation, and partnership/alliances (common with cross-sector collaboration) with a social mission, and start-ups as well as within established organizations that adopt new social business models, are all prevalent formats.Also, they point out that social entrepreneurship can take the form of starting new enterprises, growing existing social ventures, or hybrid models functioning at local and/or global levels. It can be seen in well-known well-known case-studies (e.g. microfinance, education, and health ventures), the more important point is the strategy: new model + social purpose + profit. In her research, Abeysekera (2019) stated that social entrepreneurship tries to fill the gaps in issues like poverty, education, and human rights that many businesses and governments have neglected.

Key Take Aways

Social entrepreneurship integrates the social and economic imperatives: it is not sufficient to have a social purpose and it is also not enough to have a commercially viable business and the two have to be interwoven. It seeks innovation, sustainability, scalability, and value creation (social and economic together).

2.2. Inclusive Entrepreneurship

Definition and Core Imperative

Inclusive entrepreneurship aims to broaden the risk and reward of entrepreneurial engagement to historically underserved and under-represented groups, such as women, youth, racial and ethnic minorities, and persons with disabilities. Its goal is to achieve vertical and horizontal equality in the allocation of financial and social assets, gaining equitable access to the critical resources, networks, and market access. As an example, the Organization for Economic Cooperation and Development (OECD) describes inclusive entrepreneurship as the 'missing entrepreneurs paradox' which allows wide participation of neglected demographics in entrepreneurial activities.

Yeasmin and Hasanat (2022) investigate the case around immigrant women in Northern Finland. Their paper "Understanding Inclusive Entrepreneurship: With Special Reference to Women Immigrants in Arctic Finland" details the socio-cultural and economic barriers to inclusion as well as the positive impact an inclusive entrepreneurship policy can have on the conditions of these women.

Mendoza (2023) analyzed the relation with Persons With Disabilities in "Entrepreneurial Capability and Engagement of Persons With Disabilities Toward A Framework for Inclusive Entrepreneurship" developing an interconnected framework of inclusive entrepreneurship. Hence, inclusive entrepreneurship wants to know who participates and how, rather than what the enterprise seeks to achieve.

Let us see the chief characteristics of Inclusive Entrepreneurship, which differentiates it from other strategies: Inclusive Entrepreneurship concerns access to entrepreneurial opportunities, not merely the access to business ownership. It targets the unrepresented (women, youth, people with disabilities, and ethnic minority) and the systemic barriers to access (finance, networks, skills, markets) which still remain. It aims to achieve 'equity' or 'fairness' (vertical parity = within roles/levels of the same function and horizontal parity = across different functions or multiple groups) in the entrepreneurship ecosystem.

Types/Formats

Programs with varying designs and models include:

1. **Business models supporting livelihood of needy people:** Entrepreneurship program for women, youth, immigrants, and persons with disabilities (mentoring and networks, capital and other resources access).
2. **Inclusive business models:** firms which intentionally employ or procure materials from under-represented communities (e.g., inclusive supply chains).
3. **Initiatives related to entrepreneurship for the young people:** this is one area where interest is high, but, at the same time, there are significant resource and experience shortages. (OECD: 39% of young people prefer self-employment but only ~7% in the EU were self-employed)
4. **Entrepreneurship which aligns with government policy and ecosystem interventions for marginalized people:** for example, infrastructure and tax policy, along with financial instruments, network access, and skills geared toward assimilation.

Some scholars consider inclusive entrepreneurship an ecosystem approach rather than a singular venture activity (which is, enabling access & removing barriers). It can be observed in the OECD's Women in inclusive entrepreneurship theme which shows that closing the gender entrepreneurship gap could increase the GDP by 6 to 12% in the OECD countries. The Mendoza (2023) study of persons with disabilities shows that access to credit and business information, skills and networks remain formidable barriers.

Key Take Aways

Inclusive entrepreneurship is about widening the net for participation, removing the barriers that make entrepreneurship the domain only of the elite. It is a supplement to social entrepreneurship: while social entrepreneurship emphasizes mission and model, inclusive entrepreneurship focuses on who gets to take part in the entrepreneurial activity.

2.3. Community-Based Entrepreneurship

Definition and Core Imperative

Community based entrepreneurship focuses on anchoring an enterprise within the experience of particular places and ensures ownership, strategic management, and profit-sharing of the enterprise is equitably distributed to the local people. Such businesses usually emerge from the convergence of cultural, ecological, and/or geographical affinities and seek to enhance community adaptive capacity over the long haul. As an example, Peredo & Chrisman (2006) characterise community-based enterprise (CBE) as an expression of a community acting collectively as both entrepreneur and enterprise for the attainment of the community's common good.

Suryani et al. (2022) in "Strengthening Community-Based Entrepreneurship: The significance of community capacity building and enabling ecosystem" explores the importance of local capacity and enabling networks, skills, and environment.

Let us see the chief characteristics of Community-based Entrepreneurship which can differentiate it from others. The enterprise is carried out within a locality (village, township, and/or region) and thus has strong community bonds, common culture, and collective governance. The community (employment, wealth, and capacity) reaps the benefits as opposed to the benefits being siphoned off externally. The prototype focuses on local democracy, shared governance, networked ownership, and local resource (cultural, ecological) utilization. Communities, not merely the profit or social mission, the military or other entities focus on the community's capacity to be resilient and adapt.

Types/Formats

Some of the commonly known types are:

1. **Community cooperatives or collectives:** These are organized when community members pool resources and jointly own and share the profits.

2. **Place-based social enterprises:** businesses for which their core competitive advantage is derived from local ecological, cultural, and heritage resources and context.
3. **Indigenous or rural enterprises:** those that utilize local and indigenous knowledge, materials, ecology, and culture.
4. **Development-oriented entrepreneurship:** aims at improving livelihoods and alleviating poverty through local economic development, beyond external markets.
5. **Hybrid community social enterprises:** social enterprises that have a community ownership, social purpose and market for sustainable products/services.

The systematic review by Hassan et al. (2020) identified and outlined the scope of the growing Community-Based Entrepreneurship (CBE) research. Community-based entrepreneurship is enabled by local trust and community assets, as demonstrated by Parwez's (2017) retail case study of a marginal community.

Key Take Aways

As the name suggests, Community-based entrepreneurship is important in the context of working with a specific community, addressing their needs, using locally available resources, and enabling ownership. The focus is on place, self-governance, and sustained capacity development, as opposed to mission or inclusion across groups.

When the three dimensions are deliberately combined as explained in Figure 3, SICE emerges as an integrative framework capable of generating revenue while actively redistributing assets, reinforcing local cultural and ecological identities, and advancing inclusive prosperity. Departs from the traditional profit-maximizing entrepreneurial paradigm by foregrounding collective welfare and communal advancement.

Figure 3. Dimensions of SICE

Figure 3
Dimensions of SICE

[Source: Author's own creation]

3. THEORETICAL PERSPECTIVES AND FRAMEWORK FOR SICE

To appreciate the transformative promise of socially inclusive collective entrepreneurship (SICE), one must locate it within existing analytical paradigms. The entrepreneurial event theory elucidates the antecedents, triggers, and motives that precipitate the entrepreneurial behaviour, elucidating how individuals and collectives identify opportunities and reorganise material and cognitive resources to constitute new enterprise forms. When SICE is examined through this lens, the theory posits that marginalised populations view entrepreneurial endeavour not as a narrowly framed profit-seeking, but as a mode of subsistence - the sustenance of cultural heritage, and the exercise of social agency.

When viewed through a sustainability lens, SICE's alignment with the Sustainable Development Goals (SDGs) reveals its capacity to simultaneously confront multiple, interconnected difficulties, including poverty eradication (SDG 1), gender equality (SDG 5), decent work and economic growth (SDG 8), reduced inequalities (SDG 10), and the cultivation of sustainable communities (SDG 11). Such alignment, rooted in the global policymaking arena, rescues the SDGs from mere aspirational rhetoric by tasking SICE with the responsibility of actualizing these international objectives in concrete, locally relevant initiatives. Table 1 lists types of SDGs and their functions.

Table 1. SDGs and their functions

Different Scales of SDG	Types	Functions
SDG 1	Poverty eradication	Subsistence of cultural heritage
SDG 5	Gender equality	Exercise of social agency
SDG 8, SDG 10	Decent work and economic growth	Catalytic capital
SDG 11	Reduced inequalities	Transformative capability building
Firm/Organization	Sustainable communities	Design of legal environments
	Actualizing SDGs in concrete initiatives	

3.1. Institutional and Structural Support

Achievement of SICE's aims depends critically upon institutional actors who fulfil complementary but distinct roles. Public authorities cultivate the enabling environment through coherent policies, sustained funding mechanisms, and inclusive entrepreneurship frameworks embedded within national development plans. Non-governmental organizations (NGOs) and civil society actors function as vital intermediaries, mobilizing community-level voices, driving advocacy, and implementing programs at the grassroot level. Research-intensive higher education institutions contribute towards SICE advancements through cutting-edge inquiry, innovation incubation, and human capital development, thereby equipping the next generation with the competencies and values required for socially and environmentally responsible enterprise. The private sector, meanwhile, progressively forges strategic alliances rooted in corporate-social responsibility (CSR) and shared value, thereby extending resources and networks to SICE initiatives.

By collectively orchestrating their distinct contributions, these diverse institutional actors weave a multi-tiered inclusive economically enabling framework in which

SICE can flourish. Crucially, such coordinated support transcends transactional funding; it cultivates systemic conditions in which socially and environmentally innovative enterprise ceases to treat historically marginalized populations as mere beneficiaries and, instead, affirms their position as equal actors and co-designers of the economic, social, and ecological futures - to which they are entitled.

SICE in Times of Crisis: A distinctive quality of SICE systems is their agility amid crises. Economic downturns, pandemics, and climatic catastrophes have not merely tested these initiatives; rather, they have and continue to reveal their intrinsic capacity to adapt. Anchored in persistent community engagement and an explicit commitment to inclusivity, SICE ventures attain autonomy from global supply chains and external financial injections. The consequence is a pronounced ability to absorb external shocks. Moreover, by cultivating networks of mutual aid and participatory problem-solving, they nourish both psychological and collective social resilience, rendering SICE an apparatus of economic continuity and, concurrently, an instrument of social cohesion in periods of upheaval.

Table 2. SICE Case Studies

Case (crisis & place)	SICE features / mechanisms in crisis	Concrete functions delivered (cradle→scale)	Key SDG links	Representative sources
Kudumbashree — Kerala, COVID-19 (2020)	Local women's neighbourhood networks + state linkage; rapid repurposing of micro-enterprises	Emergency food & kitchen operations; local supply chains; information dissemination; livelihood continuity	SDG 1 (poverty), SDG 5 (gender), SDG 11 (sustainable communities)	Evaluation/reports on Kudumbashree pandemic response.
SEWA & federated cooperatives — India, COVID & climate shocks (2020–2024)	Federated cooperatives, grassroots accelerators, social-enterprise support (finance, training, markets); partnerships for rapid payouts	Cash assistance & microinsurance; production (masks, food); continued market access; telehealth & capacity building	SDG 1, SDG 5, SDG 8 (decent work), SDG 13 (climate resilience)	SEWA rapid assessment reports; IDinsight/SEWA studies; Reuters coverage of 2024 heat payouts.
Mondragon cooperatives — Basque Country, 2008 & later crises	Federative governance; cross-firm solidarity funds; employment redistribution; democratic worker participation	Preserved employment; re-allocation of production; stabilised local economies; longer-term competitiveness	SDG 8 (decent work), SDG 10 (reduced inequalities), SDG 11 (sustainable communities)	Oxford Saïd case study; academic analyses of Mondragon resilience.
Mutual-aid networks — global, COVID-19 (2020–2021)	Rapid, horizontal organisation; volunteer coordination; translation of needs→resources; some formalisation into collectives	Rapid relief (food, transport, care); psychosocial support; seed networks for longer civic/enterprise forms	SDG 1, SDG 3 (health), SDG 10 (reduced inequalities), SDG 11	Fernandes-Jesus et al. (2021); Carstensen et al. (2021) mutual-aid studies.

Deriving from SICE case studies from Table 2, SICE systems integrate local democratic governance together with active membership alongside oriented or (hybrid) and economic activities to deliver hardy results. In times of crises, they function using three mutually reinforcing systems: (1) distributed governance (local ownership and federations) which allows for rapid, legitimate decision making, (2) resource pooling (informal savings, cooperative funds, catalytic grants/insurance) which maintains liquidity for livelihoods, and (3) embedded social structures (mutual aid, volunteer cadres, local leadership) that translate need into immediate action and longer-term capability building.

The case studies from Kerala's Kudumbashree, SEWA's federated cooperatives, Mondragon's solidarity mechanisms and global mutual-aid networks explain how

SICE not only cushions shocks but SICE can also catalyse longer-term transformations in local sustainable development and inclusive economic opportunities.

3.2. Transformation Opportunities for SICE

In order to develop SICE (Socially Inclusive Collective Entrepreneurship) in a different direction, three dimensions require change: First, further integration of inclusive open-innovation approaches which encourage community, business and academia collaborative problem solving (Kim & Boudreaux et al, 2017). Second, the deepening of collective governance through social entrepreneurs and their networks building-streaming entrepreneurial capital systems from the social value isolation (Szarleta, 2018) and finally, installation of sophisticated frameworks for inclusive hybrid, digital and scalable business models to help economically viable inclusive collectives to sustainably achieve social mission (Maier et al, 2014; Garcia-Jurado et al., 2024). Illustratively, community enterprises which have little to no federation of platforms need to shift focus to the use of governance systems for inter-organizational resource integration and the use of digital technologies to mitigate marginalization and equitable agency distribution in decision structures. As SICE begins these new stages, the integration of inclusive collectives into layered entrepreneurial national ecosystems built-structures and supported by relevant policy, financing, infrastructure and digital systems is the new frontier for achieving sustained local impact rather than

Integrating inclusive governance models into entrepreneurial ecosystems represents one of the key opportunities for transformation. Notably, while SICE initiatives begin with a bottom-up, grassroots approach, their sustained viability over the long term hinges on the establishment of formal governance structures that shield community ownership and foster inclusive participation. This entails a shift from poorly organized collectives to federated, multi-tiered governance arrangements that mesh local governance with regional and national governance. This kind of governance improves the pooling and allocative efficiency of resources, facilitates the transference of knowledge, and enhances the power relations of the group within the public policy arena. Furthermore, the transformation of governance also means the incorporation of transparency, participatory democracy, and gender-balanced leadership. With these values in place, SICE entities can shift from mere operational survival to impactful advocacy and policy entrepreneurship, influencing desired selectivity in developmental processes and promoting inclusiveness in the local and national entrepreneurial ecosystems.

The integration of SICE practices with eco-regenerative models represents yet another pathway of transformation. With SICE's potential to build regenerative local economies, SICE's potential to build regenerative local economies is pertinent with the increasing ecological degradation, climate change, and food insecurity, livelihood, and community destabilization. This is agroecology, sustainable forestry, community conservation, renewable energy, and circular economy with localized waste management. SICE integration of community eco governance and green finance to community enterprises and climate changes in enterprises to eco-adaptive governance is an area of priority for SICE. SICE can, if all goes as planned, be the foundation of climate and ecological restoration at the community level.

Apart from environmental changes, SICE will also benefit from digital changes which look to broaden participation and lessen structural exclusion. SICE will greatly benefit from digital technology-mobility, digital payments, blockchain, community data, AI forecasting, and most importantly, digital technology. However, inclusive innovation practices must ensure that these technologies close digital divides rather than widen. Improving digital literacy, community digital infrastructure, and designing relevant technologies are the most culturally and linguistically appropriate. For example, community digital hubs can help facilitate training, enterprise generation, and access to markets. Blockchain technologies can enhance trust and traceability within community value chains, especially in agriculture, craft, and sustainable tourist chains. Likewise, platform cooperatives-digital tools that empower workers to own and manage businesses, are positive alternatives to the exploitative models of the gig economy. Through these methods, rather than corporate consolidation, digital technology will foster collective empowerment.

The potential for change also extends to knowledge creation, research, and educational system collaborations for SICE. Communities, indigenous ways of knowing, and informal learning systems are often subjugated by conventional academic and institutional knowledge. A transformative shift means placing communities, not as research subjects, but as knowledge producers. This means involving communities in action research, documenting community knowledge, creating peer learning networks, establishing community innovation hubs, and forming collaborations between universities and community organizations.

Additionally, there are multiple ways in which adaptable and shock-responsive systems can create and strengthen resilience. With the increase in the world's volatility, including a growing number of global pandemics, climate disasters, and economic crises, SICE provides a model for creating the potential for building community resilience. However, to make the most of this opportunity, a creation of community disaster funds, a diversification of livelihood, the training of local leaders in crisis governance, the building of decentralized production networks, and risk-management systems all need to be bolstered.

SICE transformation opportunities must equally consider the socio-cultural change of the community. SICE is and has always been a product of certain cultural practices, collective identities, and community aspirations. As a community evolves due to climate stress, migration, modernization, and demographic shifts, the SICE model must adapt to evolved cultural practices while also conserving the traditional and cultural identity. It is also essential to promote cultural transformation that is socially inclusive, sustainable, and equitable. The model SICE creates acknowledges the wisdom and knowledge of the past while also embracing the potential of the future, and social transformation, along with the cultural continuity, is designed to empower the community.

CONCLUSION

This chapter thus intersects contemporary scholarly and policy discourses on entrepreneurship by rigorously theorizing and contextualizing SICE within a global frame. Utilizing secondary data from a constellation of sources—academic articles, multilateral reports, and officially circulated policy retrospectives—it weaves together the heterogeneous legacies of social, inclusive, and community-based entrepreneurship into a coalesced analytical apparatus. The chapter posits that SICE is propelled by a dual propulsion: it fortifies the circuits of local economies while advancing the broader, and interdependent, imperative of global sustainability.

Moreover, a conceptual framework unifying entrepreneurial scholarship, governance paradigms, and the Sustainable Development Goals is articulated herein. The framework delivers normative recommendations for policymakers, entrepreneurial practitioners, and the research community intent upon harnessing entrepreneurship for the construction of equitable, resilient, and sustainable economies. Through a systematic investigation of institutional architecture, collective agency, and the interplay between local and global domains, the chapter demonstrates the capacity of social, inclusive, and collaborative entrepreneurship (SICE) to function as a driver of inclusive progress that overcomes entrenched geographical, cultural, and material boundaries.

This chapter goes beyond merely describing and introducing Social, Inclusive, and Community-Based Entrepreneurship (SICE). This chapter also makes substantive contributions, both in scholarship and in practice, and relevant to policy, which attempt to redefine systems of thought concerning entrepreneurship and its measurement, pedagogy, and application in today's world. This chapter integrates multiple different theoretical, experiential, and policy-level approaches to provide a more comprehensive understanding of SICE as a complex development paradigm. This expanded section describes these contributions in detail, showing how the chapter enriches scholarship, policy, and tools for analysis available to researchers and enables action for professionals at the intersection of social justice and economic development and sustainable governance.

Reconciling three entrepreneurial traditions - social entrepreneurship, inclusive entrepreneurship, and community-based entrepreneurship - has been a major focus of this chapter. This chapter connects SICE and the Sustainable Development Goals (SDGs), arguing that various forms of collective and inclusive socially oriented enterprises are likely able to advance several of the SDGs at the same time. This chapter thus arms SICE to deal with poverty, gender inequality, and unemployment, social exclusion, and climate vulnerabilities. This association with global development frameworks makes SICE more than just a local activity. This chapter contributes to closing the global policy rhetorical gaps and the ground entrepreneurial activities of the under served.

Moreover, the chapter contributes to the discipline by providing a conceptual integration of entrepreneurial event theory, governance theory, and sustainability science to understand the intricacies of SICE. Classical entrepreneurship theories are predominantly centered around the individual: their motivation, their risk-taking, their opportunistic behaviors, and their value creation within a market. In contrast, the chapter reconceptualizes entrepreneurial events as collective processes influenced by social identity, resource pooling, cultural memory, community dynamics, and power relations. This reinterpretation of entrepreneurial events challenges the assumption of the individual as the sole entrepreneurial agent and expands the theory to include community- and equity-driven forms of entrepreneurship. This pivot represents an important theoretical contribution, providing a springboard for scholars to investigate entrepreneurship in marginalized or resource-constrained settings.

Along with the theoretical advancements in the field, the chapter is also grounded in empirical research, providing a rich array of case studies and global clippings, demonstrating the diverse applications of SICE. The chapter draws evidence from Kudumbashree in Kerala, SEWA in India, the Mondragon cooperative network in Spain, and global mutual-aid platforms, demonstrating the SICE models' robustness, flexibility, and resilience. The empirical case studies also illustrate the socio-economic stability SICE creates in times of crisis and under stress, and how it adapts and evolves.

Another significant contribution comes from the chapter's explanation of the governance and institutional conditions necessary to sustain SICE ecosystems. Using governance theories, the chapter elaborates on the multi-actor partnerships required to sustain SICE—governments, NGOs, higher education institutions, intergovernmental organizations, and the business sector. It shows how these players economically and non-economically mitigate the elements of entrepreneurial ecosystems by providing essential resources, such as capital and education, as well as reducing barriers to entry, and providing legal frameworks and social safety nets. By detailing the functions and tasks of each stakeholder group, the chapter aids policy development and institutional frameworks. It provides recommendations on how to create enabling environments that transcend singular referrals to supportive conditions and instead support sustained systemic transformations in entrepreneurial ecosystems.

Another contribution of the chapter is the conceptualization of SICE as a mechanism of building community resilience during disasters, economic recessions, and social crises. While resilience studies center on infrastructures or humanitarian responses, this chapter considers entrepreneurship as a tool of enhancing the resilience of communities by providing them with economic and social buffers. Through the SICE ventures, the chapter demonstrates the response of communities to the global crises and thereby expands the resilience scholarship and offers policy makers the response of community-based enterprises as shock absorbers and adaptive systems. This contribution is especially relevant in times of climate crises, political turmoil, migration crises, and public health crises.

The chapter also impacts how we measure and assess entrepreneurial accomplishments. Traditional metrics have focused on profitability and growth rates, with a magnified interest on the economics, not the socioeconomic and environmental profit and loss. The chapter calls for more comprehensive forms of measuring, including community empowerment, value redistribution, environmental guardianship, gender and equity, and relational resilience. This shift in development measurement standards, especially in NGOs, funding bodies, and policymakers, has profound implications. They are challenged to value the full equation of SICE. In this sense, the chapter is a pioneer in advancing tools for measuring the impact of entrepreneurship on societal development.

Lastly, this chapter strongly focuses on the entrepreneurial processes that stem from the intersection and interplay of culture, identity, and place. Whereas global entrepreneurship literature typically attempts to apply a uniform 'one-size-fits-all' model to a diverse set of communities, this chapter shines a light on the need for locally culturally informed and inclusive contextual frameworks. This is a valuable contribution to global entrepreneurship literature, as it calls for, and provides a more principled, equitable, and in-depth understanding, of how and why particular entrepreneurial models are purposely crafted, evolve and flourish in a given setting. This is a testament that sustainability and inclusion are realizable when communities are recognized and valued as active knowledge co-creators rather than passive beneficiaries.

The chapter also furthers policy innovation by providing practical guidance for governments and SICE institutions in development planning. Recommendations include inclusive entrepreneurial policy designing; social enterprise legislation; expanding cooperative frameworks; building digital inclusiveness; and gender-transformative capacity strengthening. These policy recommendations will help in bridging the gap between academia and practice. The chapter provides policymakers with a substantial integrated approach and the means to address the development of SICE facilitative frameworks and the nurturing of SICE entrepreneurial ecosystems.

The chapter also goes beyond policy development to address the need for social entrepreneurial education that goes beyond the start-up and venture capital-led profit-oriented models of most entrepreneurship curricula. It also addresses the need for community and participatory governance and ethical frameworks with systems thinking that are important in building inclusive and sustainable economies. The chapter therefore enriches educational theory and practice.

Additionally, the chapter addresses the global academic community by shedding light on the seemingly unbridgeable gap in mainstream entrepreneurship research concerning "informal, community-based, and non-capitalistic entrepreneurship". It also questions the dominant epistemic positions that are Western, market, and solo in their focus, calling for more inclusive, contextually, and socially responsive models of entrepreneurship. Such contributions are necessary for the decolonization of entrepreneurship research, and for enriching global academic discourse with a plurality of experiences and knowledge systems.

Also, the chapter contributes to practice by presenting a conceptual framework to support the implementation of SICE in a variety of settings. The framework centres on the interlinkages of governance and social value, capability development, and ecologies of market engagement and social value to assist practitioners in the design, assessment and refinement of SICE. The chapter also has practical value in helping not only academics, but also NGOs, social leaders, social entrepreneurs, public officials, and development practitioners to address structuring multidisciplinary approaches to inclusive enterprise development.

Lastly, the chapter contributes to forthcoming studies by unveiling critical underexplored areas and outlining new avenues of scholarly pursuits in the fields of collaborative entrepreneurship, inclusive digital resources, climate adaptive initiatives, gender-equitable enterprise frameworks, and ecosystem orchestration. It calls for additional empirical work such as the SICE case studies, artificial intelligence in community-driven enterprises, and the political economy of inclusive entrepreneurship. This chapter has interdisciplinary and transformative contributions, which are multilayered. They change adjustments in theory, modify policies, illuminate innovations in practices, and inspire research in the future. By framing SICE in the chapter as a conceptual paradigm and as a working strategy, it has been explained how SICE can trigger the Inclusive Development, Community Empowerment, and Global Sustainability.

Hence, the introduction reframes SICE from a mere analytical abstraction to an operational methodology targeted at effecting transformative social and economic reconfiguration. Since countries around the world are looking at strategies against global uncertainty, the benefit of SICE lies in its ability to align entrepreneurial economies with social equity, inclusiveness, and ecological preservation—offering an apt alternative towards a more peaceful, sustainable and inclusive world.

FURTHER RESEARCH SCOPE

In terms of further work on the SICE agenda to foster deeper empirical validation and methodological variations, this discourse on evidence synthesis and case illustrations suggests the construction of mixed longitudinal studies that provide characterizations of SICE ecosystems over a certain period to aid in advancing this agenda. Such and similar inquiries would be significantly enhanced by cross-regional, cross-comparative examinations of the Global North and South which can provide insights on how the configurations of institutional structures, the cultural milieu, and the political arrangements of a society, diversify SICE framework results. Perhaps a huge challenge to advancing SICE Ecosystems is the operationalization of the complex and relational metrics of community empowerment, relational resilience, and value redistribution. Developing methodology that is at once standardized and context sensitive will help SICE researchers in developing more robust empirical studies on cross-case comparative analysis as well as policy frameworks and inclusive entrepreneurial practices that have broad-based evidence.

The role of digital platforms, artificial intelligence, and data governance in either supporting or hindering community-based inclusive enterprises, as well as the political economy of SICE, are primary frontiers of SICE practice, theory, and impact. Digital platforms, artificial intelligence, reverse data governance, and the political economy of SICE by practice theory, and impact are foundational frontiers. Emerging SICE research should pay attention to the critical asymmetries and civil institutional support and explore on the potential for market and state co-opted outcomes. The efforts of this chapter and the applied movement will provide the policy, education, and practitioner frameworks to build the SICE theory. SICE should be viewed and defended as a living and adaptive methodology to address the foundational and emerging global challenges of climate change, inequality, governance deficits, democratic deficits, migration, etc.

COMPETING INTERESTS STATEMENT

The authors declare that there are no competing interests associated with this chapter.

FUNDING STATEMENT

This research received no specific grant from any funding agency in the public, commercial, or not-for-profit sectors.

PERMISSIONS STATEMENT

All figures and tables in this chapter are original and created by the authors. No copyrighted third-party material has been used.

REFERENCES

Alka, T. A., Sreenivasan, A., & Suresh, M. (2025). Entrepreneurial strategies for sustainable growth: A deep dive into cloud-native technology and its applications. *Future Business Journal*, *11*(1), 14.

Apatan, L. B., Casicas, L. E., Jarlata, J. A. P., Panga, J. R., Ugsod, I. M. B., & Teh, C. R. (2025). Technological Advancement and its Effect on Business Operations. *Research Journal in Business and Economics*, *3*(3), 103–114.

Cash, T. A. (2025). Infrastructure development, economic growth and income inequality: Evidence from India. *Indian Growth and Development Review*, •••, 1–24.

Garcia-Jurado, A., Gálvez-Gálvez, C., & Caba-Pérez, C. (2024). Social entrepreneurship, social innovation and SDGs: Digital transformation as a catalyst for inclusive development. *Administrative Sciences*, *15*(2), 55.

Hall, J., Matos, S., Sheehan, L., & Silvestre, B. (2012). Entrepreneurship and innovation at the base of the pyramid: A recipe for inclusive growth or social exclusion? *Journal of Management Studies*, *49*(4), 785–812.

Kalkanci, B., Rahmani, M., & Toktay, L. B. (2019). The role of inclusive innovation in promoting social sustainability. *Production and Operations Management*, *28*(12), 2960–2982.

Kim, K., & Boudreaux, C. (2017). Collaborative social entrepreneurship for inclusive innovation: Lessons from South Korea. *Journal of Innovation and Entrepreneurship, 6*(7), 1–16.

Knight, F. H. (1942). Profit and entrepreneurial functions. *The Journal of Economic History, 2*(S1), 126–132.

Loku, A., & Loku, N. (2025). Globalization, automation, and the future of work: Examining the impact of technological advancements on the workforce. *Calitatea, 26*(204), 88–96.

Mahajan, R., Kumar, S., Lim, W. M., & Sareen, M. (2024). The role of business and management in driving the sustainable development goals (SDGs): Current insights and future directions from a systematic review. *Business Strategy and the Environment, 33*(5), 4493–4529.

Maier, F., Meyer, M., & Steinbereithner, M. (2014). Nonprofit organizations becoming business-like: A systematic review. *Nonprofit and Voluntary Sector Quarterly, 45*(1), 64–86.

Nagdev, K., Ahtesham, S., Paliwal, S., Smith, S., & Rajesh, A. (2025). Navigating impact: A systematic review of social entrepreneurship's journey towards sustainable development. *The International Journal of Organizational Analysis*.

Szarleta, E. (2018). Community-based entrepreneurship: Fostering innovation and inclusion through local governance partnerships. *Midwest Public Affairs Conference Journal, 22*(1), 47–62.

Thomas, A. (2024). The role of women's entrepreneurship in achieving sustainable development goals (SDGs): A comprehensive review. *Journal of Biotechnology & Bioinformatics Research, 174*(6), 2–11.

ADDITIONAL READING

Bornstein, D. (2007). *How to Change the World: Social Entrepreneurs and the Power of New Ideas*. Oxford University Press.

Defourny, J., & Nyssens, M. (2010). Conceptions of social enterprise and social entrepreneurship in Europe and the United States. *Journal of Social Entrepreneurship, 1*(1), 32–53.

Elkington, J., & Hartigan, P. (2008). *The Power of Unreasonable People: How Social Entrepreneurs Create Markets That Change the World*. Harvard Business School Press.

Mair, J., & Martí, I. (2006). Social entrepreneurship research: A source of explanation, prediction, and delight. *Journal of World Business*, *41*(1), 36–44.

Nicholls, A. (2010). The legitimacy of social entrepreneurship: Reflexive isomorphism. *Social Enterprise Journal*, *6*(2), 132–152.

OECD. (2019). *The Missing Entrepreneurs 2019*. OECD Publishing.

Peredo, A. M., & Chrisman, J. J. (2006). Toward a theory of community-based enterprise. *Academy of Management Review*, *31*(2), 309–328.

Prahalad, C. K. (2004). *The Fortune at the Bottom of the Pyramid*. Wharton School Publishing.

Sen, A. (1999). *Development as Freedom*. Oxford University Press.

Smith, B., & Stevens, C. (2010). Different types of social entrepreneurship: The role of geography and culture. *Academy of Management Review*, *35*(3), 572–576.

KEY TERMS AND DEFINITIONS

Collective Governance: A democratic decision-making system where ownership, authority, and strategic choices are shared among members of an enterprise or community group.

Community-Based Entrepreneurship (CBE): Enterprise activity owned, governed, and operated by members of a specific locality to promote local well-being, resource stewardship, and equitable economic gains.

Digital Inclusion: Equitable access to digital technologies, digital skills, and internet infrastructure, enabling marginalized communities to benefit from digital transformation.

Entrepreneurial Ecosystem: A set of interconnected actors—government, academia, markets, institutions, and civil society—that collectively enable or constrain entrepreneurial activity.

Federated Cooperative Networks: Multi-tiered alliances of cooperatives or community enterprises that coordinate resources, governance, markets, and capabilities vertically and horizontally.

Hybrid Enterprise Models: Businesses that combine commercial revenue with a social or environmental mission, reinvesting profits to advance community well-being.

Inclusive Entrepreneurship: Entrepreneurial models and policies that ensure historically marginalized groups—such as women, youth, migrants, and persons with disabilities—participate fully in entrepreneurial ecosystems.

Resilience Entrepreneurship: Entrepreneurial models that enhance a community's capacity to adapt, withstand, and recover from social, economic, or environmental crises.

Social Entrepreneurship: A mission-driven form of entrepreneurship aimed at solving social, cultural, or environmental challenges using market-based or hybrid models designed for long-term sustainability.

Sustainable Development Goals (SDGs): A global agenda of 17 goals adopted by the United Nations to eliminate poverty, reduce inequality, and promote ecological sustainability by 2030.

Chapter 6

Fostering Entrepreneurial Resilience Among Urban Street Vendors Under PM Svanidhi

Poonam Verma
https://orcid.org/0009-0001-8997-4404
National Institute of Technology, Kurukshetra, India

Geeta Sachdeva
National Institute of Technology, Kurukshetra, India

Mahabir Narwal
Kurukshetra University, India

ABSTRACT

Purpose Entrepreneurship in the informal economy is highly vulnerable to systemic shocks, as evident during the COVID-19 pandemic. Urban street vendors, who constitute one of the most visible segments of India's informal workforce, faced severe livelihood disruptions due to mobility restrictions and market closures. In response, the Government of India introduced the Pradhan Mantri Street Vendor's AtmaNirbhar Nidhi (PM SVANidhi) scheme in June 2020, designed to provide collateral-free microcredit, promote digital financial inclusion, and stabilize vendor incomes. This chapter examines the implementation and impact of PM SVANidhi in the state of Haryana through secondary data analysis, positioning it within the broader discourse on entrepreneurial resilience. The purpose is twofold: (a) to

DOI: 10.4018/979-8-3373-6991-4.ch006

assess the scale and effectiveness of the scheme in Haryana compared to national trends, and (b) to link these findings with theoretical discussions on informal entrepreneurship, resilience, and financial inclusion.

1. INTRODUCTION

Informal sector plays the pivotal role of economic lifeline in most developing countries, including South Asian region where formal employment opportunities are scarce (Sultana et al., 2022). In India, approximately ninety percent of the work force is informal sector workers and the importance of this segment as a major income generator cannot be overlooked (ILO, 2018; NSSO, 2019). Informal sector contributes considerably to the country's production with some estimates suggesting that 45-50 percent of India's GDP is contributed by informal economy (NITI Aayog, 2022). "The secret of its power is that it utilizes surplus labor, stimulates entrepreneurship, and markets urban and rural masses with good quality articles at low prices!" (Henderson, 2002).

The informal economy is not just the result of metropolitan economic systems but also a key to inclusive growth, employment creation and urban resilience. Street traders are one particularly vibrant and powerful sector among these in the large informal economy (Brown & Mcgranahan, 2016). More often found in bazaars, on the sidewalk, and along transportation routes their work links urban supply with demand by providing good quality but low priced products and services to millions of consumers (Roever 2014).

Street vending is a low-cost business that can act as a point of entry to self-employment for refugee, female or other subaltern groups who are excluded from formal labor market (Bhowmik, 2012; Roever & Skinner, 2016). Vendors are "the face of informality in cities," and their daily operation ensures livelihoods, urban health and vitality as well as socioeconomic linkages. Street vendors, a population that is typically ignored in policy and planning, make a significant contribution to the Indian economy. Their work provides up to 4.2 per cent of total urban employment. Cheap modes of consumption in cities are facilitated by vendors who guarantee the constant availability of low-priced necessities, particularly for those poor families. They provide indirect support to both formal and informal supply chains including wholesalers, small producers, and transporters (Giroux et al., 2021).

The prominence of vending has been more evident because of official acknowledgment under The Pradhan Mantri Street Vendor's AtmaNirbhar Nidhi Yojana (PM SVANidhi) scheme. As of February 2022, approximately 4.95 million vendors were found in India (Lok Sabha Unstarred Question No. 3452, March 24, 2022). Uttar Pradesh contains the highest number of vendors at 849,000, and then Haryana with

117,000. It was found that street vending is not a marginal economic activity, but rather a significant aspect of India's urban economy, with great potential for job and income generation (Patel et al., 2021). Despite their significance, street vendors are continuously faced with significant threats (The Duy & Tien Thanh, 2024). They are exposed to hazardous public space tenure, repeated eviction, seizure of property, harassment by local authorities, and limited access to institutional credit. The Street Vendors (Protection of Livelihood and Regulation of Street Vending) Act, 2014, has been enforced in a patchy way and hence denied them the right to access vending locations (Kumar, 2014). Further, growth in organised retail and e-commerce has increased competition, threatening sellers' precarious livelihoods. The COVID-19 pandemic increased these systemic exposures (Banga, & te Velde, 2020). National lockdowns and travel restrictions soon halted vending activities, cutting off the single source of livelihood for millions. Vendors underwent enormous hardship since they lacked access to cash, formal protection mechanisms, or far-away employment (Hawanga, 2024). Many migrant vendors were forced to return to the villages, while others endured prolonged unemployment (Chan, 2010). The pandemic had acted as a system shock, revealing livelihoods' vulnerability in vending and throwing into sharp relief the imperative necessity for special government schemes like the PM SVANidhi scheme (Subramanian et al., 2023).

The rising appreciation of the importance of the street vending as an inseparable part of the city informal economy and the prospective necessity to assess the interventions into the city policy justify the driving force of the current research. India has experienced rapid urbanization as a result of mass rural-to-urban migration which has put a lot of pressure in formal employment opportunities and has led to growth of informal economic activities. In this regard, vending in the streets has become an important means of self-employment and earning of millions of city poor and marginalized communities. Street vendors still find themselves in the same predicament despite their significant role in the economy of urban areas, which has been marked by unpredictable regulations, absence of social security, inability to access institutional funding, and susceptibility to economic shocks.

To address these structural issues, the Government of India introduced the Pradhan Mantri Street Vendor-AtmaNirbhar Nidhi (PM SVANidhi) Scheme in 2020 that aims to create collateral-free working capital loans and encourage digital transactions, as well as increase financial inclusion of street vendors. The plan is a major policy change in the direction of formalization and empowering the informal urban labor force. Nevertheless, the realization of the policy objectives of PM SVANidhi into the concrete results of livelihoods has not been properly examined, especially on the regional level. The city of Haryana with its different municipal arrangements, administrative capability and different degrees of it can be viewed as a critical situation within which the difference of implementation can be considered in order to assess the effectiveness of the scheme.

It is based on this that the current study assumes importance as the operational performance of street vendors, financial inclusion process, business revitalization, and stability of income, adoption of digital technologies, and sustainability of the livelihoods of street vendors in general are empirically investigated. The evaluation will be conducted in a systematic review of these areas and will seek to identify the loopholes in the policy formulation and implementation on-ground and will contribute to the more developed view of the way welfare-based financial interventions are executed in informal urban settings. The findings will be beneficial to policy makers, local governments of the cities, and financial institutions involved in the design and implementation of livelihood support programs.

Academically, the research will be useful in filling the dearth of literature analyzing the nexus of public policy assessment, financial inclusion and urban informality within the Indian context. The study is attuned to the micro-level experiences of street vendors, which enables the research to close the gaps that exist in the current research concerning the multidimensional effects of PM SVANidhi. In practice, the results should be of interest to street vendors, municipal administrators, and civil society organizations because they will help identify the difficult points of implementation, best practices, and areas that will need to be improved through the policy. Finally, the research offers context-specific solutions to the area of study, enabling the development of an inclusive urban development approach and adding to the goals of the national vision of sustainable, equitable, and independent urban growth. The following Figure 1 present the framework of PMSVANidhi Scheme.

Figure 1. Framework of the PMSVANidhi Scheme

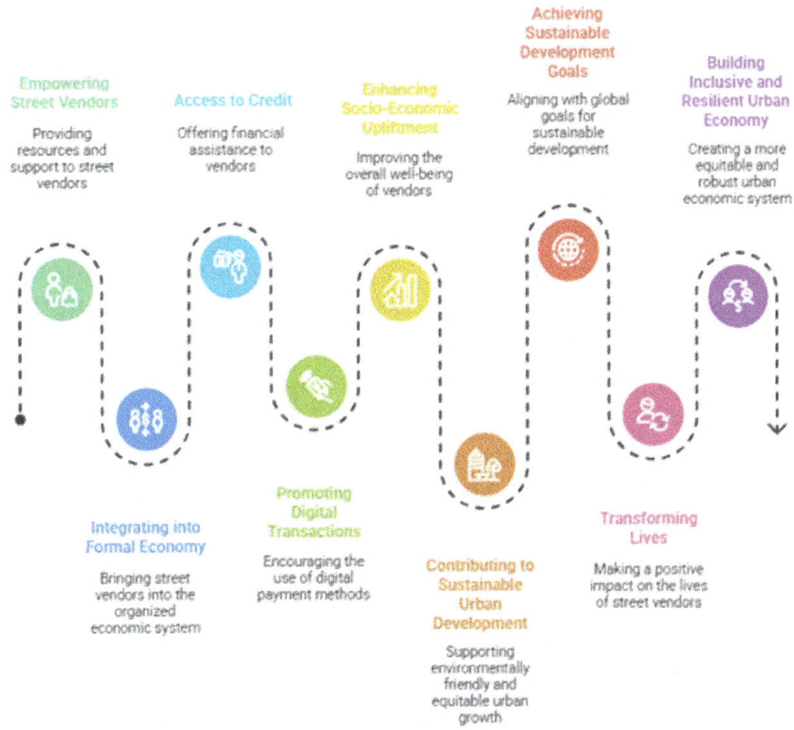

Source: Author's Own Creation

The chapter was designed in such a way that it will offer a background context regarding the topic of study, i.e., urban street vendors and the PM SVANidhi scheme. It commences by giving the extensive literature review of the study, which is the necessity of evaluating the policy interventions that are supposed to be implemented to empower the informal urban livelihoods. The development of the policy and the legal system that regulates the street vending in India is next followed by an examination of the constitutional rights and protection of street vendors. It then gives the history of the PM SVANidhi Yojana and the history of its launch and evaluates the overall developments of the scheme at the national level and the state of Haryana. The chapter also addresses major amendments and improvements made into the scheme with time such as its incorporation with the scheme of the PM SVANidhi Se Samriddhi. It also determines the key dimensions of impacts that the scheme affects the livelihoods of the urban street vendors. The chapter will end by summarizing what is known about the context of the study that will be used in the analytical framework.

2. LITERATURE REVIEW

The concept of entrepreneurial resilience is strongly becoming a critical factor to consider that helps micro-entrepreneurs, especially those involved in the informal urban economy, to survive shocks and continue in business despite unfavorable circumstances (Ayala and Manzano, 2014). As a part of the informal sector, urban street vendors are often faced with complex issues, including insecure tenancy, harassment by the government, the lack of access to credit, and sensitivity to economic changes (Bhowmik, 2012; Roever and Skinner, 2016). The lockdowns and disruptions caused by the COVID-19 pandemic particularly affected the livelihoods of the street vendors across the world forcing several to the verge of economic disintegration (Chen et al., 2021). This crisis highlights the necessity of institutional measures that would not only be used to offer solace in the short term but also create long-term entrepreneurial resilience in this risky group (Government of India Pradhan Mantri Street Vendor AtmaNirbhar Nidhi (PM SVANidhi), 2020). The scheme will help to gradually formalize activities of street vendors by means of digitization, financial inclusion, and capacity building. The multidimensional nature of PM SVANidhi, which combines financial intervention and both digital literacy and the vendor profiling, is in line with the modern definition of resilience based on interconnected financial, social, and psychological capital (Williams and Shepherd, 2016). Research indicates that access to formal financial services and especially microcredit is central in promoting the ability to withstand shocks by providing entrepreneurs with a channel to overcome liquidity crunches to invest in the enhancement of their businesses, as well as mitigating income volatility (Kumar and Roy, 2018; Mair and Marti, 2009). The fact that PM SVANidhi focuses on loans that do not require collaterals is a response to a major hindrance that street vendors formerly encountered because they did not have documentation and credit histories, which prevented their access to formal credit markets (Gupta and Das, 2022). In addition, psychosocial attitudes such as entrepreneurial self-efficacy, social networks and community support system that affect resilience are also promoted with the integration of digital payment platforms under the scheme, as it promotes transparency and financial record-keeping and increases participation in the economy (Jain and Sharma, 2022). Street vending is informal, and in most cases, it does not provide the potential the vendors to organize and fight their rights and to run the risks of being harassed and evicted (Roever & Skinner, 2016). Nevertheless, vendor networks and vendor associations have also been reported to increase resiliency at the collective level by sharing knowledge, supporting one another, and interacting with institutions of urban governance (Chen et al., 2021). In this regard, the vendor profiling and digital outreach modules of PM SVANidhi have a prospect of reinforcing social capitals by linking vendors to formal support systems and governmental benefits (Ministry of Housing and Urban Affairs,

2020).The recent empirical studies of PM SVANidhi show that they are promising but also point to the areas where improvement is needed. Jain and Sharma (2022) state that there were higher rates of loan disbursal and a positive relationship between digital transaction and loan repayment in time among beneficiaries implying greater financial discipline and strength. On the contrary, Gupta and Das (2022) spot the lack of awareness about the scheme, pending bureaucracy, and a lack of inclusion of the most marginalized vendors as the obstacles to the inclusiveness or impact of the scheme. These results support the idea that entrepreneurial resilience must be implemented in the context of a wider urban policy, which combines social protection, infrastructure access, and regulation (Roever and Skinner, 2016; Bhowmik, 2012). As an example, safe selling areas, streamlined licensing, and anti-harassment protocols can greatly decrease the structural weakness of street vendors, which will boost their ability to adapt and flourish (Chen et al., 2021). The possibility of PM SVANidhi scheme to trigger such systemic changes is in its role as a government supported platform which encourages formal recognition and financial inclusion. Nevertheless, the long-term resilience will relies on the policy commitment, multi stakeholder cooperation, and constant monitoring and evaluation of the program outcomes.Finally, the entrepreneurial resilience is to be promoted among the urban street vendors under PM SVANidhi through the combination of financial inclusion, capacity development, social support, and enabling policy environments. The available literature highlights that whereas PM SVANidhi targets the most significant financial obstacles and stimulates the process of digital formalization, it is the ability to overcome the implementation obstacles and provide social and institutional depth that will help it achieve the level of sustainable resilience. Further empirical studies using longitudinal and mixed-method designs are needed to further enhance the understanding of resilience paths and effective policy intervention strategies which would help to change the current situation in urban street vending to a more powerful and inclusive approach towards livelihood.

3. POLICY AND LEGAL FRAMEWORK EVOLUTION FOR STREET VENDORS IN INDIA

Table 1. Policy and Legal Framework Evolution for Street Vendors in India

Year	Policy	Enhanced Key Highlights
1985	"Bombay Hawkers Union and Others vs. Bombay Municipal Corporation (Supreme Court)	The Supreme Court emphasized the need for a regularized system to regulate street hawking by granting permits to vendors. To align the vendors' right to earn a livelihood with the right of walkers and convenient city movement, it directed local governments to demarcate hawking and non-hawking areas.
1989	Sodan Singh vs. New Delhi Municipal Committee	Street hawking was governed by the Indian Constitution's Article 19(1)(g) (Right to Practice Any Profession) under the Supreme Court. The right was not unrestricted, however, and could be subject to reasonable restrictions in the interest of public health, safety, and convenience. This decision was a landmark to vending as a legitimate form of independent labor.
1995	Bellagio International Declaration of Street Vendors	India signed the international declaration, which called on countries to develop national policies that are inclusive and ensure street vendors' social protection, livelihood security, and participatory planning. This was the first time informal urban labor was recognized internationally.
1998	Formationt of National Association of Street Vendors of India (NASVI)	Street vendors organized themselves to establish NASVI in order to protect their social security and rights. It played a key role in mobilizing the government, shaping national policy, and ensuring merchant representation within urban governing structures.
2004	National Policy on Urban Street Vendors, 2004 (Revised in 2009)	Street vendors were recognized as a vital part of the urban economy in the initial national policy. It advised less complex licensing arrangements, demarcation of vending areas, and Town Vending Committees (TVCs). Gender equity, inclusion, and conflict resolution mechanisms provisions were fortified in the 2009 version.
2012	Street Vendors (Protection of Livelihood and Regulation of Street Vending) Bill, 2012	Presented to Parliament for giving vendors' rights a legal backing. Through enforcement of vendor representation in decision-making, safeguarding against harassment and eviction, and rehabilitation measures in case of displacement, the Bill laid firm focus on participatory planning.
2014	Street Vendors (Protection of Livelihood and Regulation of Street Vending) Act, 2014	A landmark legislation that gives street vendors legal recognition. It mandated urban local bodies to prepare vending plans, provided protection against arbitrary eviction, and made provision for Town Vending Committees with vendor members. Around 10 million Indian vendors now have a statutory right to earn a living due to this Act.
2020	PMSVANidhi Scheme, 2020	A financial inclusion program under the Atmanirbhar Bharat Abhiyan that brings street vendors into formal credit systems through working capital loans without collateral, incentives for digital payments, and capacity building.

Source: Boruah & Aryan, 2020

The table 1 represents a chronological sequence of achieving official recognition of street vendors, starting with the judicial one in the 1980s up to the inclusion of governance and legal protection. Through the 2014 Street Vendors Act, the right to livelihood was institutionalized and the participatory approach to planning via Town Vending Committees recognised vendors. In 2020, the PM SVANidhi Scheme was a change in policy paradigm, regulation and protection gave way to empowerment and financial inclusion. The scheme enhanced livelihood security by providing easy access to microcredit, digital payment, and connecting vendors to the official financial system and introducing vendors to the notion of an inclusive, self-sustaining urban economy. Thus, the change is a paradigm shift, between controlling vendors as a threat to the stability of the urban environment to recognizing them as legitimate economic actors, and eventually empowering them to be partners in the inclusive development and digital financial revolution of India.

4. CONSTITUTIONAL RIGHTS AND SAFEGUARDS FOR STREET VENDORS

Table 2. Constitutional Rights and Safeguards for Street Vendors

Article	Provision	Relevance to Street Vendors
"Article 19(1)(g)	Right to practise any profession, or to carry on any occupation, trade, or business	Recognizes street vending as a legitimate occupation; protects vendors' right to livelihood through trade.
Article 39(a)	Citizens, men and women equally, have the right to an adequate means of livelihood	Supports equal opportunity for street vendors, ensuring their work is acknowledged as a means of livelihood.
Article 39(b)	Ownership and control of the material resources of the community are to be distributed to best serve the common good	Justifies equitable access to public spaces for vending, preventing exclusion of vendors from community resources."

Source: Boruah & Aryan, 2020

Table 2 illustrates the constitution structure of the protection of the rights of the street vendors in India. Article 19(1) (g) specifically singles out street hawking as a legitimate trade, as it keeps the right of the sellers to sell and earn a living. Also, Article 39(a) promotes the principle of equal opportunity since it recognizes vending as a respectable source of livelihood between men and women. Article 39(b) upholds this paradigm because it encourages fair allocation of community resources, such as communal spaces where vending should be permitted. A combination of all these laws empowers street hawking with a constitutional mandate that it draws upon the objective of inclusive and equitable economic growth in India and offers it legitimacy.

5. PM SVANIDHI YOJANA: BACKGROUND AND LAUNCH

On June 1, 2020, the Ministry of Housing and Urban Affairs (MoHUA) under Prime Minister Narendra Modi formally introduced the PM SVANidhi Yojana (Chattopadhyay & Kumar, 2024). It was designed as part of the AtmaNirbhar Bharat Abhiyan, a self-reliance program initiated in May 2020 to mitigate the economic impact of the COVID-19 pandemic-induced country-wide lockdown declared on March 2020. One of the worst-affected groups was street vendors, who comprise a significant part of India's unorganized economy (Chattopadhyay & Kumar, 2024). The National Sample Survey Organization (NSSO) puts the number of street vendors in urban India at approximately 1.2 crore. They make a significant contribution to local economies, though they often lack access to formal financial systems (Singh, 2018).

Their income abruptly came to an end because of the lockdown, and numerous vendors were pushed into debt traps by unlicensed moneylenders taking high-interest rates. As a response, the government launched PM SVANidhi, a microcredit program that provides low-cost, collateral-free loans to allow vendors to revive their income-earning activities. The 2014 Street Sellers (Protection of Livelihood and Regulation of Street Vending) Act, in which the rights of vendors were to be protected but which lacked funds, was the bedrock of this initiative. Though earlier, the scope were 50 lakh vendors, its success led to its extension and further expansion (Naik & Patel, 2022).

The total financing is provided by the central government for this Central Sector Scheme, which is implemented through different stakeholders like banks, Self-Help Groups (SHGs), Urban Local Bodies (ULBs), Microfinance Institutions (MFIs), and Non-Banking Financial Companies (NBFCs). SIDBI is the technical collaborator for credit guarantee and monitoring (Kandpal et al., 2023).

Objectives of the Scheme

The prime objectives of PM SVANidhi are multi-fold in nature, including economic revival, financial inclusion, and sustainable empowerment:

To Offer Collateral-Free Working Capital Loans to Street Vendors

The primary objective of PM SVANidhi scheme is to provide collateral-free working capital loans to urban street vendors to either start up or expand their microenterprises after the pandemic blowbacks The scheme will provide more credit access in the form of three tranches of loans 10,000, 20,000, and 50,000, as per credit behavior and repayment records. This form of lending is a developmental one that facilitates growth and stability of entrepreneurs and helps vendors to achieve solvency in the formal financial market (Pareek & Alok, 2024).

To Enable Economic Recovery and Foster Self-Dependence

Another important task is to enable the economic recovery of the sellers whose business was severely affected by the pandemic. The scheme allows suppliers to purchase inventory, finance working capital and maintain daily operations by injecting finance into the small and medium enterprises (Chinta, 2019). It aims to make the self-sufficient (AtmaNirbharata) by strengthening individual business possibilities, reducing dependence on illegal moneylenders, and establishing new sources of long-term sources of income (Chinta, 2019). It aligns with the vision of the country in making unofficial micro businesses to act as economic units of the city.

To Promote Digital Financial Literacy and Inclusion

PM SVANidhi intends to capture street vendors in the formal and digital financial market through rewarding digital payments and UPI-based RuPay cards (Gopal and Davidson, 2025). Digital payment is made by offering cashback to the vendors at the end of every month to motivate the behavior of buyers who have transitioned to cashless payment (Gopal & Davidson, 2025). Further, vendors are aware of digital banking and credit terms, repayment processes due to financial education training of the program to ensure financial inclusion is sustainable and accessible. Such a digital integration facilitates enhanced access to government support programs, accountability, and transparency (Aithal, 2024).

To Ensure Integration of street Vendors with Formal Credit Systems

The street vendors have traditionally relied on disorganized and high-cost loaning mechanisms that have culminated into debt traps and financial susceptibility (Labitad, 2025). The PM SVANidhi program addresses this gap by creating direct connections between street vendors and banks, microfinance organizations and non-banking financial institutions (NBFCs) (Muhammed Shafi et al., 2024). This factor in conjunction with the provision of the vendors with access to cheap funds enables them to create a credit history, which gives them access to more loans. The project merges this part with the mainstream financial system of the urban economy in India by extending its financial action into the system through regularization.

To Promote Timely Repayment and Credit Discipline

This is one of the only features of PM SVANidhi, a system of rewarding vendors when they repay the loans on time (Variyava, 2025). Other than being eligible to the next higher credit tranche, timely repayment of borrowed money by the borrowers could also enable them to be eligible to a rate rebate of 7 percent a year. The strategy reduces the chances of default, enhances financial discipline and makes borrowers feel responsible. The program makes sure that street vendors transform themselves into responsible micro-entrepreneurs in the credit system by matching financial assistance with behavioral compensations (Madhav & Majithia, 2023).

To Enhance Urban Livelihoods and Economic Resilience

For a most vulnerable group of workers, PM SVANidhi offers constant support in terms of finance and institutions, which are critical to strengthening urban livelihood resilience (Pareek & Alok, 2024). The initiative helps vendors in adapting to changing market conditions, expanding their sources of income, and damping shocks through the provision of working capital. This directly sustains the generation of jobs, microeconomic stability, and combating urban poverty, all of which align with the Indian pledge for inclusive urban development and SDG 8 (Decent Work and Economic Growth) (Dev, 2021).

Eligibility Criteria

The eligibility factors in PM SVANidhi scheme include geographical, institutional as well as financial factors which make the scheme cover all the urban street vendors. The scheme applies to those street vendors working within the boundaries of municipal localities, such as statutory towns, census towns, and peri-urban townships as stated by the respective State/UT governments. The criteria are mainly limited to the identification and certification of vendors under the terms of the Street Vendors (Protection of Livelihood and Regulation of Street Vending) Act, 2014 under which any vendor who holds a valid Certificate of Vending (CoV) or Identity Card issued by the respective Town Vending Committee (TVC) or Urban Local Body (ULB) is automatically eligible since the CoV formally accepts their right to vend in their respective locations. Moreover, all vendors that were surveyed in the ULB/TVC surveys prior to March 24, 2020, but have yet to receive a CoV, are also eligible and receive a Provisional Certificate of Vending to access loans under the scheme. Financially, to access the scheme, the applicant should be at the age of eighteen years, and have an Aadhaar-linked bank account, and the scheme is inclusive of first-time borrowers as it does not need any collateral or the history of previous borrowing. The linkages of credit are supported by Scheduled Commercial Banks, Regional Rural Banks, Small Finance Banks, Microfinance Institutions, and Non-Banking Financial Companies, and in order to maintain the transparency and effective monitoring, each qualified vendor will be assigned with an individual application number and registered on PM SVANidhi portal.

Loan Structure and Amount

The loan facility provided under PM SVANidhi scheme will be in a form of three progressive tranches to promote credit discipline and foster incremental business expansion amongst the street vendors. The initial working capital loan is the first tranche, which provides a loan of up to 10,000 to meet urgent needs including the purchase of raw materials, stock, or simple equipment to restart the vending business; this loan is not secured, not subject to collateral, a loan has a tenure of 1 year, repayable in monthly instalments (EMI), and with interest determined by the lending bank, which is usually approximately 7 percent per annum. When the first loan is fully paid and at the right time, the vendors will be entitled to the second tranche that comes with an improved loan facility of up to 20,000 to grow and increase their operations. In addition, sellers with good level of repayment record on the first two tranches are allowed to access the third tranche where they get more credit of up to 50000 which will encourage business expansion, economic stability and long term enhancement of livelihoods.

Benefits and Incentives

The PM SVANidhi program includes a variety of interest subsidies, incentives and risk mitigation mechanisms to make it more affordable, increase digital inclusivity, and motivate lenders to join. The Government of India offers an annual interest subsidy of 7 percent in order to motivate early or on-time repayment, and is done quarterly by Direct Benefit Transfer (DBT) account into the bank accounts of beneficiaries. Besides this, to encourage digital transactions, it provides monthly cashback incentives, 50 transactions, 100 transactions and 200 or more transactions in a month attract 50 cashback, 100 cashback and 100 cashback respectively. This scheme is also sustained by the powerful credit guarantee system by means of the Credit Guarantee Fund Trust of Micro and Small Enterprises (CGTMSE) which offers guarantee coverage to lending banks and minimizes their risk of credit thus encouraging loans as informal vendors with no security or previous credit record. In addition to financial incentives, the scheme also contains a number of ancillary benefits, such as integration with social security schemes such as PMSBY to provide accident insurance, PMJJBY to provide life insurance, and linkages with PMJDY to provide zero-balance accounts, as well as the SVANidhi se Samriddhi component, which links the vendors to welfare schemes like Ayushman Bharat to get health insurance. Also, the vendors enjoy the benefits of training and skill development programs including hygiene, digital literacy, and business management, and regular loan repayments to develop formal credit history, and better CIBIL scores, which will result in access to larger credits in the future; importantly, there are no processing fees and the lenders are compensated on guarantee costs, which will lead to wide institutional participation.

Application Process

Application under the PM SVANidhi scheme is meant to be easy and inclusive and with a digital first approach so that the street vendors can easily access it. Individual vendors are able to apply online using the official portal (pmsvanidhi.mohua.gov.in), the PM SVANidhi mobile application, or the UMANG app by registering with an Aadhaar-linked mobile number and by undergoing e-KYC using an Aadhaar-based OTP authentication. In addition to aadhaar (compulsory), vendor ID/ certificate of vending or letter of recommendation by the ULB, a copy of the residence such as voter ID, a bank passbook or driving license, and bank account information to transfer loans directly to the account are mandatory. The applicants are then given the option of the type of lending institution they prefer which may include a broad list of public and private banks, Regional Rural Banks, NBFCs, MFIs and Self-Help Groups and then the applications are normally processed within a duration of 30 days and the approved funds are directly deposited into the bank account of the beneficiary. In the case of vendors that do not have digital access, Common Service Centers (CSCs), Urban Local Bodies, and bank branches provide offline support to applications. The scheme is implemented in a collaborative format with the MoHUA as the policy overseer, ULBs and Town Vending Committes as the vendor identification and certification body, over 200 lending institutions as the credit delivery body, SIDBI as the technical support, dashboard monitoring and credit guarantee broker and even though the scheme was initially focused on urban areas, it was subsequently expanded to rural areas through District Urban Development Agencies (DUDA).

6. OVERALL PROGRESS OF PMSVANIDHI SCHEME IN INDIA

Table 3. Overall Progress of PMSVANidhi Scheme in India from Year 2020 to 2025

States	Eligible Loan Applications	Loans Sanctioned	Loans Disbursed	Disbursed Amount (Rs. in Crore)	Loans Repaid
Andaman and Nicobar Islands	1156	1039	1019	1.87	721
Andhra Pradesh	549345	533885	521555	783.23	248625
Arunachal Pradesh	9262	7858	7539	12.57	5132
Assam	201056	182062	179223	267.33	90760
Bihar	249929	168297	162808	209.29	68739
Chandigarh	10404	8756	8481	14.3	5238
Chhattisgarh	171694	133086	129013	188.38	66908
Delhi	377253	251840	236400	297.24	94619
Goa	3136	2785	2703	4.82	1777
Gujarat	875945	709945	692431	1030	351705
Haryana	324268	214525	206056	261.43	72126
Himachal Pradesh	11609	10185	10020	18.94	6143
Jammu and Kashmir	36346	28809	27750	46.89	17908
Jharkhand	155815	111413	109594	144.26	46393
Karnataka	677379	588429	562027	827.57	294183
Kerala	180776	157295	152783	196.62	62942
Ladakh	955	826	802	1.46	514
Madhya Pradesh	1580203	1381515	1342137	2067.55	637557
Maharashtra	1312663	1140778	1085003	1410.91	432714
Manipur	18121	14077	13975	19.96	8982
Meghalaya	7094	5283	5194	7.16	2482
Mizoram	4435	3615	3458	4.7	1692
Nagaland	7862	4877	4791	6.82	2840
Odisha	123584	103159	99488	154.59	52186
Puducherry	6207	5397	5280	8.1	2417
Punjab	249872	224345	213854	275.31	83973
Rajasthan	324220	250705	244391	312.08	131721
Sikkim	1696	1516	1481	1.74	585
Tamil Nadu	771202	577203	565552	808.07	284744
Telangana	793361	728184	720581	1227.25	428613

continued on following page

Table 3. Continued

Dadra and Nagar Haveli and Daman and Diu	3475	3329	3305	4.85	1679
Tripura	10117	8261	8104	12.13	3958
Uttar Pradesh	2066762	2015916	1993366	2810.06	919030
Uttarakhand	56885	43586	42692	65.36	21491
West Bengal	316025	242033	236639	269.84	83375
Grand Total	**11490112**	**9864814**	**9599495**	**13772.66**	**4534472**

Source: data.gov.in

Table 3 focuses on the total development of the PM SVANidhi scheme throughout India between 2020 and 2025 and brings attention to the magnitude, reach, and the financial success of the programme. On the national level, it received over 1.14 crore eligible loan applications, and 98.65 lakh loans were sanctioned and 95.99 lakh loans were disbursed with a total disbursed amount of 13,772.66 crore. This depicts high rate of eligibility to disbursement and this implies good institutional performance and the demand of formal credit among the street vendors. Also, the outstanding 45.34 lakh loans repayment indicates reasonable repayment discipline which implies that the beneficiaries can have enough to earn to repay their loans.

Inter-state analysis reveals a great variation in states. Uttar Pradesh is the best performing state in absolute terms with more than 20.6 lakh eligible applications, 19.9 lakh loans disbursed and highest disbursement of 2810.06 crore which is an indication of a big urban informal sector and high administrative penetration of the scheme. Other large states like Madhya Pradesh, Maharashtra, Telangana, Tamil Nadu, Karnataka and Gujarat also demonstrate performance of significant magnitude as each one of them spends over 800 crore as PM SVANidhi, which means that it is widely adopted in large urban economies. On the other hand, smaller states and Union Territories like Ladakh, Sikkim, Andaman and Nicobar Islands, and Goa record lower figures which is anticipated considering that they have few vendors.

Regional-wise, Haryana has a moderately, but significantly good performance with more than 3.24 lakh eligible applications, 2.06 lakh loans disbursed, and 261.43 crore released, which means that the scheme is implemented well, although there is still an opportunity to enhance it. The repayment rates in most states show that PM SVANidhi loans are being utilized to a large proportion on productive activities and this supports the argument that the scheme has facilitated income stability and resilience of livelihoods. In general, the evidence highlights PM SVANidhi as a massive, broad-based microfinance initiative that has greatly empowered financial and economic inclusion and recovery of urban street vendors in India.

REVISION OF PM SVANIDHI: TIMELINE AND ENHANCED FEATURES

The PM SVANidhi scheme, launched for the first time in June 2020, intended to provide working capital support to urban street vendors impacted by the COVID-19 pandemic (Kumar & Roy, 2018). Understanding the evolving economic needs of street vendors and the shortcomings of the initial scheme, the Union Cabinet sanctioned a new restructuring and upscaling of the scheme in August 2025. The restructuring amended the scheme's period until March 31, 2030 and introduced improvements in terms of loan structures, digital incentives, coverage, capacity building, and welfare linkages, targeting 1.15 crore street vendors, 50 lakh of whom will be new beneficiaries (Abhiyan, 2017). The revised framework benefits not only the fiscal needs of vendors but also the SVANidhi → SVANidhi se Samriddhi channel, promoting livelihood resilience and social emancipation (Madhav & Majithia, 2023).

Objectives of the Revised Loan Framework

The major goal of the modified loan framework under PM SVANidhi scheme is to provide a sustained and stress-free access to working capital to the street vendors without the need to have any security of any kind, thus catering to their short term and long term financial demands. The scheme enhances expansion and long-term development of businesses of micro-enterprises in the informal sector by gradually expanding the credit eligibility with regard to repayment performance. It also ensures that people pay in time and in the process borrow responsibly since the discipline of the credit is directly correlated with the right to borrow more loan and other incentives. At the same time, the building stimulates the usage of cashless and card-based payments, enhancing the process of digital financial inclusion of street vendors. In general, the plan is to instill a culture of discipline in credit and frequent repayment among the unorganized sector, which will allow the vendors to slowly be absorbed to the formal financial system.

Progressive Tranche-Based Credit Access

In the updated PM SVANidhi loan scheme, the credit facility is still tiered and progressive, whereby with proper behavior in repaying and performance in business, the street vendors can gradually take higher levels of finance. The first tranche provides an initial fully collateral-free loan up to 15000 rupees to all qualified vendors checked by Urban Local Bodies (ULBs) in order to be able to meet short-term working capital needs (buying goods, raw materials or small equipment); the loan has a term of 12 months, interest rate, according to the lending institutions, (usually between 7 and 12 percent interest per annum) and 7 percent interest subsidy, which is reimbursed at 7 percent per quarter through Direct Benefit Transfer (DBT The second tranche is offered to vendors that repay first tranche on time and with an acceptable repayment history to take a growth-focused loan of up to 25,000 dollars to engage in business expansion activities such as inventory improvement, product diversification, or equipment upgrades, with a flexible tenure of 12-18 months and any additional use of interest subsidies and cashback benefits provided on digital transactions. The third tranche is an expansion loan up to 50,000 rupees to the vendors who have proven themselves to have good credit discipline in the first two tranches to increase their business scale, invest long-term in the vending assets or develop their operations in a less formalized form; they provide a tenure up to 24 months and fully collateral-free and facilitated through the Credit Guarantee Fund Trust of Micro and Small Enterprises (CGTMSE).

Incentive Mechanism

The PM SVANidhi scheme of 2025 includes a significant digital transformation in the form of a RuPay Credit Card connected to UPI and provides eligible street vendors with a credit limit of up to 30,000, which will provide cashless payments, access to credit online, and better liquidity management in the short term and contribute to further financial inclusion (Kant, 2024; Silvestro and Lustrato, 2014). The new loan structure also includes a flexible repayment process to provide the expected flexibility of repayment, as the irregular income dispersion of street vendors necessitates them to have the choice to repay their loans monthly, bi-monthly, or quarterly depending on the cash flow and seasonal business patterns. The scheme, further, encourages timely repayment by providing reward points and allowing higher loan limits, and timely repayment guarantees the extension of the 7 percent annual interest subsidy, subsequent tranches of loan, better credit scores, and enhanced connection to formal financial services, all of which strengthen credit discipline and sustainable development of livelihoods in the informal-sector vendors.

7. INTEGRATION OF PMSVANIDHI WITH "PMSVANIDHI SE SAMRIDDHI"

The Ministry of Housing and Urban Affairs (MoHUA) launched PM SVANidhi se Samriddhi in January 2022 with the goal of converting the PM SVANidhi scheme from a microcredit program into a complete socio-economic upliftment program. In addition to helping street vendors recover, the word "Samriddhi," which means prosperity, represents the government of India's goal of assisting them in moving closer to long-term financial stability and social well-being.

The eight main Central Government welfare programs are systematically connected with street vendors who have taken out loans under PM SVANidhi as part of this integrated approach, guaranteeing people access to vital livelihood and social protection services. Among them are:

a) Pradhan Mantri Jeevan Jyoti Bima Yojana (PMJJBY)
b) Pradhan Mantri Suraksha Bima Yojana (PMSBY)
c) Pradhan Mantri Jan Dhan Yojana (PMJDY)
d) Pradhan Mantri Shram Yogi Maandhan Yojana (PM-SYM)
e) Pradhan Mantri Matru Vandana Yojana (PMMVY)
f) Janani Suraksha Yojana (JSY)
g) One Nation One Ration Card (ONORC)
h) Building and Other Construction Workers (BOCW) Welfare Schemes

8. IMPACT DIMENSIONS OF PMSVANIDHI

Income Stability

Income Stability is a concept that defines stability and predictability of the earnings of an individual or a household over a given time (Cutright, 1971). According to Roll et al. (2022), it represents low income volatility and is normally linked with economic stability, consumer confidence, and reduced chances of financial difficulties. Among the primary objectives of PM SVANidhi, the rapid provision of financial resources to cover the revenues of the vendors should be mentioned. Kumar and Selvam suggest that access to loans allowed merchants to experience faster recoveries amid pandemic-related financial losses, which means that they will be able to refill their inventory and resume their operations (2023). According to Mukherjee (2021), the use of predictable repayment plans and interest subsidies reduced reliance on informal lenders, the interest rates of whom were usually rose high. Prakash (2024) noted that loan vendors had Income Stability, as well as improved financial planning which led to household stability, especially in terms of monthly changes. Similarly, Paliwal et al. (2024) highlighted the psychological benefits of income security, reporting that vendors with financial support showed increased business confidence and greater willingness to invest in business upgrades. The following Figure 2 shows the component of Income Stability.

Figure 2. Components of Income Stability

Source: Author's Own Creation

PMSVANidhi Effect on the Income Stability

The literature is coherent and shows that there is a positive correlation between the PM SVANidhi scheme and Income Stability among street vendors (Shridhar, 2024; Pareek & Alok, 2024; Shukla, 2023). The program as a financial recovery measure has been at the forefront in rebuilding financial stability as well as streamlining income in the wake of economic shocks. Hasan and Alam (2015) showed that the availability of working capital loans without collaterals helped vendors to restock their inventories, stabilize their cash flow and restart operations without high reliance on informal credit sources. This change to formal borrowing helped to produce more predictable flows of income and this would reduce the risks posed by unregulated lending practices. In the same vein, Kiran and Babu (2019) have observed that the scheme was a cushion against income volatility that increased further during the pandemic enabling vendors to restore regular revenue flows and maintaining household consumption rates.

Increased entrepreneurial potential and financial self-sufficiency is also a predictor of the correlation between PM SVANidhi and Income Stability (Shridhar, 2024; Pareek and Alok, 2024; Shukla, 2023). Chakraborty and Koley (2018) remarked that access to formal credit by PM SVANidhi improved managerial and operational resources that assisted vendors to deal with inventories, expenditure planning, and customer expansion. This operational enhancement came in the form of increased income predictability and business sustainability. The findings of Apum et al. (2023) and Kumar & Roy (2018). also permit saying that PM SVANidhi was not only providing liquidity in the short-term perspective but also facilitating long-term transition to Financial Inclusion and responsible credit practices. Sellers who used to deal with informal lenders started using formal repaying methods and using digital payment, which encouraged transparency and income growth in the long-run.

This observed effect is in line with scholarly evaluations of Financial Inclusion and resilience of the informal sector (Bhowmik, 2012; 2013; Mukherjee, 2015). The previous Bhowmik studies highlighted the institutional credit limitation as the inhibitor of the ability of vendors to stabilize their income and grow their business. Formal credit under PM SVANidhi was actually a successful solution to this structural gap, as it meant that informal finance with its exploitative nature was no longer needed and a regular income could be earned. Another issue that Mukherjee (2015) raised was the fact that regular access to microfinance enables vendors to stabilize the income fluctuations and create business resilience, which are the consequences of PM SVANidhi implementation.

BUSINESS REVITALIZATION

Business Revitalization is the tactical re-creating of the activities, sales or economic stability of a firm sequentially as a response to deterioration or disturbance (Hahen & Tampe, 2021). Some of the measures are product innovation, re-entry into the market, resource optimisation, and growth-enabling activities (Ibidunni et al., 2022). Regarding resilience, reviving businesses, which is often ignored by the conventional measurement, is necessary. Over 68% of the vendors consumed the loan to replenish, enhance infrastructure (including better stalls), or more diversify their product range, according to the research of Saini et al. (2024). Setyaningsih et al. (2019) and Amiri et al. (2023) demonstrated that formal loans enhanced the quality of services of merchants, which brought in more clients. According to Sutton (2010) even these small financial boosts at critical points of time may have the significant effect on the sustainability of a micro-business, which is supported by post-pandemic recovery accounts under PM SVANidhi. Thai et al. (2021) also reported that the credit provided through the initiative improved the relationship with the local authorities and suppliers to aid in the reactivation of the companies. The Business Revitalization Strategies is shown in the following figure 3.

Figure 3. Business Revitalization Strategies

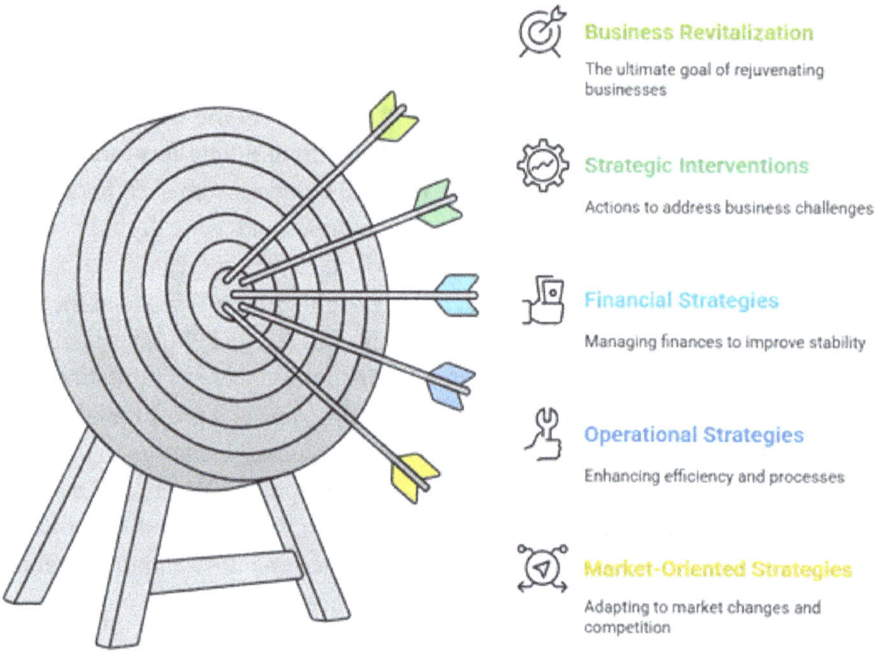

Source: Author's Own Creation

Effect of PMSVANidhi on Business Revitalization

The PM SVANidhi program has been highly perceived as a Business Revitalization stimulus of the urban street vendors especially in the post-pandemic environment (Shridhar, 2024; Gopal and Davidson, 2025). As per empirical research, the program allowed vendors to rebuild and reintegrate their businesses and was directly linked to the recovery of micro-enterprises that had suffered a serious blow (Hasan and Alam, 2015; Kiran and Babu, 2019). The scheme enhanced the functioning capabilities of vendors by funding stock replacement, refurbishing or enhancing vending infrastructure, and product diversification to enable them to recover the lost customers and stabilize their operations (Chakraborty & Koley, 2018).

The researches indicate that the ability of the vendors to redefine the business processes within the framework of PM SVANidhi is connected with the systematic financial access and gradual payment of the loans. Incremental loan cycles discovered by Selvi andVeilatchi (2020) as the vendors invested continually in the business development, such as purchasing additional stocks or providing more suitable services to their customers rather than adhering to survival strategies only. Such systematic approach facilitated a slow recovery trend that helped firms to redirect their attention on crisis response to expansion policies. Similarly, Joshi et al. (2021) reported that beneficiaries believed that the scheme was essential in rejuvenating business activity, in which the availability of credit at the appropriate time facilitated them to recover the trade operation, maintain supply chains steady, and regain trust in the market.

The study conducted by Apum et al. (2023) and Kumar & Roy (2018) also indicates the relationship between Business Revitalization and financial support. Formal credit has not just reduced the necessity to rely on informal lenders, but it also assisted the vendors to employ new mechanisms of inventory management and purchase goods of high quality and access new customer groups. This access stimulated the tactical re-investment in the businesses which advanced the Operational Efficiency and the long-term resiliency. Another point Ghosh (2024) has made is that the inclusion of the scheme in formal banking and digital solutions has facilitated better sales monitoring by vendors, expenditure control and business decision-making processes that in turn helped to revitalize micro-enterprises.

These findings are supported with historical literature on Financial Inclusion. Bhowmik and Saha (2011, 2013) emphasized that historical inability to access institutional finance limited the ability of vendors to sustain and expand their businesses most of the time leading to stagnation or deterioration. These systemic limitations are directly addressed by the infusion of structured credit under PM SVANidhi which allows vendors to turn back revenue streams lost and allows incremental business growth. In a similar claim, Mukherjee (2015) also indicated that microfinance interventions enable small scale entrepreneurs to restore operations, minimize downtime, and stabilize business processes, which are reflected in the implementation of PM SVANidhi.

FINANCIAL INCLUSION

Financial Inclusion has been defined as an accessibility and affordability of useful and affordable financial products and services to everyone and any business, including credit, savings, insurance, and digital payments (Durai and Stella, 2019). It is needed to enhance economic participation, reduce inequality, and enhance economic development (Arora, 2018). Financial Inclusion is one of the key policy pillars at PM SVANidhi. This has led to various vendors being refused access to formal banking at least in the past due to a lack of documentation or credit history. This type of exclusion cuts off access to social services of the state and vertical mobility (Kalunda, 2014; Goel and Sharma, 2017). According to Pomeroy et al. (2020), programs that link unorganized workers to formal banking and digital identities greatly expand their access to mainstream insurance and credit. For direct benefit payments, PM SVANidhi advises vendors to use their Aadhaar and Jan Dhan accounts. More than 60% of merchants used valid bank accounts to access the program, according to Amiri et al. (2023) and Saini et al. (2024). Policy links were also made possible by the fact that recipients received tailored reminders regarding further welfare payments. The following figure 4 underscore the components of Financial Inclusion.

Figure 4. Components of Financial Inclusion

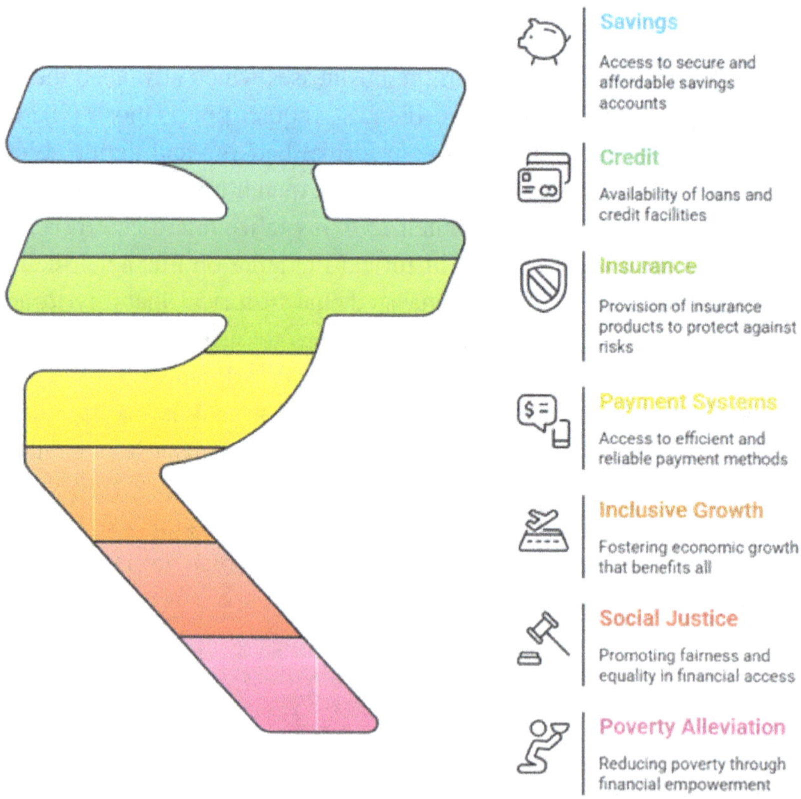

Source: Author's Own Creation

Impact of PMSVANidhi on Financial Inclusion

Financial Inclusion Financial Inclusion among urban street vendors has been greatly enhanced through the PM SVANidhi scheme, and a long-standing marginalized workforce has been incorporated into the formal banking system (Shridhar, 2024). There is empirical evidence that access to collateral-free loans and digital finances as part of the program has allowed vendors to establish formal financial connection, enhance their credit worthiness, and have sustained access to institutional finance (Apum et al., 2023; Kumar and Roy, 2018; Ghosh, 2024). The scheme promotes both financial empowerment and economic resilience by moving vendors who are in the informal credit to the formal banking system.

Bhowmik (2013) emphasized that the historical marginalization of street vendors by formal finance continued to limit businesses to high interest informal loans, limiting business growth and Income Stability. PM SVANidhi will counter such structural barriers through the creation of first time formal access to credit so that the vendors can join the banking sector and develop credit histories. Such formalization is essential as it enables vendors to advance to more lucrative loans over time, diminishes the willingness to become prey of rogue lenders, and promotes responsible finances (Hasan et al., 2015).

The campaign is also oriented to digital Financial Inclusion that is free of charge to credit access. Studies by Chakraborty and Koley (2018) and Kumar & Roy, (2018) show that the introduction of digital payment systems (i. e. QR-based transactions and online payment systems) enhances transparency, eases business, and reduces the risks of handling cash. Not only can this integration improve Operational Efficiency, but it also gives vendors access to formal financial institutions that boost financial literacy and inclusion. Apum et al. (2023) also state that the digital dimension enables the vendors to track transactions, manage cash flows, and invest in it more productively, which eventually leads to their participation in formal financial networks.

The PM SVANidhi is not only remarkably linked to the Financial Inclusion to the individual level of benefits but also to the broader socioeconomic enhancement. The scheme as Ghosh (2024) explains identifies street vendors as economic participants, which enable them to receive credit, banking services, and institutional resources. As Joshi et al. (2021) explain, these financial instruments enable beneficiaries to think that they would be free to become entrepreneurs, discipline their repayments, and get a foundation to financial planning later. All these mechanisms increase the capacity of the vendors to engage in formal economic activities, to invest in business growth, and to stabilize the flows of income, which shows how Financial Inclusion and livelihood resilience are intertwined.

DIGITAL FINANCIAL TRANSACTIONS

Digital Financial Transactions refer to the transactions carried out over an online platform, including digital wallets, UPI, online and mobile banking, and point-of-sale systems. It is valued because they are efficient, fast, open, and can promote access to financial services (Kumar & Roy, 2018). PM SVANidhi is the first effort designed to increase awareness and speed up the unorganized sector's adoption of digital currency. By facilitating onboarding through QR codes and UPI and providing cashback incentives, it incentivizes retailers to accept digital payments. Following the intervention, the adoption of digital payments among urban street vendors improved by 30–40%, as stated by Jayaraj &Bhat, 2024). Mir and Wani (2025) found that suppliers having digital footprints were more likely to be deemed "creditworthy" by banks and NBFCs. K.M. et al. (2024) found that digital payment use was greater among younger merchants and those operating in metropolitan commercial hubs. Rahman and Sadik (2024) noted that these digital practices boosted consumer happiness, increased transaction transparency, and provided real-time financial tracking. The following figure 5 presents how Digital Financial Transactions transforms informal economy.

Figure 5. Digital Finance Transforms Informal Economy

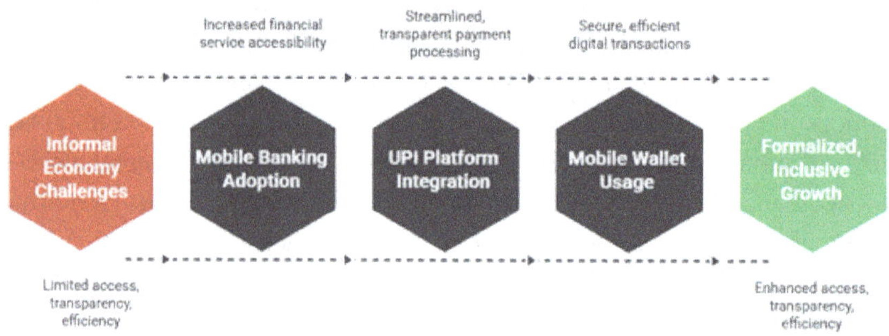

Source: Author's Own Creation

Impact of PMSVANidhi on Digital Financial Transactions

The PM SVANidhi program has played a significant role in enhancing the rate of digital financial adoption among the urban street vendors and creating a significant relationship between the technological use and Operational Efficiency. Empirical studies show that the program integration of the digital payment solutions such as-the QR-based transaction and mobile banking has made the vendors migrate to the formal digital manner of operation that will result in making their transactions more transparent and will enhance their records and financial discipline (Chakraborty and Koley, 2018; Apum et al., 2023; Kumar & Roy, 2018). The digital transformation is associated in this case with a more predictable stream of revenue and the ability to efficiently control the business, contributing to the overall revenue and business stabilization purpose.

Research indicates that the enhanced business is a direct result of the digital adoption of finances. Vendors can track the daily sales, reconcile cash flows, and plan acquiring inventory more efficiently with the assistance of mobile wallets, UPI payments, and such services as online repayment (Chakraborty and Koley, 2018). As Apum et al. (2023) also note, such tools will reduce the turnover to informal channels of credit, reduce the error in the transaction, and improve the tendency to pay in time. The net effect of these digital interventions would be the improved fusion of financial management and operational planning, which is polluting both Income Stability and Business Revitalization.

Another impact of PM SVANidhi is to extend the influence of digital financial integration to long-term financial literacy and inclusion. According to Kumar & Roy (2018). vendors that conduct transactions with digital platforms familiarize themselves with the banking mechanism, monitoring of transactions, and formal use of credit. This is the knowledge that does not just make the usage of PM SVANidhi loans effective but also prepares the vendors to provide more financial services in the future, including insurance, savings and credit of higher value of better value, hence, digital literacy becomes a part of the livelihood resilience.

Besides this, accountability and transparency that are brought about by the Digital Financial Transactions of the scheme are quite significant to the long-term expansion of the operations. Ghosh (2024) observes that via digital records, vendors and financial institutions are readily able to track the financial flows and reduce conflict and instill confidence on formal credit mechanisms. This transparency also increases the possibilities of the vendors to plan their expenditure, how they distribute their resources strategically and maximize business processes, which strengthens the relationship between digital adoption and business performance.

OPERATIONAL EFFICIENCY

Operational Efficiency is, the ability of an organization or an individual to provide goods or services using the minimum input possible and optimum output and quality. This is normally measured in terms of cost per output, turnaround time, and use of resources (Kumar & Roy, 2018Operational Efficiency is often an indirect outcome of formalization. Vendors learn about organized business administration by filling up forms, establishing their identity, and being exposed to structured repayment processes. Auramo et al. (2004) and Liu et al. (2021) show that small enterprises that adhere to core operational standards (such as stock management and sales reporting) have better revenue per transaction. Saini et al. (2024) discovered that PM SVANidhi recipients eventually followed similar practices, particularly those who advanced to the second loan tranche. Vendors also claimed to have improved their time management, financial discipline, and contacts with customers. The following figure 6 shows the components of Operational Efficiency.

Figure 6. Components of Operational Efficiency

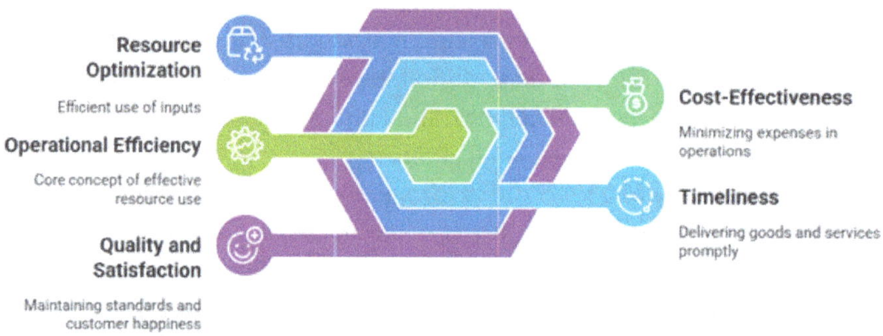

Source: Author's Own Creation

Effect of PMSVANidhi on Operation Efficiency

It has been established that the PM SVANidhi programme has had an influence on Operation Efficiency in the street vendors of the urban regions by providing centralized financial support and promoting the need to utilize digitalized means of controlling the business enterprise. Studies show that access to collateral-free working capital can facilitate the vendors in ensuring the running of day-to-day activities, the suitable amounts of inventory, and in the capacity to deliver improved response to customer demand thereby improving the performance of the operations (Hasan and Alam, 2015; Chakraborty and Koley, 2018). This scheme eases the liquidity pressures on the vendors, therefore, removing the necessity of having to use stopgap provisions or informal lending to run business operations, facilitating a more systematic planning and conduct of business operations.

There is empirical evidence of a close correlation between PM SVANidhi interventions and improved business processes. According to Selvi and Veilatchi (2020), vendors that used several loan cycles could plan supply chains, sales strategies, and minimize downtimes when there was no stock. This premeditated distribution of working capital is translated into increased productivity and easy operations, which are major signs of Operational Efficiency. Equally, Chakraborty and Koley (2018) indicated that the implementation of digital transaction under the scheme enables real time tracking of sales and expenditures, reduced errors, better control of cash flows and making of informed decisions in the daily operations of the business.

Operational Efficiency is also further promoted by the fact that the scheme focuses on the use of digital financial tools. As Kumar & Roy (2018) emphasized, QR based payments and online repayment mechanisms make transactions easier and simplify all manual bookkeeping, as well as allow the accountant to reconcile with the vendor. Such technological interventions also save time in terms of transactions giving the vendors time to concentrate on the main business operations and customers. As Apum et al. (2023) observed, vendors who used digital channels could monitor their business performance in a systematic way and determine patterns in their sales, as well as in planning seasonal or market changes, which would be directly related to the effective running of business.

Moreover, organized financial access via PM SVANidhi is aimed at optimization of the resources. According to Hasan and Alam (2015), vendors utilized the loan proceeds to stock up the products in bulk, renovate or renovate the carts and equipment, and offer more products, which leads to the better use of the available resources. Besides improving productivity, this operation factor also minimizes the variability of income by ensuring that the vendors are ready to accommodate the changing demand base without interruptions to operational activities.

9. CONCLUSION, IMPLICATIONS AND FUTURE RESEARCH DIRECTIONS

This paper attempted to critically analyze the design, implementation and results of the PM SVANidhi scheme with a particular emphasis on how it has enhanced the economic resilience of urban street vendors. Through examining the concept of eligibility norms, progressive loan schemes, interest concessions, digital incentives, credit guarantees, and repayment schemes, the paper points out how PM SVANidhi has progressed over the years as a short-term relief scheme onto a structured financial inclusion tool. The most important point that comes out of the analysis is that the tiered credit structure with the incentives to repay it on time and use digital transactions has not only alleviated the financial crunch but has also promoted formal financial conduct among the vendors who were never a part of the banking system. The digital credit facility integration and social security connections further highlight the multidimensional role in the lives of informal entrepreneurs of improving the scheme in terms of livelihoods, operational stability, and economic security in the long term. As a conclusion, the informal economy, and specifically street vending is a challenge and an opportunity to India. Although still vulnerable, unregulated, and unguarded, the sector keeps millions of people afloat, it is also a major contributor to GDP, and an enabler of urban inclusivity. It is important to learn about its dynamics, hence, to shape such interventions as PM SVANidhi that is expected to empower vendors, formalize their activities, and become a part of the great economic picture in the country.

Policy Implication on PM SVANidhi and Informal Entrepreneurship

Politically, the results indicate that PM SVANidhi is a scalable and replicable framework of assisting informal entrepreneurship in urban India. The credit-guaranteed, collateral-free structure supported by CGTMSE minimizes the risk of a lender and increases the access to institutional finance of the vendors without any formal credit history. The interest subsidy and incentives on digital transactions are good behavioral nudges that make policy goals of financial inclusion and digitalization consistent with the welfare of the vendors. The scheme can also be improved by policymakers through intensifying awareness campaigns, simplifying the implementation of the scheme at the ULB level, and widening the convergence with the skill development program, health insurance programs, and urban planning programs. These improvements can make sure that PM SVANidhi goes beyond providing credit to becoming a urban livelihood resilience model.

Entrepreneurial Insights and Resilience-Enhancing Processes

The scheme will have serious entrepreneurial implications in the case of street vendors, especially in relation to resilience building. The availability of foreseeable and increasingly large working capital allows vendors to deal with fluctuations in income and react to market shocks and invest in the growth of the business. Variable payment plans in line with the financial cycle maximize the cash flow and create sustainable behaviors in borrowing. Furthermore, the use of digital payment using UPI-based incentives and RuPay credit cards are more efficient, transparent, and bring additional customer confidence. Taken together, these processes enhance the adaptive potential of the vendors who can switch to more sustainable and expansionary micro-enterprises in the informal economy than survival-based vending.

Theoretical Contributions and Implications on Academia

This research contributes to the global body of literature on livelihood resilience, financial inclusion, and informal economy research as it shows that microcredit interventions initiated by the state can have an effect on the resilience outcomes of informal workers. The results are consistent with the resilience theory because they demonstrate the impact of access to financial, digital, and institutional resources in strengthening absorptive, adaptive, and transformative abilities of street vendors. As well, the research contributes positively to the discourse of the informal economy since street vendors are not only vulnerable but are responsive entrepreneurs who can exploit the policy support to their upward mobility. The adoption of digital finance in an informal setting also brings extended possibilities of theorize the interface between informality and formal financial structure.

Future Research Direction

Irrespective of the contributions, the study presents a number of avenues on how future research can be conducted. The longitudinal studies can evaluate the influence of PM SVANidhi on income stability, business survival, and intergenerational mobility of vendor households over time. Cross-state or urban and rural extension of the scheme could give a comparative study in the results to show contextual differences. Moreover, empirical studies that correlate the adoption of digital payment and productivity and profitability would enhance the knowledge regarding digital strength among informal entrepreneurs. Lastly, the influence of gender, social capital, and the role of a local government institution in determining effectiveness of PM SVANidhi could be investigated in future studies. By addressing these gaps, evidence-based policymaking and scholarly engagement with the resilience of the informal sector will be enhanced.

REFERENCES

Abhiyan, W. N. T. (2017). Sustainable development goals: Agenda 2030. *India 2017: a civil society report.*

Aithal, P. S. (2024). Financial literacy for economic empowerment: Microfinance initiatives in Indian SHGs. [PIJTRCS]. *Poornaprajna International Journal of Teaching & Research Case Studies, 1*(1), 80–91.

Ayala, J. C., & Manzano, G. (2014). The resilience of the entrepreneur. Influence on the success of the business. A longitudinal analysis. *Journal of Economic Psychology, 42*, 126–135.

Banga, K., & te Velde, D. W. (2020). COVID-19 and disruption of the digital economy; evidence from low and middle-income countries. *Digital Pathways at Oxford Paper Series, 7.*

Bhowmik, S. K. (2012). Street vendors in the global urban economy. Routledge.
Chen, M., Ananthakrishnan, T., & Narayan, D. (2021). Urban informal workers and COVID-19: Evidence from India. *World Development, 145*, 105509.

Boruah, J., & Aryan, S. (2020). Right to Livelihood for the Street Food Vendors in India. *Indian Journal of Socio-Legal Analysis, 1*(1).

Brown, D., & McGranahan, G. (2016). The urban informal economy, local inclusion and achieving a global green transformation. *Habitat International, 53*, 97–105.

Chan, K. W. (2010). The global financial crisis and migrant workers in China: 'There is no future as a labourer; returning to the village has no meaning'. *International Journal of Urban and Regional Research, 34*(3), 659–677.

Chattopadhyay, S., & Kumar, A. Union Budget 2024 and Inclusive Cities: An Appraisal of India's Urban Development Schemes & Policies. *Regional Centre for Urban & Environmental Studies (RCUES), Mumbai*, 1.

Chinta, S. (2019). Supply chain finance in India: current status and potentialities 2019-2020.

Cutright, P. (1971). Income and family events: Marital stability. *Journal of Marriage and Family*, •••, 291–306.

Dev, S. M. (2021). *Beyond India 75: Growth, Inclusion and Sustainability*. Indira Gandhi Institute of Development Research.

Durai, T., & Stella, G. (2019). Digital finance and its impact on financial inclusion. *Journal of Emerging Technologies and Innovative Research, 6*(1), 122–127.

Giroux, S., Blekking, J., Waldman, K., Resnick, D., & Fobi, D. (2021). Informal vendors and food systems planning in an emerging African city. *Food Policy, 103*, 101997.

Gopal, B. S., & Davidson, B. G. J. (2025). Street Vendors in India: The Beginnings of a Digital Transformation Journey. In *Evolving Landscapes of Research and Development: Trends, Challenges, and Opportunities* (pp. 365-386). IGI Global Scientific Publishing.

Gupta, R., & Das, S. (2022). Challenges in implementing PM SVANidhi scheme: A study of urban street vendors. *The Indian Journal of Public Administration, 68*(1), 45–60.

Hawanga, O. E. (2024). *The impact of COVID-19 on the livelihood of informal sector workers: A case study of street vendors in Eenhana Town, Ohangwena region, Namibia* (Doctoral dissertation, University of Namibia).

Henderson, J. (2002). Building the rural economy with high-growth entrepreneurs. *Economic Review-Federal Reserve Bank of Kansas City, 87*(3), 45–75.

Jain, S., & Sharma, P. (2022). Financial inclusion and digital transactions among street vendors: Early insights from PM SVANidhi beneficiaries. *Journal of Entrepreneurship and Innovation, 11*(2), 89–102.

Kandpal, V., Chandra, D., Dalei, N. N., & Handoo, J. (2023). MFIs and NBFCs contributions towards financial inclusion and circular economy. In *Financial inclusion in circular economy: A bumpy road towards sustainable development* (pp. 157–184). Springer International Publishing.

Kant, R. (2024). *Financial Technologies (FINTECH) in E-Commerce*. SGSH Publication.

Kumar, V., & Roy, S. (2018). Microcredit and resilience among informal urban micro-entrepreneurs in India. *International Journal of Entrepreneurship and Small Business, 34*(3), 345–360.

Labitad, J. (2025). Street Vendors' Stories: Informal Borrowing Practices and Implications on Business. *American Journal of Social Development and Entrepreneurship, 4*(1), 10–54536.

Madhav, R., & Majithia, A. S. (2023). Street Vendors and Social Solidarity Economy: Reimagining Credit and Social Security. *Socio-Legal Rev., 19*, 37.

Mair, J., & Marti, I. (2009). Entrepreneurship in and around institutional voids: A case study from Bangladesh. *Journal of Business Venturing*, *24*(5), 419–435.

Ministry of Housing and Urban Affairs. (2020). PM SVANidhi scheme guidelines. Government of India. https://pmsvanidhi.mohua.gov.in/

Muhammed Shafi, M. K., Shafi, K. M., & Saleem, S. (2024). Microfinance-Driven Banking Initiatives for Advancing Financial Inclusion; Evidences from India. In *The AI Revolution: Driving Business Innovation and Research* (Vol. 2, pp. 467–481). Springer Nature Switzerland.

Naik, A., & Patel, P. (2022). Government schemes for entrepreneurship programs. In *Agricultural microbiology based entrepreneurship: Making money from microbes* (pp. 25–40). Springer Nature Singapore.

Pareek, A., & Alok, V. N. (2024). PM SVANidhi--A Livelihood Scheme for Street Vendors in India: An Evaluation. *Nagarlok-Quarterly Journal of Urban Affairs, 56*(1).

Patel, S., Furlan, R., & Grosvald, M. (2021). A framework for enhancing the spatial urban form of informal economies in India: The case of Krishna Rajendra Market, Bangalore. *SAGE Open*, *11*(2), 21582440211023184.

Roever, S. (2014). Informal economy monitoring study sector report: Street vendors. *Cambridge, MA, USA: WIEGO, 1*(1), 1-65.

Roever, S., & Skinner, C. (2016). Street vendors and cities. *Environment and Urbanization*, *28*(2), 359–374.

Shridhar, S. (2024). An Heuristic Study on Pradhan Mantri Street Vendor's Atmanirbhar Nidhi Yojana: Context on a Micro Credit Scheme. *Asian Journal of Agricultural Extension. Economia e Sociologia*, *42*(6), 339–349.

Shukla, N. K., & Patel, A. S. Preservation of Job and Local Culture Through Sustainable Tourism: A Case Study of Uttar Pradesh With Special Reference To PM SVANidhi Scheme.

Silvestro, R., & Lustrato, P. (2014). Integrating financial and physical supply chains: The role of banks in enabling supply chain integration. *International Journal of Operations & Production Management*, *34*(3), 298–324.

Singh, B. B. (2018). Street Vendors in Food Service Activities and Their Spatial Distribution. , 37.

Subramanian, Yavana Rani & M., Govindaraj & Priya, B & Rena, Ravinder. (2023). An Empirical Study On The Impact Of Covid-19 Pandemic On Street Vendors In Karnataka Section A-Research Paper Eur. 2194-2200. .DOI: 10.48047/ecb/2023.12.si10.00263

Sultana, N., Rahman, M. M., & Khanam, R. (2022). Informal sector employment and economic growth: Evidence from developing countries in SDG perspective. *Sustainability*, *14*(19), 11989.

The Duy, D., & Tien Thanh, P. (2024). Economic challenges faced by migrant street vendors during a crisis: Implications for social inclusion development. *The International Journal of Sociology and Social Policy*, *44*(9/10), 809–825.

Variyava, K. F. (2025). Beyond the Bank Account: Financial Inclusion and Maharashtra's Microenterprises.

Williams, C. C., & Gurtoo, A. (2012). Evaluating competing theories of street entrepreneurship: Some lessons from a study of street vendors in Bangalore, India. *The International Entrepreneurship and Management Journal*, *8*(4), 391–409.

Williams, T. A., & Shepherd, D. A. (2016). Building resilience or providing sustenance: Different paths of emergent ventures in the aftermath of the Haiti earthquake. *Academy of Management Journal*, *59*(6), 2069–2102. DOI: 10.5465/amj.2014.0680

Chapter 7

The Role of Consulting Firms Easing Tensions Between Internationalization and Innovation in Startups

Lucas Cortez Costa
https://orcid.org/0009-0009-6321-2522
University of Porto, Portugal

Fábio Duarte
University of Porto, Portugal

Belem Barbosa
https://orcid.org/0000-0002-4057-360X
University of Porto, Portugal

ABSTRACT

The strategic combination of innovation and internationalization presents complex challenges and opportunities, particularly for start-ups. This study examines the role of consulting firms in helping startups navigate this process. Employing a qualitative methodology, this research draws on semi-structured interviews with start-ups that utilized consulting services for their international expansion. The findings indicate that consultants are a key resource, effectively supporting start-ups by providing critical knowledge and strategic insights derived from prior international experience.

DOI: 10.4018/979-8-3373-6991-4.ch007

INTRODUCTION

Internationalization and innovation represent critical drivers of growth for start-ups. The existing literature presents differing views on the effects of combining innovation and internationalization efforts for enterprises (Battaglia & Neirotti, 2022; Golovko & Valentini, 2011; Wu & Fan, 2025). This chapter examines the complex relationship between these strategic pursuits in the context of start-ups, focusing on the inherent tensions documented in the literature (e.g., Battaglia et al., 2018; Battaglia & Neirotti, 2022).

The primary objective, which guides the subsequent literature review, is to explore how external entities, specifically consulting firms, can mitigate these challenges.

In this chapter, we will expand our understanding of the effects of combining internationalization and innovation, as well as the role consultancy firms play in the success or failure of such pursuits, through a qualitative study that utilizes semi-structured interviews as a tool to examine real examples of start-ups' past experiences.

BACKGROUND

Innovation and Internationalization

For firms, internationalization and innovation are inherently connected activities. Entrepreneurial firms can grow by introducing new products, attracting new customers, or combining both strategies (Kyläheiko et al., 2011). In an increasingly interconnected world, international markets present both critical opportunities and significant risks for established companies and startups alike (McNaughton, 2003). Expansion into these markets requires innovation and adaptation, whether in product and service offerings, management techniques, or both (Oliva et al., 2022). For start-ups, the link to innovation is even more critical, as it is one of their defining characteristics (Ehsan, 2021). Furthermore, international expansion can provide start-ups with a means to overcome the limitations of their domestic markets (McNaughton, 2003).

A key concept in this domain is the "born global" (BG) firm, a company that internationalizes rapidly and establishes a presence in foreign markets without first developing a significant domestic footprint. BGs share many similarities with start-ups, particularly as startups with limited resources (Cavusgil & Knight, 2015). The primary distinction is the inherent international focus that BGs possess from their inception (Verbeke et al., 2014). Given the extensive body of literature on BGs and their similarities to start-ups, this review will also draw upon research on BGs, treating them as internationally focused startups.

While extensive literature addresses the relationship between internationalization and innovation (e.g., Battaglia et al., 2018; Fu et al., 2024; Golovko & Valentini, 2011; Kyläheiko et al., 2011; Wu & Fan, 2025), there is some divergence regarding the combined effect of these activities on firm performance (Battaglia & Neirotti, 2022). One perspective posits that the combination is distinctly positive and complementary, creating a dynamic, virtuous circle (see Table 1). According to this view, participation in international markets enhances organizational learning, which in turn leads to innovation. Similarly, a commitment to innovation allows a firm to enter markets with novel and better-adapted products, improving its international performance. This success, in turn, drives further investment and enhances performance in both domestic and international arenas (Golovko & Valentini, 2011). Wu & Fan (2025) corroborate this view, suggesting that the relationship between internationalization and innovation is predominantly positive.

This synergy may be even more critical for BGs (see Table 1). For these firms, simultaneously pursuing internationalization and innovation is a way to overcome domestic market constraints and capitalize on international opportunities, such as niche markets (McNaughton, 2003). Many startups in the global arena operate in high-technology sectors, where international sales are often necessary to remain viable (McDougall & Oviatt, 1996; McDougall et al., 1994). In such industries, highly specialized global niches and substantial Research & Development (R&D) costs mean that domestic sales alone are often insufficient to support the necessary investment (McDougall & Oviatt, 1996). In other words, a global presence allows BGs to increase business volume and achieve economies of scale. Furthermore, operating in foreign markets exposes a firm to diverse conditions, fostering its capacity for learning and adaptation (Autio, 2017). Indeed, high-tech BGs with higher international sales volumes tend to achieve greater market share (McDougall & Oviatt, 1996), and a positive association exists between a new venture's degree of internationalization and its profitability and growth (Schwens et al., 2018). Moreover, the international and entrepreneurial orientation of BGs, combined with the "learning advantage of newness" (Sapienza et al., 2006), enables their rapid international expansion (Love et al., 2016). Table 1 summarizes the aforementioned advantages.

Table 1. Advantages of Combining Internationalization and Innovation

General Advantages	Internationalization enhances organizational learning	(Golovko & Valentini, 2011)
	Improved product adaptation to international markets	(Golovko & Valentini, 2011)
	Creation of a virtuous circle	(Golovko & Valentini, 2011)

continued on following page

Table 1. Continued

Advantages Specific to Born Globals	Overcoming domestic market limitations	(McNaughton, 2003)
	Access to niche markets	(McNaughton, 2003)
	Positive association between internationalization and firm profitability and growth	(Schwens et al., 2018)
	Achievement of economies of scale	(McDougall & Oviatt, 1996; McDougall et al., 1994)
	Fosters management and adaptation capabilities	(Autio, 2017)
	Learning advantage of newness	(Love et al., 2016; Sapienza et al., 2006)

Source: Developed for this research.

Conversely, the combination of internationalization and innovation can have a negative impact on firm profitability (Battaglia et al., 2018). The literature recognizes several challenges associated with this combination (see Table 2). For instance, Kumar (2009) highlights the difficulty of transferring tacit knowledge and the limited absorptive capacity of firms as barriers to success. Building on this concept of limited capacity, some scholars argue that innovation efforts linked to international expansion are more complex than those targeting the domestic market (Battaglia & Neirotti, 2022; Lu & Beamish, 2004; Vuorio et al., 2020), potentially requiring a greater investment of resources. This is evident in findings of diminishing marginal returns between geographic diversification and firm success (Lu & Beamish, 2004). When internationalization is combined with innovation, the firm may experience "information overload" (Calantone et al., 2006), which can harm its profitability. Furthermore, barriers such as a lack of brand reputation in the target market, a shortage of complementary sales assets, information asymmetry, and reduced bargaining power with export intermediaries (George et al., 2005) can diminish the absorptive capacity required to efficiently leverage foreign market intelligence in the innovation process. Fu et al. (2024) reach conclusions that support this notion of trade-offs, suggesting a negative relationship between the pace of a firm's international expansion and its innovation performance.

For start-ups and Born Globals (BGs), these challenges can be even more pronounced given the resource constraints inherent to their profile (Cavusgil & Knight, 2015). In fact, firms with less than ten years of activity appear to benefit less from, or are even harmed by, the combination of internationalization and innovation activities (Battaglia et al., 2018). In addition to the challenges identified above, BGs face barriers related to their nature, such as a lack of resources, including financial, organizational, human, and marketing capabilities (Cavusgil & Knight, 2015; Leonidou, 2000).

Geographic diversification is also associated with external barriers at the political, governmental, legal, economic, procedural, sociocultural, and linguistic levels, as well as with exchange rate volatility (Roy et al., 2016). These barriers add to the complexity of both internationalization and innovation, affecting both dimensions of the combination. From this perspective, Oliva et al. (2022) identify the complexity and high costs of internationalization as the primary obstacles to the expansion of BGs. While BGs may benefit from a "learning advantage of newness" in some markets (Sapienza et al., 2006), this advantage appears less effective in countries with greater institutional distance from the firm's country of origin, that is, where these barriers are more pronounced (Love et al., 2016).

Other challenges associated with the BG profile include a lack of experience in international markets (Rutashobya & Jaensson, 2004). International market experience has a positive (though diminishing) impact on both market diversification and export intensity (Love et al., 2016); therefore, inexperience represents a significant barrier to the growth of BGs.

Internationalization can also represent a shift in the industrial paradigm. A firm that is a leader in its domestic market may expand into a foreign market where competition is more intense or where another entity is the dominant player (McDougall & Oviatt, 1996). Moreover, the competencies that generate competitive advantages in the target market may differ from those that create advantages domestically (McDougall & Oviatt, 1996).

These challenges do not affect firms in isolation. For instance, a lack of international experience and a shift in the industrial paradigm can compound the complexity of the internationalization process, which in turn exacerbates their effects. All of these challenges are further compounded by the resource constraints associated with BGs. Table 2 summarizes the aforementioned challenges.

Table 2. Challenges of Combining Internationalization and Innovation

General Challenges	Difficulty in transferring tacit knowledge	(Kumar, 2009)
	Limited absorptive capacity	(Kumar, 2009)
	Complexity of innovation processes	(Battaglia & Neirotti, 2022; Lu & Beamish, 2004; Vuorio et al., 2020)
	Information overload	(Calantone et al., 2006)
	Lack of reputation, insufficient sales-related assets, and information asymmetry with intermediaries	(George et al., 2005)

continued on following page

Table 2. Continued

Challenges Specific to Born Globals	Limited resources (e.g., organizational, marketing, financial)	(Cavusgil & Knight, 2015; Leonidou, 2000; Rutashobya & Jaensson, 2004)
	Higher probability of negative outcomes for firms under 10 years old	(Battaglia et al., 2018)
	High costs and complexity of international expansion	(Oliva et al., 2022)
	External barriers: political, governmental, legal, economic, procedural, sociocultural, and exchange rate-related	(Roy et al., 2016)
	Lack of international experience	(Rutashobya & Jaensson, 2004)
	Shift in industrial paradigm	(McDougall & Oviatt, 1996)

Source: Developed for this research.

The Role of Consulting Firms in Mitigating Tensions Between Innovation and Internationalization

Firms with dynamic capabilities are better able to navigate the complexity of these challenges by identifying, seizing, and transforming market opportunities (Teece, 2014; Teece et al., 1997). Dynamic capabilities can be defined as "the firm's ability to integrate, build, and reconfigure internal and external competences to address rapidly changing environments" (Teece et al., 1997, p. 516). Teece (2007) identifies the core of dynamic capabilities as the mechanisms of 'asset orchestration' through which firms adapt and evolve. These mechanisms refer to the processes of coordination, learning, and reconfiguration that enable firms to assimilate new technologies (Battaglia & Neirotti, 2022). In the specific case of firms seeking to expand internationally, these mechanisms involve reconfiguring both supplier and distributor networks, as well as intangible assets to respond to the unique needs of each market's consumers (Battaglia & Neirotti, 2022).

Battaglia & Neirotti (2022) suggest that firms can develop the dynamic capabilities necessary to successfully combine innovation and internationalization through two main methods. The first of these involves collaboration with external entities such as universities and research centers (see Table 3). The underlying premise is that collaborating with such partners helps firms to more easily recognize opportunities and makes the process of transforming knowledge into new products more efficient (Giudici et al., 2019). The second path to developing these dynamic capabilities focuses on the experience acquired in international markets (see Table 3). International experience exposes the firm to a greater diversity of institutional and market situations, which helps to stimulate absorptive capacity and the development of new learning methods (Lopez-Vega et al., 2016). Since it is not possible for a firm to simply receive an "injection" of international experience, a point that will be addressed later, firms can instead benefit from the international experience of hired personnel (Fletcher & Harris, 2012).

Collaboration with Universities and Research Centers

Collaboration with universities and research centers provides firms with direct access to technological and scientific knowledge (Brunswicker & Vanhaverbeke, 2015). As such, this path is more closely connected to the innovation dimension. This openness to innovative processes appears to enable firms to develop dynamic capabilities more rapidly and effectively, which the literature recognizes as necessary to mitigate the risks associated with combining internationalization and innovation (Kafouros et al., 2015; Teece, 2014; Teece et al., 2016). By collaborating with these institutions, firms can reduce the time and cost of learning (Kafouros et al., 2015) and improve their ability to develop and market products that meet the technological requirements across a geographically diverse range of markets (Battaglia & Neirotti, 2022). However, it is necessary to consider how adept firms are at receiving and processing the resulting knowledge, as well as how effectively the institutions can transfer this knowledge to the firms (Friesike et al., 2015). The smoother the knowledge transfer, the greater the reduction in research costs for the firm and the lower the risk of excessive research investment (Battaglia & Neirotti, 2022; Friesike et al., 2015).

Therefore, in addition to promoting the development of dynamic capabilities, collaboration with universities and research centers allows BGs to directly mitigate some of the challenges identified earlier. Access to scientific and technological knowledge helps firms overcome the barrier of process complexity, enabling them to better adapt their products to meet the requirements of different markets. Furthermore, the reduction in the cost and time required for innovation mitigates the negative effects of resource constraints, whether they are financial, managerial, or otherwise.

International Experience

International expansion necessitates rapid learning to overcome the institutional barriers that arise from geographic diversification (Johanson & Vahlne, 2003). As previously mentioned, a presence in foreign markets exposes firms to diverse realities, each presenting distinct challenges (Autio, 2017; Golovko & Valentini, 2011). From this perspective, international experience results in superior capabilities for identifying and capitalizing on opportunities in foreign markets, as well as for applying knowledge across diverse contexts (Battaglia & Neirotti, 2022). Indeed, according to Bai et al. (2017), the more extensive and diversified a firm's prior experience is, the lower its dependence on intermediaries.

A range of capabilities is necessary for successful international expansion (Ganotakis & Love, 2012). Knowledge can also be acquired through the existing experience of hired managers, a concept known as "grafted knowledge" (Fletcher & Harris, 2012). The principle of grafted knowledge is that firms can acquire the competencies associated with international experience by collaborating with managers who have prior experience, even if the firm itself is inexperienced (Love et al., 2016). In this way, inexperienced firms such as BGs can reap the benefits of international experience by collaborating with consulting firms. In fact, for any given level of a firm's prior international experience, grafted knowledge always represents an increase in the firm's stock of knowledge (Love et al., 2016).

Table 3 summarizes the main contributions in the literature on the role of consulting firms in mitigating tensions between innovation and internationalization.

Table 3. How Consulting Firms Mitigate Tensions Between Innovation and Internationalization

Development of dynamic capabilities		**(Teece, 2014; Teece et al., 1997)**
Collaboration with Universities & Research Centers	Provides direct access to technological and scientific knowledge	(Brunswicker & Vanhaverbeke, 2015)
	Enables faster, more effective development of dynamic capabilities	(Kafouros et al., 2015; Teece, 2014; Teece et al., 2016)
	Reduces the time and cost associated with learning	(Kafouros et al., 2015)
	Improves the ability to market products that meet diverse technological requirements	(Battaglia & Neirotti, 2022)
Direct International Experience	Exposes the firm to diverse situations and market contexts	(Autio, 2017; Golovko & Valentini, 2011)
	Builds superior capabilities to identify, seize, and apply knowledge from opportunities	(Battaglia & Neirotti, 2022)
	Reduces dependence on intermediaries	(Bai et al., 2017)
Grafted Knowledge from Consultants	Provides a range of necessary capabilities without requiring direct firm experience	(Ganotakis & Love, 2012)
	Allows knowledge to be acquired via the past experience of external experts	(Fletcher & Harris, 2012)
	Increases the firm's knowledge reservoir, regardless of its prior experience	(Love et al., 2016)

Source: Developed for this research.

METHOD

This study employs a qualitative approach to explore the benefits and challenges faced by start-ups when integrating internationalization and innovation, as well as the role of consulting firms in mitigating the resulting tensions. To this end, semi-structured interviews were conducted with representatives from start-ups that had previously collaborated with consultants for their internationalization efforts. In total, seven interviews were conducted.

Materials And Procedures

An interview protocol was developed to guide the sessions. The protocol was divided into three sequential sections. The first section aimed to understand the participants' perspectives on the process of combining internationalization and innovation, specifically to determine whether they experienced the trade-off suggested by the literature and, if so, to identify its perceived origin. The second section sought to understand the role played by the consulting firm during the process, including the nature and levels of its involvement. The third section assessed the overall outcomes of the entire process.

The interviews were conducted online via the Microsoft Teams platform, which allowed the sessions to be recorded. These recordings were subsequently used for transcription. The research process adhered to the ethical principles outlined by Bryman (2016), namely informed consent, anonymity, voluntary participation, confidentiality, and secure data storage.

Participants

A purposive sampling strategy was employed for this study. This technique allows for the identification of participants who are particularly relevant to the study's objectives (Bryman, 2016). For the sample, start-ups were selected that had previously collaborated with consulting firms for internationalization. Although purposive sampling is a non-probability method, it should not be mistaken for convenience sampling, as participants were selected based on their specific relevance to the research questions (Bryman, 2016). Accordingly, participants were identified through the public client lists of consulting firms specializing in internationalization. Table 4 provides a summary characterization of each participant.

Table 4. Participants' profiles

Participant	Sector	Prior International experience	Prior national market presence	Target Markets	Modes of Entry
P1	Cultural heritage	None	Weak	European Union	Export through a distributor
P2	Robotics	None	None	European Union	Export through a distributor
P3	Marketing	Little	None	European Union; Middle East	Direct export; Export through a distributor
P4	Management Technology	Little	Some	Spain	Export through a distributor
P5	Agri-food	None	None	European Union	Export through a distributor
P6	Civil construction	Little	Some	European Union	Direct export
P7	FinTech	None	Strong	European Union, Australia	Licensing

Source: Developed for this research.

Data Analysis Techniques

The seven interviews were recorded, transcribed, and analyzed using NVivo 15 software. The data were analyzed using a combination of inductive and deductive methods, aligning with practices used in qualitative analysis (Morgan, 2022).

Deductive coding was guided by the literature review, the creation of categories related to the advantages and challenges, the combination of internationalization and innovation, and the role of consulting firms. Inductive coding allowed themes to emerge from the interviews themselves—themes that the literature seems to neglect but that participants highlighted (Fereday & Muir-Cochrane, 2006; Morgan, 2022). The analysis process was iterative, allowing categories and subcategories to be adapted to create a comprehensive list in the final framework, presented in Table 5.

Table 5. Categories and subcategories for content analysis

Categories	Subcategories	Support	Sources	Mentions
Advantages of combining internationalization and innovation	Stimulates learning	(Autio, 2017; Golovko & Valentini, 2011; Love et al., 2016; Sapienza et al., 2006)	6	15
	Virtuous circle	(Autio, 2017; Golovko & Valentini, 2011)	6	9
	Overcoming national market barriers	(McDougall & Oviatt, 1996; McDougall et al., 1994; McNaughton, 2003)	6	11
	Firm's profitability and growth	(Schwens et al., 2018)	7	12
	Geographic diversification reduces the risk of market-specific shocks	n.a.	2	3
Challenges of the combination of internationalization and innovation	Complexity of innovation processes	(Battaglia & Neirotti, 2022; Lu & Beamish, 2004; Vuorio et al., 2020)	5	6
	Limited resources (organizational, marketing, financial)	(Cavusgil & Knight, 2015; Ehsan, 2021; Leonidou, 2000; Oliva et al., 2022; Rutashobya & Jaensson, 2004)	7	9
	Difficulty in absorbing and transferring information	(Calantone et al., 2006; Kumar, 2009)	2	4
	Lack of reputation in the target market and of sales-related assets, and information asymmetry with export intermediaries	(George et al., 2005)	4	10
	External barriers at the political, governmental, legal, economic, procedural, sociocultural, industrial, and exchange rate levels	(McDougall & Oviatt, 1996; Roy et al., 2016)	6	16
Role of consulting firms	Advantages of collaboration with universities and research centers	(Battaglia & Neirotti, 2022; Brunswicker & Vanhaverbeke, 2015; Kafouros et al., 2015; Teece, 2014; Teece et al., 2016)	2	2
	Knowledge, identification, and seizing of opportunities	(Battaglia & Neirotti, 2022; Fletcher & Harris, 2012; Ganotakis & Love, 2012; Love et al., 2016)	7	41
	Reduces dependence on intermediaries	(Bai et al., 2017)	3	5
	Requires less resource allocation	n.a.	2	4
	Trade-off between innovation and internationalization	(Battaglia & Neirotti, 2022; Battaglia et al., 2018)	5	7
	Minimization of negative impacts or leveraging of benefits	n.a.	5	7

Source: Developed for this research.

FINDINGS

The interview results show that most participants perceived both a complementary relationship (P1, P2, P3, P5, P6, P7) and trade-offs (P2, P4, P5, P6, P7) between innovation and internationalization. This apparent paradox is clarified by the fact that while complementarity can create a "virtuous circle" (Golovko & Valentini, 2011), achieving it demands financial and human capabilities that most start-ups lack (Ehsan, 2021). Supporting this, Battaglia et al. (2018) found that firms under 10 years old typically suffer when combining these efforts.

Regarding consulting firms, most participants (P1-P5) agreed they were effective in minimizing the negative impacts or leveraging the benefits of the combination; all participants reported some benefit from the collaboration. These results suggest that collaborating with consulting firms may be a viable way to overcome the capability gap required to achieve the virtuous circle.

Advantages of the Combination of Internationalization and Innovation

Participants highlighted new learning as a primary advantage of the combination. International expansion allows for "having larger [and] different projects" (P3) and "getting to know various types of clients and uses for [their] technology" (P1). This learning occurs at multiple levels (product, technology, clients, etc.) and is a well-documented phenomenon in the literature (Autio, 2017; Golovko & Valentini, 2011; Love et al., 2016; Sapienza et al., 2006). These learnings are primarily what initiate the virtuous circle (Golovko & Valentini, 2011).

Most participants also reported a complementary relationship, or virtuous circle, between innovation and internationalization: "I think it's the only way it makes sense" (P2), and "I think one even enhances the other" (P1). This virtuous circle manifests at different levels, such as new partners ("just the fact that we work with a bank [was an innovation in itself]" (P7)) or market knowledge ("this market... is telling us it is still too early to launch that" (P1)). The most predominant level, however, was the product, specifically "improving [their] product, often also preparing it for the foreign market" (P3). While participants recognize this complementarity, in line with the literature (Autio, 2017; Golovko & Valentini, 2011), they tend to disagree with the notion that the combination is *strictly* beneficial (Golovko & Valentini, 2011), as will be addressed later.

Overcoming national market barriers was cited as a key advantage and reason for international expansion. Participants described their national market as "small" (P1) and insufficient. Internationalization thus allows firms to "increase the size of the market [they] serve" (P7) as well as reach their "niche markets" (P4, P5, P6). Furthermore, foreign markets can offer "superior profitability" (P3, P5, P6), not only due to "greater financial capacity" (P6) but also because the firm expands to a "market that values" (P3, P5) its product more. This advantage is well-recognized by the literature (McDougall & Oviatt, 1996; McDougall et al., 1994; McNaughton, 2003), and participant responses reinforce that, for some BGs, this superior profitability may be necessary for survival.

All participants acknowledged that international expansion led to company growth, stating it "ends up boosting the company in a certain way" (P1). This performance improvement occurred at multiple levels, including "product" (P1, P2, P4), "visibility" (P3, P5, P7) in both foreign and domestic markets, "knowledge" (P4, P5, P6), and "internally" (P2, P3, P4, P5, P6), encompassing everything from hiring to increased productive capacity. This growth (Schwens et al., 2018) is a consequence of the previously mentioned advantages: learning from international expansion (Autio, 2017; Golovko & Valentini, 2011; Sapienza et al., 2006) enables more efficient innovation, which in turn makes internationalization efforts more efficient, creating the virtuous circle (Golovko & Valentini, 2011) that helps start-ups overcome national market barriers (McDougall & Oviatt, 1996; McDougall et al., 1994; McNaughton, 2003).

Finally, a few participants emphasized the importance of risk reduction through geographic diversification. For these participants, it is important that "in these troubled times, this dispersion [...] of potential markets allows, if there is [...] a problem in a specific market, [...] to work another that is already underway" (P1). Geographic diversification thus serves as an escape from the negative consequences of "economic cycles" (P3). While not entirely ignored by the literature (e.g., Mammen et al., 2021; Lu & Beamish, 2004), the importance of diversification for risk reduction does not receive significant attention (Mammen et al., 2021). Specifically, the literature appears to underestimate its importance for BGs, although participants who emphasized this point were in industries they perceived as more vulnerable to such risks, suggesting that this advantage may be industry-specific.

Challenges of the Combination of Internationalization and Innovation

In addition to the advantages discussed above, participants also reported challenges (see Table 5), including the complexity of innovation processes (Battaglia & Neirotti, 2022; Lu & Beamish, 2004; Vuorio et al., 2020), limited resources (Cavusgil & Knight, 2015; Ehsan, 2021; Leonidou, 2000; Oliva et al., 2022; Rutashobya & Jaensson, 2004), difficulty absorbing and transferring information (Calantone et al., 2006; Kumar, 2009), lack of reputation in the target market and sales-related assets, and information asymmetry with intermediaries (George et al., 2005), and various external barriers (McDougall & Oviatt, 1996; Roy et al., 2016). The fact that participants experienced these difficulties simultaneously with the advantages suggests that tensions between innovation and internationalization (Battaglia &

Neirotti, 2022; Battaglia et al., 2018) can coexist with the virtuous circle (Golovko & Valentini, 2011).

A large portion of participants reported difficulty navigating the complexity of innovation processes caused by international expansion. Difficulties originated from "taking a product and managing [...] to make it broad enough to meet client needs in these various countries, [...] or else having to adapt it" (P1). This need for adaptation, stemming from the "different way" (P2) people in target countries behave, meant most participants had to modify their product, from improving the "quality of the offer" (P5) to changing the "problem [...] to be solved" (P4). These results align with existing literature (Battaglia & Neirotti, 2022; Lu & Beamish, 2004; Vuorio et al., 2020), which corroborates the notion that international expansion makes innovation processes more complex.

All participants felt that their combined efforts suffered from limited resources (organizational, marketing, and financial). This access constraint heightened the "opportunity cost" (P7), leading to the realization that "in a start-up... it is not possible to go for everything" (P4). While felt at different levels, such as internal logistics requiring "a whole lot of logistics preparation" (P5), the primary constraint was "above all, I would say... financial" (P2). These results support the literature (Cavusgil & Knight, 2015; Ehsan, 2021; Leonidou, 2000; Oliva et al., 2022; Rutashobya & Jaensson, 2004), as start-ups, by definition (Ehsan, 2021), have high associated risk due to inherent resource scarcity.

Few participants highlighted difficulty in absorbing and transferring information. Those who did felt it was "difficult for the [consulting firm] to get the message across effectively" (P4) because it was a "niche business, and not one that is very simple to understand," or difficult to find "people with training who could automatically replace [an employee]" (P6). As few participants noted this, it suggests the literature (Calantone et al., 2006; Kumar, 2009) may overestimate its impact. The difficulty seems less about internal transfer (due to small teams) and more about external transfer (to consultants or new hires). It is also important to note that participants who reported this difficulty operate in niche markets, which appears to aggravate the effect.

Most participants reported a lack of reputation in the target market, sales-related assets, and information asymmetry with export intermediaries. They felt they "depended too much" (P7) on partners, especially those who were "too important" (P1) in the target market. This was aggravated by a lack of renown where "creating a portfolio [is very] important" (P6) and difficulty in "responding quickly" to market demand due to a lack of sales assets. Participants also cited a lack of "physical presence" (P1, P5, P7) needed to "provide assistance" (P1), "contact possible clients" (P5), and "manage cultural differences" (P7). These results align with the literature

(George et al., 2005), as start-ups, given their novelty, are logically more subject to these consequences.

Finally, most participants reported difficulties managing external barriers. They considered that "the cultural aspect is very important" (P2), as reflected in the "very different way" (P3) in which target markets operate. "Language" (P1, P2, P4, P5, P7) was a significant barrier; participants admitted they "underestimated the mastery of the language" (P4), finding it "difficult to implement the product" (P2) without local proficiency. Legal issues were also prominent, particularly ensuring products were "within the legislation" (P5, P6, P7). These results align with the literature (McDougall & Oviatt, 1996; Roy et al., 2016). However, the findings also suggest that the intensity of these barriers, particularly legal ones (noted in agri-food, civil construction, and fintech), is felt differently across different industries.

The Role of Consulting Firms in Alleviating the Tensions between Innovation and Internationalization

The results of this study reveal an interesting finding regarding the intervention of consulting firms in projects that combine innovation and internationalization: while all participants felt that collaborating with the consulting firm resulted in more knowledge about the target market and a superior capacity to identify and seize opportunities within it, the other benefits of the collaboration were felt by less than half of the participants (see Table 5). It is also important to note that none of the interviewees participated in open innovation projects with research centers and universities promoted by the consulting firm; those who did, did so on their own initiative. However, given the importance the literature attributes to collaboration with research centers and universities (Battaglia & Neirotti, 2022), this was also considered for the analysis.

Few participants reported involvement in open innovation projects with universities and research centers. Among those who were, two different outcomes were found. One participant considers this collaboration beneficial because they can "leverage the research development part in community funds without having to condemn the company" (P1). Conversely, another found the collaboration fruitless because "when you are part of a start-up [...] it is difficult to allocate resources to something that does not generate revenue" (P7). These results depart from existing literature. Battaglia and Neirotti (2022) suggest that collaboration with research centers and universities is one method through which firms develop dynamic capabilities (Teece, 2014; Teece et al., 2016). However, no participant recognized an improvement in these capabilities, highlighting instead the benefit of saving resources when external funding is available. The results thus suggest that for start-ups, the necessary resource allocation for such collaborations is exclusionary when funding is absent.

All participants felt the consulting firm contributed to increasing the firm's knowledge stock and helped identify and seize opportunities in the target market. As one participant noted, "The advantages... have, above all, to do with making use of highly trained structures already with superior market knowledge" (P2). Examples ranged from "generating leads" (P1) and facilitating "the cultural aspect" (P2) to "identifying [target] markets" (P3), "understanding what competition [...] existed" (P4), producing "a more realistic market prospection" (P5), "identifying the target audience" (P6), and navigating "the legislation" (P7). Most participants reported that the collaboration "significantly accelerates the processes" (P1, P2, P3, P4, P7), a celerity without which one firm "probably would not have survived" (P4). The literature suggests firms develop dynamic capabilities (Teece, 2014; Teece et al., 2016) through foreign market experience (Battaglia & Neirotti, 2022). Since start-ups, by definition (Ehsan, 2021), lack this experience, I suggest they benefit from grafted knowledge (Fletcher & Harris, 2012; Love et al., 2016) via consulting firms, thereby accessing the positive consequences of international experience while not possessing it.

Some participants reported receiving direct help from the consulting firm to "create the network" (P1) of contacts in the target country. Consulting firms seem effective in "finding distribution channels" (P4) and establishing "direct [links] with distributors and importers" (P5). This process is challenging for start-ups due to their limited reputation and information asymmetry with potential partners. The results suggest that consulting firms build "bridges" between start-ups and partners, identifying multiple intermediaries and thus reducing the start-ups' dependence on them. As the literature indicates (Bai et al., 2017), prior experience with consulting firms results in lower dependence on intermediaries—a benefit that, through grafted knowledge, can be leveraged by collaborating start-ups.

Few participants highlighted the advantage of requiring less resource allocation, though it is relevant given the inherent resource scarcity of start-ups. For some, collaboration meant "not having [...] to expend resources on market prospection" (P1). It "saves both physical and human resources" (P1) and "save[s] time" (P7), one of the "most valuable resources" (P7) for start-ups. The literature may not highlight this benefit because consulting services require an investment. However, for start-ups, this investment may ultimately save resources by streamlining areas where they would otherwise have to allocate vast (human or financial) resources.

The majority of participants recognized that the consulting firm was effective in its intervention; according to one, international expansion is "a shot in the dark without some type of support from a specialized entity" (P1). However, it is relevant to note that in some cases, participants reported that the results "would not have been" (P6) different without the consultant's support. This participant (P6) experienced great difficulty in onboarding the consulting firm, as it was "a niche product," which hindered the production of real results and ultimately yielded "no return." For the most part, these results suggest that consulting firms are capable of effectively alleviating the tensions between innovation and internationalization for start-ups.

Discussion of Findings

This study highlights the advantages and challenges of combining innovation and internationalization efforts for start-ups, as well as the role of consulting firms in leveraging the benefits and minimizing the challenges of this combination.

The results confirm that internationalization exposes firms to new realities, fostering new learning and enabling firms to overcome home market barriers. This new learning leads to improved performance in the foreign market, specifically in product or service adaptation, which leverages the benefits of international expansion. This, in turn, allows the firm to invest in its learning and innovation, creating a virtuous circle of growth. These results align with the literature on the benefits of the combination of innovation and internationalization (Autio, 2017; Golovko & Valentini, 2011; Love et al., 2016; McDougall & Oviatt, 1996; McDougall et al., 1994; McNaughton, 2003; Sapienza et al., 2006; Schwens et al., 2018).

Furthermore, the results suggest that start-ups can mitigate the risk of economic shocks through geographic diversification, a finding that has not been prominently highlighted in the literature.

However, the results suggest that, despite the potential for a virtuous circle, the barriers associated with this combination can lead to trade-offs between these two dimensions. Thus, the results contradict the notion that the combination of innovation and internationalization is strictly beneficial for firms (Golovko & Valentini, 2011), aligning instead with the findings of Battaglia and Neirotti (2022). These authors conclude that combining internationalization and innovation efforts is almost always detrimental for firms with less than 10 years of activity, as is the case for start-ups (Ehsan, 2021).

In fact, the results suggest that the combination can lead to information overload by complicating innovation processes, as acknowledged in the literature (Battaglia & Neirotti, 2022; Lu & Beamish, 2004; Vuorio et al., 2020). The results show this complexity originates primarily from external barriers, especially at the legal, procedural, sociocultural, and industrial levels. Other external barriers identified in the literature, at the political, governmental, economic, and exchange rate levels (McDougall & Oviatt, 1996; Roy et al., 2016), did not receive the same emphasis from the participants. These external barriers are particularly challenging for start-ups to overcome, given their limited international experience and access to resources. Furthermore, and in line with the literature, this lack of international experience means start-ups suffer from a lack of reputation in the target market, a lack of sales-related assets, information asymmetry with export intermediaries (George et al., 2005), and difficulties in absorbing and transferring information (Calantone et al., 2006; Kumar, 2009). However, the results suggest that the difficulty in absorbing and transferring information is not as impactful, or at least not as transversal, as a barrier. No participant reported difficulty transferring knowledge within their organization; these difficulties were felt when communicating externally with a consulting firm or a new employee. The results also suggest this barrier is especially acute for firms in niche markets.

This study suggests that one way to overcome some of these barriers is through collaboration with consulting firms. The literature suggests two approaches for firms to bridge these gaps and benefit from the combination of internationalization and innovation: prior international experience and collaboration with research centers and universities (Battaglia & Neirotti, 2022). Our results suggest a slightly different path: through their international market experience, consulting firms cultivate competencies within start-ups to navigate external barriers and the complexity of the innovation process. Moreover, their experience helps mitigate the negative effects of dependence, information asymmetry with intermediaries, and a lack of target-market reputation, as noted in the literature (Bai et al., 2017). Effectively, this allows start-ups to access the benefits associated with international experience, even when they are inexperienced.

Furthermore, according to the results, in some cases, collaboration with consulting firms allows for resource savings, both financial and human. The literature appears to place less importance on this benefit of collaboration with consulting firms; however, the results suggest that it is important for startups, especially when they are engaged in projects that combine innovation and internationalization.

It is worth noting that the results suggest consulting firms do not effectively mitigate the challenge of absorbing and transferring knowledge; in some cases, the consulting firm itself may encounter difficulties at this level.

Conversely, the results are inconclusive regarding the effect of collaboration with research centers and universities. As mentioned, the literature suggests this collaboration is one way to overcome the barriers associated with the combination of internationalization and innovation (Battaglia & Neirotti, 2022). However, few participants were involved in such collaborations. In those cases, the collaboration was not promoted by the consulting firm. Moreover, among the interviewees who did participate in such projects, there was no consensus regarding their effects.

Finally, the results suggest that the competencies consulting firms cultivate within start-ups allow them to pursue internationalization efforts independently, thanks to the knowledge gained in collaboration with the consulting firm and the experience in international markets. These results corroborate both the notion that international experience is crucial for overcoming the barriers of the combination of innovation with internationalization (Battaglia & Neirotti, 2022) and the efficacy of grafted knowledge (Fletcher & Harris, 2012; Ganotakis & Love, 2012; Love et al., 2016).

SOLUTIONS AND RECOMMENDATIONS

In addition to corroborating the benefits of the combination of internationalization and innovation highlighted by the literature, this study further suggests that internationalization represents an important risk reduction for start-ups, especially for those in industries more vulnerable to economic shocks.

Although most challenges highlighted by the literature (Battaglia & Neirotti, 2022; George et al., 2005; Lu & Beamish, 2004; McDougall & Oviatt, 1996; Roy et al., 2016; Vuorio et al., 2020) are also corroborated by the study's results, the difficulties associated with transferring and absorbing information are not as acutely felt by start-ups as the literature suggests (Calantone et al., 2006; Kumar, 2009). A possible explanation is the small size that organizations such as start-ups typically have. Furthermore, this study suggests that this difficulty may indeed be relevant for start-ups operating in niche industries.

Building on the findings of Battaglia and Neirotti (2022), this study suggests that start-ups can leverage the support of consulting firms to mitigate challenges and capitalize on the benefits associated with combining internationalization and innovation, specifically through the knowledge that consulting firms bring to the company. Even more relevant for start-ups, the support from consulting firms can result in significant time savings, which can be the difference between "life and death" for startups.

FUTURE RESEARCH DIRECTIONS

Despite this study's contributions, several constraints must be considered. First, the results should not be generalized, as they are based on a study involving seven start-ups that utilized the support of consulting firms for their internationalization efforts. Although there was diversity in business areas, experience, and size among the participants, and theoretical saturation of the data was reached, it is recommended that further studies be conducted on this topic to validate the results. Future studies should employ different methodological approaches, such as combining qualitative and quantitative methods.

Limitations in the sample pre-selection must also be noted. Specifically, only start-ups still in operation were contacted. Given that a failed project can be fatal in the early years of a new venture, integrating only active start-ups means the study does not consider cases where, hypothetically, the challenges of combining internationalization and innovation so far outweigh the benefits that the firm is now defunct.

The results also raise questions that require future exploration, notably the relevance of geographic diversification as a risk-reduction method for startups, particularly those operating in niche areas.

CONCLUSION

Throughout this chapter, various aspects of combining internationalization and innovation are analyzed. Not only were the benefits and challenges of this combination explored, but also the role of consulting firms in mitigating the latter, with a particular focus on the context of start-ups.

Through this study, it becomes clear that the challenges associated with the combination primarily stem from the concept of information overload that arises from pursuing internationalization and innovation efforts simultaneously.

Startups, for which this combination is most relevant, can mitigate the intensity of this overload by leveraging the support of consulting firms, which not only alleviate this burden but also maximize the benefits.

Thus, consulting firms represent a useful tool for the internationalization of start-ups, not only because they facilitate the international expansion process, but also because they enhance learning that may be valuable in future internationalization projects.

REFERENCES

Autio, E. (2017). Strategic entrepreneurial internationalization: A normative framework. *Strategic Entrepreneurship Journal, 11*(3), 211–227. DOI: 10.1002/sej.1261

Bai, X., Krishna, K., & Ma, H. (2017). How you export matters: Export mode, learning and productivity in China. *Journal of International Economics, 104*, 122–137. DOI: 10.1016/j.jinteco.2016.10.009

Battaglia, D., & Neirotti, P. (2022). Dealing with the tensions between innovation and internationalization in SMEs: A dynamic capability view. *Journal of Small Business Management, 60*(2), 379–419. DOI: 10.1080/00472778.2020.1711635

Battaglia, D., Paolucci, E., & Neirotti, P. (2018). The role of R&D investments and export on SMEs' growth: A domain ambidexterity perspective. *Management Decision, 56*(1), 226–246. DOI: 10.1108/MD-02-2017-0136

Brunswicker, S., & Vanhaverbeke, W. (2015). Open innovation in small and medium-sized enterprises (SMEs): External knowledge sourcing strategies and internal organizational facilitators. *Journal of Small Business Management, 53*(4), 1241–1263. DOI: 10.1111/jsbm.12120

Bryman, A. (2016). *Social research methods* (5th ed.). Oxford University Press.

Calantone, R. J., Kim, D., Schmidt, J. B., & Cavusgil, S. T. (2006). The influence of internal and external firm factors on international product adaptation strategy and export performance: A three-country comparison. *Journal of Business Research, 59*(2), 176–185. DOI: 10.1016/j.jbusres.2005.05.001

Cavusgil, S. T., & Knight, G. A. (2015). The born global firm: An entrepreneurial and capabilities perspective on early and rapid internationalization. *Journal of International Business Studies, 46*(1), 3–16. DOI: 10.1057/jibs.2014.62

Ehsan, Z.-A. (2021). Defining a startup – A critical analysis. SSRN *Electronic Journal*. http://dx.doi.org/DOI: 10.2139/ssrn.3823361

Fereday, J., & Muir-Cochrane, E. (2006). Demonstrating rigor using thematic analysis: A hybrid approach of inductive and deductive coding and theme development. *International Journal of Qualitative Methods, 5*(1), 80–92. DOI: 10.1177/160940690600500107

Fletcher, M., & Harris, S. (2012). Knowledge acquisition for the internationalization of the smaller firm: Content and sources. *International Business Review, 21*(4), 631–647. DOI: 10.1016/j.ibusrev.2011.07.008

Friesike, S., Widenmayer, B., Gassmann, O., & Schildhauer, T. (2015). Opening science: Towards an agenda of open science in academia and industry. *The Journal of Technology Transfer*, *40*(4), 581–601. DOI: 10.1007/s10961-014-9375-6

Fu, Y., Wu, X., & Wang, Z. (2024). Internationalization rhythm and innovation performance: The effects of internationalization speed, organizational slack, and competitive intensity. *International Business Review*, *33*(1), 102196. DOI: 10.1016/j.ibusrev.2024.102274

Ganotakis, P., & Love, J. H. (2012). R&D, product innovation, and exporting: Evidence from UK new technology based firms. *Oxford Economic Papers*, *63*(2), 279–306. DOI: 10.1093/oep/gpq027

George, G., Wiklund, J., & Zahra, S. A. (2005). Ownership and the internationalization of small firms. *Journal of Management*, *31*(2), 210–233. DOI: 10.1177/0149206304271760

Giudici, G., Guerini, M., & Rossi-Lamastra, C. (2019). The creation of cleantech startups at the local level: The role of knowledge availability and environmental awareness. *Small Business Economics*, *52*, 815–830. DOI: 10.1007/s11187-017-9936-9

Golovko, E., & Valentini, G. (2011). Exploring the complementarity between innovation and export for SMEs' growth. *Journal of International Business Studies*, *42*(3), 362–380. DOI: 10.1057/jibs.2011.2

Johanson, J., & Vahlne, J.-E. (2003). Business relationship learning and commitment in the internationalization process. *Journal of International Entrepreneurship*, *1*, 83–101. DOI: 10.1023/A:1023219207042

Kafouros, M., Wang, C., Piperopoulos, P., & Zhang, M. (2015). Academic collaborations and firm innovation performance in China: The role of region-specific institutions. *Research Policy*, *44*(3), 803–817. DOI: 10.1016/j.respol.2014.11.002

Kumar, M. V. S. (2009). The relationship between product and international diversification: The effects of short-run constraints and endogeneity. [REMOVED HYPERLINK FIELD]. *Strategic Management Journal*, *30*(1), 99–116. DOI: 10.1002/smj.724

Kyläheiko, K., Jantunen, A., Puumalainen, K., Saarenketo, S., & Tuppura, A. (2011). Innovation and internationalization as growth strategies: The role of technological capabilities and appropriability. *International Business Review*, *20*(5), 508–520. DOI: 10.1016/j.ibusrev.2010.09.004

Leonidou, L. C. (2000). Barriers to export management: An organizational and internationalization analysis. *Journal of International Management*, *6*(2), 121–148. DOI: 10.1016/S1075-4253(00)00022-3

Lopez-Vega, H., Tell, F., & Vanhaverbeke, W. (2016). Where and how to search? Search paths in open innovation. *Research Policy*, *45*(1), 125–136. DOI: 10.1016/j.respol.2015.08.003

Love, J. H., Roper, S., & Zhou, Y. (2016). Experience, age and exporting performance in UK SMEs. *International Business Review*, *25*(4), 806–819. DOI: 10.1016/j.ibusrev.2015.10.001

Lu, J. W., & Beamish, P. W. (2004). International diversification and firm performance: The S-curve hypothesis. *Academy of Management Journal*, *47*(4), 598–609. https://www.jstor.org/stable/20159604

Mammen, J., Alessandri, T. M., & Boyd, B. K. (2021). The risk implications of diversification: Integrating the effects of product and geographic diversification. *Long Range Planning*, *54*(5), 102047. DOI: 10.1016/j.lrp.2019.101942

McDougall, P. P., & Oviatt, B. M. (1996). New venture internationalization, strategic change, and performance: A follow-up study. *Journal of Business Venturing*, *11*(1), 23–40. DOI: 10.1016/0883-9026(95)00081-X

McDougall, P. P., Shane, S., & Oviatt, B. M. (1994). Explaining the formation of international new ventures: The limits of theories from international business research. *Journal of Business Venturing*, *9*(6), 469–487. DOI: 10.1016/0883-9026(94)90017-5

McNaughton, R. B. (2003). The number of export markets that a firm serves: Process models versus the born-global phenomenon. *Journal of International Entrepreneurship*, *1*, 297–311. DOI: 10.1023/A:1024114907150

Morgan, H. (2022). Understanding thematic analysis and the debates involving its use. *The Qualitative Report*, *27*(10), 2079–2091. DOI: 10.46743/2160-3715/2022.5912

Oliva, F. L., Teberga, P. M. F., Testi, L., Kotabe, M., Del Giudice, M., Kelle, P., & da Cunha, M. P. (2022). Risks and critical success factors in the internationalization of born global startups of industry 4.0: A social, environmental, economic, and institutional analysis. *Technological Forecasting and Social Change*, *175*, 121334. DOI: 10.1016/j.techfore.2021.121346

Roy, A., Sekhar, C., & Vyas, V. (2016). Barriers to internationalization: A study of small and medium enterprises in India. *Journal of International Entrepreneurship*, *14*, 513–538. DOI: 10.1007/s10843-016-0187-7

Rutashobya, L., & Jaensson, J.-E. (2004). Small firms' internationalization for development in Tanzania. *International Journal of Social Economics, 31*(1/2), 159–172. DOI: 10.1108/03068290410515484

Sapienza, H. J., Autio, E., George, G., & Zahra, S. A. (2006). A capabilities perspective on the effects of early internationalization on firm survival and growth. *Academy of Management Review, 31*(4), 914–933. DOI: 10.5465/amr.2006.22527465

Schwens, C., Zapkau, F. B., Bierwerth, M., & Isidor, R. (2018). International entrepreneurship: A meta-analysis on the internationalization and performance relationship. *Entrepreneurship Theory and Practice, 42*(5), 734–768. DOI: 10.1177/1042258718795346

Teece, D. J. (2007). Explicating dynamic capabilities: The nature and microfoundations of (sustainable) enterprise performance. *Strategic Management Journal, 28*(13), 1319–1350. DOI: 10.1002/smj.640

Teece, D. J. (2014). The foundations of enterprise performance: Dynamic and ordinary capabilities in an (economic) theory of firms. *The Academy of Management Perspectives, 28*(4), 328–352. DOI: 10.5465/amp.2013.0116

Teece, D. J., Peteraf, M., & Leih, S. (2016). Dynamic capabilities and organizational agility: Risk, uncertainty, and entrepreneurial management in the innovation economy. *California Management Review, 58*(4), 13–35. DOI: 10.1525/cmr.2016.58.4.13

Teece, D. J., Pisano, G., & Shuen, A. (1997). Dynamic capabilities and strategic management. *Strategic Management Journal, 18*(7), 509–533. DOI: 10.1002/(SICI)1097-0266(199708)18:7<509:AID-SMJ882>3.0.CO;2-Z

Verbeke, A., Zargarzadeh, M. A., & Osiyevskyy, O. (2014). Internalization theory, entrepreneurship and international new ventures. *Multinational Business Review, 22*(3), 246–269. DOI: 10.1108/MBR-06-2014-0023

Vuorio, A., Torkkeli, L., & Sainio, L.-M. (2020). Service innovation and internationalization in SMEs: Antecedents and profitability outcomes. *Journal of International Entrepreneurship, 18*, 92–123. DOI: 10.1007/s10843-019-00266-z

Wu, S., & Fan, D. (2025). Internationalization and innovation: A multilevel meta-analysis of national sentiments. *Journal of Product Innovation Management, 42*(2), 253–283. DOI: 10.1111/jpim.12725

KEY TERMS AND DEFINITIONS

Consulting Firm: A company that provides advice, knowledge, and guidance in a specific field or across different industries, usually to other companies.

Dynamic Capabilities: The tools through which companies are able to re-orchestrate their resources to face different challenges.

Grafted Knowledge: Knowledge and or experience that a company gains by hiring an employee or consulting firm, which the employee or consulting firm had before being hired.

Innovation: A process that begins with an idea and ends with market introduction.

Internationalization: The process through which a company expands its activity to foreign markets.

Open Innovation: A collaborative innovation framework that allows innovative ideas to be created and considered from any source, both in and out of the company.

Startup: A company that is simultaneously young, innovation-centric, associated with risk, and with large growth potential.

Chapter 8

The Strategic Shift of Management Control as a Driver of Resilience in Times of Crisis:
Evidence From Moroccan Companies

Azzouz Elhamma
https://orcid.org/0000-0003-3382-0278
Ibn Tofaîl University, Morocco

Nabila Snoussi
https://orcid.org/0009-0003-6816-0289
Ibn Tofaîl University, Morocco

ABSTRACT

This study explores the roles of management control in companies during times of crisis across five dimensions: reactivity, process improvement, strategic orientation, strategic integration, and resilience. A questionnaire survey conducted with 97 Moroccan companies, analyzed through statistical tests, reveals that management control is perceived as highly important across all dimensions, with process improvement and resilience receiving the highest ratings (96%). Post-hoc analyses confirm the strategic significance of these two dimensions for organizational adaptation. The findings highlight that management control functions as an integrated system that enhances companies' ability to respond, adapt, and remain resilient in crisis

DOI: 10.4018/979-8-3373-6991-4.ch008

contexts. The study contributes to theory by enriching the literature on the strategic role of management control and to practice by offering managers concrete guidance for prioritizing actions and strengthening organizational agility.

1. INTRODUCTION

The contemporary business environment has become increasingly volatile, uncertain, complex, and ambiguous (VUCA) (Troise et al., 2022; Erdiaw-Kwasie et al., 2023; Carayannis et al., 2025), particularly since the COVID-19 pandemic and the ongoing armed conflicts (Panneer et al., 2022; Allam et al., 2022; McKibbin & Fernando, 2023; Al-Rousan et al., 2024). This environment is further characterized by rapid technological advancements and digitalization (Carayannis et al., 2025), recurring geopolitical shocks (Cevik, 2023; Ahmed et al., 2025), and climate crises, including floods, severe droughts, and other extreme events (Pizzorni et al., 2024; European Environment Agency, 2025). Such sustained uncertainty is compelling organizations to rethink their strategies in order to adapt rapidly to market conditions and effectively manage crises (Anand et al., 2024; Garrido-Moreno et al., 2024). Organizational crises can be defined as "event[s] perceived by managers and stakeholders as highly salient, unexpected, and potentially disruptive" (Bundy et al., 2017, p. 1662). According to Hermann (1963, p. 64), an organizational crisis is characterized by three features: it "(1) threatens high-priority values of the organization, (2) presents a restricted amount of time in which a response can be made, and (3) is unexpected or unanticipated by the organization." In this context, resilience has become a priority for companies in navigating crises (Xia et al., 2024; Florez-Jimenez et al., 2024). Business resilience has been defined by Sanchis and Poler (2019) as the proactive ability of firms to respond to disruptive events, adapt to shocks, and recover from them. In contrast, less resilient firms tend to be more vulnerable when facing external shocks (Elhamma, 2025b).

Among the tools that organizations can adopt to enhance resilience during crises, and particularly to adapt to environmental changes, is management control (Jukka, 2021; Bracci & Tallaki, 2021; Martins et al., 2023). Management control is defined as "the process by which managers influence other members of an organization to implement its strategies" (Anthony & Govindarajan, 2007). Over the past several years, numerous studies have examined the potential roles of management control in times of crisis in both the public and private sectors. However, the vast majority of these studies have been conducted in developed countries, while research on this topic remains very limited, or even absent, in developing countries such as those in Africa. To address this gap, the present study aims to investigate the roles of management control as a mechanism for organizational resilience during crises in

Moroccan companies. Our research question is: To what extent does management control contribute to the resilience of companies in times of crisis?

To address our research question, a questionnaire survey was conducted among 97 Moroccan companies between April and July 2024. The results of the study show that management control is perceived as highly important during Covid-19 crisis across five key dimensions: reactivity, process improvement, strategic orientation, strategy integration, and resilience. Process improvement and resilience received the highest ratings, with nearly 96% of respondents indicating strong or very strong importance. Reactivity and strategic orientation were also valued, with around 74% rating them as strong or very strong. Statistical tests (t-tests, ANOVA, and Chi-square) confirm that all dimensions are significantly above average and that their effects are not perceived equally. Post-hoc analyses highlight that process improvement and resilience are particularly critical for organizational adaptation. Overall, the findings indicate that management control functions as an integrated system that enhances a company's ability to respond, adapt, and remain resilient in crisis contexts.

The results of this research offer both theoretical and practical contributions. Theoretically, they provide new insights into the multidimensional role of management control during crises by identifying five key missions: reactivity, process improvement, strategic orientation, strategy integration, and resilience. This enriches the existing literature on organizational resilience, demonstrating that management control actively supports the adaptation and continuity of organizational activities in times of crisis. Practically, the findings offer managers and management controllers guidance on the key dimensions to prioritize to enhance organizational resilience. In particular, they highlight process improvement and resilience as essential levers for effective adaptation.

The remainder of this paper is organized as follows. Section 2 presents the conceptual framework, reviews the relevant literature, and develops the research hypotheses. Section 3 describes the methodological design. Section 4 reports and discusses the empirical results. Finally, Section 5 concludes the study by summarizing the key findings, outlining contributions, and suggesting directions for future research.

2. CONCEPTUAL FRAMEWORK, LITERATURE REVIEW AND HYPOTHESIS DEVELOPMENT

2.1. Conceptual Definitions: Management Control, Crises and organizational resilience

Three main concepts are central to this study: management control, crises, and organizational resilience.

Management control emerged in the 1920s, yet it is surprising that no universally accepted definition exists. The first formal definition was provided by Robert Anthony in 1965. According to Anthony, management control is "the process by which managers obtain assurance that resources are obtained and used effectively and efficiently for the accomplishment of the organization's objectives". This definition emphasizes two key aspects: first, setting objectives, usually derived from strategy; and second, verifying that resources are used effectively (achieving objectives) and efficiently (minimizing resource use). Management control, in this view, is essentially concerned with avoiding waste and reflects an accounting-oriented approach, focusing on mechanical operations rather than strategic and operational management. Recognizing this limitation, Anthony redefined management control in 1988 as: "Management control is the process by which managers influence other members of the organization to implement organizational strategies". In this updated definition, the focus shifts from controlling resources to influencing behavior to achieve the company's strategy. Two complementary mechanisms arise from this perspective: a decision coordination mechanism, which enhances the efficiency of decision-making, and an animation mechanism, which guides individual behavior in line with organizational expectations.

Simons (1995) offers another perspective, defining management control as the set of "formal, information-based routines and procedures used by managers to maintain or adjust patterns in organizational activities". Simons highlights that management control can support both strategy formulation (ex-ante) and implementation. He also distinguishes between diagnostic control, which monitors outcomes against plans, and interactive control, which actively engages managers in shaping strategic processes.

Generally in the literature, a crisis is a sudden and unexpected event or period that disrupts the normal functioning, stability, or survival of an individual, organization, society, or system (Barton, 1993; Mitroff, 2001; Ciekanowski et al., 2023). In organizations, crisis management is considered essential. It is defined as a "set of factors designed to combat crises and to lessen the actual damage inflicted by a crisis" (Coombs, 2015). According to the literature on emergency preparedness, crisis management typically involves three stages: the pre-crisis phase (prevention and preparation), the crisis phase (response), and the post-crisis phase (learning and review) (Coombs & Laufer, 2018). In all three stages, management control plays an important role.

Resilience is not unique to organizations. In physics, it refers to a material's ability to return to its original form after a shock. In psychology, it describes an individual's ability to withstand trauma, recover from adversity, and remain stable despite setbacks (Bégin & Chabaud, 2010). In management sciences, organizational resilience is understood through three interconnected dimensions: (1) absorption capacity, enabling the organization to withstand shocks or unexpected events; (2) renewal capacity, allowing it to create new futures; and (3) appropriation capacity, helping it grow stronger through experience (Weick & Sutcliffe, 2007)

2.2. Literature Review and Hypothesis Formulation

The functions of management control systems go beyond improving organizational performance by integrating strategic objectives into daily operations. These systems play a crucial role in responding to sudden, unpredictable, and unprecedented events, such as crises. Crises are marked by turbulence and uncertainty, requiring companies to adapt quickly to survive and maintain performance (Teece et al., 2016). Adaptability relies on several key factors, including a flexible internal structure, rapid decision-making processes, and efficient resource management (Teece et al., 1997). In this context, management control systems are considered to enable flexibility, providing real-time data, promoting agile strategic adjustments, and ensuring business continuity in times of crisis.

Recent crises, especially the COVID-19 pandemic, have led to several empirical studies examining how management control supports organizations during times of crisis. Bracci and Tallaki (2021), using a qualitative approach in a longitudinal case study, demonstrated that management control systems (MCSs) "support adaptive behaviour and assist decision-making by providing knowledge and ready-to-use answers to cope with external shocks… MCSs played an essential role in shaping anticipatory and coping capacities". In the same vein, and based on 26 interviews with bank executives, Rikhardsson et al. (2021) studied management controls during a period of high uncertainty—the 2008 financial crisis. Their results showed that these controls served three primary purposes: to guide behavior, change perceptions, and fulfill accountability. Similarly, Leoni et al. (2021) highlight that adaptable management control systems enable organizations to transform crisis-related challenges into opportunities for internal restructuring, foster effective interdepartmental communication, and shift from a reactive to a proactive approach.

The results of a study by Geurts et al. (2022) show that organizations with flexible management control systems were particularly effective in mitigating the economic effects of the COVID-19 pandemic by quickly adapting their strategies and optimizing the use of resources. In the same vein, Bedford et al. (2022), using survey data from business unit managers in the Netherlands, examined the behavioral effects of changes in management control practices during the crisis. Their results showed that, to mitigate the negative impacts of COVID-19, companies have strengthened their budgetary controls. Similarly, Martins et al. (2023) conducted a survey of 250 large Portuguese companies to examine whether management control practices are perceived as a resource for supporting decision-making and enhancing organizational performance and competitiveness in crisis contexts. Their main findings indicate that, in an uncertain and unpredictable crisis such as the COVID-19 pandemic, organizations consider management control to have a significant impact on performance and to act as a key lever for competitiveness.

Management control plays a strategic role in the reactivity of organizations, especially during times of crisis. It provides reliable and timely information that helps anticipate threats and adjust action plans (Simons, 1995). According to Anthony and Govindarajan (2007), management control uses various mechanisms, such as monitoring costs, performance, and deviations, to quickly identify sources of problems and allocate the necessary resources. This makes it a key pillar of organizational reactivity. Therefore, we can formulate the following hypothesis:

> **Hypothesis H1**: *Management control significantly enhances organizational reactivity during crises.*

Management control plays a crucial role in improving processes during times of crisis. It enables in-depth performance analysis and the rapid detection of inefficiencies, which helps identify bottlenecks and optimize key processes (Anthony & Govindarajan, 2007). It also provides tools to align operational processes with strategic objectives, strengthening organizational coherence in uncertain contexts (Simons, 1995). In turbulent environments, management control supports managerial innovation and the adaptation of routines by integrating real-time feedback (Tessier & Otley, 2012). Furthermore, it fosters a culture of continuous improvement by linking performance measurement, gap analysis, and corrective actions (Merchant & Van der Stede, 2017). During crises, coordination between functions and hierarchical levels becomes essential for an effective organizational response (Coombs, 2015). Management control contributes to this dynamic by supporting strategic integration through the production of reliable, relevant information for decision-making (Anthony & Govindarajan, 2007). It also ensures the alignment of financial and operational resources with organizational priorities, reinforcing the coherence of actions in uncertain environments (Simons, 1995). Therefore, the following hypotheses can be formulated:

Hypothesis H2: *Management control significantly enhances process improvement during crises.*
Hypothesis H3: *Management control significantly enhances strategic orientation during crises.*
Hypothesis H4: *Management control significantly enhances strategic integration during crises.*

To ensure organizational resilience, management control plays a crucial role during crises by providing decision-makers with timely information to respond quickly to disruptions (Anthony & Govindarajan, 2007). Through performance monitoring and the detection of critical deviations, it enables organizations to anticipate risks and adjust their strategies in uncertain environments (Simons, 1995). Management control also contributes to building dynamic capabilities by fostering innovation and organizational adaptability (Merchant & Van der Stede, 2017). In turbulent times, these mechanisms support business continuity and strengthen the organization's ability to recover after a crisis (Coombs, 2015). Therefore, we can formulate the following hypothesis:

Hypothesis H5: *Management control significantly strengthens organizational resilience during crises.*

3. METHODOLOGICAL DESIGN

3.1. Data Collection and Analysis Procedures

In management science, researchers can choose between quantitative and qualitative methods (Elhamma, 2024a). This study adopts a positivist epistemological framework and a quantitative approach to test the research hypothesis. Data were collected through an online questionnaire in Morocco. Business management practices and tools in Morocco have been heavily shaped by the French model (Elhamma, 2025a). In recent years, however, Moroccan companies have increasingly adopted international frameworks, including IFRS standards (Elhamma, 2024b, 2025a, 2026), as well as modern management control tools (Elhamma, 2014, 2025c; Elhamma, & Snoussi, 2026). Moreover, the Moroccan public sector has been undergoing a long-term process of modernization (Elhamma & El-Moumane, 2025; Elhamma & Loukili, 2025).

An unstratified random sampling method was employed to ensure broad representativeness in terms of industry, company size, respondent type, and years of existence. The questionnaire was distributed online via multiple channels, including social media, personal contacts, and professional networks. The first round of distribution took place over three months, from April to July 2024, during which 130 questionnaires were sent. A total of 103 responses were received, yielding a response rate of 79%. After excluding incomplete or invalid questionnaires, 97 responses were retained, resulting in a final response rate of approximately 75%. This sample provides a solid basis for reliable analysis.

3.2. Characteristics of the Sample

Our sample consists of companies of various sizes (Table 1), representing a broad range of industry sectors (Table 2), and differing in their years of existence (Table 3).

Table 1. Distribution of Respondents by Company Size

Company size	Percentage	Number of Respondents
Large company (+200 employees and/or revenue > 175 million dirhams)	45.4%	44
Medium-sized company (50 to 200 employees and/or revenue between 10 and 175 million dirhams)	33.0%	32
Small company (10 to 50 employees and/or revenue between 3 and 10 million dirhams)	16.5%	16
Micro company (<10 employees and/or revenue <3 million dirhams)	5.1%	5
Total	100%	97

The study sample is composed mainly of large companies, which account for 45.4% of respondents, followed by medium-sized companies at 33%. Small companies represent 16.5% of the sample, while micro-enterprises are the least represented at 5.1%. This distribution appears reasonable, as formal management control is typically adopted primarily by larger companies (Elhamma, 2010; 2011; 2015; 2023; Elhamma & Lassaad, 2017).

Table 2. Distribution of Respondents by Industry Sector

Industry Sector	Percentage	Number of Respondents
Commerce	6,2%	6
Industry	17,5%	17
Technology	44,3%	43
Services	32%	31

The study sample is predominantly composed of technology companies, accounting for 44.3% of respondents. Service companies represent 32%, manufacturing accounts for 17.5%, and the retail sector is the least represented, at 6.2%.

Table 3. Distribution of Companies by Years of Existence

Years of Existence	Percentage	Number of Respondents
2 to 5 years	30,9%	30
6 to 10 years	45,4%	44
Over than 10 years	23,7%	23

The sample is composed mainly of companies aged between 6 and 10 years, representing 45.4% of respondents. Younger companies, aged 2 to 5 years, account for 30.9% of the sample, while more established companies, over 10 years old, make up 23.7%.

Table 4. Distribution of Companies by Respondent Type

Type of respondent	Percentage	Number of Respondents
Executive	33%	32
Management controller	47,4%	46
Operational Manager	13,4%	13
Financial Manager	6,2%	6

The study sample is primarily composed of management controllers, accounting for 47.4% of respondents. Executives represent 33% of the sample, operational managers 13.4%, and financial managers are the least represented, at 6.2%.

3.3. Description of Variables

In this study, to assess the roles of management control during the COVID-19 crisis, we focused on five key functions identified in the literature as essential for strengthening resilience and effectively responding to crises, namely: Reactivity; Process improvement; Strategic orientation; Strategy integration; and Resilience (Simons, 1995; Bréchet & Mevellec, 2008; Duchek, 2020; Shepherd & Williams, 2023; Weber et al., 2024; Elhamma & El-Moumane, 2025). Table 5 presents the five management control missions examined in this study during times of crisis, along with their definitions.

Table 5. Management Control Missions During Crises: Definitions and Their Relationship to Crises

	Definition
Reactivity	Reactivity is defined as an organization's ability to rapidly detect changes in its environment and adjust its actions accordingly.
Process improvement	It refers to an organization's ability to continuously review and optimize its internal processes to improve efficiency and reduce costs.
Strategic orientation	It refers to the alignment of operational and financial decisions with an organization's long-term strategic objectives.
Strategy integration	It refers to the ability to connect the different organizational levels—functional, operational, and tactical—to ensure the coherent implementation of the strategy.
Resilience	Resilience refers to an organization's capacity to absorb shocks, recover rapidly, and learn from crises to enhance its long-term sustainability.

To collect responses, participants were asked: "How do you assess the importance of management control in the following missions during the COVID-19 crisis?" Five missions were presented, each with a brief explanation: reactivity, process improvement, strategic orientation, strategy integration, and resilience. For each mission, respondents rated its importance on a five-point scale, from "very low importance" to "very high importance."

4. RESULTS AND DISCUSSION

4.1. Presentation of Survey Results

The main results of the survey are summarized in Table 6.

Table 6. Principal Results of the Survey

	Very Low Importance		Low Importance		Moderate Importance		High Importance		Very High Importance		Total	
	N.	%	N.	%	N.	%	N.	%	N.	%	N.	%
Reactivity	1	1%	4	4.1%	9	9.3%	38	39.2%	45	46.4%	97	100%
Process improvement	0	0%	1	1%	3	3.1%	31	32%	62	63.9%	97	100%
Strategic orientation	1	1%	6	6.2%	18	18.6%	40	41.2%	32	33%	97	100%
Strategy integration	0	00%	4	4.1%	10	10.3%	36	37.1%	47	48.5%	97	100%
Resilience	0	00%	1	1%	3	3.1%	30	30.9%	63	64.9%	97	100%

As shown in Table 5, the results indicate that respondents generally perceive management control as playing an important role in various tasks during a crisis. For reactivity (see graph), over 74% of respondents consider that management control contributes strongly or very strongly, whereas approximately 25% perceive its contribution as moderate or weak.

Figure 1. Importance of Management Control for Organizational Reactivity During Crises

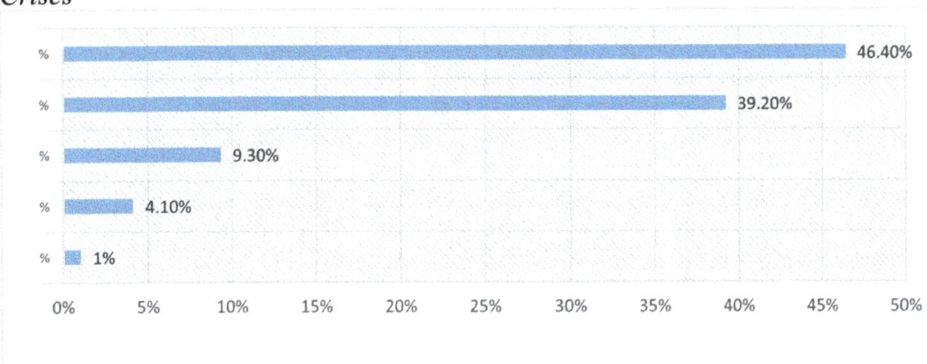

Regarding process improvement, respondents view management control as crucial during crises, with nearly 96% rating its contribution as strong or very strong. This highlights the importance of optimizing operations in a crisis context.

Figure 2. Importance of Management Control for Organizational Process Improvement During Crises

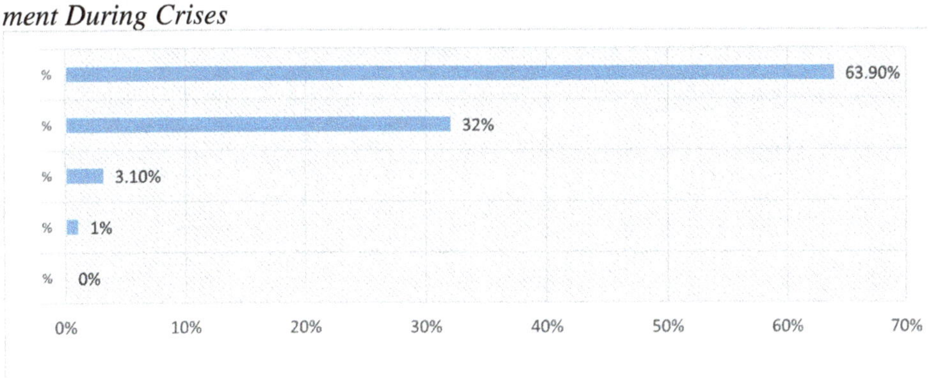

Strategic orientation is also highly valued, with approximately 74% of respondents rating its contribution as strong or very strong, demonstrating the significant role of management control as a driver of strategic alignment during crises.

Figure 3. Importance of Management Control for Organizational Strategic Orientation During Crises

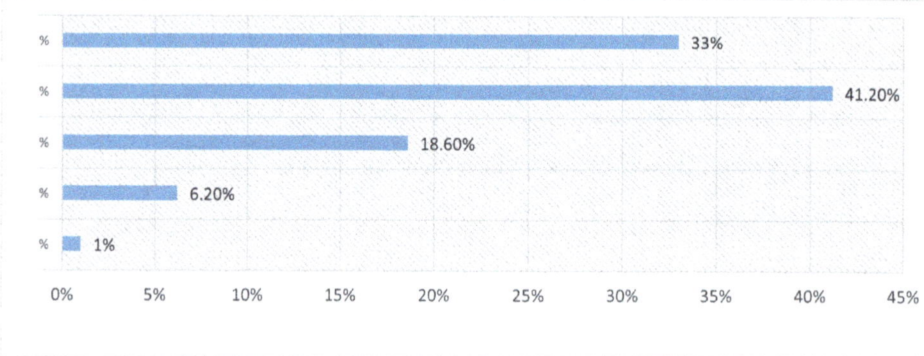

Regarding strategy integration, over 85% of respondents consider that management control plays a strong or very strong role during crises, highlighting its importance in coordinating the organization's various functions.

Figure 4. Importance of Management Control for Organizational Strategic Integration During Crises

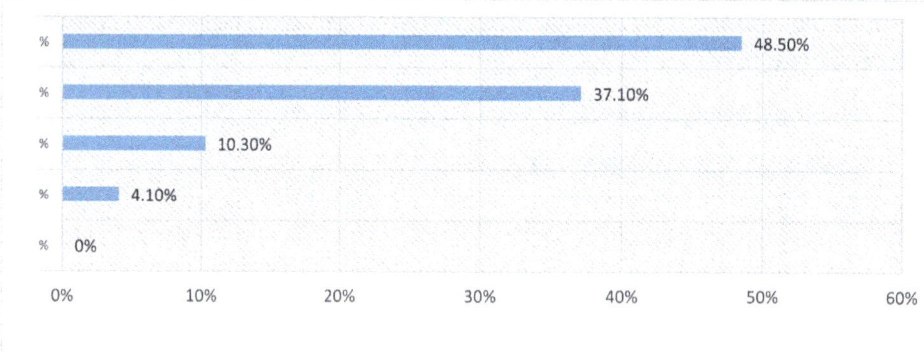

Finally, resilience is the highest-rated dimension, with nearly 96% of respondents indicating a strong or very strong contribution. This confirms that management control enhances organizations' ability to absorb shocks and adapt rapidly during crises.

Figure 5. Importance of Management Control for Organizational Resilience During Crises

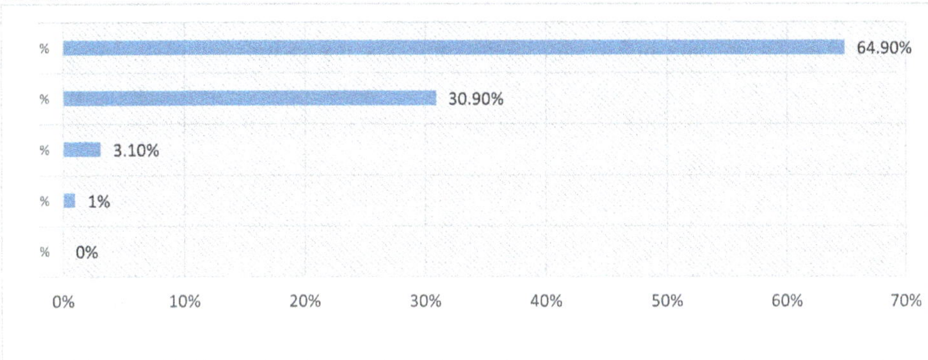

4.2. Results of Statistical Tests for Research Hypothesis Validation

In this study, five variables representing the roles of management control during crises were evaluated, namely: reactivity, process improvement, strategic orientation, strategy integration and resilience. Each variable reflects a specific aspect of management control systems in a crisis context. To test the research hypotheses, we conducted normality tests to confirm the suitability of parametric methods, followed by one-tailed t-tests, one-way ANOVA, Tukey's post-hoc tests, and Chi-square tests.

Table 7. Results of the Normality Tests

Variables	Shapiro-Wilk p-value	KolmogorovSmirnov Statistic p-value
Reactivity	0.12	0.08
Process improvement	0.15	0.09
Strategic orientation	0.05	0.04
Strategy integration	0.10	0.07
Resilience	0.11	0.09

As shown in Table 7, the results of the normality tests indicate how each variable conforms to a normal distribution. The Shapiro-Wilk test shows that all variables have p-values equal to or greater than 0.05, suggesting no significant deviation from normality. Similarly, the Kolmogorov-Smirnov test yields p-values greater than 0.05 for all variables except "Strategic Orientation" ($p = 0.04$), which shows a slight deviation. Overall, the variables "Responsiveness," "Process Improvement," "Strategy Integration," and "Resilience" approximately follow a normal distribution, while "Strategic Orientation" exhibits a minor departure from normality. These results support the use of parametric statistical methods for most variables. Moreover, since tests such as ANOVA and t-tests are robust to minor violations of normality, particularly with sufficiently large sample sizes (n > 30), this slight deviation can be considered negligible.

Table 8. t-Test Results for Differences in Means of Management Control Dimensions

Dimensions of Management Control	Mean	t-test (t-stat)	P-value (t)
Reactivity	4.24	21.96	3.25e-39 (<0,001)
Process improvement	4.58	23.03	6.94e-41 (<0,001)
Strategic orientation	3.95	10.45	1.63e-17 (<0,001)
Strategy integration	4.29	18.76	6.97e-34 (<0,001)
Resilience	4.6	27.55	2.21e-47 (<0,001)

The results presented in the table 8 show the means and one-tailed t-tests for the different dimensions of management control. The one-tailed t-tests indicate that the mean responses for each dimension are all significantly higher than 3. The high mean values, ranging from 3.95 for "Strategic Orientation" to 4.6 for "Resilience," reflect an overall positive assessment of these dimensions by the participants. Moreover, the p-values associated with each t-test are extremely low (<0.001), well below the 0.05 threshold, confirming the statistical significance of these results. This demonstrates a clear consensus among participants regarding the important role of management control in crisis management. Consequently, "Reactivity," "Process Improvement," "Strategic Orientation," "Strategy Integration," and "Resilience" are all perceived as essential and effective elements in this context.

Table 9. ANOVA Test of Mean Differences

ANOVA (F-stat)	P-value (ANOVA)
14.93	1.65e-11 (<0,001)

The ANOVA results show an F-statistic of 14.93 with an extremely low p-value (1.65e-11, <0.001), indicating that the different dimensions of management control are not perceived equally by respondents. In other words, some dimensions are considered more important than others. These findings were confirmed by a Tukey post-hoc test, which highlighted that certain dimensions of management control play a more crucial role in a crisis context. In particular, "Process Improvement" and "Resilience" were identified as key factors facilitating organizational adaptation, emphasizing their importance for effective crisis management.

Table 10. Chi-Square Test Results

Chi square (χ^2)	P-valeur (Chi square)
15.82	0.031

The Chi-square test results show a χ^2 statistic of 15.82 with a p-value of 0.031, which is below the 0.05 threshold. This low p-value indicates a significant association among the participants' responses.

The results of our analyses support all five research hypotheses, indicating that management control plays a significant role in enhancing organizational reactivity (H1), process improvement (H2), strategic orientation (H3), strategic integration (H4), and resilience (H5) during times of crisis. These findings support the idea that management control systems operate as an integrated whole, functioning coherently to facilitate organizational adaptation in a crisis context. In other words, the different dimensions of management control are not isolated but work together to enhance organizational resilience and effectiveness.

The results of this research provide empirical support for the theoretical foundations concerning the role of management control in fostering organizational resilience within turbulent environments. Specifically, the findings are consistent with the dynamic capabilities framework proposed by Teece, Pisano, and Shuen (1997), which suggests that organizations must mobilize their sensing, seizing, and transforming capabilities to adapt effectively to change and crisis conditions. The dimensions identified in this study (reactivity, process improvement, strategic orientation, strategy integration, and resilience) represent tangible manifestations of these dynamic capabilities within management control systems. Moreover, according to contingency theory (Otley, 1980), the results show that management control mechanisms are flexible (Elhamma, 2015, 2023) and adapt to the specific context of each crisis, helping organizations maintain strategic consistency and adaptability. Finally, the findings also corroborate the Levers of Control framework (Simons, 1995), which posits that management control enhances organizational resilience by balancing diagnostic and interactive levers to support strategic alignment and performance in uncertain environments.

CONCLUSION

This study aimed to examine the roles of management control in companies during times of crisis, focusing on five main functions: reactivity, process improvement, strategy orientation, strategy integration and resilience. To achieve this objective, a questionnaire survey was conducted with 97 Moroccan companies. The results, based on several statistical tests, show that management control is viewed as highly important during crises across all five dimensions. Process improvement and resilience received the highest ratings, with nearly 96% of respondents considering them highly or very highly important. Responsiveness and strategic orientation were also valued, with around 74% rating them as highly or very highly important. Statistical tests confirm that all dimensions are significantly above average, though their perceived effects differ. Post-hoc analyses reveal that process improvement and resilience are particularly critical for organizational adaptation. Overall, the findings indicate that management control functions as an integrated system that strengthens a company's capacity to respond, adapt, and remain resilient in crisis situations.

The findings of this study offer significant theoretical and practical contributions. Theoretically, it enriches the literature on management control in times of crisis by demonstrating its strategic role beyond its traditional financial steering function. It introduces an integrated framework of management control built around five dimensions—reactivity, process improvement, strategic orientation, strategic integration, and resilience—confirming their distinct contributions to organizational adaptation during crises. The results thus support the view that management control is a key driver of organizational resilience rather than merely a reporting tool. Practically, the study provides managers and management controllers with clear guidance on priority actions during periods of turbulence, particularly emphasizing process improvement and the development of resilience capabilities. It also underscores the need to invest in integrated control systems that foster organizational agility.

However, this research has certain methodological limitations that suggest avenues for improvement. First, the study is based on a questionnaire survey of 97 Moroccan companies, which limits the generalizability of the findings to other geographical or sectoral contexts. Future research could therefore include companies from other regions (e.g., Asia, Latin America) to enable comparative analysis. Second, the data collected are self-reported, which may introduce perception and social desirability biases. Future studies could mitigate this limitation by incorporating secondary data from internal company documents. Third, the research adopts a cross-sectional design, which restricts the ability to capture changes in the roles of management control over time or to establish strong causal relationships. Future research could address this by using panel data to better analyze the evolution of management control practices over time.

REFERENCES

Ahmed, F., Sohag, K., Islam, M. M., & Hassan, M. K. (2025). Navigating turbulence: How do geopolitical risks and oil price shocks shape global equity markets? A GVAR approach. *Borsa Istanbul Review*, *25*(3), 449–467. DOI: 10.1016/j.bir.2025.01.016

Al-Rousan, N., Al-Najjar, H., & Al-Najjar, D. (2024). The impact of Russo-Ukrainian war, COVID-19, and oil prices on global food security. *Heliyon*, *10*(8), e29279. DOI: 10.1016/j.heliyon.2024.e29279 PMID: 38638981

Allam, Z., Bibri, S. E., & Sharpe, S. A. (2022). The rising impacts of the COVID-19 pandemic and the Russia–Ukraine war: Energy transition, climate justice, global inequality, and supply chain disruption. *Resources*, *11*(11), 99. DOI: 10.3390/resources11110099

Anand, A., Singh, S. K., Bowen, M., & Rangarajan, D. (2024). Strategic renewal during crises: A pragmatist proposition for multinational enterprises in a globalized world. *Journal of International Management*, *30*(3), 101134. DOI: 10.1016/j.intman.2024.101134

Anthony, R. N., & Govindarajan, V. (2007). Management control systems (12e éd.). McGraw-Hill.

Barton, R. M. (1993). *Crisis management*. Oxford University Press.

Bedford, D. S., Speklé, R. F., & Widener, S. K. (2022). Budgeting and employee stress in times of crisis: Evidence from the Covid-19 pandemic. *Accounting, Organizations and Society*, *101*, 101346. DOI: 10.1016/j.aos.2022.101346

Bégin, L., & Chabaud, D. (2010). La résilience des organisations. Le cas d'une entreprise familiale. Revue française de gestion, 200(1), 127–142. https://doi.org/ DOI: 10.3166/rfg.200.127-142

Bracci, E., & Tallaki, M. (2021). Resilience capacities and management control systems in public sector organisations. *Journal of Accounting & Organizational Change*, *17*(3), 332–351. DOI: 10.1108/JAOC-10-2019-0111

Bréchet, J.-P., & Mevellec, P. (2008). L'articulation de la stratégie et du contrôle de gestion: L'apport de la modélisation en termes d'activités et de processus. Communication présentée à la 17 Conférence de l'AIMS, Nice, France. Disponible sur: https://www.strategie-aims.com/conferences/17-vieme-conference-de-l-aims/communications/1031-l-articulation-de-la-strategie-et-du-controle-de-gestion-l-apport-de-la-modelisation-en-termes-d-activites-et-de-processus/download

Bundy, J., Pfarrer, M. D., Short, C. E., & Coombs, W. T. (2017). Crises and crisis management: Integration, interpretation, and research development. *Journal of Management, 43*(6), 1661–1692.

Carayannis, E. G., Papamichail, G., & Zotas, N.. (2025). Corporate foresight: Navigating uncertainty in a VUCA world. *Journal of the Knowledge Economy*. Advance online publication. DOI: 10.1007/s13132-024-02587-4

Cevik, S. (2023). Long live globalization: Geopolitical shocks and international trade (IMF Working Paper No. 2023/225). International Monetary Fund. https://doi.org/DOI: 10.5089/9798400258169.001

Ciekanowski, Z., Nowicka, J., Żurawski, S., Czech, A., & Zdunek, M. (2023). Crisis management and crisis situation in the organization. *European Research Studies Journal, 26*(4), 339–353. DOI: 10.35808/ersj/3288

Coombs, W. T. (2015). *Ongoing crisis communication: Planning, managing, and responding* (4th ed.). SAGE Publications.

Coombs, W. T., & Laufer, D. (2018). Global crisis management – Current research and future directions. *Journal of International Management, 24*(3), 199–203. DOI: 10.1016/j.intman.2017.12.003

Duchek, S. (2020). Organizational resilience: A capability-based conceptualization. *Business Research, 13*, 215–246. DOI: 10.1007/s40685-019-0085-7

Elhamma, A. (2010). La comptabilité par activités au Maroc: Une étude empirique utilisant la théorie de la contingence. El-Bahith Review, 8(1), 39-48. Retrieved from https://elbahithreview.edu.dz/index.php/bahith/article/view/652

Elhamma, A. (2011). Impact de la taille sur le contenu des tableaux de bord dans les entreprises au Maroc: résultats d'une étude empirique. Revue Marocaine de Recherche en Management et Marketing, 4-5, 317-329. Retriever from https://halshs.archives-ouvertes.fr/halshs-00670474

Elhamma, A. (2014). Performance du Balanced Scorecard: Perception des responsables d'entreprises. *Revue Internationale de Management et de Stratégie, 5*(2), 1–9.

Elhamma, A. (2015). The relationship between budgetary evaluation, firm size, and performance. *Journal of Management Development, 34*(8), 973–986. DOI: 10.1108/JMD-06-2014-0053

Elhamma, A. (2023). The relationship between organisational decentralisation, balanced scorecard and its perceived benefits in Moroccan SMEs. International Journal of Accounting. *Auditing and Performance Evaluation, 19*(2), 185–202. DOI: 10.1504/IJAAPE.2023.132384

Elhamma, A. (2024a). Participant observation as a qualitative research method in management sciences: Interests, conditions, and limitations. In Bentalha, B., & Alla, L. (Eds.), *Applying qualitative research methods to management science* (pp. 75–91). IGI Global., DOI: 10.4018/979-8-3693-5543-5.ch004

Elhamma, A. (2024b). Determinants of national IFRS adoption: Evidence from the Middle East and North Africa region. International Journal of Accounting. *Auditing and Performance Evaluation, 20*(1-2), 69–90. DOI: 10.1504/IJAAPE.2024.135535

Elhamma, A. (2025a). A half-century of International Accounting Standards (IAS/IFRS): Assessing the mandatory adoption, impact, and Morocco's position in the convergence process. In Vardari, L., & Qabrati, I. (Eds.), *Financial reporting standards with global trade needs* (pp. 185–203)., DOI: 10.4018/979-8-3373-0887-6.ch007

Elhamma, A. (2025b). Lack of Resilience and Failure of Small and Medium-Sized Enterprises (SMEs) in Morocco: Current Situation and Key Determinants. In Dias Rouco, J. C., & Nunes Figueiredo, P. C. (Eds.), *Enhancing Resilience in Business Continuity Management* (pp. 245–266). IGI Global., DOI: 10.4018/979-8-3693-8809-9.ch008

Elhamma, A. (2025c). Digitalization of management control: Case of Moroccan companies. In Khalil, A., Bousselmi, H. E., & Ben Slimene, I. (Eds.), *Digital technologies for sustainability and quality control* (pp. 33–52)., DOI: 10.4018/979-8-3693-4373-9.ch002

Elhamma, A. (2026). The impact of mandatory IFRS adoption on foreign direct investment: Evidence from Jordan, Morocco, and the United Arab Emirates. In Elhamma, A. (Ed.), *Adoption, Impact, and Challenges of International Financial Reporting Standards* (pp. 197–222). IGI Global., DOI: 10.4018/979-8-3373-1902-5.ch007

Elhamma, A., & El-Moumane, R. (2025). The role of strategic planning in resilience and crisis management: A case study of a public organization in Morocco. In Dias Rouco, J. C., & Nunes Figueiredo, P. C. (Eds.), *Enhancing Resilience in Business Continuity Management* (pp. 433–460). IGI Global., DOI: 10.4018/979-8-3693-8809-9.ch015

Elhamma, A., & Lassaad, B. M. (2017). Liens entre participation budgétaire, taille et performance: Cas des entreprises au Maroc. *Revue Congolaise de Gestion*, *24*(2), 43–62.

Elhamma, A., & Loukili, Z. (2025). Emergence of public-private partnership policies: A comparative study of Morocco and France. In Baporikar, N. (Ed.), *Public private partnerships for social development and impact* (pp. 155–178)., DOI: 10.4018/979-8-3373-3471-4.ch007

Elhamma, A., & Snoussi, N. (2026). Challenges to the adoption of the balanced scorecard as a managerial innovation in Moroccan SMEs. In Jamil, G. L., Jamil, L. C., Paletta, F. C., Geada, N., & Vieira, A. A. P. (Eds.), *Innovation management for disruptive maturity in competitive scenarios* (pp. 249–272). IGI Global., DOI: 10.4018/979-8-3693-4030-1.ch011

Erdiaw-Kwasie, M. O., Abunyewah, M., Yusif, S., & Arhin, P. (2023). Small and medium enterprises (SMEs) in a pandemic: A systematic review of pandemic risk impacts, coping strategies and resilience. *Heliyon*, *9*(10), e20352. DOI: 10.1016/j.heliyon.2023.e20352 PMID: 37767482

European Environment Agency. (2025, July 15). Extreme weather: Floods, droughts and heatwaves. https://www.eea.europa.eu/en/topics/in-depth/extreme-weather-floods-droughts-and-heatwaves

Florez-Jimenez, M. P., Lleo, A., Danvila-del-Valle, I., & Sánchez-Marín, G. (2024). Corporate sustainability, organizational resilience and corporate purpose: A triple concept for achieving long-term prosperity. *Management Decision*, *62*(7), 2189–2213. DOI: 10.1108/MD-06-2023-0938

Garrido-Moreno, A., Martín-Rojas, R., & García-Morales, V. J. (2024). The key role of innovation and organizational resilience in improving business performance: A mixed-methods approach. *International Journal of Information Management*, *77*, 102777. DOI: 10.1016/j.ijinfomgt.2024.102777

Geurts, A., Geerdink, T., & Sprenkeling, M. (2022). Accelerated innovation in crises: The role of collaboration in the development of alternative ventilators during the COVID-19 pandemic. *Technology in Society*, *68*, 101923. DOI: 10.1016/j.techsoc.2022.101923 PMID: 36540134

Hermann, C. F. (1963). Some consequences of crisis which limit the viability of organizations. *Administrative Science Quarterly*, *8*(1), 61–82.

Jukka, T. (2021). Does business strategy and management control system fit determine performance? *International Journal of Productivity and Performance Management, 72*(5), 659–678.

Leoni, G., Lai, A., Stacchezzini, R., Steccolini, I., Brammer, S., Linnenluecke, M., & Demirag, I. (2021). Accounting, management and accountability in times of crisis: Lessons from the COVID-19 pandemic. *Accounting, Auditing & Accountability Journal, 34*(6), 1305–1319. DOI: 10.1108/AAAJ-06-2020-4784

Martins, A., Oliveira, C., Silva, R., & Castelo Branco, M. (2023). Management control practices as performance facilitators in a crisis context. *Administrative Sciences, 13*(7), 163. DOI: 10.3390/admsci13070163

McKibbin, W., & Fernando, R. (2023). The global economic impacts of the COVID-19 pandemic. *Economic Modelling, 129*, 106551. DOI: 10.1016/j.econmod.2023.106551

Merchant, K. A., & Van der Stede, W. A. (2017). *Management control systems: Performance measurement, evaluation and incentives* (4th ed.). Pearson Education.

Mitroff, I. I. (2001). *Managing crises before they happen.* American Management Association., DOI: 10.1016/S0737-6782(02)00133-9

Otley, D. T. (1980). The contingency theory of management accounting: Achievement and prognosis. *Accounting, Organizations and Society, 5*(4), 413–428. DOI: 10.1016/0361-3682(80)90040-9

Panneer, S., Kantamaneni, K., Palaniswamy, U., Bhat, L., Pushparaj, R. R. B., Nayar, K. R., Soundari Manuel, H., Flower, F. X. L. L., & Rice, L. (2022). Health, economic and social development challenges of the COVID-19 pandemic: Strategies for multiple and interconnected issues. *Healthcare (Basel), 10*(5), 770. DOI: 10.3390/healthcare10050770 PMID: 35627910

Pizzorni, M., Innocenti, A., & Tollin, N. (2024). Droughts and floods in a changing climate and implications for multi-hazard urban planning: A review. *City and Environment Interactions, 24*, 100169. DOI: 10.1016/j.cacint.2024.100169

Rikhardsson, P., Rohde, C., Christensen, L., & Batt, C. E. (2021). Management controls and crisis: Evidence from the banking sector. *Accounting, Auditing & Accountability Journal, 34*(4), 757–785. DOI: 10.1108/AAAJ-01-2020-4400

Sanchis, R., & Poler, R. (2019). Enterprise resilience assessment—A quantitative approach. *Sustainability, 11*(16), 4327. DOI: 10.3390/su11164327

Shepherd, D. A., & Williams, T. A. (2023). Different response paths to organizational resilience. *Small Business Economics, 61*(1), 23–58. DOI: 10.1007/s11187-022-00689-4 PMID: 38625189

Simons, R. (1995). *Levers of control: How managers use innovative control systems to drive strategic renewal.* Harvard Business School Press.

Teece, D., Peteraf, M. A., & Leih, S. (2016). Dynamic capabilities and organizational agility: Risk, uncertainty, and entrepreneurial management in the innovation economy. *California Management Review, 58*(4), 13–35. DOI: 10.1525/cmr.2016.58.4.13

Teece, D. J., Pisano, G., & Shuen, A. (1997). Dynamic capabilities and strategic management. *Strategic Management Journal, 18*(7), 509–533. DOI: 10.1002/(SICI)1097-0266(199708)18:7%3C509:AID-SMJ882%3E3.0.CO;2-Z

Tessier, S., & Otley, D. (2012). A conceptual development of Simons' Levers of Control framework. *Management Accounting Research, 23*(3), 171–185. DOI: 10.1016/j.mar.2012.04.003

Troise, C., Corvello, V., Ghobadian, A., & O'Regan, N. (2022). How can SMEs successfully navigate VUCA environment: The role of agility in the digital transformation era. *Technological Forecasting and Social Change, 174*, 121227. DOI: 10.1016/j.techfore.2021.121227

Weber, M. M., Pedell, B., & Rötzel, P. G. (2024). Resilience-oriented management control systems: A systematic review of the relationships between organizational resilience and management control systems. *Journal of Management Control, 35*, 563–620. DOI: 10.1007/s00187-024-00385-2

Xia, H., Liu, M., Wang, P., & Tan, X. (2024). Strategies to enhance the corporate innovation resilience in digital era: A cross-organizational collaboration perspective. *Heliyon, 10*(20), e39132. DOI: 10.1016/j.heliyon.2024.e39132 PMID: 39498084

KEY TERMS AND DEFINITIONS

A crisis: is an unexpected and disruptive event or situation that threatens the normal functioning of an organization and demands a prompt and appropriate response.

Management control: refers to a system of processes, methods, and tools implemented within public or private organizations to enable managers to plan, monitor, and assess organizational performance in order to achieve strategic objectives.

Organizational resilience: is the ability of an organization, whether public or private, to anticipate, absorb, and adapt to environmental disruptions or crises in order to prevent organizational failure.

The COVID-19 crisis: is a global health emergency caused by the rapid spread of the SARS-CoV-2 virus, resulting in significant disruptions across health, economic, and social domains, and compelling organizations to rapidly adapt their practices and strategies to manage the ensuing uncertainty.

Chapter 9

The Impact of Marketing as an Entrepreneurial Element in Fragile States: Coping Mechanisms Amid Conflict and Geopolitical Uncertainty

Konstantinos Poyiadjis
https://orcid.org/0009-0000-9748-6534
Neapolis University Pafos, Cyprus

Harry Ph. Sophocleous
https://orcid.org/0000-0002-8790-842X
Neapolis University Pafos, Cyprus

ABSTRACT

This chapter examines the role of marketing and branding as strategic tools of resilience for entrepreneurs operating in fragile states. Drawing on resilience theory, marketing scholarship, and nation branding literature, it argues that marketing transcends its traditional commercial function to become a socio-political practice that builds trust, signals legitimacy, and connects local firms to global markets. Case studies from Syria, Palestine, and sub-saharan Africa illustrate how entrepreneurs deploy marketing to navigate conflict, sanctions, and institutional weakness. Integrating insights from scholars and contemporary entrepreneurship research, the chapter highlights how branding can function as informal governance, a trust architecture, and a bridge to international solidarity and investment.

DOI: 10.4018/979-8-3373-6991-4.ch009

1.INTRODUCTION

Fragile states represent some of the most complex and precarious environments for economic activity. Characterized by weak institutions, persistent conflict, corruption, sanctions, and vulnerability to external shocks, these states are often studied from the perspectives of International Relations (IR), development, and security. International organizations such as the World Bank, OECD, and UNDP frequently classify them as countries where governance is undermined, legitimacy is contested, and social contracts are fragile. In such environments, entrepreneurs must navigate extraordinary risks while attempting to sustain their businesses and provide livelihoods.

Much of the academic and policy literature on fragile states has focused on state capacity, international aid, or peacebuilding. Comparatively less attention has been given to how micro-level entrepreneurial strategies (particularly marketing) function as mechanisms of resilience and adaptation. This chapter seeks to fill that gap by framing entrepreneurship as a survival mechanism and marketing as a resilience-building tool within fragile institutional contexts. The argument is that in conditions of extreme uncertainty, marketing does not only serve to promote products but becomes a socio-political practice: it builds trust with consumers, signals legitimacy, and bridges local firms to international markets.

An explicit research question in which the chapter tries to answer, is "*How does marketing operate as a resilience mechanism for entrepreneurs navigating fragile state environments*?"

2. THEORETICAL FRAMEWORK

2.1 Fragile States and Resilience

The concept of fragile states has become a cornerstone of interdisciplinary research at the intersection of IR, development studies, and security analysis. In academic discourse, fragility transcends the notion of administrative weakness or poor governance performance. It represents a deeper erosion of legitimacy, authority, and capacity, three interdependent pillars that underpin statehood and social order (OECD, 2022); (World Bank, 2023).

From an IR perspective, fragile states reflect the systemic inequalities of the global order, where structural dependency, colonial legacies, and asymmetric globalization reproduce internal instability (Call, 2010); (Rotberg, 2004). Fragility is not merely an outcome of internal failure, but the product of transnational power relations, in which states are embedded in complex webs of political and economic interdependence (Hameiri & Jones, 2015).

Fragile states are thus situated within what term hybrid political orders, governance arrangements in which formal institutions coexist, compete, or collaborate with traditional authorities, non-state armed groups, or informal economic networks (Boege, Brown, Clements, & Nolan, 2009). These hybrid systems often emerge as pragmatic responses to the limitations of state authority, providing social services, conflict mediation, and local legitimacy in the absence of effective central governance. Such hybrid resilience highlights the adaptability of societies under crisis rather than their collapse. Far from being "*ungoverned spaces*," fragile states embody alternative modes of political order that challenge Westphalian assumptions about sovereignty, authority, and territorial control (Chandler, 2014). In this sense, fragility does not necessarily signify total failure, but rather a reconfiguration of governance, where legitimacy and power are continuously negotiated among multiple actors operating across local and transnational levels.

2.2 Defining fragility in global governance frameworks

The term fragility has evolved from a descriptive label for weak or failing states into a core analytical category of global governance. Over the past two decades, international organizations such as the OECD, World Bank, and United Nations Development Programme (UNDP) have developed comprehensive frameworks to operationalize fragility, integrating economic, political, and social dimensions into measurable indicators (OECD, 2022); (World Bank, 2023); (UNDP, 2022). Although the terminology varies (from "*fragile and conflict-affected situations*" (FCS) to "*multidimensional fragility*") there is broad consensus that fragility encompasses more than conflict or poverty: *it reflects systemic vulnerability within states and their relationships to the global system.*

Fragility conceptualizes through five interlinked dimensions (economic, environmental, political, security, and societal) arguing that a state's exposure to risk and its capacity for resilience determine its overall level of fragility (OECD, 2022). The World Bank's Harmonized List of Fragile and Conflict-Affected Situations applies governance indicators, violence data, and institutional performance metrics to identify countries facing heightened instability (World Bank, 2023). Meanwhile, the UNDP's Human Development Reports embed fragility within broader frameworks of human security, sustainability, and inequality, emphasizing that vulnerability must be understood as both a domestic governance issue and an outcome of structural dependencies in the international political economy (UNDP, 2022).

These frameworks converge on three diagnostic pillars of state functionality (OECD, 2022); (Patrick, 2011), a) authority b) legitimacy, and c) capacity. Authority refers to the ability of state institutions to enforce laws, maintain order, and ensure security. Legitimacy involves the public's belief in fairness, inclusiveness, and accountability of political processes. Capacity captures the administrative, fiscal, and technical resources that enable service delivery. The erosion of any of these dimensions can lead to cascading instability, as institutional fragility undermines trust, fuels conflict and disrupts economic performance (Carment & Samy, 2021).

Crucially, fragility is now recognized as dynamic rather than static, a spectrum along which states move in response to governance reforms, external shocks, or peacebuilding interventions (Carment & Samy, 2021); (Brück, Naudé, & Verwimp, 2013).

This dynamic understanding challenges the older "*failed state*" paradigm (Call, 2010), emphasizing instead adaptive resilience: even fragile states possess endogenous capacities for recovery when social cohesion, entrepreneurship, and local governance networks are mobilized effectively. The growing adoption of resilience-oriented approaches by multilateral institutions marks a paradigmatic shift, from viewing fragility as a deficit to recognizing it as a condition that can be mitigated and transformed through inclusive governance, innovation, and partnership-based development (UNDP, 2022); (World Bank, 2023).

2.3 Resilience in International Relations Theory

The concept of resilience has become one of the most influential paradigms in contemporary IR symbolizing a broader epistemological shift from control to adaptation. Initially emerging in ecology and systems theory (Holling, 1973), resilience entered security and governance discourse in the early 2000s as states and international institutions sought frameworks to manage uncertainty rather than eliminate it (Chandler, 2014); (Joseph, 2013). In the IR context, resilience describes the capacity of political systems, societies, or institutions to absorb shocks, adapt to stress, and transform in response to crises while maintaining core identity and function. It marks a transition from the logic of prevention and prediction (dominant during the Cold War) to the governance of complexity in a multipolar, interdependent.

2.4 Resilience Across IR Paradigms

Within IR theory, resilience resonates differently across the major paradigms of realism, liberalism, and constructivism. From a realist perspective, resilience is rooted in the principle of *self-help*: states must rely on their own capabilities to survive in an anarchic international system (Mearsheimer J., 2001). In this view, building resilience means strengthening sovereignty, deterrence, and internal cohesion to withstand external shocks or coercion. Fragile states thus exemplify what realism warns against, overdependence on external actors and the loss of autonomous capacity. Realists therefore frame resilience primarily as strategic endurance, emphasizing military preparedness, state control, and national self-reliance.

In contrast, liberal institutionalism interprets resilience through *cooperative interdependence*. The dense web of global institutions, economic ties, and transnational networks enables collective responses to systemic stress. From this standpoint, resilience is not isolation but embedded cooperation: states strengthen their adaptive capacity through international regimes, regional organizations, and shared norms (Keohane & Nye, 1977). The EU's *Global Strategy on Resilience* and the UN's *Sustaining Peace Agenda* embody this liberal understanding, linking resilience to governance reform, development aid, and conflict prevention (European External Action Service, 2016); (UNDP, 2022).

Finally, constructivist approaches focus on *normative and ideational resilience*, the ways in which identities, beliefs, and social narratives allow societies to withstand crises. For constructivists, resilience depends on the strength of shared meanings and collective identity that sustain legitimacy during turbulence (Hoffmann, 2017). Thus, society may recover from economic collapse or war if its social fabric (trust, national identity, or moral narrative) remains intact. Constructivists therefore view resilience as a discursive process of rebuilding legitimacy, where communication and shared purpose are as vital as material resources. These theoretical perspectives provide the macro-level lenses through which the chapter interprets micro-level entrepreneurial resilience, showing how marketing behaviors, legitimacy-building strategies, and adaptation mechanisms reflect broader logics of power, cooperation, and identity.

2.5 From Risk Management to Adaptive Governance

Beyond these theoretical traditions, recent scholarship conceptualizes resilience as part of a broader transformation in global governance. The "resilience turn" represents a move away from top-down control and prediction toward *adaptive governance*, a mode of rule that values flexibility, learning, and participation.

Resilience politics reflects a "responsibilization" of actors: citizens, communities, and firms are increasingly expected to manage risks themselves rather than rely on state protection (Chandler, 2014). Extends this argument, describing resilience as a form of neoliberal governmentality, where self-organization replaces collective welfare and security provision (Joseph, 2013). Yet, this shift also empowers local actors by recognizing their agency and knowledge. In fragile states, where formal institutions are weak, such decentralized resilience practices (community networks, informal markets, or entrepreneurial adaptation) often sustain social order more effectively than central authority (Brück, Naudé, & Verwimp, 2013).

2.6 Resilience as Power and Legitimacy

The growing prominence of resilience discourse raises critical questions about power and legitimacy in world politics. Who defines what counts as "resilient," and whose interests are served? For many Global South scholars, resilience rhetoric risks becoming a depoliticized substitute for justice, transferring the burden of recovery from international institutions to vulnerable populations. However, when framed inclusively, resilience can also support empowerment, enabling societies to develop context-specific capacities that reduce dependency and enhance autonomy. In this sense, resilience is both a governance strategy and a political value: it legitimizes certain policy orientations (decentralization, self-reliance, innovation) while reflecting deeper shifts in how global order is imagined. For fragile and conflict-affected states, resilience offers a double-edged paradigm, it can justify external disengagement, but it can also nurture endogenous transformation and bottom-up peacebuilding (Bene, Godfrey, Newsham, & Davies, 2013).

2.7 Entrepreneurship and micro-level resilience

At the micro level, entrepreneurs in fragile contexts act as *adaptive governors*, compensating for public-goods deficits by supplying essential goods, services, and employment (Naudé, T., Naude, & Verwimp, 2013). Much of this entrepreneurship is necessity-driven: *entrepreneurial resilience* captures how firms diversify, cultivate informal networks, and leverage community trust to survive conflict, sanctions, and state incapacities (Bullough & Renko, 2013); (Renko, Bullough, & Saeed, 2020). These practices exemplify *everyday statecraft*, the informal enactment of governance when formal institutions falter (Richmond, 2013); (Autesserre, 2012). By keeping exchange networks alive, entrepreneurs contribute to *bottom-up stabilization* and social continuity, embedding markets in solidaristic norms that can outlast political upheaval.

2.8 Fragility, Dependence, and the Global Political Economy

Fragility is also reproduced by structures of the international political economy. Dependency and heterodox development perspectives argue that integration into global markets without robust domestic institutions can entrench vulnerability and external dependence (Amin, 1976); (Rodrik, 2011); (Stiglitz, 2018). The 1990s waves of liberalization often outpaced regulatory capacity, creating exposure to shocks. Contemporary economic sanctions further constrain domestic entrepreneurship by restricting finance, technology imports, logistics, and reputational access to markets. The literature cautions that sanctions may have heterogeneous and sometimes perverse effects on political elites versus ordinary firms (Drezner, 2011); (Early, 2015); (Peksen, 2019); (Kuersten, 2018). From a geopolitical realism lens, fragile states function as arenas where great powers project influence through aid, security cooperation, and infrastructure finance (ex. China's *Belt and Road Initiative* and Western initiatives such as *Prosper Africa* or the EU's *Global Gateway),* (Hameiri & Jones, 2015); (PIIE, 2016). In this milieu, resilience becomes politicized: external actors promote *selective resilience* aligned with their strategic preferences, potentially reinforcing asymmetric dependencies (Joseph, 2013).

2.9 From State Resilience to Societal and Entrepreneurial Resilience

Recent IR scholarship insists on a multi-scalar approach that links macro state stability with meso-level institutional robustness and micro-level adaptive behavior. In many fragile contexts, the *informal economy* sustains livelihoods and often a large share of value creation, operating through dense associational ties that provide mutual insurance and trust (Chen, Martha;, 2012). The diffusion of mobile connectivity and platforms enables entrepreneurs to build *parallel architectures of trust and transaction*, connecting with diasporas, accessing remittances, and tapping e-commerce despite degraded physical infrastructure (GSMA, 2024). Diaspora investors and transnational communities often act as *intermediary governance nodes*, providing finance, market intelligence, and reputational cover that states lack (Riddle & Brinkerhoff, 2011); (Brinkerhoff, 2012). In places like Somalia, South Sudan, or Palestine, these networks underwrite commerce, logistics, and even dispute resolution, effectively *co-producing governance* with local actors.

2.10 Resilience as Governance and Legitimacy

A key insight (and tension) in the resilience agenda is its dual character. While it valorizes local agency, it can also normalize the offloading of responsibility from international actors and state institutions onto individuals and communities (Joseph, 2013). Normatively, this requires careful design: building resilience should not substitute for building institutions. Practically, however, resilience framings can be empowered in slow-reform settings, focusing policy on capabilities for anticipation, learning, and adaptive coordination (Boin & Van Eeten, 2013). For entrepreneurs, resilience depends on legitimacy the perception by consumers, partners, donors, and regulators that a firm is credible despite systemic fragility. Here, *communication, branding, and trust architectures* become politically salient. Marketing ceases to be a mere commercial function; it becomes a *socio-political technology* of legitimacy construction and risk signaling to local and international audiences.

2.11 Bridging IR and entrepreneurship: communicative diplomacy from below

Synthesizing IR and entrepreneurship scholarship reveals that fragility and resilience are mutually constitutive: fragility conditions necessitate resilient practices, which in turn reshape political-economic orders from below. Markets in fragile states thus appear not as frictionless exchanges but as arenas where local agency negotiates with global structures (Rodrik, 2011). Within this arena, entrepreneurs increasingly engage in what can be termed *entrepreneurial diplomacy*: through branding, narrative framing, and cross-border networks, they signal credibility and project alternative images of place that counter fragility stigmas (Safranchuk, 2022); (Fatić, Korać, & Bulatović, 2011); (Nye, 2005). In this sense, marketing operates as micro-level soft power, linking economic survival to political symbolism and contributing (however modestly) to the external legitimation of fragile polities.

Viewed through IR, resilience is both a survival mechanism and a political strategy. Fragile states expose the limits of state-centric governance but also the adaptive capacities of societies and firms under chronic uncertainty. By situating entrepreneurship (and especially the communicative work of marketing) within this framework, we recognize their role in stabilizing exchange, sustaining legitimacy, and weaving transnational ties. Resilience in fragile states is therefore not only about *bouncing back*; it is about *bouncing forward* into new forms of agency, connectivity, and co-produced governance.

2.12 Marketing and Branding

Traditionally associated with promotion and consumer behavior in stable economies, marketing is increasingly seen as a strategic resource for legitimacy, trust, and communication.

Marketing is the process of identifying, communicating, and delivering value to stakeholders; in fragile states, it encompasses strategic storytelling, trust-building, and adaptive signaling to both local and international audiences. Definition – Branding: Branding refers to the creation of a distinct identity visual, narrative, and symbolic that communicates reliability, values, and legitimacy, especially critical in contexts of weak institutional trust.

Nation Branding: Nation branding is the coordinated effort of public and private actors to shape the international image and identity of a country, leveraging this image to benefit local entrepreneurs and SMEs (Sophocleous H. P., 2023). Expanded Role: Branding functions not only to communicate product quality but to construct a socio-political identity for entrepreneurs in fragile states. By embedding cultural narratives, ethical commitments, or resistance to adversity, branding provides a protective layer of meaning that shields entrepreneurs from reputational risks and enables entry into global markets (Sophocleous H. P., 2023); (Sophocleous, H. P.; Masouras, A.; Papademetriou, C.;, 2019).

Branding literature shows how identity construction can generate credibility when institutional guarantees are absent. In fragile contexts, marketing becomes less about competition for market share and more about survival through signaling reliability and forging relationships with consumers and stakeholders. Brand authenticity plays a key role in building trust and enabling forgiveness when brands face reputational crises or consumer scrutiny, which is especially relevant in fragile settings where institutional guarantees are weak (Papadopoulou, Vardarsuyu, & Oghazi, 2023).

By combining these perspectives, the chapter advances the proposition that marketing constitutes an underexplored form of resilience strategy in fragile states, connecting micro-level entrepreneurial practices with macro-level dynamics of fragility and geopolitics.

3. GEOPOLITICAL AND INTERNATIONAL RELATIONS CONTEXT

3.1 Conflict Economies and Political Fragmentation

Armed conflict fundamentally reshapes political and economic structures. In fragile and conflict-affected states, markets rarely disappear. They are reconfigured into "conflict economies", in which violence, scarcity and patronage networks structure production, distribution and accumulation (Berdal & Keen, 1997); (Ballentine & Sherman, 2003). These systems blur the boundary between licit and illicit activity as warlords, political elites and private entrepreneurs participate simultaneously in combat and commerce (Billon & Philippe, 2001); (Collier & Hoeffler, 2004). Conflict thus appears not only as a breakdown of governance, but also as a mode of governance through which power and profit are reorganised.

From an IR perspective, conflict economies expose the entanglement of domestic fragility with external intervention. They demonstrate how global processes (sanctions, arms transfers, humanitarian aid and resource trade) interact to sustain localised power structures (Duffield, 2001); (Kaldor, 2012). In Syria, for example, the protracted civil war has generated a fragmented political economy in which regime-aligned networks capture reconstruction contracts while opposition-controlled areas depend on cross-border smuggling and diaspora remittances (Haddad, 2011). Comparable dynamics exist in Libya, Yemen and the eastern Democratic Republic of Congo, where competing authorities maintain "shadow sovereignties" alongside residual state institutions. Despite pervasive insecurity, economic life persists through adaptation and informal governance. Local entrepreneurs often provide functions traditionally associated with the state, access to electricity, basic food distribution or even security (Justino, Brück, & Verwimp, 2014). These practices constitute forms of everyday state-building (Richmond, 2013): citizens assume governance roles to preserve minimum stability. Markets under fire become arenas of survival where trust, reputation and kinship substitute for legal enforcement (Brück, Naudé, & Verwimp, 2013). Entrepreneurs in conflict zones develop coping mechanisms that mirror macro-level resilience strategies: diversifying income, relying on informal and kinship networks, relocating activities and using mobile technologies for coordination and remittances (Naudé W. E., 2010); (Bullough & Renko, 2013). Digital platforms (WhatsApp, Facebook Marketplace, mobile money) facilitate micro-transactions across front lines, linking producers and consumers despite territorial fragmentation (GSMA, 2024). In Somalia or South Sudan, telecom companies and hawala systems sustain economic connectivity even when governments disintegrate. Conflict economies are therefore not economic vacuums, but reconfigured globalization under duress.

External powers often intensify these dynamics. Proxy interventions convert local wars into geopolitical marketplaces in which armed factions trade loyalty for resources and recognition. Syria, Libya and the Sahel illustrate how regional and great powers shape conflict trajectories through selective aid, arms and reconstruction contracts (Wezeman, Kuimova, & Wezerman, 2022). Realist readings interpret fragile states here as arenas of power projection (Mearsheimer J., 2001), whereas liberal and constructivist approaches emphasise transnational humanitarian, advocacy and norm-entrepreneur networks that seek to constrain violence and promote accountability (Finnemore & Hollis, 2016). For entrepreneurs, fragmented sovereignty implies multi-layered bargaining. Firms often pay multiple authorities for protection, comply with overlapping regulatory regimes, and use communication to signal neutrality or social contribution. Branding a business as community-oriented or ethically local can offer protection from predation and attract support from NGO's and diaspora investors. Marketing, in this sense, becomes an act of political positioning within conflict economies, an implicit diplomacy of survival.

The coexistence of trade and violence challenges the assumption that peace is a precondition for economic rationality. Conflict economies embody adaptive resilience: the capacity of societies to maintain production and exchange under chronic insecurity. They also complicate global policy responses. Humanitarian interventions and sanctions can inadvertently reinforce war economies by creating new rents for elites who control access to aid, border crossings or scarce goods. Understanding fragile-state entrepreneurship therefore requires acknowledging that economic agency persists within, rather than despite, fragmentation and external interference.

3.2 Sanctions, Isolation and Economic Resilience

Economic sanctions have become one of the most widely used tools of contemporary statecraft, deployed to coerce, deter or punish regimes in fragile or authoritarian contexts. They rarely operate in a vacuum. Instead, sanctions intersect with existing fragility, restructuring domestic economies and prompting adaptive behaviour that defy linear cause and effect expectations. In IR terms, sanctions are a form of economic warfare, a geoeconomic instrument that blurs the boundary between diplomacy and conflict (Blackwill, 2016). Sanctions function within the logic of weaponised interdependence (Farrell & Newman, 2019): powerful states exploit their central position in global financial, logistical and data networks to constrain others. The dominance of the U.S. dollar and the SWIFT messaging system allows Washington to project coercive power far beyond its territory (Drezner, 2011), while the EU's regulatory reach ("the Brussels effect") extends normative influence through access to its large market. These asymmetries expose fragile or sanctioned states to systemic exclusion from finance, technology and trade.

Empirical studies, however, show that broad embargoes seldom produce regime change, instead they reconfigure domestic power, empowering black-market actors, security services and rent-seeking intermediaries (Peksen, 2019); (Cortright & Lopez, 2002). Sanctions on Iraq in the 1990s, on Syria after 2011 and on Russia since 2022 illustrate the adaptability of targeted regimes, which redirect trade towards alternative partners or develop parallel payment systems (Hufbauer & Jung, 2020). The outcome is often a dual economy: a shrinking formal sector reliant on aid and a thriving informal sphere that underpins everyday survival.

At the micro level, sanctions create a paradoxical space for innovation. Entrepreneurs, cut off from conventional finance and imports, resort to substitution, localisation and digital improvisation (Brück, Naudé, & Verwimp, 2013); (Naudé W. E., 2010). In Iran, small manufacturers have built domestic supply chains and experimented with cryptocurrencies to bypass banking restrictions. In Venezuela, informal logistics networks distribute basic goods via barter and mobile applications. Palestinian firms utilise e-commerce and diaspora-based intermediaries to reach global consumers despite mobility and customs barriers. Fragility therefore reshapes, rather than eliminates, market logic.

Digital connectivity amplifies these adaptive strategies. Mobile-money systems, peer-to-peer trading platforms and encrypted communication tools constitute shadow infrastructures of exchange beyond the immediate reach of both state authorities and external regulators (GSMA, 2024). While Western policymakers often portray such mechanisms as sanctions-evasion, for local entrepreneurs they function as lifelines that preserve liquidity, cross-border trust and access to inputs.

In sanctioned environments, marketing acquires an explicitly political dimension: it becomes a medium for legitimacy signaling. Firms frame products not only as commodities but as embodiments of endurance and national identity. Iranian brands emphasize "*Made in Iran*" authenticity. Syrian small businesses highlight ethical sourcing and community solidarity to attract diaspora support (Haddad, 2011); (Götz, Gosling, & Rentfrow, 2022). Consumption is thus recast as moral participation in a collective resilience project. This resonates with constructivist claims that economic practices are embedded in normative and symbolic orders.

At the systemic level, sanctioned states exploit an increasingly multipolar environment to diversify partnerships. China's Belt and Road Initiative (BRI), Russia's regional integration schemes and South-South cooperation frameworks create alternative channels for trade and finance (Hameiri & Jones, 2015); (Bach, 2016). The growth of cryptocurrency usage and barter trade further challenges the dominance of Western-led financial governance. These developments reflect dependency-theory critiques of global capitalism (Amin, 1976); (Stiglitz, 2018), but also suggest the emergence of polycentric resilience, as weaker states navigate among competing power centres (Patrick, 2011).

For policymakers, the resilience of sanctioned economies raises difficult questions about the ethical and strategic efficacy of sanctions. Humanitarian exemptions often fail to shield civilians and small enterprises from adverse effects. Recent debates advocate more "smart" sanctions and complementary support for local economic resilience, recognising entrepreneurs as critical stabilising actors rather than collateral damage (Carment & Samy, 2021); (UNDP, 2022).

3.3 Great-Power Rivalries and the Global Political Economy

The post-cold War expectation that deep economic interdependence would marginalise traditional geopolitics has clearly not been fulfilled. Over the last decade, the international system has entered what many scholars describe as a new age of geoeconomic rivalry (Blackwill, 2016). Interdependence itself has become a strategic instrument, as states weaponize supply chains, critical technologies and financial networks. Fragile states increasingly find themselves pulled into this contest as arenas of influence rather than fully autonomous actors (Farrell & Newman, 2019); (Mearsheimer J., 2018). From a structural realist perspective, the United States, China, Russia and the European Union deploy trade policy, infrastructure finance and digital standards to compete for relative gains (Allison, 2017); (Adamic & Friedberg, 2023). Critical IPE approaches emphasise how these rivalries reproduce asymmetrical dependencies, arguing that the Global South risks renewed forms of peripheralisation under competing "hegemonic projects" (Amin, 1976); (Hameiri

& Jones, 2015). Yet, small and fragile states also exercise agency by hedging, leveraging rivalries to secure aid, investment and diplomatic recognition.

China's Belt and Road Initiative (BRI) epitomize geoeconomic statecraft. Since 2013, the BRI has pledged hundreds of billions of dollars for infrastructure and connectivity projects across Asia, Africa and parts of Europe. Official narratives stress "win-win" cooperation, but the initiative also consolidates China's strategic presence along key corridors and access to resources. In fragile states such as Pakistan, Ethiopia or Djibouti, BRI projects provide much-needed infrastructure while creating long-term financial and political dependencies (Hurley, Scott, & Gailyn, 2018); The BRI also has a technological dimension. Chinese firms such as Huawei, ZTE and Alibaba Cloud export not only hardware but digital governance models: data standards, surveillance architectures and platform ecosystems. This diffusion can be read as a form of soft power through connectivity (Nye, 2005): by embedding their systems in partner states, Chinese actors shape future options for data governance and cyber sovereignty. For fragile states seeking rapid modernization, such technology transfers bring opportunities but pose long-term dilemmas around privacy, dependence and political control.

Western powers have responded with their own connectivity and investment schemes, among them the EU's Global Gateway, Japan's Partnership for Quality Infrastructure and the U.S., led Build Back Better World (B3W) initiative. These projects combine sustainable-development rhetoric with strategic competition, positioning liberal democracies as providers of transparent, rules-based alternatives. However, they often entail stringent governance, environmental and human-rights conditionalities that fragile states struggle to meet (Patrick, 2011). The result is a bifurcated marketplace of development models: relatively unconditional Chinese finance and more norm-laden Western assistance.

Russia's reassertion of influence through energy diplomacy and security interventions adds another layer to this competitive landscape. Its actions in Syria, Libya and parts of Africa combine hard power with commercial objectives, arms sales, energy deals and private-security contracts. Energy interdependence, once seen as a stabilising factor, has become a coercive tool, as illustrated by Europe's energy crisis after 2022. For fragile states, Russian engagement may offer security support and market access but deepens entanglement in rival power blocs.

In this environment, small states pursue strategic hedging, maintaining diversified relations to avoid over-dependence on any single patron. Entrepreneurs mirror this logic at the firm level. Local companies may seek Western investors for reputational legitimacy while sourcing inputs or digital services from China and securing finance from Gulf sovereign funds. This hybridization underscores the intimate link between micro-level strategies and macro-geopolitical structures.

Ultimately, great-power rivalry redefines what resilience means for fragile states. Instead of attempting to insulate themselves from global pressures, they must learn to navigate interdependence, transforming external competition into domestic opportunity where possible. For entrepreneurs, this entails managing multiple regulatory regimes, currencies and digital ecosystems. Resilience, in the age of geoeconomic rivalry, becomes the art of balancing dependency, legitimacy and flexibility across an increasingly fragmented international political economy.

3.4 International Institutions and Multilateral Frameworks

International institutions present themselves as central pillars in managing fragility, conflict, and post-war recovery. From the Bretton Woods institutions to regional organisations and UN agencies, a dense web of actors now governs the politics of fragility through development assistance, peacebuilding, and policy conditionalities (Barnett & Finnemore, 2004). Rather than simply resolving fragility, these frameworks often reconfigure it, embedding states within transnational regimes of monitoring, benchmarking, and policy discipline that reshape domestic governance (Duffield, 2001); (Joseph, 2013).

The World Bank, OECD, and UNDP have been especially influential in conceptualising fragility as a multidimensional governance challenge. The World Bank's Harmonized List of Fragile and Conflict-Affected Situations (FCS) apply indicators of political stability, security, and economic performance to identify states at risk (World Bank, 2023). The OECD's States of Fragility framework maps fragility across economic, environmental, political, security, and societal dimensions, arguing that fragility is a structural condition requiring long-term resilience strategies rather than crisis-driven interventions (OECD, 2022). UNDP integrates fragility within broader human development and human security paradigms, defining resilience as "*the capacity of individuals, communities and institutions to anticipate, absorb, and adapt to shocks*" (UNDP, 2022); (Bene, Godfrey, Newsham, & Davies, 2013).

Collectively, these organisations promote a vision of resilience as adaptive governance, emphasizing decentralisation, transparency, participation, digital inclusion, and open markets (Carment & Samy, 2021), (Yet critics warn that this "technocratic optimism" masks power asymmetries. Development assistance and policy expertise frequently function as embedded conditionalities, aligning domestic reforms with donor priorities and global financial governance norms. Fragile states are drawn into a security-development nexus, where economic aid, stabilization, counterterrorism, and risk management become tightly intertwined (Duffield, 2001).

The IMF and WTO constitute the economic core of this governance architecture. Historically, IMF programmes and World Bank structural adjustment policies prioritized macroeconomic stability and liberalization, often at the expense of social protection and institutional cohesion (Amin, 1976); (Rodrik, 2011); (Stiglitz, 2018). Although contemporary IMF discourse emphasizes inclusive growth, many conditionalities (fiscal consolidation, subsidy reform, tax restructuring) continue to reflect international credit-market expectations (IMF, 2023). The WTO's legalistic trade regime similarly disadvantages fragile states with limited administrative capacity, constraining industrial diversification and policy experimentation.

However, institutional engagement can also provide credibility benefits. WTO membership or adherence to IMF surveillance mechanisms signals commitment to rules-based governance, reassuring donors, foreign investors, and development partners. Participation in these frameworks is thus both a constraint on autonomy and a pathway to legitimacy, external financing, and market access.

Regional organisations increasingly complement global institutions in managing fragility. The African Union (AU), Arab League, and ASEAN have developed resilience-oriented mechanisms centred on early warning, preventive diplomacy, and regional integration. The AU's Post-Conflict Reconstruction and Development (PCRD) framework links governance reforms with continental peacebuilding and local capacity-building initiatives (PCRD, 2006). Regional development banks and Islamic finance institutions similarly support SME recovery, infrastructure rehabilitation, and entrepreneurial ecosystems in fragile settings.

These transformations reflect a shift toward networked multilateralism, wherein global and regional institutions collaborate with NGOs, philanthropic foundations, and private firms. Initiatives such as the World Economic Forum's Humanitarian Investing Platform mobilize private capital for fragile contexts, explicitly positioning entrepreneurship as an instrument of resilience and peacebuilding (World Economic Forum, 2022). This aligns with the rise of development diplomacy, in which states deploy aid, investment, and trade preferences to advance foreign policy goals while promoting resilience in partner states (Brown, Grävingholt, & Raddatz, 2016). For entrepreneurs in fragile states, these institutional landscapes are decisive. Access to concessional finance, technical assistance, investment guarantees, and market preferences depends on meeting externally defined criteria. Yet institutional partnerships also create opportunities: firms that align with donor agendas (digital inclusion, gender empowerment, sustainability) gain visibility, legitimacy, and cross-border networks. In this way, local entrepreneurial resilience strategies become embedded within broader multilateral architectures, linking micro-level adaptation to global governance frameworks.

3.5 Entrepreneurial Diplomacy and the New Geoeconomic Order

The diffusion of economic and technological power beyond the nation-state has fundamentally reshaped the practice of diplomacy. Increasingly, diplomatic outcomes are influenced not only by governments but also by business leaders, start-ups, innovation ecosystems and transnational corporations. This phenomenon (conceptualise as entrepreneurial diplomacy) captures the growing involvement of private economic actors in shaping international agendas, norms and networks (Saner & Yiu, 2003). This development reflects a broader transition toward multi-stakeholder diplomacy, where states, markets and civil society collectively participate in governance. In fragile and developing states (where foreign ministries often lack resources, expertise or global reach) entrepreneurs frequently assume quasi-diplomatic roles. They attract foreign investment, engage with donors, cultivate cross-border partnerships and represent their countries at trade exhibitions, innovation summits and digital platforms. Diplomacy thus increasingly unfolds in boardrooms, incubators, supply-chain networks and online ecosystems.

Entrepreneurial diplomacy operates at the interface of soft power and economic statecraft. Soft power, according to Nye, is rooted in attraction rather than coercion (Nye, 2005). In many fragile states, successful businesses (including tech start-ups, creative industries and high-growth SMEs) project narratives of innovation, endurance and community embeddedness that counteract dominant global images of fragility (Senor & Singer, 2009) . Their products, digital presence and values publicly signal national competence and resilience.

At the same time, firms participate in economic statecraft by influencing investment flows, trade linkages, technology diffusion and the adoption of digital standards, each with geopolitical implications (Blackwill, 2016). The strategies of private actors (where they source capital, which value chains they join, what technologies they adopt) can align with or challenge broader state interests.

Within fragile contexts, entrepreneurial diplomacy performs three interrelated functions:

Legitimacy Construction: In environments where formal institutions often lack credibility, entrepreneurs use branding, certification, quality assurance and corporate-social-responsibility initiatives to signal reliability. "Brands of resilience"(firms that explicitly connect their identity to community recovery and social contribution) help rehumanize crisis-affected societies in the eyes of global audiences.

Network Bridging: Entrepreneurs act as intermediaries linking fragile domestic economies to global circuits of technology, finance and knowledge. Through diaspora networks, accelerator programmes, online marketplaces and international trade fairs, they integrate local production into global value chains. These linkages help overcome isolation caused by conflict, sanctions or limited state capacity.

Resilience Diplomacy: Entrepreneurial innovation under constraint mirrors the resilience-focused agendas promoted by UNDP, OECD and multilateral donors (OECD, 2022); (UNDP, 2022). Survival strategies (such as diversification, digital adoption, informal coordination and partnership-building) represent bottom-up stabilising forces that often provide more realistic insights than top-down policy reforms (Brück, Naudé, & Verwimp, 2013).

Tech Corporations as Geopolitical Actors: The growing influence of global tech corporations illustrates both the opportunities and risks of entrepreneurial diplomacy. Firms such as Huawei, Palantir, SpaceX, Meta and Alibaba increasingly function as geopolitical players, negotiating directly with governments, shaping digital governance and influencing contemporary conflicts through their platforms, infrastructures and algorithms.

Their expanding control over data flows, communication systems and algorithmic decision-making challenges the traditional monopoly of states over public authority and raises ethical concerns related to surveillance, accountability and human rights. The concept of algorithmic sovereignty captures this shift: private digital architecture now shape political communication and security practices at scales that rival state power (Nye, 2005).

Governments have begun formalizing engagement with private innovators. Denmark's appointment of a Tech Ambassador in Silicon Valley, the EU's expansion of digital diplomacy, and the adoption of national innovation envoys demonstrate a growing recognition that entrepreneurial actors must be integrated into foreign policy frameworks (Bradford, 2020); (OECD, 2022). Such approaches are especially relevant for small or fragile states that lack extensive diplomatic infrastructures but possess dynamic innovation communities.

Entrepreneurial diplomacy demonstrates that meaningful influence in the 21st century international system is no longer limited to great powers. Through cross-border networking, narrative framing, digital innovation and brand projection, entrepreneurs shape perceptions, mobilize resources and co-produce governance across borders.

In fragile states (where formal diplomatic institutions may be weak or constrained) these bottom-up practices complement official foreign policy by cultivating transnational ties, generating international visibility and embedding local resilience within global networks. Entrepreneurial diplomacy thus transforms micro-level innovation into macro-level geoeconomic relevance, contributing to a more polycentric and networked international order.

4. MARKETING AS A TOOL OF ENTREPRENEURIAL RESILIENCE

In this context, marketing emerges as a crucial bridge between the macro-level conditions of fragility and the micro-level strategies of entrepreneurs who must operate within them. The preceding sections demonstrated how legitimacy deficits, institutional weakness, political fragmentation and shifting geopolitical pressures shape the environment in which firms attempt to survive and adapt. At the same time, entrepreneurial resilience depends heavily on soft skills, adaptive mindsets and communicative capacities that allow actors to navigate uncertainty and construct trust in the absence of stable institutions. Marketing sits precisely at this intersection: it enables entrepreneurs to frame their value propositions, engage communities, and build relational forms of legitimacy that compensate for institutional gaps. In this way, marketing becomes not merely a commercial activity but a mechanism of resilience and informal governance within fragile contexts.

Business resilience refers to the ability of entrepreneurs and businesses to adapt positively to external shocks, institutional uncertainties, and adverse operating conditions (Becker & Kabongo, 2021); (Renko, Bullough, & Saeed, 2020). In such environments, marketing is not limited to the classic definition of commercial promotion or sales communication. Instead, it functions as a mechanism for economic and social survival: "*it helps businesses shape mental frameworks, generate legitimacy and trust, and build relationships that support their existence beyond the immediate transaction*". In other words, marketing in vulnerable countries becomes a tool for generating potential stability where formal institutions and the regulatory environment cannot provide it. Thus, value often does not come from the product itself, but from the entrepreneur's ability to "translate" it into a narrative of credibility, security, identity, and perspective. The following dimensions demonstrate specifically how marketing can function as a tool for resilience.

4.1. Communication in times of crisis as the foundation of business resilience

Communication in times of crisis is not a "secondary" support function, but the foundation of institutional and commercial resilience. A crisis (economic, health, energy, political, military, or a combination) deconstructs the mechanism that stabilizes expectations and disrupts the normality of the system. The market then ceases to function as a predictable trading environment and becomes a field of "Knightian uncertainty." In this context, communication cannot be aestheticization; it must be a tool for sensemaking and sense giving. International findings after 2020 show that organizations that activate coherent crisis communication routines see faster revenue recovery, faster restoration of trust, and less loss of market share (Kalaignanam, Tuli, Kushwaha, Leonard, & Gal, 2021). Here, then, the "quality" of communication does not simply mean more messages; it means intention, ownership, transparency, and timing.

It is vital to distinguish between two levels: a) communication as "information management" and b) communication as "meaning management." At the first level, the organisation provides timely and relevant information on availability, costs, delays, safety measures, etc. At the second level, the organisation does not simply circulate data but constructs a collective understanding of "what is happening" and "what to expect." It is this second dimension that transforms communication into an infrastructure of resilience: it activates psychological and social "cushions" on which economic recovery is based. Research shows that leaders who communicate with a focus on meaning rather than "reassuring prose" increase sales force resilience.

Empirically documents how political communication (which is the "hardest" form of meaning communication) directly influences citizen behavior, thus establishing "behavioral" resilience (Sophocleous H. P., 2024). In his research on Cypriot voters, it appears that the quality of communication (beyond content) influences the degree of engagement and ultimately the choices made (Sophocleous, H. P.; Masouras, A.; Anastasiadou, S. D.;, 2024). In another publication on the production and consumption of political communication, he reflects the same logic: communication as a process of meaning-making (rather than information provision) is the level that reconstructs behaviors (Sophocleous H. P., 2024). Furthermore, in the chapter of 2025, he clearly introduces the circular relationship between institutions, political marketing, and the electoral process (Sophocleous, Anastasiadou, & Masouras, 2025): this is precisely the core of the argument: communication changes institutional trust and institutional trust changes communication effectiveness. Therefore, communication in a crisis is not "mechanical." It is a circular feedback system.

The above has a direct practical impact on business marketing. Organisations and states that communicate clearly in a crisis: a) their intentions, b) their commitments, c) their constraints, and d) their solutions (response options), activate mechanisms of moral sympathy and risk acceptance by citizens. Thus, the citizen does not act as a "harsh judge" but as a "participant" in the survival of the organisation or the state. This is resilience as a collective quality and it can only be achieved through communication that jointly constructs meaning, not communication that simply "broadcasts" content.

4.2 Building trust and legitimacy

Building trust and legitimacy in environments of institutional weakness is a key mechanism for business resilience. When official institutions fail to provide regulatory protection, predictability, and safeguards, consumers shift their expectations of "safety" and "quality" to the private sector. In this context, organisations do not simply "communicate" to promote a product but take on the role of a "private institution" that produces, through its own means, signals of credibility, social responsibility, transparency, and accountability. Contemporary literature documents that, after 2020, trust in organisations in conditions of instability depends mainly on the quality of signaling honesty and the ability to verify claims (Kalaignanam, Tuli, Kushwaha, Leonard, & Gal, 2021). In other words, a "positive image" is not enough; the crucial element is the ability to verify compliance and consistency.

At this point, previous research (Sophocleous, H. P.; Masouras, A.; Anastasiadou, S. D.;, 2024), could be considered as relevant, because the field of political communication has gone much deeper into analyzing how "legitimacy" is constructed behaviorally. For example, in his research on political consumption in Cyprus, he shows that the quality of communication influences behavior to such an extent that it shapes the final outcome of participation/abstention (Sophocleous, H. P.; Masouras, A.; Anastasiadou, S. D.;, 2024). The specific publication on the production/consumption of political communication, highlights the role of "social legitimacy" as a result of interpretive frameworks that are disseminated to the public (Sophocleous H. P., 2024). Additionally further research documents the circular relationship between institutions, political marketing, and the electoral process and this circular model accurately reflects how communicative legitimacy can function as a substitute for institutional legitimacy (Sophocleous, Anastasiadou, & Masouras, 2025). Since the particular study documents that there is a feedback loop between trust, communication, and institutions, the same loop applies as is only in the commercial sphere, "institutions" are expected corporate behavior and "electoral results" are market behavior. Therefore, a company builds legitimacy when it provides signals that confirm that it "acts responsibly," "does not hide," "is committed," and "is accountable."

The above are not abstract concepts. They have operational implementation. Today, legitimacy is produced through: a) traceability of origin, b) ESG control, c) brand identity as an institutional signal, and d) "credence attributes." Social platforms allow for public confirmation of claims. This creates "private institutions" of credibility. Marketing therefore functions as an institutional mechanism: where the state fails to persuade, a set of signals, evidence, evaluation, and public accountability can persuade. In vulnerable markets, this process is the only stable foundation for resilience, because businesses cannot rely on regulatory trust warranties from the state. Without legitimacy, no other marketing tool can stabilize demand. So marketing here does not "sell."

4.3 Digital marketing and social media as substitute market infrastructures and a channel of resilience

Digital marketing and social media in fragile environments are not an "optional" addition to the marketing toolkit; instead, they function as "substitute infrastructures" where physical, institutional or economic infrastructures are inadequate. The rapid diffusion of smartphones and platforms (Meta, TikTok, YouTube, WhatsApp Business) allows businesses to create networks of access to audiences and markets beyond the physical boundaries of their local ecosystem. This is crucial in environments where local purchasing power collapses due to crises; the business can draw demand from elsewhere (diaspora communities, niche markets, sensitive consumer identities, ethical consumption, etc.). In this perspective, digital marketing does not simply "project". It restructures the architecture of the market, creating accessibility, network coordination and interconnection. International research after 2020 in developing economies shows that social has become the main channel of commercial intermediation, as it allows bypassing weak logistics infrastructures and weak institutions (Tamirat, 2024). The business acquires a "networked space of action" even when the physical space has collapsed.

Important but often overlooked: social media does not only create access; they also create a new form of legitimation. Social legitimacy today is often not produced by the state (regulatory legitimation), but by interactive public evaluation (rating legitimacy, professionalized self-presentation, public review). The evaluation of the brand on-line functions as a "private standardization": the business declares what it does, the public checks whether it actually does it, and this control creates the conditional institutional guarantee. This logic is very close to the political market. Sophocleous shows that political legitimacy is not only the result of message content, but also of the circular interaction of communication (trust) institutions (Sophocleous, Anastasiadou, & Masouras, 2025). This idea is directly transferred to the commercial market: platform communication does not simply "inform" but produces new institutional quality through mechanisms of social confirmation (likes, shares, reviews, direct messaging, exposure). Previous on the production and consumption of political communication documents that behavior is determined by the way the message is "understood", not by simple listening (Sophocleous H. P., 2024), this principle also applies to digital commercial marketing: the common knowledge generated around a brand on social is stronger than the brand's message itself.

Digital marketing in crisis, however, is not just about networking. It is also about learning (analytics → adaptation → new strategy). In other words, it is also a market learning infrastructure. The literature talks about marketing agility: continuous micro-experimentation, A/B testing, and leveraging small behavioral indicators for rapid adaptation (Kalaignanam, Tuli, Kushwaha, Leonard, & Gal, 2021). In a crisis, conditions change every day: so digital marketing is the only model that allows for rapid cycles of adaptation. The opposite choice (static marketing plan) leads to "paralysis". Here, research on the impact of political marketing on behavior (Sophocleous, H. P.; Masouras, A.; Anastasiadou, S. D.;, 2024) acts as a supporting argument: behavior is dynamic, not static; therefore dynamic, not static marketing is needed.

The big picture: digital marketing in a crisis is not a means of "monitoring" the market; it is a means of reconstructing the market. It transforms platforms from communication channels into mechanisms for generating legitimacy, trust, networking, and learning. Where the state fails to guarantee institutional stability, platforms create private network stabilities that allow business to survive and recover.

4.4 Market access as a resilience tool

In fragile economies, market access is not a simple technical dimension of trade (e.g. getting the product to the shelf). It is an existential dimension of survival. When domestic consumption shrinks (due to political instability, low purchasing power or institutional uncertainty), the business, in order to remain viable, must necessarily "optimize" external access. This means that marketing (especially branding origin + narrative framing) becomes a tool for producing "legitimized authenticity". Narrative campaigns such as "Made in Rwanda" or "Palestinian Fair Trade" are not simple statements of origin; they are mechanisms for converting "local hardship" into "global value".

In environments of low internal absorptive capacity (i.e. where local demand is weak, fragmented, unstable or vulnerable to political and economic shocks) market access works essentially as a "risk exit mechanism". Businesses that remain trapped in the domestic market have little capacity to absorb volatility. On the contrary, when they manage to gain access to external markets, they transform their risk exposure: from monopsony (local) to polypsony (international). This is the logic of resilience through market portfolio diversification.

But the crucial point is that this access is not achieved only with a "good product". It is achieved through narrative legitimacy: the product becomes the bearer of a framework of meaning that makes international consumers read it as a value, not just as an object. That is why "Made in Rwanda" or "Palestinian Fair Trade" campaigns are real market access mechanisms: they take the "local identity" and transform it into a marketable semantics.

This is not marketing "facelift". It is market access engineering through storytelling. And it is fully consistent with the post-2020 literature which shows that the resilience of small businesses is drastically higher when internationalization is based on brand meaning and not just on price tactics. Since it has been shown that meanings can reshape behaviors in political markets (Sophocleous, H. P.; Masouras, A.; Anastasiadou, S. D.;, 2024), then by analogy they can also reshape consumer behaviors in commercial markets. Therefore, market access through "origin branding" is in fact a resilience technique: value is transferred from the fragile local ecosystem to the more stable global ecosystem of meanings.

4.5 Business diplomacy

Business diplomacy does not simply mean "exports" or "international presence". It means that the business – often without intention and without an institutional role – acts as a carrier of the external image of its country. In fragile economies, where official state channels of public diplomacy are weak, underfunded or delegitimized, the international image of the country is often shaped through the products, brands and narratives of entrepreneurs. Recent research also documents that micro-entrepreneurs in fragile countries act de facto as "informal cultural diplomats" because they internationally transport not only products but also framed narratives of the country of origin. Entrepreneurs "export" not only value, but also a frame for who "we are" as a nation, as a culture, as a productivity. Thus, branding functions as a private tool of diplomacy: a handmade design product, a single-origin coffee, a premium agricultural product from a country in crisis - can function as an "image correction", breaking the stereotypical lens of vulnerability and replacing the "fragile state" image with an image of "creative resilience". International literature has now documented that "country-of-origin branding" is not simply about information about origin, but a process of semantic reframing of a national identity in the international field. In vulnerable ecosystems, this reframing can function as a corrective mechanism to stereotypical readings of "fragility".

This process has political consequences. It is not "neutral" or "technical" marketing. It is participation in soft power. The country does not speak through the state, but through the product. Business diplomacy does not replace official diplomacy but complement it where institutions are weak. And that is why marketing in vulnerable countries does not only have a commercial function; it has an image-making function at the international level. This logic is fully aligned with the concept of "soft power" in nation branding: the favorable image of the country is often built through commercial points of contact and not exclusively through official diplomacy.

The product becomes a vehicle for the national narrative and functions as a channel of international soft power. In some contexts, the entrepreneur ultimately represents his country more effectively than the foreign ministry. When official diplomacy is weak, commercial communication often becomes the only route to reframing the national image.

Overall, marketing in fragile and uncertain environments emerges not simply as a commercial tool but as a core mechanism of entrepreneurial resilience. It enables firms to communicate credibility, build trust, and generate forms of informal legitimacy that often substitute for weak or fragmented institutions. Through narrative framing, relationship-building and adaptive market positioning, entrepreneurs use marketing to navigate political instability, sanctions, and structural constraints while maintaining continuity of operations. In this sense, marketing acts as a form of "everyday governance from below," shaping how entrepreneurs engage with customers, communities and external stakeholders. The following case studies (or policy sections) demonstrate how these mechanisms operate in practice, showing that marketing-led resilience is most effective when it is embedded in broader social networks, institutional realities and context-specific strategies.

5. CASE STUDIES

Empirical work on micro-entrepreneurs and SMEs in fragile or turbulent environments shows how marketing and branding operate as practical tools of resilience rather than "luxury" activities. Illustrate how micro-entrepreneurs in fragile economies act as "unofficial" cultural diplomats, leveraging local culture, storytelling and place-based branding to attract tourists, donors and partners. Their market-facing activities simultaneously generate income and project informal narratives of stability, hospitality and distinct identity, effectively substituting for weak or absent official public diplomacy. Similarly, Sophocleous and colleagues (2019, 2021, 2023) show how cultural and nation branding initiatives in Cyprus can be harnessed by local organisations and SMEs as strategic assets, enabling them to align with broader narratives of place, heritage and trust.

A second stream of cases concerns SMEs competing in international markets under conditions of volatility. It demonstrate that SMEs with clearly articulated brand meaning and coherent brand narratives are better able to sustain international customer relationships during market shocks. Authenticity-based branding strategies in developing countries and the careful use of country-of-origin cues help firms differentiate themselves and maintain customer loyalty when institutional signals are weak. Market diversification, identified as a resilience strategy, further shows how firms can reconfigure their portfolios of markets and segments, reducing dependence on any single buyer, country, or channel.

A third cluster of studies focuses on communication, leadership and digital channels in turbulent contexts. Research on entrepreneurial resilience in developing and fragile economies (Becker & Kabongo, 2021); (Bullough & Renko, 2013); (Isichei, 2024); (Renko, Bullough, & Saeed, 2020). highlights the role of proactive communication with customers and communities in sustaining confidence and demand. Effective crisis communication by leaders strengthens salesperson resilience and, indirectly, customer relationships. (Tamirat, 2024) and related digital marketing work suggest that, in developing economies, low-cost online channels and social networks can provide SMEs with access to broader markets and diasporas, even when domestic conditions are unstable. Across these cases, marketing and branding are repeatedly used to absorb shocks, maintain relational ties, and open alternative pathways to revenue and legitimacy.

6. CONCLUSIONS

This chapter has demonstrated that entrepreneurship in fragile and turbulent environments cannot be understood solely through traditional economic or managerial frameworks. Instead, it must be viewed as a multidimensional process shaped by political uncertainty, institutional weakness, social fragmentation and shifting geopolitical pressures. Entrepreneurs in such settings operate within hybrid political orders, where formal institutions are inconsistent or distrusted and where informal networks, local norms and community relations play decisive roles in enabling or constraining business activity. These conditions demand a form of resilience that goes beyond financial preparedness or operational flexibility: resilience becomes a political, social and communicative practice.

Across the theoretical sections, we showed that entrepreneurial resilience is deeply intertwined with legitimacy-building, informal governance and the capacity to navigate complex political economies. Entrepreneurs must continually negotiate credibility toward customers, communities, authorities and transnational networks and this negotiation often substitutes for the stabilising functions of the state. Soft skills, adaptive mindsets and relational competencies emerge not as optional qualities but as core capabilities that allow entrepreneurs to survive and advance in unpredictable environments. Likewise, structural constraints such as sanctions, conflict legacies, institutional voids and asymmetric interdependence shape the landscape of opportunities and risks, reinforcing the need for strategic navigation rather than simple commercial adaptation.

The analysis of marketing as a tool of entrepreneurial resilience further illustrated how branding, communication and market positioning perform functions that are simultaneously economic and political. Marketing practices help entrepreneurs construct trust where institutions are weak, maintain visibility during crises, stabilise demand across fragmented markets and forge identity-based connections that endure despite volatility. In this sense, marketing becomes a form of "everyday diplomacy," allowing entrepreneurs to engage publics, shape narratives and cultivate legitimacy from below.

The case studies provided empirical depth to these arguments, showing how micro-entrepreneurs, SMEs and cultural organisations in fragile or developing contexts leverage brand meaning, authenticity, market diversification and relationship-building to withstand shocks and remain viable. Whether through cultural diplomacy, place-based branding, international market orientation or digital outreach, these actors demonstrate that resilience is rarely the result of individual toughness alone; it is built through networks, stories, relationships and the strategic use of identity.

Taken together, the chapter shows that entrepreneurial resilience in fragile contexts is a systemic phenomenon: it emerges at the intersection of individual capabilities, institutional realities, geopolitical forces and market dynamics. Supporting such resilience therefore requires interventions that go beyond technical training or financial assistance. Policy should focus on strengthening local ecosystems, enabling access to markets, supporting cultural and nation branding efforts, and cultivating the soft skills and communicative capacities that underpin legitimacy and trust. For scholars, the implication is clear: entrepreneurship in fragile settings must be studied as both an economic activity and a political practice one that illuminates how individuals and small firms contribute to stability, adaptation and informal governance in some of the world's most challenging environments.

7. POLICY RECOMMENDATIONS

Building entrepreneurial resilience in fragile and politically complex environments requires policies that recognise the interplay between markets, institutions, legitimacy and local social dynamics. Based on the analysis presented in this chapter, the following recommendations can strengthen both individual entrepreneurs and the broader ecosystems in which they operate:

7.1 Strengthen Local Market Ecosystems and Reduce Structural Barriers

Governments, development organisations and local authorities should prioritize policies that reduce uncertainty and enable predictable market participation. This includes simplifying licensing procedures, improving access to finance, supporting regulatory transparency and preventing predatory behaviour by local elites. In fragile settings, even small reductions in bureaucratic friction can significantly enhance the capacity of micro-entrepreneurs and SMEs to operate consistently and safely.

7.2 Support Cultural, Place-Based and Nation Branding Initiatives

Policies should invest in coherent place branding strategies that local firms can align with and utilise. As shown in the chapter, cultural narratives and identity-based branding significantly contribute to demand creation and informal legitimacy. Ministries of culture, tourism boards and regional authorities should provide branding toolkits, shared promotional platforms and support for community-driven cultural initiatives that enhance local reputation and visibility.

7.3 Enhance Entrepreneurial Soft Skills and Communicative Capacities

Training programmes for SMEs must prioritize soft skills (resilience, narrative framing, crisis communication, intercultural competence, negotiation and community engagement) alongside technical business skills. These abilities help entrepreneurs navigate institutional ambiguity, manage customer relationships during crises and construct trust where formal systems are weak or inconsistent.

7.4 Facilitate Market Diversification and Cross-Border Linkages

Policymakers should support SMEs in accessing new markets through export facilitation services, diaspora engagement programmes and regional trade platforms. Market diversification reduces vulnerability to domestic instability and political shocks. Diaspora communities, in particular, can play a crucial role in offering alternative market routes and legitimacy anchors.

7.5 Expand Support for Digital Channels and Low-Cost Communication Tools

Given the importance of visibility and customer engagement in fragile contexts, governments and NGOs should invest in digital literacy training, affordable internet infrastructure and e-commerce platforms accessible to micro-entrepreneurs. Digital outreach enables firms to bypass local disruptions, reach diasporas and maintain reputational continuity even in times of crisis.

7.6 Protect Entrepreneurs Operating in Hybrid or Informal Institutional Settings

Since entrepreneurs in fragile environments often rely on informal networks due to weak state capacity, policy frameworks should avoid heavy-handed formalisation that disrupts these survival mechanisms. Instead, gradual, supportive formalisation (paired with legal protections, fair taxation schemes and anti-corruption safeguards) can enhance stability without eroding the informal governance structures that entrepreneurs depend on.

7.7 Promote Inclusive, Community-Based Economic Governance

Local councils, chambers of commerce and community organisations should be involved in co-creating resilience strategies with entrepreneurs. Participatory governance improves trust, aligns interventions with local realities and ensures that policy designs resonate with lived experiences. Such collaborative structures can function as "micro-institutions" of stability in otherwise fragmented environments.

7.8 Encourage Research, Monitoring and Context-Specific Evidence

Policymakers should invest in ongoing monitoring of entrepreneurial conditions in fragile settings, including mapping informal markets, understanding local legitimacy dynamics and documenting resilience strategies. Evidence-based policy prevents the importation of inappropriate models from stable Western contexts and instead promotes contextually grounded interventions.

REFERENCES

Adamic, D., & Friedberg, A. L. (2023). Getting China Wrong. *Naval War College Review, 76*(3), 11. Retrieved 2025, from https://digital-commons.usnwc.edu/nwc-review/vol76/iss3/11

Allison, G. (2017). *Destined for War: Can America and China Escape Thucydides's Trap?* Houghton Mifflin Harcourt.

Amin, S. (1976). *Unequal Development: An Essay on the Social Formations of Peripheral Capitalism.* Sussex, England: The Harvester Press. Retrieved 2025, from https://sahistory.org.za/sites/default/files/archive-files3/unequal_development_by_samir_amin.pdf

Autesserre, S. (2012). Peaceland: Conflict Resolution and the Everyday Politics of International Intervention. *Politics of International Intervention.* doi:DOI: 10.1017/CBO9781107280366

Bach, D. C. (2016). Cross-Border Interactions and Regionalism. In D. H. Levine, & D. Nagar, *Region-Building in Africa: Political and Economic Challenges* (pp. 71-88). New York: Palgrave Macmillan. doi:https://doi.org/DOI: 10.1057/9781137586117_5

Ballentine, K., & Sherman, J. (2003). *The Political Economy of Armed Conflict: Beyond Greed and Grievance.* Lynne Rienner Pub., Retrieved 2025, from.

Barnett, M., & Finnemore, M. (2004). Rules for the World. Cornell: Cornell University Press.

Becker, T., & Kabongo, J. (2021). The resilience of entrepreneurs in developing economics. *In Research handbook on Organizational resilience*, 116-130. doi:DOI: 10.4337/9781788112215.00016

Bene, C., Godfrey, R., Newsham, A., & Davies, M. (2013, January 14). Resilience: New Utopia or New Tyranny? *Institute of Development Studies, 2012*(405), 1–61. DOI: 10.1111/j.2040-0209.2012.00405.x

Berdal, M., & Keen, D. (1997). Violence and Economic Agendas in Civil Wars: Some Policy Imp. *Millennium, 26*(3), 795–818. DOI: 10.1177/03058298970260030401

Billon, L., & Philippe. (2001). The political ecology of war: Natural resources and armed conflicts. *Political Geography*, •••, 561–584. DOI: 10.1016/S0962-6298(01)00015-4

Blackwill, B. D. (2016). *War by Other Means: Geoeconomics and Statecraft.* Harvard University Press., DOI: 10.2307/j.ctt1c84cr7

Boege, V., Brown, A., Clements, K., & Nolan, A. (2009). *On Hybrid Political Orders and Emerging States.* Berlin: Berghof Research Center. Retrieved 2025, from https://berghof-foundation.org/library/on-hybrid-political-orders-and-emerging-states-state-formation-in-the-context-of-fragility

Boin, A., & Van Eeten, M. J. (2013). The Resilient Organization. *Public Management Review, 15*(3), 429–445. DOI: 10.1080/14719037.2013.769856

Bradford, A. (2020). *The Brussels Effect.* Oxford University Press., DOI: 10.1093/oso/9780190088583.001.0001

Brinkerhoff, J. (2012). Creating an Enabling Environment for Diasporas' Participation in Homeland Development. *International Migration (Geneva, Switzerland), 50*(1), 75–95. DOI: 10.1111/j.1468-2435.2009.00542.x PMID: 22400149

Brown, S., Grävingholt, J., & Raddatz, R. (2016). The Securitization of Foreign Aid: Trends, Explanations and Prospects. *The Securitization of Foreign Aid. Rethinking International Development Series*, 1-17. doi:DOI: 10.1007/978-1-137-56882-3_11

Brück, T., Naudé, W., & Verwimp, P. (2013). Business under Fire: Entrepreneurship and Violent Conflict in Developing Countries. *The Journal of Conflict Resolution, 57*(1), 3–19. DOI: 10.1177/0022002712464846

Bullough, A., & Renko, M. (2013). Entrepreneurial resilience during challenging times. *Business Horizons, 56*(3), 343–350. DOI: 10.1016/j.bushor.2013.01.001

Call, C. T. (2010). Beyond the 'failed state': Toward conceptual alternatives. *European Journal of International Relations, 17*(2). Advance online publication. DOI: 10.1177/1354066109353137

Carment, D., & Samy, Y. (2021). *Exiting the Fragility Trap: Rethinking Our Approach to the World's Most Fragile States.* Ohio University Press.

Chandler, D. (2014). *Resilience The Governance of Complexity* (1st Edition ed.). Routledge. Retrieved from https://www.routledge.com/Resilience-The-Governance-of-Complexity/Chandler/p/book/9780415741408

Chen, M. (2012). *The Informal Economy: Definitions, Theories and Policies.* WIEGO (Women in Informal Employment: Globalizing and Organising). Working Paper No. 1. Retrieved 2025, from https://www.wiego.org/wp-content/uploads/2019/09/Chen_WIEGO_WP1.pdf

Collier, P., & Hoeffler, G. (2004). Greed and grievance in civil war. *Oxford Economic Papers, 56*(4). Advance online publication. DOI: 10.1093/oep/gpf064

Cortright, D., & Lopez, G. A. (2002). Smart Sanctions: Targeting Economic Statecraft. *International Journal (Toronto, Ont.)*, *57*(4), 647–651. DOI: 10.2307/40203698

Drezner, D. (2011). Sanctions Sometimes Smart: Targeted Sanctions in Theory and Practice. *International Studies Review*, *13*(1), 96–108. DOI: 10.1111/j.1468-2486.2010.01001.x

Duffield, M. (2001). *Global Governance and the New Wars: The Merging of Development and Security*. Zen Books., Retrieved from https://www.google.com.cy/books/edition/Global_Governance_and_the_New_Wars/BQ9kDgAAQBAJ?hl=en&gbpv=1&dq=Global+Governance+and+the+New+Wars:+The+Merging+of+Development+and+Security.+Zed+Books&printsec=frontcover

Early, B. R. (2015). *Busted Sanctions Explaining Why Economic Sanctions Fail* (1st ed.). Stanford University Press., Retrieved 2025, from.

European External Action Service. (2016). *Shared Vision, Common Action: A Stronger Europe*. Brussels: EU.

Farrell, H., & Newman, A. L. (2019). *Weaponized Interdependence: How Global Economic Networks Shape State Coercion* (Vol. 44). MIT Press., DOI: 10.1162/isec_a_00351

Fatić, A., Korać, S., & Bulatović, A. (2011). Empathy in Diplomacy. *The Review of International Affairs*, *62*(1142), 5–13. Retrieved 2025, from https://www.ceeol.com/search/article-detail?id=1071797

Finnemore, M., & Hollis, D. B. (2016). Constructing Norms for Global Cybersecurity. *The American Journal of International Law*, *110*(3), 425–479. Retrieved 2025, from https://www.jstor.org/stable/10.5305/amerjintelaw.110.3.0425

Götz, F. M., Gosling, S. D., & Rentfrow, P. J. (2022). Small effects: The indispensable foundation for a cumulative psychological science. *Perspectives on Psychological Science*, *17*(1), 205–215. DOI: 10.1177/1745691620984483 PMID: 34213378

GSMA. (2024). *The Mobile Economy Sub-Saharan Africa 2024*. London: Global System for Mobile Communications Association. Retrieved 2025, from https://prod-cms.gsmaintelligence.com/research-file-download?assetId=12080&reportId=50121

Haddad, B. (2011). *Business Networks in Syria: The Political Economy of Authoritarian Resilience*. Stanford Studies in Middle Eastern and Islamic Societies and Cultures.

Hameiri, S., & Jones, L. (2015). Global Governance as State Transformation. *Political Studies, 64*(4), 1–18. DOI: 10.1111/1467-9248.1222

Hoffmann, M. (2017). Norms and Social Constructivism in International Relations. *Oxford Research Encyclopedia of International Studies*, N/A. doi:DOI: 10.1093/acrefore/9780190846626.013.60

Holling, C. S. (1973). Resilience and Stability of Ecological Systems. *Annual Review of Ecology and Systematics, 4*, 1–23. https://www.jstor.org/stable/2096802

Hufbauer, G., & Jung, E. (2020). What's new in economic sanctions? *European Economic Review, 130*. Advance online publication. DOI: 10.1016/j.euroecorev.2020.103572 PMID: 33012831

Hurley, J., Scott, M., & Gailyn, P. (2018). *Examining the Debt Implications of the Belt and Road Initiative from a Policy Perspective*. Center for Global Development.

IMF. (2023). *United States: 2023 Article IV Consultation-Press Release; Staff Report; and Statement by the Executive Director for the United States*. Western Hemisphere. International Monetary Fund. doi:DOI: 10.5089/9798400245176.002

Isichei, E. (2024). Entrepreneurial Resilience and business survival. *The Journal of Entrepreneurship*. Advance online publication. DOI: 10.1177/09713557241233820

Joseph, J. (2013). Resilience as embedded neoliberalism: A governmentality approach. *Resilience: International Policies. Practices and Discourses, 1*(1), 38–52. DOI: 10.1080/21693293.2013.765741

Justino, P., Brück, T., & Verwimp, P. (2014). A Micro-Level Perspective on the Dynamics of Conflict. *Violence, and Development, 26*. Advance online publication. DOI: 10.1093/acprof:oso/9780199664597.001.0001

Kalaignanam, K., Tuli, K. R., Kushwaha, T., Leonard, L., & Gal, D. (2021). Marketing Agility: The Concept, Antecedents, and a Research Agenda. *Journal of Marketing, 85*(1), 35–58. DOI: 10.1177/0022242920952760

Kaldor, M. (2012). *New and Old Wars: Organized Violence in a Global Era* (3rd ed.). Stanford University Press.

Keohane, R., & Nye, J. (1977). *Power and Interdependence*. (M. Vikram, Ed.) New York, US: Pearson. Retrieved 2025, from http://slantchev.ucsd.edu/courses/ps240/05%20Cooperation%20with%20States%20as%20Unitary%20Actors/Keohane%20&%20Nye%20-%20Power%20and%20interdependence%20[Ch%201-3].pdf

Kuersten, A. (2018). Busted Sanctions: Explaining Why Economic Sanctions Fail. *Democracy and Security, 14*(2), 200–201. DOI: 10.1080/17419166.2017.1345245

Mearsheimer, J. (2001). *The Tragedy of Great Power Politics*. W W Norton and Co., Retrieved from https://samuelbhfaure.com/wp-content/uploads/2015/10/s2-mearsheimer-2001.pdf

Mearsheimer, J. (2018). *The Great Delusion: Liberal Dreams and International Realities*. Yale University Press.

Naudé, B. T., Naude, W., & Verwimp, P. (2013). Business under Fire: Entrepreneurship and Violent Conflict in Developing Countries. *The Journal of Conflict Resolution*, *57*(1), 3–19. DOI: 10.1177/0022002712464846

Naudé, W. E. (2010). Developing countries, and development economics: New approaches and insights. *Small Business Economics*, •••, 1–12. DOI: 10.1007/s11187-009-9198-2

Nye, J. (2005). *Soft Power: The Means to Success in World Politics*. Public Affairs., Retrieved 2025, from.

OECD. (2022). *States of Fragility 2022*. OECD., DOI: 10.1787/c7fedf5e-

Papadopoulou, C., Vardarsuyu, M., & Oghazi, P. (2023). Examining the relationships between brand authenticity, perceived value, and brand forgiveness: The role of cross-cultural happiness. *Journal of Business Research*, *167*. Advance online publication. DOI: 10.1016/j.jbusres.2023.114154

Patrick, S. (2011). *Weak Links: Fragile States, Global Threats, and International Security*. Oxford University Press., DOI: 10.1093/acprof:oso/9780199751501.001.0001

PCRD. (2006). *Policy on Post-Conflict Reconstruction and Development (PCRD)*. AFRICAN UNION.

Peksen, D. (2019, June 10). Sanctions Work Best? Five Key Conditions Associated with Successful Sanctions Outcomes. *Sanctions Work Best?* US, US: Center for a New American Security (CNAS). Retrieved 2025, from https://www.cnas.org/publications/commentary/when-do-economic-sanctions-work-best

PIIE. (2016). China's Belt and Road Initiative: Motives, Scope, and Challenges. Washington, D.C.: Peterson Institute for International Economics (PIIE).

Renko, M., Bullough, A., & Saeed, S. (2020). How Do Resilience and Self-efficacy Relate to Entrepreneurial Intentions in Countries With Varying Degrees of Fragility? A Six-country Study. *International Small Business Journal*, •••, 40.

Richmond, O. P. (2013). Peace Formation and Local Infrastructures for Peace. *Alternatives*, *38*(4), 271–287. Retrieved 2025, from https://www.jstor.org/stable/24569417

Riddle, L., & Brinkerhoff, J. (2011). Diaspora entrepreneurs as institutional change agents: The case of Thamel.com. *International Business Review, 20*(6), 670–680. DOI: 10.1016/j.ibusrev.2011.02.013

Rodrik, D. (2011). *The Globalization Paradox: Democracy and the Future of the World Economy*. W.W. Norton., Retrieved 2025, from.

Rotberg, R. I. (2004). *When States Fail: Causes and Consequences*. Princeton University Press., DOI: 10.2307/j.ctt7scrg

Safranchuk, I. (2022). Empathy Is the Best Strategy for Diplomacy. *The Review of International Affairs, 20*. Advance online publication. DOI: 10.31278/1810-6374-2022-20-2-54-64

Saner, R., & Yiu, L. (2003). International economic diplomacy: Mutations in post-modern times. *International Economic Diplomacy:Mutations in Post-modern Times* (p. 41). Vienna: Netherlands Institute of International Relations "Clingendael". Retrieved 2025, from https://www.clingendael.org/sites/default/files/pdfs/20030100_cli_paper_dip_issue84.pdf

Senor, D., & Singer, S. (2009). *Start-up Nation: The Story of Israel's Economic Miracle*. New York: Grand Central Publishing. Retrieved 2025, from https://ia600509.us.archive.org/7/items/TheLeanStartupErickRies/start-up_nation_the_stor.pdf

Sophocleous, H., Anastasiadou, S., & Masouras, A. (2025). The Circular Correlation Between Institutions, Political Marketing, and the Electoral Process. In *Security and Strategy Models for Key-Solving Institutional Frameworks* (Vol. 13, pp. 1-16). MDPI (IGI Global). doi:DOI: 10.4018/979-8-3693-5583-1.ch007

Sophocleous, H. P. (2023). Nation Branding as a Strategic Asset for Local SMEs: Global Developments in Nation Branding and Promotion – Theoretical and Practical Approaches. In A. Masouras, *Global Developments in Nation Branding and Promotion: Theoretical and Practical Approaches* (pp. 124-155). IGI Global Scientific Publishing. doi:DOI: 10.4018/978-1-6684-5902-7.ch006

Sophocleous, H. P. (2024). *Production and Consumption of Political Communication and Voting Behaviour*. Nova Science Publishers., DOI: 10.52305/ojbc3507

Sophocleous, H. P., Masouras, A., & Anastasiadou, S. D. (2024). The impact of political marketing on voting behaviour of Cypriot voters. *Social Sciences, 13*(3). Advance online publication. DOI: 10.3390/socsci13030149

Sophocleous, H. P., Masouras, A., & Papademetriou, C. (2019). Brand as a Strategic Asset for Cultural Organisations: A Proposal for the Forthcoming Cultural Institution of Pafos. In Kavoura, A., Kefallonitis, E., Giovanis, A., Kavoura, A., Kefallonitis, E., & Giovanis, A. (Eds.), *Strategic Innovative Marketing and Tourism* (pp. 735–743). Springer., DOI: 10.1007/978-3-030-12453-3_85

Stiglitz, J. E. (2018). *Globalization and its discontents revisited: Anti-globalization in the era of Trump*. W. W. Norton & Company., Retrieved 2025, from.

Tamirat, S. (2024). Digital Marketing in developing economies. *Journal of Marketing, 11*(21), 48–67. DOI: 10.54663/2182-9306.2023.v11.n21.48-67

UNDP. (2022). *Human Development Report 2021-22.* New York: UNDP United Nations Development Programme. Retrieved 2025, from https://hdr.undp.org/system/files/documents/global-report-document/hdr2021-22reportenglish_0.pdf

Wezeman, P. D., Kuimova, A., & Wezerman, S. T. (2022). Trends in International Arms Transfers, 2021. Stockholm International Peace Research Institute. Stockholm: SIPRI. doi:DOI: 10.55163/CBZJ9986

World Bank. (2023). *Fragile and Conflict-affected Situations*. World Bank.

World Economic Forum. (2022). *Cultivating Investment Opportunities in Fragile Contexts: Catalysing Market-Driven Solutions to Strengthen Community and Economy Resilience.* World Economic Forum. Retrieved 2025, from https://www3.weforum.org/docs/WEF_Cultivating_Investment_Opportunities_in_Fragile_Contexts_2022.pdf

Chapter 10
Exchange Rate Shocks and Entrepreneurial Resilience in Agrifood Value Chains

Georgios A. Deirmentzoglou
https://orcid.org/0000-0003-1687-0708
Neapolis University Pafos, Cyprus

Eleni E. Anastasopoulou
https://orcid.org/0000-0002-0918-8527
Neapolis University Pafos, Cyprus

ABSTRACT

Agrifood value chains operate in an increasingly turbulent global environment where exchange rate volatility interacts with climate shocks, input price surges, and geopolitical disruptions. Although agricultural trade is highly sensitive to currency movements, the implications of exchange rate shocks for entrepreneurs embedded in agrifood chains remain insufficiently examined. This chapter analyses how currency fluctuations affect costs, revenues, competitiveness, and strategic decision-making across farming, processing, and distribution activities. It highlights the uneven exposure of firms, especially small and medium-sized enterprises that rely on imported inputs and possess limited financial and organisational buffers. By integrating insights from exchange-rate economics, value-chain resilience, and entrepreneurship research, the chapter develops a conceptual understanding of how agrifood entrepreneurs sense, absorb, and adapt to exchange-rate-induced disruptions. The analysis identifies key gaps in current scholarship and outlines future research opportunities.

DOI: 10.4018/979-8-3373-6991-4.ch010

1. INTRODUCTION

1.1 Background: Global Turbulence, Currency Volatility and Agrifood Systems

Over the past two decades, agrifood systems have become more deeply embedded in global markets. Rapid trade integration, the servicification of value chains and the growing role of cross-border processing have tightened the links between farm returns, post-farmgate margins and developments in international commodity markets (Santeramo et al., 2024). At the same time, agrifood value chains remain highly vulnerable to a broad set of shocks, including climate extremes, animal and plant disease, conflict and pandemics, whose impacts cascade along supply chains and interact with broader macroeconomic disturbances such as economic crises and input price shocks (for example, energy and fertiliser price spikes) (Coral & Mithöfer, 2023; Minten et al., 2023).

A central feature of this turbulent environment is heightened volatility in agricultural and food prices and the exchange-rate channels through which global market signals are transmitted. Analyses of agricultural commodity prices over the past half-century, such as Huchet-Bourdon (2011), show that major price run-ups, notably in the 1970s and 2006–08, occurred alongside large movements in crude oil prices and in the euro–US dollar exchange rate. More recently, climate-related events and perceived climate risk have been shown to exert measurable effects on agricultural futures prices and their volatility, reinforcing the amplitude of market swings (Guo et al., 2023). In many countries, these commodity and currency dynamics have been compounded by geopolitical tensions, sanctions and trade disruptions that further destabilise agrifood markets. The result is a systemic environment in which exchange rate shocks represent not isolated disturbances but one dimension of a broader volatility complex affecting production, trade and consumption.

For agrifood systems, this context is especially consequential because of the sector's structural characteristics. Agriculture is capital-intensive in traded inputs, heavily reliant on imported machinery, fertilisers, crop protection products and energy, and deeply integrated into international markets for grains, oilseeds, livestock products and high-value horticulture. Review studies consistently find that agricultural trade flows are particularly sensitive to exchange rate movements, with volatility in real or nominal exchange rates often exerting stronger and more consistent effects on agricultural trade than on aggregate merchandise trade (Kristinek & Anderson, 2002; Wesley et al., 2012). In addition, value-chain analyses emphasise that disturbances such as market volatility or demand shocks can undermine both the supply and demand sides of agricultural chains, thereby threatening food security and rural livelihoods (Vroegindewey & Hodbod, 2018; Minten et al., 2023).

1.2 Why Exchange Rate Shocks Matter for Agrifood Entrepreneurship

Within this macro-financial landscape, agrifood entrepreneurs, such as farmers, processors, traders and service providers, face exchange rate shocks as a core component of their business environment. Exchange rate movements influence the domestic currency value of export revenues, the cost of imported inputs and capital goods, and the relative competitiveness of domestic producers vis-à-vis foreign competitors. Empirical studies of agricultural trade repeatedly show that exchange rate volatility can depress export volumes, particularly in developing and emerging economies where hedging instruments and financial markets are less developed. Kargbo (2006) analysing South African agricultural trade under policy reforms, finds that increased exchange rate volatility exerts significant negative effects on agricultural exports, even after controlling for output and income variables. For Russia, Tarasenko (2021) reports that foreign-exchange volatility reduces exports of manufactured goods and of machinery and transport equipment, with stronger negative effects where financial development is lower. Meta-regression analysis by Wesley et al. (2012) synthesises results from 351 econometric estimates and concludes that agricultural trade studies report more consistently significant and negative effects of exchange rate volatility than studies focusing on other sectors, implying that agriculture is particularly exposed to currency risk.

Yet the effects are neither uniform nor unidirectional. The broader empirical literature includes studies where exchange rate volatility has limited or insignificant impacts, or where depreciation episodes temporarily boost export competitiveness. For bilateral agricultural trade between the United States and OECD partners, Kafle (2011) finds that exchange rate volatility has a significantly negative effect on trade flows, with particularly strong impacts in the agricultural sector, while free trade agreements and the adoption of the euro are associated with higher trade volumes. Benavides Perales and Venegas Martínez (2022), examining corn and wheat trade between the United States and Mexico, find that exchange rate volatility does not significantly affect corn and wheat prices or export quantities over 1990–2017, indicating that agricultural trade in these cereals appears relatively insulated from exchange rate risk in this context.

For agrifood entrepreneurs, the mixed evidence on exchange rate effects translates into a complex and uneven risk landscape. When currencies depreciate, the domestic prices of imported fertilisers, feed, energy and machinery typically rise, compressing margins for producers and processors that sell mainly into domestic markets, even as exporters may enjoy a temporary boost in price competitiveness abroad. Whether firms can turn nominal exchange rate movements into genuine competitive gains depends on features such as their contractual arrangements, market power, scope to pass costs along the chain, and access to financial tools that help them hedge or smooth shocks. Work on agrifood value-chain resilience further shows that small and medium-sized enterprises are frequently positioned in low-bargaining-power segments and operate with constrained financial and organisational capacities, which leaves them especially exposed to sharp increases in input costs or demand contractions triggered by macroeconomic disturbances (Minten et al., 2023; Vroegindewey & Hodbod, 2018).

Against this backdrop, the purpose of this chapter is to examine how exchange rate shocks interact with the structure and institutional features of agrifood value chains to shape entrepreneurial resilience. While the literature on exchange rate volatility and trade is extensive, it has focused primarily on aggregate trade flows and macroeconomic relationships, often treating firms as homogeneous actors. At the same time, the burgeoning literature on value-chain resilience and entrepreneurial adaptation in agrifood systems has paid relatively limited attention to currency risk as a specific driver of disruption and transformation. This chapter seeks to bridge these strands by situating agrifood entrepreneurs within multi-scalar value chains that are both exposed to, and capable of responding to, exchange rate shocks.

2. UNDERSTANDING EXCHANGE RATE SHOCKS IN THE GLOBAL AGRIFOOD ECONOMY

2.1 Definitions: Nominal Vs. Real Exchange Rate Shocks

In the context of globally integrated agrifood value chains, it is essential to distinguish between nominal and real exchange rate shocks, because each operates through different mechanisms and leads to different behavioural responses by firms and farmers. The nominal exchange rate is the relative price of two currencies, typically defined as the number of units of domestic currency per unit of foreign currency. A nominal depreciation occurs when more units of domestic currency are required to purchase one unit of foreign currency, whereas a nominal appreciation implies the opposite. This is the rate most visible to market participants and is the immediate channel through which currency markets transmit shocks to cross-border prices and contracts.

The real exchange rate adjusts the nominal exchange rate for relative price levels between countries, usually via consumer price indices (CPIs) or producer price indices. In simple terms, the real exchange rate compares the price of a representative basket of goods in one country to the price of a similar basket abroad expressed in the same currency. A real appreciation indicates that domestic prices have risen relative to foreign prices (after accounting for the nominal rate), thus reducing international price competitiveness; a real depreciation has the opposite effect. Trofimov (2020), for example, defines the real exchange rate as the nominal rate multiplied by the ratio of foreign to domestic price indices, and employs this concept in assessing the J-curve effect in agricultural trade.

For agricultural and food trade, real rather than nominal exchange rate changes are more closely linked to competitiveness and trade volumes because they reflect both currency movements and inflation differentials. The USDA ERS Agricultural Exchange Rate Data Set computes bilateral real exchange rates by adjusting nominal local-currency-per-USD rates with the ratio of the trading country's price index (typically CPI) to the U.S. CPI, and aggregates these into commodity-specific, trade-weighted real exchange rate indices relevant for U.S. agricultural trade (USDA, n.a.). These indices capture how the relative cost of U.S. agricultural products changes in different foreign markets over time.

An exchange rate "shock" can be understood as an unexpected and typically sizeable change in either the nominal or real exchange rate. Such shocks may be short-lived, associated with sudden shifts in financial sentiment or persistent, reflecting structural changes in macroeconomic conditions. In empirical work, exchange rate volatility is often used as a proxy for the intensity of shocks; Steinbach (2021) measures both short-run and long-run exchange rate volatility to estimate their impact on global food supply chains. In this perspective, real exchange rate shocks are especially important for agrifood entrepreneurs because they modify the relative profitability of exporting, importing inputs, and selling on domestic markets after allowing for changes in local and foreign price levels.

Nominal shocks, however, cannot be ignored. Contracts for imported inputs such as fertilizers, feed, or machinery are frequently denominated in major currencies (e.g., the U.S. dollar or euro). When domestic currencies depreciate sharply in nominal terms, the local-currency cost of servicing foreign-currency contracts rises immediately, even before local price indices fully adjust. Bor and Dagistan (2024), for instance, use a non-linear ARDL model to show that changes in the Turkish lira–U.S. dollar exchange rate have asymmetric short-run effects on domestic fertilizer prices, underscoring how nominal exchange rate movements can rapidly affect input costs in import-dependent agrifood systems. The distinction between nominal and real shocks therefore matters empirically, yet in practice agrifood entrepreneurs often experience them jointly, as currency swings interact with inflation dynamics and price-setting behaviour along the value chain.

2.2 Sources of Volatility: Geopolitical Tensions, Commodity Price Cycles and Financialization

Exchange rate volatility in the agrifood economy is ultimately rooted in a combination of macroeconomic, geopolitical and financial forces that shape expectations about growth, inflation and risk. One major source is geopolitical tension, which influences capital flows, risk premia and trade patterns. The 2021–2022 period provides a salient example: the war in Ukraine, a major exporter of grains and fertilizers, triggered sharp swings in energy, fertilizer and food prices, while simultaneously increasing uncertainty in currency markets, especially for countries highly integrated into Black Sea trade routes. Vos et al. (2025) document how overlapping crises associated with the COVID-19 recovery and the Russia–Ukraine war produced spikes in food and fertilizer prices and contributed to an "extended period of unpredictability and volatility" in global agricultural markets. Such episodes tend to be accompanied by heightened exchange rate volatility as investors reprice country risk and as terms-of-trade expectations shift.

Commodity price cycles themselves are another structural driver of currency volatility in agrifood exporters and importers alike. Countries heavily reliant on primary commodity exports often experience "commodity–currency" dynamics in which terms-of-trade shocks feed into exchange rate movements. Huchet-Bourdon (2011), in a comprehensive analysis of agricultural commodity price volatility over the last fifty years, finds strong correlations between agricultural commodity prices, crude oil, fertilizer prices and the euro–dollar exchange rate, highlighting the intertwined nature of commodity and currency cycles. Sarris (2013) similarly emphasizes that spikes in staple food commodity prices are closely related to unpredictability in market fundamentals, such as weather-related production shocks or sudden policy changes, and that these shocks are particularly destabilizing for net food-importing developing countries. When commodity prices surge or collapse, terms of trade move sharply, and currencies of commodity-dependent economies often follow. From an international-political-economy perspective, energy security concerns and the EU's external economic relations further condition how such price shocks and currency movements propagate through production and trade systems (Deirmentzoglou et al., 2024).

A further layer of complexity arises from the financialization of food and agricultural commodity markets. The growing participation of financial investors through derivatives, index funds and exchange-traded funds has strengthened the linkages between agrifood prices, broader financial markets and exchange rates. Venegas et al. (2024) examine volatility spillovers between major agricultural commodities, agribusiness corporations and financial assets and conclude that financial speculation, especially via passive index investments, has intensified price volatility in commodity futures and increased systemic risk in the agri-food sector. When food commodities become more tightly integrated with global financial portfolios, exchange rate shocks can propagate more quickly via leveraged positions and cross-market arbitrage, amplifying volatility beyond what would be expected from physical supply-demand conditions alone.

These forces interact in non-trivial ways. Periods of loose global monetary conditions and search for yield may attract capital flows into emerging agrifood exporters, appreciating their currencies and encouraging external borrowing. Conversely, abrupt shifts in risk sentiment, triggered by geopolitical events or expectations of monetary tightening in advanced economies, can prompt rapid capital outflows and sharp depreciations. In such environments, exchange rate volatility is not merely a reflection of domestic fundamentals but the outcome of global portfolio reallocations across asset classes, including agricultural commodities. As Steinbach (2021) shows using a sectoral gravity model for 781 agricultural and food products, exposure to exchange rate risk is heterogeneous across products and stages of the value chain, with upstream segments often experiencing different trade effects than downstream, more processed products. For agrifood entrepreneurs, this implies that exchange rate shocks are shaped jointly by local macroeconomic conditions, commodity cycles and the evolving architecture of financial markets.

2.3 Transmission Channels to Agrifood Value Chains

Exchange rate shocks reach agrifood entrepreneurs through multiple, interrelated transmission channels. Three are particularly salient: fluctuations in input costs, volatility of output prices, and shifts in export competitiveness. First, the input cost channel operates primarily through imported inputs such as fertilizers, agrochemicals, feed, seeds, machinery and fuels. In many agrifood systems, especially in import-dependent countries, these inputs are denominated in major currencies. When the domestic currency depreciates, local-currency prices of imported inputs tend to rise, even if international dollar prices remain stable. Bor and Dagistan (2024) provide clear evidence of this mechanism for Türkiye: using monthly data from 2011 to 2022, they show that exchange rate movements of the Turkish lira against the U.S. dollar exert asymmetric short-run effects on domestic prices of di-ammonium phosphate and urea fertilizers, with depreciation episodes translating into rapid cost increases for farmers. More broadly, the OECD's analysis of fertilizer markets and FAO outlook reports underscore that exchange rate fluctuations, alongside freight and transaction costs, help explain why international fertilizer price declines are often only partially transmitted to prices paid by farmers.

Recent fertilizer market shocks illustrate how input-cost pressures interact with broader exchange rate dynamics. Vos et al. (2025) show that during the 2021–2022 fertilizer price spike, global fertilizer demand declined only modestly, as many commercial farmers in high-income countries absorbed higher input costs given favourable output prices and supportive policies. However, they also find that farmer profitability in low-income African countries deteriorated more sharply, partly because currency weakness and high import dependence magnified local fertilizer prices and constrained smallholders' ability to maintain application rates. These findings highlight how exchange rate shocks affecting imported inputs can erode margins, reduce input use and, in the longer run, depress yields, particularly for capital-constrained producers.

Second, exchange rate shocks influence agrifood value chains through output price volatility. Depreciation can raise domestic currency prices of tradable staples, even when world prices are stable, thereby increasing revenues for net sellers while harming net buyers. Huchet-Bourdon (2011) documents significant co-movement between agricultural commodity prices, fertilizer prices and the euro–dollar exchange rate, suggesting that exchange rate fluctuations are an integral component of overall price volatility in agrifood markets. Sarris (2013) stresses that for food-importing developing countries, exchange rate-induced spikes in import prices of staples can quickly translate into heightened food insecurity, especially where safety nets and storage systems are weak.

The relationship between exchange rate volatility and agricultural trade flows is, however, empirically nuanced. Benavides Perales and Venegas Martínez (2022), analysing corn and wheat trade between the United States and Mexico from 1990 to 2017, find that exchange rate volatility, as captured in a factor-augmented VAR framework, does not exert a statistically significant effect on bilateral agricultural trade volumes once other determinants are controlled for. Steinbach's (2021) product-level gravity analysis also reveals substantial heterogeneity: while the mean impact of short- and long-run exchange rate volatility on agricultural and food trade is modestly positive, the effects vary considerably by product sophistication and position along the supply chain, with some segments experiencing adverse trade responses. These results suggest that the output-price channel is shaped by a complex interplay between risk management strategies, pricing-to-market, and contractual arrangements along the chain, rather than a simple one-to-one mapping from exchange rate volatility to trade collapse.

Third, exchange rate shocks affect agrifood value chains through shifts in export competitiveness. Real depreciations generally enhance the price competitiveness of agricultural exporters by lowering foreign-currency unit costs of production, while appreciations erode competitiveness. The USDA ERS commodity-specific real exchange rate indices have been widely used to capture these competitiveness effects for U.S. agricultural exports, showing how changes in the dollar's value relative to trading partners can boost or dampen export performance across specific commodities. In a global perspective, Steinbach (2021) finds that exchange rate volatility has different trade effects for upstream versus downstream food products: volatility is positively associated with trade in upstream products (e.g., raw commodities) but negatively associated with trade in downstream, more processed products. This asymmetry points to the role of firm capabilities, contractual rigidities and branding in shaping how competitiveness gains or losses from exchange rate movements are transmitted along the value chain.

In parallel, there is growing evidence that exchange rate movements interact with other sources of uncertainty to influence exporters' strategic decisions. Sarris (2013) notes that high volatility in staple food prices, partly driven by exchange rate fluctuations and policy shocks, can deter investment in trade-oriented agrifood activities in developing countries, particularly when hedging instruments and risk management institutions are underdeveloped. In financialized markets, derivatives and index funds may amplify volatility in futures prices and thereby complicate price discovery for exporters and processors. For agrifood entrepreneurs, this means that exchange rate shocks and financial-market dynamics jointly influence expectations about future profitability, which in turn shape investment, contracting and market-entry decisions.

2.4 Exchange Rate Asymmetry in Agricultural Markets

The impacts of exchange rate shocks on agrifood value chains are markedly asymmetric across countries, actors and segments of the chain. At the country level, net food importers and exporters face different risk profiles. For net food-importing developing countries, volatility in food import prices—driven partly by exchange rate fluctuations—poses severe food security risks when foreign exchange reserves are limited and when policy instruments for price stabilization are weak (Sarris, 2013). By contrast, for net exporters, a real depreciation can boost export revenues and rural incomes, although this may be accompanied by higher domestic prices and distributional tensions between producers and consumers.

Within countries, exchange rate shocks also generate asymmetries between smallholders and large agribusinesses. The fertilizer market disruptions illustrate this point: while commercial farms in the United States and other major producers were generally able to absorb higher input costs associated with global price spikes, many farming households in Africa faced sharper declines in profitability, reflecting weaker access to credit, limited hedging possibilities and greater vulnerability to exchange rate-driven input cost increases (Vos et al., 2025). Bor and Dagistan's (2024) evidence of asymmetric transmission of exchange rate movements to Turkish fertilizer prices further suggests that domestic market structures can amplify adverse effects for input-dependent farmers in countries with depreciating currencies.

Firm size and position in the value chain matter as well. Large agribusinesses often have access to sophisticated risk-management instruments, such as currency hedging, diversified sourcing and long-term supply contracts, that allow them to mitigate or even exploit exchange rate volatility. Smaller agrifood entrepreneurs, especially in low- and middle-income countries, typically lack such instruments and are therefore more exposed to exchange rate-induced cost and revenue shocks. Steinbach (2021) shows that the trade effects of exchange rate volatility are heterogeneous across products and stages of the food supply chain, with upstream products generally less sensitive to adverse trade effects than downstream processed foods. This pattern suggests that firms engaged in more complex, branded or quality-differentiated products, often located downstream, may face greater challenges in passing exchange-rate-induced cost changes through to final buyers, especially in competitive retail markets.

Empirical research on export behaviour also indicates asymmetric responses to exchange rate volatility. Alegwu et al. (2017) studying Nigerian agricultural exports, identify asymmetric effects of real exchange rate volatility, finding that increases and decreases in volatility have different impacts on export volumes. Combined with the heterogeneous trade effects documented by Benavides Perales and Venegas Martínez (2022) for U.S.–Mexico grain trade, this points to a broader conclusion: the relationship between exchange rate shocks and agrifood export performance depends not only on the magnitude of volatility, but also on its direction, persistence and interaction with domestic market structures, including credit markets, infrastructure and policy regimes.

Taken together, the emerging literature suggests that exchange rate shocks in the global agrifood economy cannot be treated as symmetric "good news" for exporters and "bad news" for importers in a simplistic way. Instead, their effects are mediated by import dependence on key inputs, the availability of risk-management instruments, the degree of financialization of commodity markets, and the structural position of agrifood actors within domestic and global value chains. Understanding these asymmetries is central for analysing entrepreneurial resilience: the capacity of agrifood entrepreneurs to absorb, adapt to and transform in response to exchange rate shocks depends critically on their position in this complex web of exposures and buffers.

3. AGRIFOOD VALUE CHAINS: STRUCTURE, INSTITUTIONAL FEATURES, AND VULNERABILITIES

Agrifood value chains differ from many other manufacturing and service chains because they are deeply embedded in biological cycles, local ecologies, and social institutions. They coordinate flows of inputs, products, information, and finance from seed and fertilizer suppliers to farmers, processors, wholesalers, retailers, and ultimately consumers. This organisation is increasingly globalised, yet it remains strongly shaped by local climatic conditions, land tenure systems, and food cultures. These structural features make agrifood chains particularly vulnerable to shocks arising from climate variability, policy changes, and macroeconomic instability, including exchange rate fluctuations that alter the relative prices of traded inputs and outputs. Understanding how these chains are configured, who participates in them, and which formal and informal institutions govern transactions is therefore a prerequisite for analysing how exchange rate shocks propagate through agrifood systems and affect entrepreneurial resilience.

3.1 Characteristics of Agrifood Chains: Seasonality, Perishability, and Market Concentration

Seasonality is a defining characteristic of most agrifood chains. Crop and livestock production follows biological cycles that are constrained by temperature, rainfall, and day length, which create distinct harvest windows and off-season periods. This temporal patterning generates predictable fluctuations in supply that must be smoothed through storage, imports, or product substitution. When supply peaks, farm-gate prices tend to be depressed; during lean seasons they rise, sometimes sharply, especially where storage and cold-chain infrastructure are limited. These seasonal imbalances are well documented in empirical work on fruit and vegetable supply chains, where producers and logisticians face recurrent challenges of oversupply at harvest and deficit in the off-season, with corresponding volatility in prices and margins (Orjuela Casto et al., 2021). In such contexts, exchange rate movements can interact with seasonality: a depreciation during the off-season raises the local currency cost of imported foods and inputs, potentially exacerbating domestic price spikes, whereas an appreciation during the harvest season can compress export margins even when world prices are favourable.

Perishability further differentiates agrifood chains from those dealing in durable goods. Fresh fruits, vegetables, dairy products, meat, and many processed foods have limited shelf lives and strict temperature and hygiene requirements. These features impose tight constraints on lead times and storage options and increase the cost of buffering shocks through inventories. Studies of agri-food supply chains emphasise that perishability amplifies the consequences of logistical failures, demand shocks, and macroeconomic disturbances because unsold inventory quickly becomes unsellable, forcing actors to liquidate stocks at low prices or absorb direct losses (Kontopanou & Tsoulfas, 2022; Orjuela Casto et al., 2021) For small producers and SMEs with limited access to credit, such losses directly undermine working capital and constrain their ability to cope with exchange-rate-driven increases in input costs or decreases in export revenues.

Market concentration is another salient structural feature, particularly in downstream segments. Retail food markets and export channels in many countries have undergone consolidation, with supermarket chains, large processors, and a small number of powerful exporters exerting considerable control over procurement standards, contract terms, and pricing. Borsellino et al. (2020) show that global agri-food markets have evolved toward highly coordinated systems in which a limited number of dominant buyers set private quality and safety standards and shape the distribution of value along the chain. This concentration can have ambiguous implications for resilience. On the one hand, large retailers and processors often have better access to hedging instruments, foreign currency finance, and sophisticated risk management tools, allowing them to absorb exchange rate volatility more effectively than fragmented traditional markets. On the other hand, their buyer power can transfer a disproportionate share of the burden onto upstream suppliers, particularly smallholders and small processors, who may be forced to accept thinner margins or more volatile contract conditions when exchange rates move against them.

Recent work on agrifood supply chain resilience emphasises that these characteristics, seasonality, perishability, and increasing concentration, interact with one another and with external shocks. Kontopanou and Tsoulfas (2022) review the Triple-A and its recent extensions in the context of agrifood supply chains and argue that the time-sensitive, safety-critical nature of food products makes high agility and resilient, carefully designed sourcing strategies particularly important for managing disruptions. However, achieving such robustness is costly, especially for smaller firms, and any increase in financing costs resulting from currency depreciation may reduce the scope for maintaining redundant capacity or multiple sourcing arrangements. Thus, the structural traits of agrifood chains simultaneously create opportunities for efficiency and expose actors to heightened vulnerability when macroeconomic conditions become unstable.

3.2 The Role of SMEs, Cooperatives, and Small-Scale Producers

Despite growing consolidation in some segments, agrifood value chains remain heavily populated by small and medium-sized enterprises (SMEs) and small-scale producers. In many low- and middle-income countries, the bulk of agricultural production is carried out by smallholders, while processing, transportation, and local wholesale are often handled by micro and small enterprises. These actors typically operate with thin margins, high exposure to climatic and price risks, and limited access to formal credit and insurance. Their bargaining power is often weak vis-à-vis large buyers and input suppliers, making them particularly sensitive to exchange-rate-induced changes in input costs, interest rates, and demand conditions. Evidence from the COVID-19 period shows that agrifood entrepreneurs relied on rapid business model adjustments, diversification and digital tools to cope with these pressures, but that pre-existing structural vulnerabilities constrained many SMEs' capacity to respond (Apostolopoulos et al., 2021).

Cooperatives and producer organisations have emerged as key institutional vehicles for integrating smallholders into value chains and improving their resilience. Christian et al. (2024) show, in a case study from Eastern Cape, South Africa, that agricultural cooperatives enable smallholders to access inputs, storage, processing, and distribution services collectively and, as argued in their conceptual framework, strengthen farmers' bargaining position vis-à-vis intermediaries and buyers. They find that cooperatives provide members with lower input costs, production and marketing training, and platforms for knowledge sharing and extension, functions that strengthen smallholders' ability to cope with market and price volatility and to participate in downstream storage, processing, and distribution activities.

Beyond market access, cooperatives often contribute to sustainability and innovation within agrifood chains. Sarkar et al. (2022) show, for kiwi-fruit farmers in Meixian, China, that participation in farmers' cooperatives strengthens attitudes, subjective norms, perceived behavioural control and self-identity, which in turn significantly increase farmers' intentions to adopt environmentally friendly production technologies, suggesting that cooperative structures can play an important role in diffusing such sustainable innovations. Similarly, a recent study shows that in China's green capsicum value chain, agricultural cooperatives coordinate compliance with green food and GAP certifications and implement traceability and residue-testing systems across many small producers, thereby enabling them to supply national and overseas markets that demand stringent food-safety and environmental standards (Liu et al., 2025). These functions are directly relevant for exchange rate resilience, because they allow producers to diversify into differentiated, higher-value market segments that may be less price elastic and more insulated from pure cost-competition pressures when currencies fluctuate.

However, the capacity of cooperatives and SME-led networks to cushion exchange rate shocks is uneven. Many cooperatives remain under-capitalised and rely on members' contributions or local credit institutions that themselves may face constraints in foreign currency funding. Christian et al. (2024) report that a majority of cooperatives in their South African case study relied primarily on self-funding, with limited access to formal credit and extension services.In such settings, a sharp depreciation that raises the local currency cost of imported fertilizers, seeds, or fuel can quickly overwhelm cooperative budgets, forcing them to cut back on services or pass higher costs to members. Moreover, where cooperatives are integrated into export chains, they may bear exchange rate risk on receivables if payment terms are long and hedging options are limited. SMEs in processing and logistics face similar dilemmas: they may benefit from devaluation through improved export competitiveness, but only if they can maintain access to imported inputs and service their foreign-currency-denominated obligations.

These observations underline that the role of SMEs and cooperatives in agrifood value chains is double-edged with respect to exchange rate shocks. On the one hand, collective organisation and local embeddedness can strengthen resilience by enabling risk sharing, improving information flows, and enhancing bargaining power. On the other hand, structural financial constraints and limited access to currency risk management instruments leave these actors exposed, especially when they operate in highly globalised chains with significant foreign input content. Policies that improve cooperatives' financial literacy, access to tailored hedging instruments, and integration into inclusive financial systems are therefore crucial for enhancing entrepreneurial resilience under exchange rate volatility.

3.3 Informal Institutions: Trust Networks, PDO Systems, and Cultural Norms

In addition to formal contracts and public regulation, agrifood value chains are governed by a dense web of informal institutions that shape how transactions are organised and how risks are shared. Trust-based relationships between farmers, intermediaries, processors, and retailers are particularly important where quality is difficult to observe ex ante, where monitoring is costly, and where legal enforcement of contracts is weak. Empirical studies of localised agrifood systems show that long-standing personal relationships, reputation, and reciprocal obligations often underpin credit in kind, advance payments, and long-term supply arrangements, allowing actors to smooth shocks without resorting to formal mechanisms (Fernández-Zarza et al., 2021). In such contexts, when exchange rate shocks occur, trust networks can facilitate renegotiation of terms, temporary reallocation of liquidity, and informal risk sharing that would be hard to organise through arm's-length market transactions.

Geographical indications (GIs) and protected designation of origin (PDO) schemes occupy an intermediate position between formal and informal institutions. On the one hand, they are formal legal instruments that define standards, certification procedures, and governance bodies. On the other hand, they codify and valorise local cultural norms, production practices, and territorial identities, thereby institutionalising trust and reputation at the collective level. Research on Iberian ham and traditional chorizo value chains shows that PDO and other GI schemes are designed to signal both measurable quality and symbolic attributes linked to territory and tradition, although survey evidence suggests that many consumers rely more on brand, taste and appearance than on PDO labels when assessing quality (Fernández-Zarza et al., 2021). The certification and control systems associated with PDOs reduce information asymmetries and create reputational capital that can sustain premium prices and stable demand trajectories, even when broader market conditions are volatile.

Trust and PDO-type institutions influence how exchange rate shocks are transmitted in several ways. First, products sold under GIs and PDOs often occupy premium market niches in which consumers are less price sensitive, giving producers some degree of pricing power that can partially offset currency-induced cost increases. Second, the collective governance of these schemes, typically involving producer consortia, cooperatives, and local authorities, creates platforms for coordinated responses to shocks, such as joint marketing campaigns, temporary supply management, or collective negotiation of export contracts. Third, trusted relationships within GI systems facilitate flexible contractual adjustments; for instance, buyers may accept delayed deliveries or temporary quality deviations during crisis periods, while producers may offer more favourable terms when conditions improve.

Cultural norms around food and reciprocity also shape actors' strategies. In many traditional markets, repeated interactions in physical marketplaces, family ties, and community norms create expectations of mutual support during difficult times. These norms can translate into informal credit lines, deferred payments, and temporary price concessions that buffer the immediate impact of exchange rate-induced cash-flow shocks. At the same time, such arrangements are contingent on local social cohesion and may not extend to cross-border transactions or relationships with large corporate buyers. As agrifood chains become more globalised and mediated by digital platforms and long-distance logistics, the balance between informal trust and formal contracts is shifting, raising new questions about how social capital can be maintained or re-created in more arm's-length, transnational settings.

3.4 Exposure to Exchange Rate–Induced Risks Along the Chain

Exchange rate shocks affect agrifood value chains through multiple channels, and the distribution of risks varies systematically across upstream, midstream, and downstream stages. Upstream, farmers and input suppliers are exposed primarily through the cost of tradable inputs and capital goods. Fertilizers, agrochemicals, improved seeds, animal feed, and farm machinery are often imported or priced with reference to international markets in major currencies such as the U.S. dollar or the euro. When the domestic currency depreciates, the local price of these inputs tends to rise, sometimes sharply, raising production costs and squeezing margins unless output prices adjust fully. Evidence from agri-food global value chain analyses shows that backward participation, defined as the share of foreign value added embedded in exports, is an important channel through which countries integrate into agri-food

GVCs. Török et al. (2025) find that backward participation in agri-food sectors is driven mainly by market size and trade facilitation, while forward participation depends more on institutional quality and logistics performance. Smallholders and SMEs, who often purchase inputs on cash terms and have limited access to working capital, are especially vulnerable because they may respond to cost surges by cutting input use, with potential negative consequences for yields, product quality, and long-term soil health.

Midstream stages, processing, logistics, and storage, face a different configuration of risks. Processors and logistics providers typically operate as "margin businesses" that buy raw materials and sell processed or transported products, earning a spread between input and output prices. Exchange rate shocks can compress this spread from both sides: depreciation raises the cost of imported energy, packaging materials, and spare parts, while also affecting domestic demand conditions and export competitiveness. When processors import raw materials and sell primarily in the domestic market, depreciation can sharply increase their costs without a commensurate rise in output prices if consumers' purchasing power is constrained. Studies of price volatility transmission in agricultural markets show that shocks can propagate along farm, wholesale and retail stages, and the literature suggests that the magnitude of this transmission is shaped by factors such as market power, contractual arrangements and product characteristics, with inventory behaviour highlighted as a promising but under-researched factor (Pan et al., 2023). Perishability and limited storage capacity in midstream facilities reduce the scope for smoothing such shocks over time, particularly for fresh products that must move quickly through the chain.

Downstream stages, wholesale, retail, and exports to international buyers, are directly exposed to exchange rate movements through their impact on consumer prices and international competitiveness. For export-oriented chains, a depreciation of the domestic currency can, in principle, improve price competitiveness abroad and stimulate export volumes. However, recent gravity-model work on agricultural and food trade suggests that the trade effects of exchange rate volatility are heterogeneous across products and value-chain positions. Using highly disaggregated product-level data, Steinbach (2021) shows that both short-run and long-run exchange-rate volatility have highly heterogeneous trade effects across agricultural and food products; in the short run, processed and semi-processed goods tend to exhibit more adverse responses than bulk commodities, while long-run effects are generally small in magnitude and mixed across product groups.

Domestic retailers experience exchange rate shocks mainly through import prices and consumer purchasing power. When currencies depreciate, the local currency cost of imported foods rises, and retailers must decide how much of this increase to pass on to consumers. In highly concentrated retail markets, large supermarket chains possess substantial buying power over suppliers, which can influence how price and cost pressures are distributed along the chain, often to the disadvantage of upstream producers. In more fragmented systems, retailers may have limited ability to absorb cost increases, resulting in sharper consumer price spikes and potentially reduced demand for higher-value products. In both cases, SMEs supplying retailers, such as local processors, bakeries, and fresh produce wholesalers, may face squeeze effects if they are unable to raise their selling prices in line with their input costs.

In sum, agrifood value chains exhibit a complex mix of structural characteristics and institutional arrangements that mediate the effects of exchange rate shocks. Seasonality, perishability, and market concentration shape the physical and economic flows of products; SMEs and cooperatives provide both opportunities and vulnerabilities in terms of risk sharing and market access; informal institutions and PDO systems embed chains in networks of trust and territorial identity; and stage-specific exposures to currency movements create differentiated risk profiles along the chain. These features jointly determine the room for manoeuvre available to agrifood entrepreneurs when exchange rates move sharply, and they highlight the importance of analysing resilience not at the level of isolated firms but at the level of interconnected value chain segments and governance structures.

4. ENTREPRENEURIAL RESILIENCE IN AGRIFOOD VALUE CHAINS

4.1 Conceptualizing Entrepreneurial Resilience: Absorptive, Adaptive and Transformative Capacities

Building on broader resilience debates in food systems, resilience in agrifood value chains can be understood as the capacity of chain actors to sustain viable operations and reorganise or innovate in the face of recurrent shocks (e.g. climatic, geopolitical or market disruptions). In line with resilience theory, it is increasingly framed as a multi-dimensional capacity to cope, adapt and transform in response to shocks and stresses (Follmann et al., 2024). Absorptive capacity refers to the ability of entrepreneurs and firms to withstand shocks and maintain core functions, for example by drawing on financial buffers, inventories, or social support networks to cope with temporary input price spikes or currency depreciation. Adaptive capacity captures incremental adjustments in products, processes and market strategies that allow firms to modify their business models when volatility becomes more persistent, such as reconfiguring sourcing portfolios or switching to less import-intensive technologies. Transformative capacity relates to deeper, structural changes in the organisation of production and marketing, including the reorientation of value chains toward new markets, sustainability standards or technological regimes, when existing trajectories are no longer viable (OECD, 2025).

Although the absorptive–adaptive–transformative triad has been developed primarily in development and food-systems policy literature, it provides a useful lens for analysing entrepreneurial resilience in agrifood value chains exposed to exchange rate risk. Agrifood entrepreneurs do not only confront price and demand volatility; they operate within complex social–ecological systems where climatic, financial and institutional shocks interact. OECD work on agricultural and food-system resilience emphasises that resilience strategies must consider multiple objectives, food security, livelihoods and environmental sustainability, and acknowledges that measures that stabilise incomes in the short run may undermine long-term sustainability if they lock systems into high-emission or resource-intensive pathways (OECD, 2019; 2025) Recent conceptual work on sustainability and resilience in value chains similarly argues that resilience is a necessary condition for sustainability, but that trade-offs and tensions between these goals emerge under "multiple crises", such as climate shocks combined with geopolitical tensions and financial volatility (Follmann et al., 2024).

At the entrepreneurial level, resilience is increasingly linked to learning capabilities, strategic flexibility and the ability to recombine resources under uncertainty. Empirical research on small and medium-sized enterprises (SMEs) shows that explorative, exploitative and transformative learning significantly enhance entrepreneurial resilience by helping firms detect risks, adjust routines and reconfigure their strategic orientation.

While this work is not specific to agrifood, its insights travel well to farm and agribusiness contexts where entrepreneurs must rapidly interpret changing exchange rates, credit conditions and input costs, and then choose whether to "ride out" shocks, incrementally adjust, or fundamentally restructure their operations. In agrifood value chains, therefore, entrepreneurial resilience can be conceptualised as the conjunction of financial, organisational, relational and cognitive capacities that enable actors to absorb currency-induced shocks, adapt production and marketing models, and, where necessary, transform their position within the chain.

4.2 Micro-Level Resilience Mechanisms

At the micro level, agrifood entrepreneurs deploy a variety of strategies to manage exchange rate risk and related market volatility. One important class of mechanisms involves financial hedging and currency risk management. Firm-level studies in international trade show that larger exporters are more likely to use financial derivatives, foreign-currency borrowing and invoicing-currency choices to hedge against exchange rate fluctuations, and that hedging intensity is positively associated with exposure to foreign sales and with firm size. Although these studies typically examine manufacturing or diversified exporters, similar patterns are observed in agrifood sectors, where multinational grain traders and large agro-processors have access to sophisticated derivative markets and can combine financial hedging with "natural hedges", such as geographically diversified sourcing or multi-currency revenue streams. Smaller producers, cooperatives and SMEs usually lack direct access to complex derivative instruments, but they may engage in simpler financial practices, such as foreign-currency accounts, forward contracts with buyers, or aligning loan currencies with export revenues, that provide partial protection against adverse currency movements.

Beyond financial instruments, entrepreneurial resilience in agrifood systems is closely linked to learning and innovation. Conceptual and empirical work shows that entrepreneurial farmers and SMEs who continuously learn and experiment with new practices are better able to redeploy resources, adjust production methods and develop new market relations when conditions change, thereby sustaining livelihoods and supporting agri-food system resilience (Manyise & Dentoni, 2021) Innovation may take the form of precision agriculture technologies that reduce input intensity, climate-smart practices that stabilise yields, or new product lines that exploit emerging demand for sustainable or origin-differentiated foods. When exchange rate depreciation raises the cost of imported fertilisers or machinery, for example, entrepreneurs who have already experimented with low-input or agroecological practices may enjoy a comparative resilience advantage.

Digital technologies are another important micro-level mechanism for strengthening resilience in agrifood value chains. European initiatives on traceability and big data in agrifood emphasise that electronic platforms, interoperable data systems and data-analytics tools can reduce information asymmetries, improve transparency along the chain and support more efficient coordination between producers, processors and retailers. By expanding farmers' and SMEs' access to timely market and technical information and enabling new forms of data-driven collaboration, digital tools help lower transaction costs and enhance the capacity of value-chain actors to anticipate and respond to shocks (European Commission, 2025). However, the effectiveness of these technologies depends critically on the digital competencies of agricultural professionals; strengthening digital skills is therefore essential to ensure that farmers and SMEs can meaningfully adopt, interpret and operationalise data-driven tools as part of their resilience strategies (Petropoulos et al., 2025). In Sub-Saharan Africa, for instance, e-commerce platforms that connect smallholder farmers directly with urban consumers and institutional buyers have been shown to improve market access, raise farm-gate prices and reduce post-harvest losses (Morepje et al., 2024).

Micro-level collaboration, both vertical and horizontal, is also strongly associated with entrepreneurial resilience. Value-chain research stresses that relationships with suppliers, buyers and peers can be mobilised to share information, pool resources and coordinate responses when shocks occur. Frameworks for assessing the resilience of agricultural value chains in developing countries emphasise relational assets such as diversity of buyers, long-term contracts and the presence of producer organisations as key determinants of the capacity to withstand and recover from disruptions (Vroegindewey & Hodbod, 2018; SNV, 2022). Horizontal collaboration among farmers through cooperatives and clusters can improve bargaining power, enable joint investments in storage or quality upgrading, and provide mutual support when exchange rate movements squeeze margins. Vertical coordination, through contract farming, integrated supply-chain partnerships or participation in certified value chains, may offer more stable pricing and access to credit, albeit sometimes at the cost of reduced autonomy.

4.3 Meso-Level Resilience Mechanisms

While entrepreneurial strategies are critical, the resilience of agrifood value chains to exchange rate shocks also depends on meso-level mechanisms operating at the level of supply-chain structures and supporting institutions. Integrated and diversified value-chain configurations, linking producers, processors, logistics providers and retailers through robust coordination mechanisms, are better positioned to manage disruptions and re-route flows when costs or prices change abruptly. The resilience framework developed by Vroegindewey and Hodbod (2018), for example, highlights the importance of redundancy, diversity and connectivity across stages of the chain for maintaining functionality under shocks. Chains that rely on a single export route, a limited set of input suppliers, or a highly concentrated buyer base are more vulnerable to currency-induced cost shocks and demand contractions than those with diversified market channels and logistics options.

Institutional support and public–private partnerships (PPPs) are central meso-level mechanisms for strengthening entrepreneurial resilience. Evidence from agrifood policy and rural development literature shows that PPPs in extension services, technology dissemination and infrastructure provision can leverage the strengths of both public agencies and private actors, improving access to innovation and risk-management tools for smallholders and SMEs (World Bank, 2024; FAO & OECD, 2019). PPP-supported initiatives such as cluster-based development projects, interregional innovation partnerships around traceability and big data, and multi-stakeholder platforms for local value-chain upgrading aim explicitly to enhance competitiveness, sustainability and resilience by promoting coordinated investments and knowledge sharing across the chain. For entrepreneurs, participation in such collaborative arrangements can reduce individual exposure to exchange rate volatility by improving access to finance, infrastructure and collective marketing initiatives.

Digital platforms and e-commerce also operate as meso-level buffers against market volatility. Recent work on e-commerce and sustainable agriculture documents how online platforms expand market reach, reduce dependence on local intermediaries and support more stable demand for sustainably produced goods (Morepje et al., 2024). In parallel, emerging research on digital platforms in food supply chains argues that data-intensive e-commerce systems can enhance supply-chain resilience under exogenous disruptions by facilitating real-time information flows, flexible reallocation of orders, and semi-disintermediation models that maintain key intermediaries while reducing layers of opacity (Suali et al., 2024). For agrifood entrepreneurs facing exchange-rate-induced shocks, participation in such platforms can stabilise revenues by diversifying buyer bases, enabling dynamic price adjustments and integrating financial services such as mobile payments or embedded credit that ease liquidity constraints during periods of high input costs.

4.4 Macro-Level Institutional Enablers

Finally, entrepreneurial resilience in agrifood value chains is strongly conditioned by macro-level institutional environments. Agricultural and food-system policy analyses show that trade and agricultural support policies, together with risk-management instruments and broader macro-economic frameworks, shape the extent to which international price and currency shocks are transmitted to domestic producers and processors, and the tools they have to manage them. The choice of policy mix – including trade openness, market-stabilisation and risk-sharing instruments can either amplify or dampen the effects of international price and currency volatility on domestic markets (FAO & OECD. 2019; OECD; 2025). For example, transparent and predictable trade policies, combined with macro-prudential regulation and targeted credit guarantees for export-oriented agrifood SMEs, can mitigate financing constraints and reduce uncertainty, thereby enhancing entrepreneurs' capacity to invest in resilience-building innovations despite exchange rate turbulence.

Sector-specific support programmes also play a crucial enabling role. World Bank and FAO-linked initiatives on resilient agrifood clusters and sustainable value chains highlight the importance of coordinated investments in climate-smart technologies, post-harvest infrastructure, quality and safety systems, and rural finance in boosting both productivity and resilience (World Bank, 2024; FAO, 2021). Such programmes often promote diversification of crops and markets, support compliance with international standards and encourage the adoption of risk-transfer instruments such as index-based insurance, all of which help agrifood entrepreneurs navigate currency-induced shocks. At the same time, recent strategic roadmaps for transforming agrifood value chains emphasise the need to re-wire financial flows, redirecting capital toward more resilient and regenerative production models and away from high-risk, high-emission practices that are vulnerable to both climate and financial shocks.

Green transition and sustainability policies constitute a further macro-level dimension. Conceptual work on sustainability and resilience in agrifood value chains stresses that while resilience is a prerequisite for sustainability, poorly designed resilience policies can entrench unsustainable practices if they focus narrowly on short-term stability (Follmann et al., 2024). Emerging policy frameworks therefore increasingly aim to align resilience with climate and biodiversity objectives, for example by incentivising diversified and regenerative production systems, supporting low-carbon logistics, and encouraging circular-economy models. These policies can open new market opportunities for entrepreneurs, such as sustainability-certified exports or green public procurement, while also reducing exposure to some forms of exchange-rate-related risk by strengthening local input bases and shortening supply chains. At the same time, they may introduce new compliance costs and transition risks, which resilient entrepreneurs must anticipate and manage.

Overall, entrepreneurial resilience in agrifood value chains emerges from the interplay of micro-level capabilities, meso-level coordination and macro-level institutional frameworks. Financial hedging, innovation and digitalisation at the firm level are necessary but not sufficient; they are most effective when embedded in supportive value-chain structures and policy environments that broaden access to risk-management tools, foster collaboration and steer the sector toward sustainable, regenerative trajectories. Understanding and strengthening these multi-scalar linkages is essential for designing interventions that help agrifood entrepreneurs not only survive exchange rate shocks, but leverage them as catalysts for more robust and sustainable value-chain configurations.

5. CONCLUSION

5.1 Emerging Trends Affecting Exchange Rate Risk and Resilience

The landscape in which agrifood entrepreneurs manage exchange rate risk is being reshaped by several powerful structural trends. First, rapid digitalisation is transforming how agricultural producers and agribusinesses access information, finance and markets. Recent empirical work shows that digital technology adoption significantly raises agricultural productivity and supply-chain resilience by improving infrastructure use, market access and coordination between actors in Chinese agricultural regions (Sargani et al., 2025). Similar studies in sustainable food systems highlight that digital tools—from farm management platforms to data-driven advisory services, enhance economic resilience by enabling real-time monitoring, scenario analysis and adaptive decision-making. These developments are directly relevant to exchange-rate-related vulnerabilities because fintech and digital marketplaces expand SMEs' access to credit, payments and data-driven financial services that help them manage cash-flow and market risks, capabilities that were previously much more accessible to large corporations. Evidence from SME finance research indicates that fintech-based credit, payment and risk-management solutions can strengthen small firms' survival prospects under systemic shocks by easing liquidity constraints and improving access to tailored financial products (Zhou, & Sun, 2024; World Bank & International Finance Corporation 2022). For agrifood SMEs, digital platforms that aggregate transactions and provide transparent exchange-rate quotations can reduce transaction costs, narrow bid–ask spreads and facilitate more systematic currency risk management.

A second trend is the growing importance of sustainability pressures and green/ESG-linked finance. The expansion of green finance markets and instruments such as green bonds and green loans is reshaping how capital is channelled into agriculture and industry. Recent econometric work on East Asian economies finds that increases in green finance market value are associated with measurable improvements in indicators of sustainable development in both the agricultural and industrial sectors (Shi & Yang, 2025). Sector-specific initiatives, such as the Climate Bonds Initiative's Agriculture Production Criteria, create taxonomies and standards that allow agricultural assets and projects to be financed through labelled green or sustainability-linked debt, including instruments where interest rates are explicitly tied to ESG performance. UNEP Finance Initiative's roadmap on sustainable food systems likewise argues that financial institutions and policymakers can drive a reallocation of capital towards resilient, low-carbon food value chains through targeted de-risking, blended finance and ESG-linked credit products. For agrifood entrepreneurs, these developments imply that resilience and sustainability investments, such as energy-efficient cold chains, regenerative practices or digital traceability, are increasingly financeable through instruments that may also offer interest-rate advantages, thereby changing the calculus of how they manage both climate and exchange-rate-related uncertainties.

Climate change itself constitutes a third, overarching trend that acts as a multiplier of exchange-rate-related uncertainty. Empirical research shows that climate risk shocks, both physical risks and climate-related news, have become significant drivers of agricultural commodity price movements, in part via investors' changing risk perceptions in financialised agricultural markets (Guo et al., 2023). Other studies document how climate disasters disrupt supply chains, reduce yields and alter trade patterns, with subsequent effects on export competitiveness and terms of trade for agricultural producers (Zhang et al., 2025; Khalfaoui et al., 2024). Policy analyses by bodies such as the Network for Greening the Financial System (NGFS) emphasise that climate change is likely to increase the frequency and severity of supply shocks—especially in climate-sensitive sectors like agriculture, thereby amplifying food price volatility and interacting with broader macroeconomic and exchange-rate dynamics (NGFS, 2020). For agrifood entrepreneurs, this implies that currency risk can no longer be considered in isolation: it is entangled with climate-driven production risk, energy-price volatility and shifts in investors' appetites for commodity and currency positions.

Finally, geopolitical fragmentation and ongoing debates around de-dollarisation are reshaping the broader landscape in which agrifood trade and currencies operate. This resonates with broader evidence that geopolitical risk can reconfigure entrepreneurial intentions and opportunity recognition, suggesting that exchange-rate-related uncertainty is embedded in wider perceptions of geopolitical threat and opportunity (Deirmentzoglou et al., 2025). Recent analysis for the Geneva Reports on the World Economy argues that rising trade restrictions, financial sanctions and geopolitical tensions are fragmenting trade and financial networks, with potential long-run consequences for the geography of reserve holdings and trade-invoicing currencies (Chari et al., 2025). UNCTAD likewise highlights how the current configuration of the global financial system, with its heavy reliance on U.S. dollar liquidity, exposes developing countries to external financial cycles and limits their policy space (Demony, 2025). While the dollar remains the dominant currency for trade and finance, selected countries have started to re-anchor their currencies or trade invoicing towards the euro or other regional currencies. For agrifood value chains, such changes could gradually diversify currency exposures, alter hedging strategies and reshape patterns of price discovery for major commodities, although the transition is likely to be slow and uneven.

5.2 Policy Recommendations

These evolving trends have clear implications for policy. A central priority is to support agrifood SMEs in building financial literacy and currency risk management capabilities. Long-standing FAO and European Commission work on agricultural risk management underscores that market-based instruments, such as forward contracts, futures, options and structured financial products, can be effective tools for managing price volatility, yet uptake remains limited in many agrifood sectors because of lack of awareness, transaction costs and institutional barriers (European Investment Bank & European Commission, 2018; FAO, 2006). Policy initiatives should therefore combine training in financial literacy and risk management with the development of inclusive platforms and intermediaries that aggregate small positions and reduce the fixed costs of accessing hedging instruments. Building on recent experience with fintech-enabled SME finance, public–private partnerships can encourage the development of digital treasury and risk-management tools tailored to small agrifood firms, potentially backed by guarantee schemes that lower collateral requirements.

Strengthening institutional frameworks for food-system resilience is equally important. Recent OECD work on "Towards resilient food systems" and on practical approaches to developing resilience strategies emphasises that effective policy mixes should support not only short-term robustness but also adaptation and transformation, and should be based on inclusive, evidence-based processes that involve stakeholders across the value chain (OECD, 2023). For exchange rate–exposed agrifood sectors, this means complementing income-support or emergency measures with structural investments in climate-smart infrastructure, diversified market access, and institutional mechanisms that enable coordinated responses to shocks. Agricultural policy monitoring by the OECD further argues that resilience-oriented policies should rebalance away from distortionary price support toward targeted tools that facilitate risk management, innovation and sustainability.

Enhancing digital infrastructure is another key policy lever. As research on digital transformation in agriculture demonstrates, investment in broadband connectivity, data platforms and interoperable digital services can unlock large productivity and resilience gains by enabling precision agriculture, real-time logistics and data-driven market matching (Sargani et al., 2025; Wang et al., 2025). Public investment and regulatory frameworks should therefore ensure that rural areas and small producers can participate in digital ecosystems, including through open data standards, support for digital skills and safeguards around data governance. Digital public goods, such as climate and market information services, interoperable traceability systems, and climate–price risk dashboards, could significantly improve entrepreneurs' ability to anticipate exchange rate and price shocks and to adjust their strategies accordingly.

5.3 Future Research Directions

The analysis in this chapter points to several promising avenues for future research. First, there is a need for more granular empirical work on how fintech and digital platforms change the exchange-rate-risk profile of agrifood SMEs along different value-chain positions. While existing studies demonstrate that digital transformation enhances productivity and supply-chain resilience in agriculture and that fintech improves SME survival under shocks, they rarely link these outcomes explicitly to currency exposures or hedging behaviour. Second, more work is required to integrate climate risk and exchange rate volatility in analytical frameworks of agrifood resilience. Recent contributions in food-system resilience and climate–finance research emphasise the need to move beyond single-shock analysis and consider interacting stresses, but empirical applications that simultaneously model climate shocks, price volatility, capital flows and exchange-rate dynamics remain limited. Third, the geopolitical reconfiguration of trade and finance raises new questions about the future of agricultural currencies and de-dollarisation. Finally, consistent with calls for better evidence to inform food-system policy, future work should strengthen longitudinal and comparative research designs that track resilience outcomes over time and across contexts. Mixed-method approaches that combine quantitative indicators with qualitative insights from entrepreneurs, cooperatives and policymakers would provide a richer understanding of which combinations of micro-, meso- and macro-level strategies are most effective in sustaining agrifood value chains under exchange rate turbulence.

ACKNOWLEDGMENTS

During the preparation of this manuscript, the authors employed ChatGPT (OpenAI) solely to assist with language refinement and improvement of readability. The authors have reviewed and edited the output and take full responsibility for the content of this publication.

REFERENCES

Alegwu, F. O., Aye, G. C., & Asogwa, B. C. (2017). Asymmetric effect of real exchange rate volatility on agricultural products export: a case study. *Economia Internazionale/International Economics, 70*(3), 261-79.

Apostolopoulos, N., Ratten, V., Petropoulos, D., Liargovas, P., & Anastasopoulou, E. (2021). Agri-food sector and entrepreneurship during the COVID-19 crisis: A systematic literature review and research agenda. *Strategic Change, 30*(2), 159–167. DOI: 10.1002/jsc.2400

Baah, F. A., & Rambe, P. (2024). Exploring learning capability on entrepreneurial resilience of emerging contractor firms. *Acta Commercii-Independent Research Journal in the Management Sciences, 24*(1), 1266.

Benavides Perales, G., & Venegas Martínez, F. (2022). Impact of exchange rate volatility on agricultural trade between the US and Mexico (1990-2017). *Economía: Teoría y Practica*, (56), 131–153. DOI: 10.24275/etypuam/ne/562022/benavides

Bor, O., & Dagistan, N. (2024). The impact of fluctuating international fertiliser prices and exchange rates on domestic fertiliser prices in Türkiye. *Agricultural Economics – Czech, 70*(1), 12–23. https://doi.org/DOI: 10.17221/308/2023-AGRICECON

Borsellino, V., Schimmenti, E., & El Bilali, H. (2020). Agri-food markets towards sustainable patterns. *Sustainability, 12*(6), 2193. DOI: 10.3390/su12062193

Chari, A., Converse, N., Mehl, A., Milesi-Ferretti, G. M., & Vansteenkiste, I. (2025). Geopolitxal tensions and international financial fragmentation – Evidence and implications. Centre for economic policy research. Available at https://cepr.org/system/files/publication-files/271360-geneva_28_geopolitical_tensions_and_international_fragmentation_evidence_and_implications.pdf (Accessed on 10/12/2025).

Christian, M., Obi, A., Zantsi, S., Mdoda, L., & Jiba, P. (2024). The role of cooperatives in improving smallholder participation in agri-food value chains: A case study of one local municipality in Eastern Cape, South Africa. *Sustainability*, *16*(6), 2241. DOI: 10.3390/su16062241

Coral, C., & Mithöfer, D. (2023). The backbone of agrifood value chain resilience: Innovation in the Ecuadorian banana value chain from a historical perspective. *World Development Perspectives*, *29*, 100476. DOI: 10.1016/j.wdp.2022.100476

Deirmentzoglou, G. A., Anastasopoulou, E. E., & Sklias, P. (2024). International economic relations and energy security in the European Union: A systematic literature review. *International Journal of Sustainable Energy*, *43*(1), 2385682. DOI: 10.1080/14786451.2024.2385682

Deirmentzoglou, G. A., Anastasopoulou, E. E., & Theodorakopoulos, N. (2025). Geopolitical Risks: Threats or Opportunities in Shaping Entrepreneurial Intentions? In *European Conference on Innovation and Entrepreneurship* (pp. 184-190). Academic Conferences International Limited. https://doi.org/DOI: 10.34190/ecie.20.1.3660

del Rosario Venegas, M., Feregrino, J., Lay, N., & Espinosa-Cristia, J. F. (2024). Food Financialization: Impact of Derivatives and Index Funds on Agri-Food Market Volatility. *IJFS*, *12*(4), 1–30. DOI: 10.3390/ijfs12040121

Demony, C. (2025). Global financial system must adapt to better serve economy, UN trade agency says. Avaiable at https://www.reuters.com/business/finance/global-financial-system-must-adapt-better-serve-economy-un-trade-agency-says-2025-12-02/ (Accessed on 10/12/2025).

European Commission. (2025). *Traceability and Big Data in the agrifood value chain: S3P partnership*. Available at https://ec.europa.eu/regional_policy/policy/communities-and-networks/s3-community-of-practice/partnership_agrifood_traceability_big_data_en (Accessed on 10/12/2025).

European Investment Bank & European Commission. (2018). *Using financial instruments to reduce the impact of price volatility in agriculture*. Available at https://www.fi-compass.eu/sites/default/files/publications/Using_financial_instruments_to_reduce_the_impact_of_price_volatility_in_agriculture.pdf (Accessed on 10/12/2025).

FAO and OECD. 2019. Background Notes on Sustainable, Productive and Resilient Agro-Food Systems: Value chains, human capital, and the 2030 Agenda. Available at https://www.oecd.org/content/dam/oecd/en/publications/reports/2019/07/background-notes-on-sustainable-productive-and-resilient-agro-food-systems_e3ac2135/dca82200-en.pdf (Accessed on 14/12/2025).

Fernández-Zarza, M., Amaya-Corchuelo, S., Belletti, G., & Aguilar-Criado, E. (2021). Trust and food quality in the valorisation of geographical indication initiatives. *Sustainability, 13*(6), 3168. DOI: 10.3390/su13063168

Follmann, A., Dannenberg, P., Baur, N., Braun, B., Walther, G., Bernzen, A., & Sulle, E. (2024). Conceptualizing sustainability and resilience in value chains in times of multiple crises—Notes on agri-food chains. *DIE ERDE–Journal of the Geographical Society of Berlin, 155*(1), 29–48. DOI: 10.12854/erde-2024-692

Food and Agriculture Organization. (2006). *An introduction to market-based instruments for agricultural price risk management.* Available at https://www.fao.org/4/ap308e/ap308e.pdf (Accessed on 10/12/2025).

Food and Agriculture Organization. (2021). Sustainable agri-food value chains How policies can support the shift towards more resilient food systems. Available at https://openknowledge.fao.org/server/api/core/bitstreams/ac5cd783-8207-46b0-ab8d-b61858796fdd/content (Accessed on 10/12/2025).

Guo, K., Li, Y., Zhang, Y., Ji, Q., & Zhao, W. (2023). How are climate risk shocks connected to agricultural markets? *Journal of Commodity Markets, 32*, 100367. DOI: 10.1016/j.jcomm.2023.100367

Huchet, M. (2011). Agricultural commodity price volatility: an overview. https://dx.doi.org/DOI: 10.1787/5kg0t00nrthc-en

Kafle, K. R. (2011). *Exchange rate volatility and bilateral agricultural trade flows: the case of the United States and OECD countries*. Louisiana State University and Agricultural & Mechanical College.

Kargbo, J. M. (2006). Exchange rate volatility and agricultural trade under policy reforms in South Africa. *Development Southern Africa, 23*(01), 147–170. DOI: 10.1080/03768350600556315

Khalfaoui, R., Goodell, J. W., Mefteh-Wali, S., Chishti, M. Z., & Gozgor, G. (2024). Impact of climate risk shocks on global food and agricultural markets: A multiscale and tail connectedness analysis. *International Review of Financial Analysis, 93*, 103206. DOI: 10.1016/j.irfa.2024.103206

Kontopanou, M., & Tsoulfas, G. (2022). Analyzing new ways to adapt the triple-a supply chain model and its extensions in agri-food supply chains. *LogForum, 18*(3). Advance online publication. DOI: 10.17270/J.LOG.2022.735

Kristinek, J. J., & Anderson, D. P. (2002). *Exchange rates and agriculture: a literature review*. Agricultural and Food Policy Center, Department of Agricultural Economics, Texas Agricultural Experiment Station, Texas Cooperative Extension, Texas A & M University.

Liu, Y., Garnevska, E., & Shadbolt, N. (2025). The Role of Agriculture Cooperatives in Green Agri-Food Value Chains in China: Cases in Shandong Province. *Sustainability*, *17*(16), 7343. DOI: 10.3390/su17167343

Manyise, T., & Dentoni, D. (2021). Value chain partnerships and farmer entrepreneurship as balancing ecosystem services: Implications for agri-food systems resilience. *Ecosystem Services*, *49*, 101279. DOI: 10.1016/j.ecoser.2021.101279

Minten, B., Belton, B., & Reardon, T. (2023). Agrifood value chains: Building resilient food systems. In *Global Food Policy Report 2023* (pp. 44–51). Rethinking Food Crisis Responses., DOI: 10.2499/9780896294417_04

Morepje, M. T., Sithole, M. Z., Msweli, N. S., & Agholor, A. I. (2024). The influence of E-commerce platforms on sustainable agriculture practices among smallholder farmers in Sub-Saharan Africa. *Sustainability*, *16*(15), 6496. DOI: 10.3390/su16156496

Network for Greening the Financial System. (2020). *The macroeconomic and financial stability impacts of climate change: Research priorities*. NGFS. Available at https://www.ngfs.net/system/files/import/ngfs/medias/documents/ngfs_research_priorities_final.pdf (Accessed on 10/12/2025).

OECD. (2023). *Towards resilient food systems - Implication of supply chain disruptions and policy responses*. OECD Food, Agriculture and Fisheries paper n°205. Available at https://www.oecd.org/content/dam/oecd/en/publications/reports/2023/09/towards-resilient-food-systems_102d2ac9/f7998e46-en.pdf (Accessed on 10/12/2025).

OECD. (2025). *Practical approaches to develop resilience strategies for food systems*. OECD Food, Agriculture and Fisheries Papers, No. 217. Available at https://www.oecd.org/content/dam/oecd/en/publications/reports/2025/02/practical-approaches-to-develop-resilience-strategies-for-food-systems_97f31bb2/caa2b274-en.pdf (Accessed on 14/12/2025).

Orjuela Castro, J. A., Orejuela-Cabrera, J. P., & Adarme-Jaimes, W. (2021). Logistics network configuration for seasonal perishable food supply chains. [JIEM]. *Journal of Industrial Engineering and Management*, *14*(2), 135–151. DOI: 10.3926/jiem.3161

Pan, Z., & Zheng, X. (2023). Price volatility transmission of perishable agricultural products: Evidence from China. *Economic research-. Ekonomska Istrazivanja, 36*(1). Advance online publication. DOI: 10.1080/1331677X.2023.2180058

Petropoulos, D., Deirmentzoglou, G. A., Apostolopoulos, N., Paris, B., Michas, D., Balafoutis, A. T., & Moreira da Silva, J. F. (2025). Digital and Entrepreneurial Competencies for the Bioeconomy: Perceptions and Training Needs of Agricultural Professionals in Greece, Italy, Portugal, and Sweden. *Agriculture, 15*(10), 1106. DOI: 10.3390/agriculture15101106

Santeramo, F. G., Jelliffe, J., & Hoekman, B. (2024). Agri-food value chains and the global food dollar: The role of trade and services. *Food Policy, 127*, 102706. DOI: 10.1016/j.foodpol.2024.102706

Sargani, G. R., Wang, B., Leghari, S. J., & Ruan, J. (2025). Is digital transformation the key to agricultural strength? A novel approach to productivity and supply chain resilience. *Smart Agricultural Technology, 10*, 100838. DOI: 10.1016/j.atech.2025.100838

Sarkar, A., Wang, H., Rahman, A., Qian, L., & Memon, W. H. (2022). Evaluating the roles of the farmer's cooperative for fostering environmentally friendly production technologies-a case of kiwi-fruit farmers in Meixian, China. *Journal of Environmental Management, 301*, 113858. DOI: 10.1016/j.jenvman.2021.113858 PMID: 34607139

Sarris, A. (2013). Food commodity price volatility and food insecurity. *Bio-Based and Applied Economics, 2*(3), 213–236. DOI: 10.13128/BAE-13114

Shi, Y., & Yang, B. (2025). Green finance instruments and empowering sustainability in East Asian economies. *Humanities & Social Sciences Communications, 12*(1), 1–9. DOI: 10.1057/s41599-024-04324-3

SNV. (2022). *Resilience Conceptual Framework: Creating a common language to make it concrete and specific.* Avaialable at https://www.snv.org/assets/downloads/f/191310/2833e3a462/core-20resilience-20conceptual-20framework.pdf (Accessed on 10/12/2025).

Steinbach, S. (2021). *Exchange rate volatility and global food supply chains* (No. w29164). National Bureau of Economic Research. https://doi.org/DOI: 10.3386/w29164

Suali, A. S., Srai, J. S., & Tsolakis, N. (2024). The role of digital platforms in e-commerce food supply chain resilience under exogenous disruptions. *Supply Chain Management, 29*(3), 573–601. DOI: 10.1108/SCM-02-2023-0064

Tarasenko, I. (2021). The impact of exchange rate volatility on trade: The evidence from Russia. *Russian Journal of Economics*, *7*(3), 213–232. DOI: 10.32609/j.ruje.7.57933

Török, Á., Kovács, S., Jámbor, A., & Maró, Z. M. (2025). Understanding the Determinants of Participation in Agri-Food Global Value Chains. *Journal of Sustainability Research*, *7*(3). Advance online publication. DOI: 10.20900/jsr20250062

Trofimov, I. D. (2020). The J-curve effect in agricultural commodity trade: an empirical study of South East Asian economies. https://mpra.ub.uni-muenchen.de/id/eprint/106701

U.S. Department of Agriculture, Economic Research Service. (2025). *Agricultural Exchange Rate Data Set: Documentation*. USDA-ERS. Available at https://www.ers.usda.gov/data-products/agricultural-exchange-rate-data-set/documentation (Accessed on 10/12/2025).

Vos, R., Glauber, J., Hebebrand, C., & Rice, B. (2025). Global shocks to fertilizer markets: Impacts on prices, demand and farm profitability. *Food Policy*, *133*, 102790. DOI: 10.1016/j.foodpol.2024.102790

Vroegindewey, R., & Hodbod, J. (2018). Resilience of agricultural value chains in developing country contexts: A framework and assessment approach. *Sustainability*, *10*(4), 916. DOI: 10.3390/su10040916

Wang, Z., Pan, Z., Lai, W., Lu, S., Liu, H., Wang, X., & Wu, H. (2025). How does digital technology enhance sustainable operations in agribusiness? A case analysis of a Chinese agricultural enterprise. *Frontiers in Sustainable Food Systems*, *9*, 1718405. DOI: 10.3389/fsufs.2025.1718405

Wesley, J. D., Shen, X., Li, S., & Wilson, N. L. (2012). Agricultural Trade Bias in Exchange Rate Volatility Effect Estimation: An Application of Meta-Regression Analysis. https://doi.org/DOI: 10.22004/ag.econ.124870

World Bank. (2024). *Resilient Agri-Food Clusters Development Project (P178120): Project Appraisal Document*. World Bank, Washington, DC. Available at https://www.gafspfund.org/sites/default/files/inline-files/Resilient%20Agri-food%20Clusters%20Development%20Project%20PAD.pdf (Accessed on 12/12/2025).

World Bank & International Finance Corporation. (2022). *Fintech and SME finance: Expanding responsible access*. Available at https://openknowledge.worldbank.org/server/api/core/bitstreams/d157af2e-ad06-558f-8e1b-5bf52841d34a/content (Accessed on 12/12/2025).

Zhang, Z., Li, C., Yuan, J., & Wang, X. (2025). The impact of climate disaster risk on agricultural trade welfare and coping strategies from a global perspective. *Frontiers in Sustainable Food Systems*, *9*, 1547969. DOI: 10.3389/fsufs.2025.1547969

Zhou, N., & Sun, R. (2024). Coping with the storm: The role of fintech in SME survival. *International Review of Financial Analysis*, *93*, 103157. DOI: 10.1016/j.irfa.2024.103157

Chapter 11
The Resilience and Development of the Tourism Industry Through Foreign Direct Investment and Artificial Intelligence

Stavros G. Efthimiou
https://orcid.org/0009-0007-5840-0049
University of Piraeus, Greece

ABSTRACT

Tourism is faced with ongoing shocks—pandemics to weather risks—that undermine its capacity to innovate and sustain development. Here, this chapter argues that two levers—foreign direct investment (FDI) and artificial intelligence (AI)—combined can render the sector resilient and expand in the long term if combined with sound policy and sustainability goals. Integrating new evidence from advanced economies, small island, and transition economies, is presented how FDI increases productive capacity, improves infrastructure, and disseminates know-how as AI re-engineers demand creation, operations, and management into smarter, greener tourism. Generative AI travel companions shape trust, interaction, and the capacity to interact with travel services. This chapter recommends a framework under which sustainable vetted FDI enhances adaptive capacity. AI capabilities deploy resilience via stimulation of demand, productivity growth, and real-time risk management in supportive institutions.

DOI: 10.4018/979-8-3373-6991-4.ch011

1. INTRODUCTION

Tourism has become one of the world's most dynamic sectors, generating foreign exchange, employment, and economic diversification in developed and developing countries alike. Pre-COVID-19 pandemic, international tourist arrivals had reached over 1.5 billion, generating almost 10% of the world GDP, but the sector's vulnerability to crises such as pandemics, climate change, and geopolitical tensions has highlighted its structural fragilities (Hamcerencu, 2025; Efthimiou, 2025a). The search for resilience—attribution of tourism systems' ability to resist, adapt to, and recover from shocks—has therefore taken centre stage in academic discourse and policy making. In this search, two forces have emerged at centre stage: foreign direct investment (FDI) and artificial intelligence (AI).

FDI has long been familiar as a cornerstone of tourism development. By investing in hotels, resorts, airports, and other ancillary infrastructure, foreign investors enable destinations to achieve capacity that could not be achieved through purely domestic capital (Bhatt et al., 2024). Empirical research vouches for the strength of such linkages. Isik (2015) presented evidence of long-run bidirectional causality between tourism receipts and FDI inflows for D-7 economies, while Fauzel (2021) did the same for small island developing states, where dependence on foreign markets makes foreign capital critical to viability. In Estonia, Sokhanvar (2022) demonstrated how institutional reform and competitiveness drive attracted FDI that, in turn, boosted tourism specialization and growth. These findings suggest that FDI and tourism often complement one another, but also that the quality of institutions and governance determines the extent of positive spillovers (Nunkoo & Seetanah, 2018).

Apart from FDI, AI is increasingly revolutionizing the tourism industry. At the operational level, AI powering efficiency comes with dynamic pricing, automation, predictive analytics, and energy management (Sharma et al., 2022; Gutierriz et al., 2023). On the demand side, AI-powered chatbots and generative AI "travel companions" influence tourist behavior by providing personalized recommendations and establishing trust and engagement, with continuance intention depending to a great degree on satisfaction and technology anxiety alleviation (Bujdoso et al., 2025). At the systemic level, AI supports sustainability because it enables destinations to monitor emissions, manage tourist flows, and integrate environmental, social, and governance (ESG) frameworks into tourism planning. Isik et al. (2025) illustrate that when AI meets ESG measures, tourism contributes additional value to per-capita income, balancing out the environmental costs that usually accompany growth.

What remains unresearched, however, is the joint effect of FDI and AI. The majority of FDI studies address capital flows, infrastructure, and macroeconomic causality, while AI studies focus on consumer behavior and firm-level competitiveness. There are few recent attempts, such as Isik et al. (2025), to introduce AI into macroeconomic or sustainability models of tourism. This leaves a big gap: is still lack a general picture of how international capital and digital intelligence interact to affect resilience. Do global investments in digital platforms and smart infrastructure create synergies that accelerate crisis recovery? Can artificial intelligence make FDI-funded projects more inclusive and sustainable? What are the institutional conditions under which such forces create virtuous cycles of resilience rather than vicious cycles of dependence and vulnerability?

The present chapter tries to bridge this gap by integrating global evidence on the tourism–FDI–AI nexus and building an integrated conceptual model of resilience. Its value-add is empirical and theoretical. On the theoretical side, it does not address FDI and AI as independent variables but as complementary assets—capital and intelligence—that only achieve their highest value when mediated by good governance and aligned with sustainability goals. On the empirical side, it draws upon case studies of advanced, transition, and small island economies, as well as embryonic research on digitalization and ESG uptake, to illustrate how these dynamics unfold in practice.

The findings of this analysis extend their reach to policymakers, business leaders, and scholars. For policymakers, the study underscores that resilience is not some automatic spin-off of investment or technology but a process requiring institutions that enforce transparency, sustainability, and inclusivity. For business leaders, the takeaway is that AI supports profitability and competitiveness only if implanted in business models with trust and ethical governance at their foundation. For scholars, the paper highlights the need for longitudinal and comparative studies examining the evolving geography of FDI, the cultural dimensions of AI adoption, and digitalization's consequences for sustainability and sovereignty.

The chapter then charts the theoretical foundations and global evidence of the tourism–FDI link, followed by an assessment of how AI transforms competitiveness and resilience at both the operational and systemic levels. It then integrates these threads into a broader conceptual framework, discusses risks and trade-offs, and suggests an agenda for further research. The overall argument is that the resilience and expansion of tourism are becoming more dependent on the convergence of foreign capital and artificial intelligence, and that the trajectory of this convergence—whether virtuous or vicious—is conditioned by governance and sustainability regimes.

2. THE TOURISM–FDI NEXUS: THEORETICAL FOUNDATIONS AND GLOBAL EVIDENCE

The relationship between tourism and foreign direct investment (FDI) has been a theme of academic interest in recent years, reflecting a growing recognition that tourism is not simply a consumer service but instead an internationally traded industry that both shapes and is shaped by international capital flows. Essentially, the connection between FDI and tourism relies on the premise that tourism requires heavy capital inputs into infrastructure, facilities, and services, many of which are supplied by foreign investors (Efthimiou, 2025d). Conversely, successful tourism industries have a tendency to attract more FDI by signaling stability, profitability, and scope for expansion (Anuradha et al., 2024). The connection is therefore two-way, with complex feedback loops between host destinations, multinational corporations, and international consumers.

2.1 Historical Context and Theoretical Underpinnings

The tourism–FDI link can be positioned in two strands of economic theory: theory of international production and export-led growth theory. Domazet et al. (2024) noted that tourism, as an internationally tradable service, shares features with manufacturing exports, such as huge upfront investment, international cooperation, and exposure to global markets. Multinational corporations invest abroad to capitalize on location-specific advantages, such as natural attractions, cultural heritage, or favorable policy environments. For host countries, these investments bring in foreign exchange, technology, and access to international distribution systems.

Isik (2015) examined this connection in the D-7 nations' context, showing that FDI inflows and tourism receipts exhibit long-run bidirectional causality. Tourism development attracts new foreign investors seeking to take advantage of increasing demand, while inward FDI finances the infrastructure to support further tourism development. This correlation illustrates a virtuous circle where receipts and investment reinforce one another, resulting in overall economic growth (Efthimiou, 2025c). Theoretically, this agrees with the endogenous growth literature where capital inflows and technology transfer enhance long-run growth opportunities rather than creating short-term demand shocks.

2.2 Global Evidence of the Tourism–FDI Nexus

Empirical evidence from a range of contexts substantiates the complementarity theoretical case. Fauzel (2021), working on small island developing states (SIDS), demonstrated strong long-run relationships between FDI inflows and tourism receipts. In these economies, dependence on international markets is particularly acute, and foreign investment often funds critical infrastructure such as airports, harbors, and hotel chains. Without foreign investment, few SIDS would have the scope or the resources to have internationally competitive touristic products.

Similarly, Sokhanvar (2022) targeted Estonia and confirmed FDI as both a driver and beneficiary of tourism specialization. As Estonia improved its competitiveness and business climate, FDI inflows into tourism-related sectors increased, which supported economic diversification and export performance. In transition economies more broadly, Sokhanvar and Jenkins (2022) observed that FDI, when combined with institutional reform and openness, could significantly enhance tourism's contribution to GDP. These findings highlight the fact that while the underlying link between tourism and FDI is universally felt, its transformative intensity and potency depend on domestic institutional contexts.

2.3 Positive Contributions of FDI to Tourism Development

The benefits of FDI in tourism are numerous. Firstly, foreign investors finance infrastructure that local operators would not be able to provide, ranging from hotels and resorts to recreational and transportation facilities. This type of capital deepening enhances the ability of destinations to accommodate more tourists and to provide higher-quality services (Durani et al., 2025).

Second, FDI facilitates the transfer of technology and knowledge. International hotel chains, for example, are likely to bring in better management practices, quality control measures, and internet booking technologies. These new technologies get transferred to local businesses through supply chain connections and labor mobility, raising industry standards overall (Snyman & Saayman, 2009).

Third, FDI enhances integration into global value chains. Foreign investors have a propensity to connect destinations to their already established marketing channels, loyalty schemes, and distribution systems. This reduces host nations' barriers to entry and allows them to capture greater shares of international tourist flows (Satrovic & Muslija, 2019).

Finally, FDI is able to provide macroeconomic stability through diversifying the sources of foreign exchange revenues. Tourism receipts in the majority of developing countries are volatile and susceptible to exogenous shocks. FDI inflows, particularly if they are focused on long-term projects, are able to buffer the fluctuations by underpinning foreign exchange revenues and supporting balance-of-payments stability ((Efthimiou, 2025d)).

2.4 Challenges and Risks in the Tourism–FDI Relationship

Despite these positive impacts, FDI in tourism is not entirely beneficial. One of the problems is the ubiquity of enclave tourism, wherein foreign-invested resorts are poorly connected with local economies. Profits are often repatriated, and employment generation may be limited to low-skilled seasonal positions (Jonsson, 2022). In such a scenario, benefits to host communities are marginal, while social costs—such as cultural commodification and environmental degradation—are significant.

Another challenge is environmental vulnerability. Ibrahim (2024) noted that FDI inflows to tourism have a tendency to increase carbon emissions in developing economies, particularly when large-scale projects are not aligned with sustainability imperatives. Foreign investment-funded resorts, airports, and cruise terminals are usually energy-intensive and strain fragile ecosystems. This trade-off highlights that FDI, without strong environmental regulation, can undermine the very resilience it is meant to enhance (Khan et al., 2020).

A second limitation lies in volatility. FDI flows are highly responsive to global financial conditions. During periods of crisis, investors may disinvest or hold back investment, subjecting host economies to sudden capital flight (Efthimiou, 2025e). This volatility makes over-reliance on foreign investors a risky development strategy.

2.5 Governance as a Mediating Factor

The extent to which FDI contributes to tourism resilience positively is extremely dependent on governance. The empirical evidence suggests that in countries where institutions are competitive, transparent, and strong, FDI is more likely to create spillovers and be aligned with long-term development goals (Sokhanvar, 2022). In the context of weak governance, FDI can lead to corruption, rent-seeking, and unsustainable development patterns.

This governance dimension also determines the distribution of benefits between foreign and local actors. Policy that mandates linkages with local firms, environmental stipulations, and skills transfer can increase the developmental impact of FDI. Laissez-faire policy, on the other hand, will result in foreign domination of the sector, with limited benefits to locals (Durani et al., 2025).

2.6 Integrating FDI and AI in Tourism Resilience

While this first part has viewed the tourism–FDI nexus in its conventional form, there is a need to situate the discussion within the framework of the new role of AI. FDI is increasingly being directed into digital and technological projects, including smart hotels, AI-operated booking processes, and green energy provisions in tourism (Kamalaveni et al., 2021). These investments underpin AI adoption, which makes the tourism sector more resilient and competitive (Isik, 2015). The interplay between capital and intelligence is hence an upcoming feature of modern tourism development.

2.7 Conceptual Synthesis

The evidence theoretical and empirical points to a qualified conclusion. The relationship between tourism and FDI is symbiotic by nature: tourism development attracts foreign investment, while FDI promotes further tourism development. But the benefits are not automatic. They are mediated by governance, institutional quality, environmental governance, and absorptive capacity in host economies. FDI can establish the foundations for resilience, but in the absence of prudent management it risks creating volatility, inequality, and environmental strain.

As the subsequent sections of this article demonstrate, the introduction of AI in this nexus holds both new opportunities to overcome some of these limitations, but also introduces new challenges. The conceptual foundations explored herein provide the background for how capital and technology, together, can shape the future of tourism resilience.

3. AI-DRIVEN MECHANISMS OF RESILIENCE IN TOURISM

Artificial intelligence (AI) increasingly stands as a pillar of tourism resilience. While foreign direct investment (FDI) brings capital and infrastructure, AI brings adaptive intelligence, enabling destinations and firms to anticipate shocks, stay in business during stress, and restructure offerings for fast-changing markets (Chowdhury et al., 2024). This chapter explains the key mechanisms through which AI builds resilience in tourism, grounded in theoretical understanding and empirical practice.

3.1 Automation and Productivity Gains

One of the simplest mechanisms is automation. Hospitality and tourism are people-intensive, seasonally dependent, and low-wage workforces. This structure exposes them to labour shortages, pandemics, or sudden demand spikes. AI-driven automation—robot concierges, automated check-in kiosks, voice commands, or robot cleaning equipment—guarantees operation continuity even in the event of labor shocks (Hamcerencu, 2025).

Sharma, Jain and Dhir (2022) used a total interpretive structural modelling (TISM) methodology adjusted to frame the impact of AI on firm competitiveness. Their research provided a hierarchy: first are the AI-capable workforces, infrastructure, and policies, which enable AI technology and digital platform adoption. These enable productivity and innovation, eventually leading to tourist satisfaction and financial outcomes. This cascade demonstrates that automation does not only lower costs but also unleashes resilience by protecting firms against labor market fluctuations as well as ensuring quality service (Bujdoso et al., 2025).

3.2 Predictive Analytics and Demand Forecasting

Predictive analytics based on AI is yet another resilience approach. Tourism demand is volatile, prone to the effects of worldwide events, exchange rate variability, or mobility constraints. Machine learning algorithms could process enormous volumes of data—like booking patterns, mobility trends, and macroeconomic variables—to forecast demand more accurately than traditional methods (Gutierriz et al., 2023).

For destinations, this capability supports forward-looking resource planning: staffing levels can be adjusted to avoid overcapacity, marketing campaigns can target suitable segments, and transportation systems can prepare for peak flows. For firms, predictive analytics guide inventory management, pricing, and timing of promotions. During the COVID-19 pandemic, these models were applied to predict recovery curves and plan reopening phases (Sharma et al., 2022).

Resilience comes not only from greater efficiency but also from reduced exposure to uncertainty. The ability to anticipate downturns or surges reduces the risk of over-investment or sudden supply shortages.

3.3 Dynamic Pricing and Revenue Optimisation

Linked to forecasting is dynamic pricing—using AI algorithms to adjust room rates, air fares, or tour package prices in real time based on demand signals. Dynamic pricing smooths out revenue streams by harvesting consumer willingness-to-pay at peak demand and stimulating bookings in low-demand periods (Hamcerencu, 2025).

Revenue resilience is most important: by lowering income volatility, firms can continue to operate through crises and reinvest in recovery earlier. Empirical research shows that AI-powered pricing platforms both increase occupancy rates and profitability, providing a buffer against exogenous shocks (Gutierriz et al., 2023).

3.4 Personalisation and Tourist Satisfaction

Resilience in tourism is not only a supply phenomenon but also depends on loyalty of demand. When travelers still have trust and stay loyal during a crisis, destinations bounce back faster. AI has a contribution in this regard through personalization. Recommendation systems personalize travel suggestions, itineraries, and offers based on each person's preference. Chatbots and virtual assistants enhance pre-trip planning, and on-site AI systems personalize experiences in real time (Duong et al., 2024).

This mechanism is supported by behavioural evidence. Duong et al. (2024) demonstrate that continuance intention (CI) of tourists to use generative AI for trip planning is positively influenced by satisfaction and parasocial interaction, and technological anxiety negatively moderates the influences. This finding highlights the fact that AI enables resilience by supporting demand through greater engagement but with the proviso that tourists perceive AI to be trustworthy and user-friendly.

3.5 Smart Tourism Ecosystems and IoT Integration

AI is further amplified with the integration of the Internet of Things (IoT). Intelligent sensors deployed in airports, hotels, or tourist spots collect data on flows, occupancy, and environmental status in real-time. AI algorithms use these data to make optimization adjustments in crowd management, energy use, and service provision (Bujdoso et al., 2025).

Current literature offers the AI–IoT–ESG nexus: AI interventions interact with IoT technology and environmental, social, and governance (ESG) metrics to advance sustainability performance. Evidence shows that adoption of AI boosts the efficiency and environmental conservation of ESG-based sustainable tourism (Isik, 2015). For example, predictive maintenance of the energy industry reduces emissions, while smart crowd management prevents over-tourism and protects heritage sites.

Thus, AI not only constructs operational resilience but also enhances ecological and social resilience—essential axes in destinations vulnerable to climate risks or community opposition to mass tourism.

3.6 Financial Resilience and Fintech Integration

AI further boosts resilience through supporting fintech platforms for tourism. Reservation systems using blockchain, digital payments, and fraud control enhance financial security and reduce costs of transactions. Siddik et al. (2025) show that for top destinations, fintech and digitalisation significantly raise the favorable growth effect of tourism and FDI. During a crisis, digital payment systems provide continuity whenever physical transactions are halted, offering liquidity for firms and convenience of access for visitors.

By minimizing financial friction and increased transparency, AI-fintech integration makes it possible for both businesses and tourist-reliant national economies to improve resilience.

3.7 Governance, Ethics, and Risk Management

Whereas its advantage, AI introduces new threats: algorithmic bias, privacy infringement, cybersecurity threats, and labor displacement. Governance of these threats is included in building resilience. Duong (2008b) warned that widespread use of AI might alter global FDI flows, reducing the attractiveness of low-cost labor destinations. AI may exacerbate inequalities rather than enhancing resilience in the absence of effective governance.

Thus, there is a need for responsible AI governance: clear algorithms, data privacy, ethical norms, and inclusive policies that retrain displaced labor. The policy aspect is essential since resilience is not just technological but also institutional (Zhou & Choi, 2025).

3.8 Conceptual Synthesis

AI strengthens tourism resilience through multiple interlinked mechanisms:

- **Supply-Side**: automation, productivity, predictive analytics, and dynamic pricing.
- **Demand-Side**: personalisation, satisfaction, and continued use of AI-enabled services.
- **Systemic**: IoT integration, ESG performance, financial continuity through fintech.
- **Institutional**: risk governance, ethical frameworks, and policy support (Bujdoso et al., 2025).

Together, these mechanisms turn tourism into a more resilient, knowledge-led system that is capable of withstanding external shocks and enhancing sustainability. Coupled with FDI—providing the capital for AI take-up and growth—these mechanisms form a virtuous cycle of resilience and growth.

4. MECHANISMS OF DEVELOPMENT THROUGH FDI IN TOURISM

Foreign direct investment (FDI) has long been a cornerstone of tourism development. It introduces capital, expertise, and global connections that most destinations—particularly emerging economies—lack domestically (Domazet et al., 2024). This section summarizes the mechanisms through which FDI drives growth and resilience in tourism. It draws on both theoretical underpinnings and empirical studies of diverse contexts, from small island economies to transition economies and mature markets.

4.1 Tourism as a Priority Sector for FDI Inflows

Tourism is one of the largest export industries in the world, contributing nearly 10% to the global GDP and over 284 million jobs (Nunkoo & Seetanah, 2018). Because of its position as a source of foreign exchange, jobs, and local development, most governments aggressively seek FDI to grow their tourism industries.

FDI flows into tourism are particularly critical for capital-intensive projects such as airports, hotels, and resorts, where start-up costs exceed the resources of domestic investors (Endo, 2006; Tang et al., 2007). Transnational corporations introduce not only finance but also access to marketing outlets, global reservation systems, and management know-how (Nunkoo & Seetanah, 2018). The result is faster infrastructural growth and integration into international value chains (Efthimiou, 2025e).

4.2 Theoretical Channels of FDI in Tourism Development

The literature identifies several channels through which FDI enhances tourism development:

1. **Infrastructure Upgrading**: Inward FDI finances airports, cruise ports, and hotels, raising capacity and international attractiveness (Li et al., 2017).
2. **Technology Transfer**: Multinationals introduce new technologies, service standards, and operational practices that diffuse to local firms (Davidson & Sahli, 2015).
3. **Skill Development**: Foreign projects generate training opportunities, improving local human capital and employability (Nunkoo & Ramkissoon, 2010).
4. **Market Access**: FDI opens connections to global tour operators and distribution networks, increasing visibility and demand (Hof & Blazquez-Salom, 2015).
5. **Diversification and Risk Mitigation**: For host economies, reliance on foreign capital diversifies sources of funding, reducing vulnerability to domestic shocks (Seetanah, 2011).

Each of these mechanisms reinforces the resilience of the tourism system by building adaptive capacity, enhancing competitiveness, and broadening the base of stakeholders.

4.3 Empirical Evidence from Small Island Economies

Small island developing states (SIDS) provide a handy test ground for the tourism–FDI nexus. These economies are typically highly dependent on tourism revenues and foreign capital inflows. Fauzel (2021) employed a panel vector error correction model (VECM) on 17 SIDS between 1995 and 2018, finding a long-run positive causality between FDI inflows and foreign tourist arrivals. Importantly, the study revealed bidirectional causality: while tourism expands as FDI rises, strong tourism performance attracts additional FDI.

This observation points to a self-reinforcing vicious circle: as locations improve infrastructure and service capacity through FDI, they host more visitors, which in turn sends signals to foreign firms about investment possibilities. These loops are particularly precious for resilience in very undiversified economies.

4.4 Case study: Estonia and Transition Economies

In transition economies, FDI also plays a vital role in upgrading tourism industries. Sokhanvar (2022) applied a nonlinear autoregressive distributed lag (NARDL) model to Estonia and found that both FDI inflows and tourism specialisation exerted strong positive long-run effects on economic growth. The key finding was that the linkages withstood numerous econometric tests.

Sokhanvar and Jenkins (2022) also examined the nexus between tourism, FDI, and growth in broader transition economies and discovered that FDI enhances tourism-driven growth but only when policy stability, institutional quality, and good governance are in place. This reinforces the fact that even though FDI is resource-provisioning, host-country policy quality will determine if this resource will add to sustainable development (Zhou & Choi, 2025).

4.5 Evidence from Advanced Economies

Even for industrialized economies, FDI drives tourism upgrading. Isik (2015) tested for causality among FDI inflows, tourism receipts, and GDP for seven industrialized (D-7) countries for the years 1995-2012. The study offered evidence of long-run bidirectional causality between FDI and tourism receipts, suggesting even advanced tourist markets rely on FDI to ensure competitiveness. This implies that FDI is not only a development tool for emerging destinations but also a source of innovation and renewal for advanced ones.

4.6 FDI and Environmental Considerations

While FDI promotes tourism development, it also creates environmental sustainability issues. Ibrahim (2024) found that FDI inflows, particularly if invested in large-scale tourism establishments, can cause an increase in carbon emissions if there are no strict environmental regulations. The challenge is to attract "green FDI" that builds sustainability into investment activities.

This is particularly relevant when destinations attempt to align with the UN Sustainable Development Goals (SDGs) and climate commitments. AI can assist in this context by speeding up ESG performance (Isik, 2015), but in the absence of policy underpinnings, FDI-driven tourism's environmental impact can compromise resilience.

4.7 Distributional Effects and Community Engagement

FDI may also create uneven benefit distribution. Enclave tourism, wherein foreign-owned resorts capture receipts with minimal local linkages, can heighten inequality (Nunkoo & Seetanah, 2018). Community participation, integration of local suppliers, and skills development are therefore required to ensure that FDI enhances not only macroeconomic metrics but also social resilience.

4.8 Policy Frameworks to Maximise FDI Benefits

Policy affects the outcome of FDI-driven tourism development. Case-study evidence from Estonia (Sokhanvar, 2022) identifies the necessity to upgrade the business climate, competitiveness, and tax regimes in order to attract quality investment. Similarly, Nunkoo and Seetanah (2018) contend that governments should apply overarching policy prescriptions to drive sustainable development and safeguard cultural and environmental resources. Policy measures include:

- Offering incentives for sustainable tourism projects.
- Establishing clear regulatory frameworks to prevent over-exploitation.
- Ensuring transparent land-use planning.
- Encouraging partnerships between multinational firms and local SMEs (Efthimiou, 2024).

These measures convert FDI inflows into durable development outcomes and long-run resilience (Zhou & Choi, 2025).

4.9 Conceptual Synthesis

FDI capacitates tourism growth with capital, technology, knowledge, and market integration in theory and practice (Efthimiou, 2025e). Empirical evidence confirms the aforementioned channels across different contexts—from SIDS to transition and developed economies. However, the extent and distribution of benefits depend on governance quality, sustainability initiatives, and local integration.

FDI alone does not guarantee resilience; it must be accompanied by enabling institutions and complementary technologies such as AI. Together, these circumstances allow destinations to use FDI not solely for growth but also for adaptive capacity, sustainability, and inclusiveness.

5. THE CONVERGENCE OF FDI AND AI IN THE TOURISM VALUE CHAIN

The interface of foreign direct investment (FDI) and artificial intelligence (AI) is an imperative frontier of the reorganization of the tourism industry. Although the previous sections have examined their respective functions, this section examines how they meet within the value chain of the tourism industry (Lopez-Naranjo et al., 2025). Their complementarities can bring new efficiencies, develop adaptive capacities, and create innovative models of service provision that ensure competitiveness and resilience in a world that is increasingly uncertain.

5.1 Tourism Value Chains and Digital Transformation

Tourism value chains comprise a wide array of actors: airlines, accommodations, restaurants, travel agents, tour operators, entertainment, and local suppliers. This width makes the industry intricate and vulnerable to disruption. Digitalization, powered by AI, is disrupting these chains by enabling data-driven decision-making, real-time coordination, and customer-centric services (Gutierriz et al., 2023).

FDI plays a crucial role in financing the infrastructure of this transformation. Multinational companies introduce new technologies, create digital platforms, and integrate destinations into worldwide reservation and distribution networks. AI then scales these networks through automation, predictive analytics, and personalisation, creating more robust value chains.

5.2 FDI as a Vehicle for AI Adoption

AI technologies involve significant up-front investment in digital infrastructure, data systems, and training. The majority of local businesses—particularly in developing destinations—lack the means to adopt these innovations. In this instance, FDI acts as a vehicle for AI adoption.

For example, AI-powered booking systems, smart rooms with IoT connectivity, and robotic service delivery are invested in by international hotel chains. Biometric identification and AI-based security systems are introduced by foreign-funded airport operators. AI is used by tour operators for itinerary management, price optimisation, and logistics streamlining. Such investments transfer technological competencies to the local partners, raising the digital maturity of the destination overall (Nunkoo & Seetanah, 2018).

This echoes what Sharma, Jain and Dhir (2022) set out in their m-TISM model: infrastructure and policy provide support for AI-enabled technologies, which catalyze productivity, innovation, and satisfaction. Without FDI, most destinations could not have afforded these foundation layers.

5.3 AI as a Catalyst for FDI Returns

Just as FDI enables AI adoption, AI improves the returns to FDI. Foreign investors seek profitability, risk mitigation, and competitive advantage. AI supports these goals in multiple ways:

- **Efficiency Gains**: AI-driven automation reduces labour costs and errors, increasing operational margins (Hamcerencu, 2025).
- **Revenue Optimisation**: Dynamic pricing and targeted marketing maximise revenue per customer, enhancing return on investment.
- **Risk Management**: Predictive analytics anticipate demand fluctuations, reducing the risk of overcapacity or underutilisation.
- **Brand Differentiation**: AI-enabled personalisation strengthens brand value and customer loyalty, ensuring repeat business.

Empirical evidence confirms that AI integration enhances competitiveness. Siddik et al. (2025) found that digitalisation and fintech significantly amplify the positive impact of tourism and FDI on growth in top destinations. Thus, AI adoption not only benefits host economies but also justifies further investment from multinational firms.

5.4 Building "Tourism 4.0" Ecosystems

The confluence of AI and FDI is giving rise to Tourism 4.0—a digitally powered system characterized by smart infrastructure, seamless services, and data-driven governance. In such systems, tourists have frictionless experiences: AI-powered chatbots assist in planning, biometric boarding accelerates airport formalities, predictive analytics allocate resources optimally, and IoT-powered attractions manage tourist inflows sustainably (Bujdoso et al., 2025).

FDI becomes necessary to scale such innovations beyond the pilot stage. Multinational corporations provide the capital, global networks, and risk appetite necessary for large-scale implementation. AI, conversely, provides the layer of intelligence that optimises and integrates the system. Together, they create more resilient ecosystems that are shock-resistant yet still provide better experiences.

5.5 ESG Integration and Sustainable Investment

The convergence also operates with sustainability. Isik et al. (2025) propose an ESG indicator interacted with AI (ESG/ITA*AI) as a measure to estimate tourism activity sustainability. Based on their research, while the environmental footprint of tourism may negatively affect GDP per capita, incorporating AI with ESG applications enhances positive impacts.

FDI complements this mechanism through financing green technologies—efficient energy systems, waste management technologies, and low-carbon transport—while AI optimizes their performance. For instance, AI-driven energy management reduces consumption in overseas-owned hotels, while predictive analysis prevent overcrowding in sensitive ecosystems. What ensues is a form of green FDI supported by AI that progresses at the same pace both resilience, development, and ecological sustainability (Efthimiou, 2025e).

5.6 Case Illustrations

- **Small Island States**: FDI-financed resorts increasingly deploy AI-powered demand forecasting to manage seasonality. The synergy helps overcome vulnerability to external shocks by ensuring more stable revenue streams (Fauzel et al., 2017).
- **Transition Economies**: In Estonia, FDI and tourism specialisation contributed positively to growth (Sokhanvar, 2022). AI adoption further enhances these returns by modernising service delivery and integrating destinations into digital economies.

- **Developed Economies**: In D-7 countries, bidirectional causality between FDI and tourism receipts was observed (Isik, 2015). Here, AI adoption is reinforcing competitiveness through robotics, fintech integration, and personalised services.

These examples demonstrate that the convergence of FDI and AI is not limited to one context but is observable across different levels of development.

5.7 Risks and Potential Reversals

While useful, FDI and AI convergence is not risk-free. Duong (2008b) argued that extensive industrial applications of AI would reverse traditional FDI patterns, reducing the motives to outsource to labour-abundant developing countries. If AI substitutes the comparative advantage of cheap labour, host nations that rely solely on this determinant can lose FDI inflows.

Moreover, dependence on foreign investors for AI adoption can result in technological lock-in, where host countries are reliant on proprietary systems and have no sovereignty over data governance. If left unregulated by policy, this can undermine resilience by introducing new vulnerabilities.

5.8 Conceptual Synthesis

The convergence of FDI and AI in the tourism value chain can be understood as a mutually reinforcing relationship:

- FDI supplies the capital, infrastructure, and global connections necessary for AI adoption.
- AI enhances the profitability, efficiency, and sustainability of FDI projects.
- Together, they create adaptive, smart tourism ecosystems capable of withstanding shocks and advancing long-term growth.

But these benefits are contingent on governance. Host countries must design policies that attract sustainable and high-quality FDI, guarantee data sovereignty, and promote inclusive skills development if they are to fully reap the convergence. Without this, the risk of dependency, inequality, or environmental degradation may cancel out the gains in resilience.

6. GOVERNANCE, REGULATORY ISSUES, AND THE KNOWLEDGE ECONOMY

The intersection of artificial intelligence (AI) and foreign direct investment (FDI) in tourism presents enormous opportunities but also intricate governance and regulatory dilemmas. Though FDI introduces capital and international networks, and AI improves efficiency and responsiveness, their conjunction brings risks to equity, data sovereignty, and sustainability (OECD, 2024). This section examines how governance and regulation negotiate these tensions, and how the tourism sector can transition toward a "knowledge economy" that integrates innovation with inclusion and resilience.

6.1 The Importance of Governance in FDI and AI Outcomes

The impact of AI and FDI is rarely automatic but is mediated through host nations' institutional quality. Literature unanimously shows that bad governance leads to enclave tourism, where foreign investors capture rents with minimal local spillovers, and good governance enhances linkages, skill transfer, and sustainability (Nunkoo & Seetanah, 2018).

Similarly, AI adoption without regulatory institutions can exacerbate inequalities, present data insecurity risks, and displace labour. Ibrahim (2024) warns that FDI-driven tourism development without environmental regulation can increase carbon emissions, undermining resilience. However, Isik et al. (2025) demonstrate that AI in combination with ESG principles can align tourism with sustainable development goals, yet only when governance systems support responsible innovation.

So, governance is the pivot: it will determine if FDI–AI synergies yield strong, inclusive growth or lock in weaknesses (Sharma et al., 2022).

6.2 Regulatory Frameworks for AI in Tourism

AI deployment in tourism raises unique regulatory concerns:

- **Data Privacy and Protection**: AI applications rely heavily on customer data, including personal preferences, payment details, and biometric identifiers. Without robust data protection laws, tourists' trust in digital systems is undermined.
- **Algorithmic Transparency**: Opaque decision-making by AI systems can lead to discriminatory pricing or biased recommendations, threatening consumer rights.

- **Cybersecurity**: Tourism services increasingly depend on digital platforms vulnerable to hacking, ransomware, or system failures.
- **Labour Displacement**: Robotics and automation may displace low-skilled jobs, particularly in hotels and restaurants, unless policies facilitate retraining and upskilling.

Duong (2008a) forecasted that international FDI flows could be reshaped by the mass use of AI, reducing investment incentives in labour-surplus developing countries. The forecast emphasizes the role of policy that combines digital uptake and human capital building to prevent exclusion.

At the global level, there is also regulatory fragmentation. Destinations attract FDI with incentives, but uneven regulations on AI governance risk a "race to the bottom." Collective action—through regional agreements or international standards—would help ensure that AI application in tourism is driven by ethical and sustainability considerations.

6.3 Governance of FDI in Tourism

Governance also plays a role in the quality of FDI flows. FDI may spur tourism infrastructure, but it may lock destinations into unsustainable trajectories if it is not directed into inclusive, green investment (UNCTAD, 2007). Policy actions to promote governance are:

- **Screening and Incentives**: Governments can screen projects based on ESG performance, offering incentives for sustainable investment and discouraging environmentally damaging ventures (Ibrahim, 2024).
- **Local Linkage Requirements**: Foreign investors can be required by policies to connect with national suppliers, employ local workers, and engage the communities (Nunkoo & Ramkissoon, 2010).
- **Transparency Mechanisms**: Open contracting and project monitoring of FDI prevents corruption and balances benefits distribution.

The Estonian experience shows that institutional reforms that increase competitiveness, the tax system, and business climate reinforce the positive effects of FDI on growth and tourism development (Sokhanvar, 2022). This reflects how reforms in governance can turn inflows into real resilience.

6.4 The Knowledge Economy Dimension

AI and FDI are both pushing the shift to a knowledge economy in tourism. Unlike resource-based growth, a knowledge economy emphasizes human capital, innovation, and intangible assets. The tourism sector mirrors this shift: competitiveness is no longer solely founded on natural attractions but also on data analytics, digital marketing, and service innovation (Bhatt et al., 2024).

FDI facilitates knowledge transfer through the introduction of advanced managerial techniques and digital technologies by multinational companies. AI, however, accelerates knowledge creation and use by processing large volumes of data, recognizing patterns, and facilitating decision-making (Gutierriz et al., 2023).

Yet, Duong (2008a) emphasized the risk of AI compounding global disparities by concentrating technological competences in advanced economies. Without deliberate knowledge diffusion policies, developing destinations may be locked into low-value parts of the tourism value chain. Investment in research, education, and digital competences is therefore required to ensure that FDI and AI together support a broad-based knowledge economy rather than compounding divides.

6.5 Ethical and Social Considerations

Governance entails ethical considerations. Tourists' acceptance of AI is premised on their trust in technology. Duong et al. (2024) illustrate that continuance intention to use generative AI to plan travel depends on satisfaction and parasocial interaction but is undermined by technology anxiety. Poor governance—e.g., misuse of personal data or opaque pricing—would reduce acceptance, undermining the resilience benefits of AI.

Social inclusion is important too. For as much as AI will displace low-skill jobs, it will also demand high-skill ones in data analysis, AI maintenance, and digital marketing. Policy institutions need to facilitate reskilling and learning so that workers transition into these emerging positions rather than being excluded. In this sense, governance mediates whether AI adoption produces resilience through empowerment or fragility through exclusion.

6.6 Risks of Dependency and Lock-in

Another governance challenge is dependency risk. If destinations rely exclusively on foreign investors for AI adoption, they may find themselves locked into proprietary technologies belonging to multinational corporations. This then raises issues of technological sovereignty: who controls the data, algorithms, and platforms underpinning tourism?

In the absence of domestic capacity development, destinations stand to lose control over key assets. Ibrahim (2024) highlights how weakly regulated FDI can produce environmental weaknesses; in the same vein, weakly governed AI can yield digital weaknesses. Good governance must thus guarantee open standards, data sovereignty, and interoperability to prevent lock-in.

6.7 Policy Implications for Resilient Governance

The convergence of FDI and AI requires governance frameworks that integrate economic, technological, and social dimensions. Key recommendations include:

1. **Adopt Holistic FDI Screening**: Align investment attraction with sustainability goals and ESG metrics.
2. **Develop AI Governance Frameworks**: Ensure transparency, privacy, cyber-security, and ethical use.
3. **Invest in Human Capital**: Build digital skills, promote reskilling, and support innovation ecosystems.
4. **Promote Data Sovereignty**: Establish standards for local data storage and interoperability.
5. **Encourage Multi-Stakeholder Governance**: Involve governments, private sector, and communities in decision-making.

These measures ensure that the synergies between FDI and AI are harnessed for resilience, inclusiveness, and sustainability (Duong, 2008b).

6.8 Conceptual Synthesis

Regulation and governance are the key factors that determine whether FDI–AI–tourism nexus builds resilience or vulnerability. FDI provides resources, AI provides smarts, but only through governance grants benefits fairly distributed, risks managed, and sustainability given due importance. With the integration of ESG standards, data protection, and policies of inclusivity, places can transition to a knowledge economy that capitalises on FDI as well as AI for sustainable progress.

7. MACRO-LEVEL EVIDENCE: DIGITALISATION, TOURISM AND RESILIENCE

The micro-level and theoretical processes hitherto outlined are strongly supported by macroeconomic evidence (OECD, 2020). The recent twenty years have witnessed empirical studies progressively highlighting the systemic role of digitalisation and tourism in economic resilience, with foreign direct investment (FDI) as a complementary stimulus (Xu et al., 2024). The section here integrates macro-level evidence across diverse economies, showing how digitalisation and tourism are the main determinants of growth and stability, while AI and FDI entrench these trends.

7.1 Digitalisation as a Resilience Driver

Digitalisation has rendered tourism a more knowledge-intensive and resilient industry. Siddik et al. (2025) have examined ten leading tourism destinations between the years 2010 and 2022 with the help of econometric techniques like OLS, PCSE, FGLS, and two-step GMM. Their results show that digitalisation and tourism specialisation are the most consistent determinants of economic growth and are even more so than FDI or fintech individually.

The research shows that digitalisation enhances resilience by enabling:

- **Continuity of Operations** through e-commerce, online booking, and remote customer service.
- **Real-Time Adaptation** of tourism firms to demand fluctuations.
- **Broader Market Reach** via digital platforms, reducing dependency on single markets.

In times of crisis, such as the COVID-19 pandemic, destinations with more developed digital infrastructures recovered faster as they could transition to online marketing, digital payments, and virtual experiences (Efthimiou, 2025a).

7.2 Tourism as a Strategic Growth Engine

Tourism alone remains a powerful growth mover. There is proof that destinations strongly specialised in tourism perform better than others in foreign exchange earnings, employment creation, as well as contribution to GDP (Seetanah, 2011). However, the resilience of tourism rests on its ability to diversify markets, develop innovative products, and embrace sustainability (Bhatt et al., 2024).

Empirical proof from Estonia (Sokhanvar, 2022) indicates that specialisation in tourism adds to long-run growth, but only if it is paired with institutional reforms and competitiveness. Likewise, Sokhanvar and Jenkins (2022) show that transition economies are most aided when FDI, tourism, and policy support are all combined.

7.3 FDI as a Complementary Driver

FDI complements with infrastructure funding and knowledge transfer. Although Siddik et al. (2025) found FDI to be a less strong growth predictor than digitalisation, its contribution remained considerable. Along with tourism and digitalisation, FDI supported growth effects, indicating synergistic complementarities.

For example, Isik (2015) investigated D-7 economies over the 1995-2012 period and found long-run bidirectional causality between tourism receipts and FDI inflows. Even in developed contexts, FDI sustains tourism competitiveness, meaning that inflows still remain important for inducing innovation and quality improvement.

7.4 AI as a Catalytic Enabler at Macro Level

Artificial intelligence reinforces these macro-level interdependencies. By increasing productivity, efficiency, and sustainability, AI raises the returns to both FDI inflows and tourism specialisation (Bujdoso et al., 2025). Siddik et al. (2025) explicitly include AI adoption as part of their digitalisation index, showing that countries with greater AI penetration experienced stronger growth impacts.

At the forefront of sustainability, Isik et al. (2025) propose that AI converges with ESG-driven tourism activities, and they both have a positive impact on GDP per capita despite the environmental cost of tourism. Their empirical analysis demonstrates that an AI-augmented ESG index (ESG/ITA*AI) explains resilience outcomes more than traditional indicators, concluding that AI drives sustainable growth.

7.5 Case Studies from Diverse Contexts

- **Small Island States**: Fauzel (2021) confirmed bidirectional causality between FDI and tourism, underscoring the sector's macroeconomic importance in highly vulnerable economies. AI integration in such contexts could further reduce vulnerability by stabilising demand and optimising resource use.
- **Transition Economies**: Evidence from Estonia demonstrates how tourism and FDI jointly drive growth, with digitalisation amplifying these effects (Sokhanvar, 2022). AI adoption in transition economies has accelerated integration into the global digital economy, enhancing competitiveness.

- **Developed Economies**: Isik (2015) found that even advanced destinations rely on FDI–tourism linkages. Digitalisation and AI adoption in these markets sustain leadership in the global tourism hierarchy.

These cross-contextual findings confirm that while tourism is universally significant, its resilience is amplified when combined with FDI and AI.

7.6 Macro Evidence on Vulnerability and Recovery

Macro studies also provide information on vulnerabilities. Ibrahim (2024) showed that growth is promoted through FDI and tourism and can also promote carbon emissions when there is weak environmental governance. This comes with a paradox: growth drivers turn into risk factors unless directed through sustainable policies.

Conversely, AI holds correctives' potential. Isik et al. (2025) depict that, while AI-interacted ESG practices minimize harmful externalities, such that growth is not gained at the expense of resilience. Macro-evidences thus indicate not only the benefits of FDI and tourism but also the dangers of unsustainable channels.

7.7 Implications for Resilience Strategies

The macro evidence suggests several implications:

1. **Digitalisation First**: Digital transformation is the most robust predictor of resilience; destinations must prioritise AI adoption, digital infrastructure, and e-services.
2. **Tourism as a Base Driver**: Tourism remains a reliable growth engine, but its resilience depends on innovation, diversification, and sustainability.
3. **FDI as a Complement**: FDI is not the strongest driver alone but amplifies digitalisation and tourism when embedded in appropriate policies.
4. **AI as a Catalyst**: AI strengthens the effects of tourism and FDI, turning them into adaptive, sustainable growth pathways.
5. **Governance Matters**: Without strong environmental and institutional frameworks, growth may generate vulnerabilities rather than resilience (Efthimiou, 2025d).

7.8 Conceptual Synthesis

At a macro level, the evidence supports a *Triangular Model*:

- Tourism Specialisation drives income and employment.

- *FDI* finances infrastructure and introduces know-how.
- *Digitalisation (with AI at its core)* amplifies both, ensuring adaptability and sustainability.

This model demonstrates that resilience is not achieved through a single driver but rather through the combined effect of digitalisation, tourism, and FDI under effective governance. Those destinations that can harmonize such drivers will be able to cope better with crises, remain competitive, and achieve inclusive growth (UNCTAD, 2007).

8. BEHAVIOURAL DIMENSION: AI ADOPTION BY TOURISTS AND DEMAND EFFECTS

While the majority of the FDI and AI tourism literature emphasizes capital flows, infrastructure, and productivity at the firm level, the behavior of tourists also influences resilience. Demand stability is the basis of resilience: interested, committed, and technology-open tourists facilitate destinations to recover more quickly from crises. This section of the chapter elaborates the behavioral factor of AI adoption among tourists, such as tourists' perception and continuance intention, and impact on demand resilience.

8.1 Tourists as Co-Creators of Value in Digital Ecosystems

Consumer and service provider co-creation of tourist experiences occur. AI technologies such as generative AI companions (e.g., travel assistants on ChatGPT), recommendation engines, and chatbots shift some co-creation action to virtual spaces. The passive consumption strategy is no longer employed by tourists but instead actively construct their holidays with AI-driven platforms (Gutierriz et al., 2023).

This transformation affects resilience. Digital co-creation increases tourists' sense of control and personalization, making it more likely they will persist even when uncertain. It also provides destinations with actual-time feedback from consumers' preferences, enabling adaptive response to shocks.

8.2 Continuance Intention and Technology Acceptance

A significant behavioural theory is continuance intention (CI)—the likelihood that tourists will continue to use AI tools after initial adoption. Duong et al. (2024) provide empirical findings from a survey of 606 tourists. It illustrates that:

- *Parasocial interaction (PSI)* with AI systems strengthens CI by creating an illusion of human-like companionship.
- *Satisfaction* with AI performance directly increases CI.
- *Technology anxiety* moderates these effects negatively, reducing willingness to adopt AI tools.

These results suggest that the resilience of tourists is partly mediated by their openness to AI. Destinations and businesses that establish trustworthy, easy-to-use AI systems are likely to achieve stable demand under disruption. Poorly designed systems, however, can create annoyance or lack of trust and lower resilience.

8.3 Personalisation and Loyalty

AI-driven personalisation also enhances customer loyalty, the secret to demand resilience. By enabling personalised recommendations, itineraries, and promotions tailored to individual preferences, AI strengthens emotional connections between tourists and destinations. The literature indicates that personalised services increase repeat visitation and positive word-of-mouth, both of which enable destination recovery following crises (Sharma et al., 2022).

Personalisation also dampens demand volatility. AI systems, for example, can target domestic or regional tourists in the case of global shocks that restrict long-distance travel, preserving occupancy and revenue levels. In this way, AI increases the stickiness of demand, anchoring flows that would otherwise sever.

8.4 Generational Differences and Adoption Barriers

AI uptake in tourism remains uneven. Younger, digitally savvy tourists are more likely to embrace AI applications, but less digitally savvy or older segments remain more hesitant. Duong et al. (2024) refer to the role of technology anxiety, which is generally more pronounced in older cohorts.

Destinations must therefore design inclusive digital strategies that address uptake challenges. For example:

- Offering hybrid systems (human + AI) to ease transitions.
- Providing user education and transparent explanations of AI functions.
- Ensuring multilingual and culturally sensitive AI interfaces.

By lowering barriers, destinations can broaden adoption and avoid creating a “digital divide” in tourism demand.

8.5 Trust, Ethics, and Data Protection

Trust lies at the center of tourists' willingness to engage with AI. Issues of privacy, data security, and algorithmic fairness can be adoption inhibitors. Ibrahim (2024) and Duong (2008b) point out that governance frameworks play a crucial role in ensuring ethical application of AI and averting exploitation.

Travelers will be more inclined to utilize AI tools if they can trust that their data will be protected and openly used. Destinations that fail to address these concerns risk demand fragility, as negative publicity or scandals can immediately deter travelers. Conversely, destinations with strong data protection laws can gain a competitive edge by presenting themselves as safe digital environments.

8.6 Behavioural Resilience During Crises

The COVID-19 pandemic highlighted how the adoption of digital tools by behaviour creates resilience. Visitors increasingly depended on AI-powered platforms for rebookings, cancellations, and virtual experiences during a period of physical travel restrictions (Hamcerencu, 2025). Reassurance, information updates, and personalized advice were provided by generative AI chatbots, maintaining engagement despite limited mobility.

Such digital continuity allows destinations to retain customer relations even during periods of downturn. Once travel restrictions are lifted, tourists who have been kept engaged by AI will be more likely to return, accelerating recovery. Hence, AI adoption not only stabilises current demand but also protects future demand potential.

8.7 Implications for FDI in Demand-Side Technologies

Adoption of AI at the behavioural level also affects FDI flows. Investors are more likely to invest in digital platforms, smart hotels, or AI-powered attractions if tourists demonstrate willingness to use these technologies. Duong et al. (2024) provide evidence that demand-side acceptance creates a viable market for AI-enabled services, and this reduces investment risks.

This creates a feedback loop:

- FDI introduces new AI technologies.
- Tourists adopt them, creating stable demand.
- Stable demand attracts further FDI, reinforcing digital transformation.

Destinations that encourage adoption through education, trust-building, and inclusivity thus become more attractive to foreign investors.

8.8 Conceptual Synthesis

The behavioural element highlights the point that resilience is as much about demand flexibility as supply-side capability. The capacity of tourists to adapt to AI tools, maintain interest in the face of crises, and believe in digital systems stabilizes revenue streams and accelerates recovery.

AI strengthens demand resilience by:

- *Continuance Intention* supported by satisfaction and parasocial interaction.
- *Personalisation* that increases loyalty and repeat visitation.
- *Trust And Ethics* that mitigate adoption barriers.
- *Inclusivity Strategies* that expand adoption across demographics (Hamcerencu, 2025).

Together with FDI, which finances infrastructure to enable AI adoption, these behavioural factors ensure that the tourism industry evolves into a more adaptive, customer-oriented system.

9. ESG, GREEN TRANSITION AND THE ENERGY DIMENSION OF TOURISM UNDER FDI–AI

The convergence of artificial intelligence (AI) and foreign direct investment (FDI) in tourism is not just a matter of capital and competitiveness but also of sustainability. The global tourism industry is facing increasing criticism for its environmental and social impacts, ranging from carbon emissions and over-tourism to cultural commodification. The integration of environmental, social, and governance (ESG) factors into investment and technology design is now a prerequisite for resilience (Tong et al., 2022). This chapter explores how AI and FDI relate to each other in the context of the ESG and green transition agendas, specifically addressing the energy aspect of tourism.

9.1 The Sustainability Imperative in Tourism

Tourism accounts for nearly 8% of global carbon emissions, largely attributed to transportation, accommodation, and energy-intensive recreational activities (Efthimiou, 2025e). While it generates foreign exchange and employment, unregulated tourist growth can degrade ecosystems and reduce long-term resilience. The challenge is to align tourism with the UN Sustainable Development Goals (SDGs) by reducing environmental externalities without eroding competitiveness.

FDI can aggravate or alleviate these issues. Unregulated, large-scale tourism development financed by global capital has a tendency to strain natural resources and increase emissions. Green FDI into renewable energy, sustainable infrastructure, and sustainable business models, on the contrary, can increase resilience along with sustainability (Nunkoo & Seetanah, 2018).

9.2 AI as an Enabler of ESG Performance

AI enhances ESG outcomes by the optimisation of resource allocation, monitoring of sustainability indicators, and enabling real-time decision-making. Isik et al. (2025) designed an AI-interacted ESG tourism index (ESG/ITA*AI) and determined that although traditional tourism determinants can have an adverse effect on GDP per capita through environmental costs, AI integration supports positive outcomes. Their results show that AI transforms tourism into a more sustainable growth driver.

Certain explicit AI-enabled mechanisms are:

- **Energy Efficiency**: Smart energy management systems reduce electricity and water consumption in hotels and resorts.
- **Carbon Monitoring**: AI models track emissions across value chains, supporting compliance with climate targets.
- **Waste Reduction**: Predictive analytics optimise food supply chains, reducing waste in hospitality operations.
- **Biodiversity Protection**: AI-driven visitor management prevents overcrowding at sensitive natural or cultural sites.

These applications highlight AI's dual role: increasing operational efficiency while directly supporting ESG goals.

9.3 FDI as a Driver of Green Transition

FDI provides the financial muscle to achieve large-scale sustainability initiatives. Foreign investors are also integrating ESG factors into their decision-making, mirroring international shareholder and consumer pressure (Efthimiou, 2025d). This has two implications for tourism:

1. Destinations with strong ESG policies are more attractive to investors, as they reduce reputational and regulatory risks.

2. Investors finance the green transition, such as renewable-powered resorts, low-carbon transport systems, and eco-certification schemes.

The Estonian case shows that business environment and competitiveness are the keys to attracting such high-quality FDI (Sokhanvar, 2022). Similarly, Seetanah (2011) demonstrated that the growth impact of tourism depends on the policy and institutional setting, which now ever more includes sustainability governance.

9.4 Energy Dimension of FDI–Tourism Nexus

Perhaps most critical to sustainability in tourism is energy use. Ibrahim (2024) found that the higher FDI and tourism flows are, the more carbon emissions there are when environmental policies are loose. Green FDI through renewable energy projects such as solar-powered resorts or electric mobility corridors can, however, mitigate this.

Recent econometric findings are more nuanced. A wavelet quantile analysis yields complex interactions between FDI, trade, tourism, and consumption of renewable energy. The findings suggest that FDI and tourism can have positive impacts on the use of renewable energy under given conditions, suggesting it is within possibility for policy systems to guide investment flows towards sustainability (Durani et al., 2025).

9.5 AI and Renewable Energy Integration

Artificial intelligence complements the benefits of renewable energy integration in tourism. Smart grids with AI maximize energy exchange between solar, wind, and storage units in hotels and tourist attractions. Predictive analytics forecast energy demand, reducing the demand for fossil fuels (Bujdoso et al., 2025).

Isik et al. (2025) argue that the combination of AI with ESG activities has more sustainable macroeconomic impacts since AI ensures that investments result in measurable sustainability outcomes. Thus, AI not only promotes green FDI but also promotes performance measurement and accountability.

9.6 Social and Governance Dimensions

Beyond environmental performance, ESG also covers social and governance aspects:

- **Social**: AI-powered platforms can track labour conditions, gender equality, and community impacts of tourism projects. FDI inflows that prioritise local employment and supplier linkages contribute to social resilience (Nunkoo & Ramkissoon, 2010).

- **Governance**: AI enhances transparency through real-time monitoring of investments, but governance quality determines whether data are used effectively. Strong institutions are needed to enforce ESG commitments and prevent "greenwashing."

Here, FDI and AI converge again: foreign investors bring global ESG standards, while AI provides the tools to monitor and enforce compliance.

9.7 Risks of ESG-Washing and Dependency

Despite possible benefits, risks are present. Investors may engage in ESG-washing where they issue projects as sustainable with no significant impact. Countries that exclusively rely on foreign ESG knowledge may also become dependent, ultimately losing the capacity to develop their own sustainability guidelines. Ibrahim (2024) cautioned that outside capital may increase environmental vulnerabilities if not well regulated.

Policy interventions include stand-alone ESG certification, open data platforms for monitoring, and local stakeholder participation requirements in decision-making. These restrict dependence and ensure FDI–AI synergies have actual sustainability implications.

9.8 Policy Implications for Green Resilience

The integration of FDI and AI into ESG frameworks has several policy implications:

1. **Target Green FDI**: Incentivise investment in renewable energy, eco-tourism, and sustainable infrastructure.
2. **Mandate ESG Integration**: Require investors to adopt measurable ESG standards, monitored with AI tools.
3. **Promote AI for Resource Management**: Deploy AI in energy efficiency, carbon monitoring, and visitor management systems.
4. **Strengthen Governance**: Build institutional capacity to evaluate ESG claims, prevent greenwashing, and enforce compliance.
5. **Support Local Inclusion**: Ensure that ESG-driven projects engage local communities and share benefits equitably (Chowdhury et al., 2024).

9.9 Conceptual Synthesis

ESG, the green transition, and energy sustainability go hand in hand with tourism resilience. FDI pays for the green transition, AI enables it, and ESG frameworks hold it accountable. They are all together a vicious cycle where tourism equals not only economic growth but also climate mitigation and social inclusion.

But such an outcome is dependent upon context: poor management can make FDI a source of environmental stress, and unregulated AI can be used to enable ESG-washing. Institutions with strength, transparency, and inclusive participation are therefore imperative to make the FDI–AI–tourism nexus deliver resilience in truly sustainable form.

10. RISKS, LIMITATIONS AND TRADE-OFFS IN THE FDI–AI–TOURISM NEXUS

The nexus between foreign direct investment (FDI) and artificial intelligence (AI) offers immense potential for tourism growth and resilience but also threats, limitations, and trade-offs. While capital flows and technological change may trigger competitiveness and sustainability, they may also generate vulnerabilities if poorly managed. The following section critically assesses these issues drawing empirical evidence and theoretical perspectives.

10.1 Environmental Externalities

One of the most significant risks of tourism expansion through FDI is environmental degradation. Ibrahim (2024) illustrates that inward FDI and tourism development are typically accompanied by increased carbon emissions in host economies. Large-scale resort development, cruise terminals, and airport expansions sponsored by foreign investment consume massive energy resources and stress ecosystems.

AI can mitigate these impacts through the application of predictive analytics and smart energy management (Isik, 2015). There is, nevertheless, a compromise: the same AI applications that optimize resource use also require energy-intensive data centers, potentially negating advantages. Without the incorporation of renewables, the adoption of AI might inadvertently add to emissions, undermining the resilience that it is attempting to establish.

10.2 Socioeconomic Inequalities and Enclave Tourism

FDI may result in enclave tourism, where foreign-owned establishments and resorts appropriate the bulk of revenues with little spillovers to the local community (Nunkoo & Seetanah, 2018). The jobs created are often low-skilled and seasonal, while profits are repatriated abroad. This undermines social resilience by limiting community benefits and increasing inequality.

Similarly, AI uptake risks exacerbating gaps. Duong (2008a) warned that automation has the potential to reduce motivations for FDI in labour-abundant countries, as inexpensive human resources lose comparative advantage. Here, host nations that have relied heavily on inexpensive labour as a point of attraction for investors can witness their FDI flows reduce, further fueling unemployment.

10.3 Digital Divides and Exclusion

AI adoption in tourism is uneven. Duong et al. (2024) illustrate that continuance intention to use AI travel assistants is undermined by technology anxiety, in particular for older or less technologically sophisticated tourists. Destinations that over-emphasise AI without inclusivity undermine the risk of deterring segments of the tourist market, reducing overall demand resilience.

Moreover, in host economies, digital divides persist. Employees lacking digital skills can be excluded from new opportunities, and firms without resources to apply AI can be left out of global value chains. Such divides usher in a dual economy where only certain segments thrive, which undermines inclusiveness.

10.4 Dependence on Foreign Investors and Technological Lock-in

Reliance on FDI to adopt AI exposes countries to dependency and lock-in dangers. Multinational firms prefer to implement proprietary AI platforms, which limit host nations' control over information, algorithms, and digital infrastructure. This dependence reduces technological sovereignty and may constrain policy independence.

Ibrahim (2024) recognizes analogous risks in the environmental sector, where FDI can lock destinations into unsustainable trajectories. In the same way, dependence on foreign digital ecosystems can lock destinations into technological trajectories that are difficult to reverse. Without open standards and local capacity building, resilience is undermined by external control.

10.5 Ethical and Governance Challenges

AI in tourism raises complex ethical issues:

- **Privacy and Surveillance**: Biometric systems in airports and hotels collect sensitive data, raising privacy concerns.
- **Algorithmic Bias**: Recommendation systems may reinforce stereotypes or discriminatory pricing, eroding fairness.
- **Transparency**: Tourists often do not understand how AI decisions are made, creating trust deficits.

Duong et al. (2024) illustrate that technology anxiety reduces adoption when tourists have no trust in AI systems. Without strong governance frameworks ensuring transparency and accountability, AI adoption may compromise demand resilience instead of strengthening it.

10.6 Economic Volatility and Crisis Sensitivity

Though FDI brings in capital, it also carries exposure to financial volatility worldwide. Investors may withdraw when times are tough, leaving projects stranded or bankrupt. FDI-dependent and tourism-based economies are most vulnerable to shock stops in capital flow (Fauzel, 2021).

The Covid-19 crisis also brought this danger to the fore: numerous foreign-owned tourist infrastructure closed, with capital flight making local declines worse. AI technologies cushioned some impact by sustaining customer interface through virtual platforms (Hamcerencu, 2025), but the inherent volatility of FDI flows continues to be a structural constraint.

10.7 Governance Gaps and ESG-Washing

Governance quality determines how much FDI and AI produce sustainable outcomes. Bad governance has the potential to trigger corruption, resource misallocation, and ESG-washing, where projects are proclaimed as sustainable but lack the actual impact (Isik, 2015).

For example, investors may adopt AI-driven energy systems for branding but not reduce emissions. Foreign firms again may embark on community linkages as commitments but rely on foreign workers and vendors. These governance loopholes undermine social resilience and sustainability too.

10.8 Trade-Offs Between Efficiency and Inclusivity

AI adoption is biased toward cost savings, reducing expenses through automation. But this will work against inclusive objectives. Job losses in lower-skilled jobs can erode social resilience unless complemented by reskilling efforts. Duong (2008b) cautioned that AI would redirect FDI flows back to developed economies, leaving developing sites with less employment opportunity.

Hence, there is a balancing act to be performed: efficiency gains need to be weighed against inclusive development. Unless policy-making is done in a careful manner, resilience at the macro level (profitability and competitiveness) is at the expense of micro-level compromise (unemployment and inequality).

10.9 Policy Responses to Mitigate Risks

To address these risks and trade-offs, several policy measures are recommended:

1. **Green Conditionality**: Require FDI projects to adopt renewable energy and sustainability standards.
2. **Data Governance Frameworks**: Establish privacy laws, transparency requirements, and open standards for AI systems.
3. **Capacity Building**: Invest in digital skills and local technological ecosystems to reduce dependency.
4. **Inclusion Policies**: Support SMEs and vulnerable groups to adopt AI tools and participate in tourism value chains.
5. **Crisis Management Mechanisms**: Develop policies to prevent sudden capital flight and stabilise FDI flows (Chowdhury et al., 2024).

10.10 Conceptual Synthesis

The FDI–AI–tourism complex provides opportunities but also risks. Intelligence and capital can build resilience but bring connected vulnerability of environment, inequality, dependence, and governance. Resilience is therefore not innate but requires effective management of trade-offs.

An integrated approach is required:

- FDI should be directed toward sustainable and inclusive projects.
- AI adoption should prioritise transparency, fairness, and accessibility.
- Governance frameworks should align efficiency with equity, ensuring that resilience is not achieved at the expense of environmental or social sustainability.

It is only through such integration that FDI and AI can collectively make the tourism industry competitive as well as resilient (Chowdhury et al., 2024).

11. INTEGRATED CONCEPTUAL MODEL OF FDI–AI–TOURISM RESILIENCE

The relationship between foreign direct investment (FDI) and artificial intelligence (AI) has been shown in the preceding sections to impact the development and resilience of the tourism industry in fundamental ways. Yet, the value of this relationship is best unveiled when envisioned as an integrated system, rather than as two separate inputs into tourism development. This chapter develops a conceptual framework explaining how FDI and AI interact with one another in economic, social, and environmental domains to generate resilience. It synthesizes the structural inputs of capital and intelligence, the operational and behavioural processes through which they are manifested, the governance institutions that mediate their effect, and the feedback loops that entrench or erode resilience outcomes.

11.1 Resilience in Tourism as a Multidimensional Construct

Tourism resilience has traditionally been understood as the capacity of destinations and firms to recover from crises. However, recent scholarship formulates it as a multidimensional phenomenon that includes economic, social, and environmental systems. Economic resilience is the capacity to sustain income, employment, and competitiveness against shocks. Social resilience is the preservation of inclusivity, equity, and community well-being (Satrovic & Muslija, 2019). Ecological resilience involves minimizing environmental degradation while adhering to sustainable development imperatives in the tourism industry (Hanafiah & Zulkifly, 2019). A merged model of FDI and AI in tourism must therefore consider these three dimensions simultaneously, as a singular focus on growth can generate vulnerabilities (Hamcerencu, 2025).

11.2 Structural Foundations: Capital and Intelligence

At the core of the model are the structural resources provided by FDI and AI. FDI introduces financial capital, infrastructure, and connectivity to global markets. It allows destinations to build airports, cruise terminals, five-star hotels, and online booking systems that local investors cannot afford (Endo, 2006; Isik, 2015). AI provides an intelligence layer on top of these physical assets, allowing predictive analytics, process automation, and personalized services (Sharma et al., 2022).

These two pillars are complements, not substitutes: without FDI, most destinations lack the means to undertake extensive digital transformation; without AI, the capital channeled through FDI is not made as productive or sustainable as possible. The model thus begins with the argument that capital and intelligence are the twin bases of tourism resilience.

11.3 Translating Resources into Resilience: Operational, Behavioural, and Systemic Mechanisms

Resources do not automatically conduce to resilience. They must be translated into concrete outcomes by mechanisms operating at different levels of the tourism system. At the operational level, AI transforms FDI-funded infrastructure into responsive and efficient assets. Foreign investment-built hotels are turned into "smart hotels" as AI-powered systems reduce energy usage, personalize guest services, and automate back-office functions. airports financed through public–private partnerships are made resilient when AI-powered biometric solutions streamline passenger traffic to avert bottlenecks during times of crisis.

Relying on tourists' willingness to engage with AI-enabled technologies and to continue engaging with destinations amidst disruption at the behavioural level, Duong et al. (2024) demonstrate that satisfaction with AI technology and the sense of companionship created through parasocial interaction improve continuance intention, while technology anxiety reduces it. In this manner, the tourists themselves are active agents of resilience: if they depend on and use AI tools, demand is stabilized even in the event of external shock. FDI, in financing digital platforms and AI applications, provides the infrastructure that facilitates this behavioural engagement.

Lastly, at the systemic level, AI and FDI interact with broader economic and environmental systems. It is at this point that the integration of ESG standards is critical. Isik et al. (2025) show that AI utilized in ESG models reinforces the positive relationship between tourism and GDP per capita, negating the environmental cost that may accompany tourism expansion. FDI is the vehicle for scaling up these ESG programs, financing renewable energy investments and sustainable infrastructure. Together, they create systemic resilience through embedding sustainability in the model of tourism development.

11.4 The Enabling Environment: Governance and Institutions

Governance and regulatory quality are the mediating cross-cutting drivers that permeate all levels of the model. Good governance ensures that FDI projects deliver linkages to local economies and not in the form of enclaves, and that AI adoption follows privacy, transparency, and inclusivity (Nunkoo & Seetanah, 2018; Ibrahim,

2024). Without such frameworks, capital flows can increase inequality, and AI can reinforce digital divides or create new dependencies on exogenous platforms. The Estonian case examined by Sokhanvar (2022) illustrates this dynamic in action very nicely: competitiveness, business climate, and taxation regime reforms were central to converting FDI inflows into growth-generating impacts. Governance is therefore not an add-on but an integral part of the model, moderating the way structural assets condition resilience.

11.5 Feedback Loops and Complementarities

The integrated framework recognises that the FDI–AI–tourism nexus is dynamic in nature, as depicted through feedback loops rather than linear causality. FDI enables the uptake of AI by financing the infrastructure, training, and platforms required for digitalisation. AI, on the other hand, increases the profitability and feasibility of FDI projects, which renders destinations more attractive to additional investors. Tourists' willingness to engage with AI underpins demand for the offerings, signaling to investors that there is a robust market for digitalised tourism products. This positive feedback loop creates a virtuous cycle whereby investment, adoption, and innovation support one another (Siddik et al., 2025).

Feedback loops can, nevertheless, be negative. When there is poor governance, FDI may enter into environmentally damaging projects, while AI may be applied in a way that excludes vulnerable groups. Consumers who lack confidence in AI systems have the ability to opt out, reducing demand. In such a scenario, the system risks a vicious cycle of inequality, addiction, and environmental decay (Duong, 2008a; Ibrahim, 2024). The model thus underscores the contingent nature of resilience: results are not only a function of inputs but also of the quality of governance and social take-up.

11.6 Macro-level Validation of the Model

Empirical observation validates the integrated model across contexts. Siddik et al. (2025) show that tourism specialisation and digitalisation are the strongest predictors of growth, and FDI consolidates these effects. Isik (2015) finds long-run bidirectional causality between FDI inflows and tourism receipts in D-7 economies, confirming that FDI is both a driver and outcome of tourism development. Isik et al. (2025) demonstrate that AI applied to ESG metrics enhances positive growth outcomes, providing quantitative support for the systemic sustainability mechanisms outlined in the model. Together, these studies provide strong macroeconomic confirmation of the conceptual framework.

11.7 Policy Relevance and Applications

The model is not theoretical but offers practical guidance to policymakers. Destinations wishing to build resilience must develop investment promotion strategies that prioritize investments that embed ESG and AI capabilities. They must design digital transformation roadmaps that extend beyond multinationals to include small and medium enterprises to attain broader spillovers (Efthimiou, 2025a). Investment in human capital and digital skills is required to prevent exclusion and enable workers to transition into AI-generated new occupations. Finally, regulatory reforms are needed to enforce sustainability standards, protect data privacy, and ensure algorithmic transparency. By adopting the above policies, destinations can unchain the virtuous cycles of the FDI–AI nexus and avoid its potential pitfalls.

11.8 Conceptual Synthesis

The combined conceptual model of FDI and AI in tourism positions capital and intelligence as complementary foundations of resilience. These resources are channeled through operational, behavioural, and systemic mechanisms, all moderated by governance and expressed through feedback loops that can be either virtuous or vicious. The ultimate results are not limited to GDP growth but include inclusive development, environmental sustainability, and adaptive capacity.

This synthesis emphasizes that resilience does not necessarily ensue from investment or technology. It arises when FDI and AI are grounded in sound governance arrangements, embedded with ESG objectives, and embraced by businesses and tourists. At best, the model generates reinforcing cycles of resilience and sustainable development. At worst, it invites dependency, inequality, and environmental degradation. The challenge to industry leaders and policymakers is to steer the system towards the former, rather than the latter.

12. FUTURE TRAJECTORIES AND RESEARCH AGENDA FOR FDI–AI–TOURISM RESILIENCE

The dynamics of foreign direct investment (FDI), artificial intelligence (AI), and tourism resilience are evolving on an ongoing basis. While the above sections have mapped existing mechanisms and challenges, it is no less important that there is some articulation of emerging avenues and a research agenda able to inform policy, academia, and industry. This section does so, focusing ahead to consider the prospective evolution of the nexus over the coming decade and outstanding questions yet to be resolved.

12.1 Tourism in a Turbulent Global Context

Tourism becomes increasingly exposed to ambiguous global risks: geo-political tensions, climate change, pandemics, digital disruption, and shifting consumer behaviour. Each one of these drivers injects uncertainty into traditional patterns of growth. FDI and AI collectively offer avenues for adaptation, but risk magnifying vulnerabilities. The resilience pathway in tourism will therefore depend upon the mobilization of these tools within a changing world (Efthimiou, 2025a).

12.2 The Evolving Geography of FDI

The FDI flow geography in tourism will dramatically evolve over the coming years. Duong (2008b) contended that mass automation would lessen the investment incentive for investment in labour-surplus developing countries since the low-cost labour competitive advantage is mitigated. As AI replaces repetitive tourism work, capital can be diverted to technologically advanced economies where digital ecosystems and infrastructure already prevail.

At the same time, places that are committed to ESG principles are becoming ever more attractive to investors, a result of shareholders' and consumers' global pressure. Ibrahim (2024) shows that environmental externalities remain a necessary risk, but those that are able to manage them well have a prospect to be at a competitive advantage. This is a sign of bifurcation: those countries with strong sustainability and digital strategies will win high-quality FDI, whereas countries simply chasing low labor costs will see decreasing volumes.

12.3 AI's Deepening Role in Tourism Ecosystems

AI will further expand from operational to strategic and systemic functions. Digital transformation, as argued by Gutierriz et al. (2023), is already beginning to reshape business models, but the next step would be integrating AI into planning and governance. Predictive analytics will facilitate crisis preparedness, generative AI will create experiential travel experiences, and machine learning will facilitate sustainable resource allocation.

Behavioural studies indicate that tourists are becoming increasingly comfortable with AI, as privacy and transparency issues are resolved. Duong et al. (2024) illustrate that satisfaction and trust are positively related to AI continuance intention to use and that estimated adoption rates will be dependent on ethical governance structures. Consumer-trust-promoting destinations will benefit from resilience.

12.4 Integrating FDI, AI, and ESG for Sustainable Development

The green transition will be a characteristic hallmark. Isik et al. (2025) show the role of AI in ESG systems in making tourism development more sustainable. As the climate goals get tighter, attracting green FDI as well as using AI for resource efficiency will be a resilience-driving factor. Tourism investors may increasingly demand ESG conformity as a condition for capital inflow, giving rise to opportunities as well as challenges for new destinations (Jonsson, 2022).

This offers a new avenue of research: finding out how ESG-driven FDI overlaps with AI uptake in bulk. Subsequent research could measure the extent to which specific ESG (environment, social, governance) components interact with AI systems to determine resilience effects.

12.5 Risks and Uncertainties in Future Trajectories

Though future possibility is present, there are massive risks at stake. Overreliance on foreign investors for the adoption of AI would increase reliance and limit technological independence (Nunkoo & Seetanah, 2018). The digital divide at the transnational and national levels could persist, producing regions beyond the periphery of global value chains. Moreover, ESG-washing remains a problem: investors can apply AI tools on the exterior to market sustainability credentials yet do not make real change (Efthimiou, 2025e).

A second form of uncertainty is geopolitical. As data governance becomes a point of contention globally, destinations become potentially locked into the technology of one bloc or another and lose some measure of control. An appreciation of how geopolitical fragmentation affects FDI–AI flows into tourism will be crucial in the next decade.

12.6 A Forward-Looking Research Agenda

With these directions in mind, an integrated research agenda for FDI–AI–tourism resilience would require at least five strands:

1. Comparative Country Studies

There is a need for comparative empirical contrasts of developed, transition, and small island economies. While there are single-case studies (Isik, 2015; Fauzel, 2021; Sokhanvar, 2022), systematic cross-country examination of FDI–AI dynamics in tourism is lacking.

2. Longitudinal Analysis

Most of the available research employs short- to medium-term data. Longitudinal research is required to capture how FDI and AI affect resilience together through multiple cycles of shocks and recoveries.

3. Behavioural and Cultural Factors

While Duong et al. (2024) place importance on continuance intention, some more research into cross-cultural variations in tourist adoption of AI will be required. Understanding how cultural factors mediate trust, satisfaction, and involvement will be essential to predicting demand-side resilience.

4. ESG and Climate Resilience

Future research must integrate AI-based ESG indices with climate models to assess how far tourism can adapt to handle climate extremes, carbon pricing, and loss of biodiversity.

5. Geopolitics and Technological Sovereignty

Research also needs to examine how destinations can break away from non-domestic digital platforms, potentially through regional AI ecosystems or public–private networks that guarantee data sovereignty (Bujdoso et al., 2025).

12.7 Toward a Knowledge-Based Tourism Paradigm

Lastly, the resilience of tourism in the future rests on shifting towards a knowledge economy. As Duong (2008a) and Gutierriz et al. (2023) note, AI will reshape comparative advantage from cheap labour to innovation, digital literacy, and knowledge production. FDI will remain crucial but will increasingly flow towards destinations that have the capacity to demonstrate absorptive capacity for technology and knowledge. Tourism systems that invest in human capital, research, and digital infrastructures will be best placed to attract sustainable investment and exploit AI to benefit long-term resilience (Efthimiou, 2025b).

12.8 Conceptual Synthesis

In the future, the trajectory of FDI–AI–tourism nexus is promising but uncertain. On the one hand, interaction between capital flows and intelligent technologies could provide unprecedented resilience to infuse tourism growth with sustainability, inclusivity, and innovation. On the other, there are threats of dependency, unfairness, and ESG-washing, especially in weak-governance environments.

The research agenda therefore must aim not only to document positive outcomes but also to find impediments and to design policy frameworks to meet them. The tourism industry is at crossroads: what the next ten years bring — to open to some types of FDI, how to regulate AI, and how to add ESG — will decide if it will thrive in an era of turbulence.

13. CONCLUSION

The aim of this chapter was to examine how the confluence of foreign direct investment (FDI) and artificial intelligence (AI) can aid the resilience and growth of the tourism industry. In the previous sections, is presented how both FDI and AI provide essential inputs—capital and intelligence—that, when paired with good governance, generate synergies with the capacity to turn tourism into an even more agile, just, and sustainable sector. This conclusion integrates the major findings, highlights policy implications, and reveals the broader significance for future directions in tourism.

Tourism is especially vulnerable to exogenous shocks: pandemics, climate change, geopolitical crises, and shifting consumer attitudes all have deep-reaching implications for supply and demand. Resilience needs to be therefore defined as being multifaceted, encompassing economic stability, social inclusiveness, and environmental sustainability (Hamcerencu, 2025). The principal argument made here is that FDI and AI, strategically combined, create resilience on all three fronts.

FDI has remained a corner stone of tourism development. With capital provision, global connections, and administration experience, it finances upscale complexes such as airports, ports, and resorts (Endo, 2006; Isik, 2015). Evidences provide two-way causality between FDI inflows and tourism revenues, representing a mutual positive feedback process (Isik, 2015; Fauzel, 2021; Sokhanvar, 2022). In island countries, tourism and FDI create long-term synergies required for survival in insecure environments (Fauzel, 2021). In transition economies, institutional reforms determine whether these inflows lead to sustainable growth (Sokhanvar, 2022; Sokhanvar & Jenkins, 2022). Nevertheless, FDI is risky. It is likely to result in enclave tourism with minimal local community linkages and increase pressures on the environment in the event of weak sustainability standards (Nunkoo & Seetanah, 2018; Ibrahim, 2024). The above weaknesses highlight the imperative of governance structures to ensure that FDI enables inclusive and green growth.

AI enhances FDI by introducing adaptability and intelligence into the tourism system. It improves operation resilience through automation, predictive analysis, price dynamics, and energy efficiency (Sharma et al., 2022; Gutierriz et al., 2023). It improves demand-side resilience through increased personalisation, tourist satisfaction, and continuance intention, conditional on problems of trust and transparency (Duong et al., 2024). Mechanically, AI improves resilience through facilitating ESG frameworks, IoT network integration, and more efficient use (+). AI thus introduces the "adaptive layer" that makes FDI-funded infrastructure more efficient, profitable, and sustainable. Without AI, capital inflows may risk freezing static models; without FDI, AI implementation might remain out of reach or piecemeal. In tandem, they unleash synergies that transform tourism into a wiser and more resilient system.

Running through the analysis is the overarching role of governance. Robust institutions mediate whether FDI generates spillovers or enclaves, and whether AI implementation empowers or excludes. ESG monitoring, data privacy regulatory frameworks, and algorithmic transparency are all crucial to ensuring tourist confidence and investor trust (Ibrahim, 2024; Nunkoo & Seetanah, 2018). The Estonian experience provides an example of how competitiveness, tax reform, and institutional stability enable FDI–tourism linkages to accelerate growth positively (Sokhanvar, 2022). Conversely, bad governance creates risks: digital divides, environmental degradation, technological dependency, and ESG-washing (Isik, 2015). Resilience is not an inherent consequence of FDI or AI but an outcome of the way they are embedded in regulatory and institutional frameworks.

At the macro level, specialisation in tourism and digitalisation are the best growth predictors, while FDI and fintech are multipliers (Siddik et al., 2025). Long-run bidirectional causality is the empirical evidence found consistently between FDI inflows and tourism receipts in both developed and developing economies (Isik, 2015; Fauzel, 2021). Adoption of AI, particularly in combination in ESG measures, strengthens such associations, improving economic as well as sustainability performance (Isik, 2015). This macro evidence supports the integrated conceptual model set out in this paper and sees FDI and AI as structural foundations, mediated via governance, and passing through operational, behavioural, and systemic processes into resilience outcomes.

Despite being productive, the FDI–AI complementarities are at trade-offs. Environmental externalities persist: mass-tourism developments lead to increased emissions, and implementation of AI per se can demand considerable energy (Ibrahim, 2024). Socioeconomic inequalities may become embedded if FDI creates enclaves or if AI substitutes for unskilled workers without adequate reskilling (Nunkoo & Ramkissoon, 2010; Duong, 2008b). Digital divisions may disadvantage the excluded groups, both as consumers and as workers (Duong et al., 2024). Volatility of FDI introduces risk, as capital may leave during crises and render recovery useless

(Fauzel, 2021). Finally, foreign digital ecosystem dependence evokes reliance and technological lock-in risk, threatening sovereignty and resilience over the long term (Nunkoo & Seetanah, 2018). These limitations underscore the need for policy interventions balanced in terms of incliveness and sustainability rather than efficiency.

FDI flows in the future will shift towards destinations that have absorptive capacity to AI and ESG standards. Countries that relied solely on low-cost labor as a comparative advantage will see diminishing inflows, with automation reducing the need for outsourcing (Duong, 2008a). AI will spill over to governance, planning, and monitoring for sustainability, where digital trust and ethical adoption are essential to tourist behavior (Duong et al., 2024).

The future will be marked by research making highest priority areas out of cross-country comparisons, longitudinal examination of FDI–AI impacts, AI adoption cultural differences, inclusion of ESG models in climate models, and the geopolitical foundations of tech sovereignty (Sokhanvar, 2022; Gutierriz et al., 2023). The future stage of tourism resilience will be marked by transition towards a knowledge economy, in which innovation and digital literacy replace cheap labour as competitiveness drivers (Gutierriz et al., 2023).

The adaptability and expansion of tourism more and more depend upon the synergistic overlap of AI and FDI, under robust governance and sustainability structures. FDI supplies the capital and global linkages needed for megaprojects and global competitiveness. AI supplies the adaptive smarts that maximize these investments to be cost-efficient, profitable, and sustainable. Governance determines whether these synergies generate inclusive growth or escalate risks. This complexity is captured in conceptual model developed here: structural resources (intelligence and capital) are converted into resilience through operational, behavioural, and systemic mechanisms, conditioned by governance and activated through feedback loops. At their strongest, these interactions construct virtuous cycles of investment, adoption, and innovation which perpetuate resilience. At their weakest, they risk descending into dependency, inequality, and environmental harm. This chapter's main contribution is to show that tourism resilience is not a state of equilibrium but a process. It occurs when capital and technology are mobilized in terms reconciled with profitability and sustainability, efficiency and inclusiveness, and global integration and local empowerment. For scholars, business executives, and policymakers, the challenge is clear: to develop models that utilize FDI and AI not only for expansion, but for tourism systems that can prosper in an era of uncertainty.

REFERENCES

Anuradha, A., Chowdhury, P. R., & Biswas, A. (2024). Post-Pandemic Recovery Measures to Ensure Socio Economic Sustainability through FDI in Smart tourism. [EEL]. *European Economic Letters*, *14*(1), 1498–1509.

Bhatt, K., Seabra, C., Kumar, J., Ashutosh, K., & Kumar Kabia, S. (2024). Tourism-Led Inclusive Growth in Emerging and Developing Economies: A Systematic Literature Review. *SAGE Open*, *14*(2). Advance online publication. DOI: 10.1177/21582440241252516

Bujdoso, Z., Vida, N., Mate, B., Nagy, K., & Bringye, B. (2025). The artificial intelligence usage and benefits in tourism marketing. *Geojournal of Tourism and Geosites*, 60(2spl), 1147–1157. https://doi.org/DOI: 10.30892/gtg.602spl12-1488

Chowdhury, A. A. A., Rafi, A. H., Sultana, A., & All Noman, A. (2024). Enhancing Green Economy with Artificial Intelligence: Role of Energy Use and FDI in the United States. *Journal of Environmental and Energy Economics*, *3*(2), 55–76. DOI: 10.56946/jeee.v3i2.536

Davidson, L., & Sahli, M. (2015). Foreign direct investment in tourism, poverty alleviation, and sustainable development: A review of the Gambian hotel sector. *Journal of Sustainable Tourism*, *23*(2), 167–187. DOI: 10.1080/09669582.2014.957210

Domazet, I., Marjanovic, D., & Subic, J. (2024). Driving factors of the Montenegrin economy - FDI and tourism. *International Review (Steubenville, Ohio)*, (1-2), 117–127. DOI: 10.5937/intrev2401117d

Duong, C. D., Nguyen, T. H., Ngo, T. Q., Pham, T. T., Vu, A. T., & Dang, N. S. (2024). Using generative artificial intelligence (ChatGPT) for travel purposes: Parasocial interaction and tourists' continuance intention. *Tourism Review*, *80*(4), 813–827. DOI: 10.1108/TR-01-2024-0027

Duong, W. N. (2008a). Ghetto'ing workers with hi-tech: Exploring regulatory solutions for the effect of artificial intelligence on third world foreign direct investment. *Temple International and Comparative Law Journal*, *22*(1), 63–140.

Duong, W. N. (2008b). Effect of artificial intelligence on the pattern of foreign direct investment in the third world: Possible reversal of trend. *Denver Journal of International Law and Policy*, *36*(3 & 4), 325–334.

Durani, F., Anwar, A., Sharif, A., Hamid, A., Ali, S., & Syed, Q. R. (2025). Exploring the link between inflation, tourism, trade, foreign direct investment, and renewable energy consumption: Evidence from novel wavelet quantile correlation approach. *Clean Technologies and Environmental Policy*, *27*, 3897–3911. DOI: 10.1007/s10098-024-03073-w

Efthimiou, S. G. (2024). The impacts of COVID-19 pandemic on foreign direct investment. In Mavri, M., Mazza, P. I., Karasavvoglou, A., & Polychronidou, P. (Eds.), *Economic growth, prosperity and sustainability in the economies of the Balkans and Eastern European countries* (pp. 103–127). Springer., DOI: 10. 1007/978-3-031-58437-4_6

Efthimiou, S. G. (2025a). The trends of tourism sector after COVID-19 period: A study of strategy and implications. *Corporate & Business Strategy Review*, *6*(1), 119–133. DOI: 10.22495/cbsrv6i1art12

Efthimiou, S. G. (2025b). The role of entrepreneurship's economic adaptation to the international environment towards tourism and sustainable development of disadvantaged rural areas. *Corporate Governance and Sustainability Review*, *9*(2), 42–55. DOI: 10.22495/cgsrv9i2p4

Efthimiou, S. G. (2025c). Economic Adjustment through Foreign Direct Investments: A Literature Review. *International Journal of Applied Economics. Finance and Accounting*, *22*(1), 167–179. DOI: 10.33094/ijaefa.v22i1.2291

Efthimiou, S. G. (2025d). The contribution of foreign direct investments to the development and competitiveness of the tourism industry: Toward a sustainable growth. *Corporate Governance and Sustainability Review*, *9*(3), 24–44. DOI: 10.22495/cgsrv9i3p2

Efthimiou, S. G. (2025e). The Economic Adjustment and Regional Development of the Tourism Sector through Foreign Direct Investments. *Theoretical Economics Letters*, *15*(4), 821–850. DOI: 10.4236/tel.2025.154045

Endo, K. (2006). Foreign direct investment in tourism—Flows and volumes. *Tourism Management*, *27*(4), 600–614. DOI: 10.1016/j.tourman.2005.02.004

Fauzel, S. (2021). FDI and tourism futures: A dynamic investigation for a panel of small island economies. *Journal of Tourism Futures*, *7*(1), 98–110. DOI: 10.1108/JTF-05-2018-0026

Fauzel, S., Seetanah, B., & Sannassee, R. V. (2017). Analysing the impact of tourism foreign direct investment on economic growth: Evidence from a small island developing state. *Tourism Economics*, *23*(5), 1042–1055. DOI: 10.1177/1354816616664249

Gutierriz, I., Ferreira, J. J., & Fernandes, P. O. (2023). Digital transformation and the new combinations in tourism: A systematic literature review. *Tourism and Hospitality Research*, *25*(2), 194–213. DOI: 10.1177/14673584231198414

Hamcerencu, M. (2025). Artificial Intelligence in International Tourism. *Proceedings of the International Conference on Business Excellence*, 19(1), 1139-1151. https://doi.org/DOI: 10.2478/picbe-2025-0090

Hanafiah, M. H., & Zulkifly, M. I. (2019). Tourism destination competitiveness and tourism performance: A secondary data approach. *Competitiveness Review*, *29*(5), 592–621. DOI: 10.1108/CR-07-2018-0045

Hof, A., & Blazquez-Salom, M. (2015). Changing tourism patterns, capital accumulation, and urban water consumption in Mallorca, Spain: A sustainability fix? *Journal of Sustainable Tourism*, *23*(5), 770–796. DOI: 10.1080/09669582.2014.991397

Ibrahim, M. (2024). Foreign direct investment in tourism: A systematic review of literature. *Journal of Tourism Quarterly*, *6*(1-2), 32–38.

Isik, C. (2015). Foreign Direct Investment in Tourism: Panel Data Analysis of D7 Countries. *Athens Journal of Tourism*, *2*(2), 93–103. DOI: 10.30958/ajt.2-2-2

Isık, C., Islam, H., Ongan, S., Sengoz, A., & Usanmaz, B. (2025). Artificial intelligence (AI) interacted ESG-based sustainable tourism: Economic insights. *Tourism Economics*, *0*(0), 1–22. DOI: 10.1177/13548166251346306

Jonsson, H. C. (Ed.). (2022). *Tourism and Foreign Direct Investment: Issues, Challenges and Prospects* (1st ed.). Routledge., DOI: 10.4324/9781003155492

Kamalaveni, M. S., Suriya, A., Sakthivel, P., & Vignesh, S. (2021). Digital Transformation in Tourism. *International Journal of Advance and Innovative Research*, 8(4), ISSN 2394 – 7780.

Khan, A., Bibi, S., Lorenzo, A., Lyu, J., & Babar, Z. U. (2020). Tourism and Development in Developing Economies: A Policy Implication Perspective. *Sustainability*, *12*(4), 1618. DOI: 10.3390/su12041618

Li, X., Huang, S., & Song, C. (2017). China's outward foreign direct investment in tourism. *Tourism Management*, *59*, 1–6. DOI: 10.1016/j.tourman.2016.07.007

Lopez-Naranjo, A. L., Puente-Riofrio, M. I., Carrasco-Salazar, V. A., Erazo-Rodríguez, J. D., & Bunay-Guisnan, P. A. (2025). Artificial intelligence in the tourism business: A systematic review. *Frontiers in Artificial Intelligence*, *8*, 1599391. DOI: 10.3389/frai.2025.1599391 PMID: 40785835

Nunkoo, R., & Ramkissoon, H. (2010). Small island urban tourism: A residents' perspective. *Current Issues in Tourism, 13*(1), 37–60. DOI: 10.1080/13683500802499414

Nunkoo, R., & Seetanah, B. (2018) Foreign Direct Investment and Tourism Development: A Theoretical and Empirical Review. *The SAGE Handbook of Tourism Management: Theories, Concepts and Disciplinary Approaches to Tourism*, 556-566.

OECD. (2020). *OECD Tourism Trends and Policies 2020*. OECD Publishing., DOI: 10.1787/6b47b985-

OECD. (2024). *Artificial Intelligence and tourism: G7/ OECD policy paper. OECD Tourism Papers, 2024/02*. OECD Publishing., DOI: 10.1787/3f9a4d8d-

Satrovic, E., & Muslija, A. (2019). Causality relationship between foreign direct investment and tourism. *Uluslararası Iktisadi ve Idari Incelemeler Dergisi, 22*, 65–76. DOI: 10.18092/ulikidince.418132

Seetanah, B. (2011). Assessing the Dynamic Economic Impact of Tourism for Island Economies. *Annals of Tourism Research, 38*(1), 291–308. DOI: 10.1016/j.annals.2010.08.009

Sharma, K., Jain, M., & Dhir, S. (2022). Analysing the impact of artificial intelligence on the competitiveness of tourism firms: A modified total interpretive structural modeling (m-TISM) approach. *International Journal of Emerging Markets, 17*(4), 1067–1084. DOI: 10.1108/IJOEM-05-2021-0810

Siddik, A. B., Forid, M. S., Yong, L., Du, A. M., & Goodell, J. W. (2025). Artificial intelligence as a catalyst for sustainable tourism growth and economic cycles. *Technological Forecasting and Social Change, 210*, 123875. DOI: 10.1016/j.techfore.2024.123875

Snyman, J. A., & Saayman, M. (2009). Key factors influencing foreign direct investment in the tourism industry in South Africa. *Tourism Review, 64*(3), 49–58. DOI: 10.1108/16605370910988827

Sokhanvar, A. (2022). The Role of Tourism and FDI in the Economic Growth of EU11 Countries. *Tourism and Hospitality Management, 28*(2), 343–359. DOI: 10.20867/thm.28.2.5

Sokhanvar, A., & Jenkins, G. P. (2022). Impact of foreign direct investment and international tourism on long-run economic growth of Estonia. *Journal of Economic Studies (Glasgow, Scotland), 49*(2), 364–378. DOI: 10.1108/JES-11-2020-0543

Tang, S., Selvanathan, E. A., & Selvanathan, S. (2007). The Relationship between Foreign Direct Investment and Tourism: Empirical Evidence from China. *Tourism Economics*, *13*(1), 25–39. DOI: 10.5367/000000007779784498

Tong, L., Yan, W., & Manta, O. (2022). Artificial Intelligence Influences Intelligent Automation in Tourism: A Mediating Role of Internet of Things and Environmental, Social, and Governance Investment. *Frontiers in Environmental Science*, *10*, 853302. DOI: 10.3389/fenvs.2022.853302

UNCTAD. (2007). *FDI in Tourism: The Development Dimension*. United Nations.

Xu, A., Siddik, A. B., Sobhani, F. A., & Rahman, M. (2024). Driving economic success: Fintech, tourism, FDI, and digitalization in the top 10 tourist destinations. *Humanities & Social Sciences Communications*, *11*(1). Advance online publication. DOI: 10.1057/s41599-024-03978-3

Zhou, X., & Choi, C. H. (2025). Tourism Development, Foreign Direct Investment, and Environmental Sustainability: How Green Technology Innovations Make a Difference. *SAGE Open*, *15*(2). Advance online publication. DOI: 10.1177/21582440251331003

Chapter 12
Resilience in Tourism, Real Estate, and Mixed-Use Developments:
A KPI- and ESG-Based Framework for Managing Disruption

Ioannis Anastasopoulos
https://orcid.org/0009-0003-6430-5831
University of Piraeus, Greece

Georgios Tsoupros
https://orcid.org/0009-0001-7143-8507
University of Piraeus, Greece

Sotirios Varelas
https://orcid.org/0000-0003-4580-3256
University of Piraeus, Greece

Georgios A. Deirmentzoglou
https://orcid.org/0000-0003-1687-0708
Neapolis University Pafos, Cyprus

Eleni E. Anastasopoulou
Neapolis University Pafos, Cyprus

ABSTRACT

This chapter centers resilience in strategic decision making for tourism real estate (TRE) and mixed-use developments and proposes a concise, desk-based framework for turbulent conditions. It combines a compact set of key performance indicators

DOI: 10.4018/979-8-3373-6991-4.ch012

that pair early signals with lagging measures and link each to thresholds and managerial actions. Environmental, social, and governance practices serve as risk drivers and financing enablers, with targets for energy and water intensity, waste diversion, local employment, and governance cadence. A data-light analytics layer uses exports from property management, point-of-sale, and energy systems to trigger timely adjustments in pricing, staffing, procurement, maintenance, and capital planning. Adapting Balanced Scorecard logic at project scale, the framework ties measurement to regular review rhythms. The contribution is a repeatable system that aligns financial performance, operational reliability, sustainability outcomes, and stakeholder legitimacy. Scope is general, limitations are conceptual, and the chapter does not report new field data.

1. INTRODUCTION

Entrepreneurial activity in tourism real estate and mixed-use developments now unfolds amid persistent turbulence: abrupt demand swings, cost and interest rate volatility, supply chain fragility, climate-related disruptions, and tightening regulatory expectations. Strategy in this context cannot be designed only for steady growth; it must also be built to absorb shocks, adapt, and recover quickly, that is, to institutionalize resilience as an explicit managerial capability (Hall, Prayag and Amore, 2017). Tourism real estate is distinct from standalone hospitality because it combines accommodation with residential, retail, wellness, recreation, and public-realm elements over long horizons and with visible community footprints. These ventures are capital intensive, socially salient, and materially exposed to environmental and stakeholder risks (Keller and Bieger, 2017; Geva, & Siemiatycki, 2024).

Conventional toolkits such as financial ratios, static feasibility studies, and a narrow focus on occupancy, ADR, and RevPAR remain necessary but are no longer sufficient. They privilege lagging indicators, treat sustainability as a compliance afterthought, and offer limited guidance on how routines should change when conditions deteriorate or normalize (Assaf and Tsionas, 2018; Sainaghi, Phillips and Zavarrone, 2017). At the same time, influential perspectives in strategy and sustainability emphasize firm-specific resources and capabilities (Barney and Hesterly, 2019), stewardship of natural resources as a source of advantage (Hart, 1995), and stakeholder legitimacy as a precondition for durable performance (Freeman, 2010). Yet these perspectives often stop short of prescribing a compact, repeatable measurement-and-action system suitable for entrepreneurial teams with limited data and analytical capacity. Meta-evidence further indicates that robust environmental, social, and governance performance is positively associated with financial outcomes across a large share of empirical studies, reinforcing the treatment of ESG as both a risk lens and a financing lever in investment strategy (Friede, Busch and Bassen, 2015).

This chapter translates those insights into a concise, literature-based framework that founders, owners, and managers can use to monitor vulnerabilities, trigger timely responses, and finance improvements without heavy technical infrastructure. The framework integrates three elements. First, a disciplined set of key performance indicators that blends leading signals, such as booking-curve slope, service-failure recovery time, supplier lead-time variability, and disruption alerts, with essential lagging indicators, including revenue volatility, interest coverage, and downtime after extreme weather. Each indicator is linked to decision thresholds and preagreed actions so that early warnings lead to concrete steps in pricing, staffing, procurement, maintenance, or contingency capital spending (Phillips and Moutinho, 2014; Altin et al., 2018). Second, environmental, social, and governance practices are treated as risk drivers and financing enablers rather than add-ons. Credible targets for energy and water intensity, waste diversion, and local employment strengthen operational robustness and can improve access to capital when eligibility criteria are satisfied (Bramwell et al., 2017; Cavagnaro & Curiel, 2022; Kaplan and Norton, 2007). Third, a data-light analytics layer, assisted by simple AI tools where appropriate, prioritizes near-term demand sensing, calibrated price adjustments, basic predictive maintenance, and straightforward energy and water optimization. The emphasis is practicality: routines executable with exports from common property and energy systems and spreadsheet-level processing, escalating to advanced methods only when the incremental benefit is clear (Teece, 2007).

This resilience orientation matters for both performance and legitimacy. Ventures that lack explicit sensing and response routines often react late to demand or cost inflections, underinvest in “no-regret” preparedness such as supplier diversification and staff cross-training, and overlook financing opportunities linked to verifiable sustainability targets (Baum, 2018; Baum and Hai, 2020; Rivera, Croes and Lee, 2016). Conversely, organizations that institutionalize a small dashboard and a few well-rehearsed playbooks shorten time to decision, protect cash, preserve guest experience, and reduce recovery time after shocks (Chathoth et al., 2020; Sainaghi and Baggio, 2020). Recent contributions across hospitality performance measurement, sustainability governance, and mixed-use development converge on the need for integrated approaches that connect operations, finance, environmental stewardship, and stakeholder engagement; the framework offered here aims to make that integration operational for entrepreneurial settings (Keller and Bieger, 2017; Geva, & Siemiatycki, 2024).

Methodologically, the chapter is conceptual and desk-based. It synthesizes peer-reviewed research across entrepreneurship, tourism and hospitality management, real estate and urban development, operations and digital transformation, and sustainable finance. Sources are screened for construct clarity and measurement relevance, and evidence is organized around concepts rather than individual studies to show where findings align and where practice-oriented guidance remains under-specified. No new field data are collected, and the limitations of this approach are acknowledged.

The remainder of the chapter clarifies the constructs of resilience in tourism real estate and mixed-use development, positions ESG as both a risk lens and a financing lever, and then presents the proposed framework with its governance roles, indicator definitions, and update cadence. It links early signals to concrete operational and financial actions and closes with ecosystem enablers, specifically skills, proportionate data sharing, and finance instruments that make adoption feasible. The objective is straightforward: a clear path for ventures to detect risks earlier, adjust faster, and sustain performance under uncertainty, aligned with the volume's focus on entrepreneurial resilience in turbulent, globalized economies. This positioning is consistent with recent scholarship that reframes tourism investment as a governance hub for KPI-linked decision-making and stakeholder legitimacy in TRE and mixed-use contexts (Anastasopoulos, 2025).

2. LITERATURE REVIEW

2.1 Tourism Real Estate and Strategic Investment Context

Tourism real estate (TRE) comprises assets designed for tourism use, including hotels, resorts, second homes, and mixed-use vacation villages, whose value proposition straddles hospitality operations and property development, positioning TRE at the intersection of land use planning and tourism (Tosun and Jenkins, 1998). Over the past two decades, TRE has evolved from single purpose facilities to complex, master planned environments that curate composite experiences, embedding value in location, design, and the staged customer journey (Pine and Gilmore, 2022; Stringam, 2010). The asset class has expanded with branded communities and mixed-use complexes that can catalyze regional transformation, particularly in coastal and amenity rich destinations (; Keller and Bieger, 2017; Lowies et al., 2018). Given high capital intensity and long holding periods, TRE routinely employs hybrid financing and governance arrangements, including public-private partnerships and multi owner structures, that complicate risk allocation and performance management (DiPasquale and Wheaton, 1996; Kaplan and Norton, 2008; Grimsey and Lewis, 2004).

TRE differs from standalone hospitality through its functional breadth, combining accommodation with residential, retail, wellness, recreation, and public realm uses, and through its visible community footprint. Master planning seeks both revenue diversification and placemaking benefits, but this breadth also increases exposure to supply chain fragility, interest rate cycles, climate related shocks, and stakeholder scrutiny (Lockyer, 2005; Keller and Bieger, 2017; Geva, & Siemiatycki, 2024; Gössling, Scott and Hall, 2020; Carmona, 2021). Traditional feasibility toolkits remain necessary, such as ROI and NPV as well as ADR and RevPAR, but are insufficient on their own because they privilege lagging indicators and rarely connect measurement to timely managerial responses under turbulence. Destination competitiveness scholarship likewise stresses that long run performance depends on the coordinated quality of resources, policy, infrastructure, and management, which strengthens the case for integrated evaluation at project scale in TRE (Ritchie and Crouch, 2003).

Contemporary strategy perspectives inform a more resilient approach. The resource based view highlights firm specific assets, for example privileged sites, architectural distinctiveness, and relational capital, as sources of advantage, while dynamic capabilities emphasize sensing, seizing, and reconfiguring under change (Barney and Hesterly, 2019; Helfat and Peteraf, 2003; Grant, 2024). The natural resource based view reframes environmental stewardship, including energy and water efficiency, biodiversity protection, and circularity, as strategic capability rather than compliance (Hart, 1995). Stakeholder theory makes legitimacy a performance precondition for projects with enduring local footprints, placing structured engagement and transparent governance at the core of execution (Freeman, 2010; Clarkson, 1995). Meta analytic evidence also indicates a positive association between corporate social and environmental performance and financial performance, supporting the treatment of ESG as both a risk lens and a financing lever in TRE (Orlitzky, Schmidt and Rynes, 2003). In multi-ownership and fractional-ownership formats, governance complexity and service-quality coordination intensify, heightening the need for decision-linked metrics and codified stakeholder protocols (Warnken and Guilding, 2009; Lowies et al., 2018).

Taken together, these strands imply that TRE strategy should institutionalize resilience as an operating norm through concise, decision linked measurement and governance. In practical terms, this means replacing ad hoc monitoring with a compact KPI dashboard that blends leading signals, such as booking curve slope, supplier lead time variability, and service recovery time, with essential lagging indicators, such as revenue volatility, interest coverage, and post event downtime, each tied to predefined actions in pricing, staffing, procurement, maintenance, and contingency capital allocation. It also means treating ESG targets as risk drivers and financing enablers, not afterthoughts, and adopting a data-light analytics layer drawn from readily available system exports and spreadsheet level processing, escalating to advanced methods only when justified, to support near term demand sensing and resource optimization. Because mixed-use assets operate within destination systems, aligning project level KPIs with destination level governance and infrastructure quality improves strategic fit and long term competitiveness (Ritchie and Crouch, 2003; Keller and Bieger, 2017). This integrated stance aligns the mixed operational and asset nature of TRE with the volume's emphasis on entrepreneurial resilience in turbulent, globalized conditions.

2.2 Strategic Management in Real Estate Enterprises

In tourism real estate (TRE), effective strategy integrates three complementary lenses, namely resource-based advantage, dynamic adaptation, and stakeholder legitimacy, under governance that converts measurement into action. The resource-based view (RBV) explains persistent performance differences through firm-specific assets that are valuable, rare, inimitable, and organized, such as privileged sites, distinctive architecture, embedded regulatory know-how, and relational capital with operators, financiers, and local authorities (Wernerfelt, 1984; Barney and Hesterly, 2019). VRIO logic fits TRE portfolios where land-bank quality, design distinctiveness, and trust-based partnerships create entry barriers and pricing power. RBV alone is not sufficient for turbulent markets. Policy shifts, climate-related shocks, and demand volatility require dynamic capabilities, that is, repeatable routines by which firms sense change, seize opportunities, and reconfigure asset and operating models (Helfat and Peteraf, 2003; Teece, 2007; Eisenhardt and Martin, 2017; Grant, 2024). In mixed-use destinations, this includes repurposing space, rebalancing tenant and guest mixes, renegotiating supply contracts, and retiming capital expenditure.

A second pillar is the natural resource-based view (NRBV), which reframes environmental stewardship as strategy rather than compliance. Energy and water efficiency, biodiversity safeguards, and circularity practices reduce operating risk and volatility while differentiating the project in capital and consumer markets (Hart, 1995; Delmas and Toffel, 2008). In practice, ESG objectives should be tied to measurable targets, for example intensity metrics, diversion rates, and local procurement shares, and, where eligibility criteria are met, linked to sustainability-linked financing that can lower the cost of capital.

Third, stakeholder theory situates legitimacy as a precondition for durable performance in developments with visible community footprints (Freeman, 2010). Early, structured engagement that includes stakeholder mapping, clear benefit narratives, and transparent reporting reduces permitting friction and reputational risk, supports co-creation of public-realm amenities, and strengthens the social license to operate (Clarkson, 1995; Mitchell, Agle, and Wood, 1997; Bryson, 2018). Strategic fit then connects these lenses to context. Capabilities and ambitions must align with destination attributes, governance regimes, and demand structure across accommodation, residential, retail, wellness, and leisure components (Grant, 2024).

Operationalizing this layered perspective requires a compact, decision-linked management system rather than long checklists. We emphasize three elements. First, a KPI set that blends leading signals, such as booking-curve slope, supplier lead-time variability, and service-recovery time, with critical lagging indicators, such as revenue volatility, interest coverage, and post-event downtime, each tied to predefined playbooks in pricing, staffing, procurement, maintenance, and contingency capital expenditure. Second, ESG targets embedded as risk drivers and financing levers with documented measurement. Third, a data-light analytics layer grounded in exports from property and energy systems and spreadsheet-level processing that escalates to advanced tools only when incremental benefit is clear. In sum, TRE strategy is not merely selecting projects with attractive IRRs. It is the disciplined orchestration of resources, adaptation routines, and stakeholder governance so that resilience is institutionalized in everyday decisions (Barney and Hesterly, 2019; Helfat and Peteraf, 2003; Hart, 1995; Freeman, 2010; Eisenhardt and Martin, 2017; Delmas and Toffel, 2008; Grant, 2024; Teece, 2007).

2.3 KPIs in Tourism and Real Estate Investment Evaluation

Evaluating tourism real estate (TRE) performance requires a multidimensional indicator set that integrates financial, operational, environmental, governance, and stakeholder perspectives. Traditional financial KPIs, such as return on investment (ROI), internal rate of return (IRR), net present value (NPV), occupancy, average daily rate (ADR), and revenue per available room (RevPAR), remain foundational for feasibility and portfolio benchmarking. In volatile settings marked by demand shocks, input-cost swings, and regulatory change, static ratio analysis centered on lagging indicators is not sufficient for managerial control and timely course correction (DiPasquale and Wheaton, 1996; ; Neely, Gregory and Platts, 2005). Beyond capital returns, performance hinges on execution quality, resilience capacity, and legitimacy in the eyes of guests, employees, investors, communities, and regulators.

Contemporary TRE dashboards therefore incorporate leading indicators that anticipate pressure on cash and service quality, for example booking-curve slope, cancellation momentum, supply lead-time variability, and maintenance-backlog growth, alongside the necessary lagging indicators, for example RevPAR volatility, EBITDA-margin drift, and downtime after disruptions. Operational KPIs such as service-failure recovery time, first-contact resolution rate, and schedule variance translate day to day routines into measurable reliability (Assaf and Tsionas, 2018; Sainaghi, Phillips and Zavarrone, 2017; Bitner, 1990). Stakeholder-oriented metrics capture perceived value and social license, including guest satisfaction and Net Promoter Score (NPS), complaint-resolution cycle time, employee retention and training intensity, local procurement share, and community-sentiment signals from formal consultations (Parasuraman, Zeithaml and Berry, 1988; Barber and Scarcelli, 2010; Clarkson, 1995).

Environmental, social, and governance (ESG) indicators are increasingly treated as core risk drivers and financing enablers rather than compliance add-ons. Quantified targets for energy and water intensity per guest, greenhouse gas emissions estimates, waste diversion, ecosystem protection, and local employment link operations to measurable stewardship and to eligibility for sustainability-linked instruments when criteria are satisfied (Hart, 1995; Laine, Tregidga and Unerman, 2021; Cavagnaro & Curiel, 2022). Aligning these with relevant UN Sustainable Development Goals improves comparability across projects and clarifies trade-offs between short-term yield and long-term resilience (UNWTO, 2018).

A Balanced Scorecard logic provides a practical scaffold to integrate these perspectives into a single, repeatable measurement-and-action system that connects customer outcomes, internal processes, learning and capability development, and financial results (Kaplan and Norton, 2007, 2008; Niven, 2014). In this configuration, leading indicators trigger predefined managerial responses, such as pricing, staffing, procurement, or preventive maintenance, before financial ratios deteriorate. Governance KPIs, for example audit-closure rates, risk-register hygiene, and stakeholder-engagement cadence, reinforce accountability and shorten time to decision. Evidence from performance-measurement research consistently supports such integrated dashboards as superior to siloed financial tracking for detecting weak signals and shortening recovery after shocks (Altin et al., 2018; Marr, 2012).

In practice, data parsimony matters. Entrepreneurial TRE ventures can implement a compact dashboard sourced from existing systems, including property-management, point-of-sale, and energy meters, and spreadsheet-level processing, escalating to advanced analytics only where incremental value is clear. The aim is not maximal data collection, but a disciplined blend of leading and lagging KPIs that converts early signals into timely operational and financial actions while embedding ESG and stakeholder legitimacy as measurable pillars of long-term competitiveness.

2.4 Identified Gaps in the Literature and Rationale for the Framework

Despite substantial work on tourism, hospitality, and real estate strategy, there is no widely adopted, integrative model that translates resilience into a compact, KPI-driven system tailored to tourism real estate (TRE) and mixed-use developments. Existing strands, including project finance and market feasibility (DiPasquale and Wheaton, 1996;), resource-based and dynamic-capabilities perspectives (Barney, 2000; Wernerfelt, 1984; Helfat and Peteraf, 2003), the natural resource-based view (Hart, 1995), and stakeholder legitimacy and governance (Clarkson, 1995; Freeman,

2010), offer powerful concepts but remain fragmented at the point of managerial execution. In practice, performance management is still dominated by lagging financials, for example ROI, IRR, and RevPAR, and static feasibility studies, with limited guidance on how to connect early operational signals to pre-agreed actions or how to embed ESG into day to day control systems (Assaf and Tsionas, 2018; Sainaghi, Phillips and Zavarrone, 2017; March and Sutton, 1997).

Four gaps are recurrent. First, measurement integration is limited. The literature seldom combines leading and lagging indicators into a single, repeatable dashboard that links thresholds to operational and financial playbooks, particularly under volatility, supply-chain fragility, and climate-related shocks (Folke, Carpenter, Walker, Scheffer, Chapin, and Rockström, 2010). Second, ESG is rarely operationalized as a risk and finance lever. While stewardship and legitimacy are theorized, empirically grounded ways to embed ESG targets, for example energy and water intensity per guest and local employment, within capital decisions such as eligibility for sustainability-linked instruments are under-specified (Laine, Tregidga and Unerman, 2021). Third, governance cadence is often missing. Strategy tools like the Balanced Scorecard are acknowledged but rarely adapted to TRE's multi-actor governance and long asset horizons, where indicator owners, update frequency, and escalation paths must be defined explicitly (Kaplan and Norton, 2007, 2008; Niven, 2014). Fourth, implementation parsimony is neglected. Many prescriptions assume rich data and analytics, whereas entrepreneurial ventures need data-light routines executable from property-management systems, point-of-sale exports, and basic energy meters, escalating to advanced analytics only when incremental value is demonstrable (Marr, 2012).

The framework advanced in this chapter addresses these gaps by specifying a compact, resilience-oriented indicator set that blends leading and lagging KPIs and ties each to decision thresholds and concrete actions. It treats ESG metrics as core risk drivers and financing enablers aligned, where appropriate, with SDG-relevant themes to improve comparability and access to capital. It embeds a clear governance cadence, including roles, update frequency, and escalation, within a Balanced Scorecard logic. Finally, it prioritizes implementation parsimony so that ventures can start with existing data and spreadsheet-level processing. Grounded in established strategy and sustainability theories, including RBV, NRBV, and stakeholder governance, and informed by performance-measurement research in hospitality and TRE, the contribution is a practical, literature-based measurement-and-action system designed for volatile contexts and entrepreneurial resource constraints (Folke et al., 2010; Laine, Tregidga and Unerman, 2021; Marr, 2012; Grant, 2024).

3. PROPOSED CONCEPTUAL FRAMEWORK

This chapter advances an integrative, KPI based framework that operationalizes resilience for tourism real estate (TRE) and mixed use developments. Building on Balanced Scorecard logic that links strategy to execution (Kaplan and Norton, 2007, 2008), the framework explains how contextual inputs feed structured processes, how these processes are monitored through a parsimonious set of leading and lagging indicators, and how measured results trigger learning and recalibration. It responds to calls for sustainability aligned performance systems (Bramwell et al., 2017) by embedding dynamic capabilities, namely sensing, seizing, and transforming (Teece, 2007), together with shared value thinking (Porter and Kramer, 2011) inside governance routines suitable for multi actor, long horizon assets. The emphasis is practicality: routines are designed to run on data already available in property management system (PMS), point of sale (POS), and energy systems with spreadsheet level analytics, and only escalate to advanced tools when the marginal benefit is clear (Altin et al., 2018). The emphasis on governance cadence and parsimonious, data light routines also aligns with recent scholarship that advocates practicable, KPI anchored execution for tourism real estate and mixed-use developments (Anastasopoulos, 2025).

The framework unfolds across four interlinked stages, namely Inputs, Processes, KPIs, and Performance Evaluation, which together form a continuous management cycle. Inputs establish the strategic context and the bounds of feasible action. Internally, assets and capabilities are assessed through a resource based lens, including site control and capital structure, the quality of governance and stakeholder relationships, and know how that spans development, hospitality, and community engagement (Barney, 2000; Barney and Hesterly, 2019; Helfat and Peteraf, 2003). The natural resource based view adds environmental assets and liabilities to this picture, including exposure to climate hazards, energy and water baselines, and biodiversity constraints, and treats eco efficiency and stewardship as potential sources of advantage (Hart, 1995). Externally, inputs cover demand structure and volatility, supply chain reliability, regulatory and financing conditions, including potential eligibility for sustainability linked instruments, and the social license to operate (Freeman, 2010; Clarkson, 1995; Keller and Bieger, 2017). The output is a concise resilience brief that maps risks and capabilities, records binding constraints, and states the fit assumptions that later stages will test (Grant, 2024; Phillips and Moutinho, 2014).

Strategy formulation incorporates explicit downside scenarios; participatory planning surfaces stakeholder priorities and reduces future resistance (Freeman, 2010; Bryson, 2018); project governance allocates decision rights, escalation paths, and review cadence; and implementation proceeds through short plan, do, check, act cycles with clear contingency playbooks (Deming, 2018). Dynamic capability routines make this concrete: teams track booking curve slope and supplier lead time variability to sense change, adjust price and inventory to seize opportunities, and diversify suppliers or cross train staff to transform the operating model as needed (Teece, 2007). Structure and process are kept conceptually distinct to avoid the familiar pitfall that structure alone does not constitute organization (Waterman, Peters, and Phillips, 1980). Risk governance follows enterprise risk management principles so that indicators, limits, and responses remain coherent across functions (COSO, 2017).

A compact set of indicators spans financial, operational, sustainability, and governance domains with clear definitions, data sources, and decision thresholds. Leading indicators such as booking curve changes, service recovery times, and climate event alerts are paired with essential lagging indicators such as revenue or RevPAR volatility, interest coverage, and downtime after extreme weather. The pairing ensures that early signals translate into predefined actions in pricing, staffing, procurement, maintenance, or contingency capital expenditure (Sainaghi, Phillips and Zavarrone, 2017; Phillips and Moutinho, 2014). Sustainability metrics align with SDG relevant themes, including energy and water intensity per guest, waste diversion, and local employment, to support comparability and credibility (Cavagnaro & Curiel, 2022; Bramwell et al., 2017). Where relevant, environmental metrics follow recognized accounting guidance to enable assurance and access to sustainability linked finance (ICMA, 2020).

Results are reviewed on a fixed cadence using rolling dashboards, threshold based alerts, and scenario testing. Variances trigger root cause analysis and corrective actions, which ties measurement directly to execution (Kaplan and Norton, 2007; Niven, 2014). Transparent reporting on sustainability and governance indicators strengthens legitimacy with lenders, investors, communities, and regulators, and can support access to favorable financing when eligibility criteria are satisfied (Porter and Kramer, 2011; Kaplan and Norton, 2008; ICMA, 2020).

Within this architecture, four KPI categories provide focus without bloat. Economic indicators, including ROI, NPV, IRR, RevPAR for hospitality components, and rental or sales yields for other uses, anchor feasibility and portfolio choices across short and long horizons (Kaplan and Norton, 2008; Phillips and Moutinho, 2014). Operational indicators, such as schedule variance, cost per unit, occupancy dynamics, service recovery time, complaint resolution time, and guest experience measures like satisfaction or NPS, deliver real time feedback on execution quality (Sainaghi, Phillips and Zavarrone, 2017; Assaf and Tsionas, 2018). Sustainability indicators, including energy and water intensity, estimates of greenhouse gas emissions, waste diversion, local employment share, and supplier diversity, embed the natural resource based view into routine tracking and align with SDG relevant themes (Hart, 1995; Bramwell et al., 2017; Cavagnaro & Curiel, 2022). Governance indicators, such as compliance indices, completion of internal and external audits, the frequency and quality of stakeholder engagements, risk management maturity, and transparency measures, sustain accountability and adaptability in multi-actor settings (Porter and Kramer, 2011; Kaplan and Norton, 2007; Waterman et al., 1980; COSO, 2017).

Table 1. Overview of KPI Categories and Their Strategic Relevance

KPI Category	Example Metrics	Strategic Focus (Framework Phase)
Economic	ROI, IRR, NPV, RevPAR, rental/sales yield	Financial feasibility and portfolio value (Inputs and Evaluation)
Operational	Schedule variance, cost per unit, occupancy dynamics, service-recovery time, guest-experience indicators	Process efficiency and service quality (Processes and KPI monitoring)
Sustainability	Energy/water intensity, GHG estimate, waste diversion, local employment share	ESG integration and long-term impact (Inputs and Evaluation)
Governance	Compliance index, audit completion, stakeholder-engagement cadence, risk-maturity score, transparency indicators	Decision accountability and institutional trust (All stages)

Note. Each KPI should include a definition, data source, update frequency, and threshold-linked actions. Leading indicators are paired with lagging outcomes to shorten time to decision, protect liquidity, and reduce recovery time after shocks.

Source. Authors' synthesis of the literature (Kaplan and Norton, 2007; Teece, 2007; Sainaghi, Phillips and Zavarrone, 2017; COSO, 2017).

To translate the framework into day to day practice, management should assign clear ownership for each KPI, that is an accountable A and a responsible R, codify a review cadence that distinguishes monthly operating reviews from quarterly strategy recalibration, and maintain an action register mapping thresholds to specific interventions. Monthly reviews focus on leading indicators and service reliability, for example booking curve changes, service recovery times, and supply lead time variability, while quarterly reviews test structural assumptions via scenario and stress analysis, for example demand shocks, cost of capital shifts, and climate event downtime. A lightweight data quality protocol that covers completeness, timeliness, consistency, and basic outlier handling should accompany every dashboard refresh, with version controlled definitions and source logs to preserve reproducibility. Where eligibility criteria are met, sustainability targets, for example energy and water intensity, waste diversion, and local employment share, can be linked to sustainability linked finance, aligning operational routines with funding incentives (ICMA, 2020). This governance discipline anchors the dashboard to playbook link: early signals trigger named actions in pricing, staffing, procurement, preventive maintenance, and contingency capital expenditure, with after action reviews to reinforce organizational learning (Deming, 2018; COSO, 2017).

Following Table 1, the analysis proceeds to integrated performance evaluation, in which economic, operational, environmental, and governance results are assessed jointly rather than in isolation. In practice, management teams apply Balanced Scorecard logic. Financial indicators such as ROI and RevPAR are interpreted alongside resource efficiency metrics, for example energy and water intensity, compliance and transparency indices, and stakeholder satisfaction measures. This shifts the definition of success from narrow profitability to sustainable value, consistent with shared value reasoning and the triple bottom line perspective (Kaplan and Norton, 2007; Porter and Kramer, 2011; Cavagnaro & Curiel, 2022; Bramwell et al., 2017).

Evaluation is executed with explicit cadence and governance. Monthly operational reviews and quarterly strategic meetings use predefined thresholds for leading and lagging indicators, named accountability for each metric, and a documented action rule that links every signal to specific interventions in pricing, staffing, procurement, maintenance, taxonomy aligned and sustainability linked capital expenditures. Decisions are recorded with an audit trail to support reproducibility and organizational learning, including version controlled KPI definitions and data source logs (Niven, 2014). Basic data quality controls accompany scenario analysis and stress testing that probe sensitivities to demand shocks, cost of capital, and supply chain constraints, considerations that are especially material in capital intensive, place based developments (Assaf and Tsionas, 2018; Sainaghi, Phillips and Zavarrone, 2017).

Feedback is not limited to reporting results, it triggers resource reallocation and routine revision. Adopting a sense, seize, transform posture, teams update assumptions, refine the indicator set as conditions change, and revise playbooks accordingly, an expression of dynamic capabilities under uncertainty (Teece, 2007). Transparent disclosure of progress, particularly on ESG and governance indicators, strengthens legitimacy with investors, communities, and regulators and can facilitate access to favorable financing when eligibility criteria are met (Kaplan and Norton, 2008; Clarkson, 1995; Freeman, 2010; ICMA, 2020). Environmental performance is treated not as a compliance cost but as a strategic resource in the spirit of the natural resource based view. Credible targets for energy and water intensity, waste diversion, and local employment enhance both resilience and investment attractiveness (Hart, 1995; Keller and Bieger, 2017).

Overall, the sequence from inputs to processes, KPIs, and evaluation converts heterogeneous measures into timely managerial action. It shortens decision cycles, protects liquidity and guest experience, and reduces recovery time after shocks (Assaf and Tsionas, 2018; Sainaghi, Phillips and Zavarrone, 2017). By institutionalizing feedback, accountability, and substantive stakeholder engagement, the framework reinforces the competitiveness and credibility of tourism real estate investments, delivering not only financial returns but also durable social and environmental value (Porter and Kramer, 2011; Cavagnaro & Curiel, 2022; Bramwell et al., 2017).

Consider a mixed-use coastal development with hospitality, retail, and wellness components. Over two consecutive weeks, the booking curve slope for near term arrival windows flattens, cancellation momentum rises by 15 percent, and supplier lead time variability widens, while lagging indicators, including RevPAR and interest coverage, still appear stable. Under the framework, the monthly review flags a threshold breach on two leading indicators. The action register triggers calibrated price and inventory moves, for example targeted channel promotions and minimum stay adjustments, a temporary rebalance of labor rosters to protect service recovery times, and procurement diversification for at risk items. In parallel, the ESG dashboard shows energy intensity drift above the quarterly target. Maintenance schedules are adjusted to prioritize HVAC tuning and low cost retrofits, while a staff micro training addresses procedural causes of service failures. The next review documents outcomes, including demand pickup, service recovery normalization, and energy intensity reduction, in the audit trail and updates scenario assumptions. In this way, leading indicators consistently translate into timely interventions across operations, finance, and sustainability, while the audit trail preserves learning for subsequent cycles.

4. RESULTS

4.1 Theoretical and Practical Contributions

This subsection presents the implications and comparative advantages of the proposed KPI based framework for strategic management in tourism real estate (TRE) and mixed-use developments. It explains the framework's theoretical and practical contributions, clarifies how it diverges from existing strategic models in light of the gaps identified in Sections 2 and 3, and embeds explicit review cadences so that measurement reliably triggers action.

The framework advances strategy scholarship by making resilience, innovation, and sustainability measurable at the project level through a compact indicator system and explicit feedback loops. Whereas the Balanced Scorecard introduced multiple performance perspectives but did not fully operationalize sustainability or innovation as distinct, auditable dimensions (Kaplan and Norton, 2007), the present design integrates Environmental, Social, and Governance indicators and innovation KPIs as first class constructs aligned with triple bottom line logic (Elkington, 1997). In tourism specifically, innovation is treated not as a diffuse aspiration but as an outcome observable through the rate of new service introductions, the adoption of enabling technologies, and the cadence of structured learning, for example after action reviews, an approach consistent with accounts of tourism innovation dynamics (Hjalager, 2010) yet translated here into KPI definitions suitable for ongoing governance.

Sustainability is similarly reframed from compliance to strategic capability. Drawing on legitimacy theory and stakeholder perspectives (Suchman, 1995; Clarkson, 1995), the framework embeds metrics on energy and water intensity, estimated greenhouse gas emissions, waste diversion, local employment share, and supplier diversity, together with indicators of stakeholder engagement quality. These measures resonate with calls for integrated sustainability governance in tourism (Bramwell and Lane, 2011) and support destination scale accountability while remaining implementable at project level. By linking thresholds on these KPIs to pre agreed managerial actions and to a defined review cadence, the framework operationalizes sensing, seizing, and transforming routines within day to day decision making rather than treating them as high level aspirations.

Practically, the model equips decision makers with a unified, dashboard ready schema that spans financial viability, operational reliability, environmental performance, and stakeholder legitimacy. It enables transparent trade off analysis, for example comparing alternatives not only by NPV or RevPAR but also by resource efficiency and local employment generation, criteria that increasingly shape financing terms and community acceptance in mixed-use settings (Keller and Bieger, 2017). Because indicators are defined with data sources commonly available in property management system (PMS), point of sale (POS), and energy systems and are paired with threshold linked actions, the framework raises managerial responsiveness without presupposing heavy analytics infrastructure. In sum, it translates widely cited theoretical constructs into a repeatable measurement and action system that can be adopted by TRE ventures operating under uncertainty. This claim is consistent with hospitality performance syntheses showing that multi dimensional dashboards outperform financial only tracking for early signal detection and post shock recovery (Altin et al., 2018; Sainaghi, Phillips and Zavarrone, 2017).

4.2 Comparative Positioning of the Framework

Relative to traditional investment appraisals and destination competitiveness frameworks, the proposed KPI based framework adds project level granularity, a dynamic decision support cycle, and explicit integration of resilience, innovation, ESG, and stakeholder governance as coequal value dimensions (Kaplan and Norton, 2007; Keller and Bieger, 2017; Barney and Hesterly, 2019). Table 2 contrasts the focus and mechanics of these approaches. The intent is not to supplant established models, such as ROI and NPV feasibility analyses or destination indices (Dwyer and Kim, 2003), but to complement them with a compact, repeatable measurement and action system that is implementable by entrepreneurial teams.

Table 2. Comparative positioning of the KPI-based framework

Criterion	Traditional Investment Models (Tourism Real Estate)	Balanced Scorecard and Destination Models (Existing)	Proposed KPI-Based Framework (This Study)
Primary focus	Financial returns (ROI, NPV) and market feasibility; emphasis on short-term profitability and risk-adjusted returns (DiPasquale and Wheaton, 1996).	Multi-perspective focus (financial, customer, internal) for BSC; macro factors (resources, marketing, infrastructure) for destination models (Dwyer and Kim, 2003).	Multi-dimensional value (financial + innovation + sustainability + stakeholder) with resilience as an explicit objective; long-term value creation (Bryson, 2018; Porter and Kramer, 2011).
Innovation treatment	Largely implicit; effects inferred via financial projections; limited attention to knowledge-based assets (Hjalager, 2010).	Indirect: BSC "learning and growth" may include R&D; destination models recognize innovation but lack project-level KPIs (Pike and Page, 2014).	Explicit pillar with dedicated KPIs (e.g., new-service cadence, technology adoption, learning cycles) operationalized for governance (Altin et al., 2018).
Sustainability / ESG	Often absent or qualitative; externalities assessed only when mandated (Hart, 1995).	Emerging: Sustainability-BSC variants and destination models highlight ESG but frequently without micro-level measurement (Bramwell and Lane, 2011).	Fully embedded via measurable ESG KPIs (e.g., energy/ water intensity, GHG estimates, local employment), aligned to SDG-relevant themes (Cavagnaro & Curiel, 2022; Geva, & Siemiatycki, 2024).
Stakeholder orientation	Primarily investor-centric; other stakeholders considered if they affect returns (Freeman, 2010).	Broader but general: customers/employees (BSC); tourists/residents (destination models) with limited project specificity (Clarkson, 1995).	Multi-stakeholder metrics (investors, guests, employees, communities) with engagement cadence and legitimacy indicators (Bryson, 2018; Freeman, 2010).
Decision process	Static, outcome-oriented; go/no-go decisions on ROI/IRR thresholds (DiPasquale and Wheaton, 1996).	Dynamic execution emphasis (BSC) and macro policy/planning at destination level (Kaplan and Norton, 2007).	Dynamic, cyclical: continuous KPI monitoring, thresholds, and feedback loops that recalibrate operations and capital plans (Teece, 2007; Kaplan and Norton, 2008).

Note. The comparison highlights characteristic tendencies, implementations vary across organizations and destinations.

Source. Authors' synthesis of the literature (DiPasquale and Wheaton, 1996; Dwyer and Kim, 2003; Kaplan and Norton, 2007, 2008; Bryson, 2018; Porter and Kramer, 2011; Hjalager, 2010; Bramwell and Lane, 2011; Pike and Page, 2014; Altin et al., 2018; Cavagnaro & Curiel, 2022; Geva, & Siemiatycki, 2024; Freeman, 2010).

As Keller and Bieger (2017) underline, innovation and sustainability are now central to tourism real estate strategy. Yet both traditional appraisals and many destination models still treat these dimensions as qualitative adjuncts rather than as auditable, decision linked metrics. By aligning financial, operational, ESG, and stakeholder indicators within a unified schema, and by tying thresholds to pre agreed managerial actions, the proposed framework converts well known strategic constructs, RBV, NRBV, stakeholder legitimacy, into a practical, project scale routine (Barney and Hesterly, 2019; Hart, 1995; Freeman, 2010). In doing so, it helps bridge the long-standing gap between conceptual models and day to day investment governance in TRE (Rivera, Croes and Lee, 2016; Altin et al., 2018). This comparative positioning also reflects broader management evidence that continuous, indicator driven cycles reduce execution drift and shorten time to corrective action compared with static planning approaches (Niven, 2014; Kaplan and Norton, 2008).

4.3 Strategic Added Value for Tourism Investments

The proposed framework adds strategic value to tourism real estate and mixed-use developments by replacing single metric appraisal with a structured, multi criteria evaluation. Financial screens such as ROI, NPV, and RevPAR remain necessary, but they are read alongside indicators of stakeholder outcomes, resource efficiency, and innovation effort. This integrated view is particularly important in mixed-use and coastal settings, where externalities, place making effects, and long asset lives shape long term viability (; Keller and Bieger, 2017). By positioning non financial metrics as decision variables rather than post hoc disclosures, the framework broadens what value means at project level.

A second contribution concerns risk. By design, ESG and innovation KPIs operate as early warning signals that surface operational stress or strategic misalignment before they appear in lagging financials. Threshold linked responses, for example procurement diversification, calibrated pricing, and targeted maintenance, translate these signals into action, protecting liquidity and service quality. In parallel, the framework makes visible the intangible assets, capabilities, partner networks, and stakeholder relationships, that the resource based view identifies as foundations of sustained advantage, and it monitors their condition over time (Barney, 2000). In practical governance terms, naming an owner for each indicator and pre committing to action rules improves decision speed and auditability, which are recurrent predictors of resilience in service intensive settings (Kaplan and Norton, 2008; Niven, 2014).

Third, the framework improves strategic continuity. A single KPI spine connects board level intent with day to day execution through explicit ownership, review cadence, and decision rules. This reduces the recurring gap between strategy formulation and delivery that undermines performance in complex, multi-actor projects and supports reliability under uncertainty (Bryson, 2018). The same governance discipline underpins transparent reporting to investors, lenders, communities, and regulators, strengthening legitimacy and, where eligibility criteria are met, supporting access to favorable finance.

Finally, the framework institutionalizes benchmarking and organizational learning. Regular, evidence based reviews and documented feedback loops build cumulative knowledge and adaptive capacity, echoing findings on the role of structured knowledge processes in tourism firms' innovation and resilience (Cooper, 2006; Craig-Smith, Cooper and Ruhanen, 2004). Over successive cycles, teams refine assumptions, update indicators, and revise playbooks, yielding a repeatable measurement and action system rather than a one off assessment.

Taken together, these contributions synthesize stakeholder theory, sustainability governance, and innovation strategy into a practical apparatus for decision making in TRE. The result is a more credible path to durable performance, financial, social, and environmental, under the volatile conditions that characterize contemporary destination development (Keller and Bieger, 2017;).

5. CONCLUSION

This chapter concludes by presenting an integrative, KPI based framework that operationalizes resilience for tourism real estate and mixed-use developments, linking contextual inputs, governance processes, and a compact set of leading and lagging indicators to threshold based managerial actions. In contrast to traditional appraisals that privilege financial screens alone, the framework embeds ESG and innovation metrics as first class decision variables and ties them to explicit review cadences, shifting assessment from a static, ex post exercise to a dynamic, cyclical system of strategy execution (Kaplan and Norton, 2007, 2008; Elkington, 1997). In doing so, it aligns with calls for sustainability aligned, stakeholder aware approaches to destination development (Keller and Bieger, 2017; Bramwell and Lane, 2011).

The primary contribution is practical. The framework translates widely cited constructs from the resource based view, the natural resource based view, and stakeholder legitimacy into a repeatable measurement and action routine that can be implemented with data already available in property management system (PMS), point of sale (POS), and energy systems. Innovation is treated as an observable outcome, for example new service cadence, technology adoption, and learning cycles, and sustainability as a strategic capability, for example energy and water intensity, greenhouse gas estimates, local employment, and supplier diversity. Each indicator is linked to pre agreed actions and ownership. This enables transparent trade off analysis across financial performance, such as ROI, NPV, and RevPAR, resource efficiency, and stakeholder outcomes, improving capital allocation and legitimacy under uncertainty (Hjalager, 2010; Hart, 1995; Freeman, 2010).

A second contribution is conceptual integration. By embedding dynamic capabilities of sensing, seizing, and transforming within governance cadence and KPI thresholds, the framework specifies how organizations can shorten time to decision, protect liquidity and guest experience, and reduce recovery time after shocks. The resulting link from dashboard to playbook addresses the persistent gap between strategy formulation and delivery that undermines complex, multi-actor projects (Bryson, 2018; Teece, 2007).

Limitations are acknowledged. The design is desk based and general. Sector specific and locale specific indicator definitions and thresholds will require contextual calibration and data quality controls. Generalizability may vary by format, such as urban mixed-use versus resort communities, by regulatory regimes, and by data maturity. Transferability would benefit from multi site validation using common KPI definitions and externally benchmarked thresholds. Future research should validate the framework empirically across TRE formats and jurisdictions, develop sector specific benchmarks and resilience scorecards including reference ranges such as time to decision by asset type, test causal pathways between ESG and innovation KPI attainment and financing terms or risk adjusted returns, and examine ecosystem enablers such as skills, proportionate data sharing, and sustainability linked finance at destination scale. Comparative studies that contrast data light implementations with analytics intensive ones could clarify the marginal value of advanced tools under entrepreneurial constraints.

Overall, the framework contributes a pragmatic tool for practitioners and a structured synthesis for scholars. By coupling concise measurement with explicit feedback and accountability, it offers a credible path to durable performance, financial, social, and environmental, under the volatile conditions that characterize contemporary tourism real estate and mixed-use development (Keller and Bieger, 2017;).

REFERENCES

Altin, M., Koseoglu, M. A., Yu, X., & Riasi, A. (2018). Performance measurement and management research in the hospitality and tourism industry. *International Journal of Contemporary Hospitality Management, 30*(2), 1172–1189. DOI: 10.1108/IJCHM-05-2017-0251

Anastasopoulos, I. (2025). *Strategic management frameworks and policy approaches for tourism investment decision making: The case of tourism real estate and mixed use developments* (Doctoral dissertation, University of Piraeus). Hellenic National Archive of PhD Theses. https://doi.org/DOI: 10.12681/eadd/59316

Assaf, A. G., & Tsionas, M. (2018). Measuring hotel performance: Toward more rigorous evidence in both scope and methods. *Tourism Management, 69*, 69–87. DOI: 10.1016/j.tourman.2018.05.008

Barber, N., & Scarcelli, J. M. (2010). Enhancing the assessment of tangible service quality through the creation of a cleanliness measurement scale. *Managing Service Quality, 20*(1), 70–88. DOI: 10.1108/09604521011011630

Barney, J. B. (2000). Firm resources and sustained competitive advantage. In Baum, J. A. C., & Dobbin, F. (Eds.), *Economics meets sociology in strategic management* (pp. 203–227). Emerald Group Publishing Limited., DOI: 10.1016/S0742-3322(00)17018-4

Barney, J. B., & Hesterly, W. S. (2019). *Strategic management and competitive advantage: Concepts and cases* (6th ed.). Pearson.

Baum, T. (2018). Sustainable human resource management as a driver in tourism policy and planning: A serious sin of omission? *Journal of Sustainable Tourism, 26*(6), 873–889. DOI: 10.1080/09669582.2017.1423318

Baum, T., & Hai, N. T. T. (2020). Hospitality, tourism, human rights and the impact of COVID-19. *International Journal of Contemporary Hospitality Management, 32*(7), 2397–2407. DOI: 10.1108/IJCHM-03-2020-0242

Bitner, M. J. (1990). Evaluating service encounters: The effects of physical surroundings and employee responses. *Journal of Marketing, 54*(2), 69–82. DOI: 10.1177/002224299005400206

Bramwell, B., Higham, J., Lane, B., & Miller, G. (2017). Twenty-five years of sustainable tourism and the *Journal of Sustainable Tourism*: Looking back and moving forward. *Journal of Sustainable Tourism, 25*(1), 1–9. DOI: 10.1080/09669582.2017.1251689

Bramwell, B., & Lane, B. (2011). Critical research on the governance of tourism and sustainability. *Journal of Sustainable Tourism, 19*(4-5), 411–421. DOI: 10.1080/09669582.2011.580586

Bryson, J. M. (2018). Strategic planning for public and nonprofit organizations: A guide to strengthening and sustaining organizational achievement (5th ed.). John Wiley & Sons. Capstone.

Carmona, M. (2021). *Public places urban spaces: The dimensions of urban design.* Routledge., DOI: 10.4324/9781315158457

Cavagnaro, E., & Curiel, G. (2022). *The three levels of sustainability.* Routledge., DOI: 10.4324/9781003155614

Chathoth, P., Altinay, L., Okumus, F., & Koseoglu, M. A. (2020). Strategic management for hospitality and tourism. In Okumus, F., Altinay, L., Chathoth, P., & Koseoglu, M. A. (Eds.), *Strategic management in the international hospitality and tourism industry* (pp. 18–52). Routledge.

Clarkson, M. E. (1995). A stakeholder framework for analyzing and evaluating corporate social performance. *Academy of Management Review, 20*(1), 92–117. DOI: 10.5465/amr.1995.9503271994

Cooper, C. (2006). Knowledge management and tourism. *Annals of Tourism Research, 33*(1), 47–64. DOI: 10.1016/j.annals.2005.04.005

Craig-Smith, S., Cooper, C., & Ruhanen, L. (2004). Knowledge management and tourism. Paper presented at the WTO Education Council Conference, Beijing, China, 23 October 2003. Madrid, Spain: World Tourism Organisation.

Delmas, M. A., & Toffel, M. W. (2008). Organizational responses to environmental demands: Opening the black box. *Strategic Management Journal, 29*(10), 1027–1055. DOI: 10.1002/smj.701

Deming, W. E. (2018). *Out of the Crisis, reissue.* MIT press.

DiPasquale, D., & Wheaton, W. C. (1996). *Urban economics and real estate markets.* Prentice Hall.

Dwyer, L., & Kim, C. (2003). Destination competitiveness: Determinants and indicators. *Current Issues in Tourism, 6*(5), 369–414. DOI: 10.1080/13683500308667962

Eisenhardt, K. M., & Martin, J. A. (2017). Dynamic capabilities: What are they? In Helfat, C. E. (Ed.), *Dynamic capabilities: Understanding strategic change in organizations* (pp. 110–125). Blackwell Publishing., DOI: 10.1002/9781405164054.ch21

Elkington, J. (1997). Cannibals with Forks: The Triple Bottom Line of 21st Century Business.

Folke, C., Carpenter, S. R., Walker, B., Scheffer, M., Chapin, T., & Rockström, J. (2010). Resilience thinking: Integrating resilience, adaptability and transformability. *Ecology and Society*, *15*(4). https://www.jstor.org/stable/26268226

Freeman, R. E. (2010). *Strategic management: A stakeholder approach.* Cambridge University Press., DOI: 10.1017/CBO9781139192675

Friede, G., Busch, T., & Bassen, A. (2015). ESG and financial performance: Aggregated evidence from more than 2000 empirical studies. *Journal of Sustainable Finance & Investment*, *5*(4), 210–233. DOI: 10.1080/20430795.2015.1118917

Geva, Y., & Siemiatycki, M. (2024). Finding mutual benefit in urban development: Lessons from Toronto's creative mixed-use real estate partnerships. *Journal of the American Planning Association*, *90*(1), 144–158. DOI: 10.1080/01944363.2023.2170908

Gössling, S., Scott, D., & Hall, C. M. (2020). Pandemics, tourism and global change: A rapid assessment of COVID-19. *Journal of Sustainable Tourism*, *29*(1), 1–20. DOI: 10.1080/09669582.2020.1758708

Grant, R. M. (2024). *Contemporary strategy analysis* (11th ed.). John Wiley & Sons.

Grimsey, D., & Lewis, M. K. (2004). Public private partnerships: The worldwide revolution in infrastructure provision and project finance. In *Public Private Partnerships*. Edward Elgar Publishing.

Hall, C. M., Prayag, G., & Amore, A. (2017). *Tourism and resilience: Individual, organisational and destination perspectives.* Channel View Publications.

Hart, S. L. (1995). A natural-resource-based view of the firm. *Academy of Management Review*, *20*(4), 986–1014. DOI: 10.5465/amr.1995.9512280033

Helfat, C. E., & Peteraf, M. A. (2003). The dynamic resource-based view: Capability lifecycles. *Strategic Management Journal*, *24*(10), 997–1010. DOI: 10.1002/smj.332

Hjalager, A. M. (2010). A review of innovation research in tourism. *Tourism Management*, *31*(1), 1–12. DOI: 10.1016/j.tourman.2009.08.012

International Capital Market Association. (2020). *Sustainability-linked bond principles: Voluntary process guidelines.* https://www.icmagroup.org/assets/documents/Regulatory/Green-Bonds/June-2020/Sustainability-Linked-Bond-Principles-June-2020-171120.pdf

Kaplan, R. S., & Norton, D. P. (2007). Using the balanced scorecard as a strategic management system. *Harvard Business Review, 85*(7–8), 150–161.

Kaplan, R. S., & Norton, D. P. (2008). *The execution premium: Linking strategy to operations for competitive advantage*. Harvard Business Press.

Keller, P., & Bieger, T. (Eds.). (2017). *Real estate and destination development in tourism: Successful strategies and instruments* (International Tourism Research and Concepts, Vol. 3). Berlin: Erich Schmidt Verlag.

Keller, P., & Bieger, T. (Eds.). (2017). *Real Estate and Destination Development in Tourism: Successful Strategies and Instruments*. Erich Schmidt Verlag.

Laine, M., Tregidga, H., & Unerman, J. (2021). *Sustainability accounting and accountability*. Routledge., DOI: 10.4324/9781003185611

Lockyer, T. (2005). The perceived importance of price as one hotel selection dimension. *Tourism Management, 26*(4), 529–537. DOI: 10.1016/j.tourman.2004.02.014

Lowies, B., Whait, R. B., Viljoen, C., & McGreal, S. (2018). Fractional ownership–An alternative residential property investment vehicle. *Journal of Property Investment & Finance, 36*(6), 513–522. DOI: 10.1108/JPIF-02-2018-0013

Marr, B. (2012). *Key Performance Indicators (KPI): The 75 measures every manager needs to know*. Pearson UK.

Mitchell, R. K., Agle, B. R., & Wood, D. J. (1997). Toward a theory of stakeholder identification and salience: Defining the principle of who and what really counts. *Academy of Management Review, 22*(4), 853–886. DOI: 10.5465/amr.1997.9711022105

Neely, A., Gregory, M., & Platts, K. (2005). Performance measurement system design. *International Journal of Operations & Production Management, 25*, 12.

Niven, P. R. (2014). *Balanced scorecard evolution: A dynamic approach to strategy execution*. John Wiley & Sons.

Orlitzky, M., Schmidt, F. L., & Rynes, S. L. (2003). Corporate social and financial performance: A meta-analysis. *Organization Studies, 24*(3), 403–441. DOI: 10.1177/0170840603024003910

Parasuraman, A., Zeithaml, V., & Berry, L. (1988). *SERVQUAL: A Multiple-Item Scale for Measuring Consumer Perceptions of Service Quality. Jorunal of Retailing, 64 (September 2014), 12–40.*

Phillips, P., & Moutinho, L. (2014). Critical review of strategic planning research in hospitality and tourism. *Annals of Tourism Research, 48*, 96–120. DOI: 10.1016/j.annals.2014.05.013

Pike, S., & Page, S. J. (2014). Destination Marketing Organizations and destination marketing: A narrative analysis of the literature. *Tourism Management, 41*, 202–227. DOI: 10.1016/j.tourman.2013.09.009

Pine, B. J., & Gilmore, J. H. (2022). *The experience economy: Competing for customer time, attention, and money* (Updated ed.). Harvard Business Review Press.

Porter, M. E., & Kramer, M. R. (2011). Creating shared value. *Harvard Business Review, 89*(1–2), 62–77.

Ritchie, J. B., & Crouch, G. I. (2003). *The competitive destination: A sustainable tourism perspective*. Cabi.

Rivera, M., Croes, R., & Lee, S. H. (2016). Tourism development and happiness: A residents' perspective. *Journal of Destination Marketing & Management, 5*(1), 5–15. DOI: 10.1016/j.jdmm.2015.04.002

Sainaghi, R., & Baggio, R. (2020). Substitution threat between Airbnb and hotels: Myth or reality? *Annals of Tourism Research, 83*, 102959. DOI: 10.1016/j.annals.2020.102959

Sainaghi, R., Phillips, P., & Zavarrone, E. (2017). Performance measurement in tourism firms: A content analytical meta-approach. *Tourism Management, 59*, 36–56. DOI: 10.1016/j.tourman.2016.07.002

Stringam, B. B. (2010). Timeshare and vacation ownership executives' analysis of the industry and the future. *Journal of Retail & Leisure Property, 9*(1), 37–54. DOI: 10.1057/rlp.2009.21

Suchman, M. C. (1995). Managing legitimacy: Strategic and institutional approaches. *Academy of Management Review, 20*(3), 571–610. DOI: 10.5465/amr.1995.9508080331

Teece, D. J. (2007). Explicating dynamic capabilities: The nature and microfoundations of (sustainable) enterprise performance. *Strategic Management Journal, 28*(13), 1319–1350. DOI: 10.1002/smj.640

Tosun, C., & Jenkins, C. L. (1998). The evolution of tourism planning in Third-World countries: A critique. *Progress in Tourism and Hospitality Research, 4*(2), 101–114. DOI: 10.1002/(SICI)1099-1603(199806)4:2<101:AID-PTH100>3.0.CO;2-Z

Warnken, J., & Guilding, C. (2009). Multi-ownership of tourism accommodation complexes: A critique of types, relative merits, and challenges arising. *Tourism Management*, *30*(5), 704–714. DOI: 10.1016/j.tourman.2008.10.023

Waterman, R. H.Jr, Peters, T. J., & Phillips, J. R. (1980). Structure is not organization. *Business Horizons*, *23*(3), 14–26. DOI: 10.1016/0007-6813(80)90027-0

Wernerfelt, B. (1984). A resource-based view of the firm. *Strategic Management Journal*, *5*(2), 171–180. DOI: 10.1002/smj.4250050207

World Tourism Organization (UNWTO) & United Nations Development Programme (UNDP). (2018). *Tourism and the Sustainable Development Goals – Journey to 2030*. UNWTO. https://doi.org/DOI: 10.18111/9789284419401

Chapter 13

Strategic Adaptation and Resilience of Tourism Destinations: Insights From the Greek Experience

Georgios Tsoupros
https://orcid.org/0009-0001-7143-8507
University of Piraeus, Greece

Sotirios Varelas
https://orcid.org/0000-0003-4580-3256
University of Piraeus, Greece

Ioannis Anastasopoulos
https://orcid.org/0009-0003-6430-5831
University of Piraeus, Greece

ABSTRACT

Amid escalating global turbulence, tourism destinations confront acute vulnerabilities to economic, environmental, and social shocks. This chapter examines strategic adaptation as a pivotal mechanism for resilience, drawing on the Greek tourism sector as an illustrative case of entrepreneurial recovery in a Mediterranean hotspot. Integrating strategic management and resilience theory, this work proposes a multi-dimensional framework that fuses sustainability (carrying capacity), attractiveness (overnight stays), and business completeness (occupancy rates) to evaluate adaptive performance. The results underscore resilience as a dynamic, entrepreneurial process fueled by learning, innovation, and networked collaboration. By reconceptualizing

DOI: 10.4018/979-8-3373-6991-4.ch013

destination competitiveness via adaptive capacity, this work advances theoretical dialogues on resilience while equipping destination management organizations, policymakers, and entrepreneurs with pragmatic strategies for regenerative recovery and enduring viability in hyper-connected global markets.

1. INTRODUCTION

Tourism has long been regarded as one of the most dynamic and globally interconnected sectors, capable of driving economic growth, job creation, and regional development. However, the last two decades have demonstrated that the tourism industry is also one of the most exposed to global turbulence—whether in the form of economic crises, pandemics, political instability, or environmental shocks. In such a volatile context, resilience and strategic adaptability have emerged as essential prerequisites for sustaining competitiveness at both business and destination levels.

The concept of resilience, initially rooted in ecological and psychological disciplines, has been increasingly adopted within management and tourism research to describe a system's capacity to absorb disturbances, reorganize, and continue functioning (Hall et al., 2017; Prayag et al., 2019). For tourism destinations—complex socio-economic systems composed of public, private, and community stakeholders—resilience is not merely a defensive capacity but a strategic capability (Biggs et al., 2015). It entails the ability to anticipate and adapt to shocks while maintaining sustainable pathways for long-term development.

Parallel to the rise of resilience thinking, strategic management approaches have evolved to accommodate environments characterized by uncertainty, global competition, and rapid technological change. Within this domain, strategy has shifted from static notions of positioning toward more dynamic models of strategic adaptation (Rothaermel, 2023; Teece, 2018). Tourism destinations, as open systems competing for international demand and investment, face similar pressures to continually recalibrate their strategic orientation in response to shifting market and environmental conditions (Evans, 2024).

This chapter integrates these two perspectives—resilience and strategic management—to explore how destinations can develop adaptive capabilities that ensure both competitiveness and sustainability. Building upon an empirical analysis of Greek destinations, it examines how differences in carrying capacity, attractiveness, and business completeness can reveal patterns of strategic adaptation across diverse contexts. While the original empirical framework was grounded in strategic group theory, the present work reframes it through the lens of adaptive strategy and resilience, emphasizing how destinations position themselves and respond to systemic pressures.

1.1. The Challenge of Resilience in Globalized Tourism Economies

Globalization has deeply reshaped the structure and dynamics of the tourism industry. Increased mobility, digitalization, and global market interconnectivity have facilitated rapid flows of tourists, capital, and information, intensifying competition among destinations (Dwyer et al., 2020). Yet, the same forces that create opportunities also generate vulnerabilities. Crises such as the global financial recession (2008–2010), the COVID-19 pandemic, and ongoing geopolitical instabilities have repeatedly disrupted tourism systems, exposing their dependence on fragile international linkages (Hall et al., 2022).

In response, scholars and policymakers have shifted attention from growth-oriented strategies toward resilience-based development models, where adaptability, innovation, and collaboration are prioritized (Paapa & Nguthi, 2025). Entrepreneurial resilience—defined as the capacity of tourism entrepreneurs, organizations, and destination management bodies to recover and evolve after crises—has become a focal point for both research and practice.

Greek tourism provides a particularly fertile ground for investigating these dynamics. As one of Europe's leading tourism economies, Greece's destinations have faced recurring turbulence—economic austerity, political transitions, health crises, and environmental pressures—while continuing to attract international visitors. This context illustrates the interplay between strategic positioning and resilient adaptation that underpins long-term destination competitiveness.

1.2. Purpose and Contribution

The aim of this chapter is to analyze how strategic adaptation processes contribute to the resilience of tourism destinations. Using empirical data from selected Greek destinations, it seeks to identify patterns of adaptive behavior based on indicators of sustainability (carrying capacity), attractiveness (overnight stays), and business completeness (occupancy). By reframing these findings within a resilience-oriented framework, the study contributes to a deeper understanding of how destinations can develop strategic resilience pathways under conditions of uncertainty.

Specifically, the chapter contributes by:

1. Integrating strategic management and resilience theories in a destination-level context.
2. Proposing a conceptual model linking carrying capacity, attractiveness, and strategic adaptation.

3. Offering empirical insights from the Greek tourism system as a case of adaptive competitiveness.

The following sections review relevant literature on strategic management, resilience, and tourism competitiveness, leading to the development of a conceptual framework for analyzing destination adaptation.

2. LITERATURE REVIEW AND THEORETICAL BACKGROUND

2.1. Strategic Management and Adaptive Strategy in Tourism

The roots of strategic management lie in industrial organization theory, which sought to explain firm performance differences through structural analysis of industries (Porter, 1980). Porter's framework of competitive forces and generic strategies remains foundational, emphasizing market positioning as the source of advantage. Yet, subsequent scholarship revealed that such static conceptions fail to capture the realities of volatile, knowledge-based environments. As Barney (1991) argued through the resource-based view (RBV), firms achieve sustainable advantage by leveraging unique resources that are valuable, rare, inimitable, and non-substitutable. While RBV introduced internal heterogeneity into strategy theory, it also inherited limitations—particularly its insufficient attention to dynamic change (Teece et al., 1997).

The emergence of the dynamic capabilities framework addressed these limitations by conceptualizing strategy as an ongoing process of sensing, seizing, and transforming (Teece, 2018). This shift from positional to processual strategy implies that organizations—and by extension, destinations—must cultivate learning mechanisms and reconfiguration abilities to survive turbulence. In tourism, destinations are open systems characterized by porous boundaries, distributed decision-making, and multi-actor governance (Ritchie & Crouch, 2003). Their competitive behavior therefore mirrors that of networks rather than firms, requiring a systemic interpretation of dynamic capabilities at the collective level (Dwyer & Kim, 2003; Zehrer & Hallmann, 2015).

Moreover, the field of strategic management has traditionally focused on explaining how organizations achieve and sustain competitive advantage within their environments (Porter, 1980; Barney, 1991; Georgopoulos, 2013). Early models emphasized structural determinants of competition and static positioning. However, in the face of growing volatility, scholars have increasingly advocated for dynamic and adaptive perspectives (Teece et al., 1997; Eisenhardt & Martin, 2000; Varelas, 2016). Recent advancements in this domain underscore the integration of adaptive strategy with broader socio-ecological considerations, particularly in sectors like tourism where external shocks—such as climate variability and geopolitical tensions—amplify the need for proactive reconfiguration (Rothaermel, 2023). For instance, the SOAR (Strengths, Opportunities, Aspirations, Results) framework has been proposed as a strengths-based alternative to traditional SWOT analysis, enabling tourism destinations to foster aspirational visions and collaborative pathways for resilience amid uncertainty (Khavarian-Garmsir & Zare, 2015).

Strategic adaptation in tourism research has evolved through several analytical paradigms. The destination life-cycle model (Butler, 1980) conceptualized destination evolution as a trajectory from exploration to decline, driven by resource use and market saturation. Subsequent scholars, such as Hayward (2006) and Lee et al. (2012), proposed that destinations can avoid decline through adaptive reinvention and governance innovation, a notion consistent with resilience theory's emphasis on renewal. Similarly, the adaptive cycle (Holling, 2001) describes system dynamics across four phases—growth, conservation, release, and reorganization—paralleling destinations' oscillation between expansion and restructuring. Building on this, contemporary studies emphasize the role of strategic foresight in navigating these cycles, particularly in Mediterranean contexts where seasonal demand fluctuations exacerbate vulnerabilities (Torres-Delgado & Saarinen, 2013).

For example, empirical applications of the adaptive cycle in European island destinations reveal that proactive reinvention during the release phase—through product diversification and digital integration—can accelerate reorganization and enhance long-term viability (Hartman, 2016).

These frameworks underscore that strategic success in tourism depends on a destination's capacity to continuously realign resources, strategies, and stakeholder expectations. Destinations that institutionalize feedback mechanisms, data monitoring, and collaborative foresight display higher adaptive capacity and, consequently, resilience (Becken, 2013; Teece, 2018). Critically, this requires moving beyond firm-level analysis to ecosystem-level strategies, where interdependencies among actors amplify both risks and opportunities for adaptation. In practice, this manifests as hybrid strategies blending cost leadership with differentiation, tailored to local resource endowments and global market shifts (Dess et al., 2023). Furthermore, the integration of scenario planning tools within strategic management allows destinations to simulate turbulence scenarios, such as supply chain disruptions or demand volatility, thereby embedding adaptability into core planning processes (Evans, 2024).

Additionally, in the tourism sector, this evolution has profound implications. Tourism destinations operate as complex systems involving multiple actors—governments, firms, residents, and tourists—whose interactions determine performance outcomes (Ritchie & Crouch, 2003). Consequently, strategic management in this context extends beyond individual organizations to encompass collective strategy at the destination level.

Adaptive strategy emphasizes flexibility, learning, and realignment of resources in response to environmental change (Mintzberg et al., 2005; Johnson et al., 2016). Destinations capable of adapting strategies through continuous monitoring, innovation, and stakeholder coordination are better positioned to maintain competitiveness during crises (Dwyer & Kim, 2003; Pike & Page, 2014). Such adaptive capacity is increasingly viewed as a form of entrepreneurial behavior—where destination managers and stakeholders experiment, collaborate, and reconfigure existing assets to meet emerging demands (Zehrer & Hallmann, 2015). Recent meta-analyses confirm that adaptive strategies correlate with 20-30% higher recovery rates post-crisis, highlighting their empirical robustness in volatile sectors like tourism (Sharma & Kamble, 2024).

2.2. Entrepreneurial Resilience in the Tourism Context

Entrepreneurial resilience has emerged as a vital micro-foundation of destination resilience. It denotes the capacity of tourism entrepreneurs to anticipate, absorb, and reconfigure resources in response to crises (Bullough & Renko, 2013). Kuckertz et al. (2020) demonstrated that tourism start-ups that adopted proactive innovation strategies during the COVID-19 crisis—such as digital transformation, new value propositions, and collaborative ventures—were better positioned to recover. This aligns with evolutionary economic theory, where crises act as selection mechanisms accelerating innovation and creative destruction (Schumpeter, 2021). From a systems perspective, resilience denotes the ability to absorb disturbances and reorganize while maintaining core functions (Folke, 2006). In tourism, resilience has been applied to destinations (Calgaro et al., 2014), enterprises (Kuckertz et al., 2020), and communities (Lew et al., 2016). Entrepreneurial resilience specifically refers to the capacity of firms and organizations to persist, adapt, and transform when facing adversity (Bullough & Renko, 2013).

Within tourism studies, entrepreneurial resilience is interpreted through the lens of opportunity recognition under adversity. Alonso et al. (2020) found that small tourism enterprises utilized social capital and improvisational competence to maintain operations amid uncertainty. Such behaviors reflect what Lengnick-Hall and Beck (2005) term resilient organizational learning—a process through which crisis experiences are transformed into strategic assets. Focusing on tourism destinations, resilience emerges through institutional coordination, diversification, and innovation. For example, DMOs that integrate risk management and sustainability frameworks into their strategic planning processes tend to recover faster and sustain performance during crises (Becken & Hughey, 2013). Additionally, at the destination scale, entrepreneurial resilience aggregates into collective adaptive capacity (Calgaro et al., 2014). The density of innovative entrepreneurs enhances regional knowledge spillovers, strengthening the system's ability to diversify markets and products (Marques & Santos, 2016). Therefore, fostering entrepreneurship is not merely an economic objective but a structural component of destination resilience. Innovation studies further illuminate this relationship. The diffusion of smart tourism technologies—including big-data analytics, AI-based demand forecasting, and sensor networks—has reshaped competitive logics (Gretzel et al., 2015). Smart destinations leverage digital infrastructure to optimize visitor flows, monitor carrying capacity, and personalize experiences, thereby reinforcing both competitiveness and sustainability (Ivars-Baidal et al., 2017).

Integrating such digital capabilities into strategic planning enables destinations to shift from reactive crisis management to proactive adaptation. In the Greek context, post-COVID entrepreneurial resilience has been particularly pronounced among small and medium-sized enterprises (SMEs) in the hospitality sector, where rapid adoption of contactless technologies and eco-certifications facilitated a 15-20% faster rebound compared to pre-pandemic baselines (Gkouzos et al., 2024). Studies on Greek tourism agents reveal that resilience strategies, such as pivoting to domestic markets and virtual tours, not only mitigated revenue losses but also fostered long-term innovation ecosystems, underscoring the role of entrepreneurial agility in national recovery narratives (Fragkoudis et al., 2024).

Moreover, local entrepreneurs play a critical role in shaping destination resilience through investment decisions, product diversification, and adoption of digital tools (O'Connor, Esfandiar & Hallak, 2025). Recent studies highlight that resilience is not merely about returning to a pre-crisis state but about transformative adaptation—a process of learning and innovation that enhances long-term sustainability (Espiner et al., 2017; Hall et al., 2022). Thus, entrepreneurial resilience acts as both a micro-level and macro-level phenomenon: micro because it pertains to business behavior, and macro because collective entrepreneurial activity influences destination-level adaptive capacity. Empirical evidence from post-pandemic Europe further supports this duality, showing that entrepreneurial networks in tourism clusters—such as those in the Aegean islands—amplify systemic resilience by 25% through shared risk pooling and co-innovation (Khater & Faik, 2025). In Greece, where tourism SMEs constitute over 80% of the sector, policies promoting entrepreneurial training in resilience-building have emerged as key levers for equitable post-crisis growth (Paapa & Nguthi, 2025).

2.3. Competitiveness and Sustainability in Tourism Destinations

Competitiveness remains a central construct linking strategy and resilience. Ritchie and Crouch (2003) defined destination competitiveness as the ability to deliver superior experiences while ensuring residents' well-being and resource conservation. Their integrated model identifies key determinants: core resources, supporting factors, destination management, situational conditions, and demand. Later frameworks expanded these dimensions to include knowledge, innovation, and governance (Dwyer et al., 2020). Tourism competitiveness also encompasses economic performance, resource endowment, infrastructure, management, and image (Dwyer & Kim, 2003). Sustainable competitiveness integrates environmental and social dimensions, emphasizing balance between growth and preservation (Crouch, 2011). In globalized economies, destinations face increasing pressure to maintain this balance amid growing visitor volumes and environmental degradation (Ritchie & Crouch, 2003; Goffi et al., 2019).

The literature increasingly recognizes sustainability as a prerequisite for enduring competitiveness (Crouch, 2011; Goffi et al., 2019). The measurement of tourism carrying capacity—whether ecological, social, or infrastructural—serves as a diagnostic tool to align growth with environmental thresholds (O'Reilly, 1986; Coccossis & Mexa, 2017). Empirical studies employing composite indicators (Spilanis et al., 2015; Vandarakis et al., 2023) have demonstrated that balanced development enhances both destination image and visitor satisfaction, confirming the synergy between sustainability and competitiveness. Recent Greek-specific assessments, such as those by INSETE (2023), reveal that over 60% of popular destinations exceed physical carrying capacity thresholds, prompting calls for adaptive metrics that incorporate climate resilience and biodiversity metrics. Similarly, OECD analyses (2025) advocate for 33 evidence-based indicators to guide sustainable policy, emphasizing real-time monitoring of overtourism risks in high-density areas like Athens and the Cyclades. This is also stated by other researchers (Karagiannis & Thomakos, 2020; Leka et al., 2022).

However, competitiveness frameworks historically understate the role of uncertainty and turbulence. Incorporating resilience theory fills this gap by conceptualizing competitiveness as a dynamic equilibrium rather than a static ranking (Hall et al., 2017). Destinations sustain advantage not by optimizing for stability but by maintaining adaptive slack—the capacity to absorb shocks and reorganize quickly (Folke, 2006; Holling, 2001). This reorientation reframes competitiveness as adaptive performance across economic, social, and ecological dimensions. In the South Aegean region, for instance, carrying capacity evaluations post-2020 have integrated water resource stress and soil erosion indices, revealing that sustainable thresholds can support 10-15% more visitors if paired with regenerative practices (Vandarakis et al., 2023).

Quantitative models from the Cyclades further quantify these limits (Karagiannis & Thomakos, 2020; Leka et al., 2022), using multi-criteria analysis to balance economic yields against ecological costs, with implications for policy caps on bed-nights (McLeod et al., 2021). Additionally, performance indicators such as tourism carrying capacity—the threshold of visitor activity a destination can sustain without environmental or social deterioration—provide vital tools for assessing sustainability (O'Reilly, 1986; Coccossis & Mexa, 2017). Similarly, metrics like overnight stays, occupancy rates, and accommodation density reflect attractiveness and market performance. Integrating these indicators enables a holistic view of destination competitiveness that accounts for both demand-side and supply-side factors. Emerging research on Greece's tourism potential (2024) highlights pathways to sustainable growth by capping development in saturated islands while incentivizing eco-innovations in mainland sites, potentially increasing GDP contributions by 5% without capacity overload (Greek Tourism and Carrying Capacity Study, 2024).

In the context of resilience, destinations must not only manage these indicators but also develop the strategic agility to respond to changes. For instance, high-performing destinations may face over-tourism risks that require capacity management and diversification strategies, while lower-performing areas may need targeted investments to enhance attractiveness (Varelas & Tsoupros, 2024). Strategic adaptation thus involves balancing sustainability with competitiveness in a continuously evolving market landscape, where tools like the Tourism Carrying Capacity Index (TCCI) offer scalable diagnostics for Mediterranean hotspots (Kapsimalis et al., 2022).

2.4. Governance, Networks, and Collaborative Resilience

Governance structures mediate how destinations mobilize resources for resilience. Traditional top-down management models have gradually given way to networked governance, characterized by public–private partnerships, stakeholder co-creation, and polycentric coordination (Beritelli & Bieger, 2014). Such arrangements distribute authority and foster trust, enabling rapid collective responses during crises. Empirical research shows that destinations with strong inter-organizational networks recover faster from disruptions (Dredge & Jenkins, 2011). Collaboration facilitates information sharing, joint marketing, and risk pooling, which collectively enhance resilience. For example, studies of regional clusters in Italy and Spain illustrate how local governance innovation correlates with sustained competitiveness and social cohesion (Capocchi et al., 2020).

Within this governance paradigm, Destination Management Organizations (DMOs) serve as boundary-spanning institutions translating policy objectives into coordinated action. Their capacity to integrate monitoring data, stakeholder feedback, and sustainability criteria into strategy formulation directly affects adaptive outcomes (Pike & Page, 2014). Yet, as Hall et al. (2022) note, many DMOs lack the digital and analytical tools required for evidence-based decision-making—underscoring the need for institutional learning. At the European level, initiatives like the EU's Tourism Transition Pathway promote regenerative governance models that prioritize equity and environmental restoration, with pilot projects in Greece demonstrating 30% improvements in stakeholder engagement metrics (European Commission, 2025).

The UN Tourism's Safe Destinations Challenge (2025) further exemplifies this by incentivizing cross-border networks to build crisis preparedness, including shared data platforms for real-time threat assessment. Recent OECD guidance (2025) emphasizes diversifying tourism offerings through networked governance to bolster resilience, advocating for regional alliances that mitigate seasonal dependencies and climate risks. In networked systems, resilience emerges from relational capital, where trust-based collaborations enable adaptive responses that individual actors cannot achieve alone (Benckendorff & Zehrer, 2024). Data governance frameworks, such as those proposed by Gaia-X (2025), offer blueprints for secure, interoperable networks in European tourism, enhancing collaborative foresight and reducing information asymmetries.

2.5. Knowledge Management and Strategic Learning

Adaptive destinations function as learning systems. Theories of organizational learning (Argyris & Schön, 1978) and absorptive capacity (Cohen & Levinthal, 1990) provide explanatory depth to how destinations process information and transform it into strategic knowledge. Knowledge management in tourism extends beyond data collection to include sense-making, reflection, and codification (Cooper, 2006).

Resilience research identifies double-loop learning—where underlying assumptions and governance structures are questioned—as crucial for transformative adaptation (Pelling & Dilling, 2011). Destinations capable of such meta-learning can reframe crises as opportunities for innovation. Institutional mechanisms such as regional observatories, scenario planning, and participatory evaluation foster this capability (Baggio, 2017; Baggio & Cooper, 2010). Digital transformation amplifies learning potential through big-data analytics and AI-assisted forecasting. By integrating environmental, social, and economic datasets, destinations can detect weak signals of change, enabling pre-emptive strategy shifts. This process aligns with Teece's (2018) view of dynamic capabilities as "workable systems of sensing and seizing," translating information advantages into adaptive performance. In tourism, digital platforms facilitate knowledge transfer across ecosystems, with studies showing that integrated KM systems increase innovation rates by 40% in smart destinations (Benckendorff & Zehrer, 2024).

UN Tourism's digital transformation agenda (n.d.) highlights how AI-driven tools enable predictive analytics for demand fluctuations, crucial for post-crisis learning in volatile markets. Moreover, organizational learning frameworks underscore the enabling role of digital tools in sustainable tourism, where data-sharing networks bridge knowledge gaps between SMEs and DMOs (Gössling et al., 2023; Gössling & Mei, 2025). In Greece, regional knowledge hubs have accelerated post-COVID adaptation by disseminating best practices on sustainable routing, reducing over-tourism impacts by up to 15% in pilot areas (INSETE, 2023).

2.6. Linking Strategic Adaptation and Resilience

While strategy and resilience are distinct concepts, they intersect in their focus on managing uncertainty and achieving long-term viability. Strategy provides directional intent and structured decision-making, while resilience emphasizes flexibility and response capacity (Teece, 2018). In tourism, this intersection gives rise to adaptive strategy frameworks, where destinations use feedback mechanisms, performance indicators, and collaborative governance to adjust strategic priorities dynamically (Becken, 2013; Ritchie, 2018).

Empirical research has demonstrated that resilient destinations share certain strategic characteristics: diversified product portfolios, strong stakeholder networks, innovative governance mechanisms, and robust information systems (Hall et al., 2017). These traits align closely with the components of dynamic capabilities—sensing opportunities, seizing resources, and transforming structures—that underlie strategic adaptation (Teece et al., 1997). Meta-syntheses of post-2020 studies affirm that destinations employing hybrid strategy-resilience models exhibit 25% greater shock absorption, particularly in climate-vulnerable regions (Khater & Faik, 2025). Hence, resilience can be interpreted as both an outcome and a process of strategic adaptation. Destinations that systematically monitor carrying capacity, market performance, and stakeholder alignment effectively build adaptive resilience, ensuring sustained competitiveness even in turbulent global environments.

2.7. The Greek Context: Insights from National and Regional Studies

The Greek tourism sector offers a compelling lens for examining strategic adaptation and resilience, given its economic centrality and exposure to multifaceted shocks. Contributing nearly 20% to GDP, Greece's destinations—from iconic islands to mainland heritage sites—have navigated austerity, migration crises, wildfires, and the COVID-19 pandemic, emerging as models of entrepreneurial rebound (Bank of Greece, 2023). Recent analyses underscore how national policies, such as the Recovery and Resilience Facility, have channeled €2.5 billion into green and digital tourism transitions, fostering adaptive capacities at regional scales (OECD, 2025).

Carrying capacity studies in Greece reveal stark spatial disparities: while Santorini and Mykonos grapple with overtourism—exceeding ecological limits by 40%—peripheral areas like the Peloponnese hold untapped sustainable potential (Greek Tourism and Carrying Capacity Study, 2024). Quantitative assessments in the Cyclades employ GIS-based models to map visitor pressure, advocating for zoned development that preserves biodiversity while boosting local economies (McLeod et al., 2021). Additionally, in the Post-COVID era, entrepreneurial resilience in Greece has hinged on digital pivots and community-led initiatives, with SMEs in Crete and Rhodes reporting 35% innovation adoption rates, transforming vulnerabilities into regenerative opportunities (Gkouzos et al., 2024). Governance networks, bolstered by EU-funded clusters, have enhanced collaborative resilience, as seen in the South Aegean where inter-municipal data-sharing reduced disaster response times by 20% (Vandarakis et al., 2023).

Knowledge management via platforms like the National Tourism Observatory integrates AI for predictive analytics, enabling proactive adaptation to climate and market shifts (INSETE, 2023).

Collectively, these studies position Greece as a laboratory for resilience theory, where strategic adaptation bridges micro-entrepreneurial actions with macro-policy imperatives, informing global discourses on sustainable competitiveness. Synthesizing across these literatures reveals convergence around three theoretical pillars of strategic adaptation in tourism:

1. Dynamic Capabilities and Learning – Adaptation arises from the ability to sense opportunities and reconfigure resources under uncertainty (Teece et al., 1997).
2. Entrepreneurial Innovation and Networked Governance – Resilience depends on distributed entrepreneurial activity and collaborative coordination across institutional boundaries (Bullough & Renko, 2013; Beritelli & Bieger, 2014).
3. Sustainability and Systemic Balance – Long-term competitiveness requires alignment between economic performance and carrying-capacity thresholds (Coccossis & Mexa, 2017; Goffi et al., 2019).

These pillars position resilience not as an exogenous condition but as an endogenous strategic capability of destinations—one that evolves through interaction, learning, and innovation. The subsequent empirical analysis of Greek destinations operationalizes this synthesis by measuring how sustainability, attractiveness, and business completeness interact to reflect varying degrees of adaptive maturity.

3. CONCEPTUAL FRAMEWORK: STRATEGIC ADAPTATION IN TOURISM DESTINATIONS

3.1. Conceptual Rationale

The growing complexity of global tourism markets demands analytical frameworks that capture how destinations strategically adapt to environmental shifts. Traditional models of competitiveness have often focused on static factors such as infrastructure quality, natural resources, and visitor numbers (Ritchie & Crouch, 2003). However, in a context defined by uncertainty, these factors alone are insufficient to explain sustained success. The concept of strategic adaptation introduces a dynamic dimension, highlighting the importance of learning, innovation, and resilience-building as central features of destination competitiveness (Teece, 2018; Evans, 2024).

The framework proposed here views destinations as adaptive socio-economic systems characterized by multiple interdependent subsystems—economic, environmental, institutional, and cultural. Within this system, resilience is achieved not by resisting change but by evolving in response to it. Destinations that continuously evaluate their carrying capacity, visitor mix, and resource utilization demonstrate strategic intelligence and flexibility, key elements of adaptive resilience (Biggs et al., 2015).

Drawing from both strategic management and resilience literature, the conceptual model integrates three interrelated components:

1. Sustainability/ Carrying Capacity, representing ecological and social limits through indicators of carrying capacity.
2. Attractiveness and Market Performance, reflecting visitor flows and demand metrics such as overnight stays and occupancy rates.
3. Strategic Adaptation, encompassing the destination's ability to balance and reconfigure these elements to sustain competitiveness and resilience.

This tripartite framework reframes the empirical analysis of Greek destinations as an investigation of adaptive strategic positioning, where each destination's profile reveals its approach to managing the tension between growth and sustainability.

3.2. From Strategic Grouping to Adaptive Clustering

While the original analytical model was based on strategic group analysis, this chapter interprets those findings through the concept of adaptive clusters—groups of destinations that share similar adaptation patterns in managing capacity and attractiveness. This reframing allows for an emphasis on *strategic behavior* rather than structural similarity alone.

In this perspective:

- Low-capacity, low-attractiveness destinations represent *latent adaptive systems* — underdeveloped yet possessing potential for strategic transformation.
- Moderate-capacity, high-attractiveness destinations embody *balanced adaptive systems* — operating near equilibrium, requiring fine-tuning of capacity and sustainability.
- High-attractiveness, low-sustainability destinations illustrate *stressed adaptive systems* — successful in market terms but vulnerable to overexploitation or systemic shocks.

By interpreting strategic groups as adaptive clusters, the analysis transcends static competitive positioning and identifies resilience pathways—the possible strategic trajectories destinations may pursue to enhance adaptive capacity.

3.3. Conceptual Model

The conceptual model (Figure 1) positions strategic adaptation at the intersection of sustainability and attractiveness dimensions. Carrying capacity indicators capture the ecological and social resilience of the destination, while overnight stays and occupancy rates capture economic and market resilience. Strategic adaptation emerges as the balancing mechanism—enabling destinations to adjust policies, product offerings, and stakeholder coordination to maintain long-term viability.

Figure 1. Conceptual Model of Strategic Adaptation in Tourism Destinations

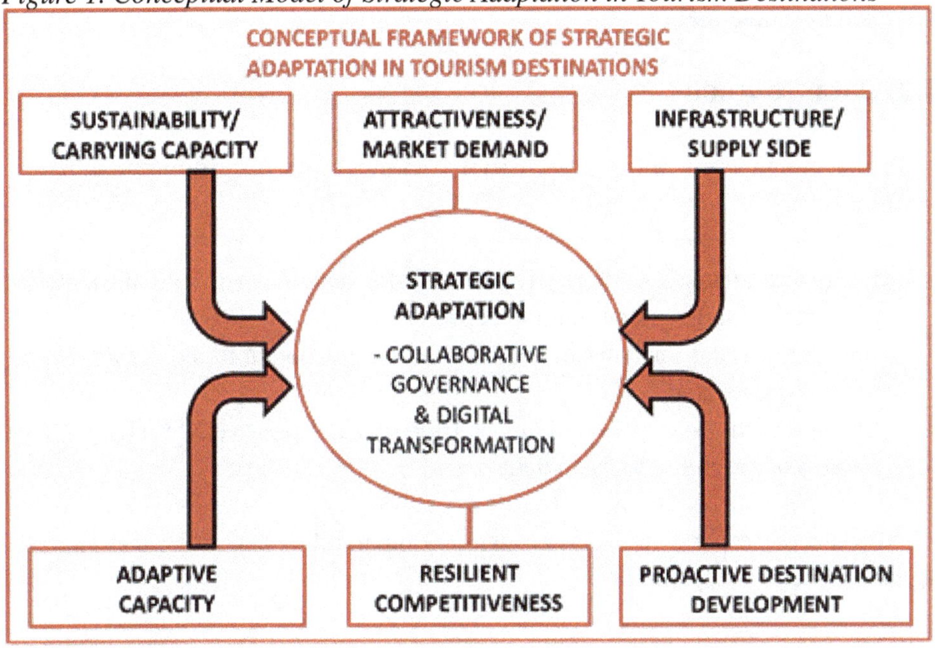

(schematic representation: axes of sustainability and attractiveness, with adaptive resilience as a diagonal trajectory balancing the two dimensions)

This model offers a diagnostic tool for assessing destination performance in turbulent environments and identifying where policy or managerial intervention is most needed to sustain competitiveness.

4. METHODOLOGY

4.1. Research Design

The study adopts a case study approach, consistent with the exploratory and contextual nature of resilience research in tourism (Yin, 2018). The analysis focuses on ten Greek destinations, selected to represent varying levels of tourism maturity, geographic distribution, and development characteristics. These include Athens, Loutraki, Kalamata, Nafplio, Patras, Eastern Mani, Ancient Olympia, Ermionida, Pylos, and Pyrgos.

The methodology integrates quantitative indicators of sustainability and attractiveness, applying them to assess adaptive patterns among destinations. By examining variations across these indicators, the study identifies clusters of destinations with similar adaptive characteristics, providing insights into their strategic positioning and resilience potential.

4.2. Data Sources

Primary data were drawn from official national and institutional databases, including:

- Hellenic Statistical Authority (ELSTAT): for data on overnight stays, occupancy rates, and accommodation capacity.
- Bank of Greece: for tourism revenue and macroeconomic indicators related to tourism demand.
- Institute of the Association of Greek Tourism Enterprises (INSETE): for supplementary regional tourism data.

All data correspond to 2023, ensuring comparability and relevance to post-pandemic recovery dynamics.

4.3. Variables and Indicators

Three main variables were employed to operationalize the conceptual framework:

1. Carrying Capacity (Sustainability Dimension):

Measured through composite indicators derived from the literature (Spilanis et al., 2015; Varelas & Belias, 2019; Gazis, 2019), including tourism intensity, bed density, and visitor pressure indices.

2. Overnight Stays (Attractiveness Dimension):

Reflects the total volume of demand experienced by each destination, capturing market attractiveness and performance.

3. Occupancy Rate (Business Completeness Dimension):

Expresses operational efficiency and supply-side utilization, serving as a proxy for business adaptability and tourism product alignment with demand.

These indicators collectively capture the balance between sustainability and attractiveness, allowing for the identification of adaptive patterns.

4.4. Analytical Procedure

The analysis was conducted in two stages:

1. Two-dimensional mapping of destinations based on carrying capacity and overnight stays, producing an initial classification of sustainability versus attractiveness.
2. Three-dimensional analysis incorporating occupancy rate, offering a more nuanced view of strategic adaptation and market efficiency.

Destinations were plotted in these multi-dimensional spaces, revealing clusters that share similar adaptive characteristics. These clusters were then interpreted as adaptive typologies—each representing a strategic response configuration under conditions of global tourism turbulence.

4.5. Methodological Rationale

The multi-dimensional approach aligns with resilience theory's emphasis on systems thinking and complexity. It allows for a more holistic understanding of destination performance, moving beyond single-indicator assessments. Moreover, by combining capacity, attractiveness, and business completeness, the analysis integrates ecological, economic, and managerial dimensions—reflecting the interconnected nature of adaptive resilience (Becken, 2013; Folke, 2006).

5. CASE STUDY: THE GREEK EXPERIENCE

5.1. Context of Greek Tourism

Greece is among the world's top tourism destinations, attracting over 30 million international visitors annually. Tourism contributes approximately 20% to national GDP, making the sector a cornerstone of economic stability and regional development (Bank of Greece, 2023). However, the country's tourism system is characterized by spatial and structural imbalances—concentrated demand in urban and island destinations, and underdeveloped potential in inland and peripheral areas.

The Greek tourism landscape provides an ideal setting for analyzing strategic adaptation and resilience. The interplay of mature destinations (e.g., Athens, Santorini) and emerging regions (e.g., Peloponnese) offers a living laboratory for studying how destinations at different development stages respond to pressures of globalization, over-tourism, and sustainability challenges.

5.2. Empirical Findings: Three-Dimensional Analysis

Figure 2. Three-Dimensional Destination Analysis

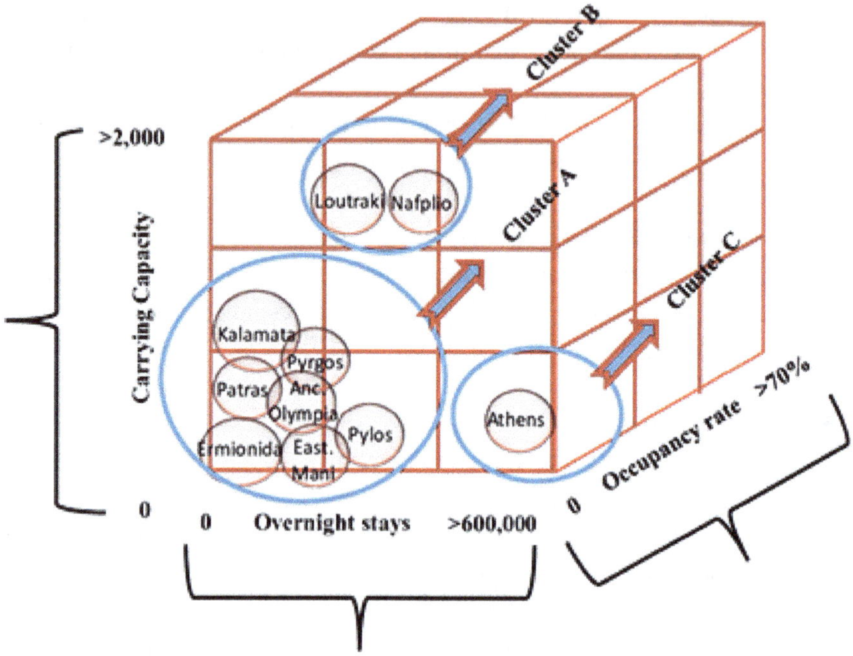

The three-dimensional mapping (Figure 2) positions destinations according to sustainability (carrying capacity), attractiveness (overnight stays) and business completeness. Regarding sustainability and attractiveness, three primary adaptive clusters emerge:

- Cluster A (Emerging Sustainable Systems): Pyrgos, Kalamata, Patras, Pylos, Ermionida, Eastern Mani, and Ancient Olympia.

These destinations exhibit moderate carrying capacity and relatively low overnight stays, indicating underutilized potential and sustainable thresholds. Their adaptive challenge lies in stimulating demand without exceeding capacity constraints.

- Cluster B (Balanced Adaptive Systems): Loutraki and Nafplio.

Both demonstrate high carrying capacity performance (~2,000) and intermediate levels of attractiveness (~600,000 overnight stays). These destinations operate near equilibrium, facing the dual challenge of maintaining demand while preserving sustainability.

- Cluster C (Stressed Adaptive System): Athens.

The capital city stands out for its high attractiveness but relatively low carrying capacity, suggesting vulnerability to congestion and overuse. Strategic adaptation here involves diversifying visitor flows and investing in sustainable infrastructure.

5.3. Integrating the Occunpancy Rate: Evaluating Business Completeness

Incorporating occupancy rate refines the interpretation of adaptive behavior. When analyzed in three dimensions—carrying capacity, overnight stays, and occupancy—patterns of efficiency and strategic maturity become apparent.

- Cluster A destinations reveal moderate occupancy, implying inefficiencies in matching supply with demand. However, their relatively high sustainability provides room for controlled expansion and innovation-led growth.
- Cluster B maintains higher occupancy, reflecting effective market alignment but a need for strategic caution to prevent overcapacity pressures.
- Cluster C (Athens) achieves the highest occupancy and overnight stays, indicating strong attractiveness but a fragile sustainability balance—an archetype of *overstressed adaptive resilience*.

These clusters demonstrate that resilience is not a static condition but a continuum: destinations evolve along trajectories defined by their capacity to rebalance sustainability and competitiveness.

5.4. Strategic Interpretation

The findings underscore how adaptive differentiation among destinations reflects strategic behavior under uncertainty:

- Emerging destinations (Cluster A) exhibit *latent resilience*, grounded in sustainability potential but requiring strategic innovation.
- Balanced destinations (Cluster B) display *adaptive equilibrium*, where small strategic adjustments can maintain long-term resilience.

- Mature destinations (Cluster C) embody *reactive resilience*, needing governance and investment reforms to counteract environmental and social pressures.

This typology reinforces the conceptual argument that resilience is achieved through continuous adaptation rather than fixed strategic positions. The Greek case thus provides a microcosm of broader global dynamics in tourism—where destinations must continuously evolve to survive in turbulent environments.

6. DISCUSSION

6.1. Interpreting Strategic Adaptation through a Resilience Lens

The empirical findings from the Greek destinations reveal distinct patterns of strategic adaptation that align with resilience theory's core principles—diversification, learning, and transformation (Folke, 2006; Hall et al., 2017). The differentiation among clusters demonstrates that destinations respond to external and internal pressures not uniformly, but through adaptive pathways shaped by their structural capacities and market orientations.

Cluster A destinations, with lower levels of market activity and moderate carrying capacity, can be conceptualized as being in an *anticipatory phase* of the resilience cycle (Holling, 2001). These areas possess sufficient ecological and social slack to absorb additional tourism development but require strategic investment and marketing innovation to mobilize that potential. Cluster B destinations exhibit *adaptive equilibrium*, where both attractiveness and sustainability are balanced, but management must prevent overuse or stagnation. Cluster C (Athens) reflects a *conservation–release phase* in which the system's success in attracting demand creates pressure that threatens its long-term stability, demanding transformative governance measures.

From a strategic management perspective, these adaptive states correspond to the dynamic capabilities framework (Teece et al., 1997). Destinations that sense environmental changes (e.g., shifts in tourist demand, emerging sustainability norms), seize opportunities (e.g., diversification into cultural or eco-tourism), and transform internal processes (e.g., governance coordination, digital integration) are more likely to sustain competitiveness in turbulent markets. Resilience, therefore, operates as both a strategic outcome and a managerial process that reinforces adaptive learning.

6.2. Strategic Balance between Sustainability and Competitiveness

The Greek case illustrates that resilience cannot be equated solely with growth or stability; it depends on a destination's ability to balance sustainability and competitiveness. Destinations with high carrying capacity but limited attractiveness risk economic inefficiency, while those with high attractiveness and low capacity face environmental degradation and declining quality of life. The strategic imperative lies in achieving dynamic balance, allowing short-term performance to coexist with long-term viability (Crouch, 2011).

Athens' high attractiveness but constrained capacity demonstrates how success can breed vulnerability. Without redistributive strategies—such as promoting nearby alternative destinations or managing visitor flows through smart mobility systems—sustained pressure on resources may erode resilience. Conversely, destinations such as Kalamata and Pylos, with underutilized potential, can strengthen resilience by selectively increasing visitation and enhancing product differentiation, provided they monitor ecological thresholds.

These findings confirm that strategic adaptation is context-dependent: resilience strategies must align with local resource bases, governance capacity, and market positioning (Becken & Hughey, 2013). A one-size-fits-all approach to resilience is ineffective; rather, destinations need bespoke strategic mixes that integrate environmental stewardship, entrepreneurship, and community engagement.

6.3. Governance, Collaboration, and Knowledge Sharing

Resilient adaptation also depends on governance structures that facilitate collective decision-making and stakeholder coordination (Dredge & Jenkins, 2011). In fragmented tourism systems such as Greece's, destination management organizations (DMOs) often operate with limited authority and resources. Strengthening institutional capacity—through public–private partnerships, knowledge networks, and data-driven planning—is essential for embedding adaptive learning within governance processes.

Inter-destination collaboration offers another avenue for resilience. Destinations within the same adaptive cluster can share best practices, jointly market complementary products, and coordinate visitor distribution. For instance, smaller Peloponnesian towns could leverage Athens' high visibility by forming regional circuits that diffuse demand and prolong visitor stays. Such cooperative strategies align with the notion of networked resilience, where interdependence becomes a resource rather than a vulnerability (Lew et al., 2016).

6.4. Innovation and Digital Transformation

Technological innovation plays a dual role in strategic adaptation: enhancing efficiency and facilitating data-driven resilience management. Digital platforms enable real-time monitoring of visitor flows, capacity utilization, and environmental indicators, allowing DMOs to make adaptive decisions (Gretzel et al., 2015). Moreover, digital marketing and virtual experiences broaden market reach and diversify revenue streams—critical for destinations recovering from crises.

Entrepreneurial actors are central to this transformation. The adoption of digital reservation systems, smart mobility applications, and sustainability certification schemes reflects micro-level adaptive behaviors that aggregate into system-wide resilience (O'Connor, Esfandiar & Hallak, 2025). Policy frameworks that incentivize innovation—through funding, training, and infrastructure—thus serve as catalysts for adaptive competitiveness.

6.5. Toward a Framework of Adaptive Maturity

Synthesizing these insights, destinations can be positioned along a continuum of adaptive maturity:

1. Foundational Adaptors – destinations in early stages of strategic development, characterized by low attractiveness but high sustainability potential; require investment in capacity building and innovation.
2. Balancing Adaptors – destinations that have achieved equilibrium between sustainability and demand; require monitoring and incremental policy adjustments to preserve balance.
3. Transformational Adaptors – mature destinations facing over-tourism or environmental stress; require transformative governance, diversification, and technological integration.

This continuum provides a heuristic for policymakers and scholars to evaluate where destinations stand in terms of resilience and to design tailored strategies for advancing along the adaptive maturity spectrum.

7. MANAGERIAL AND POLICY IMPLICATIONS

7.1. For Destination Management Organizations (DMOs)

DMOs serve as key orchestrators of resilience by integrating diverse stakeholder interests into coherent strategic plans. The study suggests that DMOs should:

- Implement dynamic monitoring systems to track carrying capacity and performance indicators in real time.
- Develop diversification strategies that reduce dependence on specific markets or seasons, promoting year-round tourism.
- Invest in human capital and digital literacy, enabling staff to respond rapidly to emerging challenges.
- Adopt participatory governance models, involving residents and local businesses in strategy formulation to enhance legitimacy and adaptive alignment.

By institutionalizing these practices, DMOs can move from reactive crisis management to anticipatory adaptation, fostering a culture of resilience within destination governance.

7.2. For Tourism Entrepreneurs and Firms

Entrepreneurial resilience is the micro-foundation of destination resilience (Bullough & Renko, 2013). Tourism enterprises can strengthen adaptive capacity by:

- Diversifying products and experiences (e.g., gastronomy, heritage, ecotourism) to attract varied market segments.
- Forming local business networks that share resources, coordinate pricing strategies, and jointly market their offerings.
- Investing in digital transformation—from data analytics to e-commerce platforms—to enhance operational flexibility.
- Engaging in corporate social responsibility (CSR) and sustainability initiatives that align business goals with community well-being.

These practices reinforce mutual dependencies between firms and destinations, embedding resilience across the tourism value chain.

7.3. For Policymakers and Regional Authorities

At the policy level, resilience requires enabling environments that balance regulation with innovation. Governments can support strategic adaptation by:

- Creating integrated regional tourism observatories that collect and disseminate performance data.
- Establishing financial incentives (tax breaks, grants) for sustainable infrastructure and innovation investments.
- Facilitating cross-regional collaboration through joint marketing and knowledge-exchange programs.
- Embedding resilience metrics within tourism planning documents and performance evaluations.

In Greece, decentralization reforms that empower regional DMOs and municipalities could enhance responsiveness and align local strategies with national resilience objectives.

7.4. Academic and Research Implications

The study underscores the need for further theoretical integration between strategic management and resilience theory in tourism. Future research should explore:

- Longitudinal analyses of destination adaptation trajectories.
- Comparative studies across countries to validate the adaptive maturity continuum.
- Quantitative modeling of resilience indicators using multi-criteria decision analysis or data envelopment analysis (DEA).
- Examination of social and cultural dimensions of resilience, including community identity and resident attitudes.

Advancing this research agenda will deepen understanding of how strategic adaptation processes operate across scales and contexts.

8. CONCLUSIONS

This chapter has explored the intersection of *strategy and resilience* within the context of tourism destination management, drawing insights from empirical analysis of Greek destinations. By reframing the traditional competitive analysis into an adaptive framework, it has demonstrated that resilience is not a static attribute but a strategic process rooted in continuous learning, innovation, and capacity balancing.

Three principal conclusions emerge:

1. Resilience as Strategic Adaptation: Destinations must continually recalibrate strategies to maintain equilibrium between sustainability and competitiveness. Adaptive capacity—the ability to sense, seize, and transform—constitutes the essence of destination resilience.
2. Differentiated Adaptive Pathways: Greek destinations exhibit diverse adaptation modes, from latent to transformational resilience. Recognizing these pathways allows policymakers and managers to design tailored interventions rather than uniform policies.
3. Integrated Governance for Resilience: Effective adaptation requires multi-level coordination, digital innovation, and participatory governance. DMOs, entrepreneurs, and public authorities must act as co-producers of resilience through data-driven decision-making and collaborative learning.

Ultimately, strategic adaptation represents the bridge between entrepreneurship and resilience in turbulent globalized economies. By embracing this paradigm, tourism destinations can transform crises into opportunities for renewal and sustainable growth. The Greek experience illustrates that even amid volatility, destinations endowed with strategic foresight, institutional learning, and collective engagement can not only survive but thrive in the face of uncertainty.

9. REFERENCES

Alonso, A. D., Kok, S. K., Bressan, A., O'Shea, M., Sakellarios, N., Koresis, A., Buitrago Solis, M. A., & Santoni, L. J. (2020). COVID-19, aftermath, impacts, and hospitality firms: An international perspective. *International Journal of Hospitality Management, 91*, 102654. Advance online publication. DOI: 10.1016/j.ijhm.2020.102654 PMID: 32863526

Argyris, C., & Schön, D. A. (1978). *Organizational learning: A theory of action perspective*. Addison-Wesley.

Baggio, R. (2017). Network science and tourism – the state of the art. *Tourism Review, 72*(1), 120–131. DOI: 10.1108/TR-01-2017-0008

Baggio, R., & Cooper, C. (2010). Knowledge transfer in a tourism destination: The effects of a network structure. *Service Industries Journal, 30*(10), 1757–1771. DOI: 10.1080/02642060903580649

Bank of Greece. (2023). *Annual report on the Greek economy*. Bank of Greece Publications.

Barney, J. B. (1991). Firm resources and sustained competitive advantage. *Journal of Management, 17*(1), 99–120. DOI: 10.1177/014920639101700108

Becken, S. (2013). Operators' perceptions of energy use and actual saving opportunities for tourism accommodation. *Asia Pacific Journal of Tourism Research, 18*(1–2), 19–33. DOI: 10.1080/10941665.2012.688512

Becken, S., & Hughey, K. F. D. (2013). Linking tourism into emergency management structures to enhance disaster risk reduction. *Tourism Management, 36*, 77–85. DOI: 10.1016/j.tourman.2012.11.006

Beritelli, P., & Bieger, T. (2014). From destination governance to destination leadership – defining and exploring the significance with the help of a systemic perspective. *Tourism Review, 69*(1), 25–46. DOI: 10.1108/TR-07-2013-0043

Biggs, D., Hall, C. M., & Stoeckl, N. (2015). The resilience of formal and informal tourism enterprises to disasters: Reef tourism in Phuket, Thailand. *Journal of Sustainable Tourism, 20*(5), 645–665. DOI: 10.1080/09669582.2011.630080

Bullough, A., & Renko, M. (2013). Entrepreneurial resilience during challenging times. *Business Horizons, 56*(3), 343–350. DOI: 10.1016/j.bushor.2013.01.001

Butler, R. W. (1980). The concept of a tourist area cycle of evolution: Implications for management of resources. *The Canadian Geographer. Geographe Canadien, 24*(1), 5–12. DOI: 10.1111/j.1541-0064.1980.tb00970.x

Calgaro, E., Lloyd, K., & Dominey-Howes, D. (2014). From vulnerability to transformation: A framework for assessing the vulnerability and resilience of tourism destinations. *Journal of Sustainable Tourism, 22*(3), 341–360. DOI: 10.1080/09669582.2013.826229

Capocchi, A., Vallone, C., Pierotti, M., & Amaduzzi, A. (2020). Correction: Capocchi, A., et al. Overtourism: A Literature Review to Assess Implications and Future Perspectives. *Sustainability* 2019, *11*, 3303. *Sustainability, 12*(4), 1541. https://doi.org/DOI: 10.3390/su12041541

Coccossis, H., & Mexa, A. (2017). *The challenge of tourism carrying capacity assessment: Theory and practice*. Routledge., DOI: 10.4324/9781315240817

Cohen, W. M., & Levinthal, D. A. (1990). Absorptive capacity: A new perspective on learning and innovation. *Administrative Science Quarterly, 35*(1), 128–152. DOI: 10.2307/2393553

Cooper, C. (2006). Knowledge management and tourism. *Annals of Tourism Research, 33*(1), 47–64. DOI: 10.1016/j.annals.2005.04.005

Crouch, G. I. (2011). Destination competitiveness: An analysis of determinant attributes. *Journal of Travel Research, 50*(1), 27–45. DOI: 10.1177/0047287510362776

Dess, G. G., McNamara, G., Eisner, A. B., & Sauerwald, S. (2023). *Strategic management: Text and cases* (11th ed.). McGraw Hill.

Dredge, D., & Jenkins, J. (2011). *Stories of practice: Tourism policy and planning*. Ashgate.

Dwyer, L., Edwards, D., Mistilis, N., Roman, C., & Scott, N. (2020). *Tourism management strategies for global competitiveness*. Channel View Publications.

Dwyer, L., & Kim, C. (2003). Destination competitiveness: Determinants and indicators. *Current Issues in Tourism, 6*(5), 369–414. DOI: 10.1080/13683500308667962

Eisenhardt, K. M., & Martin, J. A. (2000). Dynamic capabilities: What are they? *Strategic Management Journal, 21*(10-11), 1105–1121. https://sms.onlinelibrary.wiley.com/doi/abs/10.1002/1097-0266%28200010/11%2921%3A10/11%3C1105%3A%3AAID-SMJ133%3E3.0.CO%3B2-E

Espiner, S., Orchiston, C., & Higham, J. E. (2017). Resilience and sustainability: A complementary relationship? Towards a practical conceptual model for the sustainability–resilience nexus in tourism. *Journal of Sustainable Tourism, 25*, 1385–1400.

European Commission. (2025). *EU Tourism Transition Pathway: Towards a sustainable and resilient tourism sector.* European Union Publications. https://transition-pathways.europa.eu/tourism

Evans, N. (2024). *Strategic management for tourism, hospitality and events* (4th ed.). Routledge.

Folke, C. (2006). Resilience: The emergence of a perspective for social–ecological systems analyses. *Global Environmental Change, 16*(3), 253–267. DOI: 10.1016/j.gloenvcha.2006.04.002

Fragkoudis, A., Vrana, V., Karavasilis, G., & Kehris, E. (2024). Tourism Agents in Greece Recovering from COVID-19. In Kavoura, A., Borges-Tiago, T., & Tiago, F. (Eds.), *Strategic Innovative Marketing and Tourism. ICSIMAT 2023. Springer Proceedings in Business and Economics*. Springer., DOI: 10.1007/978-3-031-51038-0_40

Gazis, Z. (2019). *Η φέρουσα ικανότητα τουριστικής ανάπτυξης: Εφαρμογή στις 13 ελληνικές περιφέρειες* [Tourism carrying capacity: Its application on the 13 Greek regions] [Master's thesis, National Technical University of Athens]. http://dx.doi.org/DOI: 10.26240/heal.ntua.18183

Georgopoulos, N. B. (2013). *Στρατηγικό μάνατζμεντ* [Strategic management]. 3rd ed.). Kritiki.

Goffi, G., Cucculelli, M., & Masiero, L. (2019). Fostering tourism destination competitiveness in developing countries: The role of sustainability. *Journal of Cleaner Production, 209*, 101–115. DOI: 10.1016/j.jclepro.2018.10.208

Gössling, S., Balas, M., Mayer, M., & Sun, Y.-Y. (2023). A review of tourism and climate change mitigation: The scales, scopes, stakeholders and strategies of carbon management. *Tourism Management, 95*, 104681. DOI: 10.1016/j.tourman.2022.104681

Gössling, S., & Mei, X. Y. (2025). AI and sustainable tourism: An assessment of risks and opportunities for the SDGs. *Current Issues in Tourism*. Advance online publication. DOI: 10.1080/13683500.2025.2477142

Gretzel, U., Sigala, M., Xiang, Z., & Koo, C. (2015). Smart tourism: Foundations and developments. *Electronic Markets, 25*(3), 179–188. DOI: 10.1007/s12525-015-0196-8

Hall, C. M., Prayag, G., & Amore, A. (2017). *Tourism and resilience: Individual, organisational and destination perspectives*. Channel View Publications., DOI: 10.2307/jj.22730545

Hall, C. M., Scott, D., & Gössling, S. (2022). Pandemics, transformations and tourism: Be careful what you wish for. *Tourism Geographies*, *24*(3), 427–444. DOI: 10.1080/14616688.2020.1759131

Hayward, K. M. (2006) Legitimising the TALC as a Theory of Development in Butler, R.W. (ed.) The Tourism Area Life Cycle Volume 2 Conceptual and Theoretical Issues 29-44 Clevedon: Channelview Publications. http://books.google.co.uk/books?id=AicuoXTVrU0C&pg=PP1&dq=The+Tourism+Area+Life+Cycle+Volum e+2+Conceptual+and+Theoretical&hl=en&ei=MPpvTKPWHo774Ab-3mZHeCA&sa=X&oi=book_result&ct= result&resnum=1&ved=0CCgQ6A-EwAA#v=onepage&q&f=false

Holling, C. S. (2001). Understanding the complexity of economic, ecological, and social systems. *Ecosystems (New York, N.Y.)*, *4*(5), 390–405. DOI: 10.1007/s10021-001-0101-5

INSETE. (2023). The contribution of tourism to the Greek economy in 2023. Institute of the Association of Greek Tourism Enterprises. https://insete.gr/wp-content/uploads/2024/04/25_05_Tourism_and_Greek_Economy_2019-2023-ENG.pdf

Ivars-Baidal, J. A., Celdrán-Bernabeu, M. A., Mazón, J. N., & Perles-Ivars, Á. F. (2017). Smart destinations and the evolution of ICTs: A new scenario for destination management? *Current Issues in Tourism*, *22*(13), 1581–1600. DOI: 10.1080/13683500.2017.1388771

Johnson, G., Whittington, R., Scholes, K., Angwin, D., & Regnér, P. (2016). *Βασικές αρχές στρατηγικής των επιχειρήσεων* [Fundamentals of business strategy]. 2nd ed.). Kritiki.

Karagiannis, S., & Thomakos, D. (2020). Quantitative assessment of the tourism carrying capacity in Greece: A case study of Cyclades. *Tourism Today (Nicosia)*, *19*, 36–64. https://www.researchgate.net/publication/348049034_Quantitative_Assessment_of_the_Tourism_Carrying_Capacity_in_Greece_A_Case_Study_of_Cyclades

Khavarian-Garmsir, A. R., & Zare, S. M. (2015). SOAR Framework as a New Model for the Strategic Planning of Sustainable Tourism. *Tourism Planning & Development*, *12*, 321–332.

Kuckertz, A., Brändle, L., Gaudig, A., Hinderer, S., Reyes, C. A. M., Prochotta, A., Steinbrink, K. M., & Berger, E. S. C. (2020). Startups in times of crisis – A rapid response to the COVID-19 pandemic. *Journal of Business Venturing Insights, 13*, e00169. DOI: 10.1016/j.jbvi.2020.e00169

Lee, B. K., Agarwal, S., & Kim, H. J. (2012). Influences of travel constraints on the people with disabilities' intention to travel: An application of Seligman's helplessness theory. *Tourism Management, 33*(3), 569–579. DOI: 10.1016/j.tourman.2011.06.011

Leka, A., Lagarias, A., Panagiotopoulou, A., & Stratigea, A. (2022). Development of a Tourism Carrying Capacity Index (TCCI) for sustainable management of coastal areas in Mediterranean islands - Case study Naxos, Greece. *Ocean and Coastal Management, 216*, 105978. DOI: 10.1016/j.ocecoaman.2021.105978

Lengnick-Hall, C. A., & Beck, T. E. (2005). Adaptive fit versus robust transformation: How organizations respond to environmental change. *Journal of Management, 31*(5), 738–757. DOI: 10.1177/0149206305279367

Lew, A. A., Cheer, J. M., Haywood, M., Brouder, P., & Salazar, N. B. (2016). Visions of travel and tourism after the global COVID-19 transformation of 2020. *Tourism Geographies, 22*(3), 455–466. DOI: 10.1080/14616688.2020.1770326

Marques, J. i Santos, N. (2016). Developing business tourism beyond major urban centres: The perspectives of local stakeholders. *Tourism and Hospitality Management, 22*(1), 1–15. DOI: 10.20867/thm.22.1.3

McLeod, M., Dodds, R., & Butler, R. (2021). Introduction to special issue on island tourism resilience. *Tourism Geographies, 23*(3), 361–370. DOI: 10.1080/14616688.2021.1898672

Mintzberg, H., Ahlstrand, B., & Lampel, J. (2005). *Strategy safari: A guided tour through the wilds of strategic management* (2nd ed.). Free Press.

O'Connor, P., Esfandiar, K., & Hallak, R. (2025). Resilience for hospitality and tourism enterprises: A review and directions for future research. *Tourism Analysis, 30*(1), 5–22. DOI: 10.3727/108354224X17209729214520

O'Reilly, A. M. (1986). Tourism carrying capacity: Concept and issues. *Tourism Management, 7*(4), 254–258. DOI: 10.1016/0261-5177(86)90035-X

OECD. (2025a). *Enhancing the enabling environment for micro and small tourism enterprises in Greece*. OECD Publishing., DOI: 10.1787/48b4382b-

OECD. (2025b). *Building strong and resilient tourism destinations: Policy approaches for diversification*. OECD Publishing., DOI: 10.1787/a57c343d-

OECD. (2025c). *Strengthening the evidence base for a sustainable tourism future in Greece: A tailored set of 33 indicators*. OECD Publishing., DOI: 10.1787/6e46e845-

OECD. (2025d). *OECD diversifying tourism offerings for resilience: Guidance for regional alliances*. OECD Publishing.

OECD. (2025e). OECD Tourism Trends and Policies 2022. OECD Publishing. https://www.oecd.org/en/publications/oecd-tourism-trends-and-policies-2022_a8dd3019-en/full-report/greece_095e7405.html

Paapa, C., & Nguthi, S. (2025). Crisis Management and Resilience in Hospitality and Tourism Consulting. *African Journal of Tourism and Hospitality Management, 4*(1), 246–259. DOI: 10.37284/ajthm.4.1.3203

Pelling, M., & Dilling, L. (2011). *Adaptation to climate change: From resilience to transformation*. Routledge.

Pike, S., & Page, S. J. (2014). Destination marketing organizations and destination marketing: A narrative analysis of the literature. *Tourism Management, 41*, 202–227. DOI: 10.1016/j.tourman.2013.09.009

Porter, M. E. (1980). *Competitive strategy: Techniques for analyzing industries and competitors*. Free Press.

Prayag, G., Spector, S., Orchiston, C., & Chowdhury, M. (2019). Psychological resilience, organizational resilience and life satisfaction in tourism firms: Insights from the Canterbury earthquakes. *Current Issues in Tourism, 23*(10), 1216–1233. DOI: 10.1080/13683500.2019.1607832

Ritchie, B. W. (2018). *Crisis and disaster management for tourism*. Channel View Publications.

Ritchie, J. R. B., & Crouch, G. I. (2003). *The competitive destination: A sustainable tourism perspective*. CABI Publishing.

Rothaermel, F. T. (2023). *Strategic management* (6th ed.). McGraw Hill.

Schumpeter, J. A. (2021). The theory of economic development. Routledge. https://www.routledge.com/The-Theory-of-Economic-Development/Schumpeter/p/book/9780367705268

Spilanis, I., Kizos, T., & Karampela, S. (2015). *Νησιωτικότητα και βιωσιμότητα: Η περίπτωση των νησιών του Αιγαίου* [Insularity and sustainability: The case of the Aegean Islands]. University of the Aegean.

Teece, D. J. (2018). Business models and dynamic capabilities. *Long Range Planning, 51*(1), 40–49. DOI: 10.1016/j.lrp.2017.06.007

Teece, D. J., Pisano, G., & Shuen, A. (1997). Dynamic capabilities and strategic management. *Strategic Management Journal, 18*(7), 509–533. DOI: 10.1002/(SICI)1097-0266(199708)18:7<509:AID-SMJ882>3.0.CO;2-Z

Torres-Delgado, A., & Saarinen, J. (2013). Using indicators to assess sustainable tourism development: A review. *Tourism Geographies, 16*(1), 31–47. DOI: 10.1080/14616688.2013.867530

Tourism, U. N. (2025). Safe Destinations Challenge: Strengthening tourism resilience. United Nations World Tourism Organization. https://www.untourism.int/news/un-tourism-launches-the-safe-destinations-challenge-to-strengthen-tourism-resilience-in-europe-and-beyond

Tourism, U. N. (n.d.). Digital transformation in tourism. United Nations World Tourism Organization. https://www.unwto.org/digital-transformation

Vandarakis, D., Malliouri, D., Petrakis, S., Kapsimalis, V., Moraitis, V., Hatiris, G.-A., & Panagiotopoulos, I. (2023). Carrying Capacity and Assessment of the Tourism Sector in the South Aegean Region, Greece. *Water (Basel), 15*(14), 2616. DOI: 10.3390/w15142616

Varelas, S. (2016). *Στρατηγικές ανάπτυξης τουριστικών επιχειρήσεων: Η περίπτωση των ξενοδοχειακών επιχειρήσεων* [Tourism enterprises development strategies: The case of hotel enterprises] [Doctoral dissertation, National Documentation Centre of Greece]. http://dx.doi.org/DOI: 10.12681/eadd/39663

Varelas, S., & Belias, D. (2019). Carrying capacity assessment for tourism development: A strategic approach. In Kavoura, A., Kefallonitis, E., & Giovanis, A. (Eds.), *Strategic innovative marketing and tourism* (pp. 775–782). Springer., DOI: 10.1007/978-3-030-12453-3_100

Varelas, S., & Tsoupros, G. (2024). Key performance indicators and data envelopment analysis in Greek tourism: A strategic planning tool for destinations and DMMOs. *Sustainability, 16*(8), 3453. DOI: 10.3390/su16083453

Yin, R. K. (2018). *Case study research and applications: Design and methods* (6th ed.). SAGE Publications.

Zehrer, A., & Hallmann, K. (2015). A stakeholder perspective on policy indicators of destination competitiveness. *Journal of Destination Marketing & Management, 4*(2), 120–126. DOI: 10.1016/j.jdmm.2015.03.003

Compilation of References

Aaouid, B., Elboussadi, A., & Boubker, O. (2025). Entrepreneurial Resilience in Times of Crisis: A Bibliometric Analysis. *Entrepreneurial Business and Economics Review, 13*(3), 55–75. DOI: 10.15678/EBER.2025.130303

Aaouid, B., Elboussadi, A., Boubker, O., & Nejjari, Z. (2024). Entrepreneurial bricolage: A systematic literature network analysis and TCCM approach. *Scientific African, 26*, e02474. DOI: 10.1016/j.sciaf.2024.e02474

Abhiyan, W. N. T. (2017). Sustainable development goals: Agenda 2030. *India 2017: a civil society report.*

Adamic, D., & Friedberg, A. L. (2023). Getting China Wrong. *Naval War College Review, 76*(3), 11. Retrieved 2025, from https://digital-commons.usnwc.edu/nwc-review/vol76/iss3/11

Adenike, O. (2016). Challenges of entrepreneurship education in Nigeria. *Journal of Business and Management, 8*(3), 12–25. DOI-DOI: 10.5901/jesr.2016.v6nip208

Ahmed, A. E., Ucbasaran, D., Cacciotti, G., & Williams, T. A. (2022). Integrating psychological resilience, stress, and coping in entrepreneurship: A critical review and research agenda. *Entrepreneurship Theory and Practice, 46*(3), 497–538. DOI: 10.1177/10422587211046542

Ahmed, F., Sohag, K., Islam, M. M., & Hassan, M. K. (2025). Navigating turbulence: How do geopolitical risks and oil price shocks shape global equity markets? A GVAR approach. *Borsa Istanbul Review, 25*(3), 449–467. DOI: 10.1016/j.bir.2025.01.016

Aithal, P. S. (2024). Financial literacy for economic empowerment: Microfinance initiatives in Indian SHGs. [PIJTRCS]. *Poornaprajna International Journal of Teaching & Research Case Studies, 1*(1), 80–91.

Alegwu, F. O., Aye, G. C., & Asogwa, B. C. (2017). Asymmetric effect of real exchange rate volatility on agricultural products export: a case study. *Economia Internazionale/International Economics, 70*(3), 261-79.

Ali, I., Golgeci, I., & Arslan, A. (2021). Achieving resilience through knowledge management practices and risk management culture in agri-food supply chains. *Supply Chain Management, 28*(2), 284–299.

Alka, T. A., Sreenivasan, A., & Suresh, M. (2025). Entrepreneurial strategies for sustainable growth: A deep dive into cloud-native technology and its applications. *Future Business Journal, 11*(1), 14.

Allam, Z., Bibri, S. E., & Sharpe, S. A. (2022). The rising impacts of the COVID-19 pandemic and the Russia–Ukraine war: Energy transition, climate justice, global inequality, and supply chain disruption. *Resources, 11*(11), 99. DOI: 10.3390/resources11110099

Allison, G. (2017). *Destined for War: Can America and China Escape Thucydides's Trap?* Houghton Mifflin Harcourt.

Alonso, A. D., Kok, S. K., Bressan, A., O'Shea, M., Sakellarios, N., Koresis, A., Buitrago Solis, M. A., & Santoni, L. J. (2020). COVID-19, aftermath, impacts, and hospitality firms: An international perspective. *International Journal of Hospitality Management, 91*, 102654. Advance online publication. DOI: 10.1016/j.ijhm.2020.102654 PMID: 32863526

Al-Rousan, N., Al-Najjar, H., & Al-Najjar, D. (2024). The impact of Russo-Ukrainian war, COVID-19, and oil prices on global food security. *Heliyon, 10*(8), e29279. DOI: 10.1016/j.heliyon.2024.e29279 PMID: 38638981

Alshebami, A. S. (2025). Purpose-Driven Resilience: A Blueprint for Sustainable Growth in Micro-and Small Enterprises in Turbulent Contexts. *Sustainability, 17*(5), 2308. DOI: 10.3390/su17052308

Altin, M., Koseoglu, M. A., Yu, X., & Riasi, A. (2018). Performance measurement and management research in the hospitality and tourism industry. *International Journal of Contemporary Hospitality Management, 30*(2), 1172–1189. DOI: 10.1108/IJCHM-05-2017-0251

Amin, S. (1976). *Unequal Development: An Essay on the Social Formations of Peripheral Capitalism.* Sussex, England: The Harvester Press. Retrieved 2025, from https://sahistory.org.za/sites/default/files/archive-files3/unequal_development_by_samir_amin.pdf

Amin, M., Jolevski, F., & Islam, A. M. (2023). *The Resilience of SMEs and Large Firms in the COVID-19 Pandemic*. World Bank.

Anand, A., Singh, S. K., Bowen, M., & Rangarajan, D. (2024). Strategic renewal during crises: A pragmatist proposition for multinational enterprises in a globalized world. *Journal of International Management*, *30*(3), 101134. DOI: 10.1016/j.intman.2024.101134

Anastasopoulos, I. (2025). *Strategic management frameworks and policy approaches for tourism investment decision making: The case of tourism real estate and mixed use developments* (Doctoral dissertation, University of Piraeus). Hellenic National Archive of PhD Theses. https://doi.org/DOI: 10.12681/eadd/59316

Anthony, R. N., & Govindarajan, V. (2007). Management control systems (12e éd.). McGraw-Hill.

Anuradha, A., Chowdhury, P. R., & Biswas, A. (2024). Post-Pandemic Recovery Measures to Ensure Socio Economic Sustainability through FDI in Smart tourism. [EEL]. *European Economic Letters*, *14*(1), 1498–1509.

Anwar, I., Khan, S. Z., & Gomathi,S. (2023). Role of entrepreneurial passion and self-efficacy in fostering resilience. *Business Case Studies*, 2025.

Apatan, L. B., Casicas, L. E., Jarlata, J. A. P., Panga, J. R., Ugsod, I. M. B., & Teh, C. R. (2025). Technological Advancement and its Effect on Business Operations. *Research Journal in Business and Economics*, *3*(3), 103–114.

Apostolopoulos, N., Ratten, V., Petropoulos, D., Liargovas, P., & Anastasopoulou, E. (2021). Agri-food sector and entrepreneurship during the COVID-19 crisis: A systematic literature review and research agenda. *Strategic Change*, *30*(2), 159–167. DOI: 10.1002/jsc.2400

Argote, L., Ingram, P., Levine, J. M., & Moreland, R. L. (2000). Knowledge transfer in organizations: Learning from the experience of others. *Organizational Behavior and Human Decision Processes*, *82*(1), 1–8.

Argyris, C., & Schön, D. A. (1978). *Organizational learning: A theory of action perspective*. Addison-Wesley.

Arief, A. M. (2024). *Tantangan UMKM Bukan Digitalisasi, Tapi Daya Saing*. Katadata.Co.Id. https://katadata.co.id/berita/industri/66a0b52c6b5b5/menkop-teten-tantangan-umkm-bukan-digitalisasi-tapi-daya-saing

Asean, A. (2025). *ASEAN Strategic Action Plan for SME Development 2016-2025*. 1–10. https://asean.org/book/asean-strategic-action-plan-for-sme-development-2016-2025/

Asifulla, A., & Basha, H. M. (2023). Supply Chain Finance in SMEs A Conceptual Analysis. *Journal of Informatics Education and Research, 3*(2), 2181–2187. DOI: 10.52783/JIER.V3I2.365

Assaf, A. G., & Tsionas, M. (2018). Measuring hotel performance: Toward more rigorous evidence in both scope and methods. *Tourism Management, 69*, 69–87. DOI: 10.1016/j.tourman.2018.05.008

Audretsch, D. B., & Belitski, M. (2021). Entrepreneurial ecosystems in cities: The role of institutions. *World Bank Working Paper*.DOI:DOI: 10.1007/s10961-016-9473-8

Audretsch, D. B., Belitski, M., Caiazza, R., & Lehmann, E. E. (2020). Knowledge management and entrepreneurship. *The International Entrepreneurship and Management Journal, 16*(2), 373–385.

Audretsch, D. B., Belitski, M., & Desai, S. (2020). National business regulations and city entrepreneurship in Europe: A multilevel spatial analysis. *Entrepreneurship Theory and Practice, 44*(6), 1121–1145.

Audretsch, D. B., Belitski, M., & Desai, S. (2020). National business regulations and city-level entrepreneurship. *Small Business Economics, 54*(4), 1107–1128. DOI: 10.1007/s11187-018-01136-6

Audretsch, D. B., Lehmann, E. E., & Seitz, N. (2020). Universities as anchors of high-tech regional development: The case of university–industry knowledge transfer. *Regional Studies, 54*(7), 999–1008.

Autesserre, S. (2012). Peaceland: Conflict Resolution and the Everyday Politics of International Intervention. *Politics of International Intervention*. doi:DOI: 10.1017/CBO9781107280366

Autio, E. (2017). Strategic entrepreneurial internationalization: A normative framework. *Strategic Entrepreneurship Journal, 11*(3), 211–227. DOI: 10.1002/sej.1261

Ayala, J. C., & Manzano, G. (2014). The resilience of the entrepreneur. Influence on the success of the business. A longitudinal analysis. *Journal of Economic Psychology, 42*, 126–135. DOI: 10.1016/j.joep.2014.02.004

Baah, F. A., & Rambe, P. (2024). Exploring learning capability on entrepreneurial resilience of emerging contractor firms. *Acta Commercii-Independent Research Journal in the Management Sciences, 24*(1), 1266.

Bach, D. C. (2016). Cross-Border Interactions and Regionalism. In D. H. Levine, & D. Nagar, *Region-Building in Africa: Political and Economic Challenges* (pp. 71-88). New York: Palgrave Macmillan. doi:https://doi.org/DOI: 10.1057/9781137586117_5

Bachtiar, N. K., Setiawan, A., Prastyan, G. A., & Kijkasiwat, P. (2023). Business Resilience and Growth Strategy Transformation Post Crisis. *Journal of Innovation and Entrepreneurship, 12*(1), 1–25. DOI: 10.1186/S13731-023-00345-5/FIGURES/3

Baggio, R. (2017). Network science and tourism – the state of the art. *Tourism Review, 72*(1), 120–131. DOI: 10.1108/TR-01-2017-0008

Baggio, R., & Cooper, C. (2010). Knowledge transfer in a tourism destination: The effects of a network structure. *Service Industries Journal, 30*(10), 1757–1771. DOI: 10.1080/02642060903580649

Bai, X., Krishna, K., & Ma, H. (2017). How you export matters: Export mode, learning and productivity in China. *Journal of International Economics, 104*, 122–137. DOI: 10.1016/j.jinteco.2016.10.009

Ballentine, K., & Sherman, J. (2003). *The Political Economy of Armed Conflict: Beyond Greed and Grievance*. Lynne Rienner Pub., Retrieved 2025, from.

Balogun, M. (2023). Strategies to promote entrepreneurship education in Nigerian higher institutions. *Education Journal, 15*(2), 35–48.

Balzano, M., Marzi, G., & Turzo, T. (2025). SMEs and Institutional Theory: Major Inroads and Opportunities Ahead. *Management Decision, 63*(13), 1–27. DOI: 10.1108/MD-05-2023-0734

Banga, K., & te Velde, D. W. (2020). COVID-19 and disruption of the digital economy; evidence from low and middle-income countries. *Digital Pathways at Oxford Paper Series, 7.*

Bank of Greece. (2023). *Annual report on the Greek economy*. Bank of Greece Publications.

Baporikar, N. (2020). *Entrepreneurship Education and Training: The Issue of Effectiveness*. IGI Global.

Barber, N., & Scarcelli, J. M. (2010). Enhancing the assessment of tangible service quality through the creation of a cleanliness measurement scale. *Managing Service Quality, 20*(1), 70–88. DOI: 10.1108/09604521011011630

Barnett, M., & Finnemore, M. (2004). Rules for the World. Cornell: Cornell University Press.

Barney, J. (1991). Firm resources and sustained competitive advantage. *Journal of Management, 17*(1), 99–120. DOI: 10.1177/014920639101700108

Barney, J. B. (2000). Firm resources and sustained competitive advantage. In Baum, J. A. C., & Dobbin, F. (Eds.), *Economics meets sociology in strategic management* (pp. 203–227). Emerald Group Publishing Limited., DOI: 10.1016/S0742-3322(00)17018-4

Barney, J. B., & Hesterly, W. S. (2019). *Strategic management and competitive advantage: Concepts and cases* (6th ed.). Pearson.

Baron, D. P. (2007). Corporate social responsibility and social entrepreneurship. *Journal of Economics & Management Strategy, 16*(3), 683–717.

Bartik, A. W., Bertrand, M., Cullen, Z., Glaeser, E. L., Luca, M., & Stanton, C. (2020). The impact of COVID-19 on small business outcomes and expectations. *Proceedings of the National Academy of Sciences of the United States of America, 117*(30), 17656–17666. DOI: 10.1073/pnas.2006991117 PMID: 32651281

Barton, R. M. (1993). *Crisis management.* Oxford University Press.

Basri, Y. M., Taufik, T., Yasni, H., & Putri, R. I. (2022). Institutional Pressure and Social Entrepreneurship Orientation: Their Impact on The Performance of Social Enterprises. *Jurnal Reviu Akuntansi Dan Keuangan, 12*(3), 545–559. DOI: 10.22219/JRAK.V12I3.23425

Battaglia, D., & Neirotti, P. (2022). Dealing with the tensions between innovation and internationalization in SMEs: A dynamic capability view. *Journal of Small Business Management, 60*(2), 379–419. DOI: 10.1080/00472778.2020.1711635

Battaglia, D., Paolucci, E., & Neirotti, P. (2018). The role of R&D investments and export on SMEs' growth: A domain ambidexterity perspective. *Management Decision, 56*(1), 226–246. DOI: 10.1108/MD-02-2017-0136

Battilana, J., Leca, B., & Boxenbaum, E. (2009). 2 how actors change institutions: Towards a theory of institutional entrepreneurship. *The Academy of Management Annals, 3*(1), 65–107.

Baum, T. (2018). Sustainable human resource management as a driver in tourism policy and planning: A serious sin of omission? *Journal of Sustainable Tourism, 26*(6), 873–889. DOI: 10.1080/09669582.2017.1423318

Baum, T., & Hai, N. T. T. (2020). Hospitality, tourism, human rights and the impact of COVID-19. *International Journal of Contemporary Hospitality Management, 32*(7), 2397–2407. DOI: 10.1108/IJCHM-03-2020-0242

Becken, S. (2013). Operators' perceptions of energy use and actual saving opportunities for tourism accommodation. *Asia Pacific Journal of Tourism Research, 18*(1–2), 19–33. DOI: 10.1080/10941665.2012.688512

Becken, S., & Hughey, K. F. D. (2013). Linking tourism into emergency management structures to enhance disaster risk reduction. *Tourism Management, 36*, 77–85. DOI: 10.1016/j.tourman.2012.11.006

Becker, T., & Kabongo, J. (2021). The resilience of entrepreneurs in developing economics. *In Research handbook on Organizational resilience*, 116-130. doi:DOI: 10.4337/9781788112215.00016

Becker, G. S. (1993). *Human capital: A theoretical and empirical analysis with special reference to education* (3rd ed.). University of Chicago Press.

Bedford, D. S., Speklé, R. F., & Widener, S. K. (2022). Budgeting and employee stress in times of crisis: Evidence from the Covid-19 pandemic. *Accounting, Organizations and Society, 101*, 101346. DOI: 10.1016/j.aos.2022.101346

Bégin, L., & Chabaud, D. (2010). La résilience des organisations. Le cas d'une entreprise familiale. Revue française de gestion, 200(1), 127–142. https://doi.org/DOI: 10.3166/rfg.200.127-142

Belitski, M., Guenther, C., Kritikos, A. S., & Thurik, R. (2022). Economic effects of the COVID-19 pandemic on entrepreneurship and small businesses. *Small Business Economics, 58*(2), 593–609. DOI: 10.1007/s11187-021-00544-y PMID: 38624899

Benavides Perales, G., & Venegas Martínez, F. (2022). Impact of exchange rate volatility on agricultural trade between the US and Mexico (1990-2017). *Economía: Teoría y Practica*, (56), 131–153. DOI: 10.24275/etypuam/ne/562022/benavides

Bene, C., Godfrey, R., Newsham, A., & Davies, M. (2013, January 14). Resilience: New Utopia or New Tyranny? *Institute of Development Studies, 2012*(405), 1–61. DOI: 10.1111/j.2040-0209.2012.00405.x

Bennett, N., & Lemoine, G. J. (2014). What a difference a word makes: Understanding threats to performance in a VUCA world. *Business Horizons, 57*(3), 311–317. DOI: 10.1016/j.bushor.2014.01.001

Berdal, M., & Keen, D. (1997). Violence and Economic Agendas in Civil Wars: Some Policy Imp. *Millennium, 26*(3), 795–818. DOI: 10.1177/03058298970260030401

Beritelli, P., & Bieger, T. (2014). From destination governance to destination leadership – defining and exploring the significance with the help of a systemic perspective. *Tourism Review, 69*(1), 25–46. DOI: 10.1108/TR-07-2013-0043

Bhamra, R., Dani, S., & Burnard, K. (2011). Resilience: The concept, a literature review and future directions. *International Journal of Production Research, 49*(18), 5375–5393. DOI: 10.1080/00207543.2011.563826

Bhatt, K., Seabra, C., Kumar, J., Ashutosh, K., & Kumar Kabia, S. (2024). Tourism-Led Inclusive Growth in Emerging and Developing Economies: A Systematic Literature Review. *SAGE Open, 14*(2). Advance online publication. DOI: 10.1177/21582440241252516

Bhowmik, S. K. (2012). Street vendors in the global urban economy. Routledge. Chen, M., Ananthakrishnan, T., & Narayan, D. (2021). Urban informal workers and COVID-19: Evidence from India. *World Development, 145*, 105509.

Biggs, D., Hall, C. M., & Stoeckl, N. (2015). The resilience of formal and informal tourism enterprises to disasters: Reef tourism in Phuket, Thailand. *Journal of Sustainable Tourism, 20*(5), 645–665. DOI: 10.1080/09669582.2011.630080

Billon, L., & Philippe. (2001). The political ecology of war: Natural resources and armed conflicts. *Political Geography*, •••, 561–584. DOI: 10.1016/S0962-6298(01)00015-4

Bitner, M. J. (1990). Evaluating service encounters: The effects of physical surroundings and employee responses. *Journal of Marketing, 54*(2), 69–82. DOI: 10.1177/002224299005400206

Blackwill, B. D. (2016). *War by Other Means: Geoeconomics and Statecraft*. Harvard University Press., DOI: 10.2307/j.ctt1c84cr7

Blog, A. D. B. (n.d.). What role does human capital play in innovation? https://blogs.adb.org/blog/what-role-does-human-capital-play-innovation

Boege, V., Brown, A., Clements, K., & Nolan, A. (2009). *On Hybrid Political Orders and Emerging States*. Berlin: Berghof Research Center. Retrieved 2025, from https://berghof-foundation.org/library/on-hybrid-political-orders-and-emerging-states-state-formation-in-the-context-of-fragility

Boin, A., & Van Eeten, M. J. (2013). The Resilient Organization. *Public Management Review, 15*(3), 429–445. DOI: 10.1080/14719037.2013.769856

Bor, O., & Dagistan, N. (2024). The impact of fluctuating international fertiliser prices and exchange rates on domestic fertiliser prices in Türkiye. *Agricultural Economics – Czech, 70*(1), 12–23. https://doi.org/DOI: 10.17221/308/2023-AGRICECON

Borsellino, V., Schimmenti, E., & El Bilali, H. (2020). Agri-food markets towards sustainable patterns. *Sustainability, 12*(6), 2193. DOI: 10.3390/su12062193

Boruah, J., & Aryan, S. (2020). Right to Livelihood for the Street Food Vendors in India. *Indian Journal of Socio-Legal Analysis, 1*(1).

Borzaga, C., & Santuari, A. (2003). New trends in the non-profit sector in Europe: The emergence of social entrepreneurship. *The non-profit sector in a changing economy*, 31-59.

Bozward, D. (2024, January). Election 2024: Entrepreneurship and enterprise education policy for the English Education Ministry. Retrieved from https://david.bozward.com/2024/01/election-2024-entrepreneurship-and-enterprise-education-policy-for-the-english-education-ministry/

Bracci, E., & Tallaki, M. (2021). Resilience capacities and management control systems in public sector organisations. *Journal of Accounting & Organizational Change, 17*(3), 332–351. DOI: 10.1108/JAOC-10-2019-0111

Bradford, A. (2020). *The Brussels Effect.* Oxford University Press., DOI: 10.1093/oso/9780190088583.001.0001

Bramantyo, H. B., Sumartono, Muluk, M. R. K., & Mindarti, L. I. (2025). Public-Private Partnerships for Infrastructure in Developing Asia: A Systematic Review of Challenges and Future Research Agendas. *Lex Localis - Journal of Local Self-Government, 23*(11), 20–46. https://doi.org/DOI: 10.52152/801711

Bramwell, B., Higham, J., Lane, B., & Miller, G. (2017). Twenty-five years of sustainable tourism and the *Journal of Sustainable Tourism*: Looking back and moving forward. *Journal of Sustainable Tourism, 25*(1), 1–9. DOI: 10.1080/09669582.2017.1251689

Bramwell, B., & Lane, B. (2011). Critical research on the governance of tourism and sustainability. *Journal of Sustainable Tourism, 19*(4-5), 411–421. DOI: 10.1080/09669582.2011.580586

Branicki, L. J., Sullivan-Taylor, B., & Livschitz, S. R. (2018). How entrepreneurial resilience generates resilient SMEs. *International Journal of Entrepreneurial Behaviour & Research, 24*(7), 1244–1263. DOI: 10.1108/IJEBR-11-2016-0396

Bréchet, J.-P., & Mevellec, P. (2008). L'articulation de la stratégie et du contrôle de gestion: L'apport de la modélisation en termes d'activités et de processus. Communication présentée à la 17 Conférence de l'AIMS, Nice, France. Disponible sur: https://www.strategie-aims.com/conferences/17-vieme-conference-de-l-aims/communications/1031-l-articulation-de-la-strategie-et-du-controle-de-gestion-l-apport-de-la-modelisation-en-termes-d-activites-et-de-processus/download

Brinkerhoff, J. (2012). Creating an Enabling Environment for Diasporas' Participation in Homeland Development. *International Migration (Geneva, Switzerland)*, *50*(1), 75–95. DOI: 10.1111/j.1468-2435.2009.00542.x PMID: 22400149

Browder, R. E., Dwyer, S. M., & Koch, H. (2024). Upgrading adaptation: How digital transformation promotes organizational resilience. *Strategic Entrepreneurship Journal*, *18*(1), 128–164. DOI: 10.1002/sej.1483

Brown, S., Grävingholt, J., & Raddatz, R. (2016). The Securitization of Foreign Aid: Trends, Explanations and Prospects. *The Securitization of Foreign Aid. Rethinking International Development Series*, 1-17. doi:DOI: 10.1007/978-1-137-56882-3_11

Brown, D., & McGranahan, G. (2016). The urban informal economy, local inclusion and achieving a global green transformation. *Habitat International*, *53*, 97–105.

Brown, R., & Rocha, A. (2020). Entrepreneurial uncertainty during the Covid-19 crisis: Mapping the temporal dynamics of entrepreneurial finance. *Journal of Business Venturing Insights*, *14*, e00174. DOI: 10.1016/j.jbvi.2020.e00174

Brück, T., Naudé, W., & Verwimp, P. (2013). Business under Fire: Entrepreneurship and Violent Conflict in Developing Countries. *The Journal of Conflict Resolution*, *57*(1), 3–19. DOI: 10.1177/0022002712464846

Brunswicker, S., & Vanhaverbeke, W. (2015). Open innovation in small and medium-sized enterprises (SMEs): External knowledge sourcing strategies and internal organizational facilitators. *Journal of Small Business Management*, *53*(4), 1241–1263. DOI: 10.1111/jsbm.12120

Brush, C. G., Edelman, L. F., Manolova, T. S., & Welter, F. (2019). A gendered look at entrepreneurship ecosystems. *Small Business Economics*, *53*, 393–408.

Bryman, A. (2016). *Social research methods* (5th ed.). Oxford University Press.

Bryson, J. M. (2018). Strategic planning for public and nonprofit organizations: A guide to strengthening and sustaining organizational achievement (5th ed.). John Wiley & Sons. Capstone.

Bujdoso, Z., Vida, N., Mate, B., Nagy, K., & Bringye, B. (2025). The artificial intelligence usage and benefits in tourism marketing. *Geojournal of Tourism and Geosites*, 60(2spl), 1147–1157. https://doi.org/DOI: 10.30892/gtg.602spl12-1488

Bullough, A., & Renko, M. (2013). Entrepreneurial resilience during challenging times. *Business Horizons*, *56*(3), 343–350. DOI: 10.1016/j.bushor.2013.01.001

Bundy, J., Pfarrer, M. D., Short, C. E., & Coombs, W. T. (2017). Crises and crisis management: Integration, interpretation, and research development. *Journal of Management, 43*(6), 1661–1692.

Business Case Studies. (2025, March 16). Human Capital Theory: Education & Training. https://businesscasestudies.co.uk/human-capital-theory-education-training

Butler, R. W. (1980). The concept of a tourist area cycle of evolution: Implications for management of resources. *The Canadian Geographer. Geographe Canadien, 24*(1), 5–12. DOI: 10.1111/j.1541-0064.1980.tb00970.x

Calantone, R. J., Kim, D., Schmidt, J. B., & Cavusgil, S. T. (2006). The influence of internal and external firm factors on international product adaptation strategy and export performance: A three-country comparison. *Journal of Business Research, 59*(2), 176–185. DOI: 10.1016/j.jbusres.2005.05.001

Calgaro, E., Lloyd, K., & Dominey-Howes, D. (2014). From vulnerability to transformation: A framework for assessing the vulnerability and resilience of tourism destinations. *Journal of Sustainable Tourism, 22*(3), 341–360. DOI: 10.1080/09669582.2013.826229

Call, C. T. (2010). Beyond the 'failed state': Toward conceptual alternatives. *European Journal of International Relations, 17*(2). Advance online publication. DOI: 10.1177/1354066109353137

Canestrino, R., Magliocca, P., & Ćwiklicki, M. (2024). Digital Transformation for a Better Society: The Role of Digital Social Entrepreneurship. In *Humane Entrepreneurship and Innovation*(pp. 153-173). Emerald Publishing Limited.

Capocchi, A., Vallone, C., Pierotti, M., & Amaduzzi, A. (2020). Correction: Capocchi, A., et al. Overtourism: A Literature Review to Assess Implications and Future Perspectives. *Sustainability* 2019, *11*, 3303. *Sustainability, 12*(4), 1541. https://doi .org/DOI: 10.3390/su12041541

Carayannis, E. G., Papamichail, G., & Zotas, N.. (2025). Corporate foresight: Navigating uncertainty in a VUCA world. *Journal of the Knowledge Economy*. Advance online publication. DOI: 10.1007/s13132-024-02587-4

Carment, D., & Samy, Y. (2021). *Exiting the Fragility Trap: Rethinking Our Approach to the World's Most Fragile States*. Ohio University Press.

Carmona, M. (2021). *Public places urban spaces: The dimensions of urban design*. Routledge., DOI: 10.4324/9781315158457

Cash, T. A. (2025). Infrastructure development, economic growth and income inequality: Evidence from India. *Indian Growth and Development Review*, •••, 1–24.

Cavagnaro, E., & Curiel, G. (2022). *The three levels of sustainability*. Routledge., DOI: 10.4324/9781003155614

Cavusgil, S. T., & Knight, G. A. (2015). The born global firm: An entrepreneurial and capabilities perspective on early and rapid internationalization. *Journal of International Business Studies*, *46*(1), 3–16. DOI: 10.1057/jibs.2014.62

Certo, S. T., & Miller, T. (2008). Social entrepreneurship: Key issues and concepts. *Business Horizons*, *51*(4), 267–271.

Cevik, S. (2023). Long live globalization: Geopolitical shocks and international trade (IMF Working Paper No. 2023/225). International Monetary Fund. https://doi.org/DOI: 10.5089/9798400258169.001

Chandler, D. (2014). *Resilience The Governance of Complexity* (1st Edition ed.). Routledge. Retrieved from https://www.routledge.com/Resilience-The-Governance-of-Complexity/Chandler/p/book/9780415741408

Chan, K. W. (2010). The global financial crisis and migrant workers in China: 'There is no future as a labourer; returning to the village has no meaning'. *International Journal of Urban and Regional Research*, *34*(3), 659–677.

Chari, A., Converse, N., Mehl, A., Milesi-Ferretti, G. M., & Vansteenkiste, I. (2025). Geopolitxal tensions and international financial fragmentation – Evidence and implications. Centre for economic policy research. Available at https://cepr.org/system/files/publication-files/271360-geneva_28_geopolitical_tensions_and_international_fragmentation_evidence_and_implications.pdf (Accessed on 10/12/2025).

Chathoth, P., Altinay, L., Okumus, F., & Koseoglu, M. A. (2020). Strategic management for hospitality and tourism. In Okumus, F., Altinay, L., Chathoth, P., & Koseoglu, M. A. (Eds.), *Strategic management in the international hospitality and tourism industry* (pp. 18–52). Routledge.

Chattopadhyay, S., & Kumar, A. Union Budget 2024 and Inclusive Cities: An Appraisal of India's Urban Development Schemes & Policies. *Regional Centre for Urban & Environmental Studies (RCUES), Mumbai*, 1.

Chavira, P. C., Shamsuzzoha, A., Kuusniemi, H., & Jovanovski, B. (2023). Defining Green Innovation, Its Impact, and Cycle – A Literature Analysis. *Cleaner Engineering and Technology*, *17*, 100693. DOI: 10.1016/J.CLET.2023.100693

Chebo, A. K., & Dhliwayo, S. (2024). Scientific mapping and thematic progression of digitalization of social entrepreneurship in developing countries. *Sustainable Futures : An Applied Journal of Technology, Environment and Society*, *7*, 100153.

Chen, M. (2012). *The Informal Economy: Definitions, Theories and Policies.* WIEGO (Women in Informal Employment: Globalizing and Organising). Working Paper No. 1. Retrieved 2025, from https://www.wiego.org/wp-content/uploads/2019/09/Chen_WIEGO_WP1.pdf

Cheng, Q., Liu, Y., Peng, C., He, X., Qu, Z., & Dong, Q. (2023). Knowledge digitization: Characteristics, knowledge advantage and innovation performance. *Journal of Business Research*, *163*, 113915.

Cheng, Q., Wan, H., & Ju, H. (2025). Analysis of factors contributing to the efficiency of tackling critical technologies: From a knowledge digitisation perspective. *Technology Analysis and Strategic Management*, •••, 1–15.

Chinta, S. (2019). Supply chain finance in India: current status and potentialities 2019-2020.

Choi, N., & Majumdar, S. (2014). Social entrepreneurship as an essentially contested concept: Opening a new avenue for systematic future research. *Journal of Business Venturing*, *29*(3), 363–376.

Choudhury, T., Al Fadli, A., Butros, N., & Fadul, A. (2025). SME, Crisis and Geopolitical Risk: Lessons from COVID-19 and War. *Journal of Risk and Financial Management*, *18*(11), 645. DOI: 10.3390/jrfm18110645

Chowdhury, A. A. A., Rafi, A. H., Sultana, A., & All Noman, A. (2024). Enhancing Green Economy with Artificial Intelligence: Role of Energy Use and FDI in the United States. *Journal of Environmental and Energy Economics*, *3*(2), 55–76. DOI: 10.56946/jeee.v3i2.536

Christian, M., Obi, A., Zantsi, S., Mdoda, L., & Jiba, P. (2024). The role of cooperatives in improving smallholder participation in agri-food value chains: A case study of one local municipality in Eastern Cape, South Africa. *Sustainability*, *16*(6), 2241. DOI: 10.3390/su16062241

Ciekanowski, Z., Nowicka, J., Żurawski, S., Czech, A., & Zdunek, M. (2023). Crisis management and crisis situation in the organization. *European Research Studies Journal*, *26*(4), 339–353. DOI: 10.35808/ersj/3288

Clarkson, M. E. (1995). A stakeholder framework for analyzing and evaluating corporate social performance. *Academy of Management Review*, *20*(1), 92–117. DOI: 10.5465/amr.1995.9503271994

Coccossis, H., & Mexa, A. (2017). *The challenge of tourism carrying capacity assessment: Theory and practice*. Routledge., DOI: 10.4324/9781315240817

Cohen, W. M., & Levinthal, D. A. (1990). Absorptive capacity: A new perspective on learning and innovation. *Administrative Science Quarterly, 35*(1), 128–152. DOI: 10.2307/2393553

Collier, P., & Hoeffler, G. (2004). Greed and grievance in civil war. *Oxford Economic Papers, 56*(4). Advance online publication. DOI: 10.1093/oep/gpf064

Conduah, A. K., & Essiaw, M. N. (2022). Resilience and entrepreneurship: A systematic review. *F1000 Research, 11*, 348. DOI: 10.12688/f1000research.75473.1

Conz, E., & Magnani, G. (2020). A dynamic perspective on the resilience of firms: A systematic literature review and a framework for future research. *European Management Journal, 38*(3), 400–412. DOI: 10.1016/j.emj.2019.12.004

Coombs, W. T. (2015). *Ongoing crisis communication: Planning, managing, and responding* (4th ed.). SAGE Publications.

Coombs, W. T., & Laufer, D. (2018). Global crisis management – Current research and future directions. *Journal of International Management, 24*(3), 199–203. DOI: 10.1016/j.intman.2017.12.003

Cooper, C. (2006). Knowledge management and tourism. *Annals of Tourism Research, 33*(1), 47–64. DOI: 10.1016/j.annals.2005.04.005

Cope, J. (2011). Entrepreneurial learning from failure: An interpretative phenomenological analysis. *Journal of Business Venturing, 26*(6), 604–623. DOI: 10.1016/j.jbusvent.2010.06.002

Coral, C., & Mithöfer, D. (2023). The backbone of agrifood value chain resilience: Innovation in the Ecuadorian banana value chain from a historical perspective. *World Development Perspectives, 29*, 100476. DOI: 10.1016/j.wdp.2022.100476

Cornelius-Hernandez, T., & Clarke, A. (2024). The current state of integrating equity, diversity and inclusion into knowledge mobilization: A systematic literature review. *Equality, Diversity and Inclusion*.

Cortright, D., & Lopez, G. A. (2002). Smart Sanctions: Targeting Economic Statecraft. *International Journal (Toronto, Ont.), 57*(4), 647–651. DOI: 10.2307/40203698

Craig-Smith, S., Cooper, C., & Ruhanen, L. (2004). Knowledge management and tourism. Paper presented at the WTO Education Council Conference, Beijing, China, 23 October 2003. Madrid, Spain: World Tourism Organisation.

Crouch, G. I. (2011). Destination competitiveness: An analysis of determinant attributes. *Journal of Travel Research, 50*(1), 27–45. DOI: 10.1177/0047287510362776

Cutright, P. (1971). Income and family events: Marital stability. *Journal of Marriage and Family*, •••, 291–306.

Dabbous, A., Barakat, K. A., & Kraus, S. (2023). The impact of digitalization on entrepreneurial activity and sustainable competitiveness: A panel data analysis. *Technology in Society*, *73*, 102224. DOI: 10.1016/j.techsoc.2023.102224

Dacin, P. A., Dacin, M. T., & Matear, M. (2010). Social entrepreneurship: Why we don't need a new theory and how we move forward from here. *The Academy of Management Perspectives*, *24*(3), 37–57.

Đalic, I., & Erceg, Ž. (2024). The impact of motivation to decision on digital transformation of social entrepreneurship. *Strategic Management-International Journal of Strategic Management and Decision Support Systems in Strategic Management, 29*(3).

Damiano, R., & Valenza, G. (2025). Enacting resilience in small and medium enterprises following the sustainability path: A systematic literature review. *Strategic Change*, *34*(2), 237–252. DOI: 10.1002/jsc.2608

Darroch, J. (2005). Knowledge management, innovation and firm performance. *Journal of Knowledge Management*, *9*(3), 101–115.

Davidson, L., & Sahli, M. (2015). Foreign direct investment in tourism, poverty alleviation, and sustainable development: A review of the Gambian hotel sector. *Journal of Sustainable Tourism*, *23*(2), 167–187. DOI: 10.1080/09669582.2014.957210

De Bruin, A., Eversole, R., & Woods, C. (2024). Guest editorial: Gender and social entrepreneurship: building cumulative knowledge. *International Journal of Gender and Entrepreneurship*, *16*(1), 1–6.

De Ruysscher, C., Claes, C., Lee, T., Cui, F., Van Loon, J., De Maeyer, J., & Schalock, R. (2017). A systems approach to social entrepreneurship. *Voluntas*, *28*(6), 2530–2545.

Defourny, J., & Nyssens, M. (2017). Fundamentals for an international typology of social enterprise models. *Voluntas*, *28*(6), 2469–2497.

Deirmentzoglou, G. A., Anastasopoulou, E. E., & Theodorakopoulos, N. (2025, September). Geopolitical Risks: Threats or Opportunities in Shaping Entrepreneurial Intentions? In *European Conference on Innovation and Entrepreneurship* (pp. 184-190). Academic Conferences International Limited. https://doi.org/DOI: 10.34190/ecie.20.1.3660

Deirmentzoglou, G. A., Anastasopoulou, E. E., & Sklias, P. (2024). International economic relations and energy security in the European Union: A systematic literature review. *International Journal of Sustainable Energy, 43*(1), 2385682. DOI: 10.1080/14786451.2024.2385682

del Rosario Venegas, M., Feregrino, J., Lay, N., & Espinosa-Cristia, J. F. (2024). Food Financialization: Impact of Derivatives and Index Funds on Agri-Food Market Volatility. *IJFS, 12*(4), 1–30. DOI: 10.3390/ijfs12040121

Delmas, M. A., & Toffel, M. W. (2008). Organizational responses to environmental demands: Opening the black box. *Strategic Management Journal, 29*(10), 1027–1055. DOI: 10.1002/smj.701

Deming, W. E. (2018). *Out of the Crisis, reissue*. MIT press.

Demony, C. (2025). Global financial system must adapt to better serve economy, UN trade agency says. Avaiable at https://www.reuters.com/business/finance/global-financial-system-must-adapt-better-serve-economy-un-trade-agency-says-2025-12-02/ (Accessed on 10/12/2025).

Dess, G. G., McNamara, G., Eisner, A. B., & Sauerwald, S. (2023). *Strategic management: Text and cases* (11th ed.). McGraw Hill.

Dev, S. M. (2021). *Beyond India 75: Growth, Inclusion and Sustainability*. Indira Gandhi Institute of Development Research.

Diaz-Sarachaga, J. M., & Ariza-Montes, A. (2022). The role of social entrepreneurship in the attainment of the sustainable development goals. *Journal of Business Research, 152*, 242–250.

DiPasquale, D., & Wheaton, W. C. (1996). *Urban economics and real estate markets*. Prentice Hall.

Domazet, I., Marjanovic, D., & Subic, J. (2024). Driving factors of the Montenegrin economy - FDI and tourism. *International Review (Steubenville, Ohio)*, (1-2), 117–127. DOI: 10.5937/intrev2401117d

Dredge, D., & Jenkins, J. (2011). *Stories of practice: Tourism policy and planning*. Ashgate.

Drezner, D. (2011). Sanctions Sometimes Smart: Targeted Sanctions in Theory and Practice. *International Studies Review, 13*(1), 96–108. DOI: 10.1111/j.1468-2486.2010.01001.x

Duchek, S. (2020). Organizational resilience: A capability-based conceptualization. *Business Research, 13*, 215–246. DOI: 10.1007/s40685-019-0085-7

Duffield, M. (2001). *Global Governance and the New Wars: The Merging of Development and Security*. Zen Books., Retrieved from https://www.google.com.cy/books/edition/Global_Governance_and_the_New_Wars/BQ9kDgAAQBAJ?hl=en&gbpv=1&dq=Global+Governance+and+the+New+Wars:+The+Merging+of+Development+and+Security.+Zed+Books&printsec=frontcover

Duong, C. D., Nguyen, T. H., Ngo, T. Q., Pham, T. T., Vu, A. T., & Dang, N. S. (2024). Using generative artificial intelligence (ChatGPT) for travel purposes: Parasocial interaction and tourists' continuance intention. *Tourism Review, 80*(4), 813–827. DOI: 10.1108/TR-01-2024-0027

Duong, W. N. (2008a). Ghetto'ing workers with hi-tech: Exploring regulatory solutions for the effect of artificial intelligence on third world foreign direct investment. *Temple International and Comparative Law Journal, 22*(1), 63–140.

Duong, W. N. (2008b). Effect of artificial intelligence on the pattern of foreign direct investment in the third world: Possible reversal of trend. *Denver Journal of International Law and Policy, 36*(3 & 4), 325–334.

Durai, T., & Stella, G. (2019). Digital finance and its impact on financial inclusion. *Journal of Emerging Technologies and Innovative Research, 6*(1), 122–127.

Durani, F., Anwar, A., Sharif, A., Hamid, A., Ali, S., & Syed, Q. R. (2025). Exploring the link between inflation, tourism, trade, foreign direct investment, and renewable energy consumption: Evidence from novel wavelet quantile correlation approach. *Clean Technologies and Environmental Policy, 27*, 3897–3911. DOI: 10.1007/s10098-024-03073-w

Dwyer, L., Edwards, D., Mistilis, N., Roman, C., & Scott, N. (2020). *Tourism management strategies for global competitiveness*. Channel View Publications.

Dwyer, L., & Kim, C. (2003). Destination competitiveness: Determinants and indicators. *Current Issues in Tourism, 6*(5), 369–414. DOI: 10.1080/13683500308667962

Dziak, M. (2024). Volatility, uncertainty, complexity and ambiguity (VUCA). Retrieved from https://www.ebsco.com/research-starters/politics-and-government/volatility-uncertainty-complexity-and-ambiguity-vuca (Accessed on 20/12/2025).

Early, B. R. (2015). *Busted Sanctions Explaining Why Economic Sanctions Fail* (1st ed.). Stanford University Press., Retrieved 2025, from.

Efthimiou, S. G. (2024). The impacts of COVID-19 pandemic on foreign direct investment. In Mavri, M., Mazza, P. I., Karasavvoglou, A., & Polychronidou, P. (Eds.), *Economic growth, prosperity and sustainability in the economies of the Balkans and Eastern European countries* (pp. 103–127). Springer., DOI: 10. 1007/978-3-031-58437-4_6

Efthimiou, S. G. (2025a). The trends of tourism sector after COVID-19 period: A study of strategy and implications. *Corporate & Business Strategy Review*, *6*(1), 119–133. DOI: 10.22495/cbsrv6i1art12

Efthimiou, S. G. (2025b). The role of entrepreneurship's economic adaptation to the international environment towards tourism and sustainable development of disadvantaged rural areas. *Corporate Governance and Sustainability Review*, *9*(2), 42–55. DOI: 10.22495/cgsrv9i2p4

Efthimiou, S. G. (2025c). Economic Adjustment through Foreign Direct Investments: A Literature Review. *International Journal of Applied Economics. Finance and Accounting*, *22*(1), 167–179. DOI: 10.33094/ijaefa.v22i1.2291

Efthimiou, S. G. (2025d). The contribution of foreign direct investments to the development and competitiveness of the tourism industry: Toward a sustainable growth. *Corporate Governance and Sustainability Review*, *9*(3), 24–44. DOI: 10.22495/cgsrv9i3p2

Efthimiou, S. G. (2025e). The Economic Adjustment and Regional Development of the Tourism Sector through Foreign Direct Investments. *Theoretical Economics Letters*, *15*(4), 821–850. DOI: 10.4236/tel.2025.154045

Ehsan, Z.-A. (2021). Defining a startup – A critical analysis. SSRN *Electronic Journal*. http://dx.doi.org/DOI: 10.2139/ssrn.3823361

EIB. (2025). *EIB Investment Report 2024/2025: Innovation, Integration and Simplification in Europe*. https://www.eib.org/en/publications/20240354-investment-report-2024

Eisenhardt, K. M., & Martin, J. A. (2000). Dynamic capabilities: What are they? *Strategic Management Journal*, *21*(10-11), 1105–1121. https://sms.onlinelibrary.wiley.com/doi/abs/10.1002/1097-0266%28200010/11%2921%3A10/11%3C1105%3A%3AAID-SMJ133%3E3.0.CO%3B2-E

Eisenhardt, K. M., & Martin, J. A. (2017). Dynamic capabilities: What are they? In Helfat, C. E. (Ed.), *Dynamic capabilities: Understanding strategic change in organizations* (pp. 110–125). Blackwell Publishing., DOI: 10.1002/9781405164054.ch21

Elert, N., Henrekson, M., & Stenkula, M. (2017). *Innovation, Entrepreneurship and the Complementary Skill Structure*. 9–23. https://doi.org/DOI: 10.1007/978-3-319-55092-3_2

Elhamma, A. (2010). La comptabilité par activités au Maroc: Une étude empirique utilisant la théorie de la contingence. El-Bahith Review, 8(1), 39-48. Retrieved from https://elbahithreview.edu.dz/index.php/bahith/article/view/652

Elhamma, A. (2011). Impact de la taille sur le contenu des tableaux de bord dans les entreprises au Maroc: résultats d'une étude empirique. Revue Marocaine de Recherche en Management et Marketing, 4-5, 317-329. Retriever from https://halshs .archives-ouvertes.fr/halshs-00670474

Elhamma, A. (2014). Performance du Balanced Scorecard: Perception des responsables d'entreprises. *Revue Internationale de Management et de Stratégie*, *5*(2), 1–9.

Elhamma, A. (2015). The relationship between budgetary evaluation, firm size, and performance. *Journal of Management Development*, *34*(8), 973–986. DOI: 10.1108/JMD-06-2014-0053

Elhamma, A. (2023). The relationship between organisational decentralisation, balanced scorecard and its perceived benefits in Moroccan SMEs. International Journal of Accounting. *Auditing and Performance Evaluation*, *19*(2), 185–202. DOI: 10.1504/IJAAPE.2023.132384

Elhamma, A. (2024a). Participant observation as a qualitative research method in management sciences: Interests, conditions, and limitations. In Bentalha, B., & Alla, L. (Eds.), *Applying qualitative research methods to management science* (pp. 75–91). IGI Global., DOI: 10.4018/979-8-3693-5543-5.ch004

Elhamma, A. (2024b). Determinants of national IFRS adoption: Evidence from the Middle East and North Africa region. International Journal of Accounting. *Auditing and Performance Evaluation*, *20*(1-2), 69–90. DOI: 10.1504/IJAAPE.2024.135535

Elhamma, A. (2025a). A half-century of International Accounting Standards (IAS/IFRS): Assessing the mandatory adoption, impact, and Morocco's position in the convergence process. In Vardari, L., & Qabrati, I. (Eds.), *Financial reporting standards with global trade needs* (pp. 185–203)., DOI: 10.4018/979-8-3373-0887-6.ch007

Elhamma, A. (2025b). Lack of Resilience and Failure of Small and Medium-Sized Enterprises (SMEs) in Morocco: Current Situation and Key Determinants. In Dias Rouco, J. C., & Nunes Figueiredo, P. C. (Eds.), *Enhancing Resilience in Business Continuity Management* (pp. 245–266). IGI Global., DOI: 10.4018/979-8-3693-8809-9.ch008

Elhamma, A. (2025c). Digitalization of management control: Case of Moroccan companies. In Khalil, A., Bousselmi, H. E., & Ben Slimene, I. (Eds.), *Digital technologies for sustainability and quality control* (pp. 33–52)., DOI: 10.4018/979-8-3693-4373-9.ch002

Elhamma, A. (2026). The impact of mandatory IFRS adoption on foreign direct investment: Evidence from Jordan, Morocco, and the United Arab Emirates. In Elhamma, A. (Ed.), *Adoption, Impact, and Challenges of International Financial Reporting Standards* (pp. 197–222). IGI Global., DOI: 10.4018/979-8-3373-1902-5.ch007

Elhamma, A., & Lassaad, B. M. (2017). Liens entre participation budgétaire, taille et performance: Cas des entreprises au Maroc. *Revue Congolaise de Gestion*, *24*(2), 43–62.

Elhamma, A., & Loukili, Z. (2025). Emergence of public-private partnership policies: A comparative study of Morocco and France. In Baporikar, N. (Ed.), *Public private partnerships for social development and impact* (pp. 155–178)., DOI: 10.4018/979-8-3373-3471-4.ch007

Elhamma, A., & Snoussi, N. (2026). Challenges to the adoption of the balanced scorecard as a managerial innovation in Moroccan SMEs. In Jamil, G. L., Jamil, L. C., Paletta, F. C., Geada, N., & Vieira, A. A. P. (Eds.), *Innovation management for disruptive maturity in competitive scenarios* (pp. 249–272). IGI Global., DOI: 10.4018/979-8-3693-4030-1.ch011

Elkhidir, E., Mannakkara, S., Henning, T. F., & Wilkinson, S. (2022). Knowledge types and knowledge transfer mechanisms for effective resilience knowledge-sharing between cities–A case study of New Zealand. *International Journal of Disaster Risk Reduction*, *70*, 102790.

Elkington, J. (1997). Cannibals with Forks: The Triple Bottom Line of 21st Century Business.

Endo, K. (2006). Foreign direct investment in tourism—Flows and volumes. *Tourism Management*, *27*(4), 600–614. DOI: 10.1016/j.tourman.2005.02.004

Endress, T. (2023). Open Innovation Ecosystem in Asia. *Business and Management in Asia: Digital Innovation and Sustainability*, 35–48. https://doi.org/DOI: 10.1007/978-981-19-6418-3_3

Erdiaw-Kwasie, M. O., Abunyewah, M., Yusif, S., & Arhin, P. (2023). Small and medium enterprises (SMEs) in a pandemic: A systematic review of pandemic risk impacts, coping strategies and resilience. *Heliyon*, *9*(10), e20352. DOI: 10.1016/j.heliyon.2023.e20352 PMID: 37767482

ERIA. (2023). ASEAN's Digital Integration: Evolution of Framework Documents. *Books*. https://ideas.repec.org//b/era/eriabk/2023-10-oct-asean-digital-integration-evolution-of-framework-documents.html

Espiner, S., Orchiston, C., & Higham, J. E. (2017). Resilience and sustainability: A complementary relationship? Towards a practical conceptual model for the sustainability–resilience nexus in tourism. *Journal of Sustainable Tourism*, *25*, 1385–1400.

European Commission. (2022). Entrepreneurship and digital transformation: Policy brief. Brussels.

European Commission. (2025). *EU Tourism Transition Pathway: Towards a sustainable and resilient tourism sector.* European Union Publications. https://transition-pathways.europa.eu/tourism

European Commission. (2025). *Traceability and Big Data in the agrifood value chain: S3P partnership.* Available at https://ec.europa.eu/regional_policy/policy/communities-and-networks/s3-community-of-practice/partnership_agrifood_traceability_big_data_en (Accessed on 10/12/2025).

European Environment Agency. (2025, July 15). Extreme weather: Floods, droughts and heatwaves. https://www.eea.europa.eu/en/topics/in-depth/extreme-weather-floods-droughts-and-heatwaves

European External Action Service. (2016). *Shared Vision, Common Action: A Stronger Europe.* Brussels: EU.

European Investment Bank & European Commission. (2018). *Using financial instruments to reduce the impact of price volatility in agriculture.* Available at https://www.fi-compass.eu/sites/default/files/publications/Using_financial_instruments_to_reduce_the_impact_of_price_volatility_in_agriculture.pdf (Accessed on 10/12/2025).

Evans, N. (2024). *Strategic management for tourism, hospitality and events* (4th ed.). Routledge.

FAO and OECD. 2019. Background Notes on Sustainable, Productive and Resilient Agro-Food Systems: Value chains, human capital, and the 2030 Agenda. Available at https://www.oecd.org/content/dam/oecd/en/publications/reports/2019/07/background-notes-on-sustainable-productive-and-resilient-agro-food-systems_e3ac2135/dca82200-en.pdf (Accessed on 14/12/2025).

Farrell, H., & Newman, A. L. (2019). *Weaponized Interdependence: How Global Economic Networks Shape State Coercion* (Vol. 44). MIT Press., DOI: 10.1162/isec_a_00351

Fatić, A., Korać, S., & Bulatović, A. (2011). Empathy in Diplomacy. *The Review of International Affairs*, *62*(1142), 5–13. Retrieved 2025, from https://www.ceeol.com/search/article-detail?id=1071797

Fauzel, S. (2021). FDI and tourism futures: A dynamic investigation for a panel of small island economies. *Journal of Tourism Futures*, *7*(1), 98–110. DOI: 10.1108/JTF-05-2018-0026

Fauzel, S., Seetanah, B., & Sannassee, R. V. (2017). Analysing the impact of tourism foreign direct investment on economic growth: Evidence from a small island developing state. *Tourism Economics*, *23*(5), 1042–1055. DOI: 10.1177/1354816616664249

Fereday, J., & Muir-Cochrane, E. (2006). Demonstrating rigor using thematic analysis: A hybrid approach of inductive and deductive coding and theme development. *International Journal of Qualitative Methods*, *5*(1), 80–92. DOI: 10.1177/160940690600500107

Fernández-Zarza, M., Amaya-Corchuelo, S., Belletti, G., & Aguilar-Criado, E. (2021). Trust and food quality in the valorisation of geographical indication initiatives. *Sustainability*, *13*(6), 3168. DOI: 10.3390/su13063168

Finnemore, M., & Hollis, D. B. (2016). Constructing Norms for Global Cybersecurity. *The American Journal of International Law*, *110*(3), 425–479. Retrieved 2025, from https://www.jstor.org/stable/10.5305/amerjintelaw.110.3.0425

Fletcher, M., & Harris, S. (2012). Knowledge acquisition for the internationalization of the smaller firm: Content and sources. *International Business Review*, *21*(4), 631–647. DOI: 10.1016/j.ibusrev.2011.07.008

Florez-Jimenez, M. P., Lleo, A., Danvila-del-Valle, I., & Sánchez-Marín, G. (2024). Corporate sustainability, organizational resilience and corporate purpose: A triple concept for achieving long-term prosperity. *Management Decision*, *62*(7), 2189–2213. DOI: 10.1108/MD-06-2023-0938

Folke, C. (2006). Resilience: The emergence of a perspective for social–ecological systems analyses. *Global Environmental Change*, *16*(3), 253–267. DOI: 10.1016/j.gloenvcha.2006.04.002

Folke, C. (2016). Resilience (Republished). *Ecology and Society*, *21*(4), 44.

Folke, C., Carpenter, S. R., Walker, B., Scheffer, M., Chapin, T., & Rockström, J. (2010). Resilience thinking: Integrating resilience, adaptability and transformability. *Ecology and Society*, *15*(4). https://www.jstor.org/stable/26268226

Follmann, A., Dannenberg, P., Baur, N., Braun, B., Walther, G., Bernzen, A., & Sulle, E. (2024). Conceptualizing sustainability and resilience in value chains in times of multiple crises—Notes on agri-food chains. *DIE ERDE–Journal of the Geographical Society of Berlin*, *155*(1), 29–48. DOI: 10.12854/erde-2024-692

Food and Agriculture Organization. (2006). *An introduction to market-based instruments for agricultural price risk management.* Available at https://www.fao.org/4/ap308e/ap308e.pdf (Accessed on 10/12/2025).

Food and Agriculture Organization. (2021). Sustainable agri-food value chains How policies can support the shift towards more resilient food systems. Available at https://openknowledge.fao.org/server/api/core/bitstreams/ac5cd783-8207-46b0-ab8d-b61858796fdd/content (Accessed on 10/12/2025).

Fragkoudis, A., Vrana, V., Karavasilis, G., & Kehris, E. (2024). Tourism Agents in Greece Recovering from COVID-19. In Kavoura, A., Borges-Tiago, T., & Tiago, F. (Eds.), *Strategic Innovative Marketing and Tourism. ICSIMAT 2023. Springer Proceedings in Business and Economics*. Springer., DOI: 10.1007/978-3-031-51038-0_40

Freeman, R. E. (2010). *Strategic management: A stakeholder approach.* Cambridge University Press., DOI: 10.1017/CBO9781139192675

Friede, G., Busch, T., & Bassen, A. (2015). ESG and financial performance: Aggregated evidence from more than 2000 empirical studies. *Journal of Sustainable Finance & Investment*, *5*(4), 210–233. DOI: 10.1080/20430795.2015.1118917

Friesike, S., Widenmayer, B., Gassmann, O., & Schildhauer, T. (2015). Opening science: Towards an agenda of open science in academia and industry. *The Journal of Technology Transfer*, *40*(4), 581–601. DOI: 10.1007/s10961-014-9375-6

Frontiers in Psychology. (n.d.). Innovation capabilities and human development. https://www.frontiersin.org/articles/10.3389/fpsyg.2021.736618/full

Fu, Y., Wu, X., & Wang, Z. (2024). Internationalization rhythm and innovation performance: The effects of internationalization speed, organizational slack, and competitive intensity. *International Business Review*, *33*(1), 102196. DOI: 10.1016/j.ibusrev.2024.102274

Ganotakis, P., & Love, J. H. (2012). R&D, product innovation, and exporting: Evidence from UK new technology based firms. *Oxford Economic Papers*, *63*(2), 279–306. DOI: 10.1093/oep/gpq027

Garcia-Jurado, A., Gálvez-Gálvez, C., & Caba-Pérez, C. (2024). Social entrepreneurship, social innovation and SDGs: Digital transformation as a catalyst for inclusive development. *Administrative Sciences*, *15*(2), 55.

García-Jurado, A., Pérez-Barea, J. J., & Nova, R. J. (2021). A new approach to social entrepreneurship: A systematic review and meta-analysis. *Sustainability*, *13*(5), 2754.

Garrido-Moreno, A., Martín-Rojas, R., & García-Morales, V. J. (2024). The key role of innovation and organizational resilience in improving business performance: A mixed-methods approach. *International Journal of Information Management*, *77*, 102777. DOI: 10.1016/j.ijinfomgt.2024.102777

Gatto, A., & Sadik-Zada, E. R. (2022). Access to Microfinance as a Resilience Policy to Address Sustainable Development Goals: A Content Analysis. *Heliyon*, *8*(10), e10860. DOI: 10.1016/J.HELIYON.2022.E10860 PMID: 36267370

Gazis, Z. (2019). *Η φέρουσα ικανότητα τουριστικής ανάπτυξης: Εφαρμογή στις 13 ελληνικές περιφέρειες* [Tourism carrying capacity: Its application on the 13 Greek regions] [Master's thesis, National Technical University of Athens]. http://dx.doi .org/DOI: 10.26240/heal.ntua.18183

George, G., Wiklund, J., & Zahra, S. A. (2005). Ownership and the internationalization of small firms. *Journal of Management*, *31*(2), 210–233. DOI: 10.1177/0149206304271760

Georgopoulos, N. B. (2013). *Στρατηγικό μάνατζμεντ* [Strategic management]. 3rd ed.). Kritiki.

Geurts, A., Geerdink, T., & Sprenkeling, M. (2022). Accelerated innovation in crises: The role of collaboration in the development of alternative ventilators during the COVID-19 pandemic. *Technology in Society*, *68*, 101923. DOI: 10.1016/j.techsoc.2022.101923 PMID: 36540134

Geva, Y., & Siemiatycki, M. (2024). Finding mutual benefit in urban development: Lessons from Toronto's creative mixed-use real estate partnerships. *Journal of the American Planning Association*, *90*(1), 144–158. DOI: 10.1080/01944363.2023.2170908

Gigauri, I., Apostu, S. A., & Popescu, C. (2023). Digital transformation: Threats and opportunities for social entrepreneurship. In *Two faces of digital transformation: Technological opportunities versus social threats* (pp. 1–17). Emerald Publishing Limited.

Giroux, S., Blekking, J., Waldman, K., Resnick, D., & Fobi, D. (2021). Informal vendors and food systems planning in an emerging African city. *Food Policy, 103*, 101997.

Giudici, G., Guerini, M., & Rossi-Lamastra, C. (2019). The creation of cleantech startups at the local level: The role of knowledge availability and environmental awareness. *Small Business Economics, 52*, 815–830. DOI: 10.1007/s11187-017-9936-9

Goduni, A. (2024). Empowering growth: How economic education can drive global economic development. Academy of Economics Journal. Retrieved from https://www.abacademies.org/articles/empowering-growth-how-economic-education-can-drive-global-economic-development-17651.html#r4

Godwin, I., & Amah, E. (2013). Knowledge management and organizational resilience in Nigerian manufacturing organizations. *Developing Country Studies, 3*(9), 104–120.

Goffi, G., Cucculelli, M., & Masiero, L. (2019). Fostering tourism destination competitiveness in developing countries: The role of sustainability. *Journal of Cleaner Production, 209*, 101–115. DOI: 10.1016/j.jclepro.2018.10.208

Golovko, E., & Valentini, G. (2011). Exploring the complementarity between innovation and export for SMEs' growth. *Journal of International Business Studies, 42*(3), 362–380. DOI: 10.1057/jibs.2011.2

Gopal, B. S., & Davidson, B. G. J. (2025). Street Vendors in India: The Beginnings of a Digital Transformation Journey. In *Evolving Landscapes of Research and Development: Trends, Challenges, and Opportunities* (pp. 365-386). IGI Global Scientific Publishing.

Gössling, S., Balas, M., Mayer, M., & Sun, Y.-Y. (2023). A review of tourism and climate change mitigation: The scales, scopes, stakeholders and strategies of carbon management. *Tourism Management, 95*, 104681. DOI: 10.1016/j.tourman.2022.104681

Gössling, S., & Mei, X. Y. (2025). AI and sustainable tourism: An assessment of risks and opportunities for the SDGs. *Current Issues in Tourism*. Advance online publication. DOI: 10.1080/13683500.2025.2477142

Gössling, S., Scott, D., & Hall, C. M. (2020). Pandemics, tourism and global change: A rapid assessment of COVID-19. *Journal of Sustainable Tourism, 29*(1), 1–20. DOI: 10.1080/09669582.2020.1758708

Götz, F. M., Gosling, S. D., & Rentfrow, P. J. (2022). Small effects: The indispensable foundation for a cumulative psychological science. *Perspectives on Psychological Science, 17*(1), 205–215. DOI: 10.1177/1745691620984483 PMID: 34213378

Grant, R. M. (1996). Toward a knowledge-based theory of the firm. *Strategic Management Journal, 17*(S2), 109–122.

Grant, R. M. (2024). *Contemporary strategy analysis* (11th ed.). John Wiley & Sons.

Greer, T. W., & Egan, T. M. (2019). Knowledge management for organizational success: Valuing diversity and inclusion across stakeholders, structures, and sectors. In *Connecting adult learning and knowledge management: Strategies for learning and change in higher education and organizations* (pp. 119–136). Springer International Publishing.

Gretzel, U., Sigala, M., Xiang, Z., & Koo, C. (2015). Smart tourism: Foundations and developments. *Electronic Markets, 25*(3), 179–188. DOI: 10.1007/s12525-015-0196-8

Grimsey, D., & Lewis, M. K. (2004). Public private partnerships: The worldwide revolution in infrastructure provision and project finance. In *Public Private Partnerships*. Edward Elgar Publishing.

GSMA. (2024). *The Mobile Economy Sub-Saharan Africa 2024*. London: Global System for Mobile Communications Association. Retrieved 2025, from https://prod-cms.gsmaintelligence.com/research-file-download?assetId=12080&reportId=50121

Gul, S., Limongi, R., & Syed, H. W. U. (2024). Unraveling the nexus: Social entrepreneur intention and socioeconomic development with mediating role of entrepreneurial knowledge. *Kybernetes*.

Guo, K., Li, Y., Zhang, Y., Ji, Q., & Zhao, W. (2023). How are climate risk shocks connected to agricultural markets? *Journal of Commodity Markets, 32*, 100367. DOI: 10.1016/j.jcomm.2023.100367

Gupta, R., & Das, S. (2022). Challenges in implementing PM SVANidhi scheme: A study of urban street vendors. *The Indian Journal of Public Administration, 68*(1), 45–60.

Gutierriz, I., Ferreira, J. J., & Fernandes, P. O. (2023). Digital transformation and the new combinations in tourism: A systematic literature review. *Tourism and Hospitality Research, 25*(2), 194–213. DOI: 10.1177/14673584231198414

Haddad, B. (2011). *Business Networks in Syria: The Political Economy of Authoritarian Resilience.* Stanford Studies in Middle Eastern and Islamic Societies and Cultures.

Halberstadt, J., Timm, J. M., Kraus, S., & Gundolf, K. (2019). Skills and knowledge management in higher education: How service learning can contribute to social entrepreneurial competence development. *Journal of Knowledge Management, 23*(10), 1925–1948.

Hall, C. M., Prayag, G., & Amore, A. (2017). *Tourism and resilience: Individual, organisational and destination perspectives.* Channel View Publications.

Hall, C. M., Scott, D., & Gössling, S. (2022). Pandemics, transformations and tourism: Be careful what you wish for. *Tourism Geographies, 24*(3), 427–444. DOI: 10.1080/14616688.2020.1759131

Hall, J. K., Daneke, G. A., & Lenox, M. J. (2010). Sustainable development and entrepreneurship: Past contributions and future directions. *Journal of Business Venturing, 25*(5), 439–448.

Hall, J., Matos, S., Sheehan, L., & Silvestre, B. (2012). Entrepreneurship and innovation at the base of the pyramid: A recipe for inclusive growth or social exclusion? *Journal of Management Studies, 49*(4), 785–812.

Hamcerencu, M. (2025). Artificial Intelligence in International Tourism. *Proceedings of the International Conference on Business Excellence*, 19(1), 1139-1151. https://doi.org/DOI: 10.2478/picbe-2025-0090

Hameiri, S., & Jones, L. (2015). Global Governance as State Transformation. *Political Studies, 64*(4), 1–18. DOI: 10.1111/1467-9248.1222

Hanafiah, M. H., & Zulkifly, M. I. (2019). Tourism destination competitiveness and tourism performance: A secondary data approach. *Competitiveness Review, 29*(5), 592–621. DOI: 10.1108/CR-07-2018-0045

Hanif, R., Khalique, M., Pierotti, M., Goyipnazarov, S., Ngah, R., & Ermatov, T. (2024, December). Impact of Artificial Intelligence on Organizational Resilience and Sustainable Performance. In *Proceedings of the 8th International Conference on Future Networks & Distributed Systems* (pp. 465-471). https://doi.org/DOI: 10.1145/3726122.3726189

Han, S., & Zhou, M. (2025). Assessing the impact of climate change on entrepreneurship: Short-term and long-term effects. *Humanities & Social Sciences Communications*, *12*(1), 1–8. DOI: 10.1057/s41599-025-04763-6

Hartmann, S., Backmann, J., Newman, A., Brykman, K. M., & Pidduck, R. J. (2022). Psychological resilience of entrepreneurs: A review and agenda for future research. *Journal of Small Business Management*, *60*(5), 1041–1079. DOI: 10.1080/00472778.2021.2024216

Hart, S. L. (1995). A natural-resource-based view of the firm. *Academy of Management Review*, *20*(4), 986–1014. DOI: 10.5465/amr.1995.9512280033

Haugh, H. (2005). A research agenda for social entrepreneurship. *Social Enterprise Journal*, *1*(1), 1–12.

Hawanga, O. E. (2024). *The impact of COVID-19 on the livelihood of informal sector workers: A case study of street vendors in Eenhana Town, Ohangwena region, Namibia* (Doctoral dissertation, University of Namibia).

Hayward, K. M. (2006) Legitimising the TALC as a Theory of Development in Butler, R.W. (ed.) The Tourism Area Life Cycle Volume 2 Conceptual and Theoretical Issues 29-44 Clevedon: Channelview Publications. http://books.google.co.uk/books?id=AicuoXTVrU0C&pg=PP1&dq=The+Tourism+Area+Life+Cycle+Volum e+2+Conceptual+and+Theoretical&hl=en&ei=MPpvTKPWHo774Ab-3mZHeCA&sa=X&oi=book_result&ct= result&resnum=1&ved=0CCgQ6A-EwAA#v=onepage&q&f=false

Helfat, C. E., & Peteraf, M. A. (2003). The dynamic resource-based view: Capability lifecycles. *Strategic Management Journal*, *24*(10), 997–1010. DOI: 10.1002/smj.332

Henderson, J. (2002). Building the rural economy with high-growth entrepreneurs. *Economic Review-Federal Reserve Bank of Kansas City*, *87*(3), 45–75.

Hermann, C. F. (1963). Some consequences of crisis which limit the viability of organizations. *Administrative Science Quarterly*, *8*(1), 61–82.

Hess, S., Wurth, B., Stam, E., Giones, F., Fini, R., Cavallo, A., Wahl, A., Bosma, N., Theodoraki, C., Chabaud, D., Brem, A., & Kuckertz, A. (2025). The Future of Entrepreneurial Ecosystems Research: Toward a Policy-Oriented Research Agenda. *Journal of Business Venturing Insights*, *23*, e00538. DOI: 10.1016/J.JBVI.2025.E00538

Hjalager, A. M. (2010). A review of innovation research in tourism. *Tourism Management*, *31*(1), 1–12. DOI: 10.1016/j.tourman.2009.08.012

Hof, A., & Blazquez-Salom, M. (2015). Changing tourism patterns, capital accumulation, and urban water consumption in Mallorca, Spain: A sustainability fix? *Journal of Sustainable Tourism*, *23*(5), 770–796. DOI: 10.1080/09669582.2014.991397

Hoffmann, M. (2017). Norms and Social Constructivism in International Relations. *Oxford Research Encyclopedia of International Studies*, N/A. doi:DOI: 10.1093/acrefore/9780190846626.013.60

Hokmabadi, H., Rezvani, S. M. H. S., & de Matos, C. A. (2024). Business Resilience for Small and Medium Enterprises and Startups by Digital Transformation and the Role of Marketing Capabilities—A Systematic Review. *Systems 2024, Vol. 12, Page 220, 12*(6), 220. https://doi.org/DOI: 10.3390/SYSTEMS12060220

Hokmabadi, H., Rezvani, S. M., & de Matos, C. A. (2024). Business resilience for small and medium enterprises and startups by digital transformation and the role of marketing capabilities—A systematic review. *Systems*, *12*(6), 220. DOI: 10.3390/systems12060220

Holling, C. S. (1973). Resilience and Stability of Ecological Systems. *Annual Review of Ecology and Systematics*, *4*, 1–23. https://www.jstor.org/stable/2096802

Holling, C. S. (2001). Understanding the complexity of economic, ecological, and social systems. *Ecosystems (New York, N.Y.)*, *4*(5), 390–405. DOI: 10.1007/s10021-001-0101-5

Huchet, M. (2011). Agricultural commodity price volatility: an overview. https://dx.doi.org/DOI: 10.1787/5kg0t00nrthc-en

Hufbauer, G., & Jung, E. (2020). What's new in economic sanctions? *European Economic Review*, *130*. Advance online publication. DOI: 10.1016/j.euroecorev.2020.103572 PMID: 33012831

Hurley, J., Scott, M., & Gailyn, P. (2018). *Examining the Debt Implications of the Belt and Road Initiative from a Policy Perspective*. Center for Global Development.

Iacobucci, D., & Perugini, F. (2021). Entrepreneurial ecosystems and economic resilience at local level. *Entrepreneurship and Regional Development*, *33*(9-10), 689–716. DOI: 10.1080/08985626.2021.1888318

Iborra, M., Safón, V., & Dolz, C. (2020). What explains the resilience of SMEs? Ambidexterity capability and strategic consistency. *Long Range Planning*, *53*(6), 101947. DOI: 10.1016/j.lrp.2019.101947

Ibrahim, M. (2024). Foreign direct investment in tourism: A systematic review of literature. *Journal of Tourism Quarterly*, *6*(1-2), 32–38.

Imelda, M., & Susiang, N. (2024). Business Incubators In The Entrepreneurship Ecosystem In Indonesia Mediated By Government Support And Intellectual Capital. *Commercium : Journal of Business and Management*, 2(2), 67–81. DOI: 10.61978/COMMERCIUM.V2I2.215

IMF. (2022). *IMF Executive Board Approves Establishment of the Resilience and Sustainability Trust*. https://www.imf.org/en/news/articles/2022/04/18/pr22119-imf-executive-board-approves-establishment-of-the-rst

IMF. (2023). *United States: 2023 Article IV Consultation-Press Release; Staff Report; and Statement by the Executive Director for the United States*. Western Hemisphere. International Monetary Fund. doi:DOI: 10.5089/9798400245176.002

IMF. (2024). *Regional Economic Outlook for Europe, October 2024: A Recovery Short of Europe's Full Potential*. https://www.imf.org/en/Publications/REO/EU/Issues/2024/10/24/regional-economic-outlook-Europe-october-2024

IMF. (2025). *IMF Resilience and Sustainability Trust*. https://www.imf.org/en/Topics/Resilience-and-Sustainability-Trust

INSETE. (2023). The contribution of tourism to the Greek economy in 2023. Institute of the Association of Greek Tourism Enterprises. https://insete.gr/wp-content/uploads/2024/04/25_05_Tourism_and_Greek_Economy_2019-2023-ENG.pdf

International Capital Market Association. (2020). *Sustainability-linked bond principles: Voluntary process guidelines*. https://www.icmagroup.org/assets/documents/Regulatory/Green-Bonds/June-2020/Sustainability-Linked-Bond-Principles-June-2020-171120.pdf

Investopedia. (n.d.). Understanding human capital theory: Importance and impact. https://www.investopedia.com/terms/h/human-capital-theory.asp

Isichei, E. (2024). Entrepreneurial Resilience and business survival. *The Journal of Entrepreneurship*. Advance online publication. DOI: 10.1177/09713557241233820

Isik, C. (2015). Foreign Direct Investment in Tourism: Panel Data Analysis of D7 Countries. *Athens Journal of Tourism*, 2(2), 93–103. DOI: 10.30958/ajt.2-2-2

Isık, C., Islam, H., Ongan, S., Sengoz, A., & Usanmaz, B. (2025). Artificial intelligence (AI) interacted ESG-based sustainable tourism: Economic insights. *Tourism Economics*, *0*(0), 1–22. DOI: 10.1177/13548166251346306

Ivars-Baidal, J. A., Celdrán-Bernabeu, M. A., Mazón, J. N., & Perles-Ivars, Á. F. (2017). Smart destinations and the evolution of ICTs: A new scenario for destination management? *Current Issues in Tourism, 22*(13), 1581–1600. DOI: 10.1080/13683500.2017.1388771

Jain, S., & Sharma, P. (2022). Financial inclusion and digital transactions among street vendors: Early insights from PM SVANidhi beneficiaries. *Journal of Entrepreneurship and Innovation, 11*(2), 89–102.

Johanson, J., & Vahlne, J.-E. (2003). Business relationship learning and commitment in the internationalization process. *Journal of International Entrepreneurship, 1*, 83–101. DOI: 10.1023/A:1023219207042

Johnson, G., Whittington, R., Scholes, K., Angwin, D., & Regnér, P. (2016). *Βασικές αρχές στρατηγικής των επιχειρήσεων* [Fundamentals of business strategy]. 2nd ed.). Kritiki.

Johnson, S. (2000). *Literature Review on Social Entrepreneurship*. Canadian Centre for Social Entrepreneurship.

Jonsson, H. C. (Ed.). (2022). *Tourism and Foreign Direct Investment: Issues, Challenges and Prospects* (1st ed.). Routledge., DOI: 10.4324/9781003155492

Joseph, J. (2013). Resilience as embedded neoliberalism: A governmentality approach. *Resilience: International Policies. Practices and Discourses, 1*(1), 38–52. DOI: 10.1080/21693293.2013.765741

Jukka, T. (2021). Does business strategy and management control system fit determine performance? *International Journal of Productivity and Performance Management, 72*(5), 659–678.

Junaidi, M. (2024). *UMKM Hebat, Perekonomian Nasional Meningkat*. https://djpb.kemenkeu.go.id/kppn/curup/id/data-publikasi/artikel/2885-umkm-hebat%2C-perekonomian-nasional-meningkat.html

Justino, P., Brück, T., & Verwimp, P. (2014). A Micro-Level Perspective on the Dynamics of Conflict. *Violence, and Development, 26*. Advance online publication. DOI: 10.1093/acprof:oso/9780199664597.001.0001

Kabir, M. N. (2019). *Knowledge-based social entrepreneurship*. Palgrave Macmillan.

Kádár, B., & Jáki, E. (2024). COVID-19 and SMEs: An umbrella review of systematic literature (2020–2024) and future directions for entrepreneurship: Introduction to the "The Entrepreneurial Landscape in the Post-COVID Era: Insights, Challenges, and Future Perspectives" special issue. *Society and Economy*, *46*(4), 323–341. DOI: 10.1556/204.2024.00017

Kafle, K. R. (2011). *Exchange rate volatility and bilateral agricultural trade flows: the case of the United States and OECD countries*. Louisiana State University and Agricultural & Mechanical College.

Kafouros, M., Wang, C., Piperopoulos, P., & Zhang, M. (2015). Academic collaborations and firm innovation performance in China: The role of region-specific institutions. *Research Policy*, *44*(3), 803–817. DOI: 10.1016/j.respol.2014.11.002

Kalaignanam, K., Tuli, K. R., Kushwaha, T., Leonard, L., & Gal, D. (2021). Marketing Agility: The Concept, Antecedents, and a Research Agenda. *Journal of Marketing*, *85*(1), 35–58. DOI: 10.1177/0022242920952760

Kaldor, M. (2012). *New and Old Wars: Organized Violence in a Global Era* (3rd ed.). Stanford University Press.

Kalkanci, B., Rahmani, M., & Toktay, L. B. (2019). The role of inclusive innovation in promoting social sustainability. *Production and Operations Management*, *28*(12), 2960–2982.

Kamalaveni, M. S., Suriya, A., Sakthivel, P., & Vignesh, S. (2021). Digital Transformation in Tourism. *International Journal of Advance and Innovative Research*, 8(4), ISSN 2394 – 7780.

Kandpal, V., Chandra, D., Dalei, N. N., & Handoo, J. (2023). MFIs and NBFCs contributions towards financial inclusion and circular economy. In *Financial inclusion in circular economy: A bumpy road towards sustainable development* (pp. 157–184). Springer International Publishing.

Kant, R. (2024). *Financial Technologies (FINTECH) in E-Commerce*. SGSH Publication.

Kanyepe, J., Musasa, T., & Wilbert, M. (2025). Supply Chain Risk Factors, Technological Capabilities, and Firm Performance of Small to Medium Enterprises (SMEs). *Journal of Small Business Strategy*, *35*(1), 115–128. DOI: 10.53703/001C.125910

Kaplan, R. S., & Norton, D. P. (2007). Using the balanced scorecard as a strategic management system. *Harvard Business Review*, *85*(7–8), 150–161.

Kaplan, R. S., & Norton, D. P. (2008). *The execution premium: Linking strategy to operations for competitive advantage*. Harvard Business Press.

Karagiannis, S., & Thomakos, D. (2020). Quantitative assessment of the tourism carrying capacity in Greece: A case study of Cyclades. *Tourism Today (Nicosia), 19*, 36–64. https://www.researchgate.net/publication/348049034_Quantitative_Assessment_of_the_Tourism_Carrying_Capacity_in_Greece_A_Case_Study_of_Cyclades

Kargbo, J. M. (2006). Exchange rate volatility and agricultural trade under policy reforms in South Africa. *Development Southern Africa, 23*(01), 147–170. DOI: 10.1080/03768350600556315

Keller, P., & Bieger, T. (Eds.). (2017). *Real estate and destination development in tourism: Successful strategies and instruments* (International Tourism Research and Concepts, Vol. 3). Berlin: Erich Schmidt Verlag.

Keller, P., & Bieger, T. (Eds.). (2017). *Real Estate and Destination Development in Tourism: Successful Strategies and Instruments*. Erich Schmidt Verlag.

KEMENKO. (2021). *UMKM Menjadi Pilar Penting dalam Perekonomian Indonesia*. https://ekon.go.id/publikasi/detail/2969/umkm-menjadi-pilar-penting-%20dalam-perekonomian-indonesia

Keohane, R., & Nye, J. (1977). *Power and Interdependence*. (M. Vikram, Ed.) New York, US: Pearson. Retrieved 2025, from http://slantchev.ucsd.edu/courses/ps240/05%20Cooperation%20with%20States%20as%20Unitary%20Actors/Keohane%20&%20Nye%20-%20Power%20and%20interdependence%20[Ch%201-3].pdf

KfW. (2024). *KfW SME Panel 2024: The business environment puts pressure on companies*. https://www.kfw.de/About-KfW/Newsroom/Latest-News/Pressemitteilungen-Details_825024.html

Khalfaoui, R., Goodell, J. W., Mefteh-Wali, S., Chishti, M. Z., & Gozgor, G. (2024). Impact of climate risk shocks on global food and agricultural markets: A multiscale and tail connectedness analysis. *International Review of Financial Analysis, 93*, 103206. DOI: 10.1016/j.irfa.2024.103206

Khan, A., Bibi, S., Lorenzo, A., Lyu, J., & Babar, Z. U. (2020). Tourism and Development in Developing Economies: A Policy Implication Perspective. *Sustainability, 12*(4), 1618. DOI: 10.3390/su12041618

Khanzada, A. A., Hasnain, A., Narejo, S., Chowdhry, B. S., & Laxmi, L. (2023). Impact of digitalization on social entrepreneurship. In *Two Faces of Digital Transformation* (pp. 19–29). Emerald Publishing Limited.

Khavarian-Garmsir, A. R., & Zare, S. M. (2015). SOAR Framework as a New Model for the Strategic Planning of Sustainable Tourism. *Tourism Planning & Development, 12*, 321–332.

Khurana, I., Dutta, D. K., & Ghura, A. S. (2022). SMEs and digital transformation during a crisis: The emergence of resilience as a second-order dynamic capability in an entrepreneurial ecosystem. *Journal of Business Research, 150*, 623–641. DOI: 10.1016/j.jbusres.2022.06.048

Kim, K., & Boudreaux, C. (2017). Collaborative social entrepreneurship for inclusive innovation: Lessons from South Korea. *Journal of Innovation and Entrepreneurship, 6*(7), 1–16.

Kiptoo, M., Sambajee, P., & Baum, T. (2024). Resilience through adversity: A case of informal artisan entrepreneurs in Kenya. *International Journal of Entrepreneurial Behaviour & Research, 30*(11), 446–465. DOI: 10.1108/IJEBR-07-2023-0762

Knight, F. H. (1942). Profit and entrepreneurial functions. *The Journal of Economic History, 2*(S1), 126–132.

Kolb, D. A. (2015). *Experiential learning: Experience as the source of learning and development* (2nd ed.). Pearson Education.

Kontopanou, M., & Tsoulfas, G. (2022). Analyzing new ways to adapt the triple-a supply chain model and its extensions in agri-food supply chains. *LogForum, 18*(3). Advance online publication. DOI: 10.17270/J.LOG.2022.735

Koporcic, N., Kukkamalla, P. K., Markovic, S., & Maran, T. (2025). Resilience of small and medium-sized enterprises in times of crisis: An umbrella review. *Review of Managerial Science*, •••, 1–29. DOI: 10.1007/s11846-025-00883-0

Koporcic, N., Kukkamalla, P. K., Markovic, S., & Maran, T. (2025). Resilience of Small and Medium-Sized Enterprises in Times of Crisis: An Umbrella Review. *Review of Managerial Science*, •••, 1–29. DOI: 10.1007/S11846-025-00883-0/TABLES/2

Korber, S., & McNaughton, R. B. (2017). Resilience and entrepreneurship: A systematic literature review. *International Journal of Entrepreneurial Behaviour & Research, 24*(7), 1129–1154. DOI: 10.1108/IJEBR-10-2016-0356

Korry, P. D. P., & Wijayanti, R. (2024). Investigating entrepreneurial resilience toward sustainable competitive advantage: Does local culture matter? *Uncertain Supply Chain Management, 12*(2), 801–814. DOI: 10.5267/j.uscm.2024.1.006

KPMG. (2025). US Tariffs – Understanding the Implications for Ireland and the EU. Retrieved from https://kpmg.com/ie/en/insights/tax/us-tariffs.html (Accessed on 22/12/2025).

Kraus, S., Niemand, T., Halberstadt, J., Shaw, E., & Syrjä, P. (2017). Social entrepreneurship orientation: Development of a measurement scale. *International Journal of Entrepreneurial Behaviour & Research, 23*(6), 977–997.

Kristinek, J. J., & Anderson, D. P. (2002). *Exchange rates and agriculture: a literature review.* Agricultural and Food Policy Center, Department of Agricultural Economics, Texas Agricultural Experiment Station, Texas Cooperative Extension, Texas A & M University.

Kuckertz, A., Brändle, L., Gaudig, A., Hinderer, S., Reyes, C. A. M., Prochotta, A., Steinbrink, K. M., & Berger, E. S. C. (2020). Startups in times of crisis – A rapid response to the COVID-19 pandemic. *Journal of Business Venturing Insights, 13*, e00169. DOI: 10.1016/j.jbvi.2020.e00169

Kuersten, A. (2018). Busted Sanctions: Explaining Why Economic Sanctions Fail. *Democracy and Security, 14*(2), 200–201. DOI: 10.1080/17419166.2017.1345245

Kumar, M. V. S. (2009). The relationship between product and international diversification: The effects of short-run constraints and endogeneity. [REMOVED HYPERLINK FIELD]. *Strategic Management Journal, 30*(1), 99–116. DOI: 10.1002/smj.724

Kumar, V., & Roy, S. (2018). Microcredit and resilience among informal urban micro-entrepreneurs in India. *International Journal of Entrepreneurship and Small Business, 34*(3), 345–360.

Kyläheiko, K., Jantunen, A., Puumalainen, K., Saarenketo, S., & Tuppura, A. (2011). Innovation and internationalization as growth strategies: The role of technological capabilities and appropriability. *International Business Review, 20*(5), 508–520. DOI: 10.1016/j.ibusrev.2010.09.004

Labitad, J. (2025). Street Vendors' Stories: Informal Borrowing Practices and Implications on Business. *American Journal of Social Development and Entrepreneurship, 4*(1), 10–54536.

Laine, M., Tregidga, H., & Unerman, J. (2021). *Sustainability accounting and accountability*. Routledge., DOI: 10.4324/9781003185611

Lawrence, T., Phillips, N., & Tracey, P. (2012). From the guest editors: Educating social entrepreneurs and social innovators. *Academy of Management Learning & Education, 11*(3), 319–323.

Leadbeater, C. (1997). *The Rise of the Social Entrepreneur*. Demos.

Lee, B. K., Agarwal, S., & Kim, H. J. (2012). Influences of travel constraints on the people with disabilities' intention to travel: An application of Seligman's helplessness theory. *Tourism Management, 33*(3), 569–579. DOI: 10.1016/j.tourman.2011.06.011

Leka, A., Lagarias, A., Panagiotopoulou, A., & Stratigea, A. (2022). Development of a Tourism Carrying Capacity Index (TCCI) for sustainable management of coastal areas in Mediterranean islands - Case study Naxos, Greece. *Ocean and Coastal Management, 216*, 105978. DOI: 10.1016/j.ocecoaman.2021.105978

Lengnick-Hall, C. A., & Beck, T. E. (2005). Adaptive fit versus robust transformation: How organizations respond to environmental change. *Journal of Management, 31*(5), 738–757. DOI: 10.1177/0149206305279367

Leonidou, L. C. (2000). Barriers to export management: An organizational and internationalization analysis. *Journal of International Management, 6*(2), 121–148. DOI: 10.1016/S1075-4253(00)00022-3

Leoni, G., Lai, A., Stacchezzini, R., Steccolini, I., Brammer, S., Linnenluecke, M., & Demirag, I. (2021). Accounting, management and accountability in times of crisis: Lessons from the COVID-19 pandemic. *Accounting, Auditing & Accountability Journal, 34*(6), 1305–1319. DOI: 10.1108/AAAJ-06-2020-4784

Lestari, N. P., & Choirunissa, Z. (2025). Transformasi Digital dan Ketahanan UMKM: Systematic Literature Review (SLR). *Jambura Economic Education Journal, 7*(1), 355–372. DOI: 10.37479/JEEJ.V7I1.26333

Lew, A. A., Cheer, J. M., Haywood, M., Brouder, P., & Salazar, N. B. (2016). Visions of travel and tourism after the global COVID-19 transformation of 2020. *Tourism Geographies, 22*(3), 455–466. DOI: 10.1080/14616688.2020.1770326

Li, X., & Bosma, N. (2023). Institutional Theory in Social Entrepreneurship: A Review and Consideration of Ethics. SSRN *Electronic Journal*. https://doi.org/ DOI: 10.2139/SSRN.5043847

Linna, P. (2013). Bricolage as a means of innovating in a resource-scarce environment: A study of innovator-entrepreneurs at the BOP. *Journal of Developmental Entrepreneurship, 18*(03), 1350015. DOI: 10.1142/S1084946713500155

Liu, Y., Garnevska, E., & Shadbolt, N. (2025). The Role of Agriculture Cooperatives in Green Agri-Food Value Chains in China: Cases in Shandong Province. *Sustainability, 17*(16), 7343. DOI: 10.3390/su17167343

Liu, Y., Hu, H., & Kong, W. (2025). The Impact of Entrepreneurs' AI Literacy on Entrepreneurial Resilience: The Role of AI Anxiety and Social Support. *Behavioral Sciences (Basel, Switzerland)*. PMID: 41464084

Liu, Z., & San-Martín, S., & Others. (2019). Contextual uniqueness in entrepreneurship education: A review. *International Journal of Entrepreneurial Education*, *22*(1), 41–60.

Li, X., Huang, S., & Song, C. (2017). China's outward foreign direct investment in tourism. *Tourism Management*, *59*, 1–6. DOI: 10.1016/j.tourman.2016.07.007

Lockyer, T. (2005). The perceived importance of price as one hotel selection dimension. *Tourism Management*, *26*(4), 529–537. DOI: 10.1016/j.tourman.2004.02.014

Loku, A., & Loku, N. (2025). Globalization, automation, and the future of work: Examining the impact of technological advancements on the workforce. *Calitatea*, *26*(204), 88–96.

Lopez-Naranjo, A. L., Puente-Riofrio, M. I., Carrasco-Salazar, V. A., Erazo-Rodríguez, J. D., & Bunay-Guisnan, P. A. (2025). Artificial intelligence in the tourism business: A systematic review. *Frontiers in Artificial Intelligence*, *8*, 1599391. DOI: 10.3389/frai.2025.1599391 PMID: 40785835

Lopez-Vega, H., Tell, F., & Vanhaverbeke, W. (2016). Where and how to search? Search paths in open innovation. *Research Policy*, *45*(1), 125–136. DOI: 10.1016/j.respol.2015.08.003

Love, J. H., Roper, S., & Zhou, Y. (2016). Experience, age and exporting performance in UK SMEs. *International Business Review*, *25*(4), 806–819. DOI: 10.1016/j.ibusrev.2015.10.001

Lowies, B., Whait, R. B., Viljoen, C., & McGreal, S. (2018). Fractional ownership–An alternative residential property investment vehicle. *Journal of Property Investment & Finance*, *36*(6), 513–522. DOI: 10.1108/JPIF-02-2018-0013

Lu, J. W., & Beamish, P. W. (2004). International diversification and firm performance: The S-curve hypothesis. *Academy of Management Journal*, *47*(4), 598–609. https://www.jstor.org/stable/20159604

Luthans, F., & Youssef, C. M. (2007). Emerging positive organizational behavior. *Journal of Management*, *33*(3), 321–349. DOI: 10.1177/0149206307300814

Ma'amor, H., Badrolhisam, N. I., & Munir, R. (2025). Entrepreneurial Resilience in SMEs: A Bibliometric Perspective. *Information Management and Business Review*, *17*(3(I)), 252–265. DOI: 10.22610/imbr.v17i3(I).4701

Maalaoui, A., Le Loarne-Lemaire, S., & Razgallah, M. (2020). Does knowledge management explain the poor growth of social enterprises? Key insights from a systematic literature review on knowledge management and social entrepreneurship. *Journal of Knowledge Management*, *24*(7), 1513–1532.

Maaßen, C., Lopez, T., & Urbano, D. (2025). Institutional Enablers for Sustainable Entrepreneurship: A Configurational Analysis. *Small Business Economics*, **•••**, 1–22. DOI: 10.1007/S11187-025-01076-5/TABLES/5

Madhav, R., & Majithia, A. S. (2023). Street Vendors and Social Solidarity Economy: Reimagining Credit and Social Security. *Socio-Legal Rev.*, *19*, 37.

Mahajan, R., Kumar, S., Lim, W. M., & Sareen, M. (2024). The role of business and management in driving the sustainable development goals (SDGs): Current insights and future directions from a systematic review. *Business Strategy and the Environment*, *33*(5), 4493–4529.

Maier, F., Meyer, M., & Steinbereithner, M. (2014). Nonprofit organizations becoming business-like: A systematic review. *Nonprofit and Voluntary Sector Quarterly*, *45*(1), 64–86.

Mair, J., & Marti, I. (2009). Entrepreneurship in and around institutional voids: A case study from Bangladesh. *Journal of Business Venturing*, *24*(5), 419–435.

Malik, F. S., & Terzidis, O. (2025). Thriving in turbulence: Resilience and strategic adaptation in global business. *Review of Managerial Science*, **•••**, 1–46. DOI: 10.1007/s11846-025-00940-8

Mammen, J., Alessandri, T. M., & Boyd, B. K. (2021). The risk implications of diversification: Integrating the effects of product and geographic diversification. *Long Range Planning*, *54*(5), 102047. DOI: 10.1016/j.lrp.2019.101942

Manyise, T., & Dentoni, D. (2021). Value chain partnerships and farmer entrepreneurship as balancing ecosystem services: Implications for agri-food systems resilience. *Ecosystem Services*, *49*, 101279. DOI: 10.1016/j.ecoser.2021.101279

Maravilla, V. S.Jr, & Flores, G. (2025). Entrepreneurial competency, resilience, and financial literacy: Drivers of sustainable performance in SMEs for societal welfare. *Journal of Sustainability, Society, and Eco-Welfare*, *2*(2), 159–176. DOI: 10.61511/jssew.v2i2.2025.1374

Marques, J. i Santos, N. (2016). Developing business tourism beyond major urban centres: The perspectives of local stakeholders. *Tourism and Hospitality Management*, *22*(1), 1–15. DOI: 10.20867/thm.22.1.3

Marr, B. (2012). *Key Performance Indicators (KPI): The 75 measures every manager needs to know*. Pearson UK.

Martinelli, E., Tagliazucchi, G., & Marchi, G. (2018). The resilient retail entrepreneur: Dynamic capabilities for facing natural disasters. *International Journal of Entrepreneurial Behaviour & Research, 24*(7), 1222–1243. DOI: 10.1108/IJEBR-11-2016-0386

Martins, A., Oliveira, C., Silva, R., & Castelo Branco, M. (2023). Management control practices as performance facilitators in a crisis context. *Administrative Sciences, 13*(7), 163. DOI: 10.3390/admsci13070163

Máté, D., Estiyanti, N. M., & Novotny, A. (2024). How to Support Innovative Small Firms? Bibliometric Analysis and Visualization of Start-Up Incubation. *Journal of Innovation and Entrepreneurship, 13*(1), 1–26. DOI: 10.1186/S13731-024-00361-Z/TABLES/3

Mathuros, S., Kuljittree, S., & Wongkamhaengharn, K. (2025). *Sustainability Strategies for SME Business Development Applying ESG Concepts to Create Competitive Advantage.* Arts of Management Journal. https://so02.tci-thaijo.org/index.php/jam/article/view/278541

McDougall, P. P., & Oviatt, B. M. (1996). New venture internationalization, strategic change, and performance: A follow-up study. *Journal of Business Venturing, 11*(1), 23–40. DOI: 10.1016/0883-9026(95)00081-X

McDougall, P. P., Shane, S., & Oviatt, B. M. (1994). Explaining the formation of international new ventures: The limits of theories from international business research. *Journal of Business Venturing, 9*(6), 469–487. DOI: 10.1016/0883-9026(94)90017-5

McKibbin, W., & Fernando, R. (2023). The global economic impacts of the COVID-19 pandemic. *Economic Modelling, 129*, 106551. DOI: 10.1016/j.cconmod.2023.106551

McLeod, M., Dodds, R., & Butler, R. (2021). Introduction to special issue on island tourism resilience. *Tourism Geographies, 23*(3), 361–370. DOI: 10.1080/14616688.2021.1898672

McNaughton, R. B. (2003). The number of export markets that a firm serves: Process models versus the born-global phenomenon. *Journal of International Entrepreneurship, 1*, 297–311. DOI: 10.1023/A:1024114907150

Mearsheimer, J. (2001). *The Tragedy of Great Power Politics.* W W Norton and Co., Retrieved from https://samuelbhfaure.com/wp-content/uploads/2015/10/s2-mearsheimer-2001.pdf

Mearsheimer, J. (2018). *The Great Delusion: Liberal Dreams and International Realities*. Yale University Press.

Merchant, K. A., & Van der Stede, W. A. (2017). *Management control systems: Performance measurement, evaluation and incentives* (4th ed.). Pearson Education.

Ministry of Housing and Urban Affairs. (2020). PM SVANidhi scheme guidelines. Government of India. https://pmsvanidhi.mohua.gov.in/

Minten, B., Belton, B., & Reardon, T. (2023). Agrifood value chains: Building resilient food systems. In *Global Food Policy Report 2023* (pp. 44–51). Rethinking Food Crisis Responses., DOI: 10.2499/9780896294417_04

Mintzberg, H., Ahlstrand, B., & Lampel, J. (2005). *Strategy safari: A guided tour through the wilds of strategic management* (2nd ed.). Free Press.

Mishra, R., & Singh, R. K. (2023). A systematic literature review on supply chain resilience in SMEs: Learnings from COVID-19 pandemic. *International Journal of Quality & Reliability Management, 40*(5), 1172–1202. DOI: 10.1108/IJQRM-03-2022-0108

Mishra, V., Sharma, P., Khound, K., Mishra, V., Sharma, P., & Khound, K. (2025). Global Supply Chain Shocks and Trade Resilience: A Review Post-Covid and Ukraine Crisis. *Journal of Marketing & Social Research, 2*, 336–348. DOI: 10.61336/jmsr/25-05-38

Mishrif, A., & Khan, A. (2023). Technology Adoption as Survival Strategy for Small and Medium Enterprises during COVID-19. *Journal of Innovation and Entrepreneurship, 12*(1), 1–23. DOI: 10.1186/S13731-023-00317-9/TABLES/4

Mitchell, R. K., Agle, B. R., & Wood, D. J. (1997). Toward a theory of stakeholder identification and salience: Defining the principle of who and what really counts. *Academy of Management Review, 22*(4), 853–886. DOI: 10.5465/amr.1997.9711022105

Mitroff, I. I. (2001). *Managing crises before they happen*. American Management Association., DOI: 10.1016/S0737-6782(02)00133-9

Monllor, J., & Murphy, P. J. (2017). Natural disasters, entrepreneurship, and creation after destruction: A conceptual approach. *International Journal of Entrepreneurial Behaviour & Research, 23*(4), 618–637. DOI: 10.1108/IJEBR-02-2016-0050

Montoro-Fernández, E., Palomares-Montero, D., & Rubio-Navarro, A. (2022). Entrepreneurial resilience: A case study of university entrepreneurship education. *Sustainability, 14*(18), 11523. DOI: 10.3390/su141811523

Montoro-Fernández, M., Fernández-Muñoz, J. J., & Ruiz-Montero, M. (2022). Socio-emotional competence, self-efficacy, and resilience in higher education students. *Frontiers in Psychology*, *13*, 834521.

Morepje, M. T., Sithole, M. Z., Msweli, N. S., & Agholor, A. I. (2024). The influence of E-commerce platforms on sustainable agriculture practices among smallholder farmers in Sub-Saharan Africa. *Sustainability*, *16*(15), 6496. DOI: 10.3390/su16156496

Morgan, H. (2022). Understanding thematic analysis and the debates involving its use. *The Qualitative Report*, *27*(10), 2079–2091. DOI: 10.46743/2160-3715/2022.5912

Muhammed Shafi, M. K., Shafi, K. M., & Saleem, S. (2024). Microfinance-Driven Banking Initiatives for Advancing Financial Inclusion; Evidences from India. In *The AI Revolution: Driving Business Innovation and Research* (Vol. 2, pp. 467–481). Springer Nature Switzerland.

Nagdev, K., Ahtesham, S., Paliwal, S., Smith, S., & Rajesh, A. (2025). Navigating impact: A systematic review of social entrepreneurship's journey towards sustainable development. *The International Journal of Organizational Analysis*.

Naik, A., & Patel, P. (2022). Government schemes for entrepreneurship programs. In *Agricultural microbiology based entrepreneurship: Making money from microbes* (pp. 25–40). Springer Nature Singapore.

Naudé, W. E. (2010). Developing countries, and development economics: New approaches and insights. *Small Business Economics*, •••, 1–12. DOI: 10.1007/s11187-009-9198-2

Nautiyal, S., & Pathak, P. (2023). Resilience through the lens of entrepreneurship: A bibliometric analysis and network mapping of the emerging research field. *The International Journal of Organizational Analysis*. Advance online publication. DOI: 10.1108/IJOA-12-2022-3540

Ndou, V. (2021). Social entrepreneurship education: A combination of knowledge exploitation and exploration processes. *Administrative Sciences*, *11*(4), 112.

Neely, A., Gregory, M., & Platts, K. (2005). Performance measurement system design. *International Journal of Operations & Production Management*, *25*, 12.

Network for Greening the Financial System. (2020). *The macroeconomic and financial stability impacts of climate change: Research priorities*. NGFS. Available at https://www.ngfs.net/system/files/import/ngfs/medias/documents/ngfs_research_priorities_final.pdf (Accessed on 10/12/2025).

Newman, A., Mole, K. F., Ucbasaran, D., Subramanian, N., & Lockett, A. (2018). Can your network make you happy? Entrepreneurs' business network utilization and subjective well-being. *British Journal of Management*, *29*(4), 613–633. DOI: 10.1111/1467-8551.12270

Niven, P. R. (2014). *Balanced scorecard evolution: A dynamic approach to strategy execution*. John Wiley & Sons.

Nonaka, I., Toyama, R., & Konno, N. (2000). SECI, Ba and leadership: A unified model of dynamic knowledge creation. *Long Range Planning*, *33*(1), 5–34.

North, D. C. (1990). *Institutions, Institutional Change, and Economic Performance*. Cambridge University Press., https://doi.org/https://doi.org/10.1017/CBO9780511808678

Nunkoo, R., & Seetanah, B. (2018) Foreign Direct Investment and Tourism Development: A Theoretical and Empirical Review. *The SAGE Handbook of Tourism Management: Theories, Concepts and Disciplinary Approaches to Tourism*, 556-566.

Nunkoo, R., & Ramkissoon, H. (2010). Small island urban tourism: A residents' perspective. *Current Issues in Tourism*, *13*(1), 37–60. DOI: 10.1080/13683500802499414

Nye, J. (2005). *Soft Power: The Means to Success in World Politics*. Public Affairs., Retrieved 2025, from.

O'Connor, P., Esfandiar, K., & Hallak, R. (2025). Resilience for hospitality and tourism enterprises: A review and directions for future research. *Tourism Analysis*, *30*(1), 5–22. DOI: 10.3727/108354224X17209729214520

O'Reilly, A. M. (1986). Tourism carrying capacity: Concept and issues. *Tourism Management*, *7*(4), 254–258. DOI: 10.1016/0261-5177(86)90035-X

OECD. (2020). *OECD Tourism Trends and Policies 2020*. OECD Publishing., DOI: 10.1787/6b47b985-

OECD. (2021; 2024). Education and Skills: OECD Education at a Glance. Paris.

OECD. (2022). *States of Fragility 2022*. OECD., DOI: 10.1787/c7fedf5e-

OECD. (2023). *Towards resilient food systems - Implication of supply chain disruptions and policy responses*. OECD Food, Agriculture and Fisheries paper n°205. Available at https://www.oecd.org/content/dam/oecd/en/publications/reports/2023/09/towards-resilient-food-systems_102d2ac9/f7998e46-en.pdf (Accessed on 10/12/2025).

OECD. (2024). *Artificial Intelligence and tourism: G7/ OECD policy paper. OECD Tourism Papers, 2024/02*. OECD Publishing., DOI: 10.1787/3f9a4d8d-

OECD. (2024). *Education at a glance 2024: OECD indicators*. OECD Publishing., DOI: 10.1787/eag-2024-en

OECD. (2024, December 18). Human capital and educational policies. https://www.oecd.org/education/human-capital-and-educational-policies.htm

OECD. (2025), Economic Security in a Changing World, New Approaches to Economic Challenges, OECD Publishing, Paris. https://doi.org/DOI: 10.1787/4eac89c7-en

OECD. (2025). *Practical approaches to develop resilience strategies for food systems*. OECD Food, Agriculture and Fisheries Papers, No. 217. Available at https://www.oecd.org/content/dam/oecd/en/publications/reports/2025/02/practical-approaches-to-develop-resilience-strategies-for-food-systems_97f31bb2/caa2b274-en.pdf (Accessed on 14/12/2025).

OECD. (2025a). *Enhancing the enabling environment for micro and small tourism enterprises in Greece*. OECD Publishing., DOI: 10.1787/48b4382b-

OECD. (2025b). *Building strong and resilient tourism destinations: Policy approaches for diversification*. OECD Publishing., DOI: 10.1787/a57c343d-

OECD. (2025c). *Strengthening the evidence base for a sustainable tourism future in Greece: A tailored set of 33 indicators*. OECD Publishing., DOI: 10.1787/6e46e845-

OECD. (2025d). *OECD diversifying tourism offerings for resilience: Guidance for regional alliances*. OECD Publishing.

OECD. (2025e). OECD Tourism Trends and Policies 2022. OECD Publishing. https://www.oecd.org/en/publications/oecd-tourism-trends-and-policies-2022_a8dd3019-en/full-report/greece_095e7405.html

OECD. (n.d.). International compendium of entrepreneurship policies. Retrieved from https://www.oecd.org/en/publications/international-compendium-of-entrepreneurship-policies_338f1873-en.html

Okolie, J.. (2023). Impact of entrepreneurship education on competencies of Nigerian university students. *American Journal of Entrepreneurship*, *5*(4), 77–90.

Oliva, F. L., Teberga, P. M. F., Testi, L., Kotabe, M., Del Giudice, M., Kelle, P., & da Cunha, M. P. (2022). Risks and critical success factors in the internationalization of born global startups of industry 4.0: A social, environmental, economic, and institutional analysis. *Technological Forecasting and Social Change*, *175*, 121334. DOI: 10.1016/j.techfore.2021.121346

Oluwafunmilola, R. O. (2024). The contemporary issues and technological gaps in entrepreneurship education in Nigerian higher institutions. *European Journal of Business and Innovation Research, 12*(5), 80–89.

Organisation for Economic Co-operation and Development (OECD). (2021). *Entrepreneurship Education: A Road to Success*. OECD Publishing.

Orjuela Castro, J. A., Orejuela-Cabrera, J. P., & Adarme-Jaimes, W. (2021). Logistics network configuration for seasonal perishable food supply chains. [JIEM]. *Journal of Industrial Engineering and Management, 14*(2), 135–151. DOI: 10.3926/jiem.3161

Orlitzky, M., Schmidt, F. L., & Rynes, S. L. (2003). Corporate social and financial performance: A meta-analysis. *Organization Studies, 24*(3), 403–441. DOI: 10.1177/0170840603024003910

Orth, D., & Schuldis, P. M. (2021). Organizational learning and unlearning capabilities for resilience during COVID-19. *The Learning Organization, 28*(6), 509–522. DOI: 10.1108/TLO-07-2020-0130

Otley, D. T. (1980). The contingency theory of management accounting: Achievement and prognosis. *Accounting, Organizations and Society, 5*(4), 413–428. DOI: 10.1016/0361-3682(80)90040-9

Oyinlola, M. (2024). Entrepreneurship and innovation in Nigerian universities. *Journal of African Educational Research, 9*(1), 105–125.

Ozanne, L. K., Chowdhury, M., Prayag, G., & Mollenkopf, D. A. (2022). SMEs navigating COVID-19: The influence of social capital and dynamic capabilities on organizational resilience. *Industrial Marketing Management, 104*, 116–135. DOI: 10.1016/j.indmarman.2022.04.009

Paapa, C., & Nguthi, S. (2025). Crisis Management and Resilience in Hospitality and Tourism Consulting. *African Journal of Tourism and Hospitality Management, 4*(1), 246–259. DOI: 10.37284/ajthm.4.1.3203

Panneer, S., Kantamaneni, K., Palaniswamy, U., Bhat, L., Pushparaj, R. R. B., Nayar, K. R., Soundari Manuel, H., Flower, F. X. L. L., & Rice, L. (2022). Health, economic and social development challenges of the COVID-19 pandemic: Strategies for multiple and interconnected issues. *Healthcare (Basel), 10*(5), 770. DOI: 10.3390/healthcare10050770 PMID: 35627910

Pan, Z., & Zheng, X. (2023). Price volatility transmission of perishable agricultural products: Evidence from China. *Economic research-. Ekonomska Istrazivanja, 36*(1). Advance online publication. DOI: 10.1080/1331677X.2023.2180058

Papadopoulou, C., Vardarsuyu, M., & Oghazi, P. (2023). Examining the relationships between brand authenticity, perceived value, and brand forgiveness: The role of cross-cultural happiness. *Journal of Business Research, 167.* Advance online publication. DOI: 10.1016/j.jbusres.2023.114154

Parasuraman, A., Zeithaml, V., & Berry, L. (1988). *SERVQUAL: A Multiple-Item Scale for Measuring Consumer Perceptions of Service Quality. Jorunal of Retailing, 64 (September 2014), 12–40.*

Pareek, A., & Alok, V. N. (2024). PM SVANidhi--A Livelihood Scheme for Street Vendors in India: An Evaluation. *Nagarlok-Quarterly Journal of Urban Affairs, 56*(1).

Patel, S., Furlan, R., & Grosvald, M. (2021). A framework for enhancing the spatial urban form of informal economies in India: The case of Krishna Rajendra Market, Bangalore. *SAGE Open, 11*(2), 21582440211023184.

Patrick, S. (2011). *Weak Links: Fragile States, Global Threats, and International Security.* Oxford University Press., DOI: 10.1093/acprof:oso/9780199751501.001.0001

PCRD. (2006). *Policy on Post-Conflict Reconstruction and Development (PCRD).* AFRICAN UNION.

Peksen, D. (2019, June 10). Sanctions Work Best? Five Key Conditions Associated with Successful Sanctions Outcomes. *Sanctions Work Best?* US, US: Center for a New American Security (CNAS). Retrieved 2025, from https://www.cnas.org/publications/commentary/when-do-economic-sanctions-work-best

Pelling, M., & Dilling, L. (2011). *Adaptation to climate change: From resilience to transformation.* Routledge.

Pennetta, S. (2025). Redefining Entrepreneurial Resilience for Global Business. *The Journal of Entrepreneurship, 34*(2), 221–267. DOI: 10.1177/0971355720957889

Pennetta, S., Anglani, F., Reaiche, C., & Boyle, S. (2025). Entrepreneurial agility in a disrupted world: Redefining entrepreneurial resilience for global business success. *The Journal of Entrepreneurship, 34*(2), 221–267. DOI: 10.1177/09713557251352283

Pérez-Barea, J. J. (2025). The Evolution of Social Entrepreneurship: Broadening the Framework for the Digital and Sustainable Era. *Administrative Sciences, 15*(2), 55.

Persada, A. R., Mulyadi, H., Jajang, A., Mahri, W., & Furqon, C. (2025). Digital Transformation and Business Incubation on SME Performance in Indonesia. *Jurnal Ilmiah Manajemen Kesatuan, 13*(4), 2183–2194. DOI: 10.37641/JIMKES.V13I4.3441

Petropoulos, D., Deirmentzoglou, G. A., Apostolopoulos, N., Paris, B., Michas, D., Balafoutis, A. T., & Moreira da Silva, J. F. (2025). Digital and Entrepreneurial Competencies for the Bioeconomy: Perceptions and Training Needs of Agricultural Professionals in Greece, Italy, Portugal, and Sweden. *Agriculture, 15*(10), 1106. DOI: 10.3390/agriculture15101106

Petropoulou, A., Angelaki, E., Rompogiannakis, I., Passas, I., Garefalakis, A., & Thanasas, G. (2024). Digital Transformation in SMEs: Pre- and Post-COVID-19 Era: A Comparative Bibliometric Analysis. *Sustainability 2024, Vol. 16, Page 10536, 16*(23), 10536. https://doi.org/DOI: 10.3390/SU162310536

Phillips, P., & Moutinho, L. (2014). Critical review of strategic planning research in hospitality and tourism. *Annals of Tourism Research, 48*, 96–120. DOI: 10.1016/j.annals.2014.05.013

PIIE. (2016). China's Belt and Road Initiative: Motives, Scope, and Challenges. Washington, D.C.: Peterson Institute for International Economics (PIIE).

Pike, S., & Page, S. J. (2014). Destination Marketing Organizations and destination marketing: A narrative analysis of the literature. *Tourism Management, 41*, 202–227. DOI: 10.1016/j.tourman.2013.09.009

Pine, B. J., & Gilmore, J. H. (2022). *The experience economy: Competing for customer time, attention, and money* (Updated ed.). Harvard Business Review Press.

Piva, M., &Vivarelli, M. (2018). Technological change and employment: Is Europe ready for the challenge? *Economics of Innovation and New Technology, 27*(2), 95–113. Doi: https://DOI: 10.1007/s40821-017-0100-x

Piva, M., & Vivarelli, M. (2018). Technological change and employment: Is Europe ready for the challenge? *Economics of Innovation and New Technology, 27*(1), 1–19. DOI: 10.1080/10438599.2017.1250189

Pizzorni, M., Innocenti, A., & Tollin, N. (2024). Droughts and floods in a changing climate and implications for multi-hazard urban planning: A review. *City and Environment Interactions, 24*, 100169. DOI: 10.1016/j.cacint.2024.100169

Pomerantz, M. (2003). The business of social entrepreneurship in a down economy. *In Business, 25*(3), 25–30.

Poolsawat, P., & Rinthaisong, I. (2025). The Mediating Role of Entrepreneurial Resilience and Self-Efficacy in Enhancing SMEs Performance in Thailand. *Journal of Business* [JBIS]. *Innovation and Sustainability, 20*(2). Advance online publication. DOI: 10.71185/JBIS.2025.276235

Portales, L. (2019). Social innovation: Origins, definitions, and main elements. In *Social innovation and social entrepreneurship: fundamentals, concepts, and tools* (pp. 1–14). Springer International Publishing.

Porter, M. E. (1980). *Competitive strategy: Techniques for analyzing industries and competitors*. Free Press.

Porter, M. E. (1990). *The competitive advantage of nations*. Free Press.

Porter, M. E., & Kramer, M. R. (2011). Creating shared value. *Harvard Business Review*, *89*(1–2), 62–77.

Prasannath, V., Adhikari, R. P., Gronum, S., & Miles, M. P. (2024). Impact of Government Support Policies on Entrepreneurial Orientation and SME Performance. *The International Entrepreneurship and Management Journal*, *20*(3), 1533–1595. DOI: 10.1007/S11365-024-00993-3

Prayag, G., Spector, S., Orchiston, C., & Chowdhury, M. (2019). Psychological resilience, organizational resilience and life satisfaction in tourism firms: Insights from the Canterbury earthquakes. *Current Issues in Tourism*, *23*(10), 1216–1233. DOI: 10.1080/13683500.2019.1607832

Rae, D. (2010). Entrepreneurial learning: Educating for ambition and aspiration. *Education + Training*, *52*(8/9), 722–740.

Renko, M., Bullough, A., & Saeed, S. (2020). How Do Resilience and Self-efficacy Relate to Entrepreneurial Intentions in Countries With Varying Degrees of Fragility? A Six-country Study. *International Small Business Journal*, •••, 40.

Rey-Martí, A., Ribeiro-Soriano, D., & Palacios-Marqués, D. (2016). A bibliometric analysis of social entrepreneurship. *Journal of Business Research*, *69*(5), 1651–1655.

Richmond, O. P. (2013). Peace Formation and Local Infrastructures for Peace. *Alternatives*, *38*(4), 271–287. Retrieved 2025, from https://www.jstor.org/stable/24569417

Riddle, L., & Brinkerhoff, J. (2011). Diaspora entrepreneurs as institutional change agents: The case of Thamel.com. *International Business Review*, *20*(6), 670–680. DOI: 10.1016/j.ibusrev.2011.02.013

Rikhardsson, P., Rohde, C., Christensen, L., & Batt, C. E. (2021). Management controls and crisis: Evidence from the banking sector. *Accounting, Auditing & Accountability Journal*, *34*(4), 757–785. DOI: 10.1108/AAAJ-01-2020-4400

Ritchie, B. W. (2018). *Crisis and disaster management for tourism*. Channel View Publications.

Ritchie, J. B., & Crouch, G. I. (2003). *The competitive destination: A sustainable tourism perspective*. Cabi.

Rivera, M., Croes, R., & Lee, S. H. (2016). Tourism development and happiness: A residents' perspective. *Journal of Destination Marketing & Management, 5*(1), 5–15. DOI: 10.1016/j.jdmm.2015.04.002

Rodrik, D. (2011). *The Globalization Paradox: Democracy and the Future of the World Economy*. W.W. Norton., Retrieved 2025, from.

Roever, S. (2014). Informal economy monitoring study sector report: Street vendors. *Cambridge, MA, USA: WIEGO, 1*(1), 1-65.

Roever, S., & Skinner, C. (2016). Street vendors and cities. *Environment and Urbanization, 28*(2), 359–374.

Rose, A. (2017). Defining and measuring economic resilience to disasters. *Disaster Prevention and Management, 26*(1), 2–13. DOI: 10.1108/DPM-02-2016-0043

Rose, A. (2017). *Economic resilience: Definition and measurement. Community and Regional Resilience Institute (CARRI) Research Report*. Oak Ridge National Laboratory.

Rose, A. (2017). *Human capital and recovery after disaster: Evidence and policy implications*. ADB Blog.

Rotberg, R. I. (2004). *When States Fail: Causes and Consequences*. Princeton University Press., DOI: 10.2307/j.ctt7scrg

Rothaermel, F. T. (2023). *Strategic management* (6th ed.). McGraw Hill.

Roundy, P. T. (2022). Artificial intelligence and entrepreneurial ecosystems: Understanding the implications of algorithmic decision-making for startup communities. *Journal of Ethics in Entrepreneurship and Technology, 2*(1), 23–38. DOI: 10.1108/JEET-07-2022-0011

Roundy, P. T., Brockman, B. K., & Bradshaw, M. (2017). The resilience of entrepreneurial ecosystems. *Journal of Business Venturing Insights, 8*, 99–104. DOI: 10.1016/j.jbvi.2017.08.002

Roy, A., Sekhar, C., & Vyas, V. (2016). Barriers to internationalization: A study of small and medium enterprises in India. *Journal of International Entrepreneurship, 14*, 513–538. DOI: 10.1007/s10843-016-0187-7

Rutashobya, L., & Jaensson, J.-E. (2004). Small firms' internationalization for development in Tanzania. *International Journal of Social Economics*, *31*(1/2), 159–172. DOI: 10.1108/03068290410515484

Saad, M. H., Hagelaar, G., Van Der Velde, G., & Omta, S. W. F. (2021). Conceptualization of SMEs' business resilience: A systematic literature review. *Cogent Business & Management*, *8*(1), 1938347. DOI: 10.1080/23311975.2021.1938347

Saebi, T., Foss, N. J., & Linder, S. (2019). Social entrepreneurship research: Past achievements and future promises. *Journal of Management*, *45*(1), 70–95.

Safranchuk, I. (2022). Empathy Is the Best Strategy for Diplomacy. *The Review of International Affairs*, *20*. Advance online publication. DOI: 10.31278/1810-6374-2022-20-2-54-64

Sainaghi, R., & Baggio, R. (2020). Substitution threat between Airbnb and hotels: Myth or reality? *Annals of Tourism Research*, *83*, 102959. DOI: 10.1016/j.annals.2020.102959

Sainaghi, R., Phillips, P., & Zavarrone, E. (2017). Performance measurement in tourism firms: A content analytical meta-approach. *Tourism Management*, *59*, 36–56. DOI: 10.1016/j.tourman.2016.07.002

Sakib, Md. N., & Rahman, Md. M. (2024a). Mitigating the Impact of COVID-19 on SMEs Through Government Policy Intervention: A Systematic Literature Review and Bibliometric Analysis. *Future Business Journal 2024 10:1*, *10*(1), 1–11. https://doi.org/DOI: 10.1186/S43093-024-00346-0

Salma, D. F., Nuryartono, N., & Purwanto, B. (2023). Sharia Financial Inclusion to Build Economic Resilience of Micro Small Enterprises During COVID-19. *Jurnal Manajemen Dan Organisasi*, *14*(4), 430–439. DOI: 10.29244/JMO.V14I4.47631

Sanchis, R., & Poler, R. (2019). Enterprise resilience assessment—A quantitative approach. *Sustainability*, *11*(16), 4327. DOI: 10.3390/su11164327

Saner, R., & Yiu, L. (2003). International economic diplomacy: Mutations in post-modern times. *International Economic Diplomacy:Mutations in Post-modern Times* (p. 41). Vienna: Netherlands Institute of International Relations "Clingendael". Retrieved 2025, from https://www.clingendael.org/sites/default/files/pdfs/20030100_cli_paper_dip_issue84.pdf

San-Martín, S.. (2019). The effectiveness of entrepreneurship education programs. *Education + Training*, *61*(7/8), 872–887.

Santeramo, F. G., Jelliffe, J., & Hoekman, B. (2024). Agri-food value chains and the global food dollar: The role of trade and services. *Food Policy*, *127*, 102706. DOI: 10.1016/j.foodpol.2024.102706

Santos, F. M. (2012). A positive theory of social entrepreneurship. *Journal of Business Ethics*, *111*(3), 335–351.

Santos, S. C., Liguori, E. W., & Garvey, E. (2023). How digitalization reinvented entrepreneurial resilience during COVID-19. *Technological Forecasting and Social Change*, *189*, 122398. DOI: 10.1016/j.techfore.2023.122398 PMID: 36778643

Sapienza, H. J., Autio, E., George, G., & Zahra, S. A. (2006). A capabilities perspective on the effects of early internationalization on firm survival and growth. *Academy of Management Review*, *31*(4), 914–933. DOI: 10.5465/amr.2006.22527465

Sarfo, C., Zhang, J. A., O'Kane, C., & O'Kane, P. (2024). Perceived Value of Microfinance and SME Performance: The Role of Exploratory Innovation. *International Journal of Innovation Studies*, *8*(2), 172–185. DOI: 10.1016/J.IJIS.2024.02.003

Sargani, G. R., Wang, B., Leghari, S. J., & Ruan, J. (2025). Is digital transformation the key to agricultural strength? A novel approach to productivity and supply chain resilience. *Smart Agricultural Technology*, *10*, 100838. DOI: 10.1016/j.atech.2025.100838

Sarkar, A., Wang, H., Rahman, A., Qian, L., & Memon, W. H. (2022). Evaluating the roles of the farmer's cooperative for fostering environmentally friendly production technologies-a case of kiwi-fruit farmers in Meixian, China. *Journal of Environmental Management*, *301*, 113858. DOI: 10.1016/j.jenvman.2021.113858 PMID: 34607139

Sarris, A. (2013). Food commodity price volatility and food insecurity. *Bio-Based and Applied Economics*, *2*(3), 213–236. DOI: 10.13128/BAE-13114

Satar, M. S., Aggarwal, D., Bansal, R., & Alarifi, G. (2023). Mapping the knowledge structure and unveiling the research trends in social entrepreneurship and inclusive development: A bibliometric analysis. *Sustainability*, *15*(7), 5626.

Satrovic, E., & Muslija, A. (2019). Causality relationship between foreign direct investment and tourism. *Uluslararası Iktisadi ve Idari Incelemeler Dergisi*, *22*, 65–76. DOI: 10.18092/ulikidince.418132

Scheidgen, K., Günzel-Jensen, F., & Schmidt, S. L. (2025). Entrepreneurial Resourcefulness Throughout Crisis. *Entrepreneurship Theory and Practice*, *49*(2), 502–538. DOI: 10.1177/10422587241269067

Schumpeter, J. A. (2021). The theory of economic development. Routledge. https://www.routledge.com/The-Theory-of-Economic-Development/Schumpeter/p/book/9780367705268

Schwab, K. (2023). The Global Competitiveness Report 2023. World Economic Forum. https://www.weforum.org

Schwens, C., Zapkau, F. B., Bierwerth, M., & Isidor, R. (2018). International entrepreneurship: A meta-analysis on the internationalization and performance relationship. *Entrepreneurship Theory and Practice*, *42*(5), 734–768. DOI: 10.1177/1042258718795346

Scott, W. R. (1987). The Adolescence of Institutional Theory. *Administrative Science Quarterly*, *32*(4), 493. DOI: 10.2307/2392880

Scuotto, V., Lemaire, S. L. L., Magni, D., & Maalaoui, A. (2022). Extending knowledge-based view: Future trends of corporate social entrepreneurship to fight the gig economy challenges. *Journal of Business Research*, *139*, 1111–1122.

Seelos, C., & Mair, J. (2005). Social entrepreneurship: Creating new business models to serve the poor. *Business Horizons*, *48*(3), 241–246.

Seetanah, B. (2011). Assessing the Dynamic Economic Impact of Tourism for Island Economies. *Annals of Tourism Research*, *38*(1), 291–308. DOI: 10.1016/j.annals.2010.08.009

Senor, D., & Singer, S. (2009). *Start-up Nation: The Story of Israel's Economic Miracle*. New York: Grand Central Publishing. Retrieved 2025, from https://ia600509.us.archive.org/7/items/TheLeanStartupErickRies/start-up_nation_the_stor.pdf

Shalhoob, H., & Hussainey, K. (2022). Environmental, Social and Governance (ESG) Disclosure and the Small and Medium Enterprises (SMEs) Sustainability Performance. *Sustainability 2023, Vol. 15, Page 200*, *15*(1), 200. https://doi.org/ DOI: 10.3390/SU15010200

Sharma, K., Jain, M., & Dhir, S. (2022). Analysing the impact of artificial intelligence on the competitiveness of tourism firms: A modified total interpretive structural modeling (m-TISM) approach. *International Journal of Emerging Markets*, *17*(4), 1067–1084. DOI: 10.1108/IJOEM-05-2021-0810

Shepherd, D. A., & Williams, T. (2020). Entrepreneurship responding to adversity: Equilibrating adverse events and disequilibrating persistent adversity. *Organization Theory*, *1*(4), 2631787720967678. DOI: 10.1177/2631787720967678

Shepherd, D. A., & Williams, T. A. (2023). Different response paths to organizational resilience. *Small Business Economics, 61*(1), 23–58. DOI: 10.1007/s11187-022-00689-4 PMID: 38625189

Shi, Y., & Yang, B. (2025). Green finance instruments and empowering sustainability in East Asian economies. *Humanities & Social Sciences Communications, 12*(1), 1–9. DOI: 10.1057/s41599-024-04324-3

Shojaee, S., & Mirzaei, I. (2024). The Impact of Financial Flexibility on the Resilience of Small and Medium Enterprises in the Face of Economic Shocks. *Business, Marketing, and Finance Open, 1*(2), 150–159. DOI: 10.61838/bmfopen.1.2.13

Shore, A., Tiwari, M., Tandon, P., & Foropon, C. (2024). Building Entrepreneurial Resilience during Crisis Using Generative AI: An Empirical Study on SMEs. *Technovation, 135*, 103063. DOI: 10.1016/J.TECHNOVATION.2024.103063

Short, J. C., Moss, T. W., & Lumpkin, G. T. (2009). Research in social entrepreneurship: Past contributions and future opportunities. *Strategic Entrepreneurship Journal, 3*(2), 161–194.

Shridhar, S. (2024). An Heuristic Study on Pradhan Mantri Street Vendor's Atmanirbhar Nidhi Yojana: Context on a Micro Credit Scheme. *Asian Journal of Agricultural Extension. Economia e Sociologia, 42*(6), 339–349.

Shrivastav, S. K., Bag, S., & Bhattacharya, R. (2025). Sustainable knowledge management in the digital era: Leveraging natural language processing to identify trends, challenges and future directions. *Journal of Knowledge Management, 29*(9), 2843–2872.

Shukla, N. K., & Patel, A. S. Preservation of Job and Local Culture Through Sustainable Tourism: A Case Study of Uttar Pradesh With Special Reference To PM SVANidhi Scheme.

Siddik, A. B., Forid, M. S., Yong, L., Du, A. M., & Goodell, J. W. (2025). Artificial intelligence as a catalyst for sustainable tourism growth and economic cycles. *Technological Forecasting and Social Change, 210*, 123875. DOI: 10.1016/j.techfore.2024.123875

Silvestro, R., & Lustrato, P. (2014). Integrating financial and physical supply chains: The role of banks in enabling supply chain integration. *International Journal of Operations & Production Management, 34*(3), 298–324.

Simons, R. (1995). *Levers of control: How managers use innovative control systems to drive strategic renewal.* Harvard Business School Press.

Singh, B. B. (2018). Street Vendors in Food Service Activities and Their Spatial Distribution. , 37.

Smith, I. H., & Woodworth, W. P. (2012). Developing social entrepreneurs and social innovators: A social identity and self-efficacy approach. *Academy of Management Learning & Education, 11*(3), 390–407. DOI: 10.5465/amle.2011.0016

SNV. (2022). *Resilience Conceptual Framework: Creating a common language to make it concrete and specific.* Avaialable at https://www.snv.org/assets/downloads/f/191310/2833e3a462/core-20resilience-20conceptual-20framework.pdf (Accessed on 10/12/2025).

Snyman, J. A., & Saayman, M. (2009). Key factors influencing foreign direct investment in the tourism industry in South Africa. *Tourism Review, 64*(3), 49–58. DOI: 10.1108/16605370910988827

Sokhanvar, A. (2022). The Role of Tourism and FDI in the Economic Growth of EU11 Countries. *Tourism and Hospitality Management, 28*(2), 343–359. DOI: 10.20867/thm.28.2.5

Sokhanvar, A., & Jenkins, G. P. (2022). Impact of foreign direct investment and international tourism on long-run economic growth of Estonia. *Journal of Economic Studies (Glasgow, Scotland), 49*(2), 364–378. DOI: 10.1108/JES-11-2020-0543

Solomon, G. T., Alabduljader, N., & Ramani, R. S. (2019). Knowledge management and social entrepreneurship education: Lessons learned from an exploratory two-country study. *Journal of Knowledge Management, 23*(10), 1853–1873. DOI: 10.1108/JKM-12-2018-0743

Sophocleous, H. P. (2023). Nation Branding as a Strategic Asset for Local SMEs: Global Developments in Nation Branding and Promotion – Theoretical and Practical Approaches. In A. Masouras, *Global Developments in Nation Branding and Promotion: Theoretical and Practical Approaches* (pp. 124-155). IGI Global Scientific Publishing. doi:DOI: 10.4018/978-1-6684-5902-7.ch006

Sophocleous, H., Anastasiadou, S., & Masouras, A. (2025). The Circular Correlation Between Institutions, Political Marketing, and the Electoral Process. In *Security and Strategy Models for Key-Solving Institutional Frameworks* (Vol. 13, pp. 1-16). MDPI (IGI Global). doi:DOI: 10.4018/979-8-3693-5583-1.ch007

Sophocleous, H. P. (2024). *Production and Consumption of Political Communication and Voting Behaviour*. Nova Science Publishers., DOI: 10.52305/ojbc3507

Sophocleous, H. P., Masouras, A., & Anastasiadou, S. D. (2024). The impact of political marketing on voting behaviour of Cypriot voters. *Social Sciences, 13*(3). Advance online publication. DOI: 10.3390/socsci13030149

Sophocleous, H. P., Masouras, A., & Papademetriou, C. (2019). Brand as a Strategic Asset for Cultural Organisations: A Proposal for the Forthcoming Cultural Institution of Pafos. In Kavoura, A., Kefallonitis, E., Giovanis, A., Kavoura, A., Kefallonitis, E., & Giovanis, A. (Eds.), *Strategic Innovative Marketing and Tourism* (pp. 735–743). Springer., DOI: 10.1007/978-3-030-12453-3_85

Spilanis, I., Kizos, T., & Karampela, S. (2015). *Νησιωτικότητα και βιωσιμότητα: Η περίπτωση των νησιών του Αιγαίου* [Insularity and sustainability: The case of the Aegean Islands]. University of the Aegean.

tefan, S. C., Popa, I., & Breazu, A. (2025). A new framework for the artificial intelligence entrepreneurship ecosystem. *Journal of Innovation & Knowledge, 10*(6), 100850. DOI: 10.1016/j.jik.2025.100850

Steinbach, S. (2021). *Exchange rate volatility and global food supply chains* (No. w29164). National Bureau of Economic Research. https://doi.org/DOI: 10.3386/w29164

Steiner, S., Brock, D., Pittz, T., & Liguori, E. (2018). Multi-disciplinary involvement in social entrepreneurship education: A uniquely threaded ecosystem. *Journal of Ethics and Entrepreneurship, 8*, 73–91.

Stiglitz, J. E. (2018). *Globalization and its discontents revisited: Anti-globalization in the era of Trump*. W. W. Norton & Company., Retrieved 2025, from.

Stringam, B. B. (2010). Timeshare and vacation ownership executives' analysis of the industry and the future. *Journal of Retail & Leisure Property, 9*(1), 37–54. DOI: 10.1057/rlp.2009.21

Suali, A. S., Srai, J. S., & Tsolakis, N. (2024). The role of digital platforms in e-commerce food supply chain resilience under exogenous disruptions. *Supply Chain Management, 29*(3), 573–601. DOI: 10.1108/SCM-02-2023-0064

Subramanian, Yavana Rani & M., Govindaraj & Priya, B & Rena, Ravinder. (2023). An Empirical Study On The Impact Of Covid-19 Pandemic On Street Vendors In Karnataka Section A-Research Paper Eur. 2194-2200. .DOI: 10.48047/ecb/2023.12.si10.00263

Suchman, M. C. (1995). Managing legitimacy: Strategic and institutional approaches. *Academy of Management Review, 20*(3), 571–610. DOI: 10.5465/amr.1995.9508080331

Sultana, N., Rahman, M. M., & Khanam, R. (2022). Informal sector employment and economic growth: Evidence from developing countries in SDG perspective. *Sustainability*, *14*(19), 11989.

Supari, S., & Anton, H. (2022). The Impact of the National Economic Recovery Program and Digitalization on MSME Resilience during the COVID-19 Pandemic: A Case Study of Bank Rakyat Indonesia. *Economies 2022, Vol. 10, Page 160, 10*(7), 160. https://doi.org/DOI: 10.3390/ECONOMIES10070160

Syahribulan, S., Lasaksi, P., Samuddin, S. F., Souisa, W., & Hafid, A. (2024). Entrepreneurial Resilience and Adaptation in Times of Crisis: A Bibliometric Study on Business Continuity in SMEs. *West Science Social and Humanities Studies*, *2*(05), 728–738. DOI: 10.58812/WSSHS.V2I05.875

Szarleta, E. (2018). Community-based entrepreneurship: Fostering innovation and inclusion through local governance partnerships. *Midwest Public Affairs Conference Journal*, *22*(1), 47–62.

Tamirat, S. (2024). Digital Marketing in developing economies. *Journal of Marketing*, *11*(21), 48–67. DOI: 10.54663/2182-9306.2023.v11.n21.48-67

Tang, S., Selvanathan, E. A., & Selvanathan, S. (2007). The Relationship between Foreign Direct Investment and Tourism: Empirical Evidence from China. *Tourism Economics*, *13*(1), 25–39. DOI: 10.5367/000000007779784498

Tarasenko, I. (2021). The impact of exchange rate volatility on trade: The evidence from Russia. *Russian Journal of Economics*, *7*(3), 213–232. DOI: 10.32609/j.ruje.7.57933

Taskan, B., Junça-Silva, A., & Caetano, A. (2022). Clarifying the conceptual map of VUCA: A systematic review. *The International Journal of Organizational Analysis*, *30*(7), 196–217. DOI: 10.1108/IJOA-02-2022-3136

Teece, D. J. (2007). Explicating dynamic capabilities: The nature and microfoundations of (sustainable) enterprise performance. *Strategic Management Journal*, *28*(13), 1319–1350. DOI: 10.1002/smj.640

Teece, D. J. (2014). The foundations of enterprise performance: Dynamic and ordinary capabilities in an (economic) theory of firms. *The Academy of Management Perspectives*, *28*(4), 328–352. DOI: 10.5465/amp.2013.0116

Teece, D. J. (2018). Business models and dynamic capabilities. *Long Range Planning*, *51*(1), 40–49. DOI: 10.1016/j.lrp.2017.06.007

Teece, D. J., Peteraf, M., & Leih, S. (2016). Dynamic capabilities and organizational agility: Risk, uncertainty, and entrepreneurial management in the innovation economy. *California Management Review*, *58*(4), 13–35. DOI: 10.1525/cmr.2016.58.4.13

Teece, D. J., Pisano, G., & Shuen, A. (1997). Dynamic capabilities and strategic management. *Strategic Management Journal*, *18*(7), 509–533. DOI: 10.1002/(SICI)1097-0266(199708)18:7<509:AID-SMJ882>3.0.CO;2-Z

Tessier, S., & Otley, D. (2012). A conceptual development of Simons' Levers of Control framework. *Management Accounting Research*, *23*(3), 171–185. DOI: 10.1016/j.mar.2012.04.003

The Duy, D., & Tien Thanh, P. (2024). Economic challenges faced by migrant street vendors during a crisis: Implications for social inclusion development. *The International Journal of Sociology and Social Policy*, *44*(9/10), 809–825.

Thomas, A. (2024). The role of women's entrepreneurship in achieving sustainable development goals (SDGs): A comprehensive review. *Journal of Biotechnology & Bioinformatics Research*, *174*(6), 2–11.

Todt, G., Wolf, B., & Maisch, B. (2024). Navigating Peaks and Valleys-Fostering Resilience via Entrepreneurial Life Design. *CERN ideaSquare Journal of Experimental Innovation*, *8*(3), 28–35. DOI: 10.23726/cij.2024.1578

Tong, L., Yan, W., & Manta, O. (2022). Artificial Intelligence Influences Intelligent Automation in Tourism: A Mediating Role of Internet of Things and Environmental, Social, and Governance Investment. *Frontiers in Environmental Science*, *10*, 853302. DOI: 10.3389/fenvs.2022.853302

Topcu, M., & Gulsen, M. A. (2025). Governance Quality Vs. Stimulus Size: Fiscal Policy Effectiveness During the COVID-19 Pandemic. *Public Sector Economics - Submission Site*, *49*(2), 251–272. https://doi.org/DOI: 10.3326/PSE.49.2.4

Török, Á., Kovács, S., Jámbor, A., & Maró, Z. M. (2025). Understanding the Determinants of Participation in Agri-Food Global Value Chains. *Journal of Sustainability Research*, *7*(3). Advance online publication. DOI: 10.20900/jsr20250062

Torres-Delgado, A., & Saarinen, J. (2013). Using indicators to assess sustainable tourism development: A review. *Tourism Geographies*, *16*(1), 31–47. DOI: 10.1080/14616688.2013.867530

Tosun, C., & Jenkins, C. L. (1998). The evolution of tourism planning in Third-World countries: A critique. *Progress in Tourism and Hospitality Research*, *4*(2), 101–114. DOI: 10.1002/(SICI)1099-1603(199806)4:2<101:AID-PTH100>3.0.CO;2-Z

Tourism, U. N. (2025). Safe Destinations Challenge: Strengthening tourism resilience. United Nations World Tourism Organization. https://www.untourism.int/news/un-tourism-launches-the-safe-destinations-challenge-to-strengthen-tourism-resilience-in-europe-and-beyond

Tourism, U. N. (n.d.). Digital transformation in tourism. United Nations World Tourism Organization. https://www.unwto.org/digital-transformation

Tracey, P., & Phillips, N. (2007). The distinctive challenge of educating social entrepreneurs: A postscript and rejoinder to the special issue on entrepreneurship education. *Academy of Management Learning & Education*, *6*(2), 264–271.

Trofimov, I. D. (2020). The J-curve effect in agricultural commodity trade: an empirical study of South East Asian economies. https://mpra.ub.uni-muenchen.de/id/eprint/106701

Troise, C., Corvello, V., Ghobadian, A., & O'Regan, N. (2022). How can SMEs successfully navigate VUCA environment: The role of agility in the digital transformation era. *Technological Forecasting and Social Change*, *174*, 121227. DOI: 10.1016/j.techfore.2021.121227

Tunçalp, D. (2025). Entrepreneurial Resilience in Polycrisis: Adaptation Via Improvizational Action, Institutional Workarounds, and Strategic Reconfiguration. *Journal ofManagement & Organization*, •••, 1–23. DOI: 10.1017/JMO.2025.10040

U.S. Department of Agriculture, Economic Research Service. (2025). *Agricultural Exchange Rate Data Set: Documentation*. USDA-ERS. Available at https://www.ers.usda.gov/data-products/agricultural-exchange-rate-data-set/documentation (Accessed on 10/12/2025).

UNCTAD. (2007). *FDI in Tourism: The Development Dimension*. United Nations.

UNDP. (2022). *Human Development Report 2021-22*. New York: UNDP United Nations Development Programme. Retrieved 2025, from https://hdr.undp.org/system/files/documents/global-report-document/hdr2021-22reportenglish_0.pdf

Uygur, U., & Marcoux, A. M. (2013). The added complexity of social entrepreneurship: A knowledge-based approach. *Journal of Social Entrepreneurship*, *4*(2), 132–152.

Vandarakis, D., Malliouri, D., Petrakis, S., Kapsimalis, V., Moraitis, V., Hatiris, G.-A., & Panagiotopoulos, I. (2023). Carrying Capacity and Assessment of the Tourism Sector in the South Aegean Region, Greece. *Water (Basel)*, *15*(14), 2616. DOI: 10.3390/w15142616

Varelas, S. (2016). *Στρατηγικές ανάπτυξης τουριστικών επιχειρήσεων: Η περίπτωση των ξενοδοχειακών επιχειρήσεων* [Tourism enterprises development strategies: The case of hotel enterprises] [Doctoral dissertation, National Documentation Centre of Greece]. http://dx.doi.org/DOI: 10.12681/eadd/39663

Varelas, S., & Belias, D. (2019). Carrying capacity assessment for tourism development: A strategic approach. In Kavoura, A., Kefallonitis, E., & Giovanis, A. (Eds.), *Strategic innovative marketing and tourism* (pp. 775–782). Springer., DOI: 10.1007/978-3-030-12453-3_100

Varelas, S., & Tsoupros, G. (2024). Key performance indicators and data envelopment analysis in Greek tourism: A strategic planning tool for destinations and DMMOs. *Sustainability*, *16*(8), 3453. DOI: 10.3390/su16083453

Vargas-Zeledon, A. A., & Lee, S. Y. (2024). Configurations of Institutional Enablers that Foster Inclusive Entrepreneurship: A Fuzzy-Set Qualitative Comparative Analysis. *Journal of Innovation and Knowledge*, *9*(4). Advance online publication. DOI: 10.1016/J.JIK.2024.100549

Variyava, K. F. (2025). Beyond the Bank Account: Financial Inclusion and Maharashtra's Microenterprises.

Vasi, M., Sansone, G., & English, V. (2024). Exogenous Crises and SMEs Resilience: The Dynamic Open Innovation Funnel. *Technovation*, *129*, 102886. DOI: 10.1016/J.TECHNOVATION.2023.102886

Vázquez-Parra, J. C., García-González, A., & Ramírez-Montoya, M. S. (2020). Social entrepreneurship competency: An approach by discipline and gender. *Journal of Applied Research in Higher Education*.

Vega, B. (2025). Empowering growth: How economic education can drive global economic development. *Journal of Economics and Economic Education Research*, *26*(S3), 1–3. https://www.abacademies.org/articles/empowering-growth-how-economic-education-can-drive-global-economic-development-17651.html#r3

Verbeke, A., Zargarzadeh, M. A., & Osiyevskyy, O. (2014). Internalization theory, entrepreneurship and international new ventures. *Multinational Business Review*, *22*(3), 246–269. DOI: 10.1108/MBR-06-2014-0023

Vizcaíno, F. V., Cardenas, J. J., & Cardenas, M. (2020). A look at the social entrepreneur: The effects of resilience and power distance personality traits on consumers' perceptions of corporate social sustainability. *The International Entrepreneurship and Management Journal*, *17*, 83–103.

Vos, R., Glauber, J., Hebebrand, C., & Rice, B. (2025). Global shocks to fertilizer markets: Impacts on prices, demand and farm profitability. *Food Policy*, *133*, 102790. DOI: 10.1016/j.foodpol.2024.102790

Vroegindewey, R., & Hodbod, J. (2018). Resilience of agricultural value chains in developing country contexts: A framework and assessment approach. *Sustainability*, *10*(4), 916. DOI: 10.3390/su10040916

Vuorio, A., Torkkeli, L., & Sainio, L.-M. (2020). Service innovation and internationalization in SMEs: Antecedents and profitability outcomes. *Journal of International Entrepreneurship*, *18*, 92–123. DOI: 10.1007/s10843-019-00266-z

Wahrudin, B., & Sutrisno. (2025). Public Policy Strategies for Enhancing Innovation and SME Competitiveness in Emerging Economies. *International Journal of Economics and Development*, *1*(1), 63–78. https://journal.as-salafiyah.id/index.php/ijed/article/view/348

Wallace, S. L. (1999). Social Entrepreneurship: The role of social purpose enterprises in facilitating community economic development. *Journal of Developmental Entrepreneurship*, *4*(2), 153–174.

Wang, M., Rasoolimanesh, S. M., & Kunasekaran, P. (2022). A review of social entrepreneurship research in tourism: Knowledge map, operational experiences, and roadmaps. *Journal of Sustainable Tourism*, *30*(8), 1777–1798.

Wang, Z., Pan, Z., Lai, W., Lu, S., Liu, H., Wang, X., & Wu, H. (2025). How does digital technology enhance sustainable operations in agribusiness? A case analysis of a Chinese agricultural enterprise. *Frontiers in Sustainable Food Systems*, *9*, 1718405. DOI: 10.3389/fsufs.2025.1718405

Warnken, J., & Guilding, C. (2009). Multi-ownership of tourism accommodation complexes: A critique of types, relative merits, and challenges arising. *Tourism Management*, *30*(5), 704–714. DOI: 10.1016/j.tourman.2008.10.023

Waterman, R. H.Jr, Peters, T. J., & Phillips, J. R. (1980). Structure is not organization. *Business Horizons*, *23*(3), 14–26. DOI: 10.1016/0007-6813(80)90027-0

Weber, M. M., Pedell, B., & Rötzel, P. G. (2024). Resilience-oriented management control systems: A systematic review of the relationships between organizational resilience and management control systems. *Journal of Management Control*, *35*, 563–620. DOI: 10.1007/s00187-024-00385-2

Wernerfelt, B. (1984). A resource-based view of the firm. *Strategic Management Journal*, *5*(2), 171–180. DOI: 10.1002/smj.4250050207

Wesley, J. D., Shen, X., Li, S., & Wilson, N. L. (2012). Agricultural Trade Bias in Exchange Rate Volatility Effect Estimation: An Application of Meta-Regression Analysis. https://doi.org/DOI: 10.22004/ag.econ.124870

Wezeman, P. D., Kuimova, A., & Wezerman, S. T. (2022). Trends in International Arms Transfers, 2021. Stockholm International Peace Research Institute. Stockholm: SIPRI. doi:DOI: 10.55163/CBZJ9986

White House. (2025). Further Modifying the Reciprocal Tariff Rates. Retrieved from https://www.whitehouse.gov/presidential-actions/2025/07/further-modifying-the-reciprocal-tariff-rates/ (Accessed on 22/12/2025).

Williams, C. C., & Gurtoo, A. (2012). Evaluating competing theories of street entrepreneurship: Some lessons from a study of street vendors in Bangalore, India. *The International Entrepreneurship and Management Journal*, *8*(4), 391–409.

Williams, T. A., & Shepherd, D. A. (2016). Building resilience or providing sustenance: Different paths of emergent ventures in the aftermath of the Haiti earthquake. *Academy of Management Journal*, *59*(6), 2069–2102. DOI: 10.5465/amj.2014.0680

World Bank & International Finance Corporation. (2022). *Fintech and SME finance: Expanding responsible access*. Available at https://openknowledge.worldbank.org/server/api/core/bitstreams/d157af2e-ad06-558f-8e1b-5bf52841d34a/content (Accessed on 12/12/2025).

World Bank. (2020). *The Human Capital Index 2020: Human capital in the time of COVID-19*. World Bank Publications.

World Bank. (2020). *The human capital project 2.0: Investing in people to build resilience and productivity*.

World Bank. (2020). *The Human Capital Project 2.0: Investing in people to build resilience and productivity*. World Bank Publications., DOI: 10.1596/978-1-4648-1520-3

World Bank. (2020). *World Development Report 2020: Trading for Development in the Age of Global Value Chains*. World Bank Group.

World Bank. (2022). *World Development Report 2022: Finance for an Equitable Recovery*. https://www.worldbank.org/en/publication/wdr2022

World Bank. (2023). *Fragile and Conflict-affected Situations*. World Bank.

World Bank. (2024). *Resilient Agri-Food Clusters Development Project (P178120): Project Appraisal Document*. World Bank, Washington, DC. Available at https://www.gafspfund.org/sites/default/files/inline-files/Resilient%20Agri-food%20Clusters%20Development%20Project%20PAD.pdf (Accessed on 12/12/2025).

World Bank. (2025). *World Bank SME Finance*. https://www.worldbank.org/en/topic/smefinance

World Economic Forum. (2022). *Cultivating Investment Opportunities in Fragile Contexts: Catalysing Market-Driven Solutions to Strengthen Community and Economy Resilience*. World Economic Forum. Retrieved 2025, from https://www3.weforum.org/docs/WEF_Cultivating_Investment_Opportunities_in_Fragile_Contexts_2022.pdf

World Economic Forum. (2023). Seizing the Momentum to Build Resilience for a Future of Sustainable Inclusive Growth (White paper). World Economic Forum & McKinsey & Company. Retrieved from https://www3.weforum.org/docs/WEF_Resilience_Consortium_2023.pdf (Accessed on 23/12/2025).

World Economic Forum. (2023). The global competitiveness report. https://www.weforum.org/reports/global-competitiveness-report-2023/

World Economic Forum. (2025, June 21). Youth innovation builds workforce resilience through entrepreneurship. Retrieved from https://www.weforum.org/stories/2025/06/youth-innovation-builds-workforce-resilience-through-entrepreneurship/

World Tourism Organization (UNWTO) & United Nations Development Programme (UNDP). (2018). *Tourism and the Sustainable Development Goals – Journey to 2030*. UNWTO. https://doi.org/DOI: 10.18111/9789284419401

Worsham, E. L. (2012). Reflections and insights on teaching social entrepreneurship: An interview with Greg Dees. *Academy of Management Learning & Education, 11*(3), 442–452.

WTO. (2025). *The WTO in brief*. https://www.wto.org/english/thewto_e/whatis_e/inbrief_e/inbr_e.htm

Wu, S., & Fan, D. (2025). Internationalization and innovation: A multilevel meta-analysis of national sentiments. *Journal of Product Innovation Management, 42*(2), 253–283. DOI: 10.1111/jpim.12725

Xia, H., Liu, M., Wang, P., & Tan, X. (2024). Strategies to enhance the corporate innovation resilience in digital era: A cross-organizational collaboration perspective. *Heliyon, 10*(20), e39132. DOI: 10.1016/j.heliyon.2024.e39132 PMID: 39498084

Xu, A., Siddik, A. B., Sobhani, F. A., & Rahman, M. (2024). Driving economic success: Fintech, tourism, FDI, and digitalization in the top 10 tourist destinations. *Humanities & Social Sciences Communications, 11*(1). Advance online publication. DOI: 10.1057/s41599-024-03978-3

Yin, R. K. (2018). *Case study research and applications: Design and methods* (6th ed.). SAGE Publications.

Zahra, S. A., Gedajlovic, E., Neubaum, D. O., & Shulman, J. M. (2009). A typology of social entrepreneurs: Motives, search processes, and ethical challenges. *Journal of Business Venturing, 24*(5), 519–532.

Zehrer, A., & Hallmann, K. (2015). A stakeholder perspective on policy indicators of destination competitiveness. *Journal of Destination Marketing & Management, 4*(2), 120–126. DOI: 10.1016/j.jdmm.2015.03.003

Zhang, Z., Li, C., Yuan, J., & Wang, X. (2025). The impact of climate disaster risk on agricultural trade welfare and coping strategies from a global perspective. *Frontiers in Sustainable Food Systems, 9*, 1547969. DOI: 10.3389/fsufs.2025.1547969

Zhao, M. (2021). Social entrepreneurship for systemic change: The case of Southeast and South Asian countries. *Journal of Asian Public Policy, 14*(2), 225–250.

Zhao, X., & Zhang, L. (2025). How to Improve the Financing Availability of Transport Smes? A Survey Based on Supply Chain Relationship-Logistics Capability-Information Traceability. *Research in Transportation Business & Management, 62*, 101421. DOI: 10.1016/J.RTBM.2025.101421

Zhou, N., & Sun, R. (2024). Coping with the storm: The role of fintech in SME survival. *International Review of Financial Analysis, 93*, 103157. DOI: 10.1016/j.irfa.2024.103157

Zhou, N., & Sun, R. (2024). Coping with the Storm: The Role of Fintech in SME Survival. *International Review of Financial Analysis, 93*, 103157. DOI: 10.1016/J.IRFA.2024.103157

Zhou, X., & Choi, C. H. (2025). Tourism Development, Foreign Direct Investment, and Environmental Sustainability: How Green Technology Innovations Make a Difference. *SAGE Open, 15*(2). Advance online publication. DOI: 10.1177/21582440251331003

Zimmermann, V., & Köhler-Geib, F. (2023). Impact of the COVID-19 Pandemic on Different Groups of SMEs in Germany and Their Recovery. *Inter Economics, 58*(6), 333–341. DOI: 10.2478/IE-2023-0068

About the Contributors

Georgios Deirmentzoglou is an Assistant Professor in International Entrepreneurship, Technology, and Sustainable Development at Neapolis University Pafos (Cyprus). He holds a PhD in Business Administration, an MBA with a specialization in Total Quality Management and a BSc in Industrial Management and Technology. Before joining NUP, Georgios served as an Adjunct Lecturer at the University of Piraeus and other colleges in Greece in partnership with UK and French universities. Georgios has extensive experience as a Scientific Coordinator in EU-funded projects, primarily focusing on digital transformation and sustainable development. His research interests focus on entrepreneurship, technological innovation, sustainable development, and tourism.

Eleni E. Anastasopoulou is a Lecturer in Sustainable Entrepreneurship at Neapolis University Pafos. She holds a Ph.D. in Sustainable Agri-food Entrepreneurship, an M.Sc. in Pharmacognosy and Chemistry of Natural Products, and a B.Sc. in Agriculture with a specialization in Food Science and Technology. Her research focuses on sustainable development, innovation in the agri-food and tourism sectors, and rural policies at national and European levels. She has published in high-impact journals, co-edited academic volumes, authored book chapters, and presented at international conferences. She also serves as Local Coordinator for the European University Alliance EMERGE and has extensive experience in EU-funded research projects.

Valeska V. Geldres-Weiss is an Associate Professor of Marketing at the Department of Business and Economics, Faculty of Law and Business, Universidad de La Frontera, Chile. She holds a Ph.D. in Business Administration and Marketing from the University of Seville (Spain) and completed postdoctoral studies at the University of São Paulo (Brazil). Her academic and professional expertise lies in international business and marketing, export competitiveness, sustainability in global markets, and innovation in the agri-food sector. She has led and participated in interdisciplinary research projects with a strong publication record in high-impact journals. Dr. Geldres-Weiss has designed and delivered postgraduate courses in Chile, Poland, and Bolivia, focusing on international business strategy, trade data analysis, and sustainability standards. Her teaching integrates real-world tools such as TradeMap, Export Potential Map, and Market Access Map, fostering applied learning in multicultural environments. In 2025, she teaches the course Practical Business Creation (University Spin-Offs), part of the Entrepreneurship Minor offered by Universidad de La Frontera, which equips students with competencies to create technology-based enterprises from academic research. She served as the founding Dean of the Faculty of Law and Business at Universidad de La Frontera (2014–2020) and was the first woman to preside over the Chilean Association of Senior Executives of Business Schools (ASFAE). In the private sector, she co-founded and managed a Born-Global agrifood firm, successfully exporting to Europe and the Middle East. Her career bridges academia, policy, and practice in international business.

Bojan Jovanovski holds a doctorate in Technical sciences in the field: Industrial Engineering and Management with a focus on Innovation Management, awarded by Ss. Cyril and Methodius University in Skopje. He is currently a Professor (FH) at the Institute of International Management at FH JOANNEUM in Graz, Austria, where he teaches and conducts research in innovation, particularly in the areas of small business competitiveness and sustainability innovation. entrepreneurship, and entrepreneurial learning, since 2006. He was involved in the development of the Ss. Cyril and Methodius Business Start-up Centre and later co-founded the NGO National Centre for Development of Innovation and Entrepreneurial Learning – Skopje. In 2024, Dr. Jovanovski founded the Startup Hub at FH JOANNEUM, which he is coordinating since. In the academic year 2024–2025, he is also the interim head of the Transfer Center at the Institute of International Management and Entrepreneurship at FH JOANNEUM. In recognition of his contributions to science and society, he became a member of the European Academy of Science and Arts in 2025. His publication record includes over 80 bibliographic units, such as scientific papers, teaching materials, research reports, and handbooks, and he has presented at more than 30 international conferences. His academic contributions also include participation in over 50 international and numerous national and industry projects. His activities have resulted with support of more than 50 start-ups, the development of high-school curricula on national level in North Macedonia, and the delivery of training programmes for companies, young professionals, entrepreneurs, and educators.

Andreas Masouras is an Associate Professor of Communication and Marketing in the Department of Economics & Business at Neapolis University. He holds a

PhD with distinction from the Department of Political Science and International Relations at the University of the Peloponnese. The title of his doctoral dissertation is "Entrepreneurship and Competitiveness through the Lens of Institutional Analysis: The Case of Cyprus," which is available in the National Archive of Doctoral Dissertations. He coordinates the following programs: the conventional MBA, the distance MBA (English-speaking), and the MBA in Tourism (distance learning). He is actively writing scientific articles and participates in international conferences. His book, "Entrepreneurship in Small and Medium-Sized Enterprises", published by the American publishing house Nova, has been indexed in the Scopus book list.

***

Konstantina K. Agoraki is an Assistant Professor in the Department of Business Administration, University of Piraeus. She holds a PhD from the Department of Business Administration, University of Piraeus and a Master's degree (MSc) in International Economics and Finance, Athens University of Economics and Business. Dr. Agoraki has taught in the Department of Tourism Studies, University of Piraeus, as well as at the University of Peloponnese, at both undergraduate and postgraduate levels. Additionally, she has taught at the postgraduate level at the Athens University of Economics and Business and the Open University of Cyprus. Her research interests include, among others, Knowledge Management, Innovation and Technology Management, Entrepreneurship and Social Entrepreneurship. She has published in high-quality international scientific journals such as the Journal of International Money and Finance, International Journal of Innovation and Technology Management, Social Responsibility Journal and has participated in international scientific conferences. She is also a reviewer in international scientific journals.

Akhil Anand has done MBA (2022-2024 Batch) from Indian Institute of Technology Jodhpur

Ioannis E. Anastasopoulos is a civil engineer and tourism-management scholar focusing on strategic decision-making for tourism investments, tourism real estate, and mixed-use developments. He holds a PhD in Tourism Studies from the University of Piraeus (2025), an MSc in Governance and Public Policy (2016), and a BEng in Civil Engineering (2014). He has served as Technical Consultant at the University of Piraeus and as a research team member on the ELIDEK-funded "Tourism Knowledge Base" project. His interests include KPI-based strategy, ESG-aligned governance, destination carrying capacity, and sustainable port and destination policy.

Belem Barbosa received her PhD in Business and Management Studies – Specialisation in Marketing and Strategy from the University of Porto, Portugal. She is an Associate Professor at the School of Economics and Management of the University of Porto. She is a full researcher at CEF.UP Center for Economics and Finance at the University of Porto and an invited researcher at LIAAD INESC TEC. Her research interests lie primarily in the areas of digital marketing and consumer behavior.

Lucas Cortez Costa holds a Master's in Internationalization Economics and Management from the University of Porto. He has experience in business consulting. His main research interest is business internationalization.

Fabio Duarte (PhD) is the author or co-author of several scientific papers, including publications in Small Business Economics, European Financial Management, Journal of Business Finance and Accounting, Financial Research Letters, Financial Innovation, among others. His research interests focus on banking financing conditions for SMEs and on microcredit tools as an instrument to promote the financial inclusion of microentrepreneurs. Enthusiastic about emerging areas, such as crypto assets.

Stavros G. Efthimiou is a Postdoctoral Researcher (Postdoc) and Academic Fellow at University of Piraeus. He holds a Ph.D. from the Department of International and European Studies– University of Piraeus at the field of International Economics.

Prajna Jha is Assistant Professor in Department of Computer Science in Amity University, Mumbai

Ioannis Katsanakis is an Assistant Professor at the Department of Tourism Studies of the University of Piraeus in the field of Information Systems Management in Enterprises and Organizations with a focus on Business Process Management. His research interests focus on the application of new technologies in business, the strategic use of new technologies, information systems evaluation, system analysis, e-business, knowledge management, e-learning, business forecasting, quantitative methods in decision-making, data analytics and fraud examination and analytics. He has worked in entrepreneurship, ICT and e-learning research programs at the University of Piraeus.

Aradhana Kumari is an Assistant Professor of Economics with over 10 years of teaching experience. She specializes in Mathematical Economics, Microeconomics, and Development Economics. Alongside her academic career, she has extensive experience in content writing and developing academic materials in Economics. Her work reflects a blend of analytical rigor and applied economic perspectives.

Vaishali Mogha, from New Delhi, is an Assistant Professor with a strong foundation in technology and education. She holds a B.Tech in Electronics & Communication, an M.Tech in IoT and Sensors, and a B.Ed, reflecting her passion for both innovation and teaching. Known for her clear guidance and student-focused approach, she strives to inspire young learners and contribute meaningfully to the academic and tech community.

Mahabir Narwal is Professor and Chairperson, Department of Commerce, Kurukshetra University Kurukshetra, having 28 years of teaching experience.

Laveena Pareek holds a Ph.D. in Entrepreneurship and is NTA-NET qualified in Commerce. She is an accomplished and dedicated academician with a strong commitment to academic excellence and student success. With demonstrated expertise in entrepreneurship, marketing, and digital marketing, she is known for her ability to design impactful curricula and deliver engaging, student-centered instruction. Her work reflects a passion for mentoring students, fostering critical thinking, and creating inclusive learning environments. Dr. Pareek has actively contributed to research and publication in the areas of Marketing Management, Women and Youth Entrepreneurship, and Digital Transformation in Business. She is also deeply involved in preparing students for industry through soft skills and communication training. Her qualifications include a Master's in Commerce and a Postgraduate Diploma in Business Administration, along with strong competencies in communication, leadership, and academic writing. Driven by a desire to create meaningful academic impact, she continues to engage in research that bridges academic theory with real-world entrepreneurial practice.

Konstantinos M. Poyiadjis is a scholar and media commentator specializing in international relations, strategy, and security studies. He holds a BSc in Mathematics from University of Portsmouth, and postgraduate degrees an MBA, an MPA, and an MSc in International Relations, Strategy & Security from Neapolis University Pafos. His research focuses on geopolitics, AI-driven foreign policy decision-making, automated deterrence systems, strategic stability, and emerging security architectures. He has authored over 150 analytical publications and contributed peer-reviewed chapters through IGI Global. He also serves as a reviewer for the publisher, providing editorial and peer-review expertise in international political economy and strategic analysis. As an International Relations Specialist, he regularly appears as a public figure on national TV and radio panels, engaging in key foreign policy and security debates.

Geeta Sachdeva is an Assistant Professor in the Department of Humanities and Social Sciences at the National Institute of Technology (NIT), Kurukshetra, where she has been serving since 2013. With over 15 years of academic experience in Management, she holds a Ph.D. from UGC-NET qualified. Her research expertise spans Human Resource Management, Workplace Spirituality, Green HRM, Employee Behavior, and Digital Workplaces. She has published extensively in Scopus-indexed and ABDC-listed journals and has presented her work at prestigious national and international conferences, including IIMs, IITs, and global academic forums. Dr. Sachdeva is currently the Principal Investigator of an ICSSR-sponsored research project on the PM SVANidhi scheme. She has supervised and guided several Ph.D. scholars in emerging HR domains. She has also contributed as a content writer for the MHRD's NME-ICT initiative, developing academic modules in Human Resource Management.

Apostolos Skotis is an Assistant Professor in the Department of Business Administration at the University of Piraeus. He holds a PhD in Decision Support Information Systems. His teaching focuses on information systems and applications for business management, business simulations, and knowledge management. His research interests include big data–driven decision support making, unstructured data analytics, behavioral analytics in digital environments, information management, and customer knowledge management. He has extensive industry experience in business analytics, management information systems, risk analytics and management, IT project implementation, model development and validation, and data quality assessment.

Georgios Tsoupros is a Research Economist and a PhD candidate at the University of Piraeus. He has gained work experience as a Research Analyst and a Teaching Assistant in the same university. Moreover, he holds a Master of Business Administration from the University of Piraeus and a Bachelor of Economics from the University of Peloponnese, where he was honored by the State Scholarships Foundation as the first-ranked graduate of 2021-2022. His research interests focus on Hospitality Strategic Management, Performance Measurement & Sustainability.

Sotirios Varelas is an Associate Professor at the Department of Tourism Studies of the University of Piraeus with the subject "Hospitality Business Strategy and Tourism Organizations". He holds a PhD from the Department of Business Administration of the School of Economics, Business and International Studies of the University of Piraeus. He has 15 years of professional experience as a scientific consultant to tourism organizations and is the creator and manager of a start-up company on virtual tourism www.netourwork.com. In the past he was a scientific consultant at the Ministry of Tourism, the Greek Tourism Organisation and the Peloponnese Region. Within his responsibilities he has designed and implemented destination management and marketing activities at national- regional level (airline recruitment, digital marketing, participation in b2b events, fam press trip, consultations, experiential products, identity creation, etc). He has authored and participated in more than 40 study projects on topics such as Tourism Observatories, Sustainability, Destination Management, Destination Strategy, DMMO, Destination Marketing and Branding. He has collaborated with several research centres such as the Institute of Regional Development, the University of Peloponnese, the Laboratory of Policy Evaluation and Programme Development and the Research Centre of the University of Piraeus. He teaches in the Postgraduate Programmes in Tourism Business Administration and Business Administration at the University of Piraeus and in the Undergraduate Programme in Tourism Management at the Hellenic Open University. Since 2010 he has taught at several academic and professional institutions such as the University of Piraeus, the University of West Attica, the University of Peloponnese, the University of Piraeus, the Institute of the Hellenic Tourism Business Association (INSEETE), the Hellenic Society of Business Administration (HSE) and the Air Force War College. He has been appointed by the Assembly of the Department as the student internship coordinator and coordinator of the academic advisors of the Department of Tourism Studies. Dr. Varela was the creator and coordinator of the Graduate Program in Tourism Business Administration and the Center for International Tourism Research at Neapolis University. His scientific papers have been published in several international journals and he is a member of the editorial board of several journals and conferences. He frequently writes articles and participates as a speaker on issues related to tourism and tourism business.

Poonam Verma is currently working as a Research Assistant in the Department of Humanities and Social Sciences at NIT Kurukshetra. She has completed her Ph.D. from the Haryana School of Business, Guru Jambheshwar University of Science & Technology, Hisar, Haryana (India). A dedicated and enthusiastic scholar, she has published several research papers in reputed national and international journals and has presented her work at various academic conferences. She has also served as an Editorial Assistant for the HSB Research Review Journal. Her academic and research experience reflects her strong commitment to advancing knowledge in the field of social sciences.

Muskan Wadhwa is an Assistant Professor in French at IMS Noida, with expertise in French language instruction, intercultural communication, and curriculum development. She has experience teaching in different programs, with a focus on enhancing global readiness and business communication through language.

Her pedagogical approach integrates communicative methodologies, multimedia tools, and differentiated instruction tailored to varied learner profiles. She has actively contributed to academic life by organizing French cultural events under the Institution Innovation Council and conducting industry-linked guest lectures. She has presented research at an international conference on "The Evolution of French: From Elite Circles to University Curriculum."

Wahyu Wibowo is a graduate student in the Master's Program in Shariah Economics at UIN Sunan Kalijaga Yogyakarta. His academic interests include the Halal industry, Islamic philanthropy, and economic literacy. He received four DIKTI-funded PKM grants (2012–2014), three of which focused on community service—ranging from Jarimatika training to literary-mathematical education for orphans, one of which was selected as a national finalist. He also initiated an entrepreneurship project titled IBU SASTIKA (Innovative Mathematical Literature Book) that combines educational innovation with creative content.

Index

A

B

C

D

E

L

M

N

O

P

R

S

T

U

V

www.ingramcontent.com/pod-product-compliance
Lightning Source LLC
LaVergne TN
LVHW062332300926
849161LV00007B/1669
9798337369914